A Guide of our **Blessed Virgin Mary**

PART I . . . 20th Century apparitions

Peter Heintz
Introduction by Fr. Raymond Skonezny, STL, SSL

GABRIEL PRESS
Sacramento, California

Acknowledgments

I wish to thank M Fernandez and J Colby for their faithfulness in typing and organizing this work — to R Jewell, J Colby and S & I Coonley for their loving effort in editing this work — and finally to S & I Coonley for producing the graphics.

© 1993, 1994, 1995 by Peter Heintz
ISBN 0-9645506-0-1
Library of Congress Catalog Card Number: 95-75624
Published by Gabriel Press
All rights reserved

With the exception of short excerpts for critical reviews, no part of this book may be reproduced in any manner whatsoever without permission in writing from the publisher. Write:
**Gabriel Press
PO Box 601001
Sacramento, CA 95860**

ISBN 0-9645506-0-1
Printed **June 25, 1995** in the United States of America

Dedications

- First, to Our Blessed Mother, under every title by which She appears, guiding us to Her Divine Son Jesus.

- Then to granddaughters: Tara, Erin, Lacey and Heather. Thank you for your inspiration and for your honest love for Our Blessed Mother and for Her most holy rosary.

- Finally, to all the faithful who pray the holy rosary daily.

Story of the Cover Picture

The artist, a novice, had difficulty completing the nose and chin in the original painting. After praying for help, he applied a white brush stroke to the nose, which instantly popped out. Then he applied a white brush stroke to the chin intending to feather it and complete the chin the next day. However, the next day the light and shadow of the chin had been feathered, and the painting was completed, without the application of brush or paint.

DECLARATION

In conformity with the decree of Pope Urban VIII, we have no intention of anticipating on the judgment of the Holy Apostolic See and of the Church to which we are faithfully submissive.

CANON LAW

Since the abolition of Canon 1399 and 2318 of the former Code of Canon Law by Pope Paul VI in AAS (*Acta Apostolicae Sedis 1909, Apostolicam Actuositatem 1966*) 58 (1966) pg. 1186, publications about new apparitions, revelations, prophecies, miracles, etc., have been allowed to be distributed and read by the faithful without the express permission of the Church, provided they contain nothing which contravenes faith and morals. This means no imprimatur is necessary.

POPE URBAN VIII ABOUT CONTEMPORARY MESSAGES

"In cases which concern private revelations, it is better to believe than not believe, for, if you believe, and it is proven true, you will be happy that you have believed, because our Holy Mother asked it. If you believe, and it should be proven false, you will receive all blessings as if it had been true, because you believed it to be true."
His Holiness, Pope Urban VIII, 1623-44

Heavenly Father, help us never to cease having recourse to the Blessed Virgin Mary. Let us keep ever in mind that She is Your Blessed Daughter, Spouse of the Holy Spirit, and Mother of Your Son.

"God sent forth his Son born of woman, born under the law, to deliver from the law those who were subjected to it."
Galatians 4:4-5

"God has decreed that the whole of Redemption should be accomplished through Mary, with Mary, and in Mary. Just as nothing was created without Christ, so nothing is recreated without the Virgin Mary."
St. John of the Cross

"The Blessed Virgin directs to us all acts that every mother lavishes on her children. She loves us, watches over us, protects us and intercedes for us."
Pope John XXIII

"Blessed are those who abandon themselves into Our Lady's hands. Their names are written in the Book of Life."
St. Bonaventure

"The salvation of the whole world began with the *'HAIL MARY.'* Hence, the salvation of each person is also attached to this prayer."
St. Louis Grignion de Montfort

"Let Mary never be far from your lips and from your heart. Following Her, you will never sink into despair. Contemplating Her, you will never go wrong."
St. Bernardine of Siena

"What a wondrous book is the heart of Mary! Blessed are those who read with intelligence what is written therein, for they will learn the science of salvation."
St. John Eudes

"So pleasing to God was Mary's humility that He was constrained by His Goodness to entrust to Her the Word. His only Son. And it was that dearest Mother who gave Him to us."
St. Catherine of Siena

"Read attentively the book of purity that is Mary, written entirely by the finger of God. Read the holiness, the love, the kindness, the humility - in short, read the vast fullness of all the virtues."
St. Thomas of Villanova

"Mary's grace has given glory to heaven, a God to earth, and faith to the nations. She has conferred death on vices, order on life, and a rule on morals."
St. Peter Chrysostom

"Go to Mary and sing Her praises, and you will be enlightened. For it is through Her that the true Light shines on the sea of this life."
St. Ildephonsus

"Do you wish to know the most intimate perfections of Jesus and the most hidden attractions of His Love? Then seek them in the heart of Mary!"
St. Peter Eymard

"Human beings will never comprehend sufficiently the anguish and immensity of Mary's sorrows. Very few Christians partake of those sufferings and even fewer offer any consolation to Her."
St. Bridget

"The Blessed Virgin Mary is the Mother and Dispensatrix of all graces. There is not a single servant of this great Queen who can fail to declare: 'It is my devotion to Mary that accounts for the growth of everything good in me.'"
St. Antoninus

"Those who want to prevent their heart from being pervaded by the evils of earth should entrust it to the Blessed Virgin, Our Lady and Our Mother. They will then regain it in heaven, freed from all evils."
St. Francis de Sales

"The heart of our good Mother Mary is all love and mercy. She desires nothing else but our happiness. We need only have recourse to Her and we will be heard."
St. John Vianney

"Mary is an arsenal of graces and She comes to the aid of Her clients. She sustains, strengthens, and revives us by the heavenly favors that She heaps on us."
St. Paulinus

"While remaining the Mother of our Judge, Mary is a mother to us, full of mercy. She constitutes our protection. She keeps us close to Christ, and She faithfully takes the matter of our salvation into Her charge."
St. Peter Canisius

"During the end times, Jesus Christ will transfer all His power received from the Father to Mary, Jesus wishes to act through Her..."
St. Louis Grignion de Montfort

"Oh you whoever you are, if you understand that in the whirlpool of this life you are very far from walking on solid ground, instead you are buffeted by storms and tempests. Do not turn your eyes away from this sparkling Star, if you do not wish to be engulfed by the hurricane. If the wind of temptations rises up, if you strike the reefs of tribultaions, look to the Star, invoke Mary, *'respice Stellam, voca Mariam!'*
If you are shaken by the waves of pride, ambition, criticism, or of jealousy, look to the Star and invoke Mary!
If anger, avarice or the seductions of the flesh shake the frail skiff of your soul, cast a look toward Mary, *'respice ad Mariam'*.
If, troubled by the enormity of your crimes, confused by the ugliness of your conscience, frightened by the fear of the judgment incurred, you feel yourself slipping into the gulf of sadness and into the abyss of despair, then think of Mary - *'cogita Mariam'*. In dangers, anguishes, perplexities, think of Mary, invoke Mary. May Her name be constantly on your lips, that it does not leave your heart..."
St Bernard

INTRODUCTION

Many studies of the major shrines and accompanying apparitions have been done over the past hundred years or so, especially after the events at Lourdes. The author of this work has limited his scope of attention to the apparitions 'essentially from Fatima to the present.' Even then, choices had to be made concerning the authenticated and alleged apparitions that have occurred since that time.

The author's work is a massive one and a very welcome beginning to what I believe will be a major area of study in the Church as we enter the new millennium of Christianity. To aid in this study the author has provided us with a tool, namely, a set of categories. In our age of computers the categorizations used — *thirty-three* — of them are of immeasurable help in comparing, analyzing, and weighing the purpose, content, development and commonality of the apparitions, theology, spirituality, prophetic nature, and above all, the continuing unceasing compassionate love of a mother for her straying children.

It is this last and continuous repetition of a mother's warnings and appealing calls for repentance, echoing that of John the Baptist, that catches one's attention. As the Father sent John the Baptist to warn His people, so He sends today the Mother of His Son to warn, awaken and reinvigorate His people to the realization that one age is coming to an end in a purifying process so that a new period of God's love will be evident to all. A mother's love moves Her to repeat the message of the Father on the Mount of Transfiguration and Baptism, "This is My Beloved Son. Listen to Him." (Mk. 17:8)

No ordinary messenger was sent to Mary at the Annunciation. It was an archangel. We have no ordinary messenger here. It is the Mother of God concerning whom Pius IX will write in the Apostolic Constitution, Ineffabilis Deus, the following: "Wherefore, far above all the angels and saints so wondrously did God endow Her with the abundance of all heavenly gifts poured from the treasury of His Divinity that this Mother ever absolutely free of all sin, all fair and perfect, would possess that fullness of Holy Innocence and sanctity which, under God, one cannot imagine anything greater, and which, outside of God, no mind can succeed in comprehending fully." [1]

Both the dignity of the messenger and the contents of the messages demand from us an attentive hearing and acquiescence of mind, heart and will. The major problem in all matters of 'private revelation' is one of credibility. [2] The two extremes of credulousness and a rationalism that denies the supernatural are errors to be condemned. The Church is adamant in stating that 'public revelation', to which we are bound, ended with the Apostolic Age. However, God's activity in the world did not end there. The criterion that the Church uses in judging so-called 'private revelation' is the Bible and Tradition. The Magisterium, or teaching authority within the Church, repeats the words of the Epistle to the Hebrews, "At various times in the past and in various different ways, God spoke to our ancestors through the prophets; but in our own time, the last days, He has spoken to us through His Son, the Son that He has appointed to inherit everything and through whom He made everything there is." (Heb. 1:1-2) This is the definitive revelation. All that comes after this period, at best, is seen as containing nothing that is against Her faith and morals.

This does not mean to say that the Church doesn't express tacit or explicit approval of sites and 'messages' alleged to come from God in one manner or another. Local ecclesiastical approval and the 'good fruits' accompanying these acclaimed apparitions or messages bear weight to their authenticity.

The words of Our Lord, "a good tree bears good fruit," and "by their fruits you shall know them" reveal their full force at the major shrines of the Church. Any investigation of alleged apparitions must take this into account. Jesus' response to His accusers that He did his works by the power of Beelzebub was: "Every kingdom divided against itself is heading for ruin, and a household that is divided against itself collapses. So, too, with Satan: if he is divided against himself, how can his kingdom stand?" (Lk. 11:17-18). To visit the Shrines of Our Lady of Guadalupe, Lourdes, Fatima and yes, too, those of today being investigated at Medjugorje and Betania, for example, is to witness the faithful committing themselves to God, praying to Our Lord, honoring His Mother, going to confession, Communion, beginning a new life directed to God. These are all fruits of grace, of the Holy Spirit, to live in and for the kingdom we all pray to be a part of in the 'Our Father'.

This is truly a worldwide phenomenon today. "Surely this phenomenon is embraced in the 'signs of the times', a phrase biblical in origin, and used in Vatican II's document." [3] Many people independent of each other and living on different continents claim to be experiencing apparitions from Our Blessed Mother, Our Lord and from Our Father. Which ones and to what degrees they are authentic is a matter of grave concern for the Church. 'Private' in one sense they may be, but in another they are very public and affect the lives of millions. The ones producing an abundance of 'good fruit' merit serious consideration. Otherwise we could be ignoring the abundant grace associated with these events. The evil in the world today is enormous. So, too, must be the grace of God.

In general, the themes of all these occurrences are the great ones of conversion, warning, heaven, hell, judgment, the love and mercy of God for His children, the imminence of God's manifest activity in the world and in souls, the sheer beauty of the Mother to whom God has given so much love and Her overwhelming concern for the spiritual alienation of man from God today by sin and its tragic consequences. The urgency of our times is reflected in the messages. The Father sends Her as a last resort to proclaim a time of mercy before justice falls on those who reject this mercy.

Among others these themes tie together these varied apparitions. They provide a patterned plea for vigilance, spiritual awakening, a casting aside of all torpor and apathy to welcome the coming 'Day of the Lord.'

This volume, used properly, is a mine of spiritual riches. The author has included as a category the prayers of the various messages that are so beautiful and simple. We have, for example, the prayer the Blessed Mother asked the children to say at Fatima at the end of each decade of the rosary, "Oh, my Jesus, forgive us our sins, save us from the fires of hell; lead all souls to heaven, especially those in most need of Thy mercy." (July 13, 1917) How profound and yet how simple are the words of Our Lady of Peace at Medjugorje (March 27, 1986): "Dear Children, I wish to thank you for all your sacrifices and I also call you to the greatest sacrifice, the sacrifice of love. Without love, you will be unable to accept either Me or My Son. Without love, you will not be able to convey your experiences to others. Therefore, dear children, live love within your hearts. We are in the truth that God is love."

In conclusion, this volume enriches the mind and heart of anyone who uses it for study or spiritual reading. May Our Lord and His Blessed Mother pour out their graces on the author and those who take the time to read and meditate in prayer the contents of this work.

Fr. Raymond Skonezny, STL, SSL

1. **"Our Lady"** (Papal teachings arranged by the Benedictine Monks of Solesme and printed by the Daughters of St. Paul, 1961; pg. 61).

2. One of the simplest and clearest analyses of apparitions is that of Fr. Albert J. Hebert, S.M. entitled **"The Discernment of Visionaries and Apparitions Today"** and can be obtained from the author himself at the following address:
    Albert J. Hebert, S.M.
    P.O. Box 309
    Paulina, LA 70763

3. **Pastoral Constitution on the Church in the Modern World, #4.**

FORE-WORD

This work is intended to provide the reader with a more comprehensive grasp of the ever-increasing frequency and duration of reported apparitions of the Blessed Virgin Mary occurring during this 20th century, as well as a comparison of elements and messages of the various apparitions.

This work essentially, commences with the apparitions occurring at Fatima in 1917 — which was arbitrarily chosen as a starting place primarily because Fatima was the first major apparition to occur in this century.

The 33 headings or categories contained under each separate apparition site were also somewhat arbitrarily chosen. Other headings could be added, some could be deleted or for that matter an entirely different approach could have been used. These categories were chosen primarily because they seemed to require individual recognition at Fatima.

We trust this approach will not be an undue burden for the reader. A time line graph and world map is included at the end of this work. These should permit easy and instant review and comparison of the different apparitions.

For our purposes, an apparition is a manifestation of God, angels or the dead, appearing under a form that surprises the senses. Here we are primarily focused on apparitions of the glorified person of the Blessed Virgin Mary. An authentic apparition is not purely subjective, but is the result of real and objective intervention of a higher power. We do not purport to analyze or establish the authenticity of the apparitions.

Apparitions of Our Blessed Lady during the 20th century have been reported from every continent on our globe. The durations of the apparitions have been from one brief appearance to daily or (almost daily) apparitions for an uninterrupted span of some fourteen years (Medjugorje, Yugoslavia).

Apparitions have been reported occurring during the same time frame in many locations in many countries. Sometimes the apparitions occur in remote areas of the world, other times the apparitions occur in large cities, in public areas, in private homes, forests, fields, caves, at sites of existing shrines, inside chapels and churches, above churches, at convents, at monasteries or other places.

Often the seers are children (or one child). On the other hand, the seers have been adults from many walks of life, including religious, clergy, and one bishop. The reported range of age of those receiving the apparitions has been from mere toddlers to octogenarians.

This work is not intended to be exhaustive, nor could it be, if for no other reason than that some persons, perhaps many, have had apparitions which were never recorded nor revealed. Other apparitions may be privately recorded yet not reported nor revealed.

Additionally, the sheer volume of messages does not permit the full context of all messages to be reported here. Of course many books are available concerning and reporting many of these apparitions.

Neither does this work purport to cover other apparitions, visions, occurrences, locutions, images, dreams, messages and/or messengers from heaven such as:

1. Apparitions of Jesus, saints or angels.
2. Statues of Jesus, Our Lady, the Holy Family or saints which reportedly weep human tears and/or human blood and/or oil.
3. Icons, pictures, images, photographs of Jesus, Our Lady, the Holy Family or saints which reportedly weep human tears and/or tears of blood and/or pure olive oil.
4. Photographs, recordings, motion pictures and/or video tapes which contain images or depictions of Jesus, Our Lady, the Holy Family, saints and/or angels, etc., which images did not manifest to the viewer at the scene when the picture was taken.
5. Images, purportedly of Jesus, Our Lady, the Holy Family, saints and/or angels which appear or are formed in the sky, in churches, or other places, for which there seems to be no natural cause or explanation.
6. Locutions received by anyone, whether on one occasion only, or whether repeated or ongoing.
7. Dreams and/or visions of Jesus, Our Lady, the Holy Family, saints and/or angels whether occurring during sleep or in the waking state or otherwise.
8. Any other phenomena not included in the seven (7) categories above.

Nevertheless a selected group of reported visions and locutions occurring during this century are included in this work.

Most likely some saintly persons - (and some not so saintly) - now living on this planet with us, have had one or more of the above experiences. Perhaps most of us at some point during our lifetime have had, or will have, an experience or vision or dream, which we believe (we just know) is from the other world.

As can be gleaned from the numerous messages reported by the seers, the messages plead that the human family must amend its ways, return to

God, love and forgive one another, and live the life of Jesus, outlined for us during His days on earth.

Some of the messages purport to warn us of imminent dangers, some contain prophecies of future chastisements. Yet these same messages seem to say that these very chastisements can be averted, or at least diminished, if we convert now, pray daily, especially the daily rosary, fast and do penance, go to frequent confession, attend Mass frequently, receive the Eucharist often and consecrate ourselves, our families and our countries to the Sacred Heart of Jesus and the Immaculate Heart of Mary, and observe the devotion of the nine (9) First Fridays and five (5) First Saturdays in reparation for sins committed and for the conversion of all sinners — and to do so from the heart.

The messages assure us that Jesus and Mary always love us, will always love us, will always be with us while we are here on earth and They want each of us to go to heaven and be with Them forever in heaven — and be saved from hell. We have been assured, through the messages, that now is the time for our conversion, that the immense mercy of Jesus is now open and abundantly available to us all.

Physical proof (for those who accept it as such) of various apparitions has been given at various locations, i.e. the 'Dance of the Sun' phenomenon (at Fatima, Portugal) witnessed by many thousands; the Living Spring (at Lourdes, France); the Miraculous Image of Our Lady of Guadalupe (at Mexico City); the Weeping Statue of Our Lady (at Akita, Japan); the Miracle of the Eucharist (at Garabandal, Spain). It has been said: "for those who believe, no proof is necessary, and for those who do not believe, no proof is possible".

The Catholic Church has prudently been cautious to approve, disapprove or condemn reported apparitions. Generally, studied apparitions are classed as "not worthy of belief," "not contrary to the Faith" or "worthy of belief."

Prior to any classification, the local bishop, if deemed appropriate, appoints a committee or commission to take testimony, investigate, study and report its findings to the local bishop. In some such instances the local bishops have accepted the findings and proclaimed and reported that the apparitions cannot be proven to be of supernatural origin, or are not worthy of belief, or that further study is required, or that there is nothing contrary to the Faith in the messages or apparition, or that the messages and apparition are worthy of belief.

This criteria is not covered in this work. Nonetheless, if the message of an apparition is at variance with revealed doctrine or teaching of the Church, this is a clear sign of its non-authenticity. In some instances the Church has prohibited the clergy from going on pilgrimage to these places of apparition.

It is true that the Deposit of Faith consists of Sacred Scripture and

Tradition which closed upon the death of the last Apostle. We are obliged to profess our belief in the Deposit of Faith – public revelation – to which nothing may be added and from which nothing may be removed. The Magisterium faithfully guards and interprets the Deposit of Faith – public revelation. Therefore, from time to time a dogma is later defined which necessarily existed as part of public revelation (our Deposit of Faith) such as, defining the Dogma of the Assumption of the Blessed Virgin Mary.

On the other hand, private revelations — such as apparitions of Our Blessed Virgin Mary — do not become part of the Deposit of Faith. For this reason the Church does not oblige us to believe in private revelations, even when the Church declares them to be authentic.

Though graces and conversions and other fruits may flow from these private revelations the Church does not command the faithful to have an inner assent of faith or to believe in these private apparitions; nevertheless when the Church interdicts (condemns) the apparitions, the faithful are then also bound to disbelieve. In no way could Our Blessed Mother work against revealed doctrine of the Church of Her Son Jesus. We can be certain that Our Blessed Mother is only permitted to appear on this earth and give messages, if She is sent by Jesus, ie God. We can further be certain that Her will necessarily always coincides with the will of God. Therefore, any and all messages which Our Blessed Mother truly gives to a visionary upon this earth are messages from God.

Certain confusions and distractions may arise which require careful and prayerful discernment by the Church; and by each of us. The goal of discernment is to sift out, retain and embrace only those messages truly from God; and to reject and discard all others.

This work does not purport to cover the process the Church employs in discernment; yet that same process is to be our own guide in helping us discern.

There are official Church documents as well as other books, documents and information available to the reader to aid in the process of discernment. But most of all our prayers for discernment are essential.

Reference is made to the booklet 'Mystics, Prophets, and Seers,' by Fr. Felix Bourdier. Another booklet entitled 'The Church and Apparitions, Their Status and Function, Criteria and Reception,' by Father Rene Laurentin, guides one through the steps the Church takes in considering apparitions (discernment). A more recent publication entitled 'A Still, Small, Voice' authored by Father Benedict J. Groeschel, CFR and published by Ignatius Press, is useful as a practical guide for discerning reported apparitions and messages. Broadly, there are certain general categories from which these messages/apparitions may originate:

1) Some messages/apparitions may be totally fabricated by the alleged visionaries, either intentionally or otherwise. These are not accepted by the Church. If these are investigated by the Church they would surely be

condemned. Likewise, we are bound to disbelieve if the Church acts to condemn any messages/apparitions.

(2) Other messages/apparitions are contaminated either because some portions of the messages/apparitions have been exaggerated or fabricated; or because the visionary is under an impediment, be it physical, mental, emotional or spiritual, which renders the messages/apparitions suspect. Of course these cases are the most difficult and also probably constitute the majority of cases investigated by the Church and undoubtedly require intensive discernment in search for the truth. Some of these messages may be found to be authentic and others not truly from God. The Church wisely refrains from making hasty decisions. Again if the Church condemns any of these messages/apparitions we are also bound to disbelieve and discard the same without further ado. On the other hand, when the Church proclaims the messages/apparitions to be worthy of belief, we may, but need not believe in them.

Probably most messages/apparitions in this second category have not been definitively acted upon by the Church. So long as they are not condemned we are free to believe or not to believe, or we need not decide either way. If the Church declares the messages/apparitions genuine and worthy of belief; even though we need not assent in our own belief, we must not berate the messages/apparitions once declared true and valid by the Church.

(3) Sacred Scripture alerts us to 'false prophets' and 'wolves in sheep's clothing'. There have been, and may be in the future, messages/apparitions whose origins began through demonic influences. These, the Church will never embrace and will always strongly condemn. It is our duty and our blessing to follow the Church and discard these without a second thought.

(4) Finally, there are the true appearances by, and messages from, Our Blessed Mother. It is these cases which the Church embraces and treasures as a great reservoir of graces to be distributed to the people. Examples of this category are Lourdes, Fatima and Guadalupe (Mexico City). Once again, though we are not bound to believe, yet we must not disparage these messages/apparitions which the Church has declared authentic. Further it would seem that many graces may be lost if the people do not believe. Praying for discernment would seem to be equally important in cases declared authentic by the Church as in other cases where we pray for help in discerning the truth.

There have been many reported miracles, cures and healings (physical, mental, spiritual) at various apparition sites and at other places, some of which are documented by medical or other evidence.

Needless to say, many people, Christian and non-Christian alike, are interested in these phenomena. Several of the reported apparitions of the Blessed Virgin Mary have been witnessed by Catholics, other Christians, Moslems, Jews and nonbelievers. At some locations, reports of immediate conversions and baptisms occurred, eg, Hrushiv.

In the great majority of apparitions, the seers reportedly received messages from Our Lady, audible to the seers at least. On the other hand, there have been silent apparitions reported at Knock, Ireland; at Zeitun, Egypt; and at Pontmain, France.

Our Lady has appeared in a marvelous and dazzling mode of attire and has announced Herself under a variety of titles and has asked that chapels be built in Her honor. In each case, it seems the seers report that She is indescribably beautiful, that Her voice is certainly from heaven, and that She appears at times happy, sad, or serious. Nevertheless, She is always kind, loving and caring. She is usually reported being 15 to 20 years old, yet announces that She is the Mother of us all.

Our Lady usually arrives surrounded by light which is sometimes preceded by one or more light flashes given as a signal. Often there is definite movement when She arrives and when She departs, although at other times She appears and simply fades away when the apparitions are concluded. At times a sweet fragrance can be detected.

Sometimes, She announces future apparitions in advance and makes predictions of future events and happenings. She announces that She is from heaven.

We all know She was a human being, not a god, yet Her close association with God, with Jesus, and the residents of Paradise naturally capture our interest, our imagination, our love and our hope. We naturally aspire to achieve Her degree of holiness and sanctity so as to share in the reward Jesus promised to all the faithful.

Undoubtedly, some people are interested in the apparitions from a position of curiosity alone; others from a prophetic point of view; still others wish to learn about the messages in order to help their own spiritual life or that of other people. Some may have different reasons yet.

Although this work is aimed at 20th century apparitions of the Blessed Virgin Mary, it really begins during Mary's lifetime since She was reportedly honored by the Apostles and even by the angels during Her own lifetime; witness, for example, the miraculous statue of Our Lady of the Pillar. Even more accurately, this work begins at the Annunciation when Mary Herself received a message from the Angel Gabriel, to whom Mary proclaimed the big *"YES"*. In another sense, the true beginning is when Mary was first conceived ~Immaculately Conceived in the womb of Her earthly mother, Saint Anne ~yes; and even prior to that because Mary was singled out from the Beginning to become the earthly Mother of Jesus Christ, true God and true man.

We are so blessed and so privileged. Amen.

– **Peter Heintz**

CATEGORIES

I Place
II Dates of First and Last Apparition
III Seer(s)
IV Total Number of Apparitions
V Dates and Locality of Each Apparition
VI Description of Our Lady
VII Title(s) of Our Lady
VIII Brief Factual Review
IX The Primary Messages
X Signs Preceding the Apparitions
XI Other Visions During Apparitions
XII Prayers Taught to the Seer(s)
XIII Special Devotion Given to the Seer(s)
XIV Requests Made by Our Lady
XV Specific Bible References
XVI Secrets Given to the Seer(s)
XVII Miracles Promised by Our Lady
XVIII Miracles Performed
XIX Miracles Promised not yet Performed
XX Signs Promised
XXI Signs Given
XXII Predictions/Promises
XXIII Prophecies/Warnings of Chastisement
XXIV Method of Appearance
XXV Method of Departure
XXVI Confrontation w/Civil Authorities
XXVII Confrontation w/Church Authorities
XXVIII Request Chapel/Shrine Built
XXIX Free Will/Choice
XXX Seer(s)' Suffering/Sacrifice
XXXI Healings Reported
XXXII Action Taken by the Church
XXXIII Bibliography

CONTENTS

Section	Dates	Page
Acknowledgments		ii
Dedications		iii
Declaration		iv
Introduction		ix
Fore-Word		xiii
Categories		xix
Table of Contents		xxi
Ode to Mary		xxiv
Rosary		xxv
Feast Days of Our Lady		xxvi
1 Le Pailly, France	1909-1930	1-13
2 Brussels, Belgium	1911-1922	14-21
3 Fatima, Portugal	1917	22-38
4 Portiers, France	1920-1923	39-49
5 Tuy/Pontevedra, Spain	1925-1929	50-56
6 Beauraing, Belgium	1932-1933	57-67
7 Banneux, Belgium	1933	68-75
8 Piotrowicza, Poland	1934-1986	76-84
9 Heede, Germany	1937-1940	85-90
10 Kecskemet, Hungary	1939-1986	91-99
11 Amsterdam, Holland	1945-1959	100-114
12 Zagreb, Yugoslavia	1945-1976	115-121
13 Marienfried, Germany	1946	122-130
14 Tre Fontane, Italy	1947-1980	131-138
15 Montichiari/Fontanelle, Italy	1947-1983	139-150

CONTENTS CON'T

Section		Dates	Page
16	Lipa, Philippines	1948	151-164
17	Consenga, Italy	1950-1961	165-175
18	Rome, Italy	1953-1983	176-183
19	Sabana Grande, Puerto Rico	1953	184-197
20	Fostoria, Oh., USA	1954-1984	198-208
21	Seredne, Ukraine	1954-1955	209-215
22	Budapest, Hungary	1955-1988	216-223
23	Eisenberg, Austria	1955-1982	224-241
24	Turzovka, Czechoslovakia	1958	242-255
25	Garabandal, Spain	1961-1965	256-265
26	Kespest, Hungary	1961-1981	266-274
27	San Damiano, Italy	1964-1970	275-286
28	Porto San Stefano, Italy	1966-1979	287-295
29	Imo State, Nigeria	1972-1989	296-307
30	Akita, Japan	1973	308-319
31	Milan, Italy	1973-present	320-333
32	Binh Loi, Vietnam	1974-1982	334-350
33	Eastern Canada	1974-1987	351-361
34	Betania, Venezuela	1976-present	362-370
35	Le Frechou, France	1977-present	371-377
36	Philadelphia, Pa., USA	1978-present	378-383
37	Cuapa, Nicaragua	1980	384-395
38	El Escorial, Spain	1980-1992	396-403
39	Medjugorje, Yugoslavia	1981-present	404-424
40	Kibeho, Rwanda	1981-1989	425-441
41	Damascus, Syria	1982-1992	442-451

CONTENTS CON'T

Section		Dates	Page
42	San Nicolas, Argentina	1983-1990	452-464
43	Kinshasa, Zaire	1984-1988	465-477
44	Oliveto Citra, Italy	1985-1989	478-490
45	Naju, Korea	1985-1994	491-504
46	Inchigeela, Ireland	1985-1987	505-513
47	Melleray, Ireland	1985	514-522
48	Seven Hills, Oh., USA	1985-present	523-533
49	Undisclosed USA	1987	534-544
50	Hrushiv, Ukraine	1987	545-558
51	Bessbrook, N. Ireland	1987-1988	559-566
52	Ballindaggin, Ireland	1987-1989	567-574
53	Gortnadreha, Ireland	1988-1992	575-585
54	Santa Maria, Ca., USA	1988-present	586-599
55	Cuenca, Ecuador	1988-1990	600-611
56	Agoo, Philippines	1989-1993	612-628
57	Scottsdale, Az., USA	1989-present	629-642
58	Litmanova, Slovakia	1990-present	643-652
59	Hillside, Il., USA	1990-present	653-663
60	Denver/Golden, Co., USA	1991-present	664-673

After-Word		xxxi
Time-Line		xxxiv
Location-Map		xxxvii
Topical Index		xxxix

ODE TO MARY

- Peter Heintz

O Blessed Mary
   Immaculate Virgin
Most holy and pure
   free of all sin

Mother of God
   and all mankind
Loving and gentle
   sweet and kind

Full of grace
   and merciful
Perpetual Help
   and prayerful

Our Lady of Sorrows
   so sorrowful
Soul eternally spotless
   so beautiful

Messenger of God
   our intercessor
Perfect human
   our protector

To save mankind
   reveal Your faces
at Knock, Tre-Fontane
   and other places

At La Salette
   and at Pontmain
At Rue du Bac
   and at Beauraing

Lady of Carmel
   and Guadalupe
Lady of Fatima
   and Medjugorje

Lady of the Rosary
   and of Lourdes' Shrine
Lily of the Valley
   Torch of Love sublime

Cape of Juan Diego
   Song of Bernadette
Miracle at Fatima
   the world dare not forget

Queen of Peace
   and of Heaven above
Queen of Earth
   And Queen of Love

You gave us the grace
   of First Saturday
And specially taught us
   the rosary to pray

Please help us convert
   and help us to pray
To open our hearts
   to do penance each day

To love one another
   and do every good deed
To respond from our hearts
   Your teachings to heed

Draw us ever closer
   to Your Divine Son
That we may become holy
   and our hearts become one

For your are the Handmaid
   of the Lord
You live eternally
   according to His Word

Rosary

- Peter Heintz

Tonic for the heart
   adventure for the soul
Nine and fifty beads a-strung
   a prayer that makes us whole

Dominic was first taught
   the rosary to recite
With love and deep devotion
   steeped in Our Lady's light

Peace and war may alternate
   through time and centuries past
Yet power of the rosary grows
   and will triumph at last

Some learn the beads in early years
   great joy is theirs for life
Others finally pray through tears
   or in a time of strife

Promise made to all mankind
   who persevere each day
Eternal bliss and happiness
   who do the rosary pray

Urgent is Our Mother's plea
   to pray more, one and all
Prepare our hearts on bended knee
   respond to Mary's call

PLEASE PRAY THE ROSARY EVERY DAY!

FEAST DAYS OF THE BLESSED VIRGIN MARY

Every Saturday: throughout the year.
Special Devotion: First Saturday of each month -
{Reparation to the Immaculate Heart of Mary}

January

✝ 1 Solemnity of Mary, Mother of God
{maternity of the Blessed Virgin Mary}
12 Feast of the Holy Family
23 Mary's Wedding

February

★ 2 Purification of the Blessed Virgin Mary
{Presentation of Our Lord}
◆ 11 Feast of Our Lady of Lourdes
20 Our Lady of Tears

March

✝ 25 The Annunciation of the Blessed Virgin Mary
Movable Feast - Feast of the Seven Sorrows of Mary
{Friday before Palm Sunday}

April

26 Mary, Mother of Good Counsel

May {the month of Mary}

8 Mary, Mediatrix of All Graces
13 Our Lady of the Most Blessed Sacrament
13 First Apparition of Our Lady at Fatima
15 Mary, Comfort of the Afflicted
21 Mary, Mother of Light
24 Mary, Help of Christians
24 Mary of the Path
31 Mary, Queen of All Saints
★ 31 Visitation of the Blessed Virgin Mary
31 Our Lady of the Most Holy Mountain

FEAST DAYS OF THE BLESSED VIRGIN MARY

May con't

31 Mary, Mother of Wonderful Love
   Movable Feast - Mary, Queen of the Apostles
       {Saturday during the Octave of Ascension Day}

June

9 Mary, Mother of Grace
27 Our Lady of Perpetual Help
◆ Movable Feast - Feast of the Immaculate Heart of Mary
       {Saturday following the second Sunday after Pentecost}

July

5 Feast of the Seven Joys of Mary
9 Mary, Queen of Peace
9 Mary, Miraculous Mother
13 Feast in honor of Rosa Mystica {The Mystical Rose}
◆ 16 Our Lady of Mt. Carmel {Mary's Scapular Feast Day}
17 Feast of Mary's Humility
   Movable Feast - Mary, Mother of Mercy
       {Saturday before the fourth Sunday in July}

August

2 Mary Queen of the Angels
5 Reported Birth Day of Our Lady {1 of 2}
◆ 5 Dedication of St. Mary Major
5 Feast of Our Lady of Snows
13 Mary, Refuge of Sinners
✝ 15 Assumption of the Blessed Virgin Mary
☉ 22 Queenship of Mary
22 Feast of Our Lady of Beauraing
   Movable Feast - Mary, Health of the Sick
       {Saturday before the last Sunday in August}
   Movable Feast - Feast of Mary, Comfort of the Afflicted
       {Sunday after the Feast of St. Augustine}

FEAST DAYS OF THE BLESSED VIRGIN MARY

September

    3 Mary, Mother of the Good Shepherd
☆   8 Nativity of Our Lady {1 of 2}
  12 The Holy Name of Mary
☉ 15 Our Lady of Sorrows
  24 Our Lady of Ransom
  27 Mary, Protector of Orphans

October {the month of the Holy Rosary}

☉   7 Feast of Our Lady of the Rosary
  11 Feast of the Motherhood of Mary
  12 Our Lady of the Pillar {Saragossa, Spain}
  16 Feast of Mary's Purity
  20 Mary, Wonderful Mother
      Movable Feast - Mary, Mother of the Dying
          {Fourth Sunday in October}

November

    8 Feast of Mary, Our Shelter
☉ 21 Presentation of the Blessed Virgin Mary
  27 Feast of the Miraculous Medal
      Movable feast - Our Lady of All Graces
          {Saturday after All Saints day}
      Movable Feast - Mary Mother of Divine Providence
          {Saturday before third Sunday in November}

December

✝   8 The Immaculate Conception
  10 Our Lady of Loreto
☆ 12 Our Lady of Guadalupe
  18 The Expectation of the Blessed Virgin Mary

- ✝ **Solemnity** - The highest liturgical rank of a feast in the ecclesiastical calendar. Of the 14 solemnities, four are dedicated to the Blessed Virgin Mary.
- ★ **Feast** - Days set apart by the Church to give special honor to God, the Savior, angels, saints, sacred mysteries and events.
- ☼ **Memorial** - Festivals of the third order liturgical rank in the ecclesiastical calendar.
- ◆ **Optional** - Festivals which are fourth in the order of dignity and are non-prescribed memorials.

Chapter 1

LE PAILLY, FRANCE
(1909 - 1930)

I Place - Le Pailly, France

II Dates of First and Last Apparition

First: September 9, 1909
Last: September 8, 1930

III Seer(s) - 1

Name: Father Pere Lamy (John Edward Lamy),
            (Oblates of St. Francis de Sales)
Birth: June 23, 1853
Age at first apparition: 56
Status: Deceased - December 1, 1931

IV Total Number of Apparitions - 6

V Dates and Locality of Each Apparition

1909: September 9th in the Chapel at Gray
1912: May 18th inside St. Lucian Church at La Courneuve
1914: Inside the Chapel of Our Lady of the Woodlands, (Boise Guyotte)
1915: February inside the Chapel of Our Lady of the Woodlands, (Boise Guyotte)
1920: October in St. Michael des Batignolles Church in Paris
1930: September 8th inside the chapel at Notre Dame de Chambourg

VI Description of Our Lady

At Gray (September 9, 1909) the Blessed Virgin Mary descended from the ceiling to the altar during Holy Mass. Her hands were joined and She was throned in Her Great Glory (surrounded by a brilliant furnace of light). Her Glory penetrated everything gradually - the candles, the chalice, the altar vestments, and the seer. Our Lady was dressed in a deep blue gown with a white veil and sleeves gathered at the wrists. Her eyes were periwinkle, that is not brown and not altogether blue. Her ears were visible as was the start of Her hair on Her forehead. She was in bare feet and stood upright never touching the floor. Her demeanor was very simple and She looked the seer straight in the face.

On Her dress, near Her Heart, was a rosary, with beads of white pearl, with the Pater and Ave, all arranged heart-shaped. (Pere understood this to signify that the rosary was close to Our Lady's Heart.)

When Our Blessed Lady spoke as a Mother, She spoke tenderly and kindly. It was then that She wore a crown made of sprays of flowers. But, on the other hand, when Our Lady condemned modernism She wore a regal crown of matchless beauty. This crown was made of clusters of jewels and light all harmoniously arranged with sparkling lights inset between the stones. Our Lady wears this crown when She speaks as a Sovereign Lady.

VII Title(s) of Our Lady - 1

On September 9, 1909 at Gray, Our Lady said: *"I am the Mother of God."*

VIII Brief Factual Review

John Edward Lamy was born on June 23, 1853 at Le Pailly, France, a village in the Langres Diocese situated in east-central France. He was baptized the following day. His parents John and Mary were devout Catholics, the father worked his own land and also did masonry work. It is reported that John's (Pere) grandmother used to hide outlawed priests during the Napoleonic persecutions.

Pere was an altar boy and used to serve Mass for Msgr. Darboy, Archbishop of Paris, who was later shot by the communists. Le Pailly was an idyllic community when Pere grew up. Many pious souls helping each other and giving respect and assistance to their priests. Pere was always very prayerful during these years. The people at that time traveled often by foot - Pere himself traveled to Gray to attend Mass some 28 miles from Le Pailly.

Pere felt his vocation to become a priest the day of his First Communion. His parents had set aside money for the seminary—but a terrible fire ruined the family home. They had to start over and Pere had to defer his priesthood studies.

He was taken to serve a term in the military. It was during this term in the military that Our Lady gave him a miraculous and instant cure of an advanced state of eczema at Gray. He promised Our Lady to visit Gray as often as he could. It was also while he was in the military service that an exploding rifle shot caused him to lose the sight of one eye.

After his military service he again pressed to become a priest. Finally the Oblates of St. Francis de Sales promised him a priesthood if he would sign a 15 year engagement. This he did which led him to his first assignment as head of the youth movement at Troyes. Here he stayed for 14 years, while studying for the priesthood. Once while he was deep in his studies, he felt that he would never become a priest. He despaired and was going to give up. It was then that St. Joseph appeared to him in the Chapel at Troyes and spoke: *"Be a priest, be a good priest."* Pere was ordained a priest on December 12, 1886.

In 1892 he became Curate of St. Ouen. Then in 1900 he became the parish priest at La Courneuve, where he remained some 20 plus years. He retired in 1923 to the rest home Marie-Therese in Paris and died on December 1, 1931 at Jouy-en-Josas.

Many priests and higher ranking clerics chose Pere as their personal confessor. He was a holy man and a devoted priest and pastor for his flock.

During his lifetime, Pere had apparitions of Jesus, Our Blessed Mother, St. Joseph, the Holy Family, many saints and multitudes of angels, including his own guardian angel and Angel Gabriel, and also of the devil.

Pere was a true mystic who received numerous and miraculous signs and visions, not the least of which was the vision of the Mystical Lamb. It is reported by testimonies that Pere bilocated on many occasions. He was given to speak prophecy, and predicted both World War I and World War II. He was also given secrets. Many miracles were attributed to Pere.

It is reported that more than 2500 miracles are set down in the Golden Book at Our Lady of the Woodlands Shrine attributed to Our Blessed Mother through Pere. When asked about miraculous cures he simply says: "The Blessed Virgin works the cures. She does it. I pray. I pray to Her that the cure may not happen in the chapel on the spot (but later). . . but She would prefer to work a miracle on a soul."

It was reported that Pere could **"smell sin"** in the confessional, even above any perfume being worn.

Our Blessed Mother commissioned him to found Our Lady of the Woodlands Society. She told him of the hard times that would fall on that Society during his lifetime. All came to pass as Our Lady had said. In

1930 that Society known as the Congregation of the Servants of Jesus and Mary was officially established, the Rule was approved by the Church, and it has grown and thrives to this day. Pere loved to pray the rosary. He said that Our Blessed Mother is filled with mercy. Once She said: *"If in God's wrath, He should smash the world, I would bring Him all the pieces."*

It is said that he lived his life for Our Blessed Mother. It is also reported that Pere became radiant when he spoke of the Majesty of Jesus or of the Holy Priesthood. He always said he wanted to die owning no money or goods. This did happen, for when he died he had only money collected that day for Masses to be said the next day. His books of account were always open for all to inspect. Our Blessed Lady had shown him the room in which he would die (in a vision). When he first entered that room after his retirement he immediately recognized it.

Now we may review the apparitions of Our Blessed Virgin Mary. But first Pere did admit that Our Lady appeared to him when he was 10-11, around the time of his First Holy Communion. Once someone asked Pere how he saw the Blessed Virgin and he answered: "I see Her as I see you."

(1) The first reported apparition of Our Lady occurred on September 9, 1909. Pere had traveled to Gray, as he did nearly every year since Our Blessed Mother cured him. This time he was accompanied by the parish priest of Violot. Abbe Lemoine was on the kneeler as Pere began the Mass. Suddenly Our Blessed Mother appeared descending from the ceiling. She was followed by Lucifer. During the descent Our Lady said: *"Is that you?"* And the Devil responded: *"I have leave from the Father."* Then Our Lady: *"So be it. You know how to obey the Father."* The parish priest was so overcome he put his hands over his face and his face into his book. Pere was so startled that he said to himself. "If you are the Blessed Virgin show me." It was then that Our Lady said: *"I am the Mother of God"*—and Pere believed Her. The Mass server asked Pere "Is it the Blessed Virgin, Father?" Pere responded: "Don't talk you will make Her go away." As the server carried the Book from the Epistle side to the Gospel side, Our Blessed Mother looked at him with motherly tenderness, and then She stayed aside so he could pass as he carried the book. Then She took Her place again in the middle of the altar. During certain parts of the Mass, Pere bowed to Our Lady and She returned the bow. Even so he became so upset that he made a mistake when he muddled the Credo. Our Lady took over and finished the Credo for him. Pere later remarked: "She knows Her prayers well." At the Memento (Prayers of the Faithful), when Pere was concluding, Our Lady urged him to ask for more: *"There is a great store, and still greater to be given."*

Our Blessed Mother had candid style conversation with the devil which Pere overheard. Some of these words referred to Pere himself. Our Blessed Mother said: *"He would like very much for Me to cure him, but I will not cure him, it will keep him humble."* This Our Blessed Mother said referring to Pere's blindness and while looking at his glasses lying on the altar. Our Blessed Mother asked for penance, for conversion and for a return to God, for holiness in family life and for prayer. She strongly condemned modernism and predicted World War I in very sorrowful tones. She said about five millions will be killed. Pere was shown a vision of how the war was to start and was also shown the countries to be involved. He said he thought he saw Belgrade.

Pere was also given a vision of how and where he was to set up Our Lady of Woodlands sanctuary.

Our Lady reminded Pere to do what is laid down to obtain the Sabbatine Privilege. Pere later said: "She is very strict to respect the Pope's orders."

Our Lady said to Pere: *"While I am on earth, ask Me all that you will, I will grant it."* To this Lucifer broke in: *"Suppose he asks you for infused knowledge?"* And Our Lady: *"I can give it to him, but he does not ask it."* Then, Lucifer: *"If he asks for wealth, honor."* Our Lady: *"He does not."* Lucifer: *"The gift of miracles."* Our Lady: *"He does not."*

Of some interest it is reported that as Lucifer was accusing Pere of some sin while addressing Our Lady, She answered Lucifer: *"That is a very small sin, it is human weakness."* Contrariwise Our Blessed Mother does not excuse the sin of pride. Nothing comes from us, everything has been given us by God. We can take absolutely no credit for our very existence, nor our talents, nor our family, nor our situation in life, including graces received. These are all granted to us freely by God.

Then Our Lady spoke of Pere's death, reviewed the meaning of events which occurred in his life and told him She would assist Pere at his death. Then incredibly Our Lady said to the fiend: *"Now that we have no more business here let us go."* The devil left first, then Our Lady disappeared.

Pere was later to say: "The fiend is behind the Mother of God. If you let Her go by, you find the fiend."

The bishop of Langres was astounded upon hearing the familiar dialogue between Our Blessed Mother and the devil, but Pere responded: "She speaks as She chooses. She is not high-falutin." She told me, (Pere, that is): *"I am coming into the family circle."*

Finally it is reported that Jesus appeared at the Consecration of the Mass and simply said to Pere: *"A year from now."* As it happened Jesus did again appear to Pere one year later while Pere was saying Mass at this same chapel.

(2) On May 18, 1912 the Blessed Virgin appeared to Pere at La Courneuve inside St. Lucian, the parish church, of which Pere was pastor.

It was 5 AM, the inside of the church was dirty, and Pere had decided to clean it. He donned a patched blue apron which tied around the waist. He was on the floor on all fours in the process of picking up some discarded paper and had decided to lean against the small harmonium to say one Hail Mary.

Just then the archangel appeared and announced: *"Look out, you are going to pray before the Virgin Mary."* When Pere looked there was the Blessed Virgin Mary, with St. Lucian accompanied by more saints and some sixty angels. They surrounded Pere who remained on his knees. He was so embarrassed at his attire and condition of the Church that he "wanted to sink into the floor." Later he said that if he had started an hour earlier Our Lady would not have seen the mess and confusion. Now he tried to untie his blue apron but the more he tried the tighter it got. He later explained: "There is a kind of magnetism where She is." Our Blessed Mother kindly glanced at the untidy places in the Church but made no remarks. She said to the saints around Her: *"—but he minds too much."* She wanted to show Pere that She did not mind seeing him in this situation. Pere later remarked: "The Blessed Virgin is an extremely good housekeeper, She is not stingy but likes things well done. She is very gracious. She makes no remarks."

Our Blessed Mother said to the saints (overheard by Pere): *"When you were judged, I gave you all that a certain person could have, or could earn, of merits."* The saints replied: *"We are very grateful."* The conversation went on about other intimate matters. Then Our Lady said: *"Yes I will give him a great deal."*

Before She left, Our Blessed Mother recounted out loud, what a certain lady (now deceased) had donated to the Church including the choir candlesticks and payment for the crown on a statue of Our Lady. Pere noticed the demon was in the corner watching Our Lady, when She said to the demon: *"You shall give Me up that soul."* The enraged demon responded: *"I shall have to."*

Our Lady appeared to Pere on other occasions while at La Courneuve. It was usually at times when Pere felt exhausted: "I can no more." When She appeared on these occasions She reminded him that: *"I am always with you—I am always in the gap."* These visits gave the old priest renewed strength.

When Pere was once asked how he could sense Our Blessed Lady, he responded: "Oh, Her presence is easily felt. She is to the soul what perfume is to the body."

(3) Our Lady appeared to Pere in the chapel at Our Lady of the Woodlands on at least two reported occasions. Once in 1914 and once again in February 1915. There were probably more appearances at this favorite shrine of Our Blessed Mother.

The first time they were ringing for a Baptism, Our Blessed Mother appeared in the vestibule behind Her own statue.

The other appearance was during the First World War, February 1915. Pere had a small crown, which was given to him, and which he was attempting to place on Our Lady's statue but the globe on the statue was too short thus preventing the crown from fitting. Pere asked Our Lady for help and She responded. The globe was drawn out so that the crown fit perfectly. As Pere dusted the statue he felt he was touching a human face, She was smiling! She said a few words and departed.

(4) In October 1920 Our Blessed Mother appeared to Pere in the Church of St. Michael de Batignolles in Paris. The Church was in the construction stage, not yet finished. Pere had come to Vespers for a Novena to St. Michael, after which the parish priest showed Pere around the church. The priest showed Pere a statue of the Virgin and Child done by a well known artist. The statue showed the Blessed Virgin with Her robe open at the neck, the Child was quite naked, and She was holding the Child with a piece of cloth.

Just then Our Blessed Mother appeared to Pere and said: *"Take care, Lucifer is after you like a dog tracking down a hare."* She signified Her own displeasure with the statue, however, when Pere was about to speak condescendingly about the statue, She asked him to be very careful with his words. Pere then said: "The statue did not answer the great dignity of the Mother of God and the statue did not please me." (Please Pere that is).

(5) On September 8, 1930 the Blessed Virgin appeared to Pere in the chapel of the convent of Notre Dame de Chambourg. Disappointing events were occurring in Pere's life, the greater number of novices in the Society had left, his own health was worsening and barriers appeared between Pere and his superior. He was to leave the convent.

Our Blessed Mother appeared early in the morning before Mass and said: *"Stay here."* She was wearing a white veil but Her face was sad. She said: *"Don't worry."* Then She told Pere that the troubles were not at an end for the Society, that as long as Pere was alive the Community shall be in misfortune, but afterwards things will get better. Our Blessed Lady said: *"I will intervene".*

In response to this light and guidance received, Pere released the novices and postulants in early 1931. The Archangel Gabriel and Pere's own guardian angel, appeared to him and told him to bow to the storm. Pere was obedient and did that. Our Lady answered Pere that She wanted the Congregation—and it has survived and flourished. Today the Society of Jesus and Mary is strong in many countries around the world.

IX The Primary Messages - 4

(1) **Rosary** - September 9, 1909 (Apparition at Gray). Our Lady appeared with a pearl rosary heart-shaped on Her breast. Up above the rosary there was a little open wound in the region of the Heart. From this opening rushed a red flame and a green flame which rose and fell as Our Blessed Mother breathed. Pere was led to understand from Our Blessed Mother that the rosary is a symbol of Faith, the red flame of Charity and

the green flame of Hope. Then Pere was led to understand that prayer in unison with the Blessed Virgin has great power over the Heart of God.

Also during this same apparition Our Lady said: *"When you meditate on the Passion, I give almost as much as to the saints in heaven."*

Pere himself was immersed in perpetual recitation of the rosary. Pere relates that the recitation of the holy rosary is what knocks Lucifer flat — and Lucifer is the sworn enemy of the rosary.

(2) Prayer - Our Blessed Mother urged prayer when She appeared in 1909 at Gray and when She predicted the outbreak of World War I. Pere preached this warning and urged prayer and conversion, but no one listened to him. Our Lady said: *"I hear the lowly and trusting prayer of the little one."*

(3) Conversion / Penance - On September 9, 1909 Our Blessed Mother asked for penance, for conversion, return to God, and for holiness in family life. She asks us to give up disorder and go back to orderly lives and then all will be restored. *"God does not demand more for forgiveness."*

(4) Modernism - Although the report is brief, Our Blessed Mother did specifically condemn modernism during the apparition at Gray on September 9, 1909.

(**Note:** It may be remembered that Our Holy Popes have also condemned modernism and have spelled out this pernicious threat in greater detail.)

X Signs Preceding the Apparitions

Our Blessed Mother is preceded by and enveloped in a great furnace of light, which is Her Glory.

XI Other Visions During Apparitions

(1) Jesus appeared during Our Lady's apparition at Gray on September 9, 1909. Jesus also appeared to Pere at other times including one occasion while Pere was saying the Mass. Jesus appeared and allowed Pere to place his hands with the Consecrated Host onto the breast of Jesus. Pere later remarked, about the gown Jesus was wearing: "It is good cloth, fine thick wool."

(2) The Archangels Raphael and Gabriel appeared to Pere.

(3) St. Lucian appeared with Our Lady at La Courneuve in St. Lucian's Church.

(4) Some sixty angels appeared with Our Lady at La Courneuve. Angels also appeared to Pere at other times. He even heard the angels sing.

(5) Pere's guardian angel appeared too and conversed with him on more than one occasion.

(6) St. Joseph appeared to Pere and told him to *"be a good priest."*

(7) Lucifer appeared at Gray during Our Lady's apparition and also at La Courneuve.
(8) Our Lady showed Pere Her Immaculate Heart at Gray.
(9) In addition to these apparitions Pere was also shown many visions including the vision of the Mystical Lamb.

XII Prayers Taught to the Seer(s) - Not Reported

XIII Special Devotion Given to the Seer(s)

(1) **Sabbatine Privilege** - Although Our Lady did not give this Special Devotion to Pere, She nonetheless reminded him of its importance and told Pere: *"You must do what is laid down."*
(2) **Congregation of the Servants of Jesus and Mary** - At Gray on September 9, 1909 Our Lady requested that Pere found the Sanctuary of Our Lady of the Woodlands. She showed him a vision of the woods and the place of the Sanctuary. It came to pass as She showed him. She also told Pere to start the Society of the Congregation of the Servants of Jesus and Mary. She told Pere that the Society would fall on hard times during his lifetime but would later flourish. The Congregation of the Servants of Jesus and Mary was established in 1931 and has thrived and is doing well today.

XIV Requests Made by Our Lady

(1) During the apparition at Gray, Our Lady requested that Pere ask for more graces and blessings from Our Lord, because: *"There is a great store, and still greater to be given."*
(2) Our Lady requested that Pere found Our Lady of the Woodlands Sanctuary—this was done successfully.
(3) Our Lady requested that Pere establish the Congregation of the Servants of Jesus and Mary. This was established in 1931 and thrives to this day.

XV Specific Bible References - Not Reported

XVI Secrets Given to the Seer(s)

It is reported that Our Lady gave secrets to Pere. She forbade him to speak about them except to *"a few pious souls."*

XVII Miracles Promised by Our Lady - NR

XVIII Miracles Performed

(1) Pere was instantly and miraculously cured of eczema at Gray.
(2) The globe on a statue of Our Lady was miraculously stretched so that the crown, which Pere obtained, would fit onto the statue.
(3) Some 2,500 miracles are attributed to Our Lady worked through Pere, all written up in the Golden Book at Our Lady of the Woodlands Shrine.

XIX Miracles Promised not yet Performed - NR

XX Signs Promised

Our Lady always appeared bare footed to Pere. On one occasion (at Gray) when She said She would not cure his eye problem—Pere said to Our Lady: "I wish I had lovely feet like those." Our Lady responded: *"You will."*

Sure enough and true to Her word—upon Pere's death when they laid him out to make everything ready—they were surprised to see that the feet on Pere's body were small and lovely, just like Our Lady's.

XXI Signs Given

(1) **Mystical Lamb** - When Pere was only 10 years old while minding his parents cows, there appeared to him the Mystical Lamb. Pere describes the incident by saying the whole hill was lighted up. The lamb was standing up, holding in his left foot the standard cross bent towards Chalindrey, with a white pennant floating from it. The Lamb's head was turned toward Le Pailly. The eyes of the Lamb were clearly visible although the vision was some two miles away.

(2) **World War I** - When Our Blessed Mother predicted this war, Pere was also shown a vision: a sign of the different countries to be involved in the War.

(3) **Sanctuary of Our Lady of the Woodlands** - Again during the apparition at Gray, Our Lady showed Pere, in great detail, the woods and the house where She wanted Our Lady of the Woodlands to be set up. Pere did take Our Lady's statue and did set up Our Lady of the Woodlands Shrine as he saw in the vision.

(4) **Luminous Statue** - Our Lady also showed Pere a statue of Our Lady in a shop and which Pere was to purchase and take on pilgrimage and set it up in the Woodlands. In 1912 Pere spotted this statue in a shop in the Red Cross Square. The statue was ugly and was displayed with other more beautiful statues of Our Lady. He wanted to choose the nicer one, but

decided to ask the shopkeeper to show him the 'ugly' one. When the shopkeeper handed the statue to Pere, the statue suddenly became luminous and radiant. After some hesitation the shopkeeper did sell the statue to Pere. He kept it at his residence until he took it on pilgrimage to the Woodlands on April 18, 1914 as Our Lady had requested. It became luminous at other times and also changed to become 'nice looking.'

(5) **Pilgrimage to the Woodlands** - In the early days of April 1914 Pere heard the angels saying: *"He is going to carry the statue of Our Queen to the Woodlands. We must get him a fine day."* This they did. When Pere placed the statue in the Shrine of Our Lady of the Woodlands, it again became luminous.

Also at that very moment Pere saw a procession of saints from the neighboring villages. He knew many of them. There were men, women and children. His own parents and grandparents were in the procession. The saints were three or four yards above the ground, each was barefoot and they walked along without disturbing the trees or any of the branches. The women in black, the virgins in white and the men in brown. The children were also in white. Our Lady also appeared and Her Glory went right through the saints, although each saint had their own lesser glory. While this was going on Pere was saying the rosary. When finished Pere stopped atop a rock and blessed France with Our Lady's statue. Just then the saints were gone as was Our Lady and the statue was no longer luminous.

(6) **Sacred Scripture** - The Book was often seen by Pere surrounded by light.

(7) **Lovely Small Feet** - Pere's feet were terribly disfigured from service in the Army. Our Lady always appeared barefoot to him. Once he said: "I wish I had lovely feet like those." Our Lady said: *"You will."* His feet changed to become small lovely feet with no disfigurement of any kind and all the corns disappeared instantly. This was well known amongst all those close to him. When they laid him out upon his death they examined his feet and confirmed this fact.

(8) **Statue Weeps** - The statue of Our Lady in the Chapel at Chambourg, wept tears in the presence of Pere and several postulants.

XXII Predictions/Promises

(1) Our Lady predicted World War I and predicted that it would set all Europe on fire and there would be about 5 million killed.

(2) Our Lady also predicted that the Germans would not advance to Le Pailly. It happened as predicted.

(3) Our Lady promised to give Pere *"a great deal"*. This She surely did. She also told Pere, however, that his last days would be full of pain. This also came true as predicted. She told Pere that the Congregation of the Servants of Jesus and Mary would have troubles before Pere's

death but would later thrive. This also came true as predicted.
(4) Our Lady predicted World War II (as did Jesus to Pere). The War will begin in Poland and *"When it is over you will not be on velvet."* China and Japan would become involved in the war, which will be universal. It will start in 1939. Our Lady spoke very sorrowful when She said these things. At Gray She also showed Pere visions of countries and places that would be affected by these wars.

XXIII Prophecies/Warnings of Chastisement

Our Blessed Mother foretold the First World War and the Second World War. She warned that these wars would occur unless people did penance, converted and returned to God, and placed holiness in family life. Pere faithfully preached the message, but he complained no one would listen. Instead the people complained because his homilies always included this warning and plea to follow Our Lady's request. Only after the war started did people say "If we had only known."

XXIV Method of Appearance

Pere describes a great light surrounding Our Lady as She appears (Her Glory).

XXV Method of Departure - Not Reported
XXVI Confrontation w/Civil Authorities - NR
XXVII Confrontation w/Church Authorities - NR

XXVIII Request Chapel/Shrine Built

Our Lady requested that Pere establish the Shrine of Our Lady of the Woodlands. This was done.

XXIX Free Will/Choice - Not Reported

XXX Seer(s)' Suffering/Sacrifice

(1) Pere suffered much from skin eczema, though he was later cured by Our Lady.
(2) Likewise, he suffered due to loss of sight in one eye and later from declining eyesight.
(3) He struggled and sacrificed financially, never having sufficient funds and always relying on donations to survive.

Le Pailly, France

(4) His greatest suffering may have been the extensive problems presented to him upon establishing the Congregation of the Servants of Jesus and Mary. Most of the Postulants left, some of them betraying Pere and creating much ill will and causing people to despise Pere.

XXXI Healings Reported

(1) Pere himself was cured of painful eczema by Our Lady.
(2) He was also cured of badly disfigured feet by Our Lady.
(3) More than 2,500 miraculous cures are recorded in the Golden Book at the Shrine of Our Lady of the Woodlands. Some people used the water, others the statue of Our Lady or made novenas to Our Lady.
(4) One report of January 16, 1924 lists an interesting case of a girl aged 18-19. She drank of the water and asked that her front teeth be given to her. She had lost them all. Her top front teeth began to grow back and she eagerly reported this to Pere. He remarked: "What good are those teeth to you. You cannot eat, go back and ask the Blessed Virgin for the lower teeth." The girl went back and the lower teeth also began to grow back.

XXXII Action Taken by the Church - NR

XXXIII Bibliography

Pere Lamy 1973
By: Comte Paul Biver
Published by: Tan Books & Publishers

Chapter 2

BRUSSELS, BELGIUM
(1911—1922)

I Place - Brussels, Belgium

II Dates of First and Last Apparition

First: September 17, 1911
Last: In the year 1922

III Seer(s) - 1

Name: Berthe Petit
Birth: January 23, 1870
Age at first apparition: 41
Status: Deceased - March 26, 1943

IV Total Number of Apparitions - 4

V Dates and Locality of Each Apparition

1911: September 17th, Brussels, Belgium
1911: March 24/25, Brussels, Belgium
1912: Brussels, Belgium
1922: Brussels, Belgium

VI Description of Our Lady

On September 17, 1911 Our Lady appeared to Berthe showing Our Lady's forehead pierced and bleeding, with Her hands and Heart transfixed. Our Lady said: *"You have the understanding of the sorrows that My Heart endured, of the sufferings of all My being for the salvation of the world."*

VII Title(s) of Our Lady - 2

On March 24/25, 1911 Our Lady said: *"I am called The Immaculate Conception. With you, I call Myself the Mother of the Sorrowful Heart."*

VIII Brief Factual Review

Belgium is located on the Western Coast of Europe, adjacent to France, Germany, Luxembourg and Holland. Brussels is the capital of Belgium.

Berthe Petit was born January 23, 1870 at Enghien, Belgium. She was the third daughter to a Catholic family. She was well educated for her day, spending 1886-1887 (the last 2 years of her schooling) as a resident in a convent school at Olliguies (Hainaut). Soon after leaving the convent school, Berthe's father suffered financial reverses. Although Berthe had asked Our Lord for a religious vocation at the time of her First Holy Communion, she was now needed to work in order to help support the family.

Her first vision of Our Lady occurred when she was but four years old. Her first vision of Jesus was sometime later in the convent chapel, when the tabernacle opened and the Child Jesus came out to her. He made the sign of the cross on her forehead and said: *"You will suffer always, but I shall be with you."* She suffered much during her lifetime as predicted by Jesus. She was given the last rites of the Church seven times. When she was 10 she received her First Holy Communion directly from Jesus. It was at this time she asked Jesus for a religious vocation—later when her confessor told her she must work and forego the religious vocation—she requested of Our Lady that one priestly vocation would be permitted in place of her own vocation. This request was granted and later Berthe was given the knowledge of this priest's identity and met this priest, who in fact provided great assistance to her and became her spiritual advisor. This priest was Father Louis Decorsant.

It was while attending Fr. Decorsant's Midnight Mass on Christmas 1909 that she saw the wounded Heart of Jesus closely united to the Heart of Mary, pierced with a sword. At the same time she heard these words: *"Cause My Mother's Heart, transfixed by sorrows that rent Mine, to be loved."* This was to be Berthe's special calling and mission.

This vision and message was repeated on December 31, 1909 and again on January 30, 1910. On February 7, 1910 Berthe saw the hearts of Jesus and Mary *"interpenetrating"* one another, partly fused together. Hovering over the two Hearts was a Dove, symbol of the Holy Spirit. Our Lord told Berthe *"to spread love and My Mother's Heart so wholly united with Mine."* Her visions increased in frequency. Jesus told Berthe *"the world must be dedicated to the Sorrowful and Immaculate Heart of My Mother, as it is dedicated to Mine."* Later Our Lord guided Berthe in drawing a picture of the Sorrowful and Immaculate Heart of Mary, and instructed the invocation *"Sorrowful and Immaculate Heart of Mary, pray for us,"* be added.

On September 17, 1911 Our Lady instructed Berthe on this devotion and said: *"You have the understanding of the sorrows that My Heart endured, of the sufferings of all My being for the salvation of the world."*

At Holy Hour on March 24th Our Lady said *"I am called the Immaculate Conception. With you, I call Myself the Mother of the Sorrowful Heart; this title, that My Son wants is the dearest to Me of all My titles and it is through it that shall be granted and spread everywhere graces of mercy, of conversion, and of salvation."* During this vision Our Lady miraculously healed Berthe of a serious condition of an ulcer on her foot accompanied by periostitis. Our Lady told Bertha that a torrent of grace was ready to spring from Her wounded heart. Our Lord told Berthe *"it is in co-redemption that My Mother was above all great; that is why I ask that the invocation, as I have inspired it, should be approved and diffused throughout the whole Church . . . by consecration to the Sorrowful and Immaculate Heart of My Mother, the Church shall be uplifted and the world renewed."* None of the Popes ever approved the consecration, although indulgences were granted for reciting the invocation. Cardinal Mercier of Belgium and Cardinal Bourne of England did accept the new devotion and did consecrate their countries. The new devotion has never been condemned by the Church on doctrinal grounds.

July 12, 1912 marked the beginning of another phase of Berthe's mystical life. From that date forward she received not only religious messages, but also messages and revelations concerning political matters and world events. The first revelation of July 12, 1912 occurred during Holy Communion. Our Lord told the mystic that the heir to the Catholic Empire of Austria/Hungary would be assassinated; a double murder. This came to pass when Archduke Ferdinand was killed, which triggered World War I. Berthe spent the years of World War I in Switzerland. She constantly predicted various events occurring during the war. In 1918 Our Lord told Berthe that without Our Lord's intervention obtained by Cardinal Bourne's consecration of England to the Sorrowful and Immaculate Heart of Mary, the victory would have belonged to the other side: *". . . material force would have prevailed over justice".*

Brussels, Belgium

Commencing with Armistice Day, Berthe received messages from Our Lord during the years between World War I and II.

In 1919 she received this message: *"It will soon become apparent how unstable is a peace set up without Me and without the intervention of him who speaks in My name, the Pope. The nation which is thought to be conquered, but whose strength is only temporarily diminished, remains a threat to your nation and to France. Trouble and danger will spread to all countries. It is because this peace is none of Mine that wars will blaze up again everywhere: civil wars, racial wars, what should have been so great, so true, so beautiful, so durable, is delayed . . . Humanity is rushing toward a dreadful storm, which will divide the nations more and more. All human plans will be annihilated, the pride of the Lords of the moment will be broken. It will be clearly shown that nothing can subsist without Me and that I remain the sole master of the destiny of nations."*

While in Switzerland, Berthe was received into the Third Order of St. Francis. In addition to physical suffering, Berthe also received the invisible Stigmata. She was physically attacked by the devil. She did not eat during the last 35 years of her life, except for the reception of the Holy Eucharist. She was frequently in touch with souls in purgatory, especially the souls of priests.

As World War II approached Berthe received more messages. During the conduct of World War II Berthe again received messages which predicted events, which did in fact occur.

In 1941 Our Lord said: *"By confident consecration to My Mother, the devotion to My Heart will be strengthened and, as it were, completed."*

On April 25, 1942 Our Lord gave Berthe this message: *"A frightful torment is in preparation. It will be seen that the forces launched in such fury, will soon be let loose. It is now or never, the moment for all of you to give yourselves to the Sorrowful Heart of My Mother. By Her acceptance of Calvary, My Mother has participated in all My sufferings. Devotion to Her Heart united to Mine will bring peace, that true peace so often implored and yet so little merited."*

The picture of Our Lady of Olliguies, with the invocation indulged by Cardinal Mercier: *"Sorrowful and Immaculate Heart of Mary, pray for us who have recourse to you"* became widely spread by Berthe and her friends. After Berthe's death the spread of this devotion was carried on by her friend Miss A. de V----.

Towards the end of Berthe's life she experienced spiritual desolation, the dark night of the soul. On March 25, 1943 she said with a smile, *"it will be done,"* in speaking of the consecration of the world to the Sorrowful and Immaculate Heart of Mary. Although the consecration requested by Our Lord has not been accomplished, the devotion to the Sorrowful and Immaculate Heart of Mary is spreading.

IX The Primary Messages - 1

The primary message is devotion to the Sorrowful and Immaculate Heart of Mary.

X Signs Preceding the Apparitions - Not Reported

XI Other Visions During Apparitions

Jesus appeared and spoke to Berthe. She also had visions and locutions from Jesus.

XII Prayers Taught to the Seer(s)

Jesus instructed Berthe to affix this invocation to the picture of Our Lady: *"Sorrowful and Immaculate Heart of Mary, pray for us."*

XIII Special Devotion Given to the Seer(s)

Consecration of the world, and devotion to, the Sorrowful and Immaculate Heart of Mary.

XIV Requests Made by Our Lady

Spread devotion to the Sorrowful and Immaculate Heart of Mary and request the consecration of the world to the Sorrowful and Immaculate Heart of Mary.

XV Specific Bible References - Not Reported

XVI Secrets Given to the Seer(s)

Jesus gave Berthe many revelations which came true as predicted.

XVII Miracles Promised by Our Lady - NR

XVIII Miracles Performed

On the night of March 24-25, 1911, Our Lady healed Berthe instantly of an ulcer on her foot. During the night compresses of Lourdes water were applied to her foot. Our Lady comforted and reassured Berthe during Holy Hour, and as Our Lady departed She blessed Berthe. At that instant Berthe's ulcer was healed.

XIX Miracles Promised not yet Performed - NR
XX Signs Promised - Not Reported

XXI Signs Given

Berthe received the invisible Stigmata.

XXII Predictions/Promises

(1) In 1922 Our Lady assured Berthe with these words: *"Events have taken place, acts have been accomplished which will prove to be the unassailable foundations of work which you serve. It will attain its end with the full amplitude which is God's will."*

(2) In 1919 Our Lord told Berthe: *"It will soon become apparent how unstable is a peace set up without Me . . . Trouble and danger will spread to all countries. It is because this peace is none of Mine that wars will blaze up again everywhere: civil wars, racial wars . . . Humanity is rushing toward a dreadful storm, which will divide the nations more and more. All human plans will be annihilated, the pride of the Lords of the moment will be broken."*

XXIII Prophecies/Warnings of Chastisement

(1) Commencing on July 12, 1912 Our Lord began to give prophetic messages to Berthe concerning political matters and world events. These messages continued during World War I as well as during the period between World War I and World War II. In fact they continued during World War II until Berthe died.

(2) On July 2, 1940 Our Lord told Berthe: *"Recourse to My Mother under the title I wish for Her universally is the last help I shall give before the end of time."*

XXIV Method of Appearance - Not Reported
XXV Method of Departure - Not Reported
XXVI Confrontation w/Civil Authorities - NR

XXVII Confrontation w/Church Authorities

Berthe's priest, Fr. Decorsant, spent much time communicating with the Church hierarchy informing them of her visions and attempting to get approval and promotion of the devotion to the Sorrowful and Immaculate Heart of Mary.

Cardinal Mercier of Belgium granted an indulgence and contacted Pope Pius X and attempted to win approval for the devotion. That Pope said Berthe must be satisfied with the indulgence for now. Seventeen petitions in all were made to Pope Pius X. The devotion was not approved, nor was it condemned.

Pope Benedict XV was also approached to grant approval of the devotion. Although the Pope granted an indulgence of 100 days for every recitation of the emancipation to the Sorrowful and Immaculate Heart of Mary, approval for the devotion was not forthcoming. Pope Pius XI was never approached concerning the devotion.

Two of the most influential cardinals of the Roman Curia always opposed the official acceptance by the Church of this new Marian devotion. A number of cardinals personally accepted the devotion.

Cardinal Mercier of Belgium sent a Pastoral letter announcing he had privately consecrated his diocese, and as far as he was able his whole country, to the Sorrowful and Immaculate Heart of Mary.

Cardinal Bourne of England went even further and did consecrate England to the Sorrowful and Immaculate Heart of Mary. Berthe received messages from Jesus stating His approval of Cardinal Bourne's consecration of England. Although the consecration of the world as requested by Jesus has not yet been done, the devotion has spread worldwide.

XXVIII Request Chapel/Shrine Built - NR

XXIX Free Will/Choice

Both Our Lord and Our Lady told Berthe she has been given a special mission and would suffer greatly. She accepted the mission and the suffering, exercising her own free will.

XXX Seer(s)' Suffering/Sacrifice

The seer suffered much emotional distress in not being successful in having the Church approve the devotion as Our Lord requested.

XXXI Healings Reported

Berthe herself was healed of an ulcer on her foot on March 24/25, 1911.

XXXII Action Taken by the Church

(1) Cardinal Mercier granted an indulgence each time the prayer or invocation was said.
(2) Pope Benedict XV also granted an indulgence.
(3) Cardinal Mercier and Cardinal Bourne consecrated their own countries to the Sorrowful and Immaculate Heart of Mary.

XXXIII Bibliography

The Immaculate Heart of Mary   1976
By: Fr. Joseph A. Pelletier, A.A.
Published By: Assumption Publication

Chapter 3

FATIMA, PORTUGAL
(1917)

I Place - Fatima, Portugal

II Dates of First and Last Apparition

First: May 13, 1917
Last: October 13, 1917

III Seer(s) - 3

Name: Jacinta Marto
Birth: March 11, 1910
Age at first apparition: 7
Status: Deceased - February 20, 1920

Name: Francisco Marto
Birth: June 11, 1908
Age at first apparition: 8
Status: Deceased - April 4, 1919

Name: Lucia de Jesus dos Santos
Birth: March 22, 1907
Age at first apparition: 10
Status: Living - Sister Maria das Dores (Mary of the Sorrows)

IV Total Number of Apparitions - 6

V Dates and Locality of Each Apparition

1917: May 13th, Cova da Iria.
1917: June 13th, Cova da Iria.
1917: July 13th, Cova da Iria.
1917: August 15th, Valinhos.
1917: September 13th, Cova da Iria.
1917: October 13th, Cova da Iria.

VI Description of Our Lady

The children saw, at a Holm oak tree, a beautiful lady clothed all in white, more brilliant than the sun, shedding rays of light clear and stronger than a crystal glass filled with the most sparkling water pierced by the burning rays of the sun. Her face was indescribably beautiful, not sad, not happy, but serious. Her hands as in prayer at Her breast were pointing up with rosary beads hanging down from between the fingers of Her right hand. Her garment made solely of the same white light, a single tunic falling to Her feet, and over it a mantle from Her head to the same length, its edge made of fiercer light that seemed to glitter like gold. Neither Her hair nor Her ears could be seen. It was almost impossible to look steadily at Her face, it dazzled, and hurt the eyes, and made the children blink or look away. The children were so near to Her that they were actually within the light which the beautiful Lady radiated from Her person; a distance of about three feet. Her age was 15-18, about 17.

VII Title(s) of Our Lady - 1

Our Lady Of The Rosary (given October 13, 1917)

VIII Brief Factual Review

Fatima is a small village located in central Portugal, northeast of Lisbon. Of the three seers, Jacinta and Francisco Marto were sister and brother, Lucia dos Santos was their cousin. They each came from devout Catholic families and together their families tended sheep in the hills.

During 1916 the Angel of Peace appeared to the three children. The first appearance was in springtime, the next in midsummer and the final appearance of the angel was in late September or October of that same year.

(1) 1st Apparition of the Angel - In the spring of 1916, the three children were tending the sheep and had sought shelter among the rocks from the rain. When the sky cleared, suddenly they saw a strange light coming toward them from the east. When it drew near they saw it was a young man about 14-15, whiter than snow, transparent as crystal when the sun shines through it, and of great beauty. He drew closer and spoke to them and taught them a prayer.

Message and Prayers:

The Angel: *"Fear not I am the Angel of Peace, pray with me."*

Prayer: *"My God, I believe, I adore, I trust and love Thee. I ask pardon for those who do not believe, do not adore, do not trust and do not love Thee!"*

The Angel: *"Pray thus, the Hearts of Jesus and Mary are attentive to the voice of your supplications."*

(2) 2nd Apparition of the Angel - In the summer of 1916 the three children were playing near the well behind Lucia's house. Suddenly the same angel appeared to them and spoke to them, asking them to pray and make sacrifices.

The Angel: *"What are you doing? Pray, pray a great deal! The Hearts of Jesus and Mary have designs of mercy for you. Offer up prayers and sacrifices to the Most High."*

Message: *"Make everything you do a sacrifice and offer it as an act of reparation for the sins by which He is offended, and in supplication for the conversion of sinners. Bring peace to your country in this way. I am its Angel Guardian, the Angel of Portugal. Above all, accept and bear with submission the sufferings sent you by Our Lord."*

(3) 3rd Apparition of the Angel - In the autumn of 1916 the same angel appeared to the three children again, while the children were prostrate on the ground praying the prayer the angel had earlier taught them. This time the angel was holding a Chalice in his left hand, with a Host suspended above it from which some drops of blood fell into the Chalice. Leaving the Chalice and Host suspended in the air, the angel again prostrated himself and taught them another prayer. Then the angel arose and took the Chalice and Host into his hands and gave the Host to Lucia and the contents of the Chalice to Jacinta and Francisco. He spoke to them, prayed and departed.

Prayer: *"Most Holy Trinity, Father, Son and Holy Spirit. I adore Thee profoundly. I offer Thee the most precious Body, Blood, Soul and Divinity of Jesus Christ, present in all tabernacles of the world, in reparation for the outrages, sacrileges and indifferences by which He is offended. And through the infinite merits of His most Sacred Heart, and of the Immaculate Heart of Mary, I beg the conversion of poor sinners."*

The Angel: *"Take and drink the Body and Blood of Jesus Christ, horribly outraged by ungrateful men. Make reparation for their crimes and console your God."*

On Sunday, May 13, 1917 about noon, while tending their sheep, a flash of lightning drew the attention of the children; then they saw a brilliant light and a figure appearing over the trees at the Cova da Iria. This was the first apparition of Our Lady to the three seers. Our Blessed Mother requested that they come again to the Cova da Iria on the 13th day of each succeeding month for 6 consecutive months at the same hour. True to Her word, Our Lady again appeared to the 3 seers on June 13, July 13, September 13, with a final appearance on October 13, 1917. The children were in jail on August 13 and were therefore unable to meet Our Lady at the Cova da Iria on that date. She appeared to them instead on August 15, 1917 at a place nearby called Valinhos.

On the date of the final apparition, October 13, 1917 Our Lady performed a great miracle just as She promised. On that day a celestial phenomenon took place when the sun spun in the sky in a colorful symphony and seemed to tumble from the sky and crash towards earth, then retreat to its proper place in the sky. This is the day the **"Sun Danced at Fatima"**, an event witnessed by tens of thousands.

During each of the apparitions Our Lady gave messages to the children; She showed them visions of hell; She gave them prophecies and warnings of great chastisements to come unless mankind returns to God; She spoke of the Devotion to the Immaculate Heart of Mary; and finally She gave three secrets to the seers. The secrets have been revealed except for the third secret which was written on a paper by Lucia and is now in the hands of the Vatican. Instructions were that this secret was to be revealed to the world no later than 1960. Thus far the third secret has not been revealed.

These apparitions have been approved by the Church, and many extraordinary graces have been received by multitudes of souls – and are still being received, throughout the world. Fatima has become a high bench mark for Marian apparitions, the subject of much study and discussion, the topic of many books and articles, a direct catalyst producing vast amounts of good spiritual fruits.

Both Francisco and Jacinta died at a young age as predicted by Our Blessed Mother; Blessed Francisco in 1919, and Blessed Jacinta in 1920. Both of their causes have advanced to Beatification.

Lucia, on the other hand was told by Our Lady that God wanted her to stay on earth and carry out a special mission. This mission was later given to Lucia; Consecration of Russia to the Immaculate Heart of Mary, and Communion of Reparation of the Five First Saturdays to the Immaculate Heart of Mary. Both of these causes have been successfully advanced.

IX The Primary Messages - 5

(1) **Prayer**
(2) **Rosary**
(3) **Sacrifice/Penance**
(4) **Conversion**
(5) **Communion of Reparation of the Five First Saturdays**

First Apparition of Our Lady - May 13, 1917 Our Lady said: *"I am from heaven. I come to ask you to come here for six successive months, on the 13th day at the same hour. Later I will tell you what I want. And I will return a seventh time."*

Our Lady also promised that the three children will go to heaven but Francisco must pray many rosaries first.

Then Our Lady said: *"Do you wish to offer up to God all the sufferings He desires to send you in reparation for the sins by which He is offended, and in supplication for the conversion of sinners?"* The seers said: "Yes we do."

Then Our Lady said: *"Go then, for you will have much to suffer, but the grace of God will comfort you. Pray the rosary every day in order to obtain peace for the world and the end of the war."*

Second Apparition of Our Lady - June 13, 1917 Our Lady said: *"I want you to come here on the 13th of the next month. I want you to pray the rosary every day, and learn to read. Later I will tell you what else I want."*

Our Lady also said to Lucia: *"I will take Jacinta and Francisco soon, but you must remain here some time longer. Jesus wishes to make use of you to make Me known and loved. He wants to establish in the world devotion to My Immaculate Heart."*

Third Apparition of Our Lady - July 13, 1917 Our Lady said: *"I want you to come here on the 13th of next month. Continue to pray the rosary every day, in honour of Our Lady in order to obtain peace for the world and the end of the war, because only She can obtain it. In October, I will tell you who I am and what I want, and I will perform a miracle so that all may believe. Sacrifice yourselves for sinners, and say often, especially when you make some sacrifice: 'O Jesus, this is for love of You, for the conversion of sinners, and in reparation for the sins committed against the Immaculate Heart of Mary'.*

Then Our Lady showed the children avision of hell. *"You have seen hell where the souls of poor sinners go. In order to save them, God wishes to establish in the world devotion to My Immaculate Heart. If you do what I tell you, many souls will be saved, there will be peace, the war will end. But if men do not cease offending God, another and more terrible war will break out during the pontificate of Pius XI.*

*"When you see a night lit up by an unknown light, know that it is the sign God gives you that He is about to punish the world for its crimes by means of war, hunger, and persecution of the Church and the Holy Father. In order to prevent this, I shall come to ask for the Consecration of Russia to My Immaculate Heart, and the Communion of Reparation on the Five First Saturdays. If My wishes are fulfilled, Russia will be converted and there will be peace. If not, Russia will spread her errors throughout the world, promoting wars and persecution of the Church. The good will be

martyred, the Holy Father will have much to suffer, and various nations will be annihilated. But finally, My Immaculate Heart will triumph. The Holy Father will consecrate Russia to Me and it will be converted, and a time of peace will be conceded to the world. In Portugal the Dogma of Faith will always be preserved. [Here the third secret was given] . . . Do not tell this to anybody. You may tell it to Francisco."*

Then Our Lady added: *"When you recite the rosary, after each mystery say: 'Oh my Jesus, forgive us our sins, save us from the fires of hell; lead all souls to heaven, especially those most in need of Thy mercy.'"*

Fourth Apparition of Our Lady - August 15, 1917 Our Lady said: *"I want you to continue going to the Cova da Iria on the 13th, and to continue praying the rosary every day. In the last month I will perform a miracle so that all will believe. Pray, pray very much and make sacrifices for sinners, for many souls go to hell because they have nobody to pray and make sacrifices for them."*

Fifth Apparition of Our Lady - September 13, 1917 Our Lady said: *"Continue to pray the rosary in order to obtain the end of the war. In October Our Lord will come, and also Our Lady of Dolorous and Our Lady of Carmel. Saint Joseph will appear with the Child Jesus to bless the world. God is pleased with your sacrifices, but He does not want you to sleep with the cord on, only to wear it during the daytime. In October, I will perform a miracle so that all will believe."*

Sixth Apparition of Our Lady - October 13, 1917 Our Lady said: *"I want to tell you that I wish a chapel to be erected here in My honor, for I am the Lady of the Rosary. Continue to say the rosary every day. The war will soon end, and the soldiers will return to their homes. Do not offend God Our Lord any more, for He is already deeply offended."*

X Signs Preceding the Apparitions

The seers saw one or two flashes of lightning immediately before each of the six apparitions.

XI Other Visions During Apparitions

(1) July 13, 1917 - As Our Lady said these words: *"Sacrifice yourselves for sinners and say often especially when you make some sacrifice: 'Oh Jesus, this is for love of You, for the conversion of sinners, and in reparation for the sins committed against the Immaculate Heart of Mary . . . .'"* She opened Her hands as She had done during the two previous months. The light from Our Lady's hands seemed to penetrate the earth, and the children saw a sea of fire. Immersed in this fire were demons and lost souls that looked like transparent embers, some black or bronze, in human form, driven about by the flames that issued from within themselves, together with clouds of smoke. They were falling on all sides, just as sparks cascade from great fires, without weight or equilibrium, amid cries of pain and despair which horrified the children so that they trembled with fear and terror. The demons were horrible, terrible, loathsome and nauseous and unknown animals, but transparent as live coals in a fire.

Terrified, and as if to plead for succor, the children raised their eyes to Our Lady for help, who said kindly but sadly: *"You have seen hell where the souls of poor sinners go."*

(2) October 13, 1917 - At the conclusion of Her message this day Our Lady opened Her hands, She made them reflect on the sun. While She ascended the reflection of light from Her own person was projected onto the sun itself.

When Our Lady disappeared in the immense distance of the firmament, near the sun, the children saw St. Joseph with the Child Jesus and Our Lady robed in white with a blue mantle. St. Joseph and the Child Jesus seemed to bless the world, for they made the Sign of the Cross with their hands. A little later this vision vanished, and the children saw Our Lord and Our Lady who appeared to be Our Lady of Sorrows. Our Lord seemed to bless the world in the same manner as St. Joseph. This apparition disappeared and the children saw Our Lady again. This time resembling Our Lady of Mt. Carmel.

XII Prayers Taught to the Seer(s)

(1) July 13, 1917 Our Lady said: **Prayer**: *"O Jesus, this is for love of You, for the conversion of sinners, and in reparation for the sins committed against the Immaculate Heart of Mary."*

(2) July 13, 1917 Our Lady said: *"When you recite the rosary, after each mystery say:"* **Prayer**: *"Oh my Jesus, forgive us our sins, save us from the fires of hell; lead all souls to heaven, especially those most in need of mercy."*

(3) During the apparitions of the Angel of Peace in 1916 the angel taught the children these prayers:

1st Apparition, Spring 1916 Prayer: *"My God, I believe, I adore, I trust and I love Thee. I ask pardon for those who do not believe, do not adore, do not trust and do not love Thee."*

3rd Apparition, October or late September 1916 Prayer: *"Most Holy Trinity, Father, Son and Holy Spirit, I adore Thee profoundly. I offer Thee the most precious Body, Blood, Soul and Divinity of Jesus Christ, present in all the tabernacles of the world, in reparation for the outrages, sacrileges and indifferences by which He is offended. And through the infinite merits of His most Sacred Heart, and of the Immaculate Heart of Mary, I beg the conversion of poor sinners."*

Fatima, Portugal

XIII Special Devotion Given to the Seer(s)

(1) June 13, 1917 Our Lady said: *"Jesus wishes to make use of you* (Lucia) *to make Me known and loved. He wants to establish in the world devotion to My Immaculate Heart."*

(2) June 13, 1917 Our Lady said: *"In order to save them* (sinners) *God wishes to establish in the world devotion to My Immaculate Heart. In order to prevent war, hunger, persecution of the Church, I shall come to ask for the Consecration of Russia to My Immaculate heart, and for the Communion of Reparation on the First Saturdays."*

(3) December 10, 1925 Our Lady and Child Jesus appeared to Lucia and requested the Five First Saturday Reparation Devotion to the Immaculate Heart of Mary.

(4) February 15, 1926 the Child Jesus again appeared to Lucia asking Lucia if she had spread the Devotion of Reparation to the Immaculate Heart of Mary.

(5) June 1929 Our Lady again appeared to Lucia and said: *"The moment has come when God asks the Holy Father in union with all the bishops of the world, to make the Consecration of Russia to My Heart, promising to save it by this means."*

XIV Requests Made by Our Lady

(1) Pray the Rosary

May 13, 1917: *". . . Pray the rosary. Offer up to God all sufferings."*
June 13, 1917: *". . . I want you to pray the rosary every day."*
July 13, 1917: *". . . Continue to pray the rosary every day. Sacrifice yourselves for sinners."*
August 15, 1917: *". . . Continue praying the rosary every day. Pray, pray very much and make sacrifice for sinners."*
September 13, 1917: *". . . Continue to pray the rosary. God is pleased with your sacrifices."*
October 13, 1917: *". . . Continue to say the rosary every day. Do not offend God Our Lord any more, for He is already deeply offended."*

(2) Penance and Conversion

May 13, 1917: *". . . Are you willing to offer yourselves to God and bear all the sufferings He wills to send you, as an act of reparation for the sins by which He is offended and in supplication for the conversion of sinners?"* The children answered in the affirmative.
July 13, 1917: *". . . Sacrifice yourselves for sinners, and say many times, especially whenever you make some sacrifice, 'O Jesus it is for love of You, for the conversion of sinners and in reparation for the sins committed against the Immaculate Heart of Mary.'"*

August 15, 1917: *". . . Pray, pray very much and make sacrifices for the sinners, for many souls go to hell because there are none to sacrifice themselves and to pray for them."*

October 13, 1917: As a condition for obtaining graces for certain persons mentioned by Lucia, Our Lady said: *"They must amend their lives, and ask forgiveness for their sins."*

And Our Lady said to all: *"Do not offend the Lord our God any more, because He is already so much offended."*

(3) **Return to Apparition Site** - Our Lady asked the children to return on six consecutive months on the thirteenth day of each month.

XV Specific Bible References - Not Reported

XVI Secrets Given to the Seer(s)

A total of three secrets was given to the seers.

(1) June 13, 1917: Revelation of the Immaculate Heart of Mary encircled and pierced with thorns. Our Lady did not specify this as a secret, nonetheless the children felt obliged to keep this a secret.

(2) July 13, 1917:

First Secret—Vision of hell. (This was later revealed to the public.)

Second Secret—Establish devotion to the Immaculate Heart of Mary. Consecration of Russia to the Immaculate Heart of Mary. Our Lady's intercession can obtain salvation from God for souls who would otherwise be condemned. Warnings of war. (These were later revealed to the world.)

Third Secret—This secret has never been revealed to the public. However, Lucia wrote this secret on a single piece of paper sometime between January 2, 1944 when Our Lady appeared to Lucia and confirmed the request to write the secret as coming from God, and January 9, 1944 when Lucia wrote to Bishop de Silva announcing that she had written down the secret. On December 8, 1945, Bishop de Silva placed Lucia's envelope containing the secret into another envelope.

Realizing that Bishop de Silva resolved not to open the secret during his lifetime, Lucia made him promise to open and read the secret to the world at Lucia's death or in 1960 whichever first occurs.

In 1957 the Holy Office asked for the text of the secret. Later on April 16, 1957 the secret, in the sealed envelope, arrived at the Vatican and was placed by Pope Pius XII into a little box entitled 'Secret of the Holy Office.' Both Cardinal Ottaviani and Msgr. Capovilla (Secretary to Pope John XXIII) affirm that the envelope had remained sealed when Pope John XXIII opened it in 1959, which was one year after the death of Pope Pius XII. Pope John XXIII did not reveal the secret to the public.

Pope Paul VI, elected on June 21, 1963 also read the secret. On February 11, 1967 Cardinal Ottavani made a declaration in the name of the Pope, to explain that the third secret would not yet be divulged.

Pope John Paul I did not disclose the secret. Following the assassination attempt on Pope John Paul II on May 13, 1981 the Pope asked the help of a Portuguese interpreter/ translator to help to grasp the sense of the secret in the Portuguese language. It seems Pope John Paul II read it. Cardinal Ratzinger announced that he (the Cardinal) learned the contents of the secret. He spoke of it on two occasions (October 1984 and June 1985).

Our Lady asked of Lucia that the third secret be revealed in 1960, because, as Lucia told Cardinal Ottavani: "In 1960 the message will appear clearer." Thus far the third secret remains a secret and has not been revealed to the general public.

XVII Miracles Promised by Our Lady

(1) July 13, 1917: *"In October I will perform a miracle so that all may believe."*
(2) August 15, 1917: *"In the last month I will perform a miracle so that all will believe."*
(3) September 13, 1917: *"In October I will perform a miracle so that all will believe."*

XVIII Miracles Performed

October 13, 1917, as Lucia (and the two other children) observed the apparitions of Our Lord and Our Lady beside the sun, the spectators were amazed and overcome by the miracle in the sky. The sun stood forth like a great silver disc, which though bright as any sun they had seen, they could look straight at it without blinking. While they gazed, the sun began to "dance". The sun whirled rapidly like a gigantic fire-wheel. After doing this awhile, it stopped and then rotated again, with dizzy, sickening speed. Finally there appeared on the rim a border of crimson, which flung across the sky as from a hellish vortex. Blood-red streamers of flame, reflecting to the earth lit the trees and shrubs and upturned faces and clothes, with all sorts of brilliant colors in succession; green, red, orange, blue, violet and the whole color spectrum. The sun madly gyrated in this manner three times, it seemed to shudder and tremble then plunge toward earth in a zigzag pattern toward the crowd. Then the sun retreated and returned to its place in the sky. A fearful cry broke from the mouths of the crowd, many of whom thinking the end of the world had come. Some cried out, said prayers, confessed sins, and fell on their faces and broke into sobs. Many cried: "Miracle, miracle, the children were right . . ."

It had been raining and the ground was a vast morass of mud, suddenly people were making the discovery that their drenched clothes were now completely dry in some unexplained manner. This was the great miracle promised by Our Lady and came to be called: '**The Miracle of the Sun**.'

XIX Miracles Promised not yet Performed

None known unless contained in the third secret yet unrevealed.

XX Signs Promised

July 13, 1917: *". . . When you see a night lit up by an unknown light, know that it is the sign God gives you that He is about to punish the world for its crimes by means of war, hunger, and persecution of the Church and the Holy Father."*

XXI Signs Given

(1) On January 25/26, 1938 Sr. Lucia saw the Great Northern Lights when an unusual light appeared in the skies above the Northern Hemisphere of the world. Lucia confirmed this as the sign promised during the July 13, 1917 apparition.

(2) The angel gave the Host to Lucia and then gave the contents of the chalice to Jacinta and Francisco.

XXII Predictions/Promises

(1) May 13, 1917: *"Go then, for you will have much to suffer, but the grace of God will comfort you."* (This prediction has been fulfilled).

(2) June 13, 1917: *"Yes, I will take Jacinta and Francisco soon, but you* (to Lucia) *must remain here some time longer . . ."* (This prediction has been fulfilled).

(3) July 13, 1917: *"In October I will tell you who I am and what I want, and I will perform a miracle so that all may believe."* (This prediction has been fulfilled).

(4) August 15, 1917: *"In the last month I will perform a miracle so that all will believe."* (This prediction has been fulfilled).

(5) September 13, 1917: *"In October Our Lord will come, and also Our Lady of Dolorous and Our Lady of Carmel. St. Joseph will appear with the Child Jesus to bless the world."* (This prediction has been fulfilled).

(6) October 13, 1917: *"The war will soon end, and the soldiers will return to their homes."* (This prediction has been fulfilled).

Fatima, Portugal

XXIII Prophecies/Warnings of Chastisement

July 13, 1917: *"You have seen hell where the souls of poor sinners go. In order to save them, God wishes to establish in the world devotion to My Immaculate Heart. If you do what I tell you, many will be saved, there will be peace, the war will end. But if men do not cease offending God, another and more terrible war will break out during the pontificate of Pius XI.*

"When you see a night lit up by an unknown light, know that it is the sign God gives you that He is about to punish the world for its crimes by means of war, hunger, and persecution of the Church and the Holy Father. In order to prevent this, I shall come to ask for the Consecration of Russia to My Immaculate Heart, and the Communion of Reparation of the First Saturdays.

"If My wishes are fulfilled, Russia will be converted and there will be peace. If not, Russia will spread her errors throughout the world, promoting wars and persecution of the Church. The good will be martyred, the Holy Father will have much to suffer, and various nations will be annihilated. But finally, My Immaculate Heart will triumph."

XXIV Method of Appearance

At each appearance, May 13, 1917 through October 13, 1917 Our Lady comes from the East, preceded each time by one or two flashes or reflexes of lightning, and emerges from a ball of light, standing over the Holm Oak tree.

XXV Method of Departure

At each departure, May 13, 1917 through October 13, 1917 Our Lady serenely ascends going up towards the East, the light that surrounds Her seems to open up a path before Her, until She finally disappears in the immensity of space.

XXVI Confrontation w/Civil Authorities

Arthur de Oliveira Samos, then mayor of the district of Vila Nova de Qurem as well as deputy judge of the district, had long been a Freemason. Plotting to take secret action against these Fatima events, he eventually persecuted the three children and later carried out persecutions against some pilgrims.

On August 13, 1917 the mayor, by fraud and trickery, physically took the children against their will to the Vila Nova de Qurem. At Qurem the children were locked in a room and told they could not leave until they told the secret. They were offered pieces of gold to reveal the secret. They refused to tell the secret. They were then taken back to court and threatened they would be boiled alive in oil if they did not tell the secret. The children were summoned one by one and told the boiling oil was awaiting them. The children believed they were going to their deaths, but held fast and refused to tell the secret. Finally after a couple of days the children were released and left at the priest's house.

Meanwhile at the appointed time at noon on August 13, 1917 Our Lady apparently appeared at the Cova da Iria, as witnessed by the crowd at the Cova, who suddenly heard a clap of thunder followed by a flash of lightning. Many saw a small white cloud above the holm oak tree, which cloud soon disappeared. Our Lady did later appear to the three children on August 15, 1917 at Valinhos (there has been some disagreement on this date: some reporting it to have been August 19, 1917).

XXVII Confrontation w/Church Authorities

Sometime after the June 13 apparition, Tio Marto, the father of Jacinta and Francisco, took his 2 children to Fr. Ferreira who examined the children. Later, Lucia was also taken to prior, Fr. Ferreira by her mother so that Lucia might confess the truth. After completing his examination, Fr. Ferreira seemed convinced that the children told the truth as to what they said they saw and heard. Yet he said: "It doesn't seem to me like a revelation from heaven. It may be a deception of the devil, you know. We shall see. We shall see. We shall give our opinion later on."

The possibility of the devil prompting the apparition of Our Lady had never occurred to Lucia or to her mother. Lucia became terrified. She suffered day and night and announced to Jacinta and Francisco that she would not return to the Cova again. This distressed Francisco and Jacinta who pleaded with Lucia that the apparitions were from God and not from the devil. It was not until July 13, 1917 when Lucia had a strong interior desire that nearly dragged her to the Cova, that she went to the Marto home and found both Jacinta and Francisco weeping bitterly at their beds and wailing: "We don't dare go out without you." Lucia responded: "We'll I've changed my mind, and I'm going."

XXVIII Request Chapel/Shrine Built

(1) August 15, 1917: " . . . *and whatever is over is to help toward the building of a Chapel . . .* " (speaking of donations left by the pilgrims).
(2) October 13, 1917: *"I want to tell you that I wish a chapel to be erected here in My honor, for I am the Lady of the Rosary."*

The First Chapel was built.

On October 13, 1921 permission was granted to celebrate the first Mass

at the Chapel of the Apparitions. On March 6, 1922 the Chapel was destroyed by dynamite, the work of disbelievers.
(3) In 1928 the first stone of the Sanctuary was laid which was later completed.

XXIX Free Will/Choice

May 13, 1917 Our Lady said: *"Do you wish to offer up to God all the sufferings He desires to send you in reparation for the sins by which He is offended, and in supplication for the conversion of sinners?"*
Lucia said: *"Yes we do."*
Our Lady said: *"Go then for you will have much to suffer, but the grace of God will comfort you."*

XXX Seer(s)' Suffering/Sacrifice

Lucia's family did not believe her when she reported the apparitions. As a consequence Lucia had much to suffer, both physical and emotional from her own family. When Fr. Ferreira stated the apparitions may be from the devil, Lucia suffered greatly emotionally and spiritually to the point where she had refused to ever go to the Cova again.
Likewise, Jacinta and Francisco suffered from their families (although not from Tio Marto, their father), as well as from their local priests' treatment.
The three children suffered during their ordeal of July 13-15 when they were taken prisoner by the mayor. Jacinta and Francisco both suffered (as predicted by Our Lady) prior to their early deaths. Lucia has suffered much in being required to remain silent and see Our Lady's and Our Lord's wishes being frustrated, hindered and delayed.

XXXI Healings Reported

(1) Many physical, emotional and spiritual healing have occurred and are still occurring.
(2) Starting on June 13, 1917 Lucia transmitted to Our Lady numerous requests for cures. Our Lady said: *"I will cure some, but not others ."*
(3) One of the first cures, where an inquiry was done officially, was that of Maria do Carmo. In July 1917 her doctor declared she had another fortnight to live. She was a victim of tuberculosis and she was declining every day. She lived in Maceira, some 35 kilometers from Fatima. She went to Fatima on August 13, again on September 13 and finally on October 13, 1917. At the moment of the apparition on October 13, she was suddenly cured.

(4) Canon Formigao's work cited some 24 cases of marvelous cures which had already taken place from 1917 through 1922.
(5) The publication Voz Da Fatima described 800 cases of cures which took place from 1922 to 1942.
(6) One absolutely amazing case is that of Margarida de Jesus Rebelo who was cured on May 13, 1944. She had Pott's disease in a very advanced state, located on a fracture of the spine, and which had been diagnosed by X-rays. Her condition was complicated by a fistula or ulcer of the kidneys, which required permanent draining. She was totally paralyzed. At the moment of the Benediction of the Blessed Sacrament she was instantly cured. At one stroke all the symptoms of her disease disappeared, she was able to get up, walk and take food. All her functions had been instantly restored, the ulcer which only an hour before had been giving off tuberculous puss had disappeared and instantaneously closed up, leaving in its place, completely new skin.

XXXII Action Taken by the Church

(1) On May 3, 1922 the bishop of Leiria nominated a Commission of Inquiry. In 1927 the Holy See granted the privilege of a Votive Mass at Fatima.
(2) On October 13, 1930 the bishop of Leiria published a Pastoral Letter approving the Cult of Our Lady of Fatima and declaring the apparitions worthy of belief.
(3) On May 13, 1931 the great Pilgrimage of the bishops of Portugal to Fatima, and the Consecration of Portugal to the Immaculate Heart of Mary occurred.
(4) On May 13, 1946 the Papal Legate crowned the statue of Our Lady of Fatima as **"Queen of Peace and of the World."**
(5) On October 13, 1951 the Pontifical Legate closed the 1950 Holy Year at Fatima.
(6) On May 13, 1967 Pilgrimage to Fatima of (the future) Pope Paul VI on the occasion of the Golden Jubilee of the apparitions.
(7) On May 13, 1982 Pilgrimage to Fatima by Pope John Paul II, one year after the attempt on his life in St. Peter's Square. On this date the Collegial Consecration of Russia to the Immaculate Heart of Mary took place.

XXXIII Bibliography

The Apparitions of the Blessed Virgin Mary Today   1990
By: Fr. Rene Laurentin
Published by: Veritas

Our Lady of Fatima   1990
By: Wethan Thomas Walsh
Published by: Image Books Doubleday

A Woman Clothed in the Sun   1990
Edited by: John J. Delaney
Published by: Image Doubleday

Fatima Way of Peace   1989
By: Antonio Martins, S.J.
Published by: Augustine Publishing Company

Meet the Witnesses   1988
By: John M. Haffert
Published by: AMI Press

Fatima Revealed and Discarded   1988
By: Bro. Michel de La Sainte Trinite
Published by: Augustine Publishing Company

Fatima: The Full Story   1986
By: Fr. John De Marchi, IMC
Published by: AMI Press

The Sun Danced at Fatima   1983
By: Fr. Joseph A. Pelletier, A.A.
Published by: Image Books

Fatima Today   1983
By: Fr. Robert J. Fox
Published by: Christiandom Publication

Jacinta, the Flower of Fatima   1982
By: Rev. Joseph Galamba Oliviera
Published by: AMI Press

Fatima   1981
By: Frs. Severo Rossi and Aventino de Oliveira
Published by: Consolata Missions Publications

1917 Red Banners White Mantle   1981
By: Warren H. Carroll
Published by: Christiandom Press

The Secret of Fatima, Fact and Legend 1979
By: Joaquin Maria Alonso, CMF
Published by: The Ravengate Press

Fatima the Great Sign 1979
By: Francis Johnston
Published by: Tan Books and Publishers Inc.

The Immaculate Heart of Mary 1976
By: Fr. Joseph A. Pelletier, A.A.
Published by: Assumption Publications

Fatima In Lucia's Own Words 1976
Edited by: Fr. Louis Kondor SVD
Published by: Postulation Centre

More About Fatima 1960
By: Rev. Fr. V. Montes De Oca, CSSp
Published by: The Newman Press

Mother of Christ Crusade 1947
By: Fr. John de Marchi, I.M.C.
Published by: Mother of Christ Crusade, Inc.

Chapter 4

PORTIERS, FRANCE
(1920 - 1923)

I Place - Portiers, France
(Les Feuillants at the old monastery of the Sacred Heart at Portiers, France; also at Marmoutier, France).

II Dates of First and Last Apparition

First: October 3, 1920
Last: December 15, 1923

III Seer(s) - 1

Name: Sister Josefa Menendez (Society of the Sacred Heart)
Birth: February 4, 1890
Age at first apparition: 30
Status: Deceased - December 29, 1923

IV Total Number of Apparitions - 71

V Dates and Locality of Each Apparition

(All apparitions occurred at Les Feuillants unless otherwise stated.)

1920: October 3, 5, 8 (twice), 15; December 6, 7, 8, 10, 18, 25.
1921: January 24; March 5, 11, 25; April 9, 22; May 9, 14, 17; June 13, 20, 29; July 1, 22, 27; September 3; October 25; November 22; December 6.

1922: January 11; February 12, 24; March 3; May 3; June 16; July 16, 21, 26, 27, 30; August 15; September 9, 15; October 16, 25; December 3, 8, 26.

1923: January 21; February 17; March 15, 16, 21; April 1, 19; May 6 and 16, (Marmoutier); June 19, 20; July 15, 16; August 15, 17, 20; October 9 and 20 (Rome); December 4, 8, 12, 15.

VI Description of Our Lady

(1) October 3, 1920 Josefa heard light footsteps, then saw a lady standing beside her bed, clothed in white and wrapped in a long veil. Her features were fine, Her hands crossed, She looked tenderly at Josefa.

(2) December 25, 1920 Our Lady appeared with the Christ Child. Our Lady wore a white tunic, a very pale rose mantle, and a veil of the same color, but it was of much finer stuff, the Holy Child's raiment was of a material as light as foam. An aura of radiance surrounded His Head and Our Blessed Lady had the same.

(3) March 25, 1921 Our Lady was clothed in a very dark purple tunic and veil, She held in Her hand the Crown of Thorns, all covered in blood. (Our Lady brought the Crown of Thorns and pressed it onto Josefa's head on several occasions.)

(4) February 12, 1922 Our Lady appeared surrounded by light. Before She departed Our Lady made the sign of the cross on Josefa's forehead, and gave Her hand for Josefa to kiss. Then Our Lady vanished. (Our Lady permitted Josefa to kiss Her hand more than once.)

(5) On July 16, 1922 and again on August 15, 1922 Our Lady appeared with a diadem crowning Her head. Her hands were crossed on Her breast, as they usually were during other apparitions.

(6) On March 21, 1923 Our Lady came to entrust the Cross of Jesus to Josefa saying: *"Now keep this precious treasure and pray for souls."*

(7) August 15, 1923 Our Lady appeared and recalled to Josefa, Our Lady's lifetime on earth. She stated that as She was about to enter Her 73rd year, Her soul passed like a flash from earth to heaven. At the end of three days the angels fetched Our Lady's body and brought it to Her soul in triumph to heaven.

(8) On December 8, 1923 Our Lady came clothed as usual and surrounded with dazzling light and standing on a crescent of azure blue clouds which were very airy and ethereal. On Her head She wore a long pale blue veil, transparent as gossamer, which was lost in the clouds on which Her feet rested.

VII Title(s) of Our Lady - 6

(1) June 29, 1922 Our Lady said: *"I am the Refuge of Sinners."*

(2) February 12, 1922 Our Lady said: *"I am the Immaculate Mother of Jesus Christ, the Mother of Your Redeemer and Your God."*

(3) December 8, 1923 Our Lady said: *"My choicest title of glory is that being Immaculate at the same time as being Mother of God. But My greatest joy is to add to this title that of Mother of Mercy and Mother of Sinners."*

VIII Brief Factual Review

Josefa Menendez was born on February 4, 1890 in Madrid, Spain. She was the eldest child of the family of four girls and two boys.

She was confirmed at the early age of five. Her pastor, Fr. Rubio, who was also her confessor for a period of time, taught her to use ejaculatory prayer and to meditate. At age 11 she received First Holy Communion. While the nuns were preparing her for First Communion, she promised Our Lord ever to remain a virgin, even though she did not totally understand what this meant. She repeated the promise that day and heard a voice say to her: *"Yes, little one, I want you to be all mine."* On the very day of her First Communion, March 19, 1901 she wrote out and signed a Promise and a Petition which she prepared promising Jesus to remain a virgin always.

In 1907 her father and mother both became invalids and one of her sisters died. Josefa took care of her parents, who both did recover. Josefa now did dressmaking to support the family. She attended Sacred Heart Free School in Madrid run by the nuns. The nuns at the Sacred Heart School helped the family in their needs. Josefa's desire was to become a nun in the Society of the Sacred Heart.

Her wish finally came true when she entered the Society as a novice at Les Feuillants, Portiers, France in 1920. Les Feuillants was an ancient monastery closed during the French Revolution and now operated by the Society of the Sacred Heart.

Our Lord gave Josefa the mission to enlighten the world through His Sacred Heart; to be an Apostle of His Love and Mercy. In addition Josefa willingly became a victim soul to suffer for the sins of others. Her sufferings included participation in the passion of Christ as well as persecution and abuse by diabolical forces. At one point God permitted the devil to take her down into hell. During one period of time the devil carried her off almost daily and the other sisters would find her at various locations in the convent.

The messages she received were of Love and Mercy. The Sacred Heart and the overwhelming love of Jesus for mankind are brought out in the messages in a striking manner, as is the infinite mercy of Jesus. Josefa lived the messages and under obedience faithfully kept a diary of all her visions and messages from Jesus and from Our Blessed Mother. Like St. Margaret Mary, Jesus also took Josefa into His Sacred Heart, into His special place of refuge.

During July and August 1920 Jesus appeared to Josefa with six thorns in His Sacred Heart. When He later returned only one thorn remained and He asked Josefa to remove this thorn caused by the sins of a religious. Josefa prayed to Our Blessed Mother for help. On August 15, 1920 Josefa spent the day in union with Our Blessed Mother, begging Her to take charge of that soul and draw out the thorn that Jesus asked to be removed. Then On August 25, 1920 Jesus appeared to Josefa in glory. The remaining thorn had been removed from His Sacred Heart.

Commencing October 3, 1920 Our Lady began to appear to Josefa more frequently. Jesus's part however remained paramount, while Mary helped when there was a question to reassure Josefa or to bring Josefa's will into line with God's will. Our Lady acts as a warning, sometimes as a support, She initiates Josefa into Our Lord's plans and prepares her for His coming and She teaches Josefa how to guard against the snares of the devil.

The Foundress of the Society, Saint Madeleine Sophie, also appeared to Josefa many times in the monastery, usually in the cell which St. Madeleine Sophie occupied when she was alive.

Many suffering souls in purgatory appeared to Josefa and pleaded for prayers and sufferings to alleviate their own sufferings in purgatory.

IX The Primary Messages - 5

The primary messages given to Josefa were of course those given to her directly by Jesus. The Primary Messages given by Our Lady were:

(1) **Prayer** - December 8, 1920: *"Pray humbly and confidently when you feel lonely and given up to temptation, when your soul is cold and you have no courage to go on, do not give up prayer."*

(2) **Humility** - December 8, 1920: *"Humble yourself."* May 16, 1923: *"Be humble but do not lose courage."*

(3) **Sufferings** - September 9, 1922: *"Suffer with courage and energy."* January 24, 1921: *"Love and suffering can obtain anything."*

(4) **Reparation** - February 24, 1922: *"See how His Heart is outraged in the world. Do not lose any chance of making reparation these days, offer up everything for souls, and suffer with great love."*

(5) **Love** - October 25, 1921: *"There is one thing you must do, Josefa: Love! Love! Love!"*

X Signs Preceding the Apparitions

Usually Our Lady came in response to a great sorrow or distress which Josefa was then suffering, and comforted the seer. (*"I am here because I heard your call."* October 25, 1921) No repeated sign preceding the apparitions is reported.

XI Other Visions During Apparitions

Jesus appeared sometimes alone and sometimes with Our Lady. St. John the Evangelist appeared to the seer, as did the Foundress Saint Madeleine Sophie; Satan also appeared to Josefa in human and other forms.

XII Prayers Taught to the Seer(s)

(1) October 8, 1920 Our Lady taught the seer this:
  Prayer: *"O Father, make me worthy to accomplish Thy Holy Will, for I belong to Thee."*
(2) October 15, 1920 Our Lady taught the seer this:
  Prayer: *"O Father, merciful and good, look upon Thy child, and make her so entirely Thine own, that she may lose herself in Thy Heart. May her one desire, O Father, be to accomplish Thy holy will."*
(3) March 16, 1921 Our Lady taught the seer these: *"What pleases My Son most is love and humility; so write:"*
  Prayer: *"O sweet and dearly loved Jesus, wert Thou not my Savior, I should not dare to come to Thee, but Thou art both my Savior and my Bridegroom, and Thy Heart loves me with the most tender and burning love, as no other Heart can love. Would that I could correspond with this love of Thine for me. Would that I had for Thee, who art my only love, all the ardor of the seraphim, the purity of the angels and virgins, the holiness of the blessed who possess Thee and glorify Thee in heaven.*

  "Were I able to offer Thee all this, it would still be too little to honour Thy goodness and mercy. That is why I offer Thee my poor heart such as it is, with all its miseries, its weakness and good desires. Deign to purify it in the Blood of Thy Heart, to transform and inflame it Thyself with an ardent and pure love. Thus the poor creature that I am, who can do no good but is capable of every evil, will love and glorify Thee as do the seraphim who in heaven are consumed with adoring love.

  "Lastly, I ask of Thee, O gentle Jesus, to give my heart the very sanctity of Thy Heart, or rather to plunge it in Thy Divine Heart, that in it I may love and serve and glorify Thee, and lose myself in Thee for

all eternity. I beg this same grace for all those whom I love. May they render Thee for me the glory and honour of which my sins have deprived Thee."

Then Josefa shyly asked this most kind and indulgent Mother to tell her of an ejaculatory prayer she could repeat over and over again while at her work. *"Say these words which He will love,"* said Our Lady:

Prayer: *"'O my Beloved, who art also my God, make my heart a flame of pure love for Thee.' And every evening before you fall asleep, say with much respect and confidence,"* continued Our Lady:

Prayer: *"O Thou who knewest all my misery before Thine eyes were fixed on me; Thou didst not turn away from my wretchedness but because of it Thou didst love me with a love more sweet and tender. I beg pardon for having corresponded so little to Thy love . . . I beg Thee to forgive me, and to purify my actions in Thy Divine Blood. I am deeply grieved at having offended Thee, because Thou art infinitely Holy. I repent with heartfelt sorrow and I promise to do all in my power to avoid these faults in the future.*

"After which in all tranquillity and joy take your rest," so Our Lady concluded.

Even more amazing Our Lord Himself dictated a prayer (to Josefa) directed to Our Holy Mother. *"Josefa,"* He said to her that night, *"is it true that you would like something to say to My Mother that would please Her? Write what I tell you."* Then in ardent, burning, even enthusiastic words, the seer noted, He said this prayer:

Prayer: *"O tender and loving Mother, most prudent Virgin, Mother of my Redeemer, I come to salute You today with all the love that a child can feel for its mother.*

"Yes, I am indeed Your child, and because I am so helpless I will take the fervor of the Heart of Your Divine Son; with Him I will salute You as the purest of creatures, for You were framed according to the wishes and desires of the thrice-holy God.

"Conceived without sin, exempt from all corruption, You were ever faithful to the impulses of grace, and so Your soul accumulated such merit that it was raised above all other creatures.

"Chosen to be Mother of Jesus Christ, You kept Him as in a most pure sanctuary, and He who came to give life to souls, Himself took life from You, and received nourishment from You.

"O incomparable Virgin! Immaculate Virgin! Delight of the Blessed Trinity, admiration of all angels and saints, You are the Joy of Heaven. Morning Star, Rose blossoming in springtime, Immaculate Lily, tall and graceful Iris, sweet-smelling Violet. Garden enclosed kept for the delight of the King of heaven . . . You are my Mother, Virgin most prudent, Ark most precious containing every virtue! You are my Mother, O Refuge of sinners! I salute You and rejoice at the

sight of the gifts bestowed on You by the Almighty, and of the prerogatives with which He has crowned You!

"Be blessed and praised, Mother of my Redeemer, Mother of poor sinners! Have pity on us with Your Motherly protection.

"I salute You in the name of all men, of all saints and all angels.

"Would that I could love You with the love and fire of the seraphim, and this is too little to satisfy my desires . . . and to render You filial homage constant and pure for all eternity.

"O incomparable Virgin, bless me, since I am Your child. Bless all men! Protect them and pray for them to Him who is Almighty and can refuse You nothing.

"Adieu, tender and sweet Mother; day and night I salute You, in time and for eternity."

"Now, Josefa, praise the Mother with the words of the Son, and the Son with those of His Mother," concluded Jesus.

(4) August 20, 1923 Our Lady urged Josefa to repeat often the prayer of St. Ignatius:

Prayer: *"Take, O Lord, and receive all my liberty, my memory, my understanding and my will . . ."*

(5) October 9, 1923 Our Lady taught Josefa the following prayer to defend against Satan's attacks:

Prayer: *"Begone, Satan, I will have nothing to do with you who are delusion and falsehood. I belong to Jesus who is truth and life."*

XIII Special Devotion Given to the Seer(s)

(1) Jesus gave Josefa a definite mission to suffer with love and to spread devotion to His Sacred Heart.
(2) On July 1, 1921 the Feast of the Precious Blood, Our Lady urged the seer: *"Adore the Precious Blood of My Son, daughter, and beg Him to pour It on that soul, that he may be touched, forgiven and purified."*

XIV Requests Made by Our Lady

(1) December 8, 1920 Our Lady told the seer: *"'My child,' She said, 'never be afraid of suffering or of sacrifice; such are God's ways. If you want to come out victoriously from the assaults of the devil, pay attention to two things: first, humble yourself, for you are nothing and deserve nothing . . . everything comes to you as a grace from God. Second, when you feel lonely and given up to temptation, when your soul is cold and you have no courage to go on, do not give up prayer. Pray humbly and confidently, and go at once to seek guidance from her whom God has given you for that purpose. Believe Me, child, if you do this, you will make no mistakes. Let*

Me bless you, for I am your Mother.'"

(2) June 13, 1921 Our Lady said, (after the devil had assaulted Josefa): *"Listen, daughter, do not pay any attention to what you feel. Believe Me, the sharper your repugnance, the greater your merit in the eyes of your Master. Be on guard about these three points by which the enemy of souls will endeavor to make you fail."*

"First — Never give in to scruples which he suggests to you in order to make you give up Holy Communion."

"Second—When My Son asks anything of you - be it an act of humility or some other act - do it with great love, telling Him all the time Lord, Thou seeth how much it costs me but Thou first, and I afterwards.'"

"Third — Pay no attention to the artifice of the devil who tries to persuade you that the confidence you have in your Mother subtracts something from your tenderness for Jesus. If he is able to master you in this matter, he will have gained everything."

(3) On several occasions Our Lady brought the Crown of Thorns and pressed it onto Josefa's head, requesting the seer guard it.

(4) July 15, 1923 Our Lady said, (after Josefa was taken down into hell): *"You must not be afraid, for every time Jesus allows you to endure those torments He means for you to draw from them a threefold fruit:* **Firstly:** *Great love and deep gratitude to the Divine Majesty, who in spite of your faults prevents you from falling eternally into hell.* **Secondly:** *Boundless generosity and ardent zeal for the salvation of souls, with the desire of saving many for Him by your sacrifices and even your tiniest acts, for you know how much these please Him.* **Thirdly:** *The sight of such innumerable crowds of souls lost for ever . . . of souls, of which not one can so much as make an act of love, ought to make you who can love, send up unceasingly to Him echoes of love's clamour to drown the blasphemous vociferations of that impious abode."*

"Therefore, great generosity for the salvation of souls, daughter, and much love . . . Let My Son use you as He wills . . . Let Him finish His work."

Then Our Lady blessed the seer and permitted the seer to kiss Her hand, and then She disappeared.

XV Specific Bible References - Not Reported

XVI Secrets Given to the Seer(s)

On August 20, 1923 Our Lady revealed to Josefa that she would soon travel to Rome in order to carry a secret personal message to the Mother General. The contents of this secret are not reported.

XVII Miracles Promised by Our Lady - NR
XVIII Miracles Performed - Not Reported
XIX Miracles Promised not yet Performed - NR
XX Signs Promised - Not Reported

XXI Signs Given

On October 16, 1922 Our Lady appeared and took Josefa's rosary by the cross, slowly dropped the rosary into Josefa's hand, then pressed the cross onto Josefa's forehead three times. A few minutes later a novice noticed three drops of blood on the coif where Our Lady pressed the cross onto Josefa's forehead. This was repeated on March 15, 1923.

Both coifs are preserved to this day at the convent, each containing the blood stains on the coif.

XXII Predictions/Promises

(1) On January 11, 1922 Our Lady predicted the seer's death: *"You will die in France, in the House of Portiers, and that before ten years are out, and then . . . heaven!"* This occurred. Josefa died December 29, 1923 in the House of Portiers.

(2) On December 3, 1922 Our Lady predicted that the seer would transmit Our Lord's words to the bishop of Portiers, then added: *"You will see him three times before your death."* This also came true as predicted.

(3) On April 19, 1923 Our Lady predicted and revealed that the seer would leave Portiers, much to the distress of Josefa. Our Lady said: *"Jesus wants you to make the sacrifice of this House."* This came to pass as predicted when Josefa was sent to live in the House at Marmoutier, France. She later returned to Portiers.

(4) On August 20, 1923 Our Lady told Josefa that she would travel to Rome on a mission for Jesus. This occurred as predicted.

XXIII Prophecies/Warnings of Chastisement -NR

XXIV Method of Appearance

Our Lady usually appeared when Josefa was in distress and called on Our Lady. Our Lady appeared in different attire, sometimes with the Child Jesus, sometimes with the Crown of Thorns for Josefa, yet no repeated method of appearance is reported.

XXV   Method of Departure

Our Lady would often permit Josefa to kiss the hands of Our Lady, and then Our Lady would touch Josefa's forehead and give her a special blessing before She departed.

XXVI   Confrontation w/Civil Authorities - NR
XXVII   Confrontation w/Church Authorities - NR
XXVIII   Request Chapel/Shrine Built - NR

XXIX   Free Will/Choice

Josefa's diary contains many reported messages where Our Lady either asks for Josefa's acceptance or tells her that she has a choice; free will.

(1) On October 5, 1920 Our Lady said: *"If you refuse to do My Son's will, you will wound His heart."*
(2) On December 7, 1920 Our Lady said: *"If you want to be a comfort to Jesus, I will tell you what gives Him pleasure ."*
(3) On December 18, 1920 Our Lady said: *"I beg you not to refuse My Son anything He asks of you."*
(4) On September 3, 1921 Our Lady said: *"The more Jesus asks of you, the more you must rejoice, My child."*
(5) On March 3, 1922 Our Lady said: *"Do not be unhappy, My daughter, if you are willing Jesus will go on drawing comfort from you."*
(6) On December 8, 1922 Our Lady said: *"My child, if you want to give much glory to Jesus and save many souls . . . let Him do as He likes with you and give yourself up to His love."*
(7) On August 20, 1923 Our Lady said: *"Have no fear, Jesus who loves you so specially will Himself tell you His wishes - and all will be carried out easily, simply and humbly."*

XXX   Seer(s)' Suffering/Sacrifice

(1) Josefa suffered great physical, emotional and spiritual pain as a victim soul.
(2) In particular she suffered greatly at the hands of Satan.
(3) She suffered great distress firstly in the delay in becoming a religious, also later in being transferred from her beloved Community at Portiers.
(4) Josefa was so sensitive to the presence of, and wishes of, Jesus that she suffered greatly at the thought that she did, or may have done, anything against the Holy Will of Jesus.

XXXI Healings Reported

Josefa's mission as a victim soul was to suffer for the conversion of sinners. Her diary is replete with requests made by Jesus for her to suffer for others; then the reports of the suffering she endured; and finally the messages from Jesus that the souls for whom she had suffered had been converted, a true spiritual healing.

XXXII Action Taken by the Church

Cardinal E. Pacelli, later to become Pope Pius XII, gave his consent to publish her diary. Josefa kept the diary in which she wrote and reported the messages from Jesus and Mary, at the special request of Jesus and Mary.

XXXIII BIBLIOGRAPHY

The Way of Divine Love   1981
By: Sister Josefa Menendez
Published by: Tan Books and Publishers Inc.

Chapter 5

Tuy/Pontevedra, Spain
(1925-1929)

I Place - Tuy/Pontevedra, Spain

1925: Tuy, Spain - Convent of Sisters of St. Dorothy.
1929: Pontevedra, Spain - Convent of Sisters of St. Dorothy.

II Dates of First and Last Apparition

First: December 10, 1925.
Last: June 13, 1929.

III Seer(s) - 1

Name: Lucia de Jesus dos Santos
Birth: March 22, 1907
Age at first apparition: 17
Status: Sister Maria das Dores (Mary of the Sorrows)

IV Total Number of Apparitions - 2

V Dates and Locality of Each Apparition

1925: December 10, Tuy, Spain, Dorothean convent in Lucia's room.
1929: June 13, Pontevedra, Spain, chapel in convent of Sisters of St. Dorothy.

VI Description of Our Lady

(1) December 10, 1925 Our Lady appeared to Lucia with the Child Jesus by Her side, elevated on a cloud of light. Our Lady rested one hand on Lucia's shoulder while in Her other hand Our Lady held a heart surrounded by sharp thorns. It was the same 'Lady of Fatima' who had appeared to Lucia (and the two other children) in 1917 at Fatima.

(2) June 13, 1919 while Lucia was praying the holy hour in the chapel, suddenly the whole chapel was illuminated by a supernatural light. In this apparition Lucia saw the mystery of the Trinity. Our Lady was standing beneath the right arm of the cross and in Her hand was Her Immaculate Heart (it was Our Lady of Fatima, with Her Immaculate Heart in Her left hand without sword or roses, but with a crown of thorns and flames).

VII Title(s) of Our Lady - 1

December 10, 1925 and June 13, 1929 - *Our Lady of Fatima*

VIII Brief Factual Review

Our Lady of Fatima again appeared to Lucia:

(1) December 10, 1925 Our Lady appeared to Lucia while Lucia was in her room at the convent. The Child Jesus was at Our Lady's side elevated upon a cloud of light. Our Lady rested one of Her hands on Lucia's shoulders while Our Lady held in Her other hand a heart surrounded by sharp thorns. Both the Child Jesus and Our Lady spoke to Lucia and gave messages.

Although the Child Jesus again appeared to Lucia and spoke to her on February 15, 1926 Our Lady did not then appear.

In 1927 while praying in the convent chapel in Tuy, Spain, Lucia received permission from heaven to reveal the first two parts of the secret, ie the vision of hell and the urgent need for Devotion to the Immaculate Heart of Mary.

Sr. Lucia tells us that on May 29-30, 1920 during the night, Our Lord informed her of the reason for the Five First Saturdays Devotion.

(2) June 13, 1929 Sr. Lucia had obtained permission from her superiors and confessor to make Holy Hour in the chapel from 11:00 PM until midnight every Thursday night. Being alone one night, she knelt near the altar rails in the middle of the chapel prostrate praying the Prayer of the Angel. Feeling somewhat tired, Lucia stood up and continued to say the prayers with her arms in the form of a cross. The only light was that of the sanctuary lamp. Suddenly the whole chapel was illuminated by a supernatural

light and above the altar appeared a Cross of Light reaching to the ceiling. In brighter light on the upper part of the Cross, Lucia could see the face of a man and his body as far down as the waist; upon his breast was a dove of light; nailed to the Cross was the body of another man. A little below the waist of the man on the Cross, Lucia could see a Chalice and a large Host suspended in the air, into which drops of blood were falling from the Face of Jesus crucified and from the wound in His side. These drops of blood ran down onto the Host and fell into the Chalice. Beneath the right arm of the Cross was Our Lady and in Her left hand was Her Immaculate Heart, without sword or roses, but with a crown of thorns and flames. Under the left arm of the Cross, large letters, as if of crystal clear water which ran down upon the altar, formed these words: 'Graces and Mercy.' Lucia understood that it was the mystery of the Most Holy Trinity which was shown to her.

IX The Primary Messages - 2

(1) Devotion of Reparation of Five First Saturdays - December 10, 1925 Our Lady said: *"My daughter, look at My Heart encircled with the thorns with which ungrateful men pierce it at every moment by their blasphemies and ingratitude. Do you at least try to console Me and announce in My name that I promise to assist at the hour of death with graces necessary for salvation all those who, on the First Saturday of five consecutive months, go to confession and receive Holy Communion, recite the rosary and keep Me company for a quarter of an hour while meditating on the mysteries of the rosary with the intention of making reparation to Me."*

The Child Jesus also spoke to Lucia and gave her messages on this occasion.

On February 15, 1926 the Child Jesus again appeared to Lucia and gave her messages. Our Lady did not appear at this time.

(2) Consecration of Russia to the Immaculate Heart of Mary - June 13, 1929 Our Lady said: *"The moment has come in which God asks the Holy Father, in union with all the bishops of the world, to make the Consecration of Russia to My Immaculate Heart, promising to save it by this means. There are so many souls whom the justice of God condemns for sins committed against Me, that I have come to ask reparation, sacrifice yourself for this intention and pray."*

X Signs Preceding the Apparitions

June 13, 1929; suddenly the chapel was illuminated by a supernatural light.

XI Other Visions During Apparitions

(1) December 10, 1925 the Child Jesus appeared by Our Lady's side elevated on a cloud of light.
(2) June, 13, 1929 Lucia was given to see the Holy Trinity in the form of God the Father, a man above the Cross from the waist up, God the Son as Jesus crucified on the Cross and God the Holy Spirit in the form of a dove, together with the Chalice, dripping blood from the wounds of Jesus onto the Host and into the Chalice, as well as the words: **'Graces and Mercy.'**

XII Prayers Taught to the Seer(s)

It is reported that while Sr. Lucia was in the Chapel in Rianjo, Spain, praying for the conversion of Spain, Portugal, Europe, Russia, and of the world, that Our Lord spoke to Lucia. Jesus told Lucia that He was pleased with her prayer and requested that Lucy ask this grace also of *"My Mother."* Jesus then gave Lucia two prayers:

Prayer: *"Sweet Heart of Mary, be the salvation of Russia, Spain, Portugal, Europe and the whole world."*

Prayer: *"By Thy pure and Immaculate Conception, O Mary, obtain for me the conversion of Russia, Spain, Portugal, Europe, and the whole world."*

XIII Special Devotion Given to the Seer(s)

(1) December 10, 1925 — Five First Saturdays of Reparation to the Immaculate Heart of Mary.
(2) June 13, 1929 — Consecration of Russia to the Immaculate Heart of Mary.

XIV Requests Made by Our Lady

(1) December 10, 1925 — Five First Saturdays of Reparation to the Immaculate Heart of Mary. Go to Confession and receive Holy Communion, recite the rosary and keep Our Lady company for 15 minutes while meditating on the rosary with the intention of making Reparations to the Immaculate Heart of Mary.
(2) June 13, 1929 — Holy Father in union with all the bishops in the world make the consecration of Russia to the Immaculate Heart of Mary. Sacrifice yourself for this intention and pray.

XV Specific Bible References - Not Reported

XVI Secrets Given To The Seer(s)

December 10, 1925 — Five First Saturdays Devotion of Reparation to the Immaculate Heart of Mary.

XVII Miracles Promised by Our Lady - NR
XVIII Miracles Performed - Not Reported
XIX Miracles Promised not yet Performed - NR
XX Signs Promised - Not Reported
XXI Signs Given - Not Reported
XXII Predictions/Promises - Not Reported
XXIII Prophesies/Warnings of Chastisement - NR

XXIV Method of Appearance

(1) December 10, 1925; Mary appeared to Lucia with the Child Jesus at Her side on a cloud of light, while the seer was in her room at the convent.
(2) June 13, 1929; suddenly the chapel in the convent was illuminated by a supernatural light and the apparition became visible to Lucia.

XXV Method of Departure - Mary disappears

XXVI Confrontation w/Civil Authorities - NR
XXVII Confrontation w/Church Authorities - NR
XXVIII Request Chapel/Shrine Built - NR

XXIX Free Will/Choice

(1) December 10, 1925; *"Do you at least try to console Me and announce in My name . . ."*
(2) June 13, 1929; *"Sacrifice yourself for this intention and pray."*

XXX Seer(s)' Suffering/Sacrifice

(1) On February 15, 1926 the Child Jesus again appeared to Lucia and asked her if she had spread this Devotion to the Immaculate Heart of Mary. Lucia told the Lord of the difficulties she had in convincing her superiors and those in the hierarchy of the Church to spread this Devotion to the Immaculate Heart of Mary; all to Lucia's great suffering.

Tuy/Pontevedra, Spain

(2) Likewise, Lucia was informed by Jesus that the first Consecration of Russia to the Immaculate Heart of Mary was incomplete. She made several communications to superiors endeavoring to have the Consecration of Russia to the Immaculate Heart of Mary that would please heaven. Apparently this was accomplished on May 13, 1982.

XXXI Healings Reported

Many physical, mental and spiritual healings are reportedly attributed to Fatima.

XXXII Action Taken by the Church

(1) December 10, 1925 - Devotion of Reparation to the Immaculate Heart of Mary. September 13, 1939 the bishop of Leiria made public the Devotion of Reparation to the Immaculate Heart of Mary.

On December 8, 1942 Pope Pius XII personally consecrated his own diocese of Rome to the Immaculate Heart of Mary.

On May 8, 1944 the Holy See established the Feast of the Immaculate Heart of Mary as a universal Feast Day for the whole Church.

On May 1, 1948 Pope Pius XII issued his Encyclical Auspicia Quaedam which asked for the consecration of dioceses, parishes and families to the Immaculate Heart of Mary.

On October 11, 1954 Pope Pius XII by the Encyclical Ad Caeli Reginam decreed and instituted the Feast of Mary as Queen to be celebrated throughout the world on May 31st.

On May 13, 1967 Pope Paul VI came to the shrine in Fatima and took part in the 50th Anniversary celebration. He invited Sr. Lucia to stand beside him before the great crowd. He promulgated Signum Magnum asking members of the Church to renew their personal consecration to the Immaculate Heart of Mary.

Today the devotion of Reparation to the Immaculate Heart of Mary is practiced throughout the world — spearheaded by the Blue Army.

(2) June 13, 1929 - Consecration of Russia to the Immaculate Heart of Mary. October 31, 1942 Pope Pius XII first consecrated Russia (by veiled allusion to Russia) to the Immaculate Heart of Mary, of which Lucia says: "was incomplete according to HIS wishes."

July 7, 1952 Pope Pius XII issued an apostolic letter Sacro Vergente Ano by which document he again consecrated Russia to the Immaculate Heart of Mary.

October 11, 1954 Pope Pius XII issued the Encyclical Ad Caeli Reginam by which he consecrated the whole human race to the Immaculate Heart of Mary.

On November 21, 1964 Pope Paul VI proclaimed Mary the Mother of the Church and renewed the October 31, 1942 consecration of the world to the Immaculate Heart of Mary.

On May 13, 1981 the Holy Father John Paul II was shot and injured at St. Peter's Square in Rome. Pope John Paul II stated he would personally travel to Fatima to thank Our Lady for saving his life. This he did on May 13, 1982. Sr. Lucia was on the platform with Pope John Paul II during the Mass. At the end of the Mass the Pope consecrated Russia to the Immaculate Heart of Mary in collegial union with all the pastors of the church.

June 28, 1982, Pope John Paul II spoke to the Sacred College of Cardinals in Rome and invited them to join him collegially as he repeated the last paragraph in the Act of Consecration he pronounced at Fatima on May 13, 1982.

XXXIII Bibliography - [See Fatima Bibliography]

Chapter 6

BEAURAING, BELGIUM
(1932-1933)

I Place - Beauraing, Belgium
(Academy at the Convent of Sisters of Christian Doctrine.)

II Dates of First and Last Apparition

First: November 29, 1932
Last: January 3, 1933

III Seer(s) - 5

Name: Gilberte Voisin
Birth: Unknown
Age at first apparition: 13
Status: Unknown

Name: Fernande Voisin
Birth: Unknown
Age at first apparition: 15
Status: Unknown

Name: Albert Voisin
Birth: Unknown
Age at first apparition: 11
Status: Unknown

Name: Andre Degeimbre
Birth: Unknown
Age at first apparition: 14
Status: Unknown

Name: Gilberte Degeimbre
Birth: Unknown
Age at first apparition: 9
Status: Unknown

IV Total Number of Apparitions - 27

V Dates and Locality of Each Apparition

(All apparitions occurred inside the Academy under the Hawthorne tree unless otherwise stated.)

1932: November 29, 30 and December 1 (three apparitions occurred above the viaduct at the Academy); December 2, 4, 5, 7, 8, 9, 10, 11, 12, 14, 17, 21, 23, 24, 28, 29, 30, 31.
1933: January 1, 2 and 3.

VI Description of Our Lady

Our Lady appeared to be 18 or 20. Her eyes are a beautiful deep blue. Rays of light radiated from Her head. Our Lady's smile lighted up Her features and the garb She wore was a long white, heavily pleated gown without a belt. The dress reflected a kind of blue light.

She was walking on air, through the folds of Our Lady's robe the children could see the movements of Our Lady's knees as She walked. Her feet were hidden by a little cloud.

From November 29, 1932 through December 5, 1932 Our Lady carried no rosary; beginning on December 6, 1932 and during each apparition thereafter, Our Lady had a rosary on Her right arm.

On December 29, 1932 Our Lady opened Her arms in the usual gesture of farewell, and when She did so, the seer saw a brilliant heart of gold. The heart was near the center of Her chest, at the place where Our Lady held Her hands. The gold heart was surrounded by little glittering rays, finer than those coming from Our Lady's head. The ends of rays tapered away from the gold heart. This occurred and was seen by one or more of the seers six times (December 29, 30, 31 and January 1, 2, 3).

VII Title(s) of Our Lady - 3

"I am the Immaculate Virgin." - December 2, and 21, 1932.
"I am the Mother of God." - January 3, 1933.
"I am the Queen of Heaven." - January 3, 1933.

VIII Brief Factual Review

Beauraing, Belgium is a village of about 2000 people in Walloon, a (French speaking) part of Belgium.

Hector and Marie Louise Voisin were nominal Catholics and were not practicing their religion. Three of their children and two of the children of Germaine Degeimbre, a widow and a practicing Catholic, were the seers who received these apparitions and messages. Mrs. Degeimbre, as well as Mr. and Mrs. Voisin, each received a strong conversion and thereafter supported the children — although first they were skeptical. Likewise Mother Superior was so disturbed by these events and especially the ruckus caused by the crowds that she barred the children from coming onto Academy grounds. Once she saw that the children were obedient to her demands, she opened her heart, permitted the children to return and she herself believed.

On November 29, 1932 the three Voisin children were joined by the two Degeimbre children as they proceeded to the Academy. They rang the bell and waited for the Sisters to answer the door. It was then that Albert turned and announced that he saw the Blessed Virgin Mary dressed in white walking over the bridge. The other children also saw Her. The children became frightened. Later they told the Sisters and their parents, none of whom believed the children.

Our Lady appeared to the children nearly every day from November 29, 1932 until January 3, 1933. The first six apparitions through December 1, 1932 were silent. Commencing on December 2, 1932 Our Lady gave messages to one or more of the children. Also starting December 2nd the children would instantly fall onto their knees and begin praying and talking in high pitched voices when Our Lady appeared.

Prior to December 6th Our Lady did not carry a rosary, however, beginning December 6, 1932 Our Lady appeared each time with a rosary on Her right arm. Our Lady showed Her Heart of gold (Immaculate Heart) to one or more of the children on six different occasions, namely December 29, 30, 31, and January 1, 2, and 3. Our Lady identified Herself as the Immaculate Virgin, as the Mother of God, and as the Queen of Heaven.

She requested of the children that a chapel be built and that they *"pray, pray very much."* Her first words to the children were *"always be good"* and Her message to Andre on Her last appearance was *"I will convert sinners."* On that last appearance of January 3, 1933 Our Blessed Mother gave secrets to Gilberte Voisin, to Gilberte Degeimbre and to Albert Voisin. Our Lady's last words were to Fernande Voisin when Our Lady said: *"Do you love My Son? Do you love Me?"* After Fernande answered "Yes," Our Lady then said *"Then sacrifice yourself for Me,"* and *"Good-Bye"* as She disappeared.

These apparitions have been approved by the Church.

IX The Primary Messages - 5

1) **Prayer**
2) **Sacrifice**
3) **Conversion of Sinners**
4) **Rosary**
5) **Devotion to the Immaculate Heart of Mary**

December 2, 1932: (First message). Albert asked: "Are you the Immaculate Virgin? Our Lady smiled and nodded Her head. Next, Albert asked "What do you want?" Our Lady's first words were: *"Always be good."*

December 2, 1932: (Third appearance). In reference to the question: "What do you want from us?" Our Lady said: *"Is it true you will always be good?"* "Yes," cried Andre, "We will always be good."

December 4, 1932: Albert Voisin again asked: "Are you the Immaculate Virgin?" Again Our Lady nodded Her head. Fernande Voisin asked: "What day must we come?" Our Lady replied: *"The day of the Immaculate Conception."* (December 8). Fernande Voisin asked: "Should we have a chapel built?" Our Lady responded: *"Yes."*

December 6, 1932: Our Lady appeared for the first time with a rosary over Her right hand. During this apparition the children first began to say the rosary during or while awaiting the apparition. Our Lady wore a rosary during every subsequent apparition.

December 8, 1932: The children crashed to their knees and prayed in a high pitched voice, while the observers and medical men present performed tests on the children, such as applying an open flame to the hands of Gilberte Voisin and Gilberte Degeimbre. Other doctors pinched, slapped and pricked the 5 children. Flashlights were shined in their eyes. There was no reaction, the children were in ecstasy. When it was over no burns nor injury had occurred to the children.

December 9, 1932: Commencing this date the children were kept separated during the apparitions, yet they all fell to their knees at the same instant and all changed into high pitched voices when Our Lady arrived, and all told the same story after the apparitions.

December 17, 1932: The children asked Our Lady, upon the suggestion of a priest: "On behalf of the clergy, we ask what we must do for you?"

The Lady replied: *"A chapel."*

December 21, 1932: The children asked the vision: "Tell us who you are," Our Lady answered: *"I am the Immaculate Virgin."*

December 23, 1932: Fernande asked: "Why do you come?" Our Lady answered: *"That people might come here on pilgrimages."*

December 28, 1932: Our Lady said: *"Soon I shall appear for the last time."*

December 29, 1932: The children had planned to ask Our Lady: "And now what must we do?", but Our Lady opened Her arms in the usual gesture of farewell and when She did so Fernande saw in the Virgin's chest a Heart of Gold surrounded by glittering rays. The other four children did not see it on this occasion.

December 30, 1932: In addition to showing Her Gold Heart again to three of the children, namely Fernande, Andre, and Gilberte Voisin, Our Lady said to the children: *"Pray, pray very much."*

December 31, 1932: Our Lady appeared and showed Her Heart to all five of the children.

January 1, 1933: Our Lady said to Gilberte Voisin: *"Pray always."* Again Our Lady showed Her Heart.

January 2, 1933: Our Lady said: *"Tomorrow I will speak to each one of you separately."* Our Lady showed Her Heart of Gold to the children for the fifth time.

January 3, 1933: On the final appearance Our Lady first spoke to Gilberte Degeimbre: *"This is between you and me, and I ask you to speak of it to no one."* Then Our Lady told Gilberte a secret which has never been revealed and then said: *"Good Bye."*

Our Lady next spoke to Gilberte Voisin these words which are considered the Great Promise of Beauraing: *"I will convert sinners."* Then Our Lady gave Gilberte a secret and said: *"Good Bye."*

Our Lady told Albert a secret and said: *"Good Bye."*

To Andre Our Lady said: *"I am the Mother of God, the Queen of Heaven, pray always."* and *"Good Bye."*

Fernande was crushed when Our Lady left without telling her a secret. However, Our Lady dramatically reappeared to Fernande and said: *"Do you love My Son?"* Fernande said: "Yes." Our Lady said: *"Do you love Me?"* Fernande said: "Yes." Our Lady then said: *"Then sacrifice yourself for Me."* Extending Her arms Our Lady showed Her Heart to Fernande and said *"Good Bye."*

X Signs Preceding the Apparitions

January 3, 1933. After Our Lady had appeared to the other children, Fernande could not see Her, yet Fernande refused to leave the area and continued to pray and plead with Our Mother — Suddenly a crack of thunder shot through the evening sky, followed by a ball of fire, which landed on the Hawthorne tree. Everyone could see it. The crowd froze, then Fernande broke into a smile. The Immaculate Virgin had heard her prayer and appeared to Fernande again.

XI Other Visions During Apparitions

Our Lady did show Her Gold Heart on six occasions.

XII Prayers Taught to the Seer(s) - Not Reported

XIII Special Devotion Given to the Seer(s)

(1) Though no express devotions were stated — the Immaculate Virgin did show Her gold heart on six occasions, which certainly was meant to bring to mind devotion to Her Immaculate Heart.
(2) Also, commencing on the 6th apparition (December 2nd) Our Lady held a rosary on Her right arm each time — again a strong reminder to pray the rosary.

XIV Requests Made by Our Lady

(1) December 2, 1932: *"Always be good."*
(2) December 23, 1932: Our Lady said She came *". . . so that people might come here on pilgrimages."*
(3) December 6, 1932: Our Lady silently requested that we pray the rosary, by appearing with a rosary on Her right arm during all apparitions after December 1st.
(4) Our Lady silently urged the devotion to Her Immaculate Heart by showing Her Gold Heart on six separate occurrences.

XV Specific Bible Reference Given - Not Reported

XVI Secrets Given to the Seer(s)

On January 3, 1933 Our Lady gave secrets to three of the seers, namely; Gilberte Degeimbre, Gilberte Voisin, and Albert Voisin. These secrets have never been revealed; although it is reported that when Albert Voisin was questioned about the secret Our Lady had confided in him, he said that it contained only a few words and that the message was sad to him.

Beauraing, Belgium

XVII Miracles Promised by Our Lady

December 8, 1932: Because Our Lady asked the children to come to the apparition site on this Feast Day of the Immaculate Conception, the crowd expected a miracle. The unusual occurrence was the testing done to the children with open flames, flashlights shined into their eyes and sensory tests, all of which did not disturb the children nor cause pain or injury.

XVIII Miracles Performed - Not Reported
XIX Miracles Promised not yet Performed - NR

XX Signs Promised

January 2, 1933 Our Lady promised to speak to each seer separately on the following day. She kept Her promise on January 3, 1933.

XXI Signs Given

January 3, 1933 Our Lady disappeared after appearing and speaking to 4 children. Then suddenly She reappeared to Fernande. This was preceded by a crack of thunder and a ball of fire which landed on the Hawthorne tree and was visible to everyone present.

XXII Predictions/Promises

(1) **On December 4, 1932** and probably also on December 6th Our Lady asked the children to come to the apparition site on December 8th, thus silently stating that Our Lady would appear on December 8th, Her Feast Day of the Immaculate Conception. This prediction came true as Our Lady did appear to the children on December 8th.

(2) **On December 28, 1932** Our Lady said: *"Soon I shall appear for the last time."* This promise came true on January 3, 1933.

(3) **On January 2, 1933** Our Lady said: *"Tomorrow I will speak to each one of you separately."* This promise came true on January 3, 1933.

(4) **On January 3, 1933** Our Lady said *"I will convert sinners."* This prediction came true promptly and continues to be played out by the Immaculate Virgin. Witness the return to the faith of Mrs. Degeimbre, and the fervent embrace of the faith by Mr. and Mrs. Voisin after years of not attending Mass or receiving the sacraments.

Among the most famous of the converts was a young man who had given up his faith and became a communist. He became editor of the Belgium communist newspaper, Le Drapeau Rouge (The Red Flag). During the German occupation he was imprisoned. While in prison he promised Our Lady he would return to the faith if he was freed from prison. He was freed.

Later in September 1945 he had an urge to visit Beauraing and found himself standing before the Hawthorne tree. Suddenly he was thrown to the ground "I was trying to protect myself from the fall." he said "and I fell, hanging onto the back of the last bench. For a long time I saw nothing but the figure of Our Lady in the Hawthorne tree. A complete transformation was produced in me. I cried over my past life. But I also cried for joy, conscious that something new had entered my soul!" The next day this former editor went to confession and received Holy Communion. He now receives Communion every day. It was through him that the Legion of Mary was established in Belgium.

XXIII Prophecies/Warnings of Chastisement - NR

XXIV Method of Appearance

(1) The first appearances of Our Lady were outside the Academy when Our Lady suddenly appeared to the children, by walking above the viaduct.
(2) The balance of the apparitions occurred under the lower branch of the Hawthorne tree on the Academy grounds where Our Lady had also suddenly appeared.
(3) It was only at the final appearance to Fernande on January 3, 1933 when a loud clap of thunder followed by a ball of fire which landed on the Hawthorne tree, observed by all present, that Our Lady's method of appearance was so dramatic and different from Her other appearances.

XXV Method of Departure

(1) Her usual departure was by opening Her arms in a gesture of farewell.
(2) Six times She also showed Her Gold Heart as She opened Her arms in the typical farewell gesture. (December 29, 30, 31, and January 1, 2 and 3).
(3) On January 3, 1933 She also said: *"Good Bye!"* to each of the children separately.

XXVI Confrontation w/Civil Authorities

There was great opposition to these apparitions from the socialist press, the police, teachers and from government members. Many books were written to disparage the apparitions. Little by little this opposition lost its force.

XXVII Confrontation w/Church Authorities

At first the parish priest was reserved and hesitant. Mother Superior was outright hostile. However, they both became strong believers.

XXVIII Request Chapel/Shrine Built

On December 4, 1932 and again on December 17, 1932 Our Lady requested a chapel be built. On December 23, 1932 She asked: *"That people might come here on pilgrimages."*

XXIX Free Will/Choice

(1) December 2, 1932 Our Lady said: *"Is it true you will always be good?"* and the children said: "Yes."
(2) January 3, 1933 Our Lady said to Fernande: *"Do you love My Son?" "Do you love Me?"* Fernande said: "Yes." Then Our Lady said: *"Then sacrifice yourself for Me."*

XXX Seer(s)' Suffering/Sacrifice

The families of the seers, together with their friends and neighbors did not believe the children and were rude to them at first.
Mrs. Degeimbre thought the children were playing a trick on everyone. At one point, armed with a stick, she thrashed about the bushes where the apparitions occurred looking for the person playing these tricks.
On December 3rd, Mother Superior banned the children from coming to the Academy. It was only after the crowd heckled her that she relented. She said that because the children had obeyed her and stayed away on December 3rd, she thereafter permitted the children to come to the street outside the garden at dusk.
All this served to cause great pain and anxiety to the children.

XXXI Healings Reported

(1) There have been at least two cures recognized as miraculous. Many other cures are reported.
(2) One among many cures is that of Maria Van Loer of Turnhout, Belgium, who had been a helpless invalid for 16 of her 33 years, with a tubercular condition. Her spinal column was deformed, one of her legs was diseased and had large tumors which had developed into open sores. The doctors said an operation would be fatal, and they held no hope for her recovery. Miss Van Loer was taken to Beauraing on June 23,

1933 and her stretcher was taken to the Hawthorne tree. She also saw and spoke with Gilberte Degeimbre and returned a second time to the Hawthorne tree where she found herself able to move for the first time. Later that day, when she arrived at her home in Turnhout, she was completely cured. No pain, no tumors, no sores, and no deformities. Maria Van Loer is today Sister Prudentia of the Franciscan Sisters of the Holy Family, where she leads an active life.

XXXII Action Taken by the Church

(1) In 1935 the bishop of Namur in the diocese in which Beauraing is located, appointed an Episcopal Commission to investigate the facts. This bishop died, but the investigation continued.

(2) On February 2, 1943 the bishop authorized public devotions to 'Our Lady of Beauraing.'

(3) July 2, 1949 the bishop released two documents:

(a) An Episcopal Decree declaring that two cures of the many cures were authentic miracles credited to Our Lady of Beauraing (one was Miss Van Loer).

(b) A letter from the bishop to the clergy of his diocese, wherein the bishop said: "We are able in all serenity and prudence to affirm that the Queen of Heaven appeared to the children of Beauraing during the winter of 1932-33 especially to show us in Her Maternal Heart the anxious appeal for prayer and the promise of Her powerful mediation for the conversion of sinners."

XXXIII Bibliography

A Woman Clothed with the Sun   1990
By: John J. Delaney
Published by: Image Books/Doubleday

The Woman Shall Conquer   1986
By: Don Sharkey
Published by: AMI Press

Dictionary of Mary   1985
By: various contributors
Published by: Catholic Book Publishing Co.

The Immaculate Heart of Mary 1976
By: Fr. Joseph A. Pelletier, A.A.,
Published by: Assumption Publication

The Many Faces of Mary 1987
By: Bob and Penny Lord
Published by: Journeys of Faith

Chapter 7

BANNEUX, BELGIUM
1933

I Place - Banneux, Belgium
(in the garden at seer's home and at the spring)

II Dates of First and Last Apparition

First: January 15, 1933
Last: March 2, 1933

III Seer(s) - 1

Name: Mariette Beco
Birth: March 21, 1921
Age at first apparition: 11
Status: Unknown

IV Total Number of Apparitions - 8

V Dates and Locality of Each Apparition

The location of the apparitions listed below is in the garden at the seer's home.

1933: January 15, 18, 19, 20; February 11, 15, 20; March 2nd.

VI Description of Our Lady

Mariette the seer saw a light in the small garden in front of her house, within this light was a lovely Lady seeming to be all light. The Lady was young, beautiful and had a most gracious smile. Her head and shoulders were slightly bent to the left looking towards the seer.

A great oval light enveloped Her body. Her gown was spotless and dazzling white, chastely closed at the collar and falling in the simple dignity of broad pleats. Her sash, an unforgettable sky blue, was loosely fashioned around the waist and terminated in two streamers at Our Lady's left knee. Covering Our Lady's head, shoulders, and arms was a veil as completely white as Her gown, but of a transparent material. Our Lady was inclined to the left and forward, with the hem of Her dress slightly lifted, exposing Her right foot which was crowned with a golden rose. On Her right arm hung a rosary of diamond-like brilliance, whose golden chain and cross reflected in the light. Our Lady's hands, folded together, as is usual in prayer, imparted an air of familiarity as their fingers pointed downward, not upward. Later apparitions showed Her hands pointed upward in prayer.

Our Lady's head was surrounded by rays of light that resembled long and short 'pencils'. She resembled Our Lady of Lourdes.

VII Title(s) of Our Lady - 3

(1) January 19, 1933: *"I am The Virgin Of The Poor"*
(2) March 2, 1933: *"I am The Mother of the Savior."*
(3) March 2, 1933: *"I am The Mother Of God"*

VIII Brief Factual Review

Banneux, Belgium is a small hamlet located about 15 miles from Liege.

Mariette Beco, age 11, was the oldest of seven children living at home with their parents. The world was in the midst of a great depression and the Beco family was poor. Neither of the Beco parents practiced their Catholic faith. Mariette had dropped from her religious instruction class preparing her for First Holy Communion.

On the evening of January 15, 1933 Mariette and her mother were at home busy with household chores. Mariette was awaiting dinner for her brother Julien, who was due home. As Mariette waited at the window she lifted the sheet (which doubled as a curtain) from the window and suddenly saw a lovely Lady seeming to be all light, in the garden. Thinking she was being tricked, Mariette moved the oil lamp but the luminous Lady remained. Mariette informed her mother "There's a woman in the garden". Mrs. Beco at first said, "Nonsense," however to silence Mariette, Mrs. Beco looked out the window and saw a white light in the general form of a person of normal size, slightly bent to the left and wearing what appeared to be a sheet over her head. She could not make out the distinct features Mariette had announced, so with some alarm she declared "It's a witch!"

Mariette started to pray the rosary that she had found earlier by chance along the road. After several decades, Our Lady's lips began to move in prayer and Our Lady placed Her left hand on Her breast, lifted Her left hand to the level of Her head and beckoned Mariette with Her index finger. Mariette attempted to go outside but Mrs. Beco covered the window with the sheet and bolted the door. When Mariette again looked out the window the light was gone.

Later Mariette told one of her friends who promptly informed the parish priest. The following day Mr. Beco experimented with lanterns but was unable to duplicate the light reported by Mariette. He also accompanied Mariette the following evening when she went to the garden at 7:00 PM to kneel and pray the rosary in the cold freezing weather, awaiting Our Lady's visit.

On all subsequent appearances Mariette would extend her hands and fall hard to her knees (if standing), then her voice and the pace of her rosary quickened when Our Lady arrived. It was in this way that onlookers could tell when Our Lady appeared. Also during all subsequent appearances Mariette observed Our Lady appear from between the top of two pine trees, gradually becoming larger and soon standing but five feet away from the seer, resting on a smokish grey cloud about one foot off the earth. Our Lady's head was surrounded by rays of light.

When Our Lady directed Mariette to the Spring, Our Lady floated on the cloud, gliding through openings in the fence onto the road.

On January 18, 1933 Mr. Beco witnessed the second apparition, which was also the first time Our Lady led Mariette to an unknown Spring in a ditch some 300-400 feet away, along the road. The next day, Mr. Beco went to confession and Holy Communion, which was the first time he had done so since he made his First Holy Communion as a child. He now believed.

Our Lady appeared four times in a six day period, then after some time elapsed she appeared four times more. She gave a secret to Mariette and gave messages every time except on the first occasion. On two occasions Our Lady blessed Mariette with imposition of Her hands and the Sign of the Cross, and each time Mariette collapsed.

During the second appearance Our Lady showed Mariette the Spring and said: *"Dip your hand in the water. This Spring is set aside for Me,"* and again on January 19, 1933 Our Lady said: *"This Spring is set apart for all countries, to help the sick,"*

On each occasion Our Lady bid Mariette *"Good Bye for now"* (Au Revoir) except on the last visit when Our Lady simply said: *"Good Bye"* (Adieu).

It is interesting to note that on the evening of January 15, 1933 while Our Lady was appearing to Mariette for the first time; that meanwhile in Liege, Bishop Kerkhof was consecrating his diocese to the Immaculate Heart of Mary, in fulfillment of Our Lady of Fatima's request.

Also of interest was the February 15, 1933 appearance when Mariette (at the priest's direction) inquired of Our Lady: "Holy Virgin, Father told me to ask a sign from you". Our Lady responded: *"Trust Me. I will trust you."* These apparitions have been approved by the local bishop.

IX The Primary Messages - 4

(1) Prayer
(2) To relieve suffering
(3) Help the poor
(4) Pray the Rosary

January 15, 1933 - No messages were given to the seer. The Holy Virgin, in resplendent light, prayed, smiled on Mariette and motioned her to come closer.

January 18, 1933 - After praying for some time Our Lady led Mariette to the Spring and said: *"Dip your hands in the Water. This Spring is set apart for Me. Good Evening. Good Bye for now."*

January 19, 1933 - Mariette asks: "Who are you Beautiful Lady?" The Holy Virgin replies: *"I am the Virgin of the Poor."* Then Our Lady led the seer to the Spring again. Kneeling at the source Mariette said: "Beautiful Lady, yesterday you said 'This Spring is for me' Why for me?" Our Lady seemed amused and said: *"This Spring is reserved for all nations — to relieve the sick".* Then Our Lady said *"I will pray for you. Good Bye for now."*

January 20, 1933 - Mariette asks: "What do you wish, my Beautiful Lady?" The Holy Virgin replies: *"I would like a small chapel."* Then Our Lady, just before departing, unfolded Her hands from their prayerful position, imposed them on Mariette, then with Her right hand, blessed Mariette with the Sign of the Cross. At this point Mariette collapsed.

February 11, 1933 - The Feast day of Our Lady of Lourdes. For a third time Our Lady led the seer to the Spring and said: *"I come to relieve suffering. Good Bye for now."*

February 15, 1933 - It was during this apparition that Mariette said: "Holy Virgin, Father told me to ask a sign from you." The Holy Virgin replied: *"Trust Me. I will trust you."* Then Our Lady confided a secret to Mariette and added: *"Pray much. Good Bye for now."*

February 20, 1933 - For a fourth time Our Lady led Mariette to the Spring. Our Lady appeared grave and unsmiling and said: *"My dear child, pray much. Good Bye for now."*

March 2, 1933 - Our Lady said: *"I am the Mother of the Savior, Mother of God. Pray much."* Mariette answered: "Yes, yes." Then Our Lady again imposed Her hands on Mariette and blessed her with the Sign of the Cross. Our Lady said: *"Adieu"*.

X Signs Preceding the Apparitions - Not Reported

XI Other Visions During Apparitions

Although no other visions were reportedly received by Mariette, nonetheless, Mrs. Beco did see a white light in the general form of a person of normal size, slightly bent to the left, and wearing what appeared to be a sheet over her head, which prompted her to exclaim: **"witch!"**

XII Prayers Taught to the Seer(s)

(1) Although no new prayers were taught to Mariette, yet Our Lady is seen in prayer by Mariette during the apparitions.
(2) Our Lady said on three occasions: *"Pray much"* and told Mariette on January 19, 1933, *"I will pray for you"*.

XIII Special Devotion Given to the Seer(s) - NR

XIV Requests Made by Our Lady

(1) On January 19, 1933 Our Lady identified Herself as: **"The Virgin of the Poor"** and later on February 11, 1933 Our Lady said: *"I come to relieve suffering"*. It seems She requests us to help the poor.
(2) Pray much, February 15, 20 and March 2, 1933.
(3) A Spring; Our Lady led Mariette to the Spring during four apparitions and requested Mariette to dip her hands into the water, and said that the Spring was set apart for all countries, to help the sick.
(4) Build chapel — On January 20, 1933 Our Lady said: *"I would like a small chapel."* The chapel was built. A basilica was later built.
(5) On February 15, 1933 Our Lady said: *"Trust Me. I will trust you"*.

XV Specific Bible References - Not Reported

XVI Secrets Given to the Seer(s)

On February 15, 1933 Our Lady confided a secret to Mariette which has never been revealed.

XVII Miracles Promised by Our Lady - NR
XVIII Miracles Performed - Not Reported
XIX Miracles Promised not yet Performed - NR

XX Signs Promised

On January 18, 1933 and on subsequent appearances, Our Lady led Mariette to an unknown Spring. On January 19, Our Lady said: *"This Spring is set apart for all countries, to help the sick".* Many healings have been reported.

XXI Signs Given

(1) Spring: Our Lady led Mariette to discover a Spring that was set apart for all countries, to help the sick.
(2) When requested to give a sign on February 15, 1933 Our Lady said: *"Trust Me. I will trust you."*

XXII Predictions/Promises

(1) January 19, 1933 Our Lady said: *"I will pray for you".*
(2) On February 15, 1933 Our Lady said: *"Trust Me. I will trust you."*

XXIII Prophecies/Warnings of Chastisement - NR

XXIV Method of Appearance

The Holy Virgin, all-luminous, appeared descending between the tops of two pine trees, gradually becoming larger and soon standing but five feet from the seer, resting on a smokish grey cloud about one foot above the earth. Upon Our Lady's arrival Mariette would open her arms and usually say: "Here She is."

XXV Method of Departure

As in Her appearances, Our Lady departed by ascending above the pines and becoming smaller as She traveled in Her chariot of light and finally disappeared.

XXVI Confrontation w/Civil Authorities - NR

XXVII Confrontation w/Church Authorities

The local pastor, Abbe Louis Jamin, did not believe in the truth of the apparitions, and was skeptical throughout the apparitions. Yet he was the one who requested an interview with Mariette and her family and reported to his bishop. Soon his skepticism faded and he too believed.

XXVIII Request Chapel/Shrine Built

On January 20, 1933 Our Lady requested that a small Chapel be built. The Chapel was completed on August 15, 1933. Later, a basilica was built—the Chapel remains.

XXIX Free Will/Choice

February 15, 1933 Our Lady said: *"Trust Me. I will trust you."*

XXX Seer(s)' Suffering/Sacrifice

Mariette's parents did not believe her, neither did her parish pastor. Her own grandmother and aunt, ridiculed her. Of course this caused great distress and grief to Mariette. On top of that she was abused and mocked by some of the boys at her school who would mock her by genuflecting to her. Once these boys physically beat her. Likewise some of the girls in her school would give vulgar imitations of Our Lady and then jeerfully sing out: "Good Morning Bernadette".

XXXI Healings Reported

(1) Both of Mariette's parents were converted and became devout practicing Catholics. Mariette herself, who had dropped out of her First Communion class, attended and devoted such sincere effort that she alone was permitted to receive First Communion at an earlier date.

(2) The rosary has been recited in Banneux each evening at seven o'clock since the Holy Virgin first appeared, praying for the poor, the suffering, and for peace among nations.

(3) Almost immediately miraculous cures and conversions took place. As a matter of fact because of the great number of miracles that took place at the little shrine the church was caught by surprise. In Bishop Kerkhof's work (Notre-Dame de Banneux) he lists 20 miraculous cures which took place at Banneux between May 21, 1933 and 1938.

(4) One of the most spectacular cures was that of Benito Pelegri Garcia who lived in Spain. His right arm was so severely injured in an

explosion that he was unable to work. His wife, a Belgian, heard of Banneux and insisted they travel to Banneux. They walked from Barcelona, Spain to Banneux under the hot midsummer sun, and had given up wine and tobacco during the journey as a penance.

Once in Banneux, Benito plunged both hands into the Spring. His left hand found the water pleasantly cool, but his right hand found it boiling hot. Withdrawing his hands he said: "If you are the Virgin of the Poor, prove it. Here is a man who has come all the way from Spain." He thrust his right hand into the pool a second time. Then he withdrew the drain tube from the wound. Before the amazed eyes of everyone present, the wound closed, the flesh became sound and the arm was completely healed.

XXXII Action Taken by the Church

(1) March 1942, Bishop Kerkhof sent a pastoral letter to his diocese informing the people of clearance from Rome.
(2) In 1942, during the German occupation, the bishop authorized the Cult of Our Lady of Banneux.
(3) On the Feast of the Immaculate Heart of Mary in 1949, the Church through the bishop, officially recognized the reality of the apparitions at Banneux.

XXXIII Bibliography

A Woman Clothed with the Sun   1990
Edited by: John J. Delaney
Published by: Doubleday/Image

The Many Faces of Mary, *A Love Story*   1987
By: Bob and Penny Lord
Published by: Journeys of Faith

Dictionary of Mary   1985
By: various contributors
Published by: Catholic Book Publishing Co.

The Woman Shall Conquer   1976
By: Don Sharkey
Published by: AMI Press

Chapter 8

PIOTROWICZA, POLAND
(1934-1986)

I Place - Piotrowicza, Poland

II Dates of First And Last Apparition

First: 1934
Last: 1986 (last reported)
Note: These apparitions may be ongoing.

III Seer(s) - 1

Name: Wladyslaw Biernacki
Birth: November 10, 1922
Age at first apparition: 12
Status: Unknown

IV Total Number of Apparitions - 6

V Dates and Locality of Each Apparition

It is reported there were a total of 31 apparitions of Our Lady, and some 67 of Jesus; with only a few identified with dates and/or places.
1934: When the seer was 12; his mother recovered from an illness.
During World War II: Our Lady said: *"Don't kill anyone."* Our Lady protected the seer from harm on different occasions.
1945: She appeared and/or spoke to him.
1950's: Our Lady and Our Lord appeared together.
1973: Monastery of Jasna Gora.
1985: July 28, Piotrowicza, Poland.

VI Description of Our Lady

Our Lady is not described in the English translation.

VII Title(s) of Our Lady - Not Reported

VIII Brief Factual Review

Wladyslaw Biernacki was born on November 10, 1922 in eastern Poland in a place named Alexsandrouska. His father was a farmer and also painted religious icons. His father died when Wladyslaw was six. Two years later his mother remarried and they had two children together (one boy and one girl).

The seer began to have mystical experiences at an early age. In 1934 when he was only twelve, his mother became seriously ill. He became distressed and ran away to the forest where he spent three days and nights. It was here that the Blessed Virgin Mary first appeared to him, and assured him that his mother had recovered and was preparing his dinner. He went home and happily found this to be true.

Wladyslaw longed to become a priest, however the hardship of the coming war prevented him from doing so. During World War II he fought in guerrilla units alongside the Russians against the Nazis, and later in the Polish People's Army. About the time when the Second World War broke out he received a locution from Our Lady. She said: *"My son, always remember this: DON'T KILL ANYBODY, and you won't be killed yourself."* He took this admonition to heart and purposely aimed away so as not to kill any enemy soldiers. For this he was often rewarded and protected from harm during the course of the war.

It is reported that on several occasions Our Blessed Mother protected him from certain death, among them:

(1) On one occasion they were involved in very fierce fighting. Out of 1,000 men in his battalion, Wladyslaw was the only one to come out completely unscathed.

(2) On another occasion, he was dressed as a civilian when a German soldier shot at him from a distance of less than ten feet, and missed. The soldier then seized Wladyslaw, brought him before the mayor and declared that Wladyslaw was a robber. The mayor ordered him to be executed by a six man firing squad immediately. Just before the command to fire was given, he heard a voice say: *"Don't be scared."* Then, a German Colonel came by and stayed the illegal execution of a civilian. Wladyslaw was released.

(3) In 1941 enemy troops surrounded Wladyslaw's house. He tried to escape but the enemy, some 70 troops, were in hot pursuit, when he

heard these words: *"Throw yourself into the water and breathe through the stem of a reed and you won't be found."* He looked around, saw a large bomb crater full of water with reeds growing around the water. He did as the voice said and was never discovered.

(4) Another time he heard the voice of Our Blessed Mother tell him exactly where to hide in a cornfield so he would be safe from his intended captors.

(5) In 1945 he was in a Soviet-run political prison, Gliwice Polska, and had been sentenced to be shot to death at 10:00 AM the next day. During the night at 4:30 AM, the Virgin Mary appeared to Wladyslaw in his cell. She told him: *"Get up my son."* In some way he cannot explain, Our Lady made him invisible and he just walked out of prison. She led him to safety after his escape.

In 1945 after the war, Wladyslaw came to live in Swinowjscie for about a four year period. He was harassed by the Secret Police and pressured to join the Communist Party, which he refused to do. In 1953 he married Krystyna Mackiewicz and moved to a farm near the village of Piotrowicza. They have four children, all of whom live nearby. Wladyslaw and his wife live a simple life on the farm. He also does well-drilling for income and then spends much of his time giving talks to various groups for which he never takes money. He and his wife are both faithful Catholics. Yet his wife does not fully understand or share his gifts of healing and prophecy. Wladyslaw is quoted as saying: "I am inclined to treat life as a pilgrimage and so do not get too preoccupied about this."

It is reported that once when Wladyslaw was having difficulties reconciling his family duties with his wider mission, Jesus and St. Peter appeared to him and said: *"You are the husband, and head of the household, and so you have the right to be obeyed by your wife, by your children, and even by all your domesticated animals. You must not antagonize your wife in any way, but you must carry out Our orders. If you do this faithfully, you'll one day be seated here beside us. We too had families in our times, and suffered what you suffer now, but we chose to listen, not to our wives, but to Christ; and to follow and serve Him. So do the same yourself. Even though your path will be hard, it will lead you to eternal life, to salvation."*

Nowadays Krystyna creates no difficulties for Wladyslaw and they live in harmony.

Wladyslaw was given the gifts of healing and prophecy. He is ridiculed by some of his neighbors for these gifts, yet he is lauded for his expertise in well-drilling and for his personal integrity.

He first discovered that he was given the gift of healing in 1973. This was at the monastery of Jasna Gora where Our Lady appeared to him and told him he had been chosen by Almighty God for this work. He claims that for healings to occur the person to be healed must have great faith and must have a great desire to be healed. At the time of laying on of hands no metal objects should be on the person, and the person should not watch television nor smoke for the first two weeks thereafter.

Wladyslaw conducts healing services throughout Poland at local churches by authority of the local parish priest and bishop. Sometimes the number of people attending run into the thousands and the services sometimes go on until two or three in the morning.

He has been successful in healing every type of sickness or disease except for venereal diseases and acute infections. He explains that there are instant cures which take from two to ten minutes, and regular healings that take from one day to months for complete healing. It is reported that during his healing services conducted in Poland, the cure rate is often as high as 97%; and of those, half or so are instantly cured. In 1983 his own bishop, Jan Nowak of Czestochowa, was cured of a primary hepatoma.

Wladyslaw also was given the gift of prophecy. The prophetic messages were first given to him by Jesus Himself in 1973, later also by Our Blessed Mother, and at other times by Bishop Bilewica, formerly the bishop of Lvov, who died in 1973.

Jesus has appeared to Wladyslaw some 67 times and Our Lady has appeared to him 31 times. Several saints and Apostles have also appeared to him. In addition Satan has appeared to Wladyslaw and harassed him.

The prophetic messages received are in great detail and generally relate to the great chastisement, World War III, three days of darkness and an era of peace.

During 1985 and 1986 he traveled to England for healing and speaking engagements at the specific request of Jesus. On Easter Sunday, April 7, 1985 it is reported that Jesus showed purgatory to Wladyslaw and took him down into hell. This is described in some detail and was well remembered by the seer.

The bishops of Poland have given Wladyslaw their unanimous backing! One example of the high esteem in which the bishops of Poland hold the seer is reported, when in 1979 Cardinal Stefan Wyszynski died unexpectedly, a successor had to be found. Thereupon a delegation from the bishops came to the seer's home and found him working in the garden digging potatoes. The delegation presented the seer a list of seven names of potential successors to Cardinal Stefan. Wladyslaw discounted each name except the final name Glemp and said: "This man is not perfect but he is the best of the lot." A few days later this priest was appointed as the new Archbishop of Warsaw. It is reported that the seer and Pope John Paul II have been friends since the 1970's when Pope John Paul II was then Karol Wojtyla, the Archbishop of Krakow.

Although the seer is nearly entirely unknown in the West, now books of the seer's life, healings and prophecies have been translated into several languages. Some 700,000 audio cassettes of his prophecies have been circulated in Poland, to which are added about 5,000 a week. It is further reported that he does not derive one single penny from the sale of these books or cassettes.

IX The Primary Messages - 3

(1) **Prayer**
(2) **Penance**
(3) **Rosary**

As Jesus told the Seer: *"My people, come to your senses before twelve o'clock strikes! Take refuge beneath My Cross, because it is only through the Cross that you will ever attain Eternal Salvation. Humble your hearts before the majesty of God. I have opened for you the gates of heaven and I want to lead you all to Eternal Happiness, and would love to meet every one of you there! Do penance, pray, pray the rosary, and show love towards everyone. The holy rosary is the great scourge of Satan, of this seducer of the people of God."*

X Signs Preceding The Apparitions

None reported, although the apparitions reported usually occurred during a time of significant trial in the seer's life.

XI Other Visions During Apparitions

(1) Jesus appeared to the seer some 67 times.
(2) Bishop Bilewica appeared to the seer and gave him some prophecies.
(3) Saint Peter and other saints and apostles appeared to the seer.
(4) The seer was shown hell on Easter Sunday, 1985.

XII Prayers Taught to the Seer(s) - Not Reported

XIII Special Devotion Given to the Seer(s)

Although no new devotion is given; yet it is reported that:
(1) The seer predicted a period of 20 years of peace after the chastisement, when there will be a triumphant reign of the United Hearts; that is the Sacred Heart of Jesus and the Sorrowful and Immaculate Heart of Mary.
(2) The seer is reported to say that his prophecies are nothing less than personal pleadings of Jesus and Mary to avoid sin, practice virtues, and consecrate ourselves to Our Lord and to Our Blessed Mother who will lead us all to the Eternal Happiness of Heaven.

XIV Requests Made by Our Lady

The first request made of the seer was *"not to kill anyone."* The seer faithfully complied and in turn was saved from harm.

XV Specific Bible References

(1) Apocalypse 9:3-6
(2) Apocalypse 20:4-6
(3) Apocalypse 21:8

XVI Secrets Given to the Seer(s)

Wladyslaw alludes to secrets given to him by Jesus when he states that he can only tell certain things about his trip to hell on Easter Sunday 1985.

XVII Miracles Promised by Our Lady

Our Lady promised to, and in fact did, keep the seer safe from harm during the war.

XVIII Miracles Performed

(1) Our Lady kept Her promise and intervened to miraculously protect the seer and save him from certain harm on several different occasions.
(2) God performed many miraculous cures and healings through the seer— and continues to do so through his healing powers.

XIX Miracles Promised not yet Performed - NR

XX Signs Promised

It is reported that some years ago the bishops of Poland tried to pressure the seer to change some of his prophecies. He refused; and today the bishops accept the messages as they are.

XXI Signs Given

Our Lady gave the seer many signs during the war when She protected him from harm.

XXII Predictions/Promises

(1) In 1934 Our Lady predicted that the seer's mother had recovered from an illness. It was true just as stated.
(2) The record is replete with numerous detailed predictions of future events and happenings. Most have to do with the coming chastisement.
(3) Our Lord told the seer: *"One day you will die as a martyr."*

XXIII Prophecies/Warnings of Chastisement

A great portion of the reported prophecies have to do with warnings of great natural catastrophes, wars, three days of darkness, the chastisement and the ensuing era of peace, among which are briefly:

(1) The world is going to be devastated (during the next few years) by a series of quite un-predicted natural disasters.
(2) During the same time there is going to take place a worldwide political and military upheaval, culminating in a Third World War.
(3) He predicts three days of darkness and the earth spinning off its axis.
(4) Due to these occurrences, the population of the planet will have been reduced to one-quarter of its present level.
(5) Pope John Paul II will reign for 16 years and suffer much until 1994. After him will come only two more popes.
(6) He predicts East Germany will defect from the Warsaw Pact, a revolution will break out in Poland, the once-great Soviet empire will become extinct six weeks after the restoration of order to Poland, the Ukranian national groups will try to drive off Russian armies, Hungary and Romania will experience anticommunist uprisings, and that China, the United States, England and Canada (among others) will take part in World War III.
(7) He predicts there will be great hardships and famine throughout North America with plagues and epidemics raging unchecked. There will be a sudden breakdown in law and order in the United States, due to widespread uprisings fomented by communists. The nation will be completely divided; brother will fight brother, the poor will murder the rich farmers and factory owners everywhere, looting and burning their property.
(8) Great Britain will have grave civil disturbance much like those predicted for the USA.
(9) After the three days of darkness there will be a great calm. The great centers of population will now be just gigantic graveyards.
(10) He states that if there is sufficient repentance, these chastisements can be lessened and mitigated in certain places.
(11) He states that the Anti-Christ was born in 1977 near the border of Israel and Egypt.

(12) That upon the Second Coming of Christ everyone in the world will see Him, the evil people will have either died or have been converted, and only the good will remain for the period of Great Peace.

XXIV Method of Appearance - Not Reported
XXV Method of Departure - Not Reported

XXVI Confrontation w/Civil Authorities

(1) It was reported that the seer was pressured to join the Communist Party which he refused to do.
(2) It is also reported that he was ridiculed by his neighbors and others who didn't believe in the truth of the prophecies.

XXVII Confrontation w/Church Authorities

Likewise it is reported that the bishops of Poland tried to pressure the seer to change some of the prophecies. He refused and they have accepted the prophecies as received.

XXVIII Request Chapel/Shrine Built - NR

XXIX Free Will/Choice

It is reported several times that the seer was given messages like *"now is the time to come to your senses"*, which clearly indicates that we are to use our free will and choose to return to God.

XXX Seer(s)' Suffering/Sacrifice

(1) The seer was ridiculed by his neighbors and others which undoubtedly grieved him.
(2) Also, when the bishops of Poland tried to pressure Wladyslaw to change his prophecies, this must have caused him great distress.

XXXI Healings Reported

(1) Wladyslaw received the gift of healing. It is reported that up to 97% of the people attending his healing sessions in Polish churches were healed; about half of those experienced instant healings.
(2) It is reported that a great variety of diseases and conditions were healed through the seer; everything except venereal disease and acute infections.

Wladyslaw even healed his own bishop.
(3) Conversions are reported as a result of the miraculous healings and also as a result of the prophecies which were fulfilled.

XXXII Action Taken by the Church

(1) It is reported that the Polish bishops are unanimously in support of the seer.
(2) Also it is reported that the Pope is favorably impressed with the seer; and has known the seer since the 1970's. In 1984 a copy of the life of Wladyslaw was publicly presented to Pope John Paul II in the Vatican. The Holy Father reportedly responded by immediately kissing the book solemnly.

XXXIII Bibliography

Prophecies 1986
Translated by: Henryk Szewczyk
Published by: Fraternity Publications

Chapter 9

HEEDE, GERMANY
(1937-1940)

I Place - Heede, Germany

II Dates of First And Last Apparition

First: October 1, 1937
Last: November 3, 1940

III Seer(s) - 4

Name: Margaret Gansferth
Birth: Unknown
Age at first apparition: Unknown
Status: Unknown

Name: Greata Gansferth
Birth: Unknown
Age at first apparition: Unknown
Status: Unknown

Name: Anna Schulte
Birth: Unknown
Age at first apparition: Unknown
Status: Unknown

Name: Susanna Bruns
Birth: Unknown
Age at first apparition: Unknown
Status: Unknown

IV Total Number of Apparitions - 3
(Plus an undetermined number of other apparitions.)

V Dates and Locality of Each Apparition

The dates of the first and last apparition is reported. The dates of other apparitions are not reported.

1937: October 1 - Heede, Germany.
1937 - 1940: During this period Our Lady appeared to the children near their homes, in a meadow, and at other places.
1940: November 3 - Heede, Germany.

VI Description of Our Lady

It is reported when Our Blessed Lady first appeared She was holding the Divine Child in Her arms.

VII Title(s) of Our Lady - Not Reported

VIII Brief Factual Review

Heede is a small village with a population of about 1500 people located in what was West Germany near the Dutch border. It is located in the diocese of Osnabrick which dates back to the time of Charlemagne in 787.

Our Lady first appeared to the seers, four little girls, outside the parish church. The reports are unclear whether the four girls were all sisters, since different last names are given. Our Lady spoke and gave messages, during Her first appearance, meant for each of the girls individually. Before Our Lady disappeared, She invited the seers to return to the same place again. Other apparitions followed.

It is reported that it was obvious to everyone that the seers' lives were being transformed. After the initial apparition, they displayed more piety and devotion to the holy rosary.

At first the parish priests, and other clergy, along with the seers' parents refused to believe the girls. However the children's perseverance through all kinds of trials, their undeniable sincerity and the amazing cures that took place gained everyone's credence.

Germany was under the rule of Hitler, the Nazis and the gestapo during the time when these apparitions of Our Lady occurred. It was not long before the gestapo, arrested the four girls, declared them to be mental patients and confined them to an asylum.

However, after many weeks of seclusion and medical examinations the girls were found to be perfectly normal and sent back to their families.

The gestapo was prompt to intervene again. This time it expressly forbade the girls to return to the place of the apparitions. However the Blessed Mother was not bound by these restrictions and reportedly She appeared to the seers near their home, in a meadow, and anywhere else She pleased.

It is reported that Our Lady became the educator of the seers, trained them in prayer and often enjoined them to pray for the conversion of sinners. Our Lady also confided to each of the four seers separately, a secret to be transmitted to the Holy Father in Rome through the medium of their parish priest.

Under strict government dictatorship nothing was allowed to be published about these apparitions. Soon the war set in and Germany was successful in conquering Poland in 1939 and then took over France and the low countries up to the Atlantic Ocean in 1940. Our Lady's last apparition to the girls was on November 3, 1940.

It is reported that the four children saw the Angels of Justice and were told of the coming of a "minor judgment".

The war ended in 1945 with Germany's total defeat and the disappearance of Adolf Hitler. It was in the year 1945 that Our Lord is reported to have appeared to one of the seers, namely Margaret Gansferth, also in Heede, where Our Lady had earlier appeared.

Our Lord's messages are reported in summary that mankind had ignored the Fatima messages and it was for this reason that Jesus Himself was now coming in person in this last hour to warn and exhort mankind. People must repent, turn away from sin, appease God's anger, especially by reciting the rosary. Pleasure parties and entertainment must come to an end. Our Lord told the seer (Margaret Gansferth) to tell the parish priest to announce from the pulpit that the upcoming dance set for October 21, 1945 must be forbidden.

The priest complied with this request, the dance fell through and it is reported that no dances have taken place in Heede since that time.

The parish stated that there were undeniable proofs of the seriousness and authenticity of these manifestations. However it is not reported what action has been taken; nor what decisions, if any, have been given by the Church.

IX The Primary Messages - 3

(1) Prayer
(2) Conversion
(3) Rosary

The seers were told that the rosary has "unmeasurable power." It is reported that Our Lady Herself became the teacher of the children when

She appeared to them secretly after the seers were forbidden to go to the place of the original apparition.

X Signs Preceding the Apparitions - Not Reported

XI Other Visions During Apparitions

(1) At the first apparition Our Lady appeared with the Divine Child Jesus in Her arms.
(2) Jesus appeared to one of the seers, Margaret Gansferth in Heede in the year 1945. Jesus gave messages to this seer.
(3) It is reported that the seers saw the Angels of Justice.

XII Prayers Taught to the Seer(s) - Not Reported
XIII Special Devotion Given to the Seer(s) - NR

XIV Requests Made by Our Lady

During the first appearance Our Lady invited the seers to come to the place of apparitions again.

XV Specific Bible References - Not Reported

XVI Secrets Given to the Seer(s)

It is reported that Our Lady confided, to each of the four seers separately, a secret to be transmitted to the Holy Father through their parish priest. The contents of the secrets are not reported.

XVII Miracles Promised by Our Lady - NR
XVIII Miracles Performed - Not Reported
XIX Miracles Promised not yet Performed - NR
XX Signs Promised - Not Reported

XXI Signs Given

When the gestapo had forbidden the four seers to go to the place of the apparitions; it may well be said that Our Lady gave a sign by appearing to the girls several times at different locations in spite of the gestapo's orders.

XXII Predictions/Promises

It is reported that the coming of a 'minor judgment' was predicted by the Angel of Justice.

XXIII Prophecies/Warnings of Chastisement

(1) The seers were reportedly told of a coming 'minor judgment.'
(2) Jesus told the children that because mankind has ignored His Mother's message at Fatima, that He Himself was coming in person in this last hour to warn and exhort mankind that these times are very serious; that people must repent at last, turn away from sin with all their souls and appease the anger of God; and to do so especially by reciting the rosary.

XXIV Method of Appearance - Not Reported
XXV Method Of Departure - Not Reported

XXVI Confrontation w/Civil Authorities

(1) Firstly, the gestapo arrested the seers, declared them to be mental patients then confined them in an asylum.
(2) After the girls were released the gestapo again intervened and forbade the seers from returning to the place of the apparitions. The gestapo of course could not stop Our Lady from appearing to the girls at other locations of Her own choice.
(3) Under strict censorship by the government, nothing was allowed to be published about these apparitions.

XXVII Confrontation w/Church Authorities

It is reported that at first the parish priest and other clergy did not believe in these apparitions. It was only after the children persevered under all trials, and displayed their sincerity and after several wonderful cures occurred, that the clergy was supportive of the children.

XXVIII Request Chapel/Shrine Built - NR
XXIX Free Will/Choice - Not Reported

XXX Seer(s)' Suffering/Sacrifice

(1) First off their own parents and parish priest did not believe them.
(2) Then the gestapo arrested them, declared them to be mental cases and had the children confined in an asylum.
(3) After their release the gestapo continued to keep an eye on them and even forbade them to return to the place of apparitions. Undoubtedly this caused stress to the seers.

XXXI Healings Reported

It is reported that it was only after wonderful cures occurred that the parish priest and other clergy supported the seers and believed in these apparitions. The details of the various healings are not reported.

XXXII Action Taken by the Church

The bishop of Osnabrick at the time the apparitions commenced, appointed a new parish priest and a new curate. The new priest declared in writing that there "are undeniable proofs of the seriousness and authenticity of these manifestations of Our Lord". No other Church action is reported.

XXXIII Bibliography

The Final Hour 1992
By: Michael H. Brown
Published by: Faith Publishing Company

Vers Demain Magazine 1971
By: Louis Even
Published by: Vers Demain

Chapter 10

KECSKEMET, HUNGARY
(1939-1986)

I Place - Kecskemet, Hungary

II Dates of First and Last Apparition

First: 1939
Last: January 25, 1986

III Seer(s) - 1

Name: Sr. Maria Natalia (Order of Sisters of St. Magdalene)
Birth: 1901
Age at first apparition: 38
Status: Deceased - April 27, 1992

IV Total Number of Apparitions - 20

There were a minimum of 20 apparitions, visions & locutions reported.

V Dates and Locality of Each Apparition

All apparitions occurred at Kecskemet, Hungary unless otherwise noted.

1939: Feast of Christ the King.
1940: Feast of Christ the King.
1944: Feast of Christ the King.
1945: Feast of Christ the King.

After World War II.
Prior to 1985
1985: Spring; September 8; Autumn.
1986: January 25.

VI Description of Our Lady

(1) In 1939 on the Feast of Christ the King, Natalia saw Our Lady being carried by the angels on a heavenly throne, Our Lady wore a royal mantle and a triple crown. In one hand She held a scepter and in the other hand the globe. During this same vision Jesus appeared as King and Our Lady stood on His right as the Queen of the World.

(2) On another occasion Our Lady again appeared as Queen of the World, She seemed very young. She wore a royal crown on Her head and Her feet were covered with shining clouds. She blessed the world.

(3) On another occasion Our Lady wore a snow white dress with a blue sash around Her waist, over the dress was a scarlet mantle connected by a shining gold buckle. From the mantle a transparent turquoise blue veil waved down. The features of Her face were tender and infinitely lovely.

(4) On another occasion in 1944 Natalia saw Our Lady as Queen of the World. Her clothing was white with a scarlet mantle. Her whole figure was covered with a transparent black veil. On Her head was a crown of thorns. Her hands were folded in prayer and tears rolled from Her eyes.

VII Title(s) of Our Lady - 1

Victorious Queen Of The World

VIII Brief Factual Review

Sr. Maria Natalia was born in 1901 near Pogsong, Hungary, which later became Bratislana, Czechoslovakia. Today Czechoslovakia is broken into Czech and Slovakia.

She was one of nine children. When she was young she learned to speak German from her parents. She also spoke the Hungarian and the Slovakian languages. Later she learned French. Her messages were received in Hungarian.

Natalia received First Holy Communion at age six. At fourteen she took the vows as a Third Order Franciscan. She was seventeen when she entered the cloister. At age 33 she was transferred to Belgium and eventually returned to serve in the cloisters at Budapest and Kecskemet, Hungary. It was here she received messages for Hungary and for the world.

Kecskemet, Hungary

She recorded the messages and supernatural events in her diary between 1939 and 1943. Then there was a gap until 1981 when she resumed writing again in her diary.

Terrible events occurred after 1943. Hungary was overrun by the Red Army. The Catholic Church was persecuted in Hungary and many clerics were martyred and many religious went into hiding, including Sr. Natalia.

Apparently an early experience with Our Blessed Mother occurred when a stranger came to Natalia's home and requested to spend the night. The next day Natalia went to church with this Lady who had spent the entire night talking to Natalia about heaven. The priest reported that when this Lady received Communion the next day, the Host flew out of his hand into her mouth, all the while her face radiated light - light even came out of her mouth. Natalia was sure this was Our Blessed Mother. On another occasion Our Lady showed Natalia what was to be Natalia's garment of eternal life.

When Natalia was 33, Jesus gave her the choice of being taken to heaven then or living a prolonged life as a victim to suffer to save sinners. Of course she chose to suffer for souls.

Like most other victim souls, Natalia was tormented by Satan. She was also taken to and shown the souls in purgatory by Jesus. Jesus appeared to Natalia frequently and gave her the life mission to suffer for sinners and thereby save souls. Jesus specifically requested Natalia to suffer for priests, and Jesus also gave her messages of warning for priests.

She was also shown the individual judgment which occurs upon death — the guardian angel is present and Satan is also present, and Our Blessed Mother pleads for the poor sinners.

In 1939 Natalia had a vision which included Our Lady as Queen of the World. On one occasion Our Lady appeared to Natalia and said: *"Make reparation, make reparation, make reparation, because only in this way will you be worthy of the graces."* She also received messages especially for Hungary, demanding that a Chapel for Reparation be erected and continuous prayer, sacrifice, and penance be made in reparation for men's sins.

Natalia was told of the coming chastisement by both Jesus and Mary. Our Lady also told the mystic that the time of the chastisement is only known to the Father.

Jesus gave Natalia the Double Great Novena accompanied by 33 amazing promises.

In more recent messages (1985-1987) Our Lady allowed Natalia to know that the greatest epidemic spreading throughout the world is the denial of the Real Presence in the Holy Eucharist.

Natalia died April 27, 1992. No Church decision is reported.

IX The Primary Messages - 3

(1) **Reparation** - On one occasion Our Lady said: *"Make reparation! Make reparation! Make reparation! Because only in this way will you be worthy of the graces!"*
   Another time in the Spring 1985 Our Lady said: *"The reparations done in Hungary, and throughout the world, which were initiated in Hungary, are pleasing to God."*
(2) **Prayer** - Our Lady appeared more than once with Her hands folded in prayer. On one occasion in 1945 Our Lady ordered Natalia to ceaselessly pray for the new Prelate of Hungary, Cardinal Mindszenty. On another occasion Our Lady called on us to trust Her and Jesus and to make reparation, life offering and prayers.
(3) **Holy Eucharist** - In the fall of 1985 Our Lady told Natalia that the greatest epidemic that is spreading wide throughout the world is the denial of the Real Presence in the Holy Eucharist, and that this false teaching is coming from modern theologians who mislead people.

X Signs Preceding the Apparitions - Not Reported

XI Other Visions During Apparitions

Jesus appeared and gave messages to Natalia frequently. Jesus accompanied Natalia when He showed her purgatory.

XII Prayers Taught to the Seer(s)

Jesus taught the seer this prayer to be said on First Saturdays:
Prayer: *"Most Sacred Heart of Jesus I offer You this Holy Communion through the Immaculate Heart of Mary, to console You for all the sins committed against You."*

XIII Special Devotion Given to the Seer(s)

The Great Double Novena consists of making the Nine First Fridays and Nine First Saturdays **(instead of five)** for nine consecutive months, in reparation for sins committed, all the while performing all that is necessary to comply with the First Friday and the First Saturday Devotion, including confession, Communion, prayers for the Holy Father, and visits with Our Lady for 15 minutes in the church on each of the First Saturdays. The intention should be to console the Sacred Hearts of Jesus and Mary.
   On August 15, 1942 Jesus gave Natalia 33 promises for those persons

who complete the great Double Novena for nine consecutive First Fridays and First Saturdays in honor of the Sacred Heart of Jesus and the Immaculate Heart of Mary.

The 33 Promises:

1) All that they ask of Me through the Heart of My Mother - provided the request is compatible with the will of My Father - I will grant during the novena.
2) They will experience in every circumstance the extraordinary help of My Mother, together with Her blessings.
3) Peace, harmony, and love will reign in their souls and in the souls of the members of their families.
4) I will protect their families from scandals, disappointments, and injustice.
5) Married couples will stay together, and if one has already left, he or she will return.
6) The members of their families will understand each other and persevere in faith.
7) Expectant mothers will experience My Mother's special protection and will receive what they ask for themselves as well as for their children.
8) The poor will receive room and board.
9) I will lead them to love prayer and suffering. They will learn to love God and their fellow man.
10) Sinners will be converted without special difficulty, even if someone else completes this novena for them.
11) Sinners will not fall back into their previous state. Not only will they receive forgiveness for their sins, but through perfect contrition and love they will regain baptismal innocence.
12) Those who complete this novena in their baptismal innocence (especially children) will not offend My Heart with serious sin through the time of their deaths.
13) Sinners who sincerely repent will escape not only hell but even purgatory.
14) Lukewarm believers will become fervent believers, and they will persevere and reach perfection and saintliness in a short time.
15) If parents or other members of a family complete this novena, nobody from that family will be condemned to hell.
16) Many young people will receive the calling to religious life, including priesthood.
17) Unbelievers will become believers, and those who wander without direction (fallen-away Catholics) will return to the Church.
18) Priests and religious will remain faithful to their vocations. The unfaithful will receive the grace of sincere contrition and the possibility of return.
19) Parents and leaders will receive help in both spiritual and material needs.

20) The body will be freed from temptations of the world and of Satan.
21) The proud and the arrogant will become humble; the hot-tempered will become loving.
22) Fervent souls will experience the sweetness of prayer and sacrifice; they will never be tormented by uneasiness or doubt.
23) Dying persons will depart without agony and without the attacks of Satan. They will escape sudden, unexpected death.
24) The dying will experience tremendous longing for eternal life; thus they will surrender to My will and will depart from life in the arms of My Mother.
25) They will experience the extraordinary protection of My Mother at the Last Judgment.
26) They will receive the grace to have compassion and love toward My suffering and that of My Mother.
27) Those who strive to be perfect will obtain as a privilege the main virtues of My Mother: humility, love, and purity.
28) They will be accompanied with certain external and interior joy and peace, throughout their lives, be they sick or healthy.
29) Priests will receive the grace to live in the presence of My Mother without any hardship.
30) Those who advance in unity with Me will receive the grace to experience this unity. They will know what it means: not that they live any more, but that I will live in them. That is: I will love with their hearts, I will pray with their souls, I will speak with their tongues, I will serve with their whole beings. They will experience that what is good, beautiful, holy, humble, meek, obedient, valuable, and admirable in them is Me, the Omnipotent, the Infinite, the only Lord, the only God, the only Love.
31) The souls of those who complete this novena will be radiant like white lilies around the Heart of My Mother in eternity.
32) I, the Divine Lamb of God, united with My Father and the Holy Spirit, will rejoice forever seeing these souls who, through the Immaculate Heart of My Mother, will gain the glory of eternity.
33) Priestly souls will always advance in faith and virtue.

XIV Requests Made by Our Lady

(1) Our Lady ordered Natalia to pray ceaselessly for the new prelate of Hungary.
(2) Our Lady requested that the seer establish a Chapel for Reparation.

XV Specific Bible References - Not Reported
XVI Secrets Given to the Seer(s) - Not Reported
XVII Miracles Promised by Our Lady - NR

XVIII Miracles Performed - Not Reported
XIX Miracles Promised not yet Performed - NR
XX Signs Promised - Not Reported

XXI Signs Given

(1) Our Lady showed Natalia what her garment of eternal life was to be.
(2) Our Lady appeared as Queen of the World in crowned regal splendor on more than one occasion.

XXII Predictions/Promises

(1) Our Lady predicted that Natalia would become a nun.
(2) Our Lady predicted victory over Satan and Her own participation as the Victorious Queen of the World. She stated the decisive victory will end the saturation of the world with lies and open the way of the promised holy peace. This will come about when Satan will have gained power everywhere and when he will have seduced most souls and when he will feel in his haughtiness that he can ruin God's plan. True faith and light will live only in a few souls because all the unstable will have gone over to Satan. It is then that the victory will come suddenly and unexpectedly.

XXIII Prophecies/Warnings of Chastisement

(1) Our Lady said only the Eternal Father knows the date of the chastisement: *"The Age of World Peace is not delayed; the Heavenly Father wants to give time to those who are able to convert; and the world received an extension of time because of reparation and self-sacrifice offered throughout the world."*
(2) Jesus also gave messages of the coming chastisement: *"The right hand of My Father will annihilate all those sinners, who, despite the warnings and the period of grace and the tireless efforts of the Church, will not convert."*
(3) And Jesus also told Natalia: *"My daughter, tell My priests and the whole world, if they do not convert, then because of the multitude of sins, the world will be ruined. My words are true! Whoever listens to My words will live; but those who dismiss them will be lost."*

XXIV Method of Appearance

Generally, Our Lady appeared with Her hands clasped in prayer; sometimes as the Victorious Queen. On some occasions She was sad.

XXV Method of Departure

Generally, She blessed Natalia and the world before disappearing.

XXVI Confrontation w/Civil Authorities

World War II brought about the invasion of Hungary, and resulted in Natalia (and many other religious) going into hiding to avoid persecution.

XXVII Confrontation w/Church Authorities - NR

XXVIII Request Chapel/Shrine Built

Our Lady asked the seet to have a Chapel for Reparation prepared.

XXIX Free Will/Choice

The messages from Our Lady and from Jesus warn of consequences if mankind does not turn from sinful ways; the choice is clearly ours.

XXX Seer(s)' Suffering/Sacrifice

(1) Firstly, Natalia suffered very much, as did other clerics and religious in Hungary. After Hungary was invaded, many were forced underground in order to survive.
(2) Jesus gave Natalia the mission to make reparation to save souls, through her suffering. She was faithful to this mission and suffered much as a victim soul.
(3) Our Lady requested reparation for Hungary especially. She told Natalia that when King St. Stephen's son, St. Emeric died, that St. Stephen gave the country (Hungary) to Our Blessed Mother, and that Our Lady accepted this inheritance.

XXXI Healings Reported

Many conversions are reported through the prayers and sufferings and reparations made; especially in Hungary.

XXXII Action Taken by the Church

In 1954, Pope Pius XII designated May 31st as a Feast Day for Mary as Queen of the World.

XXXIII Bibliography

The Victorious Queen of the World 1988
By: Stephen A. Foglein MS (translator)
Published by: Two Hearts Books and Publishers

Chapter 11

AMSTERDAM, HOLLAND
(1945-1959)

I Place - Amsterdam, Holland

II Dates of First And Last Apparition

First: March 25, 1945
Last: May 31, 1959

III Seer(s) - 1

Name: Miss Ida Perleman
Birth: Unknown
Age at first apparition: Unknown
Status: Living

IV Total Number of Apparitions - 56

Fifty-six apparitions during the period of March 25, 1945, to May 31, 1959. Additionally, the seer had Eucharistic experiences from July 17, 1958 through 1984.

V Dates and Locality of Each Apparition

1945: March 25; April 21; July 29; August 29; October 7.
1946: January 3, February 7, 25; March 29; June 9.
1947: January 4; August 30; December 7, 26.
1948: March 28.

Amsterdam, Holland

1949: May 7; October 1; November 19; December 16.
1950: February 14; May 27; August 15; November 16; December 10.
1951: January 25; February 11; March 4, 28; April 1(twice in Germany); 29; May 31; July 2; August 15; September 20; November 15; December 31.
1952: February 17; March 19; April 6; June 15; October 5; December 8.
1953: March 20; May 10; October 11; December 3.
1954: April 4; May 31.
1955: May 31, (St. Thomas Aquinas Church).
1956: May 31.
1957: May 31, (St. Thomas Aquinas Church).
1958: February 18/19; May 31.
1959: May 31.

Eucharistic Experiences

These are continuations of the messages of Our Lady of All Nations. On May 31, 1958 Our Lady of All Nations told the seer: *"The contact will remain."* All these Eucharistic experiences occurred during Holy Mass inside a church.

1958: July 17;
1959: March 11; August 30; September 9; October 11, 18.
1960: January 31; March 25; May 31; October 30.
1961: January 15; February 26; March 25; May 31.
1962: May 31.
1963: May 23, 31.
1964: May 31.
1965: May 31.
1966: May 31, June 19.
1967: May 31.
1968: May 31.
1969: May 31.
1970: March 25; May 31; August 15.
1971: February 28; March 14, 25; May 31; August 31, December 8.
1972: February 2, 11; March 25; May 31; December 8.
1973: February 2, 11; March 25; May 31; August 15, September 8; November 29; December 8, 30.
1974: February 2, 11; March 25; May 31; June 9, 13; August 15; September 8; November 24; December 8.
1975: January 7, 8; February 2, 11; March 25; May 31; August 15; September 8; October 7; November 5/6 (Vision at Home); December 8.
1976: February 2, 11; March 25; May 8, 31; May 31 / June 1 (dream); August 15; September 8; October 7 and 29/30 (dream); December 8, 9.
1977: January 1, 2; February 2, 11; March 25; April 7, 10; May 5-6 (Vision at Home); May 12, 19, 29, 31; August 15, 27; October 7; December 8.

1978: January 1; February 2, 11; March 23, 25; April 3; May 31; June 11; August 15, 17; September 28, 29; October 7, 15, 16, 22; December 8.
1979: February 2, 11; March 23, 24, 25; April 12; May 15, 31; June 22, 23; August 15; September 2, 8; October 7; December 8.
1980: January 6; February 2; March 25; April 3; May 25, 31; August 15; September 8; December 8.
1981: February 2, 11; March 25; April 16; May 15, 31; June 23; August 15.
1984: March 25.

VI Description of Our Lady

(1) March 25, 1945 - first apparition. The seer was in her home and found herself drawn by an inner force to an adjoining room from where she suddenly saw a light coming forth. She went into the adjoining room and from the corner of the room saw a light coming nearer to her. The wall and all disappeared and out of the light a living female figure moved forward. The figure was clad in white and wore a sash, stood with Her arms lowered and the palms of Her hands turned outward toward the seer, and spoke to her, saying: *"repeat what I say"*.

(2) Thereafter, Our Lady appeared in various modes, sometimes smiling, sometimes sad, serious, compassionate, suffering, and sometimes in tears. On occasion She shook Her head, clenched Her fist, struck a table with Her fist and once She collapsed and wept bitterly. She appeared once clad in mourning. On two occasions Our Lady blessed the seer.

(3) Commencing with the 24th apparition on Nov 16, 1950 Our Lady appeared standing on the globe. This occurred thereafter on several occasions. She announced Her title as: *"Our Lady of All Nations"*. She detailed Her Image in several later apparitions and invited the seer to study well the image of Our Lady standing on the globe with both feet planted firmly and to look closely at Her hands, face, feet, hair and veil. She is standing in front of the Cross. Snow is falling around Her and flocks of sheep emerge around the foot of the globe. In a semicircle above the Cross are printed letters to form these words: 'The Lady of All Nations'.

VII Title(s) of Our Lady - 2

(1) **Our Lady of All Nations.** (Also shown as, *'The Lady of All People'* in a book of that same title translated from the French by Earl Massecar.)

On November 16, 1950 Our Lady first identified herself as: *"Our Lady of all Nations"*. She later reiterated this many times.

Previously, during the first five years of apparitions, no mention

of this title was given to the seer.
(2) **Co-Redemptrix, Mediatrix, Advocate.** April 15, 1951 and during other later apparitions Our Lady named this title.

VIII Brief Factual Review

It was 1945 and World War II was raging in Europe. Holland was occupied by the Nazi forces.

The apparitions and messages of Our Lady of All Nations first occurred in Amsterdam, Holland to a single anonymous woman on March 25, 1945 the Feast of the Annunciation. Some 20 of the apparitions occurred while the seer was in Germany. Two messages occurred in a public church, St. Thomas Aquinas, in Amsterdam, Holland. The apparitions lasted until May 31, 1959 the Feast Day of the Queenship of Mary. In addition the seer received Eucharistic experiences from July 17, 1958 through March 24, 1984.

The seer resided with her sister in Amsterdam when the first apparition occurred on March 25, 1945. She was surprised to see a brilliant light come from an adjoining room. She went into that room to find a light coming nearer to her. The walls and background disappeared. Then she saw the form of a female figure made of light, which the seer understood to be the Blessed Virgin Mary. The figure of light spoke and said: *"Repeat what I say."* The seer repeated this aloud. The seer's sister and her spiritual director, Father Freke O.P., were present when this first apparition took place. They wrote down this message (and also subsequent messages). After the message was given, the figure withdrew very slowly. Only then did the light also disappear and everything returned as it was.

The seer once asked: "Are you Mary?" The figure answered: *"They will call Me Mary, Mother."*

During the period from March 25, 1945 to May 31, 1959, Our Lady appeared during 55 apparitions and gave the seer some 60 messages. The first group of messages (No. 1 - No. 23) from March 25, 1945, to August 15, 1950 paint a background onto which Our Lady will later place Her Title, Her Prayer, Her Image, Her Worldwide Movement and the announcement of the Last Marian Dogma.

(1) Her title is: *"Our Lady of All Nations."*
(2) Her Prayer is: *"Lord Jesus Christ, Son of the Father, send forth now Thy Spirit over all the earth. Let the Holy Ghost live in the hearts of All Nations, that they may be preserved from moral decline, disasters and war. May the Lady of All Nations, who once was Mary, be our Advocate. Amen."*
(3) Her Image was shown and explained in great detail to the seer on various separate appearances recorded in the messages.
(4) Worldwide movement to spread Her Image (picture) and prayer

throughout the world is stressed in many messages.

(5) The last Marian Dogma proclaiming Mary as Co-Redemptrix, Mediatrix and Advocate. Our Lady said this Dogma would be resisted, and that the worldwide action of the spread of the Prayer and the Image will precede the Dogma. She also announced that the Dogma of the Assumption had to be proclaimed before the Last Marian Dogma would be declared by the Church.

Interestingly, the first message concerns a new prayer, the second message concerns a new image (picture), the third message concerns the worldwide spreading of the prayer and image and the fourth message concerns the Last Marian Dogma. Of course other messages also dealt with each of these subject matters.

Our Lady gave messages to apply to the whole world. Some messages are directed to the Pope and to priests and also to the Church at large. She gave warnings to nations and continents. She gave prophecies, some of which have already come to pass.

As in many other Marian Apparitions, Our Lady spoke of the moral decline of the world, of people being led astray by false prophets, of the world degenerating with calamitous effects and of future disasters. Yet She also promised to bring that true peace now lacking in the world and announced that She would obtain spiritual unity. She came to teach us to invoke the coming of the 'Holy Spirit of Peace' into the world.

IX The Primary Messages - 9

(1) **Eucharist**
(2) **New prayer**
(3) **New image**
(4) **World wide spreading of prayer and image**
(5) **Last Marian Dogma**
(6) **Messages of warnings to nations and continents**
(7) **Prophecies**
(8) **Unity of Christians**
(9) **Priests and Religious**

(1) **Eucharist:** October 5, 1952 Our Lady tells the seer that Amsterdam was chosen, being the City of Miracles, referring to the Miracle of the Blessed Eucharist which took place in Amsterdam on March 25, 1345 exactly 600 years before the first apparition to this seer. She again restated this in an apparition on March 20, 1953. Our Lady stated that Our Lord Jesus Christ gave a daily miracle to the nations of the whole world, yet many people pass it by, and She stresses that the daily Sacrifice must return into the midst of this degenerate world.

(2) **New Prayer:** Lord Jesus Christ, Son of the Father send forth now

Your Spirit over all the earth. Let Thy Holy Spirit live in the hearts of all nations, that they may be preserved from moral decline, disasters and war. May the Lady of All Nations, who once was Mary, be our Advocate. Amen.

On February 11, 1951 Our Lady gave this new prayer to the seer and said, *"My child, this prayer is so short and simple that each one can say it in his own tongue, before his own Crucifix; and those who have no Crucifix, repeat it to themselves. This is the message which I have come to give you today, for I have now come to tell you that I want to save the souls. Let all men cooperate in this great work for the world! If only everybody tried to follow this for himself!"*

(3) **New Image:** On November 16, 1950 Our Lady appeared to the seer standing on the Globe, the details of this image were shown to the seer in later apparitions. On March 4, 1951 Our Lady said: *"Look at My picture and study it well".* Then again: *" I am standing on the globe and both My feet are firmly fixed upon it. You can also clearly see My hands, My face, My hair, and My veil."* Our Lady was standing in front of the Cross.

Then again: *"I am the Lady standing in front of the Cross. My head, hands and feet are like those of a human being. The triangle, however, belongs to the Spirit."*

"I am standing upon the globe because this message concerns the whole world."

Then Our Lady said: *"Have this picture of Me painted and together with it spread the prayer I have taught you."*

In a semi circle over the picture are printed the words 'Lady of All Nations'.

The image was painted by the German painter, Heinrich Repke.

(4) **World Wide Spreading of Prayer and Picture:** On March 4, 1951 Our Lady said She wanted Her Image reproduced and the prayer spread and done in many languages. She insisted there must be a worldwide movement with the prayer and message to be spread to all peoples, even into countries cut off from the others.

On April 15, 1951 Our Lady said: *"Are you afraid? Don't I help you? You will find that the prayer will spread as of its own accord. You are on the right road. It must and will be done."*

Within one year after She gave Her Prayer and Her Image, the picture was painted, the prayer and a copy of the image were approved by ecclesiastical authority and printed, and the picture and prayer began to be spread among the people.

Our Lady promised to procure graces for soul and body, according to the will of the Son, for all who will pray before the image and ask the help of Mary, *"The Lady of All Nations".*

(5) **The Last Marian Dogma:** On May 31, 1951 Our Lady said: *"... for*

it is the wish of the Father and the Son to send Me into the world in these times as the 'Co-Redemptrix, Mediatrix and Advocate'. This will constitute a new and last Marian Dogma. This picture will go before it. The Dogma will be much disputed and yet it will prevail."

Then Our Lady said; *"Now look at My hands and relate what you see."* The seer then saw in the palms of Our Lady's hands what appeared to be wounds already healed and from these, rays of light streamed out, three from each hand, and diffused themselves upon the sheep. Smiling, the Lady said: *"These three rays are Grace, Redemption, and Peace."*

On October 5, 1952 Our Lady said: *"Never has 'Marian' or 'Mary' in the Community, the Church, been officially called 'Co-Redemptrix-Mediatrix'. Never has She been officially called 'Advocate'. These three thoughts are not only closely connected, they form one whole. Therefore this will be the keystone of Marian history, it will become the Dogma of Co-Redemptrix, Mediatrix and Advocate."* Then again on August 15, 1951 Our Lady said: *"The Dogma of the Assumption had to precede it. The last and greatest Dogma will follow."*

On July 2, 1951 Our Lady said further: *"Now watch well and listen. The following is an explanation of the New Dogma: 'As Co-Redemptrix, Mediatrix and Advocate, I am standing on the globe in front of the Cross of the Redeemer. By the will of the Father the Redeemer came on earth. To accomplish this, the Father used the Lady. Thus, from the Lady, the Redeemer received only — I am stressing the word only — flesh and blood, that is to say, the body. From the Lord and Master the Redeemer received His Divinity. In this way The Lady became Co-Redemptrix."*

Later on June 15, 1952 Our Lady said, *"Only on the departure of the Lord Jesus Christ did Co-redemption have its beginning. Only when the Lord Jesus Christ went away did She become the Mediatrix and Advocate."*

On April 4, 1954 Our Lady said: *"I am not bringing a new doctrine, I am now bringing old ideas. Because the Lady is Co-Redemptrix, She is also Mediatrix and Advocate, not only because She is the Mother of the Lord Jesus Christ, but,* **and mark this well**, *because She is the Immaculate Conception."*

On May 31, 1954 Our Lady appeared and said: *"I have given you the explanation of the Dogma. Work and ask for this Dogma. You should petition the Holy Father for this Dogma."* Then She added: *"I have chosen this day (May 31). On this day the Lady will be crowned. When the Dogma, the last Dogma in Marian history, has been proclaimed, the Lady of All Nations will give peace, true peace to the world. The nations, however, must say My Prayer in unison with the Church. They must know that the Lady of All Nations has come as Co-*

Redemptrix, Mediatrix, and Advocate. So be it!"

(6) Messages and Warnings to Nations and Continents: Our Lady gave warnings to many nations and also to entire continents. These are contained in many different messages. Selected messages are given:

America - The seer sees America and Europe lying side by side. After this the seer sees writing: *"Economic warfare, boycotts, currency crises, catastrophes."* (December 26, 1947)

On May 7, 1949 Our Lady said: *"Come along to Russia; they are making chemicals, America be warned - Intervene, do intervene. It is not human lives alone that are involved here but higher powers."*

Again on February 14, 1950 Our Lady said speaking of the role of the Church, *"The attack is no longer directed against nations, but against the mind of man,"* and then Our Lady continues, *"There will be a great struggle, America and Russia, that is coming."*

"To America I say: 'Do not push your policies too far; seek after truth.' I am glad that America is better disposed to the Faith at the moment."

On November 15, 1951 Our Lady angrily said: *"America, where do you stand? Dare you carry through? It is 'The Lady of All Nations' who asks you this."*

Again on December 31, 1951, Our Lady said: *"America, remember your Faith. Do not sow wrong ideas and confusion among your people and abroad. The Lady of All Nations exhorts America to remain what it has been."*

On July 29, 1945 Our Lady said: *"England will find her way back to Me. So will America."*

Africa - On February 11, 1951 Our Lady said: *"For Africa I say, 'Let it be known that I desire a seminary there. I shall assist the Dominicans.'"*

England - On February 7, 1946 Our Lady said: *"England, make no mistake as to your task. England you will have to go back to the highest. 'The Highest'."* And again on August 15, 1950, Our Lady places Her foot on England (on the globe) and moving Her finger to and fro in warning, She says: *"Why so slow to change? Can you not turn to what is normal?"* Then Our Lady 'said' to England: *"I shall return England."* (February 11, 1951).

Europe - Our Lady said: *"There will be a conflict in all Europe and beyond. It is a heavy spiritual struggle."* (January 3, 1946)

Again, *"Europe must be on her guard, warn the Peoples of Europe."* (February 7, 1946)

On December 16, 1949 Our Lady said: *"Europe, take warning, unite in the good cause. This is not merely an economic warfare; the aim is to corrupt the spirit. It is a politico-Christian warfare."*

Then on December 31, 1951 Our Lady said: *"Europe, you should seek to establish peace among yourselves. Help those who are in need; in spiritual need. Get ready for the combat; the spiritual combat."*

Finally on March 20, 1953 Our Lady said: *"It is the Lady of All Nations who calls on you to do so; not as though you would want to destroy your enemy, but so that you might win him over to your side. Just as you are striving to achieve political unity, so you must also be of one mind in the True, Holy Spirit."*

France - On December 10, 1950 Our Lady said: *"France is in a very sad plight. France, you have fallen off badly, in the military, economic and spiritual sense. Where are your glory and your pride? And yet so very little would be necessary to make people see the error of their ways."*

And again on November 15, 1951 Our Lady said: *"France you will be and have been destroyed in your faith. France - and now I am addressing the great ones - you will save your country only by taking it back to the Cross and 'Notre Dame'. Your people must be guided back to the Lady of All Nations."*

Germany - On November 19, 1949 Our Lady said: *"Do warn Germany and Italy, they can be saved yet. You must tell them to work against the degeneration of Germany. The people are good, but they are the prey of circumstances. We must bring the Cross there again and place it in the Center. Beginning with youth, they must work up the Faith and instill it again."*

Again, *"Child, I will give you another message for Germany. It must be saved. Let the bishops work! They must get their priests to work especially amongst the young, against humanism - modern paganism."* (December 31, 1949)

"Do ask that the Pope send directives, for Germany has so great a need of the right Spirit and it is through these that it can receive it." (February 14, 1950)

On November 16, 1950 Our Lady said: *"Germany must start to regain unity. Let a beginning be made by everyone for himself in his own home. The children must be reunited with father and mother. Let them kneel down together again and say the rosary."*

On February 11, 1951 Our Lady spoke in German when She said: *"I am greatly concerned about Germany. The Mother of God weeps for the children of Germany."*

Holland - On November 19, 1949 Our Lady said: *"Holland too starts sliding down. They stand on a downward slope."*

Again, *"Holland is on the brink of total degeneration."* (August 15, 1951)

On November 15, 1951 Our Lady said: *"Holland, look out! Your people too, Holland, have taken the wrong turning."* And again, *"Holland is on the way to ruin."* (October 5, 1952)

Israel - On April 21, 1945 Our Lady said: *"Yahweh is ashamed of His people."* And *"Israel will rise again."*

Italy - On November 19, 1949 Our Lady said: *"In Italy more must be done against communism. Do warn Germany and Italy, they can be saved yet."*

Again on February 11, 1951 *"To Italy I say, Great ones of Italy, do you realize what it is you have to do?"*

On November 15, 1951 Our Lady said: *"Italy, you have had your crosses. Remain on guard. Rome, remember your poor people."*

Japan - On December 10, 1950 Our Lady said: *"Japan too, must be on guard. I am telling you all this, for you will live to see it."*

Again on February 14, 1950 Our Lady said: *"Japan will be converted."*

Korea - On August 15, 1950 Our Lady said: *"The fighting in Korea is an omen and the beginning of great distress."* And again, *"My child, I told you that it was an omen. By this I meant that there would be periods of apparent tranquillity, which, however, do not last."* (December 10, 1950)

China - Our Lady said: *"Manchuria; there will be a tremendous insurrection."* (December 10, 1950)

Then again on Dec 31, 1951 Our Lady said: *"China will turn to the Mother Church"* - pause - *"after much conflict."*

Russia - On February 14, 1950 Our Lady said: *"There will be a great struggle, America and Russia, that is coming."* Again on November 16, 1950 Our Lady says: *"The Russians will not leave things the way they are at present."*

On May 7, 1949 Our Lady said: *"Russia will try to deceive everyone in everything she does. There will be a complete revolution."*

On December 10, 1950 the seer was shown Russia up to the left and then the seer *"saw a hellish light. It seems to explode from the ground upwards."* Our Lady then said: *"And then you see nothing anymore."* The seer now sees a burnt out plain.

Balkans - On October 1, 1948 Our Lady appeared and showed the seer several visions. Then suddenly the seer saw the Balkans. Our Lady said: *"Child there will be a fierce struggle. We have not seen the end of this struggle yet. Economic disasters will come. . ."*

Then on August 15, 1950 Ida saw Our Lady and was shown several visions. The seer reports: "Then I see the Balkans and Greece surrounded by a big chain, East Germany is inside also. The Lady seems to tie all those countries up in the chain. I notice that part is still free, and in the background I discern a sitting figure leaning his head on his hand. The voice says to me, *'These are the people that plan and bring about the destruction of the world.'"*

Note: It should be mentioned here that Yugoslavia is a country located in the Balkans, with its western boundary being the Adriatic Sea, across from Italy. The country has been divided into separate states. Zagreb is the Capital of Croatia, one of the separate states. A terrible and destructive war has been raging in this country for the past several years — and true peace has not yet come to the region.

Medjugorje, the site of the apparitions of Our Blessed Mother is located in Bosnia-Herzogovina, another one of the separate states of the former Yugoslavia where war has raged.

There were also warnings pertaining to Asia, Egypt, Greece, Indonesia, Austria, Persia and Turkey.

(7) **Prophecies:** Our Lady prophesied struggle within the Church and stated great changes would take place in the Church. These prophecies were contained in several different messages.

Certainly these were borne out, especially since Vatican II. A struggle has arisen within the Church and many changes were made, such as: Host in the hand, turned altar, and Mass in the vernacular.

On February 19, 1958 Our Lady said: *"I am going to tell you something you are not to mention to anyone; this is the communication: Listen, the present Holy Father Pope Pius XII will be taken up among our number at the beginning of October of this year."* (Pope Pius XII died on October 9, 1958)

(8) **Unity of Christians:** The messages are replete with pleas for Christian unity.

(9) **Priests and Religious:** Likewise the messages contain various messages and statements directed to priests and to all clergy and religious.

X Signs Preceding the Apparitions

(1) The first apparition was preceded by a brilliant light coming from the adjacent room.
(2) Generally an approaching light preceded later apparitions. The seer reports: "I see a bright light and then I see the Lady standing there."

XI Other Visions During Apparitions

(1) Our Lady appeared to the seer several times standing on the globe in front of a Cross. These were mostly the times when Our Lady instructed the seer on the 'Last Marian Dogma.'
(2) The seer received certain Eucharistic experiences from July 17, 1958 to March 25, 1984. These were not experienced during the reported Marian Apparitions but were events occurring inside the church during Mass, when Jesus appeared to the seer and spoke to her.

XII Prayers Taught to the Seer(s)

On Sunday, February 11, 1951 during the 27th apparition, Our Lady taught the seer a prayer and requested that the prayer and Her Image be spread worldwide.

Prayer: Lord Jesus Christ, Son of the Father send forth now Your Spirit over all the earth. Let the Holy Spirit live in the hearts of all nations, that they may be preserved from moral decline, disasters and war. May The Lady of All Nations, who once was Mary, be our Advocate.   Amen.

XIII Special Devotion Given to the Seer(s)

(1) Our Lady gave an Image of Herself standing on the globe in front of a Cross. She requested this Image be produced and distributed, along with Her Prayer, all over the world.

(2) Our Lady also told the seer that the "*Last Marian Dogma*" would be proclaimed by the Church; that of Mary as Co-Redemptrix, Mediatrix, and Advocate. This likewise was given over several messages.

XIV Requests Made by Our Lady

(1) Our Lady requested the Prayer be spread along with Her Image.
(2) Our Lady requested that She be known under the title of 'Our Lady of All Nations.'
(3) Our Lady requested that the 'Last Marian Dogma' be proclaimed by the Church, being that of Mary as Co-Redemptrix, Mediatrix and Advocate.

XV Specific Bible References

(1) Our Lady made reference to both the Old and New Testament.
(2) The seer was made to see representations of biblical characters and events during some apparitions.

XVI Secrets Given to the Seer(s)

On February 19, 1958 Our Lady gave the seer a message to be kept secret, which predicted the death of Pope Pius XII "*at the beginning of October this year*". Pope Pius XII died October 9, 1958.

XVII Miracles Promised by Our Lady - NR
XVIII Miracles Performed - Not Reported
XIX Miracles Promised not yet Performed - NR

XX Signs Promised - Not Reported

XXI Signs Given

On May 31, 1957 Our Lady said: *"My signs are contained in My words."*

XXII Predictions/Promises

(1) Our Lady (correctly) predicted the death of Pope Pius XII.
(2) Our Lady predicted struggles within the Church and great changes to take place within the Church. Vatican II seems to bear this out.
(3) Our Lady said, in part, about Russia, *"There will be a complete revolution."* (December 10, 1950)

XXIII Prophecies/Warnings of Chastisement

The messages are replete with warnings to different named nations of catastrophes, violence, disasters, insurrection and great threatening dangers hanging over the world.

XXIV Method of Appearance

Usually the seer saw a bright light and then Our Lady appeared.

XXV Method of Departure

Usually Our Lady slowly disappeared at the end of the apparition.

XXVI Confrontation w/Civil Authorities - NR

XXVII Confrontation w/Church Authorities

(1) **Prayer:** The Church authorities had trouble with the words "once was Mary" in the prayer. Our Lady explained this phrase to the seer in detail. It was later approved and the prayer-picture has been spread to millions of people.
(2) **Last Marian Dogma:** This doctrine has not been proclaimed by the Church. Our Lady herself said controversy would arise within the Church, but in the end the New Dogma will be proclaimed. She urges the Church to act and rallies the theologians to move forward. There

Amsterdam, Holland

is at the present time serious and concerted effort being presented to the Vatican to proclaim this Last Marian Doctrine.

(3) **Image:** The seer had the Image painted by a German painter, Henrick Repke. The original was installed in the Chapel at St. Thomas Aquinas Church in Amsterdam. However in 1955 Msgr. JP Harlbers, the bishop of Haarlem, withdrew the permission, thus requiring that the original painting be removed, pending the inquiry into the genuineness of the apparitions.

XXVIII Request Chapel/Shrine Built

There are numerous instructions and directions contained in the messages concerning the site and construction of Her requested church. On May 31, 1956 Our Lady showed the seer the site where the church is to be built. It is a place called: "ZUIDELIZKE WANDELWEIG" in Amsterdam, Holland.

XXIX Free Will/Choice - Not Reported

XXX Seer(s)' Suffering/Sacrifice

(1) All throughout the messages the seer complains of pain in her hands and otherwise.
(2) Undoubtedly she suffered emotional distress and agonized over the struggle about the Prayer and the Image. Furthermore Our Lady requested the seer to have the Pope proclaim the New Marian Dogma, which has not been accomplished, all to the seer's anxiety.

XXXI Healings Reported - Not Reported

XXXII Action Taken by the Church

The local Church did approve the form and dissemination of the New Prayer and The Image. Later the bishop withdrew his permission to keep the original painting in St. Thomas Aquinas Church pending the inquiry into the genuineness of the apparitions. A commission is established, no final word has been given.

Incidentally the statue of Our Lady of Akita, Japan which shed tears 101 times, was carved from a piece of wood using the Image of 'Our Lady of All Nations' as a model. The apparitions in Akita, Japan have been approved by the local bishop.

XXXIII Bibliography

The Messages of the Lady of All Nations 1987
Edited by: Josep Kunzli
Published by: Miriam-Verlag

Eucharistic Experiences 1987
Edited by: Josef Kunzli
Published by: Miriam-Verlag

The Lady of All Peoples 1978
Translated by: Earl Massecar
Published by: Les Presses Lithographiques Inc.

Chapter 12

ZAGREB, YUGOSLAVIA
(1945-1976)

I Place - Zagreb, Yugoslavia (and other places)

II Dates of First and Last Apparition

First: 1945
Last: 1976

III Seer(s) - 1

Name: Julia
Birth: Unknown
Age at first apparition: Unknown
Status: Unknown

IV Total Number of Apparitions - 100

Visions, locutions, and apparitions are reported to have occurred at least 100 times. This information is from the diaries of Julia.

V Dates and Locality of Each Apparition

The exact dates of each apparition (or vision) is usually not reported for the period **1945-1975**. Some dates are reported for **1975** and **1976**.

VI Description of Our Lady

(1) During one vision occurring during 1973-1975 Our Lady was referred to as being of indescribable beauty. She looked young; 13 years old. Her eyes shone like stars. She was dressed in white.

(2) Another time Our Lady wore a white dress with blue coat. Her headwear was white and from Her belt hung three ribbons, blue, pink and yellow. On Her chest showed the Immaculate Heart, within which was a poesy of flowers of various colors. The petals shimmered like gold.

VII Title(s) of Our Lady - 3

(1) *"I am the Mother of Exalted Love of God's Creatures."*
(2) *"I am the Mother of Pure Love."*
(3) *"I am Queen of Heaven and Earth."*

VIII Brief Factual Review

Julia, the eldest daughter of 13 children, was born into a poor but truly Christian family. She was very fond of the rosary and of the Cross of Our Lord Jesus.

She had supernatural experiences in her early childhood and thought that everyone had these experiences. When she was about 17 Our Blessed Lady appeared to her dressed in white.

Julia longed to become a nun but her father could not provide a dowry. She did become married. Two sons were born to her, one died shortly after birth. Her husband was killed during a bombing raid toward the end of World War II. She became a widow at 24.

Thereafter while kneeling before the picture of the Sacred Hearts of Jesus and Mary, Julia vowed to live a life of chastity for the remainder of her years on earth. At that time Jesus spoke to her and thrice asked her: *"Julia, will you serve me?"*

Our Lord instructed Julia that in heaven the Sign of the Cross is made in this way: *"In the name of God the Father, who made me in His Love, in the name of God the Son, who redeemed me by His bitter sufferings, in the name of God the Holy Spirit, who sanctified me by His Grace..."*

Jesus commissioned Julia to pray much for His people who sin very much and to make reparation for their sins. Our Lord also told Julia to distribute all her belongings to the poor. Jesus showed heaven to Julia, and also took her to purgatory and arranged meetings with souls in purgatory. God the Father and the Holy Spirit also appeared to Julia.

Various saints appeared to Julia and spoke to her, among them: St.

Juliana, St. Joseph, St. Anthony, St. Barbara, St. Francis, St. Peter, St. Paul, St. Clare, St. John, St. Stephen, Pope Leo the Great, St. Martin, St. Thomas Aquinas, St. Anne, St. Elizabeth, St. Catherine, St. Mary Magdalene, as well as some angels.

The devil also appeared to Julia and tormented her.

Jesus appeared to Julia many times and gave her many messages and instructions, and said to her: *"You must write down all that I have revealed and said to you for My Faithful on the earth."* In 1952 Julia received God's command to convey the messages to the church, however, every effort she made to do so was met with silence.

In 1973 Fr. Rudolf visited Julia and thereafter they traveled to Rome together to deliver the messages. Along the way they visited at many Marian shrines including San Damiano where they saw Mama Rosa. They also went to Rimini to visit the visionary Elvira. It was here the Blessed Virgin Mary appeared while they were in chapel. Julia had many other visions and apparitions while on this journey.

Our Lady often appeared to the visionary during Mass at the altar, especially on certain Feast Days. She usually floated down from heaven. During Holy Mass Julia had visions and saw events from the life of the Blessed Virgin Mary. Julia often received an explanation from Our Lady or from Our Lord as to the meaning of the vision she had experienced. Our Lady sometimes appeared as Queen.

On one occasion while Julia was praying after Mass before the statue of Our Lady of Fatima she noticed the rosary on the statue, in the hands of Our Lady, moved back and forth. Then Our Lady said: *"This happy movement of the rosary in My hands means that the call of My appearances at Fatima has been spread over the whole world."*

Both Jesus and Mary often gave Julia sermons and lengthy teaching messages on a variety of subject-matters. Jesus gave Julia many messages concerning the church, the priesthood and also several detailed messages of the coming chastisement and the era of peace to follow. She had several visions where she saw the terrible chastisements.

These messages have not been approved by the Church.

IX The Primary Messages - 5

(1) **Julia's Mission** - given to her by Jesus; and augmented by Our Lady includes: **Reparation, Penance, Prayer** for the conversion of sinners.

(2) **Prayer** - During one vision given to Julia Our Lady announced to the congregation: *"Pray, for the bitter hour is near! I will defend all those who walk in My ways."*

On another occasion Our Lady said: *"My heart is very happy when you open your mouths in prayer, to praise the Lord and honor Me. My heart is united with your hearts."*

Again, Our Lady said on September 10, 1976: *"Pray to Our Lord, so that you may soothe His sufferings, which He endures through the offenses of His people. Pray in these times of afflictions."*

(3) **Pray the Rosary** - *"When you are saying the rosary you shall all be protected by Me,"* says Our Lady. On June 19, 1976 Our Lady said: *"My dear children! Recite the rosary to praise God our Triune Lord, and in My honor, your Mother, so I can be amongst you in the hour of chastisement to take you under My protection."*

(4) **Chastisement** - On June 21, 1976 Our Lady said: *"My dear children! I am hurrying to take you into the care of My Heart and to shield you with My mantle in the days of the chastisement."*

On August 27, 1975 Julia had a vision of the great chastisement; A great calamity, together with demons, plunged to the earth. After this began an indescribable horror. The people struck and killed each other mercilessly. The air was filled with screams, lamentations and cries for help. The mountains were raised, fell over and disappeared into the abyss, etc.

September 22, 1974 during a vision Julia saw a great trial threaten the earth, but Our Heavenly Mother prevented it from reviling the earth.

(5) **Holy Mass** - Many visions of Our Lady, Our Lord and a multitude of saints occurred at the altar during Holy Mass. On June 23, 1975 Our Lady said: *"Blessed is the House where the Sacrifice of Our Lord Jesus Christ, My Son is offered. Blessed are those who believe and stay with their belief and do not doubt the presence of Our Lord Jesus Christ."*

X Signs Preceding the Apparitions

(1) Most frequently in the visions of Julia, Our Lady is seen descending from heaven, sometimes this occurs during Mass when Our Lady descends to the altar.
(2) Often a statue of Our Lady, at a shrine or in a church, will glow and Our Lady appears; out of the statue.

XI Other Visions During Apparitions

During the visions, Julia saw Jesus, the Holy Spirit, God the Father, the Holy Trinity, as well as a multitude of saints and angels.

XII Prayers Taught to the Seer(s)

Our Lady admonished the visionary to pray much, to pray to Our Lord. However, no specific prayer is reported as given to the seer.

XIII Special Devotion Given to the Seer(s)

On September 10, 1976 Our Lady said: *"Pray to My Sorrowful Heart."*
This is apparently to remind us to practice the devotion to the Sorrowful Heart of Mary given at an earlier time to another seer.

XIV Requests Made by Our Lady

(1) On November 9, 1975 Our Lady requested Julia to go with Her to visit heaven.
(2) Thereafter, Our Lady requested that Julia accompany Her to purgatory.

XV Specific Bible References - Not Reported
XVI Secrets Given to the Seer(s) - Not Reported
XVII Miracles Promised by Our Lady - NR
XVIII Miracles Performed - Not Reported
XIX Miracles Promised not yet Performed - NR
XX Signs Promised - Not Reported

XXI Signs Given

(1) There are numerous reports of many signs given to Julia during the visions. Likewise in many instances Our Lady (as well as Our Lord) explained the meaning of these signs.
(2) One such sign occurred on September 10, 1976 when Our Lady appeared and under Her feet the letter "V" appeared as large as a person. The sign played in colors blue, white, pink, yellow and violet. Our Blessed Mother proclaimed: *"Those who venerate My Heart shall gain VICTORY, the Glory with Me for all Eternity."*
Our Lady further declared: *"Blue signifies heaven; pink signifies prayer, the rosary; white signifies purity, chastity of the spirit; violet signifies the clergy, the hearts of those who glow with love for My Heart, for God the Father, the Son, and the Holy Spirit; yellow signifies the glory of heaven."*

XXII Predictions/Promises

On November 11, 1975 Our Lady promised to all present: *"Our Help, Mine and that of Our Lord, will protect you in difficult times. I will take your prayer to Our Lord."*

XXIII Prophecies/Warnings of Chastisement

(1) Jesus gave Julia several messages concerning the coming of the great chastisements. Jesus once told Julia: *"A small Last Judgment is coming."*
(2) Julia had visions of terrible chastisements and suffering of the people, and then of an era of peace.
(3) Several visions which Julia experienced, showed Our Heavenly Mother protecting us from a great danger. On June 21, 1976 Julia saw something long and black come towards the Earth. It looked like a comet. Our Dear Mother rushed past it to help us. While Our Lady spoke the comet stood still in space.

XXIV Method of Appearance

Most often Our Lady descended from heaven onto the altar during Holy Mass.

XXV Method of Departure

Usually Our Lady would bless Julia, and all those present, before departing. Then a delightful fragrance was detected by those present.

XXVI Confrontation w/Civil Authorities - NR

XXVII Confrontation w/Church Authorities

In 1952 Julia received God's command to convey messages and visions to the Church. Several times, Julia asked the heads of the relevant dioceses for an official hearing. Regrettably the answer was always silence.

XXVIII Request Chapel/Shrine Built - NR

XXIX Free Will/Choice

From the beginning when Our Lord first appeared to Julia and asked her three times: *"Julia will you serve me?"*, it was always clear that Julia had the discretion to use her own free will and was invited to do so by Jesus.

XXX Seer(s)' Suffering/Sacrifice

(1) When Julia was requested to go on a journey to Rome — she was told that she would suffer; and she did.

(2) As a victim soul she suffered greatly for the sins of others during most of her lifetime.
(3) Julia describes her sufferings during and after some of her visions; especially those revealing the terrible catastrophes of the great chastisement.

XXXI Healings Reported - Not Reported

XXXII Action Taken by the Church

(1) No definitive action by the Vatican is reported.
(2) Fr. Rudolf, who accompanied Julia on her trip to Rome, as well as other clerics, have confidence in the truth of the visions and messages reported by Julia.

XXXIII Bibliography

Jesus Calls Us   1985 - V1
By: Julia/Fr. Rudolf Skunca
Published by: Haupt Cristi - Verlag

Jesus Calls Us   1988 - V2
By: Julia/Fr. Rudolf Skunca
Published by: In Wahreit und Treue

Jesus Calls Us   1988 - V3
By: Julia/Fr. Rudolf Skunca
Published by: In Wahreit und Treue

Chapter 13

MARIENFRIED, GERMANY
(1946)

I Place - Marienfried, Germany

II Dates of First and Last Apparition

First: April 25, 1946
Last: June 25, 1946

III Seer(s) - 1

Name: Barbara Reuss
Birth: May 13, 1934
Age at first apparition: 12
Status: Living

IV Total Number of Apparitions - 4

V Dates and Locality of Each Apparition

All reported apparitions occurred at Marienfried, Germany.

1946: April 25 (twice); May 25, June 25.

VI Description of Our Lady

The seer reports that during prayer, Our Lady, suddenly appeared unspeakably beautiful, brilliant and full of light — a blinding vision of most pure light and radiance. Our Lady's eyes had a characteristic luster. Above Her head were rays formed over one another so that they had the appearance of a three-tiered crown. During the blessing She became as transparent as crystal completely blinding the seer. When the seer looked again Our Lady was gone.

VII Title(s) of Our Lady - 3

(1) Mediatrix of Graces
(2) All Wonderful Mother
(3) The Sign of The Living God

VIII Brief Factual Review

During World War II the parishioners of the local parish in Marienfried, Germany promised to build a Chapel in the nearby woods if their parish was protected and saved from harm. The parish was protected and was not harmed.

It was on April 25, 1946 that Barbara Reuss, age 12 years, and 2 other girls went out to the woods to the place where the Chapel was to be built, in order to arrange for the erection of a little wayside shrine. The exact spot for the Chapel had not been determined as there were 2 acceptable locations. They discussed different legends of Shrines where Our Lady had left signs. They prayed the rosary together and began to work on the clearing. Suddenly Barbara announced: "Someone called me!" This happened again. Our Lady then appeared and Barbara asked the others to come and see. But Our Lady disappeared before the others could see Her.

No sooner had Barbara commenced her work when she was again called and Our Lady appeared to her. Our Lady told Barbara of a very personal experience that happened to this seer when she (the seer) was only 6 years old (May 13, 1940). The other girls did not see Our Lady but heard Barbara's side of the conversation. During this apparition Our Lady told the seer: *"I am the Sign of the Living God. I place My sign on the foreheads of My children, (those who consecrate themselves to My Immaculate Heart). The star* (Lucifer) *will persecute the Sign. But My Sign will conquer the star."*

On May 25, 1946 an angel who had previously appeared to Barbara, announced that he was *"the Angel of the Great Mediatrix of Graces".* He requested that Barbara go to the woods after Mass that day. The seer resisted but after speaking with her friends, relented and did go to the woods that day.

Our Lady appeared again and gave a lengthy message to Barbara. She said that She was the *"Powerful Mediatrix of Graces."* She complained because men do not live up to the consecration of the world to Her Immaculate Heart. She warned of the Great Chastisement to befall mankind: *"The world will have to drink the cup of wrath to the dregs because of the countless sins through which His Heart is offended."* She exhorted the world to pray, make sacrifice and pray the rosary. Our Lady requested that Barbara return again on the Feast of Holy Abbott William. Our Lady gave a secret to the seer and told the seer that as a sign of the reality of the visions the seer was to go to Beuren and that on the way she would find a man who needed help, she was to bring him to this place and Our Lady would help him. Barbara did find a man at the designated place who was distraught and was contemplating hanging himself. She brought him to the site where he stayed alone for a time, he then abandoned the idea of suicide.

The angel, present throughout this apparition of May 25, 1946 began to pray and taught the girls a prayer. When the angel finished praying he told the girls, both Anne and Barbara, to kneel down. Thereupon Our Lady blessed the seer and Anne. Anne could see a bit of Our Lady, she only heard Barbara's voice. During the blessing Our Lady became transparent as crystal. Barbara was completely blinded by the radiance and had to look away. When she could look again Our Lady was gone.

The final apparition occurred on June 25, 1946 which was the date Our Lady had requested Barbara to return, the Feast Day of Holy Abbot William. The two sisters again accompanied Barbara to the site and said the rosary on the way. Once again Our Lady urged us to pray, to make sacrifices and to pray the rosary. She again warned of the Purification to come: *"The Father pronounces a dreadful woe upon all who refuse to obey His will."* She also said many people would refuse to believe these apparitions but a loyal group would accept them.

When Barbara asked if a Chapel was to be built, Our Lady said: *"I have fulfilled your wish, now you also accomplish your vow."*

After Our Lady completed the message, a group of angels knelt and prayed a prayer to honor the Most Holy Trinity. Our Lady then blessed the seer. While Our Lady prayed She became increasingly brilliant and again the seer had to look away. When the seer looked again Our Lady was gone.

A Chapel has been completed on the site. The Blue Army in Germany holds national meetings and ceremonies at Marienfried. His Eminence Cardinal Ribeiro of Lisbon, Portugal participated in one such national meeting. Other Church dignitaries have spoken well of Marienfried. No Church action or decision has been given, although the Church offices of the diocese have made an investigation. Some bishops have come out in favor and others against these happenings. It is reported that Barbara received the Stigmata on Good Friday 1947, which she kept for two years. She asked Jesus to take it away and it is now reported to be invisible.

Although these messages are not widely circulated in the USA, ecclesiastical permission has been given to publish the messages in the United States. Barbara is married and has children. It is reported she lives an ordinary life as a good Christian wife and mother.

IX The Primary Messages - 4

(1) Prayer - On May 25, 1946 Our Lady said: *"Pray, make sacrifices for sinners; Pray not so much for external things, weightier things are at stake in these times."*
Again on June 25, 1946 Our Lady implored: *"Pray and offer sacrifices through Me. Pray always, pray the rosary. Make all your entreaties to the Father through My Immaculate Heart. Offer your prayer to Me as sacrifices. Be not seekers of self. Many prayers should be offered for sinners."*

(2) Sacrifice - On June 25, 1946 Our Lady spoke: *"Upon you it depends to shorten the days of darkness. Your blood and your sacrifices shall destroy the image of the beast, bring many sacrifices and offerings to Me! Be prepared to carry the cross that peace may soon be achieved."*
Again on May 25, 1946 Our Lady said: *"The devil has power over all people who do not trust in My Heart. Wherever people substitute My Immaculate Heart for their sinful hearts, the devil has no power. But he will persecute My children, they will be despised, but he can do them no harm."*

(3) Pray the Rosary - *"Pray the rosary!"* Our Lady pleaded on May 25, 1946 and again on June 25, 1946.

(4) Consecrate Ourselves to the Immaculate Heart of Mary - On April 25, 1946 Our Lady said: *"I am the sign of the Living God. I place My Sign on the forehead of My children, those who consecrate themselves to My Immaculate Heart."*

Then on May 25, 1946 She said: *"Have unreserved confidence in My Immaculate Heart! Substitute My Immaculate Heart in place of your hearts. Then it will be I who will draw the power of God, and the love of the Father will renew the fullness of Christ in you."*

Also on June 25, 1946 Our Lady said: *"People must believe that I am the permanent Bride of the Holy Ghost and the faithful Mediatrix of All Graces. God wants it so!"* Then again: *"Keep the Saturdays which have been dedicated to Me, as I have requested. Apostles and priests should consecrate themselves to Me especially, so that the great sacrifices which the Inscrutable One demands above all from them may be placed in My Hands, increase in sanctity and worth."*

X Signs Preceding the Apparitions

Just before the apparitions of April 25, 1946 Barbara heard her name being called. However this did not occur in the following apparitions of May 25 or June 25, 1946.

XI Other Visions During Apparitions

(1) On May 25, 1946 an angel, who previously had already appeared frequently to Barbara, appeared again announcing that he was *"the Angel of the Great Mediatrix."* The angel taught Barbara a prayer.

(2) On June 25, 1946 after Our Lady had completed Her message a host of angels prayed a prayer in Honor of the Holy Trinity.

XII Prayers Taught to the Seer(s)

(1) The following two prayers were taught to the seer by Our Heavenly Mother:

Prayer: Miraculous Mother, replace our hearts with Your Immaculate Heart, so that in this way Your Divine Son may work in me. Listen to my supplication, powerful and faithful Mediatrix of all Graces. Amen.

Prayer: My dear Jesus replace my sinful heart with Your Divine wounded Heart, that the Holy Spirit may work in me; that You may grow in me with Your merciful love. My good and faithful loving Jesus, listen to my prayer that soon You may reign on this earth as the King of Peace. Amen.

(2) On May 25, 1946 the angel taught Barbara this prayer:

Prayer: Act as the Mother of Grace, Act as the Thrice Miraculous Mother, the Thrice Admirable Mother of Grace, Thou Great Mediatrix of Graces.

(3) Then on June 25, 1946 the angels said this prayer:

Prayer: We salute Thee, Most High Sovereign Lord, Living God, Eternal Existence, awe-inspiring and Just Judge, our always good and merciful Father. Adoration, praise, honor, and glory be to Thee, now and forever, through Thy spotlessly Pure Daughter our Wonderful Mother!

We salute Thee, immolated God-Man, Bloody-Lamb, King of Peace, Tree of Life, Firstborn of the Living, Eternal Sovereign reigning in Thy own right! Splendor and jubilation, grandeur and adoration, expiation and praise, be to Thee now and forever through Thy Immaculate, and our own admirable Mother!

We salute Thee, Spirit of the All-Holy God, Who proceeds eternally from Its Sanctity. Deluge of Fire from the Father to the Son, Thou Radiant Stream from which strength and light and ardour flow into the members of Eternal Love! Thou perpetual Bond of Love, Figure

Marienfried, Germany

of the Essence of the Godhead's eternal Love. Thou ruddy Stream of Fire from the Ever Living to mortals! To Thee, now and in eternity, be praise and exaltation and benevolence through Thy Star-crowned Bride, our Wonderful Mother! Amen.

XIII Special Devotion Given to the Seer(s)

(1) On May 25, 1946 Our Lady said: *"It is true the world was consecrated to My Immaculate Heart, but this consecration has become a fearful responsibility to many men. I demand that the world live this consecration."*

(2) June 25, 1946 Our Lady said: *"In your prayers implore graces for individual souls, for the community, for the nations, so that all may come to love and honor the Divine Heart. Keep Saturdays, which have been dedicated to Me, as I have requested. Apostles and priests should consecrate themselves to Me especially."*

XIV Requests Made by Our Lady

(1) On May 25, 1946 Our Lady requested that Barbara return to the apparition site again on the Feast of 'Holy Abbot William' (celebrated on June 25, 1946). Our Lady did appear to the seer on June 25, 1946.

(2) Also on May 25, 1946 Our Lady requested of the seer: *"On the way to Pfaffenholen from Beuren, there is a man in great distress. You must help him. Send him here. He will be helped."*

Barbara found the man as foretold, brought him to the place and he was helped.

XV Specific Bible References - Not Reported

XVI Secrets Given to the Seer(s)

On May 25, 1946 Our Lady entrusted a secret to Barbara which she was to keep to herself. There is no report that this secret has ever been divulged.

XVII Miracles Promised by Our Lady - NR
XVIII Miracles Performed - Not Reported
XIX Miracles Promised not yet Performed - NR

XX Signs Promised

(1) On April 25, 1946 Our Lady said: *"I place My Sign on the foreheads of My children."*
(2) Then on May 25, 1946 Our Lady told Barbara that as confirmation of the reality of the visions, Barbara was to bring a certain man to this place who she was to find on the way from Pfaffenholen to Beuren. This occurred.
(3) Interestingly enough, when on June 25, 1946 Barbara begged Our Lady for an outward sign, Our Lady said: *"I have already given many signs and spoken often to the world, but people have not taken them seriously. On account of these outward signs the 'Great Multitude' do not even grasp the essential things. Outward signs only succeed in annoying many who do not draw the necessary conclusions from them."*
(4) Again on May 25, 1946 Our Lady said: *"Expect no signs or wonders. I shall be active as the powerful Mediatrix in secret."*

XXI Signs Given

(1) On May 25, 1946 Our Lady promised a sign by way of the man that Barbara was to find and bring to the place to be helped. This sign was given as promised and Barbara did find and bring the man to this place where he was helped.
(2) On two separate occasions Our Lady blessed Barbara, hands on.
(3) Barbara received the Stigmata on Good Friday, 1947, and kept it for two years. Now the Stigmata is reported to be invisible.

XXII Predictions/Promises

(1) On May 25, 1946 Our Lady predicted that the seer would find a man on the way to Beuren. This occurred as promised.
(2) Again on May 25, 1946: *"Wherever people substitute My Immaculate Heart for their sinful hearts, the devil has no power."*

XXIII Prophecies/Warnings of Chastisement

(1) On May 25, 1946 Our Lady said: *"The world will have to drain the cup of wrath to the dregs because of the countless sins through which His Heart is offended. The Star of the infernal regions will rage more violently then ever and will cause frightful destruction, because he knows that his time is short and because he sees that already many have gathered around My sign. Over these he has no power, although he will kill the bodies of many, but through these sacrifices bought for Me, My power to lead the remaining host to victory will increase. Some have already*

allowed My sign to be impressed on them, their number will keep growing. But I want to tell you, My children, not to forget that the very cross of those bloody days is a grace."

(2) On June 25, 1946 Our Lady said: *"The Father pronounces a dreadful woe upon all who refuse to obey His will."* She said that upon our prayers depends the shortening of the days of darkness.

XXIV Method of Appearance - Not Reported

XXV Method of Departure

On two reported occasions Our Lady blessed the seer, while increasing in a brilliant radiating light, then disappeared.

XXVI Confrontation w/Civil Authorities

On June 25, 1946 Our Lady foretold that many minds will be divided concerning these revelations, that a large number will be scandalized, but there will be a small group who would correctly understand and carry out the messages. This is what occurred, many people now follow these messages and visit the site of the apparitions. It is reported that for a time, even now, these apparitions were forgotten by many.

XXVII Confrontation w/Church Authorities

After Barbara received the Stigmata on Good Friday 1947 some bishops in Germany issued public statements in favor of these apparitions. Others were not favorable. The investigation of the reported apparitions did not produce a decision. These messages and apparitions have been all but forgotten by many.

XXVIII Request Chapel/Shrine Built

(1) The parishioners of the parish at Marienfried had promised to build a Chapel in the nearby woods if their parish was protected during World War II. Their town was protected and the Chapel was built.
(2) It was during the vision of June 25, 1946 when Barbara asked Our Lady if she desired a Chapel to be constructed, that Our Lady responded: *"I have fulfilled your wish, now you also accomplish your vow."*

XXIX Free Will/Choice

(1) On June 25, 1946 Our Lady said: *"Choose My sign."*

(2) Throughout the messages it is clear that Our Lady implores and even begs us to pray, sacrifice and practice devotion to the Sacred Heart and to the Immaculate Heart, always respecting our free will to choose Her way or to refuse to follow Her.

XXX Seer(s)' Suffering/Sacrifice

(1) Barbara was beset by fits of doubt on two occasions. She did not want to return to the site of the apparition, even though Our Lady Herself had made the request. We need only imagine the severe spiritual and emotional distress suffered by the seer.

(2) It is reported that many people did not believe in the apparitions; Clergy and religious too; this undoubtedly caused more stress and suffering to the seer. We must always pray for the seers.

XXXI Healings Reported

The man found by the seer on the way to Beuren was apparently healed spiritually and emotionally when he was brought to the place of the apparitions after the word given to Barbara by Our Lady on May 25, 1946.

XXXII Action Taken by the Church

(1) First the local church authorities did conduct an investigation, the result of which is not reported.

(2) After Barbara received the Stigmata on Good Friday 1947 some bishops issued public statements in favor of the apparitions; some against.

(3) The Chapel is completed. There are no prohibitions against these apparitions.

(4) It is reported that little by little the Marienfried Shrine has become a center of the Apostolate of the Blue Army of Germany who have had National Blue Army meetings and ceremonies at Marienfried.

XXXII Bibliography

Divine Love (magazine) #86   1981
By: Rev. Martin Rumpf
Published by: Apostolate of Christian Action

Chapter 14

TRE FONTANE, ITALY
(1947-1980)

I Place - Tre Fontane, Italy

II Dates of First and Last Apparition

First: April 12, 1947
Last: April 12, 1980

III Seer(s) - 4

Name: Bruno Cornacchiola
Birth: May 9, 1913
Age at first apparition: 34
Status: Living

Bruno Cornacchiola's 3 children:

Name: Gianfranco
Birth: Unknown
Age at first apparition: 4
Status: Living

Name: Isola
Birth: Unknown
Age at first apparition: 10
Status: Living

Name: Carlo
Birth: Unknown
Age at first apparition: 7
Status: Living

IV Total Number of Apparitions - 4

V Dates and Locality of Each Apparition

All reported apparitions occurred at Tre Fontane, Italy.

1947: April 12, May 16, 30.
1980: April 12.

VI Description of Our Lady

April 12, 1947: She was standing on a rock in the cave and wore a green mantle that covered Her head and fell to Her feet. Her hair was black, Her dress was of a brilliant whiteness and a pink sash went around Her waist to fall down Her side. In Her hands She carried a dark colored book held close to Her heart. Beside Her on the floor, was a black cassock and near it a broken cross.

VII Title(s) of Our Lady - 1

The Virgin of Revelation.

VIII Brief Factual Review

Bruno Cornacchiola was born on May 9, 1913. He was one of five children in a poor godless home in the slums of Rome, Italy. It was in this home with an alcoholic father and a quarreling and violent environment that Bruno spent his first years.

Bruno left his home and survived on the streets. A lady found him on the street and arranged to have him prepared for First Holy Communion. After receiving Communion he went home to share his joy with his parents. A quarrel ensued. Bruno discarded his prayer book and rosary and left home for good.

Years later during the Spanish Civil War, Bruno met and was influenced by a German Lutheran who violently opposed the Catholic Church. Bruno became an Adventist and Freemason.

Although Bruno's wife Iolanda was a good Catholic, he forbade his family to follow the Church. He destroyed all holy pictures in their home, broke the home Crucifix across his knees, ordered his children to spit on priests, forbade prayers to Our Lady, ridiculed the Real Presence in the Blessed Sacrament, and told his family to despise the Pope. His wife had a devotion to the Sacred Heart of Jesus. As a last resort she made a deal with Bruno. If he would make the Nine First Fridays with her, she would consider becoming an Adventist if this devotion did not change him. He was not changed. His wife, however, honored her promise to him. He thus led his family away from the Church.

Eventually Bruno completed a plan to assassinate the Pope. He also prepared writings of bitter criticism of Our Lady. It was during a time when he was in this mood, that Bruno, with his three children, went to Tre Fontane on April 12, 1947 for an outing. Tre Fontane (three fountains) is a place where tradition has it that St. Paul was beheaded and his head rolled causing "three fountains" or springs to appear. The children were playing and lost their ball they used while playing. Bruno searched for the ball and suddenly saw his son Gianfranco kneeling before a cave, staring into the cave and repeating: *"Beautiful Lady! Beautiful Lady!"* Bruno was unable to distract his son. He now called his daughter Isola. When she came to the cave she likewise dropped to her knees and exclaimed: *"Beautiful Lady!"* Next Bruno called Carlos, who also fell to his knees upon reaching the cave and murmured: *"Beautiful Lady!"*

Now Bruno panicked, he could not budge the children. Thinking this to be a trick of a priest hiding in the cave, he entered and found it empty. In desperation he cried out: *"My God, save us!"*

Instantly he saw two white hands coming towards him. The hands touched his face twice, and it felt like a band had been wrenched from his eyes; now he was blind. Then there was a pinpoint of light that grew larger and brighter; the light illuminated the cave. At its most brilliant point it was surrounded by dazzling rays of gold, and within that setting Bruno saw a woman of celestial beauty.

She spoke to Bruno: *"I am the one who is in the Blessed Trinity. I am the Virgin of Revelation. You persecute Me. Enough of this. Come back into the sacred fold, the Heavenly Court on earth. The Nine First Fridays you made in reparation to the Sacred Heart of My Son, before you went further on the road of sin, have saved you. Every Hail Mary recited with faith is a golden arrow reaching the Heart of Jesus."*

The children did not hear this message. She also requested daily recitation of the rosary, prayer for sinners and unbelievers and for the unity of Christians. Our Lady told Bruno, that with the earth on this hallowed spot, She would work miracles. Our Lady promised that the soil of Tre Fontane would have healing power similar to that of the water at Lourdes. The reported healings and abandoned crutches testify to this truth.

She gave Bruno a sign that would identify the priest who would accompany Bruno to visit the Pope and deliver a secret message for the Pope.

Our Lady also told Bruno: *"My body could not and did not decay. I was taken up to heaven by My Son and His angels."* The Dogma of the Assumption of the Blessed Virgin Mary in fact was declared on November 1, 1950 by Pope Pius XII.

After She departed, the cave was filled with a sweet eternal perfume. Bruno was instantly converted and went directly to the church and later confessed his sins.

Later on December 9, 1949 he personally handed over to the Holy Father, the very dagger which Bruno had schemed to use to kill the Pope. He had engraved on the dagger: "Death to the Pope!"

Our Lady appeared to Bruno several more times and predicted great healings and conversions. In 1980 Our Lady said She would appear and work a great miracle within the year, to convince unbelievers of the truth of these apparitions. On April 12, 1980, 33 years after the first apparition, the Miracle of the Sun was witnessed by many during an outdoor Mass celebrated at Tre Fontane. Many conversions and healings were reported at that time.

Bruno has dedicated his life to the service of Our Lady; as an ardent disciple at Tre Fontane.

The story of Tre Fontane really began in 1937, when a young woman named Gina Sinapi, a mystic and victim soul, went to Tre Fontane where Our Lady appeared to her and told her: *"Within 10 years, I shall appear again in this very same place and make use of a man who today persecutes the Church and intends to kill the Pope"*. Gina gave the message (and others she received) to Cardinal Pacelli, who was to become Pope Pius XII.

For this reason, Pope Pius XII immediately showed interest in Bruno's reported apparitions of Our Lady - 10 years later - and in fact received Bruno in private audience.

Also a nun by the name of Sister Raffaela Somma had a dream where she received the identical message Bruno received on April 12, 1947. In her dream she also predicted four personal happenings for herself and for Bruno's future. These have all occurred.

IX The Primary Messages - 4

    (1) Recitation of the daily rosary
    (2) Prayer for sinners, unbelievers and the unity of Christians
    (3) Declared the true facts of the Assumption
    (4) Stated great spiritual value of Nine First Fridays

X Signs Preceding the Apparitions

The cave is lit by celestial light and in the midst of this splendor Our Lady appears.

XI Other Visions During Apparitions - Not Reported
XII Prayers Taught to the Seer(s) - Not Reported

XIII Special Devotion Given to the Seer(s)

(1) No new devotions were given to the seer. Our Lady said however: *"making the Nine First Fridays"* saved Bruno. No doubt She urges us to practice this Devotion to the Sacred Heart of Jesus.
(2) Our Lady said that praying the Hail Mary is like sending golden arrows to Jesus.

XIV Requests Made by Our Lady

(1) April 12, 1947 Our Lady requested Bruno to personally deliver a secret message to Pope Pius XII. This was accomplished.
(2) April 12, 1947 Our Lady requested that Bruno and his entire family go to confession. Their confessions were heard by their parish priest, Fr. Carniel, on May 17, 1947.
(3) May 30, 1947 Our Lady requested that Bruno go to the pious Philippine teachers and tell them to pray for unbelievers of their neighborhood. This was also accomplished.

XV Specific Bible References - Not Reported

XVI Secrets Given to the Seer(s)

On April 12, 1947 Our Lady gave Bruno a secret for the Pope, which Bruno (in the company of a selected priest) was to personally deliver to the Pope. This occurred just as Our Lady said.

XVII Miracles Promised by Our Lady

In 1980 Our Lady told Bruno that within that year (1980) She would work a miracle to convince unbelievers of the truth of the Tre Fontane apparitions. This occurred on April 12, 1980.

XVIII Miracles Performed

True to Her promise, on April 12, 1980 exactly 33 years after Her first apparition to Bruno, upon the elevation of the Host during Mass, an amazing solar phenomenon occurred at Tre Fontane. The sun seemed to melt in the sky and throw out colored circles. It's glare dimmed until it could be looked at with the naked eye. The sun then stood out as a white disc, carrying embossed in it the letters **IHS** against a cross. Scintillating rays of light flowed from this vision of the Host. Further below the sun there appeared a crown of twelve stars. Now the circles thrown out by the sun began to form rings of fire. The letter **M** and a heart surrounded by glowing globes, like illuminated beads in a rosary, appeared in the sky. Within the grotto itself, there came a soft diffused light which seemed to flow from the mantle of the statue of Our Lady of Revelation. Thousands of people witnessed and photographed this phenomenon. This amazing miracle of the sun has also occurred on subsequent anniversaries (April 12th of subsequent years).

XIX Miracles Promised not yet Performed - NR

XX Signs Promised

(1) On April 12, 1947 Our Lady told Bruno to go forth and address some priest with the words: *"Father I want to speak with you."* To the priest who answers with the words: *"Ave Maria, what do you want to say?"* Bruno must tell whatever at that moment comes to his lips. In turn this priest would then refer Bruno to yet another priest with the precise words: *"This priest is meant for you."* Then this final priest would help Bruno on his path to salvation and prove the authenticity of the apparitions.

(2) On April 12, 1947 Our Lady gave Bruno a secret which was to be personally delivered to Pope Pius XII. (This is the very Pope who Bruno hated and plotted to assassinate). Our Lady told Bruno a priest would accompany him to deliver the secret to the Pope. A priest, she told Bruno, would say to him: *"I feel chained to you."* That would be the priest who would accompany Bruno to deliver the secret to the Pope.

XXI Signs Given

(1) After the apparition of April 12, 1947 Bruno went directly to the nearby church and retracted all his hatred and heresy. After days of searching for the priest who would give the correct response, Bruno was dejected. At the urging of his wife, Bruno went to his own church where two priests entered and walked by him. One was the parish priest, the other a visiting priest, Fr. Frosi. Because Bruno was ashamed of his past behavior and did not want to speak to his parish priest, he said to Fr. Frosi: "I want to speak with you." Fr. Frosi replied: "Ave Maria, my son, what do you want to say?" At this Bruno was elated and said the first thing that came to his lips: "Father you have restored to me my life with those words. Then it is true, I am certain." Fr. Frosi replied: "See that priest who is changing in the sacristy. Go to him. He is the priest for your case."

Bruno entered the sacristy and told Fr. Carniel, the local pastor, the entire story. Later on May 17, 1947 Fr. Carniel heard the confessions of Bruno and his entire family.

(2) Many people wanted proof of the apparitions. One such person was Fr. Sfoggia. On one occasion he observed Bruno during an apparition and saw Bruno go into ecstasy. Fr. Sfoggia became aware of an exquisite aroma, and turning to Bruno, he said: "I feel chained to you." Just as Our Lady had promised, this was the priest who accompanied Bruno to personally deliver the secret message to the Pope.

XXII Predictions/Promises

(1) On April 12, 1947 Our Lady predicted the priest who would help Bruno on his way to salvation, and prove the authenticity of the apparition. This came true.
(2) On April 12, 1947 Our Lady also predicted the priest who would accompany Bruno to deliver the secret message to the Pope. This also came true as predicted.
(3) In 1980 Our Lady predicted that She would work a great miracle during 1980. This came true on April 12, 1980 when the Miracle of the Sun occurred before many witnesses.

XXIII Prophecies/Warnings of Chastisement - NR

XXIV Method of Appearance

The grotto (cave) suddenly was lit with dazzling light, from which Our Lady appeared.

XXV Method of Departure

An exquisite perfume filled the air as Our Lady departed.

XXVI Confrontation w/Civil Authorities - NR
XXVII Confrontation w/Church Authorities - NR

XXVIII Request Chapel/Shrine Built

There was no request, yet a magnificent grotto and sanctuary has been erected.

XXIX Free Will/Choice

On April 12, 1947 Our Lady spoke with Bruno for one hour and twenty minutes. She said: *"You persecute Me. Enough of this. Come back into the sacred fold, the Heavenly Court on earth..."*

Thus clearly Bruno was requested to change his behavior and return to God. This Bruno did of his own choice.

XXX Seer(s)' Suffering/Sacrifice

Bruno undoubtedly suffered emotionally and spiritually when Our Lady first spoke to him on April 12, 1947 admonishing him for his behavior towards Our Lady and towards the Pope. In addition he suffered shame and fear when he searched for the priest that was to help him and also when he was to deliver a message to the very Pope whom Bruno had plotted to kill.

It is also reported that many people demanded proof of the apparitions; this frequently occurs and nearly always gives distress to the seer.

XXXI Healings Reported

(1) First off, Bruno and his entire family were spiritually healed.
(2) Many healings and conversions were promised by Our Lady and have already occurred. The Grotto is evidenced with many abandoned crutches.

XXXII Action Taken by the Church

The church permits public worship at the Grotto and Sanctuary. Clergy and religious are permitted to visit the Sanctuary. Bishops and cardinals have been there, including Cardinal Wojtyla (now Pope John Paul II) who visited the Sanctuary. An official paper of the Vatican lists Tre Fontane as one of the Marian Sanctuaries.

No decision has been made by the Church.

XXXIII Bibliography

The Virgin of the Revelation
By: Fr. Giuseppe Tomaselli
Published by: (Not Given)

Tre Fontane
By: Francesco Spadafora
Published by: Mediatrix BVM (coordinator)

Chapter 15

MONTICHIARI/FONTANELLE, ITALY
(1947-1983)

I Place - Montichiari and Fontanelle, Italy

II Dates of First and Last Apparition

First: Montichiari; Spring 1947.
Last: Montichiari; December 8, 1947.

First: Fontanelle; April 17, 1966.
Last: Fontanelle; August 6, 1966.

Later Apparitions - (In seer's home chapel at Montichiari)
First: October 12, 1968.
Last: March 24, 1983.

III Seer(s) - 1

Name: Pierina Gilli
Birth: August 3, 1911
Age at first apparition: 35
Status: Unknown

IV Total Number of Apparitions - 35

First Phase: Early Montichiari - 7
Second Phase: Early Fontanelle - 4, Later Montichiari - 24

V Dates and Locality of Each Apparition

First Phase - *All apparitions occurred at Montichiari.*
1947: Spring (hospital room); June 13 (hospital room); October 22 (chapel in hospital); November 16 & 22 (parish church); December 7 and 8 (parish church).
1966: February (once in seer's home chapel in Montichiari when Our Lady announced that She would appear in Fontanelle).
Second Phase - *All apparitions occurred at well in Fontanelle.*
1966: April 17, May 13, June 9, August 6.
Further Apparitions - *The following apparitions took place in the seer's home chapel in Montichiari.*
1968: October 12, 13.
1970: February 14, May 19.
1971: January 17, July 25.
1972: August 5.
1973: July 22.
1974: May 15, June 29, September 3.
1975: January 30, April 8, July 3, August 31, November 23.
1975: January 6, February 13, April 20, June 6, September 3.
1979: June 12.
1982: May 13.
1983: March 24.

VI Description of Our Lady

(1) At the first apparition in a hospital room in Montichiari Our Lady appeared as a beautiful Lady, dressed in a violet dress with a white veil around Her head. She was very sad, Her eyes filled with tears which fell to the floor. The seer saw Our Lady's heart (breast) pierced by three swords.

(2) Thereafter commencing on June 13, 1947 Our Lady appeared several times dressed in white, with three roses, instead of three swords on Her breast, a white rose, a red rose and a golden rose. On June 13, 1947 Our Lady explained to the seer the meaning of the three swords and the three roses.

(3) On December 8, 1947 Our Lady appeared in the parish Church in Montichiari. She appeared on a big white staircase which was decorated on both sides with white, yellow and red roses. Our Lady descended the stairs.

(4) During the second phase commencing on April 17, 1966 Our Lady appeared in Fontanelle above the well. Our Lady followed the seer to the well and touched the water at two places with Her own hands. As Our Lady arose into the air to leave She opened Her arms and Her

cloak, which filled an immense space in the universe. From Her arms hung a white rosary.

(5) On May 19, 1970 Our Lady appeared as usual in a white mantle, Her heart adorned with three roses, white, red and golden. Over Her right arm She wore a big rosary which ended, not in a cross, but in a medal. Our Lady spread Her arms and showed the front and reverse of the medal to the seer.

(6) Our Lady often appeared unexpectedly and in a magnificent light.

VII Title(s) of Our Lady - 6

(1) She announced Her title as *"Rosa Mystica, the Mystical Rose"* and requested a Feast Day on July 13 and Special Devotion and Veneration under that title.

(2) On December 8, 1947 She said: *"I am the Immaculate Conception, I am Mary of Grace, that is, full of Grace, Mother of My Divine Son Jesus Christ"*.

(3) On September 8, 1974 She said: *"I am Mary, the Mother of the Church."*

(4) On June 6, 1976 Our Lady said: *"I am Mary, the Mediatrix of Grace."*

VIII Brief Factual Review

Montichiari, Italy is a small town located in Northern Italy at the foot of the Italian Alps, also near Brescia which was the home town of Pope Paul VI.

The seer, Pierina Gilli was born August 3, 1911. She was 35 when the apparitions commenced in the Spring of 1947. She worked then as a nurse in the local hospital.

At the first appearance Our Lady appeared to the seer in a room in the hospital, dressed in violet with a white veil around Her head. This was the only time She wore violet. Every time thereafter She was dressed in white. On this first occasion She was very sad, Her eyes were filled with tears which fell to the floor.

Our Lady wore three swords on Her breast (in Her heart). Her first words were: *"Peace - Penitence - Expiation"*.

At the second appearance of June 13, 1947 Our Lady had three roses over Her heart (instead of three swords), a white one, a red one and a golden one. Our Lady explained the meaning of the three swords and the three roses to Pierina: **First sword:** means loss of vocation as a priest or monk. **Second sword:** means priests, monks and nuns who live in deadly sin. **Third sword:** means priests and monks who commit the treason of Judas.

While on the other hand, **White rose:** means the spirit of prayer. **Red rose:** means the spirit of expiation. **Yellow (golden) rose:** means the spirit of penitence.

On this second appearance, Our Lady also told the seer of a new Marian Devotion for religious communities: That of the 13th of each month, the Day of Mary. On the 12 previous days special prayers and preparation should be made. She also said She wished July 13th of each year to be celebrated in honor of the 'Rosa Mystica', the Mystical Rose.

On the third apparition Our Lady appeared in the Chapel at the hospital and thereafter She appeared in the parish Church in Montichiari through December 8, 1947.

On November 22, 1947 Our Lady appeared and predicted She would appear again on December 8, 1947 at noon which will be an **Hour of Grace.** On December 7, 1947 Our Lady said: *"Tomorrow I shall show you My Immaculate Heart which human beings know so little."* She requested that the devotion of the 'Rosa Mystica' together with the veneration of Her Immaculate Heart, be increased in the religious and monastic communities in Montichiari. On December 7, 1947 Our Lady was accompanied by Jacinta and Francisco of Fatima. At this time Our Lady gave a secret to the seer.

True to Her promise Our Lady appeared at noon on December 8, 1947. She announced: *"I am Mary of Grace, that is, the Full of Grace, Mother of My Divine Son Jesus Christ. I come here to Montichiari because it is My wish to be appealed to and venerated as 'Rosa Mystica'."* Our Lady showed the seer Her Heart. There were three notable healings which occurred on December 8, 1947 during the Hour of Grace.

The second phase of the apparitions occurred in Fontanelle, which is a suburb of Montichiari. The first appearance there occurred on April 17, 1966 while the seer walked up and down a path above the well praying the holy rosary. Our Lady asked the seer to kiss the steps leading to the well as a sign of penance and purification. Then Our Lady went near the well and said: *"Take mud, dirt in your hands, then wash with the water! This is to show that sin becomes mud and dirt in the hearts of My children. When it is absolved in the water of grace, souls become clean again and worthy of grace."* Then the Mother of Our Lord bowed down and touched the water of the well in two places with Her own hands.

Our Lady asked that the sick and all Her children come to the 'Spring of Grace' and further that a basin be built to immerse the sick in the water and that the other part of the well was to be reserved for drinking.

On June 9, 1966 the Feast of 'Corpus Christi', Our Lady appeared above the well and came down to earth with Her feet on a ripening wheat field. The faithful present watched in silence as Our Lady touched the ripening wheat field and said: *"How very much I wish that this wheat would be Eucharistic Bread in many Communions of Reparation. It is My wish that this wheat be baked into Holy Wafers, be brought to Rome and that the wafers reach Fatima for the 13th of October."*

Then Our Lady said She wanted a statue built facing the well and roofed over, and that the statue is to be brought to the well on October 13th in procession.

During the very next apparition on August 6, 1966 Our Lady said that Her Divine Son Jesus sent Her to ask for a world union of Communion of Expiation, to be held on October 13, 1966 for the first time and every October 13th thereafter. She promised an abundance of graces.

By order of the bishop, the seer, Pierina Gilli has not been allowed to go to Fontanelle since 1966. Our Lady, however, is not bound by this order. Beginning on October 12, 1968 She appeared to the seer in the seer's home chapel in Montichiari several times through March 24, 1983. Our Lady pleads that we pray, pray the holy rosary and do penance.

On May 19, 1970 Our Lady requested a medal be struck and distributed, with the inscription on front 'Rosa Mystica' and on the reverse 'Mary, Mother of the Church'. She also explained the meaning of Her appearance as 'Rosa Mystica'.

On September 8, 1974 Our Lady showed the seer a vision of a great church with five round arches and requested that such a church be built in Fontanelle. Our Lady explained that the five arches signify that Jesus would like to enfold all five continents in His arms.

The parish priest had arranged for statues of the 'Rosa Mystica' to be carved by a family of carvers working on their knees. On August 31, 1975 Our Lady told the seer that, Our Lady, through the Pilgrim Madonna statues, is accompanied by whole hosts of holy angels who praise the Lord and that wherever She stays as the Pilgrim Madonna, and where She is invoked, and where many prayers are said, that Her Divine Son Jesus Christ causes great graces to flow down onto every such place.

On May 29, 1984 at St. John of God's Church in Chicago, Illinois a pilgrim statue of the 'Rosa Mystica' wept tears. Thereafter there have been many reported weepings of the pilgrim 'Rosa Mystica' statues.

No final Church action is reported.

IX The Primary Messages - 8

(1) Prayer, Penitence, Expiation - These words were the first and only words spoken by Our Lady on Her first apparition in the Spring of 1947. Thereafter She repeated this request many times from 1947 through 1976.

(2) Rosary - Our Lady pleads: *"Pray the rosary"* (January 17 and July 25, 1971 and also August 5, 1972).

(3) Devotion to 'Rosa Mystica' - Our Lady requested a new Marian Devotion, especially for religious, consisting of the Day of Mary, on the 13th day of each month and with special prayer and purgation during the 1st twelve days.

Also July 13th of each year is to be celebrated in honor of 'Rosa Mystica' the Mystical Rose. (Requested by Our Lady on: June 13, 1947, December 7 and 8, 1947 and July 22, 1973).

(4) Hour of Grace at Noon on December 8th - Our Lady requested a special Hour of Grace at noon on December 8th when great graces would be given to Her children who faithfully keep this devotion. (December 8 and November 22, 1947).

(5) World Wide Communion of Reparation - Our Lady requested this prayer and devotion on October 13th of each year commencing October 13, 1966. (June 9 and August 6, 1966).

(6) Medal Honoring 'Rosa Mystica' - On May 19, 1970 Our Lady said to the seer: *"It is My wish that a medal be struck like the one which I am showing you. With the inscription on the front: 'Rosa Mystica', and on the reverse: 'Mary, Mother of the Church'."*

(7) Rosa Mystica Statue - On June 9, 1966 Our Lady requested a statue to be made of the 'Rosa Mystica' and brought in procession to Fontanelle on October 13.

She also stated on August 31, 1975: *"That wherever My Pilgrim Madonna goes there I am accompanied by the holy angels who praise God. Where I stop as Pilgrim Madonna, where I am invoked, and where many prayers are said, My Divine Son Jesus Christ, in every such place, causes special graces to flow down into souls."* On another occasion She said: *"When I am brought as a Pilgrim, as the 'Rosa Mystica' to people, I shall come with the holy angels and saints and will stand by them always protecting and blessing them. Similarly, when I am accepted with joy and love in houses, religious or secular, I will bless them and those who live in them; but quite specially, I shall be near them with graces of God and My mother-love, at the hour of death."*

(8) Angels - On June 29, 1974 Our Blessed Mother said: *"Happy is the man who commends himself to his guardian angel, and follows his imitations."*

X Signs Preceding the Apparitions - Not Reported

XI Other Visions During Apparitions

(1) On December 7, 1947 Our Lady was accompanied by Jacinta and Francisco, two of the children from Fatima. Our Lady said: *"Jacinta and Francisco, they will be your companions in all your afflictions. They too have suffered; though they were much younger than you. Look, this is how I would like you to be; simple and good, as these children used to be."*

(2) On June 29, 1974 Our Lady was accompanied by the holy angels and the seer heard the angels singing.

XII Prayers Taught to the Seer(s) - Not Reported

XIII Special Devotion Given to the Seer(s)

(1) Devotion to the 'Rosa Mystica' especially for religious, and for the Day of Mary on the 13th day of each month, with special prayers and preparation for the previous 12 days. Also that the 'Rosa Mystica' should be venerated on July 13th of each year.
(2) World Day of Communion of Reparation on October 13th of each year commencing October 13, 1966.
(3) Hour of Grace at Noon before the Blessed Sacrament (or at home) on December 8th of each year.
(4) Medal honoring the 'Rosa Mystica' with the inscription on front 'Rosa Mystica' and on the reverse 'Mary, Mother of the Church.'

XIV Requests Made by Our Lady

(1) Devotion of the 'Rosa Mystica' with Day of Mary on the 13th day of each month and feast of the Rosa Mystica on July 13th of each year.
(2) Communion of Reparation on October 13th of each year starting October 13, 1966.
(3) Hour of Grace at Noon on December 8th of each year.
(4) Medal honoring 'Rosa Mystica'.
(5) Statue of 'Rosa Mystica' be made and distributed and also brought to the well by procession on October 13th.

XV Specific Bible References - Not Reported

XVI Secrets Given to the Seer(s)

Our Lady gave the seer a mystery or secret during the apparition of December 7, 1947 and again on December 8, 1947.

XVII Miracles Promised by Our Lady

The seer asked Our Lady to perform a miracle. Our Lady answered: *"The most evident miracle will be the ungodly souls, who for some time, especially during the last war, became lukewarm so that they were unfaithful or even betrayed their vocations."*

XVIII Miracles Performed

(1) Many healing miracles and conversions were performed beginning December 8, 1947 during the Hour of Grace.
(2) The 'Miracle of the Sun' was seen by many witnesses in Montichiari on April 20, 1969. This 'Miracle of the Sun' was witnessed by about 120 persons, which dazzling display included clear signals of light in code, three short, three long and again three short for SOS: "Save Our Souls".

XIX Miracles Promised not yet Performed

A secret was given to Pierina on December 8, 1947 and Our Lady then promised to come again and tell her when the moment would come to reveal it.

XX Signs Promised - Not Reported

XXI Signs Given

(1) The 'Miracle of the Sun' was reported by different groups of witnesses occurring at different times at Montichiari; including the reports of April 20, 1969 and Dec 8, 1969.
(2) Many Pilgrim 'Rosa Mystica' statues from around the world have been reported to weep human tears.

XXII Predictions/Promises

(1) On November 22, 1947 and again on December 7, 1947 Our Lady promised to appear in the church at Montichiari at noon on December 8, 1947 for the Hour of Grace. She did appear on December 8, 1947 as promised.
(2) On March 24, 1983 Our Lady said that the five dome church She wants built in Fontanelle will become a reality.

XXIII Prophecies/Warnings of Chastisement

The messages contain warning of punishment due humanity for sins committed, together with pleas for prayer and penance in reparation for sins and for conversion of sinners, as well as words of Our Dear Lady's intercession on our behalf.
(1) November 16, 1947 - *"Our Lord, My Divine Son, is tired of the many offenses, the severe offenses, the sins against holy purity. He wants to*

send another flood of punishment. I have interceded that He may be merciful once more. Therefore I ask for your prayer and penitence to expiate these sins."
(2) **May 13, 1966** - *"The world is approaching ruin. Once more I have obtained mercy for you."*
(3) **August 5, 1972** - *"Times become dark, full of confusion and horror, but if people pray and do penance, this Heart of the Mother will once more get light, love and peace for the whole world from the Lord, My Divine Son Jesus Christ."*
(4) **January 30, 1975** - *"The times are getting worse and worse; a terrible danger is threatening; the Church too, is in great danger. Things will get so bad that people will think all is lost, but I am after all a Mother who has a Living Heart for Her children and would save them. As you can observe for yourself, human pride has resulted in confusing those in the highest offices of the Church."*
(5) **April 8, 1975** - *"The prayers, offerings and penance of so many people prevent the true judgment of God from falling upon mankind. In My love I am always pleading with My Son Jesus Christ."*
(6) **June 14, 1975** - *"The times grow ever more calamitous through the effect of a satanic and godless delusion, which strives to undermine and destroy the work of the Divine Redeemer, the Lord of the whole universe."*
(7) **November 23, 1975** - *"The world ought to have been visited by a great judgment because of its hardening in sin. His great and endless mercy has triumphed once again."*

XXIV Method of Appearance

(1) There seems to have been no special method of appearance during Stage One and Stage Two. Except for the first appearance, when Our Lady appeared in a violet dress, each time thereafter She appeared in a white mantel.
(2) On December 8, 1947 Our Lady appeared on a big white staircase decorated on both sides with white, red and yellow roses. She descended the staircase with great majesty.

XXV Method of Departure

(1) Usually Our Lady said a parting remark of love and took leave.
(2) On April 17, 1966 Our Lady rose into the air and opened Her arms and Her cloak, which filled an immense space in the universe. From Her arm hung a rosary. Below and on the right side of Her cloak the seer could see the church of Montichiari and the Castle of St. Mary. This method of departure was repeated on other occasions.

XXVI Confrontation w/Civil Authorities - NR

XXVII Confrontation w/Church Authorities

(1) The bishop of Brescia, Monsignore Giacinto Tredici, made his order forbidding the seer to go to Fontanelle commencing in 1966. The seer complied. Our Lady appeared to the seer thereafter in the seer's home chapel in Montichiari.

(2) The same bishop appointed a commission to investigate, which commission returned a negative report. However, it is reported that the commission did not investigate any reported miracles, did not interrogate any witnesses, and rejected every medical report except one negative report from one physician.

(3) This same Bishop Tredici is said to personally believe in the apparitions but was afraid of his adversaries.

(4) Monsignore Abate Rossi, who was the parish priest of Montichiari for 22 years *(1949-1971)*, believed in the genuineness of the apparitions. He ordered the statue of Mary to be carved according to the message and later to be placed in the church at Montichiari. He built the chapel in Fontanelle, and ordered the big statue of the Madonna. He also had the roof over the statue built and also a basin as Our Lady said She desired.

(5) The seer made a report to the Holy Father, Pope Pius XII and that Pope granted a private audience to the seer on August 9, 1951.

(6) The Church has not approved the apparitions at Montichiari or Fontanelle, however, there is no formal or definite prohibition in effect.

XXVIII Request Chapel/Shrine Built

(1) Our Lady requested a Chapel/Shrine, to be built in Fontanelle, which was done.

(2) On September 8, 1974 Our Lady showed the seer a vision of a church with five round arches. Later on Aug 31, 1975 Our Lady said: *"This picture* (of the church with five arches) *will become a reality."*
Again on March 24, 1983 Our Lady said of the vision of the church with five arches: *"Truly! One day this will become a reality."*

XXIX Free Will/Choice

Throughout the apparitions Our Lady pleaded for prayer, penance and conversion. Obviously we are free to choose or reject the graces distributed by Our Mother. As an instance on Dec 8, 1947 Our Lady said: *"I have an abundance of graces ready for all those children who hear My voice and take My wishes to heart."*

XXX Seer(s)' Suffering/Sacrifice

(1) First off the bishop forbade the seer to go to Fontanelle starting in 1966, which undoubtedly caused her great anxiety and distress.
(2) The commission investigating these apparitions appointed a doctor to examine her. That medical doctor reported that the seer was addicted to morphine. All other medical opinions were ignored. Again this caused her severe distress.

XXXI Healings Reported

On December 8, 1947 at noon during the Hour of Grace, a boy of 5 or 6 who was suffering from polio and could not stand or walk; also a woman of 26 who suffered since age 12 from severe tuberculosis, were both completely healed at the same 'Moment of Grace' inside the church. The woman who had been unable to speak for nine years, now broke out and sang a song of praise to the Lord. She could speak perfectly now; she became a pious nun. The boy thereafter married.

A third miraculous healing happened at the same time but not inside the church. A woman of 36 was healed in her own home at the time of the Hour of Grace in the church. This woman had severe physical and mental problems. She could not speak and she had no control over her bodily functions. The woman's sister-in-law stayed at home with her while the woman's father went to the cathedral for the anticipated appearance of Our Lady during the Hour of Grace. The sister-in-law prayed the holy rosary at the time of the Holy Hour and exclaimed: "Our Dear Lady, if you are really present in the church at Montichiari, please heal this poor sick girl." In that same moment the sick woman was healed completely. These miraculous healings caused a sensation.

There are many reported cases of dramatic conversions. Healings are reported at the sites where 'Rosa Mystica' statues have been reported to weep. Healings continue.

XXXII Action Taken by the Church

(1) Commission appointed by the bishop of Brescia gave a negative report.
(2) Pope Pius XII gave the seer a private audience.
(3) The parish priest of the church at Montichiari for 22 years, believes in the genuineness of the apparitions and has done things to carry out Our Lady's requests.
(4) These apparitions do not have Church approval, but no definite, formal prohibition exists against these apparitions.

XXXIII Bibliography

Mary the Mystical Rose   1988
By: Rev. A.M. Weigl
Published by: Rev. Raymond J. Fasinski, St. John of God Church

Rosa Mystica   1986
By: Franz Spechbacher
Published by: Mediatrix-Verlag
English Distribution: Our Lady of the Roses Charitable Trust

Chapter 16

LIPA, PHILIPPINES
(1948)

I Place - Lipa, Philippines
(At the Carmelite Monastery known as Carmel)

II Dates of First And Last Apparition

First: August 18, 1948
Last: November 12, 1948

III Seer(s) - 1

Name: Teresita Castillo (Novice)
Birth: July 4, 1927
Age at first apparition: 21
Present: Living

IV Total Number of Apparitions - 19

Note: It is reported that since 1991, Teresita has been receiving locutions and messages again.

V Dates And Locality of Each Apparition

The apparitions occured in the convent garden unless otherwise noted.

1948: August 18, 19 (twice in seer's convent cell); September 12, 13, 14, 15, 16, 17, 18, 19, 20, 21, 22, 23, 24, 25, 26 & November 12.

VI Description of Our Lady

(1) When Our Lady first appeared to the seer in August in the cell of the seer, it is reported that Teresita entered her cell and saw a very bright light and saw Our Lady in white, Her hair seemed silvery, and She was very beautiful.

(2) In September, Our Lady appeared in the garden by the vine on a cloud, dressed in white, hands clasped at Her breast, and a golden rosary hanging from Her right hand. Her dress was very white, very simple, and around Her cincture a narrow belt was tied. She was radiant with beauty.

VII Title(s) of Our Lady - 2

(1) *"I am Mary, Mediatrix of All Grace."* (September 26, 1948)
(2) *"I am your Mother, I am the Mother of My Son, Jesus."* (September 13, 1948)

VIII Brief Factual Review

The city of Lipa is located just one hour's drive south of Metro Manila in the Southern Tagalog Province of Batangas, Philippines, and was formerly a center of world culture and glamour. Lipa was once the world's sole supplier of coffee beans.

During World War II, the Japanese invaded Lipa and established a district headquarters there. Sixteen thousand men, women, and children reportedly were herded into a diocesan seminary (converted into a prison), and were bayoneted to death. This seminary was later to become the Carmelite Convent of Lipa, the scene of the reported apparitions and other supernatural events involving the seer Teresita Castillo.

Teresita Castillo was born into a prominent family, her father having been governor of the Province of Batangas. Influenced by convent school values, "Teresing" (as she is affectionately called), nurtured a secret desire to join the Carmelites.

On her 21st birthday, July 4, 1948 Teresita fled her home and entered Carmel, the Convent of Discalced Carmelites, in Lipa. Of course, when her family learned of her action they attempted to dissuade her by promises and threats. But all to no avail. She was determined to become a Carmelite novice.

Within one month of her arrival at the convent, on the night of July 31st, 1948 Satan visited Teresita in her cell and attempted to convince her to leave the convent. She rejected Satan, but he did not give up—rather Satan appeared to her three more times, again trying to force her to leave the convent through fear and threats. A foul odor accompanied Satan.

In contrast when Our Lady first appeared to Teresing in August, She was surrounded by an overpowering and pleasant fragrance. Our Lady appeared to the seer three times during August, then for fifteen consecutive days in September at the vine in the convent garden, with one final appearance on November 12, 1948.

The seer was amazed at this rapid succession of supernatural occurrences. It is reported that Teresita asked: "Why is it like this? Is life in Carmel really like this?"

On August 18th Our Lady requested that the seer wash the feet of the Prioress Mother Cecilia, and drink some of the water. When this was reported to the prioress, she was "dubious." However, Our Lady's request was repeated again the next day, August 19th. This time Mother Cecilia received a locution from Our Lady telling her that the seer would carry a sign of confirmation. This sign occurred when Mother Cecilia next saw the seer with circles of blood around the seer's eyes. The feet washing event occurred that very day. That evening, Our Lady appeared to the seer disguised as a nun and said: *"Your Mother made a wise decision in obeying Me. Now that you have given Me proof of your humility, and your Mother of her simplicity, I can now proceed. Both of you will always remain under My mantle."*

The very next day, August 20th, the seer saw showers of rose petals fall for the first time. This phenomena was repeated many times both inside the convent and outside in the garden. Many clergy, religious, and pilgrims witnessed these rose petal "showers." The rose petals contained miraculous images of Jesus and the Blessed Mother and other holy scenes, and were collected and cherished and saved by many, even to this day.

It was two days later on August 22nd that the evil one physically attacked the seer. Mother Cecilia became physically involved in this incident. When it was over the seer became blind. Teresita regained her eye sight on September 7th. Mother Cecilia had a prophetic locution predicting that the seer would regain her eye sight. The seer suffered many times during the period of these apparitions, and it is reported that Mother Cecilia received locutions and prophetic messages of these sufferings before they occurred.

The messages started on September 12th while Teresing was praying in the garden when suddenly a vine began to shake. Then Our Lady appeared to the seer and requested that she kiss the earth and return to this same spot for fifteen consecutive days. The seer complied and messages were given to Teresita.

Our Lady requested the vine be blessed which has also been done. Later She also requested a statue (Image) be placed at the site of the apparition. This was also accomplished.

The messages stressed humility, penance, prayers, especially prayer for priests and nuns, and to pray the rosary. Teresita was given secrets. The seer reports there was one secret for herself, one for the community at Lipa Carmel, one for the world and one for China, none for Russia.

Our Lady appeared sad during some of the apparitions because two nuns refused to believe. One nun had a miraculous healing some forty years later which she attributed to Our Lady—then she believed.

On September 22nd Our Lady said: *"To My daughter who does not believe Me, I do not oblige you to believe. It is enough that you do not believe. But do not block nor debase My secret place, nor despise My words. I do not oblige you to listen, nor to obey them if you do not wish to, for you have free will. Neither should you honor Me on Saturdays if you are not inclined to . . ."*

On September 26th (the last of the fifteen consecutive appearances), Our Lady requested that a Mass be held on the 12th day of every month and asked that the community consecrate themselves to Her. Before departing, She identified Herself as: *"I am Mary, Mediatrix of All Grace."* There are accounts of a blue bird appearing at the vine before each apparition, accounts of the spinning sun, heavy fragrance of roses, and, of course, the "showers" of rose petals. Incredibly, whole roses were manifested out of thin air. Some people reported seeing the statue of Our Lady come to life.

Warnings of persecutions, unrest, and bloodshed for *"your country"* were given by Our Blessed Mother during Her last apparition at the vine. She also said: *"The Church will suffer much."* Just before She departed Our Lady said: *"What I ask here is the same I asked at Fatima. I bless this community in a very special blessing. All these can be revealed now."*

Many cures have been reported using the rose petals, including some remarkable instantaneous cures. There are reports of the blind being cured as well as other amazing cures.

In one instance, a baby (Soccorro Mendoza Dichoso), born in December, 1948 with a hole in her skull experienced an amazing cure. The parents reportedly applied "rose petals" from the "shower" to the baby's skull on January 28, 1949. The child was cured, the hole in the skull closed and the brain receded. This was confirmed by X-rays.

Another reported healing occurred on December 24, 1950 when the Last Sacraments were administered to a girl dying of cerebral hemorrhage. Fr. Casey applied a Lipa rose petal to the girl's forehead, when instantly, upon the ringing of the Angelus bell, the girl suddenly woke up as if nothing was wrong. She was cured.

One cure that is outstanding occurred to a child named Menania Maria Sungo who was born in 1940 with a severely deformed right foot. The sole of the foot was curled up, she could not wear a shoe on it and the leg had atrophied, shortened, and wasted away. In 1949, when the child was nine years old, her uncle brought to her family a bottle of water which had been placed overnight beside the statue of Our Lady (Mary, Mediatrix of All Grace). The child's mother rubbed this water on the child's foot every evening for one week and offered many prayers. Then one morning, the child awoke to discover that her foot was normal; totally cured. This caused a sensation amongst friends and neighbors. Neighbors remarked they experienced a strong fragrance of flowers around the child's home. Meanwhile, the family of the Sungo household was shocked when a shower of rose petals fell inside their own home.

The statue of Our Lady Mediatrix of All Grace has been on several pilgrimages, traveling to Spain, to the United States and to other places. Smaller replicas of the statue have been distributed.

It is also reported that Teresita received the Host for Holy Communion on her tongue from an angel on an occasion when she was unable to attend Mass because she was sick in bed. Teresita had other mystical experiences including visions of the Sacred Heart, of a multitude of angels and saints, of Saint Cecilia and Saint Terese of Lisieux. The seer was also seen to go into a state of unconsciousness, and then, while lying on the floor, enact the agony of Christ on the Cross. This phenomenon was witnessed by the prioress, by Bishop Obviar, and by members of the Carmel Community at Lipa. As one nun put it: "The seven words would be reenacted and we really did see it!"

On January 23, 1949 the cornerstone was laid for the church known as the Chapel of Our Lady Mediatrix of All Grace, officiated by Bishop Obviar. Some twenty to fifty thousand people were present. The church has been completed and was funded entirely by public donations.

The Bishop of Lipa, Alfredo Verzosa, ordered the Carmelite sisters to withdraw the statue of Our Lady from public veneration because of all the commotion. He personally went to the convent on November 19, 1948 determined to do so himself. When he opened the door and entered the convent a shower of rose petals fell on him. He fell to his knees and could not utter a word. Thereafter, Bishop Verzosa supported these apparitions and applied his Imprimatur to an official account of the apparitions at the vine.

Soon the events were commercialized by some, and fake rose petals were being sold. The Carmel at Lipa suffered a series of attacks. On January 23, 1950 Bishop Verzosa was suddenly transferred from Lipa and virtually all power of the Lipa Diocese was placed into the hands of an Apostolic Administrator. Shortly thereafter, on February 27, 1950 Mother Cecilia was suddenly replaced. Bishop Obviar was also relieved of his duties. It was reported that many people distrusted the "showers" of rose petals and accused the nuns of somehow orchestrating these "showers."

The seer was interviewed and interrogated by a psychologist, Fr. Blas, who reportedly attempted to have her renounce. She refused to do so. Then Dr. Pardo, a psychiatrist, reportedly intimidated the seer seeking to have her admit insanity in her family. There are also reports that they submitted false documents for Teresita to sign and again she refused. However, the written report of Fr. Blas states that: "Fr. Blas believes she is perfectly normal and is not suffering from hallucinations."

In April 1951 the official investigation by the Church produced a negative report and was signed by six bishops; some of whom would later say they were coerced into signing under threat of excommunication. The investigation appears to have been lacking. Neither Bishop Obviar nor Bishop Verzosa were questioned by the investigators. Of some interest is that the bishops who signed the verdict that there was no supernatural intervention at Lipa Carmel, nevertheless, kept the rose petals from Lipa given to them. One or more bishops announced on his deathbed that he was forced to sign the verdict against his own free will.

After the Church's decision was released, the nuns were ordered to destroy all materials connected with the apparitions. They burned Teresita's diary as well as Mother Cecilia's diary. The statue of the Mediatrix was also ordered destroyed; however, the nuns managed ways and means to save it from destruction.

Our Lady had warned of persecutions. All those centrally connected with these apparitions were made to suffer. Stringent sanctions were imposed on the Community of Lipa. The doors of Lipa were closed, not only to applicants to the religious life, but also to hired help and to all outside assistance. The nuns were not allowed to see members of their own families.

For a long time, Sr. Elizabeth single-handedly supported the community by begging. She was the only nun permitted to go outside the community and to attend to the community's needs.

In February 1990 a strange new phenomenon was reported in the Granja District of Lipa, a few blocks from the Carmel. A white luminous outline of a female in prayer began to appear in the evenings on one of the leaves of a tall coconut tree. The silhouette was visible for ninety consecutive evenings.

Then on May 21, 1990 the day after the silhouette ceased, Sr. Alphonse pleaded on her deathbed that the statue of Mediatrix be again exposed in the Chapel of Carmel. The following day, Archbishop Gaviola instructed the statue be again displayed, the first time in forty years!

Shortly thereafter, on January 24, 1991 the rose petals reportedly began to fall again at Lipa Carmel. Teresita and two other people were inside the church in front of the statue of Mediatrix when rose petals suddenly began to fall. The rose petals were pure white this time.

Soon other happenings were reported. A few days later, six children playing in the garden at Carmel saw the statue come to life. They reported "I saw Her eyes tear and Her feet come closer together; I held Her hand and it was soft; I saw Her dress blow in the breeze; I held Her dress and it was soft; When I kissed Her feet, I felt them move."

Petal showers have occurred with some regularity inside Teresita's home and other places, too. Several witnesses, including a priest, were present when full roses materialized out of thin air and landed on the stairs, altar, and bedroom of the seer's own home.

Teresita now reports that she has begun to receive messages from Mary again.

On July 16, 1991 Archbishop Gaviola declared the statue of Mediatrix would be exposed to the public at Lipa Carmel, during his entire term as archbishop. A secret new commission has been set up by the archbishop and he asks for a speedy investigation and report.

Teresita left Carmel, never to return to the order. At present she works assisting in the production of the English-Tagalog dictionary.

Very negative media articles together with sham dealers in 'Rose Petals' helped turn public opinion against these apparitions. This, together with the Church's negative report, submerged these apparitions for some forty years. Recent efforts of television investigative reporter, June Keithley, helped bring some of the true, overlooked or suppressed facts to the attention of the people and of the Church. As a consequence the Church has now set up a new committee to investigate these apparitions.

IX The Primary Messages - 5

Teresita reports the emphasis of the messages was on humility, simplicity, penance, and prayer.

(1) Prayer - On September 21, 1948 Our Lady said: *"Pray, pray, pray for a soul, My daughter."*

At the last appearance on November 12, 1948 Our Lady said: *"People do not believe My words, pray, My child, pray much because there will be persecutions. Pray for priests. Pray for the conversions of sinners throughout the world. What I ask here is exactly what I asked at Fatima."*

(2) Penance - *"Do penance for those who do not believe . . ."* (November 12, 1948)

Again, *"Do penance for priests and nuns, but be not afraid, for the love of My Son will soften the hardness of hearts, and My Motherly love will be their strength to crush the enemies of God."*

(3) Humility and Simplicity - On September 26, 1948 Our Lady said: *". . . Be humble and simple because humility and simplicity are the two virtues I love most . . ."*

(4) Rosary - *". . . Spread the meaning of the rosary because this will be the instrument for peace throughout the world. Tell the people that the rosary must be said with devotion."*

(5) Devotions - *"Propagate the devotion to My Immaculate Heart."* (November 12, 1948)

On September 21, 1948 Our Lady said: *"I ask you to honor Me on Saturdays especially in these devotions:*
    1) **Our Lady of Mount Carmel**
    2) **Our Lady of Snow**
    3) **Our Lady of the Holy Rosary**
    4) **Our Lady of Perpetual Help**
    5) **Immaculate Heart of Mary**
    6) **Our Lady of the Abandonment and Refuge of Sinners**
    7) **Our Lady of Lourdes**
    8) **Our Lady of Peace and Good Voyage**
    9) **Our Lady of Good Counsel**
    10) **Holy Name of Mary**
    11) **Our Lady of Loreto**
    12) **Our Lady of Remedy**
    13) **The Seven Dolors**

X Signs Preceding The Apparitions

(1) At the first visit of Our Lady on August 18, 1948 Teresita was surrounded by an awesome fragrance and upon entering her cell she saw Our Blessed Mother.

(2) It is reported that often a blue bird would appear at the vine before or during the apparitions. The bird was as large as a dove but blue in color and people reported hearing it sing. It had a real voice.

XI Other Visions During Apparitions

(1) **Satan** - Satan appeared and spoke to Teresita on four separate occasions, each time trying to persuade the seer to leave Carmel. She refused. The first occurred on July 31, 1948 when she was startled by three loud knocks on her cell door, then a foul odor, then a harsh voice which frightened her. When the seer showed her rosary to him, he departed leaving a soot-covered hoof print on the floor. On two occasions, Satan appeared with fire around his head and around his body. Again, she resisted him. Once Satan awoke the seer from her sleep by violently rocking her bed. One final encounter occurred on August 22, 1948 when the seer awoke and felt unseen hands trying to strip her of her clothing. She struggled, broke free and fled to the stairway leading to the cell of the prioress. The prioress heard the commotion and came and helped free the seer.

(2) **Angels** - On September 16th the seer saw Our Lady arrive accompanied by little angels. The angels disappeared one by one. At other times, angels are reported to have visited Teresita in her cell.

(3) **Saints** - St. Therese of Lisieux, also called 'Little Flower', accompanied

Our Blessed Mother during some of the apparitions. (Recall St. Therese's words: *"From the Heavens I will let fall a Shower of Roses."*)

St. Cecilia - It is reported Teresita had visions of St. Cecilia and other saints and angels as well as visions of the Sacred Heart.

XII Prayers Taught to the Seer(s) - Not Reported

XIII Special Devotion Given to the Seer(s)

(1) Although no new devotion as such is reported, Our Lady requested the seer to *"propagate the devotion to My Immaculate Heart."* (November 12, 1948)

(2) On September 21st Our Lady requested that She be honored on Saturdays, especially in specified devotions: **1)** Our Lady of Mount Carmel **2)** Our Lady of Snow **3)** Our Lady of the Holy Rosary **4)** Our Lady of Perpetual Help **5)** Immaculate Heart of Mary **6)** Our Lady of the Abandonment and Refuge of Sinners **7)** Our Lady of Lourdes **8)** Our Lady of Peace and Good Voyage **9)** Our Lady of Good Counsel **10)** Holy Name of Mary **11)** Our Lady of Loreto **12)** Our Lady of Remedy **13)** The Seven Dolors

XIV Requests Made by Our Lady

(1) **Wash feet of Prioress** - Our Lady requested the seer to wash the feet of the prioress and to kiss her feet, and to drink some of the water (August 18, 1948). This was done, and later revealed by Our Lady to have been a lesson and test for humility and obedience.

(2) **Kiss the earth and return to the vine** - On September 12, 1948 Our Lady requested the seer to kiss the earth and return to this place (the vine) for fifteen consecutive days. This was also done and Our Lady appeared to the seer each of the fifteen days.

(3) **Blessing** - On September 14th Our Lady requested the place of the apparitions be blessed in the presence of the community. This was likewise accomplished.

(4) **Request for Statue/Image** - Our Lady requested Her Image be struck and placed at the site of the apparition and that it become a shrine for prayer. The statue was enshrined (September 15th and 16th).

(5) **Mass on 12th of the month** - On September 26th Our Lady asked that a Mass be held on the 12th of each month.

(6) **Consecration to the Immaculate Heart** - On September 25th Our Lady said: *"I wish you all to consecrate yourselves to Me on October 7th and be My slaves."* Again on September 26th She reminded the community to consecrate themselves to Her.

XV Specific Bible References - Not Reported

XVI Secrets Given to the Seer(s)

Our Lady gave the seer several secrets: one for herself, one for the prioress, one for the community, and one for China.

XVII Miracles Promised by Our Lady - NR

XVIII Miracles Performed

(1) **Shower of Petals** - The first shower of rose petals occurred on August 20, 1948 which phenomenon was to be repeated many times and witnessed by many clergy, religious and others, in addition to the seer. Images of Jesus, Mary, Holy Family, and other religious scenes were imaged on these rose petals. The images remained on the petals and the people gathered and saved these petals.
(2) **Communion from the Angel** - Teresita was ill and unable to attend Mass. The angel brought her Communion.
(3) **Whole roses manifested** - Several witnesses were present when whole roses manifested out of thin air inside the seer's home.

XIX Miracles Promised not yet Performed - NR

XX Signs Promised

When Our Lady requested the seer to wash and kiss the feet of the prioress, Our Lady gave the prioress a locution that she, the prioress, would be given a sign. This sign was given; for when the prioress next saw Teresita's face, there was a circle of blood around the seer's eyes. This was the promised sign.

XXI Signs Given

(1) When Our Lady requested the seer to wash and kiss the feet of the prioress, Our Lady also gave the prioress a locution that she, the prioress, would be given a sign; this was given for when the prioress next saw Teresita's face, there was a circle of blood around the seer's eyes. This was the promised sign.
(2) The 'showers' of rose petals impressed with holy images of Our Lord, Our Lady, the Holy Family and others, surely were signs of the presence of Our Lady. These "showers" were witnessed by many who collected and saved the petals.

(3) The appearance of the blue bird at the apparition site (the vine) before and during the apparitions.
(4) Reports of a spinning sun, of a strange light on top of the vine, of plants in the garden turning to face the apparition site, of the strong fragrance of roses.
(5) Entire roses materializing out of thin air before witnesses.
(6) The Statue of the Mediatrix of All Grace was the center of attraction during one period, when the following was reported by witnesses:
    A - The statue moved inside its glass case.
    B - The eyes of the statue raised and were gazing into the distance.
    C - The rosary on the statue moved as if the statue was praying the rosary.
    D - Little children saw the dress of Our Lady move, they touched Her dress and Her feet which were soft, and when they kissed Her feet the toes wiggled.
(7) When the nuns at Carmel burned the petals and other material as ordered, a blue flame arose four feet above the pyre and lingered until all was consumed.
(8) In 1990 a silhouette of what appeared to be a woman in prayer appeared in a luminous white outline on one of the leaves of a tall coconut tree. This phenomenon occurred for ninety consecutive evenings.
(9) On one occasion the seer received the Sacred Host on her tongue from an angel.

XXII Predictions/Promises

Mother Cecilia received messages from Our Lady predicting the date the seer, Teresita would lose her eyesight, as well as the date she would regain her sight. All occurred as predicted.

XXIII Prophecies/Warnings of Chastisement

At Her final apparition of November 12, 1948 Our Lady said: *"There would be persecutions, unrest and bloodshed in your country. The enemy of the Church will try to destroy the faith which Jesus had established and died for. The Church will suffer much."* It seems some of these things have already come to pass.

XXIV Method of Appearance

(1) During the August apparitions of Our Lady, it is reported that Teresita saw her cell engulfed in light, then she saw Our Lady.
(2) On September 16, 1948 Our Lady descended in company of little angels who then vanished one by one.

XXV Method of Departure

Usually Our Lady announced blessings on all those present and took Her leave by simply disappearing.

XXVI Confrontation w/Civil Authorities

(1) It is reported that many people distrusted the "showers" of rose petals and accused the nuns of somehow orchestrating these showers.
(2) Very negative media articles together with people who dealt in sham "Rose Petals" helped turn public opinion against these apparitions. This, together with the Church's negative report, submerged these apparitions for some forty years. The efforts of television investigative reporter, June Keithley, helped bring some of the true, overlooked or suppressed facts to the attention of the people and the Church. As a consequence the Church has now set up a new committee to investigate these apparitions.

XXVII Confrontation w/Church Authorities

(1) Monsignor Alfredo Verzosa, Bishop of Lipa, was suspicious of the events of Lipa and was determined to close Lipa Carmel and keep the crowds away. On November 19, 1948 he hurried to Lipa Carmel, intent on closing the convent. When he opened the door and entered a shower of rose petals fell on him. He picked up one petal and looked to see from where it came, then he fell to his knees, speechless. He told the nuns he lifted all prohibition against the crowds coming to Carmel and told them they could display the statue as before.

He now believed and would publish an official account of the apparitions with his Imprimatur on December 8, 1948. However, about a year after the first "shower" of petals, Lipa Carmel was to suffer much at the hands of Church authorities.
(2) On January 2, 1950 Bishop Verzosa was relieved as bishop of Lipa.
(3) An Apostolic Administrator took over the powers of the diocese.
(4) Bishop Obviar, a strong supporter of these apparitions, was also relieved of his duties.
(5) Mother Cecilia was transferred out of Carmel.
(6) Teresita herself was forced to leave Lipa Carmel.
(7) A commission was set up by Bishop Verzosa's successor, Msgr. Santos. The commission reportedly intimidated the seer and offered her a false document to sign. They never interviewed Bishop Verzosa or Bishop Obviar. The negative decision was signed by six bishops—several of whom stated on their deathbed that they were forced to sign the verdict

under threat of excommunication from the Papal Administrator.
(8) The Church's decision required all petals and documents to be burned and the statue to be destroyed. The available petals were burned along with the diaries of Teresita and Mother Cecilia; however, the statue was saved.

The convent was ordered sealed from outside contact, no novice applicants, no employees and no services were permitted to enter the convent. One of the nuns was permitted to go outside daily and beg for money and food to sustain the community.
(9) Some forty years later on January 24, 1991 rose petals were reported to have fallen again at Lipa Carmel. After some in-depth investigation and after statements from witnesses of these events were publicized and brought to the attention of Church authorities, another and new commission has been established. This is not yet the end of Lipa Carmel.

XXVIII Request Chapel/Shrine Built

(1) Our Lady requested the statue be formed and placed at the site of the apparitions. This has been done.
(2) It is further reported that a church known as the Chapel of Our Lady Mediatrix of All Grace has been built and totally financed by public donations.

XXIX Free Will/Choice

On September 21, 1948 Our Lady said in part: *". . . To My daughter who does not believe, I do not oblige you to believe. It is enough that you do not believe. But do not block nor debase My sacred place nor despise My words. I do not oblige you to listen nor to obey them if you do not wish to, for you have free will. Neither should you honor Me on Saturdays if you are not inclined to . . . "*

XXX Seer(s)' Suffering/Sacrifice

(1) Certainly the initial contest with the seer's own family when she first entered Carmel on her 21st birthday, caused her much fear, anguish, and suffering.
(2) Her several encounters with Satan caused her terror, fear and suffering.
(3) Her bouts with blindness also caused her to suffer.
(4) The intimidation during the course of the investigation caused more fright and suffering to the seer.
(5) The forced departure from Lipa Carmel was devastating to the seer. Teresita said that she cried and cried for two years.
(6) The entire handling of the investigation, the transfer of Bishop Obviar

and the separation and transfer of Mother Cecilia were perplexing and painful to the seer.
(7) It is reported that to this very day, Teresita has had to contend with accusations of insanity and fraud.
(8) On November 5, 1948 Sr. Teresita suffered the passion of Jesus. This began at exactly 12 noon.

XXXI Healings Reported

(1) Teresita's blindness was healed on September 7, 1948 as Our Lady pre-told the prioress. When the prioress made the sign of the cross on both of the seer's eyes, suddenly Teresita could see again.
(2) The rose petals were the trigger for physical healings as well as conversions. A report of November 1948 states that a rose petal fell in front of a man in the crowd. He picked it up and an instant conversion occurred. He had been a member of the Masonic Lodge.
(3) Amazing physical healings occurred when rose petals were applied to ailing victims. In some instances water which had the rose petals dipped into it was the catalyst for cure.

XXXII Action Taken by the Church

(1) Bishop Obviar was closely involved and believed in the apparitions. He allowed the nuns to commission a statue, he approved release of the messages to the public, and blessed the ground-breaking for the new chapel.
(2) The first investigation ended with a negative verdict. Since that time, however, the bishop has permitted the statue to again be displayed in Lipa Carmel.
(3) In 1993 a new commission was established to investigate the Lipa occurrences. This was after reports that the "showers" of rose petals had resumed and that more miraculous cures were reported. This was also after reports of interviews with original witnesses were publicized and brought to the Church's attention. Only time will tell the outcome. These apparitions have not been given Church approval as of now.

XXXIII Bibliography

Lipa 1992
By: June Keithley
Published by: Cacho Publishing House, Inc.

Chapter 17

CONSENGA, ITALY
(1950-1961)

I Place - Consenga, Italy

II Dates of First and Last Apparition

First: April 7, 1950 (Good Friday)
Last: 1961 (Good Friday)

III Seer(s)

Name: Sister Elena Aiello
Birth: Unknown
Age at first apparition: Unknown
Status: Deceased: 1961

IV Total Number of Apparitions - 11 Reported

V Dates and Locality of Each Apparition

All apparitions occurred in Consenga, Italy unless otherwise noted.

1950: April 7, Good Friday.
1951: March 23, Good Friday.
1954: April 16, Good Friday.
1955: April 8, Good Friday.
1956: December 8, Immaculate Conception.

1958: July 2, Feast of the Immaculate Heart of Mary.
1959: Feast of the Immaculate Heart.
1960: Good Friday.
1960: Feast of the Immaculate Heart, and August 22.
1961: Good Friday.

VI Description of Our Lady

On Good Friday April 16, 1954 Our Blessed Lady appeared dressed in black, with seven swords piercing Her Immaculate Heart, with an expression of profound sorrow, and with tears on Her cheeks. Yet, the seer reported that Our Blessed Mother appeared majestic even with tears on Her cheeks.

VII Title(s) of Our Lady - 1

Our Lady appeared as 'Our Lady of Sorrows'.

VIII Brief Factual Review

Sister Elena Aiello was well known in Italy and in much of Europe. She had many visitors come to her, similar to the crowds that visited Padre Pio or Theresa Neumann. High Church officials as well as government officials came to see the 'miracle of the bleeding panel'. It is reported Sister Aiello founded homes for orphaned children in Italy. For many years her messages were not distributed because people, and editors, thought the warnings contained in the messages were too frightening, too disturbing and too 'doomsday' sounding. In 1964 an English edition of the book 'The Incredible Life Story of Sister Elena Aiello' by Msgr. Francesco Spadafora, was published (unfortunately a copy was not available to use or report from for this work).

In 1940 Jesus directed Sister Elena to deliver a message to Premier Benito Mussolini telling him not to join with Hitler in World War II, otherwise Italy would suffer a terrible defeat and Mussolini would be punished by Divine Justice and have a speedy downfall. She sent the message but he ignored the warning. All that was foretold did come to pass. Sister Elena had the Stigmata and suffered the passion of Christ much as Padre Pio and Theresa Neumann before her. She bore the Wounds of Christ on her hands, feet and side. Her suffering and bleeding were most severe during passion week and especially on Good Friday.

On September 29, 1955 Feast of St. Michael the Archangel, an image of Jesus miraculously appeared on a masonite panel near the seer's bedside; the image was of the face of Jesus and was formed by human blood. Over the years the blood (tested as human blood) would form various images on this panel.

Our Blessed Lady of Sorrows first appeared to Elena on Good Friday, 1950 and the last reported apparition and message from Our Lady was on Good Friday 1961.

Our Lord also appeared to Sister Elena and gave her messages (April 16, 1954 and in 1959).

Our Lady told Elena to spread the messages that she received from both Jesus and Mary: *"Let this warning be known to all, because it will help save many souls and prevent much destruction in the Church and in the world."* Sister Elena died in 1961.

IX The Primary Messages - 5

(1) Prayer - On April 16, 1954 Our Lady said: *"Prayers and penances are necessary because men must return to God and to My Immaculate Heart. Cry out these things to all, like the very echo of My voice! Let this be known to all, because it will help save many souls, and prevent much destruction in the Church and in the world."*

On Good Friday 1960 Our Lady said: *"Pray and lose no time, lest it be too late since dense darkness surrounds the earth and the enemy is at the doors!"*

(2) Penance and Sacrifice - In 1959 Our Lady said: *"The only valid means for placating Divine Justice is to pray and do penance, return to God with sincere sorrow for the faults committed."*

Again on Good Friday 1960: *"In these tragic hours, the world needs prayers and penance, because the Pope, the priests and the Church are in danger."*

(3) Rosary - On Good Friday March 23, 1951 Our Lady said: *"The only salvation is a complete repentance and return to God; particularly in the daily recitation of the rosary."*

Then on August 22, 1960 Our Lady said: *"Do not fear, for I will accompany with maternal protection My faithful ones, and all those who accept My urgent warnings, and they, especially by the recitations of My rosary, will be saved."*

(4) Reparation - Repeatedly during these messages Jesus and Mary implored us to make reparation for the sins of the world in order to avoid or lessen the chastisements which God is ready to send on all humanity. These messages are repeated and are very strong and urgent.

(5) Evil in the World Today and Warnings of Punishments - In the messages given to Elena, both Jesus and Mary repeat over and over the following information and requests:

(a) Mankind has become mired in sin; is turning away from God; and refuses to heed the many warnings of Our Lady, such as those given at Fatima. Men must amend their lives and turn back to God and to a Christian way of living.

(b) Youth is being corrupted everywhere. Many homes are no longer havens of love and prayer; and many parents are leading their own children along the paths of moral destruction.

(c) The leaders of major governments speak much about peace, but prepare for war with terrible weapons that can and will destroy peoples and nations.

(d) Just punishments are to come upon the world in three ways:

First - From the hand of God through major disturbances of nature, as a warning for men to repent, or even worse disasters will befall the earth. Specifically mentioned several times are; major earthquakes, frightening hurricanes, vast floods and overflowing of the streams and the seas, droughts, famines, epidemics and plagues.

Second - Because most people will not repent, there will follow bloody revolutions throughout the world. Russia will launch World War III in Europe, unleashing frightful destruction, particularly in Italy. The Holy Father and the Church will suffer much.

Third - When all seems lost, heaven will intervene in the affairs of men with a purifying deluge of fire, in which the ungodly will be destroyed. This will be the promised triumph of the Immaculate Heart of Mary, with its victory of the forces of good over the forces of evil.

(e) If souls will consecrate themselves to the Immaculate Heart of Mary, Queen of the Universe, Mother of Mercy, and Mediatrix of men to God, through prayers and penance, particularly the praying of the daily rosary, then Our Lady will be able to draw down God's Mercy; the power of Satan will be lessened, and the predicted punishments will be mitigated and shortened.

X Signs Preceding the Apparitions - Not Reported

XI Other Visions During Apparitions

(1) On April 7, 1950 Our Lady showed Elena souls falling into hell while giving this message: *"Satan reigns and triumphs on earth! See how the souls are falling into hell. See how high the flames are, and the souls who fall into them like flakes of snow look like transparent embers! How many sparks! How·many cries of hate and of despair! How much pain! See how many priestly souls! Look at the sign of consecration in their transparent hands."* (In the palms of their hands the sign of the cross, in more vivid fire, could clearly be seen!) *"What torture My daughter, in My maternal heart! Great is My sorrow to see that men do not change! The Justice of the Father requires reparation; otherwise many will be lost!'*

(2) Also on Good Friday April 7, 1950 Our Lady showed Elena another vision and gave her a message: *"See how Russia will burn!"* (Elena saw an immense field covered with flames and smoke, in which souls were submerged as in a sea of fire!) *"And all this fire is not that which will fall from the hands of men, but will be hurled directly from the angels!"*, thus concluded Our Lady.

(3) Then on Good Friday 1961 Our Lady showed Elena yet another vision, with a message: *"Russia, spurred on by Satan, will seek to dominate the whole world, and by bloody revolutions, will propagate her false teachings throughout all the nations, especially in Italy. The Church will be persecuted, the Pope and the priests shall suffer much."* (Then Sr. Aiello saw a "Horrible Vision"). A great revolution was going on in Rome! The revolutionaries were entering the Vatican, and the Pope was alone, praying. They took the Pope by force and held him, then they knocked him down to the floor. They tied him and then she saw them kicking the Pope. Just then Our Blessed Mother drew near, and the evil men fell to the floor like corpses. Our Lady helped the Pope up on his feet and taking him by the arm, She covered him with Her mantle saying: *"Fear not."* Then the flags flying the red flag over St. Peter's dome and elsewhere collapsed and their power was gone. Yet these atheists were heard to shout: *"We don't want God to rule over us, we want Satan to be our master!"*

XII Prayers Taught to the Seer(s)

On Good Friday April 8, 1955 Our Lady said: *". . . I ask that the prayer of Maternal Refuge be spread as a most useful means to obtain graces and salvation for poor sinners. Say often with your arms crossed:"*

Prayer: Queen of the Universe, Mediatrix of Men to God, Refuge of all our hopes, Have mercy on us!

XIII Special Devotion Given to the Seer(s)

Although no new devotion is reported, Our Lady repeatedly implored us to renew with fervor the devotion to the Immaculate Heart of Mary.

On March 23, 1951 Our Lady said: *"How can the world be saved from the disaster that is about to crash down upon the misleading nations, if man does not repent of his errors and failings? The only salvation is a complete repentance and return to God, and a true devotion to My Immaculate Heart, particularly in the daily recitation of the rosary."*

Again on April 8, 1955 *"Priests must unite by prayers and penance. They must hasten to spread the devotion to the Two Hearts. The hour of triumph is close at hand. The victory will be accomplished through the love and mercy of the Heart of My Son, and of My Immaculate Heart; the Mediatrix between men and God. By accepting this invitation and by* uniting their tears to those of My Sorrowful Heart, priests and religious will obtain great graces for the salvation of poor sinners."

In 1959 after Jesus first appeared to Elena all dripping with blood, Our Sorrowful Mother then said: *"In order to save souls, I wish that there be propagated in the world the consecration to the Immaculate Heart of Mary, Mediatrix of men, devoted to the Mercy of God, and to the Queen of the Universe."*

On the Feast of the Immaculate Heart of Mary, August 22, 1960 Our Lady again said: *"Spread the devotion to My Immaculate Heart, in order that many souls may be conquered by My Love, and that many sinners may return to My Maternal Heart."* Earlier in 1959 Our Sorrowful Mother said *"Humanity will never find peace if it does not return to My Immaculate Heart as Mother of Mercy and Mediatrix of men, and to the Heart of My Son Jesus".*

XIV Requests Made by Our Lady

(1) Spread the Devotion to the Immaculate Heart of Mary and the Sacred Heart of Jesus.
(2) Say often the Maternal Refuge prayer.
(3) Spread the messages and cry out these things to all!

XV Specific Bible References - Not Reported
XVI Secrets Given to the Seer(s) - Not Reported
XVII Miracles Promised by Our Lady - NR

XVIII Miracles Performed

The remarkable events reported were not attributed to the intervention of Our Blessed Virgin Mary, but rather due to, and concerning, Sister Elena's devotion to the Holy Face of Jesus.

It is reported that on September 29, 1955 the Feast of St. Michael the Archangel, Sister Elena was in her bed. Near her bed was a section of masonite paneling placed there to protect her from cold air drafts. Suddenly one of the sisters who attended Sister Elena was startled by a flash of light on the lower corner of the panel. Greatly surprised, both Sister Elena and the other sister looked closely at the panel and saw blood dripping down the panel. Later as cotton tufts and linen clothes were applied to wipe away the blood, several forms or designs showed through, such as a cross, a crown, a heart and the face of Jesus. Photographs of these were taken and sent to the Vatican.

It is reported that this phenomenon of dripping blood took place many times during the next years, and especially on the Feast Days of Our Lord, such as on the Feast Days of the Holy Cross, the Sacred Heart and the Most Precious Blood of Jesus.

Consenga, Italy

On July 8, 1956 Sister Elena washed the panel with a caustic soda, trying to wipe the blood away, but in vain. The image remained unmistakable. Many tests were made by physicians, chemists and others. They all agreed it was human blood that formed the image, and there was no explanation for what was taking place.

Sister Elena confided that she felt the blood indicated the need for more reparation for the crimes of our day, and further that this sign tied in with the grave messages she was receiving.

XIX Miracles Promised not yet Performed - NR
XX Signs Promised - Not Reported

XXI Signs Given

(1) The visions Sister Elena received
(2) The message Sister Elena gave to Mussolini
(3) The bleeding panel
(4) Elena received the Stigmata

XXII Predictions/Promises

(1) In 1940 Our Lord gave Sister Elena a message for Benito Mussolini; not to join Hitler or Italy would suffer a terrible defeat and Mussolini would have a speedy downfall. He ignored the warning and Italy did suffer a terrible war and defeat. Mussolini was publicly and swiftly cut down.
(2) Several times Our Lady warned that Russia would march on Europe and take over Rome unless mitigated by prayers and reparations.

XXIII Prophecies/Warnings of Chastisement

These messages are alive and explode with repeated warnings of the chastisement to come to mankind; unless people return to God:

(1) Here is Our Lady's Message of Good Friday March 23, 1951: *"My daughter, the scourge is near. Much is spoken of peace, but all the world will soon be at war, and the streets will be stained with blood! No gleam of light is seen in the world, because men live in the darkness of horror, and the enormous weight of sin angers the justice of God.*

"All nations will be punished, because sin has spread all over the world! Tremendous will be the punishments, because man has arrived at an insupportable contest with his God and Father, and has exasperated His Infinite Goodness!

"My heart bleeds for Italy also, which will be safe only in part for the Pope! Oh! What grief to see the representative of Christ on earth hated,

persecuted, outraged!

"He, who is the Spiritual Father of the people, the defender of the Faith and of truth, whose face, radiant with light, shines upon the world, is greatly hated.

"He, who personifies Christ on earth, doing good for all, becomes thus outraged with impunity!

"Many iniquitous and wicked leaders of the people, who live and drag along with them their people outside the Laws of God, showing themselves in sheeps' clothing, while being rapacious wolves, have ruined society, stirring it up against God and His Church.

"How can the world be saved, from the disaster that is about to crash down upon the misleading nations, if man does not repent of his errors and failings? The only salvation is a complete repentance and return to God, and a true devotion to My Immaculate Heart, particularly in the daily recitation of My rosary.

"Once there was the chastisement by water, but if there is not a returning to God, there will come the chastisement by fire, which will cover the streets of the world with blood.

"My daughter, cry out loudly, and let it be known to all, that, if they do not return to God, Italy too, will only in part be safe for the Pope.

"My Heart of Mother, and Mediatrix of men, close to the mercy of God, invites, with many manifestations and many signs, the people to penance and to pardon. But they respond with a storm of hate, blasphemies and sacrilegious profanities, as if blinded by an infernal rage. I wish prayers and penance, in order that I may again obtain mercy and salvation for many souls - otherwise they will be lost."

(2) On April 16, 1954, Our Lady appeared to Elena and said: "My Heart is sad for so many suffering in an impending world in ruin. The justice of Our Father is most offended. Men live in their obstinacy of sin. The wrath of God is near. Soon the world will be afflicted with great calamities, bloody revolutions, frightful hurricanes, and the overflowing of streams and the seas.

"Cry out until the priests of God lend their ears to My voice, to advise men that the time is near at hand, and if men do not return to God with prayers and penances, the world will be overturned in a new and more terrible war. Arms most deadly will destroy peoples and nations! The dictators of the earth, specimens infernal, will demolish the churches and desecrate the Holy Eucharist, and will destroy things most dear. In this impious war, much will be destroyed of that which has been built by the hands of man.

"Clouds with lightning flashes of fire in the sky and a tempest of fire shall fall upon the world. This terrible scourge, never before seen in the history of humanity, will last seventy hours, godless persons will be crushed and wiped out. Many will be lost because they remain in their obstinacy of sin. Then shall be seen the power of light over the power of darkness.

"Be not silent, My daughter, because the hours of darkness, of abandonment, are near.

"I am bending over the world, holding in suspension the justice of God. Otherwise these things would already have now come to pass. Prayers and penances are necessary because men must return to God and to My Immaculate Heart; the Mediatrix of men to God, and thus the world will be at least in part saved.

"Cry out these things to all, like the very echo of My voice. Let this be known to all, because it will help save many souls, and prevent much destruction in the Church and in the world."

(3) On Good Friday April 8, 1955 Our Lady spoke: "My daughter, it is thy Mother speaking to thee. Listen attentively and make known all that I tell thee, because men, in spite of repeated warnings, are not returning to God. They refuse grace, and are not listening to My voice. You must have no doubt about what I am making known to you, because My words are very clear, and you must transmit them to all.

"Dark and frightful days are approaching! Mankind is obscured by a thick fog, as a result of the many grievous sins, which are well nigh covering the whole earth. Today, more than ever, men are resisting the calls from heaven, and are blaspheming God, while wallowing in the mire of sin.

"My daughter, look upon My heart, pierced by the thorns of so many sins; My face, disfigured by sorrow; My eyes, filled with tears. The cause of such great sadness is the sight of so many souls going to hell, and because the Church is wounded - inwardly and outwardly.

"The rulers of nations make so much ado and speak of peace. But instead, the whole world will soon be at war, and all mankind will be plunged into sorrow, because the justice of God will not be delayed in fulfilling its course, and these events are near. Tremendous will be the upheaval of the whole world, because men as at the time of the Deluge have lost God's way and are ruled by the spirit of Satan.

"Priests must unite by prayers and penance. They must hasten to spread the devotion to the Two Hearts. The hour of My triumph is close at hand. The victory will be accomplished through the love and mercy of the Heart of My Son, and of My Immaculate Heart; the Mediatrix between men and God. By accepting this invitation, and by uniting their tears to those of My Sorrowful Heart, priests and religious will obtain great graces for the salvation of poor sinners.

"Launch forth into the world a message to make known to all that the scourge is near at hand. The justice of God is weighing upon the world. Mankind, defiled in the mire, soon will be washed in its own blood, by disease; by famine; by earthquakes; by cloudbursts, tornadoes, floods, and terrible storms; and by war. But men ignore all these warnings, and are unwilling to be convinced that My tears are plain signs to serve notice that tragic events are hanging all over the world, and that the hours of great trials are at hand.

"If men do not amend their ways, a terrifying scourge of fire will come down from heaven upon all the nations of the world, and men will be punished according to the debts contracted with Divine Justice. There will be frightful moments for all, because heaven will be joined with the earth, and all the ungodly people will be destroyed. Some nations will be purified, while other nations will disappear entirely.

"You are to transmit these warnings to all, in order that the new generation will know that men had been warned in time to turn to God by doing penance, and thus could have avoided these punishments."

Sr. Elena asked Our Lady: "But when will this all come about?"

"My daughter," answered the Blessed Mother, "the time is not far off. When men least expect it, the course of Divine Justice will be accomplished.

"My Heart is so big for poor sinners and I make use of every possible means that they may be saved. Look at this mantle, how big it is. If I were not bent over the earth to cover it with all My maternal love, the tempest of fire would already have broken upon the nations of the world!"

Then the seer exclaimed, "My lovely Mother, never before have I seen Thee with such a large mantle." And the Blessed Virgin, holding Her arms wide, answered: "This is the mantle of mercy for all those who, having repented, come back to My Immaculate Heart. See? The right hand holds the mantle to cover and to save poor sinners, while with the left hand I hold back the Divine Justice, so that the time of Mercy may still be prolonged. To help Me in this, I ask that the prayer, maternal refuge, be spread as a most useful means to obtain graces and salvation for poor sinners. Say often with your arms crossed: 'Queen of the universe, Mediatrix of men to God, refuge of all our hopes, have mercy on us.'"

(4) July 2, 1958 Our Lady warned that God has no choice but to send the punishment because there is more sin now (in proportion) then at the time of the deluge and evil surpasses the good; Italy will be washed in her own blood, France will be covered with rubble and much of the United States will be in the hands of communists, except an area which has turned to the rosary.

(5) In 1959 Our Lady said: *"The world will be once more afflicted with great calamity, with bloody revolutions, with great earthquakes, with famines, with epidemics, with fearful hurricanes, with floods from rivers and seas. But if men do not return to God, purifying fire will fall from the Heavens, like snowstorms, on all peoples, and a great part of humanity will be destroyed."*

(6) Again on Good Friday 1960 Our Lady warned: *"Great calamities will come upon the world, which will bring confusion, fears, struggles and pain. Great earthquakes will swallow up entire cities and countries, and will bring epidemics, famine and terrible destruction; especially where the sons of darkness are."*

(7) August 22, 1960 Our Lady spoke: *"If people do not recognize in the scourge* (of nature) *the warnings of Divine Mercy, and do not return to God with truly Christian living, another terrible war will come from the East to the West. Russia with her secret armies will battle America and will overrun Europe. The river Rhine will be overflowing with corpses and blood. Italy also will be harassed by a great revolution and the Pope will suffer terribly."*

XXIV Method of Appearance

Our Lady is reported looking sad during most appearances. Once She was dressed in black.

XXV Method of Departure - Not Reported
XXVI Confrontation with Civil Authorities - NR
XXVII Confrontation w/Church Authorities - NR
XXVIII Request Chapel/Shrine Built - NR

XXIX Free Will/Choice

The messages state that the great punishment would come unless mankind turned back to God; thus implying our free will to choose.

XXX Seer(s)' Suffering/Sacrifice

Sister Elena must have suffered very much since she had the wounds of Christ; the Stigmata.

XXXI Healings Reported - Not Reported
XXXII Action Taken by the Church - Not Reported

XXXIII Bibliography

Divine Love (magazine #86) 1981
By: Divine Love Apostalate
Published by: Divine Love Apostalate

Urgent Warning From Heaven (pamphlet)
By: Two Hearts Books and Publishers
Published by: Two Hearts Books and Publishers

Chapter 18

ROME, ITALY
(1953 - 1983)

I Place - Rome, Italy

II Dates of First and Last Apparition

First: March 21, 1953
Last: October 9, 1983

III Seer(s) - 1

Name: Elena Patriarca Leonardi (Sister Elena della Croce)
(Maid of Jesus in the Most Holy Sacrament of the Altar)
Birth: November 4, 1910
Age at first apparition: 42
Status: Deceased

IV Total Number of Apparitions - 49

V Dates and Locality of Each Apparition

All apparitions occurred at the seer's home unless otherwise noted.

1953: March 21.
1955: February 1, April 21, December 31.
1957: January, 1, May 21, May 27.
1958: April 6.
1960: July 11.

1961: July 18.
1962: July 24.
1963: September 4.
1964: August 15.
1965: July 13, (inside church); September 20, (vision, church of St. Mary of Grace); 1st Thursday in October (vision); 1st Friday in October; 8 days later (vision).
1968: April 22.
1969: April 15.
1970: January 31.
1971: January 22 (vision, St. Mary of Grace Church); April 17.
1973: May 9, July 18.
1974: July 20, August 15.
1975: January 20, March 2, July 22, December 28.
1976: April 2, July 28, September 30, November 4.
1977: February 13, March 6, April 10, May 28, July 6, August 18, October 14, December 12.
1978: March 26, July 22, September 25, December 29 (vision).
1979: January 17, February 12, March 23 and 29, April 5 and April 8(vision, inside Church of Divine Love); April 10 and 14.
1980: March 13.
1983: June 21, October 9.

VI Description of Our Lady

(1) Our Lady appeared dressed in white with a long, light-ivory veil over Her head. She was wearing a scarf-like sash as blue as the sky. (September 25, 1978)
(2) Sometimes She held the Child Jesus in Her arms.
(3) On May 28, 1977 Our Lady appeared all dressed in black.

VII Title(s) of Our Lady - 2

(1) On July 22, 1978 Our Lady said: *"I am the Mother Of God and of Justice."*
(2) On April 14, 1979 Our Lady said: *"I am the Mother of All Peoples."* She repeated this on March 13, 1980.

VIII Brief Factual Review

Elena Patriarca Leonardi was born on November 4, 1910 in Avezzano, Italy. In 1915 a great earthquake upset Avezzano. Elena's family home collapsed and little Elena was trapped in the rubble for 8½ hours.

When Elana was 6½ her mother died. Little Elena never did see the coffin, so she set out searching for her mother. Guided by her guardian angel she found herself inside the (locked) church near her own home. There she addressed a statue of the Virgin of Carmel: "Will you be my mommy?" Elena received an affirmative response and Elena's life unfolded to evidence this response.

Her family consisted of herself and five little brothers, an aunt, and later also a stepmother. Her early years were full of sacrifice and difficulty. Her schooling consisted of primary school only. When she was only 15 she set up her own tailor shop and worked hard at it.

At the age of 20 she married. She has a son, and now a grandson. Her husband died. Thereafter she was consecrated by Padre Pio as Sister Elena della Croce, Maid of Jesus in the Most Holy Sacrament of the Altar.

Elena had a special relationship with Padre Pio, beginning on November 12, 1919 when Elena was only nine and continuing until Padre Pio's death on September 23, 1968. And continuing thereafter as Padre Pio appeared to the seer many times after his own death, sometimes alone and sometimes with Jesus and/or Mary.

On April 22, 1968 Elena was involved in a serious accident when she was struck by an automobile while she was a pedestrian. After the accident Elena devoted her full time towards the realization of a work, pre-announced to her by Padre Pio on February 4, 1947 and afterwards confirmed to her by Our Lady. This mission was also later confirmed by Our Lord on January 20, 1975 as set forth in the messages. The mission entrusted to the seer by Our Lady and Our Lord was the foundation of the 'House of the Kingdom of God and Reconciliation of Souls.' This is a refuge and place of prayer where people from all over the world could come to pray. On February 13, 1977 Our Lady named this House during one of the apparitions. The essential goals of the 'House' are:

1) Prayer, the practice of prayer and diffusion of prayer.
2) Evangelization.
3) Reconciliation of all mankind with God.

These goals are sought through the means of participation at Holy Mass, reception of the Sacraments, recitation of the holy rosary, adoration of the Blessed Sacrament, community prayer and offering of all small daily sacrifices. With the particular help of Our Lady, the House has been purchased and completely renovated. It has two chapels on the ground floor richly adorned with statues, religious objects, and sacred vestments. On the upper floors there are dormitories for the 'servants' destined for prayer.

More recently Sister Elena has been entrusted by Our Lady with another mission, namely; the realization of a 'Casa d'Accoglienza' (House of Reception), a house where the elderly, lonely and ill priests will be received.

Premonitions and other spiritual experiences seemed to begin in 1919,

Rome, Italy

when Elena met Padre Pio and continued thereafter. During the period from March 21, 1953 till the death of Padre Pio she received locutions, visions and messages from Jesus, the Blessed Virgin and Child, Padre Pio, St. Joseph and St. Anthony.

The seer apparently saw Padre Pio dead in his coffin on September 19, 1968 four days prior to his death. Padre Pio died on September 23, 1968.

The locutions, apparitions and messages continued until October 9, 1983 on an irregular basis, although apparitions did occur more frequently through the years, on certain dates.

The messages are replete with warnings of chastisement by fire, and the messages become more graphic and more urgent. Similarly, the messages contain many references to the formation of the House of Prayer. Sister Elena has since died. The Church has not approved these messages.

IX The Primary Messages - 8

(1) **Prayer**
(2) **Rosary**
(3) **Penance**
(4) **Eucharist**
(5) **Mass**
(6) **Sacrifice**
(7) **Warnings of Chastisement**
(8) **Establish House of Prayer**

(1) **Prayer** - Nearly every message during the 10 year period 1973-1983 contains exhortations for prayer, such as: *"Pray for the postponement of the divine punishments and for the conversion of the world."* (July 20, 1974) Again on February 12, 1979: *"I am a mother who is calling on Her children. I do not want you to perish in the eternal fire. With tears in My heart, I am calling everyone to pray and make others pray."*

(2) **Rosary** - In many, if not most, of the messages in the final ten years (1973 - 1983), Our Lady pleads with us that we pray the rosary, and *"to make chains of rosaries."* (April 10, 1977)

(3) **Penance** - Again the messages are filled with urgent requests to do penance. Our Lady says: *"Mankind must do penance, pray, say the holy rosary, receive Holy Communion, attend Holy Masses, go to confession and do penance! My mercy is great if you repent and do penance, but humanity walks at Satan's side."* (July 6, 1977)

(4) **Eucharist** - This is another major and repeated message given to the seer, such as: *"participate in the holy sacrifice of the Mass, together with Holy Communion, atone, do penance, pray the holy rosary."* (March 2, 1975)

(5) **Mass** - Our Lady's urgent appeal to attend Holy Mass is repeated in many of the messages. On December 28, 1975 Our Lady said: *"Say the holy rosary; attend Holy Mass and receive Holy Communion."*

(6) Sacrifice - This is another oft repeated request throughout the messages. On July 22, 1975 Our Lady said: *"Sacrifice and atone, and make others atone. In this way God's anger will be appeased."*

(7) Warnings of Chastisement - The messages contain many grave warnings of chastisements, which will befall mankind, unless mankind converts. Some of the messages give a detailed narrative of the terrible punishment to be visited on mankind, unless we repent and return to God.

On April 2, 1976 Our Lady warns: *"If men do not cease offending My Son, Divine Justice will send to earth, in the not too distant future, its due punishment. It will be the worst punishment ever seen in human history. An unforeseen fire will descend over the whole earth, and a great part of humanity will be destroyed."*

Again on March 13, 1980 Our Lady said: *"Repent! Come back to the sheepfold, to the truth and the light. My children, listen to My call of Love, the call of your Merciful Mother. How can I save you if you do not listen to Me? Flames will fall from heaven, and cause suffering for the godless: cave-ins and earthquakes upon humanity that does not repent; the earth will open under its very feet, and there will be no mercy. The terrible calamity never before seen in man's history, will last for seventy hours..."*

(8) Establish House of Prayer - In several messages in 1975 Our Lady requested the seer to establish a House of Prayer.

In the message of February 17, 1977 Our Lady said: *"Build My house, you must call it House of the Kingdom of God and Reconciliation of Souls."*

Later Our Lady and Our Lord both 'commanded' the seer to establish this House of Prayer.

X Signs Preceding the Apparitions

Usually, but not always, the seer first sees a dazzling light or ball of light before the apparition.

XI Other Visions During Apparitions

There are reported visions of Jesus, Madonna and Child, Padre Pio, St. Joseph, St. Anthony, Archangel Michael and Archangel Gabriel and other angels.

The most frequent appearances are those of Jesus and Padre Pio, each of whom gave messages to the seer during some apparitions.

XII Prayers Taught to the Seer(s)

On July 22, 1978 Our Lady said: *"Say frequently: 'Mother of Divine Mercy and Refuge of Sinners!'"*

XIII Special Devotion Given to the Seer(s)

(1) Although Our Lady exhorted the seer to practice devotion to the Sacred Heart of Jesus and to the Immaculate Heart of Mary, this was not a new devotion.
(2) Likewise Our Lady requested the seer to set up the House of Prayer, which is not a devotion.

XIV Requests Made by Our Lady

(1) Our Lady requested, even commanded, the seer to establish the House of Prayer and even gave the seer, in a message, the name: 'House of the Kingdom of God and Reconciliation of Souls.' Our Lord also made this request.
(2) Our Lady also requested the seer to establish a House of Reception (Casa d'Accoglienza) where elderly, lonely and ill priests will be received.

XV Specific Bible References - Not Reported
XVI Secrets Given to the Seer(s) - Not Reported
XVII Miracles Promised by Our Lady - NR
XVIII Miracles Performed - Not Reported
XIX Miracles Promised not yet Performed - NR

XX Signs Promised

(1) On April 2, 1976 Our Lady said: *"When an extraordinary sign appears in the skies men will know that the world's punishment is near. The lash is near, and the hour of darkness approaches."*
(2) Also during the same apparition: *"Many signs never before seen will occur in the world as a warning to men to tell them that the measure is filled. There will come a fearful moment when My Son will speak with His Judge's voice, and pronouncing the verdict over an anxious and drugged humanity."*

XXI Signs Given

(1) The seer was shown Padre Pio dead in his coffin on September 19, 1968. Padre Pio died on September 23, 1968.
(2) The seer was shown on September 25, 1978 the coffin where Pope Luciani was placed. Pope Luciani was Pope John Paul I who died on Sept. 28, 1978.

XXII Predictions/Promises

Just days before the death of Padre Pio and also days before the death of Pope Luciani (John Paul I) the seer saw them in their coffins even though they were still alive.

XXIII Prophecies/Warnings of Chastisement

The messages are replete with repeated, graphic and very detailed and sobering warnings of chastisements to come to people on earth, unless we convert and turn back to God. Primary emphasis is placed on fire from the heavens, a punishment more severe than mankind has ever seen. The punishment and darkness is to last for 70 hours. *"Five nations will be completely destroyed"* (December 28, 1975).

The good news is that the chastisement can be lessened by prayer and conversion, and by this chastisement the earth will be cleansed. Those who remain will find God's mercy in Our Lady's power and protection and they will be saved.

XXIV Method of Appearance

The messages do not indicate a pattern or regular method of appearance. Instead sometimes a dazzling light proceeds, sometimes a voice, sometimes an angel and fragrance of roses occur at the beginning of the apparition.

XXV Method of Departure

Usually Our Lady departs as She blesses the seer.

XXVI Confrontation w/Civil Authorities

Other than the problems encountered in arranging for the purchase of the building for the House of Prayer (located at #29B Via Gracchi), there are no reported confrontations with civil authorities.

XXVII Confrontation w/Church Authorities - NR

XXVIII Request Chapel/Shrine Built

House of Prayer - Our Lady told the seer to build the House of Prayer, (April 14, 1979). On the night of June 25-26, 1979 during a vision, the seer was led to a location and was shown a house (#29) which she was to acquire. Later the House located at 29B Via Gracchi was purchased and became the permanent location of the House of Prayer.

XXIX Free Will/Choice

Free will is implied in various messages. On December 28, 1975 Our Lady said: *"Nobody goes to hell without his own consent."*

XXX Seer(s)' Suffering/ Sacrifice

(1) The events concerning medical attention, and lack thereof, after the seer's accident certainly caused her great distress.
(2) The severe warnings of chastisement given to the seer by Our Lady undoubtedly caused the seer great stress.

XXXI Healings Reported

Through prayer, many spiritual graces, conversions and surprising cures have been obtained at the House of Prayer.

XXXII Action Taken by the Church

The parish of 'Santa Croce in Gerusalemme' Rome, which is the seer's own parish, lauds the 'prayer group' which regularly meets at the House of Prayer. No decision is made on the authenticity of the apparitions.

XXXIII Bibliography

Mary's Triumph
By: Mother Elena Patriarca Leonardi
(House of the Kingdom of God and Reconciliation of Souls)
Published by: House of the Kingdom of God and
              Reconciliation of Souls

Chapter 19

SABANA GRANDE, PUERTO RICO
(1953)

    I Place - Barrio Rincon, Sabana Grande, Puerto Rico

    II Dates of First and Last Apparition

First: April 23, 1953
Last: May 25, 1953

    III Seer(s) - 3

Name: Juan Angel Collado (male)
Birth: Unknown
Age at first apparition: 8
Status: Living

Name: Ramonita Belen (female)
Birth: Unknown
Age at first apparition: 7
Status: Living

Name: Isidra Belen (female)
Birth: Unknown
Age at first apparition: 9
Status: Living

    IV Total Number of Apparitions - 33

V Dates and Locality of Each Apparition

All apparitions occurred at the well and schoolroom in Sabana Grande, Puerto Rico, unless otherwise noted.

1953: April 23, 24, 25, 26, 27, 28, 29, 30; May 1, 2, 3, 4, 5, 6, 7, 8, 9, 10, 11, 12, 13, 14, 15, 16, 17, 18, 19, 20, 21, 22, 23, 24, 25.

VI Description of Our Lady

April 23, 1953 - A most beautiful Lady about 18-20 years old, was standing on a small cloud. She wore a long white gown and Her head was covered by a long blue mantle. At Her neck She wore a brooch, around Her waist a brown strap like a belt. She held a rosary in Her hands. Seven stars floated about Her head, each more brilliant than the sun. There was one large star above Her forehead and three smaller stars on each side of Her head.

VII Title(s) of Our Lady - 5

(1) On April 25, 1953 and again on April 26, 1953 Our Lady said: *"I am the Virgin of the Rosary"*
(2) *"Mother of the True Way to the Father,"* given in the message disclosed in 1978.
(3) In the 4th message disclosed May 25, 1992 Our Blessed Mother said: *"I am the Major Angel, envoy of these times, the Virgin of Light, the Virgin Mary, the Spouse of God."*

VIII Brief Factual Review

Puerto Rico is located in the West Indies, an island chain consisting of Cuba, Haiti/Dominican Republic, Jamaica and Puerto Rico, southeast from the State of Florida, USA.

Sabana Grande is a small village situated on high hills overlooking fields of sugar cane, coffee and tropical fruit and is located in the southwest corner of Puerto Rico.

In 1953, Ramonita Belen was seven years old and in the first grade. Her sister, Isidra Belen, was nine and in third grade. Juan Angel Collado was eight years old and in the second grade.

Approximately three kilometers from Sabana Grande, on a hill in Barrio Rincon, sits a small school house (first, second, and third grades). The school is named Lola R de Tio. The school teacher in 1953 was Josefa Rios. As was the practice, every day at 11:00 AM some of the children were selected to go to the bottom of the hill to fetch water from the small well 'pocito' which was used by the school children for cooking and drinking.

On April 23, 1953 Juan Angel and a friend were chosen to fetch water. When they got to the well, suddenly the friend yelled for Juan. When Juan turned to his friend he saw his friend's hand frozen in mid air holding a tin cup over the bucket. From the tin cup, into the bucket, poured out the most beautiful rainbow-colored water. Juan's friend became frightened, dropped the bucket and tin cup and ran back to the school. Juan meanwhile felt the entire world had come to a standstill. When Juan turned and looked above the hill from the well he saw a most beautiful Lady. She was standing on a small cloud. She appeared to be 18-20 and was wearing a long white gown, while Her head was covered by a blue veil that nearly touched the cloud on which She stood. Floating a few inches above Her head were seven stars. She looked directly into Juan's eyes and smiled. When he realized his friend was gone, he too ran back to school. He told several friends of the events, who scoffed at him. He did not then tell the teacher.

The next day, April 24, 1953 the two Belen sisters accompanied Juan to the well to fetch water. Our Beautiful Lady appeared again; this time to all three children. Immediately Isidra fell to her knees and began praying. Our Lady did not speak to the children. When they returned to the schoolhouse the girls told the teacher. The teacher did not believe them and told them not to tell anyone about it and to forget it. However, word quickly spread throughout Sabana Grande.

April 25, 1953 was a Saturday and there was no school. The three children, however, had an urge to go to the well at 11:00 AM. When they arrived many local people were already there. Our Lady appeared for the third time. This time Our Lady smiled at the children, stepped down from the cloud and began walking towards them. When the children backed off, Our Lady said: *"Be not afraid, I am the Virgin of the Rosary."* She went back to the cloud and disappeared.

Our Lady appeared again on April 26, 1953. This time Ramonita blurted out: "People want to know who you are and what you want." The beautiful Lady answered: *"I am the Virgin of the Rosary and what I want is for everyone to pray the rosary to obtain peace in the world and for the conversion of sinners."*

On April 27, 1953 Our Lady appeared again and told the children She would be taking over the classroom from that date until Her last appearance May 25, 1953 and that She would teach the children the lessons they needed to learn.

Thereafter every day Our Lady would appear to the three children at the well at 11:00 AM, then lead them to the schoolhouse. Our Lady would then sit in the teacher's chair and ring the little bell to bring them to attention. By this time many people gathered outside the schoolroom. Some witnessed the little bell rising above the desk and ringing. It is reported that the birds eagerly listened to Our Lady teach. The teacher, Josefa Rios, remembers the children would announce Our Lady's presence, at which time she would give up her chair to Our Lady.

It is reported that Our Lady taught the children the importance of the Holy Eucharist and the rosary. She emphasized the value of prayer and sacrifice. She told them about the Sacraments. In order for the children to better understand, Our Lady made the lessons very simple. She used the number seven in teaching them. She always surrounded herself with seven different items, and explained these to the children in this manner:

(1) **The Seven Stars** - Besides representing the seven Sacraments, they also represent the seven virtues which She is asking us to live by: Humility, Generosity, Chastity, Patience, Temperance, Charity and Diligence.

(2) **Her Blue Mantle** - She told the children that She will always protect us with Her blue mantle if we pray daily and listen to Her Son.

(3) **Her White Gown** - A symbol of our own priesthood and purity. She invites us to spend more time for God and with God. We are the new apostles of these latter days.

(4) **The Brooch** - The brooch at Her neck symbolizes Her reign as Queen of all Her new apostles. She will help us to bring many other souls to the service of God.

(5) **The Holy Rosary** - The rosary in Her hands was always there to remind us to pray the rosary with fervor and from the heart on a daily basis for the rest of our lives. She asked that seven rosaries be prayed at the sanctuary of Sabana Grande when anyone visits there. This is to be done for two intentions: for the conversion of sinners and to bring peace to the world.

(6) **Her Strap or Belt** - This symbolizes the true obedience to our Church. We must always remain firm, obedient and strong to the true Church founded by Her Son Jesus Christ. Even if we falter or sin or fail along the way, we must always remain faithful to our Church.

(7) **Her Sandal** - This symbolizes our own pilgrimage and our walk with God. This will always lead us to sanctity. She is inviting us to take that first step towards our own spiritual growth.

Our Lady requested that everyone who came to the well should pray seven rosaries before leaving the area.

It is reported that the Blessed Virgin showed the children heaven and walked them through purgatory, but She declined to show them hell, because: *"You are too small to show you what hell is like."*

A large policeman named Dario Garcia was assigned to protect and help the children through the crowd. Once he fell and split his finger. In the presence of the children Our Lady miraculously healed his finger.

Our Lady requested a small chapel be built. Later on May 25, 1953 the day of the great miracle, the teacher, Josefa Rios, saw a vision of the chapel to be built in great detail, in the sky. The chapel shown to her had seven sides. It was completed in 1967 just as she had seen it.

Our Lady appeared 33 times and told the children this was to symbolize the 33 years Jesus lived on earth. She told the children that the number seven signifies plenitude. The Blessed Virgin gave the children a total of seven messages to be divulged to the world at a later date as ordered by God. Four of these messages have already been revealed. Juan Angel has been chosen by the Virgin Mary to release the other three messages at a later date.

The three visionaries have each married. Ramonita Belen married Michael Hanly from Tennessee. Isidra Belen married Luis Angel Sierra. Juan Angel Collado married Zulma. The three visionaries get together annually at the chapel, and at the well during the anniversary celebrations on April 23rd and May 25th.

An association has been formed to preserve and celebrate anniversaries of the apparitions and the miracle. The rosary is prayed at the chapel every Saturday evening at 7:30 PM. Water from the well, 'pocito' can be obtained free. The first Mass was celebrated in the new chapel in 1967.

The children suffered much due to false accusers; especially did Juan Angel suffer much. He still gets ridiculed.

Many healings have been reported. One spectacular healing took place at the moment of the miracle on May 25, 1953 at high noon, to a Greek lady by the name of Georgina Politis. On April 23, 1991 on the anniversary of the apparitions, the 'Miracle of the Sun' was witnessed by some 100,000 people. No Church action is reported.

IX The Primary Messages - 4

(1) **Pray the rosary daily**
(2) **Prayer**
(3) **Repent**
(4) **Penance for conversion of sinners**

(1) The following is the beginning of the message delivered by the Virgin Mary during Her apparition in Barrio Rincon, Sabana Grande, Puerto Rico in 1953. It was to be announced to the world when the fulfillment of certain predictions indicated the appropriate moment. This message was made known to the public in 1978. *"Go out into the world and when you are the most deeply submerged in darkness and after having denied My name, you will receive a messenger who will remind you of the TRUE WAY. Satan will knock at the doors of your house and you will drive him away in anger. This is the sign that the time has come to make known the following promise:*

"I promise to make available the graces necessary for salvation, before

the Hour of death, to all those who, in times of confusion and in defining the way to My most Beloved Son, promulgated My name as Mother of the True Way to the Father."

(2) The following is the second message announced by Our Lady on Her visit to Barrio Rincon, Sabana Grande, Puerto Rico in 1953. It was made known publicly on February 13, 1984 after the predicted indications duly took place: *"The hour will come when the spiritual and moral deterioration of the shepherds of My Son's flock will be a matter of public knowledge. The indifference of God's children will prevent them from seeing the great danger which lies in wait. The pain in My heart will be all the more piercing, since it will be these specially beloved sons who forsake Me. This will be the sign that the time has come for making known the following message:*

"Difficult and confused those times will be. Spiritual growth will become very, very difficult for the sons and daughters of God. There will come further times when such growth will seem almost impossible. So be alert My new children because your indifference and confusion will prevail along the way and throughout the world.

"Strange ideas and new philosophies will enshroud the true way in greater darkness. The teachings of My most Beloved Son, the order established by the Father and truth itself, will be set aside in favor of these new and strange beliefs. The selfishness of God's children will give rise to conflicts and divisions which will intensify My pain. You must realize that the shepherds of the flock are men as well. Pardon their faults and assist them, for they represent My Son.

"Remain steadfast in the true way to the Father; in the Church of My Son; for times of great testing are drawing near. Suffering will be necessary. Prayer and sacrifice will be almost mandatory, almost definite.

"Take refuge under My mantle and live in My virtues. Plenitude is what I desire. For it is this that My Son has entrusted to Me. Seven will be the young shoots and seven the swords. Seven will be the generations. After that, they will become innumerable. Two ways will open up before these generations; casting down or building up; defeat or victory.

"Plenitude and My promise: This is the restoration of the way."

(3) The following is the third message left by the Virgin Mary on Her visit to Sabana Grande in April 1953. This message was divulged on April 26, 1987 after certain events had been completed: *"In those days, the Holy Father, the true and chosen son of the Father for our times will have visited this land."* (Note: Pope John Paul II visited Puerto Rico in October 1984.) *"These will be times of depression and persecution for all who proclaim My name as Mother of the True Way to the Father. In these moments of tribulation there will be a great surge of hope. Millions of My sons will*

unite themselves in a great demonstration of true love. They will unite their hearts with Mine asking supplication from My beloved Son. This is the sign that it is time to make known the following message:

"Humanity has submerged itself in a very deep and profound indifference; it lacks faith, hope and love. The ego, selfishness, materialism and blasphemous murmurs have corrupted the hearts of many. My dear children, be careful of the ego. This demon has penetrated the very souls of many men on their true way.

"My dear children, this is the hour when all men must unite themselves in one continuous prayer supplicating mercy from My Son. It is necessary that the Holy Father call all priests, religious, bishops, chosen ones, and together with all the children of the Church, pray the holy rosary for the conversion of all men.

"My new children, please ask the Father for the transformation of all humanity. Above all, for those who are isolated and far away from God, especially the leaders of the Church.

"It is time that everyone be converted by the true voice of My Son, who is The Way. Through their voices an example will be shown and they will proclaim the love of My Son. The Church must always be open to all men on earth, because My Son died for all the sinners of this earth.

"At eleven o'clock in the morning, I visited you for the first time. I made you aware that the hour and time is very near. A very great danger is threatening humanity. My new children, be alert. Plenitude is what I desire.

"I will promise you My maternal protection. I will cover you with My mantle and I will facilitate to all mankind the necessary graces to all those who in difficult moments have said and prayed at least five decades of the rosary.

"I will always protect you under My mantle and you shall live in My virtues. Plenitude is what I desire because My Son has charged Me with this virtue.

"Plenitude and My promise and the reestablishment of the true way."

(4) The following is the fourth message left by the Virgin Mary on Her visit to Sabana Grande in April 1953. This message was divulged on May 25, 1992 after certain events had been completed: *"Those will be difficult times of great social and moral deterioration, but above all, of spiritual deterioration. Men's selfishness will reign. Those consecrated to My most Beloved Son Jesus, through My call to promulgate a new breed of true Christians, will be persecuted. Some new children, consecrated to My small reign, will thrust My Heart with the Sword of Treason and the deterioration of their promise to Our Lord Jesus Christ. Nevertheless, the message of restitution will be accepted and promulgated beyond the sea,*

where I have set My right foot. In the moments of greater tribulation and persecution, I will send the angel that will show you the way, again. This is the sign that the time has come to make the following message known:

"Thousands of souls are lost daily, dragged by sin and infidelity away from My most Beloved Son. The social, moral, and spiritual deterioration darkens humanity that populates the earth. The prophesied times in which parents and children destroy themselves have arrived. Humanity is plunged in a great crisis of faith hardly noticed. Most men do not keep their Christian commitments. Driven by selfishness and pride, they have fallen in the deceit of appearances and superficiality of human demands.

"Some priests, ministers of My Son as shepherds of the flock are irreverent in the celebration of Holy Sacraments; they become allies of the enemy by the infidelity to their consecrated life, their attachment to money, the search for recognition and their unrestraint to pleasures. They are responsible for the loss of faith, they motivate falling away and engender antagonism and violence. If they do not repent and start a life of penance, they will lose their souls forever. I remind you, My children, that they have the task to represent My Son on earth and as Christians you should love and help them. Offer your prayer and sacrifice for their conversion. I assure you that My Son's love and mercy are great for those who make restitution. The elixir of My Son's merciful love protects and revives those who are faithful, who keep their commitment.

"It is the hour in which, because you have not responded to My warnings, the prophecies will start to come true. My children, protect yourselves under My mantle and live in My virtues. I warn you that one day the vault of heaven will be totally orange and dark, there will be an intense cold and a great tribulation and desperation will fall over mankind. It will be as if hell had settled upon earth. Parents, children and all human beings will fight among themselves and will want to kill each other. They will hurt each other till death...

"All that I have warned can be avoided and the crisis of faith could come to an end if the chosen ones become converted and start living a life of intense prayer, dedicating themselves to penance, subjecting themselves to fasting and abstinence, practicing mortification of the senses, and paying special attention to the participation of the Sacraments. These will be received with great devotion and fervor, each one according to their condition and directions, living in My virtue, and observing the teachings of My Most Beloved Son Jesus' Church...

"One last word of advice, My children, the devil will try to destroy My work and My manifestation to the world. There will be such a relaxation for the divine that vain and superficial messages will be spoken

of everywhere. Many will the alleged apparitions be. Some will be genuine and others will be the work of the evil one that with sagacity and a disguise of light, will involve many. Some of these apparitions that will not be My manifestations, will be supported by shepherds and hierarchs of the Church of My Son Jesus. Others, where I am present, will be persecuted and repressed, but this should not be cause of frustrations and loss of faith; so much the better. Then, stay firm in the Church of My Son, love it more intensely, love your shepherds and priests, make an effort to live in harmony and common union with the shepherds. This will be a sign that you are with Me, you are in Me and belong to My Son Jesus, the Christ.

"I will give you a sign: there where I will be, I will ask for prayer, I will ask for penance, with special attention to fasting, and I will ask for much sacrifice. Above all, I will ask a special love for My Large Star, My Son, the Eucharist.

"I am the Major Angel, envoy of these times, the Virgin of Light, the Virgin Mary, the Spouse of God."

(There are three more messages yet to be revealed at a later date by Juan Angel Collado, when certain events occur and as ordained by God.)

X Signs Preceding the Apparition

The first three times Our Lady appeared She was standing on a cloud at 11:00 AM at the well.

XI Other Visions During Apparitions

Our Lady took the children to heaven and purgatory.

XII Prayers Taught to the Seer(s) - Not Reported

XIII Special Devotion Given to the Seer(s)

The first message given in 1953 and revealed to the world in 1978 states: *"I promise to make available the graces necessary for salvation before the hour of death, to all those who, in times of confusion and in defining the way to My most beloved Son, promulgate My name as Mother of the True Way to the Father."*

XIV Requests Made by Our Lady

That all pilgrims who come to the site of the apparition pray seven rosaries before leaving the area.

XV Specific Bible References

On one occasion Juan Angel went home totally exhausted. A friend Andrea Nagario was with him. Suddenly Juan asked Andrea to write as Juan began to dictate the entire history of this earth from its creation to the present time. He also told and interpreted verses from the Bible, using names and titles. He related to Andrea the entire life of Jesus, including His birth and childhood, His life with His foster father, St. Joseph, His death and also His Resurrection. Andrea wrote and filled three tablets. He was shocked. Juan was only eight and could barely read and never had a Bible in his hands before this date.

XVI Secrets Given to the Seer(s)

The seers received a total of seven messages with directions to reveal them when they received word from God. Four messages have since been revealed.

XVII Miracles Promised by Our Lady

The Virgin Mary promised the children a big miracle that would take place on May 25, 1953. This did occur when many people witnessed the Miracle of the Sun. This is when the teacher, Josefa Rios, saw the chapel to be built as well as the faces of Jesus and Mary in the sky. Then the rain fell in rainbow colors. When it was over everyone was dry, but the shirts and blouses worn that day retained the speckled colored dots of the miraculous rainbow rain.

XVIII Miracles Performed

(1) May 25, 1953 Our Lady performed the Miracle of the Sun. (This was repeated in April 23, 1991). In addition She performed the miracle of the rainbow colored rain.
(2) The policeman assigned to protect the children, namely, Dario Garcia, fell and accidentally cut his index finger wide open. The children announced that the Blessed Virgin was applying something green onto Dario's finger. This not only immediately stopped the blood flow, but instantly healed the wound.

XIX Miracles Promised not yet Performed - NR

XX Signs Promised

(1) Our Lady promised a great miracle to occur on May 25, 1953. This did occur. The 'Miracle of the Sun' and the rainbow colored rain.

(2) In the message revealed on May 25, 1992 Our Lady said She will give a sign that Her messages are true; because She will ask for penance, for prayer, for sacrifice and for a special love for the Eucharist.

XXI Signs Given

(1) Rainbow colored water during the first apparition.

(2) May 25, 1953 Miracle of the Sun and rainbow colored rain.

(3) On another occasion, a newspaperman from San German came to see Juan Angel and told him bluntly: "If you say you can see the Virgin Mary, why doesn't She allow me to photograph Her, so that I can believe and my readers can also believe?" Juan Angel lowered his head, listened to the Virgin Mary talking to him and said, *"The Virgin Mary says She will appear in a movie soon."* No one knew what that meant. A few days later, the three visionaries and a group of followers were invited to the house of Dr. Lassise to see a home movie that had been made of the visionaries and the crowds during one of the apparitions at the well; the visionaries saw themselves at the well in the movie. As the camera panned the crowds and sky, there in the clouds, to their amazement, was the Virgin Mary in the movie. Her words again were true.

XXII Predictions/Promises

(1) Our Lady predicted a great miracle would occur on May 25, 1953. This occurred as predicted.

(2) In the message disclosed on April 26, 1987 Our Lady promised all necessary graces in difficult moments to those who have said five decades of the rosary.

(3) In the message revealed May 25, 1992 Our Lady predicted and warned of false apparitions and messages which come from the evil one and which will confuse many.

XXIII Prophecies/Warnings of Chastisement

(1) In the third message given in April 1953 and revealed to the world on February 13, 1984 Our Lady said: *"...The moment of great trial is drawing near; suffering will be necessary, sacrifice will be mandatory."*

(2) In the fourth message given in 1953 and revealed on May 25, 1992 Our Lady said in part: *"It is the hour which, because you have not responded to My warnings, the prophecies will start to come true, I*

warn you that one day the vault of heaven will be totally orange and dark, there will be an intense cold and a greater tribulation and desperation will fall over mankind. It will be as if hell had settled upon earth. All that I have warned can be avoided and the crisis of faith could come to an end, if the chosen ones become converted and start living a life of intense prayer."

XXIV Method of Appearance

During the first three appearances Our Lady appeared standing on a cloud. Thereafter She appeared at the well daily at 11:00 AM for 30 consecutive days.

XXV Method of Departure

It is reported that at the end of each apparition She just disappeared.

XXVI Confrontation w/Civil Authorities

(1) The teacher, Josefa Rios at first did not believe. Later she became, not only a believer, but a strong supporter of the children. After she saw the vision of the chapel on May 25, 1953 she was a supporter for the construction of the chapel. The chapel has been built in detail just as she saw it on that date.

(2) Many people, doubters and disbelievers came to the apparition site. Some attempted to trick the children. (Yes some even tried to trick Our Lady.)
One day someone came to the place early and buried a rosary along the path that the Virgin Mary would lead the children from the well to the schoolhouse. When Our Lady began to walk She stopped suddenly and told the visionaries to tell the people who buried the rosary to take it up, as She would not step over the rosary. Someone did pick up the rosary. Our Lady then admonished everyone never to treat a rosary in jestful ways or as a plaything.

XXVII Confrontation w/Church Authorities

(1) There is one incident reported concerning a priest who apparently had doubts. It seems that one day, a priest disguised himself as a layman in ordinary clothes. He asked one of the visionaries to ask Our Lady to help him. He claimed to have lost his own mother in the crowds for three days and couldn't find her. If She was really the Virgin Mary, She should know exactly where his mother could be found. The Virgin

Mary told the visionary to tell this 'priest' that his mother had died years ago and was in heaven with Her.
(2) There were some priests who openly, even from the pulpit, accused Juan Angel of lying about seeing the Virgin Mary.

XXVIII Request Chapel/Shrine Built

(1) During the apparitions of April 1953 Our Lady asked that a small chapel be built at the apparition site by the 'pocito', the little well. A temporary chapel was built almost immediately.
(2) The visionaries kept telling the teacher that the Virgin Mary wanted a chapel built there. The teacher prayed for guidance. On May 25, 1953 the day of the great miracle, God allowed Josefa Rios to see a clear vision of the chapel in the sky. The Virgin Mary was pointing to the chapel and Josefa saw the chapel in great detail. The chapel was built in 1967 exactly as shown in that vision.

XXIX Free Will/Choice

Seven messages were given by Our Lady to the visionaries in 1953 which were to be revealed only after certain predicted indications had taken place. The seers are responsible to keep the messages secret until the proper time; obviously free to chose to comply with Our Lady's instructions. We are requested to follow the messages and to choose God and to convert.

XXX Seer(s)' Suffering/ Sacrifice

(1) At first the teacher did not believe the children, which caused them some distress.
(2) Doubters, unbelievers and even priests caused the children to feel pain and rejection.
(3) Juan Angel, who is given the task of revealing the messages when certain indications are given, is especially rejected and criticized.

XXXI Healings Reported

Many healings have been reported, and healings are still occurring. Two spectacular healings are reported:
 a) Mrs. Nora Freyre, a well known artist-painter from Mayaquez was totally paralyzed and had been confined to a wheel chair for eight years. On May 19, 1953 she was helped to the well by a policeman. She took a glass of water and drank it. Her whole body felt cold, then

she felt warm. She embraced a crucifix which her brother had put on her chest. Some of the water had spilled onto her legs. Suddenly in one instant, she stood up, began walking, then running up the hill. After she came down the hill unassisted, she then walked all the way to Sabana Grande and back. Thousands of people witnessed this miraculous healing and shouted praises to God. Mrs. Freyre lived a normal and healthy life for over 33 years after her healing. She never used a wheel chair again until the day she died of natural causes on June 13, 1986.

b) Mrs. Georgina Politis was a paraplegic and also confined to a wheel chair. Her whole body was supported by many wires and mechanical straps. During the early days she used to come by the school and look through the windows during the apparitions. On May 25, 1953 the day of the great miracle, about noon, she stood up and dropped all her mechanical wires and supports. She was instantly and completely healed. She later moved to Miami, Florida.

c) Many conversions are reported.

XXXII Action Taken by the Church

(1) In 1967 the chapel was completed.
(2) The first Mass was celebrated in the chapel by Fr. Jose Herrando on October 1, 1967.
(3) In February 1987 the bishop ordered the Blessed Sacrament to be removed from the sanctuary of the chapel.
(4) The bishop undertook an investigation and when the final report was given to him two years later he was not ready to make any comments or details on the report. The people accept with obedience and pray for guidance by the Holy Spirit, while they await the Church's decision.

XXXIII Bibliography

The Virgin of the Rosary Visits Puerto Rico
By: Tony Zuniga
Published by: (Not Given)

Mary's Newsroom (article of text of the fourth message)   1992
Published by: Mary's Newsroom

Chapter 20

FOSTORIA, OHIO, USA
(1954-1984)

I Place - Fostoria, Ohio, USA

II Dates of First and Last Apparition

First: November 8, 1954
Last: January 3, 1984

III Seer(s) - 1

Name: Sister Mildred Mary Neuzil
    (Cloistered Sisters of the Precious Blood)
Birth: Unknown
Age at first apparition: Unknown
Status: Living

IV Total Number of Apparitions - 42

There were at least 42 apparitions of the Blessed Virgin Mary. There may have been additional apparitions recorded in Sr. Mildred's diary and not otherwise reported.

Also Sr. Mildred received messages from Jesus starting in the 1940's and continuing into the 1950's.

V Dates and Locality of Each Apparition

All apparitions occurred in the convent at Fostoria unless otherwise noted.

1954: November 8.
1956: September 25, 26 and 27; October 5 and 13; November 15.
1957: January; February 3; March; April; August 5, 22; September 26, 27; October 7; November 22, 23.
(All the following apparitions occured while the seer was cloistered.)
1958: February 11, 12; March 11; June.
1959: February 23; July 18; December 20.
1960: April 4, 6.
1961: April 21.
1967: June 25.
1972: February 22; September 18.
1980: July 18; August 14; September 19; November 22; December 10.
1981: January 23; April 3, 18.
1982: Several apparitions.
1983: Several apparitions.
1984: January 3.

VI Description of Our Lady

(1) On September 25, 1956 the seer felt the presence of Our Lady and saw part of Her white gown and a small portion of Her blue sash.

(2) Usually Our Lady suddenly appeared enveloped in a soft glow of light. She wore a white veil reaching almost to the waist and a mantle and robe of pure white with no decoration. An oblong-shaped clasp or brooch held the ends of the mantle together at the top. The clasp was gold as was the high and brilliant crown She wore. Her hair and eyes seemed medium brown. Her feet were bare and sometimes covered by the moving clouds upon which Our Lady stood. She held a lily in Her right hand. With Her left hand She slightly held the upper part of Her mantle, exposing Her Immaculate Heart, encircled with red roses and sending forth flames of fire.

(3) On some occasions She held the world in Her hands and tears from Her eyes were flowing upon the world. At other times Her hands were clasped in prayer. On October 8, 1957 She appeared with a blue rosary of glass-like quality hanging from Her right hand.

(4) On November 22, 1957, and again on November 23, 1957 Our Lady appeared standing on a globe, Her right foot resting on crescent or quarter moon, Her left foot was on the snout of a rather small and very ugly looking dragon. Fire was coming out of the dragon's jaws but not much because of the pressure from Our Lady's foot. The dragon looked somewhat black and again green.

Our Lady was all in white. Her veil was so long that it seemed to envelope the globe halfway, sometimes the veil appeared transparent so that Our Lady's hair could be seen through it. Her hair seemed to be sparkling with the light of many stars. At times the edges of the veil, sleeves, and garments seemed to be outlined in light. The veil was held about Her head by a wreath of white roses. Her feet were bare, but on each foot was a large white rose. The roses, both on Her feet and on the crown, were of such dazzling whiteness that the outlines of the petals could barely be seen, sometimes not at all.

Our Lady slowly raised Her hands and crossed them on Her breast, while so doing She bent Her head slightly forward, revealing on Her breast, through the veil, the Triangle and the Eye (which is often depicted as the symbol of the Divine Indwelling). A strong beam of light streamed from the Divine Presence within Our Lady onto the globe at Her feet. Then in a half circle halfway around the figure of Our Lady and above Her head appeared a scroll on which was written in letters of gold the words: **All the Glory of the King's Daughter is within.**

VII Title(s) of Our Lady - 3

(1) Our Lady of America
(2) Our Lady of the Divine Indwelling
(3) Immaculate Virgin

VIII Brief Factual Review

Ohio is a state located in the industrial northeast section of the USA, and is bounded on the north by Lake Erie. Fostoria is located in Seneca County, which is in the northwestern region of Ohio.

Sister Mildred Mary was professed a religious in 1933. She received her assignments to work in various houses of the congregation, mostly in domestic work. Later, in 1958 she was cloistered.

About 1938 she began to have mystical experiences. After some years she began to write them down. Finally in 1954 she began to receive frequent apparitions and messages from Our Lord Jesus and from Our Lady.

It was on November 8, 1954 that Our Lady first spoke to the seer, and on September 25, 1956 Our Lady first appeared to the seer.

Our Lady announced Herself as Our Lady of America and stated Her great concern for the youth and called on Americans to live a life of purity.

The Blessed Mother also taught the seer of the Indwelling of the Holy Trinity and stated: *"I am Our Lady of the Divine Indwelling, Handmaid of Him who dwells within."* She taught the seer a Prayer to the Immaculate Conception (October 5, 1956), and also a prayer to the Indwelling Most Holy Trinity. Our Lady also instructed the seer to cause a medal to be struck and distributed. The details and explanation of the meaning of the medal was explained to Sister Mildred by Our Blessed Lady.

Fostoria, Ohio, USA

Our Lady further gave warnings of a coming Chastisement unless the people have an inner conversion and reform their lives. The seer was permitted to see Our Lady's Immaculate Heart and also to see the Eye enclosed within a triangle on Our Lady's breast, the symbol of the Divine Indwelling.

St. Joseph, St. Michael the Archangel, Archangel Gabriel, Angel Sultra and Archangel Sardus appeared to the seer and gave messages to her.

No Church action is reported.

IX The Primary Messages - 5

(1) Life of Purity - Our Lady requested that Her children honor Her, especially by the purity of their lives. She said to the seer on September 26, 1956: *"My child, I entrust you with this message that you must make known to My children in America. I wish it to be the country dedicated to My purity. The wonders I will work will be wonders of the soul. They must have faith and believe firmly in My love for them. I desire that they be the children of My Pure Heart. I desire, through My children of America, to further the cause of faith and purity among peoples and nations.*

"Let them come to Me with confidence and simplicity, and I, their Mother, will teach them to become pure like My Heart, that their own hearts may be more pleasing to the Heart of My Son."

Again on September 25, 1956: *"Behold, O My children, the tears of your Mother. Shall I weep in vain? Assuage the sorrow of My Heart over the ingratitude of sinful men by the love and chasteness of your lives. Will you do this for Me, beloved children, or will you allow your Mother to weep in vain? I come to you, O children of America, as a last resort. I plead with you to listen to My voice. Cleanse your souls in the Precious Blood of My Son. Live in His Heart, and take Me in that I may teach you to live in great purity of heart which is so pleasing to God. Be My Army of Chaste Soldiers, ready to fight to the death to preserve the purity of your souls. I am the Immaculate One, Patroness of your Lord. Be My faithful children as I am your faithful Mother."*

Again: *"My Immaculate Heart desires with great desire to see the kingdom of Jesus My Son established in all hearts"* (March 1957).

(2) Prayer and Sacrifice - On February 3, 1957 Our Lady said: *"My Son asks of souls, love, that true love waiting to sacrifice itself in the one loved. Man fears to sacrifice himself because he is selfish".*

On December 20, 1959 Our Lady said: *"Oh, penance. How little My children understand it! They give Me many words but sacrifice themselves they will not. It is not Me that they love but themselves. Weep, then with your Mother over the sins of men. Intercede with Me before the Throne of Mercy, for sin is overwhelming the world and punishment is not far away.*

"There is no true love unless there is sacrifice." (Given during 1982).

(3) Divine Indwelling - On November 22 and November 23, 1957 Our Lady presented Herself and said: *"I am Our Lady of the Divine Indwelling; Handmaid of Him who dwells within."*

Again on February 11, 1958: *"The Spirit of Christ will dwell in the hearts of men. Those in whom this Spirit is NOT found will be condemned to eternal hell-fire."*

Our Lady made known to the seer that Our Blessed Mother is particularly interested in the youth of our nation. It is the youth who are to be the leaders of this movement of renewal on the face of the earth. But the youth must be prepared, and this must be done by instilling into them, not only the knowledge of the Divine Indwelling, but a serious study of it, a living it in such a way that the Divine Presence becomes, as it were, an intimate and necessary part of their life and daily living. From this will flow a great love, a conflagration that will envelope the world in the flames of Divine Charity. This is what Our Lady is working for, because this is the great desire of Her Divine Son, and it is to the youth of America that She is holding out this challenge.

On November 8, 1954 Our Lady said: *"The Divine Trinity will dwell in your midst only if you are faithful in practicing the virtues of Our life at Nazareth, then, you also, My children, you also will become another Paradise. God will then walk among you and you will have peace."*

Our Lady inspired the seer to pen a prayer to the Indwelling Most Holy Trinity.

(4) Medal - Our Lady showed and gave directions to the seer to cause a medal of Our Lady of America to be produced and distributed, and promised those who wore the medal with great faith and fervent devotion to Our Lady, they will receive the grace of intense purity of heart and the particular love of the Holy Virgin and Her Divine Son.

(5) Family Rosary - On October 7, 1957 the evening of the feast of the Most Holy Rosary, Our Lady appeared. Hanging from Her right hand was a blue rosary of a glass-like quality. Our Lady said: *"Making the rosary a family prayer is very pleasing to Me. I ask that all families strive to do so. But be careful to say it with great devotion meditating on each mystery and striving to imitate in your daily lives the virtues depicted herein. Live the mysteries of the rosary as I lived them, and it will become a chain binding you to Me forever. They who are found in the circle of My rosary will never be lost. I Myself will lead them at death to the throne of My Son, to be eternally united to Him."*

X Signs Preceding the Apparitions - Not Reported

XI Other Visions During Apparitions

(1) Jesus appeared to the seer and gave her messages. (May 22, 29 and

July 11, 12, 13, 14, 15 of 1954)
(2) Our Lady showed the seer the image She requested to be shown on the medal and explained its meaning.
(3) Archangel Michael appeared and gave messages to the seer. (Autumn 1954; November 7, 1954; and May 8, 1957)
(4) Archangel Gabriel appeared and gave messages to the seer. (Nov 20, 1955)
(5) St. Joseph - In October 1956 St. Joseph gave interior messages to the seer. On March 11, 1958 Our Lady told the seer that St. Joseph would visit. St. Joseph came to the seer as promised. Then on March 19, 1958 St. Joseph appeared again to the seer and gave messages. St. Joseph also came again on March 30, 1958 as he had promised.
(6) Angel Sultra (meaning Power of God) appeared as a vision of light and gave messages to the seer. (August 22, 1981)
(7) Archangel Sardus (meaning Strength of God) also appeared as a vision of light. (August 22, 1981)

XII Prayers Taught to the Seer(s)

(1) Prayer to the Indwelling Most Holy Trinity

Prayer: O my Love, my only Good, Most Holy Trinity, I adore You, hidden in the depths of my soul. To You, to Your honor and glory, I dedicate my life. May every thought, word and deed of mine be an act of adoration and praise directed towards Your Divine Majesty enthroned in my heart.

O Father, Infinite Goodness, behold Your child, clothed in the likeness of Your Son. Extend to me Your arms that I may belong to You forever.

O Son, Divine Lord, made man, crucify me with Yourself that I may become, in union with You, a sacrifice of praise for the glory of Your Father.

O Holy Spirit, Fire of Everlasting Love, consume me on the altar of Divine Charity, that at the end of life nothing may remain but that which bears the likeness of Christ.

O Blessed Trinity, worthy of all adoration, I wish to remain in spirit on my knees, to acknowledge forever Your reign in me and over me, to Your everlasting glory.

Through the Immaculate Heart of Mary and the pure heart of St. Joseph, I consecrate my life to Your adoration and glory.

At the moment of death, receive me, O my Triune Love, that I may continue my adoration of love through all eternity. Amen.

(2) Prayer to The Immaculate Conception
(Inspired during an apparition on October 5, 1956)

Prayer: O Immaculate Mother, Queen of our country, open our hearts, our homes, and our Land to the coming of Jesus, Your Divine Son. With Him, reign over us, O Heavenly Lady, so pure and so bright with the radiance of God's light shining in and about You. Be our Leader against the powers of evil set upon wrestling the world of souls, redeemed at such a great cost by the sufferings of Your Son and of Yourself, in union with Him, from that same Savior, Who loves us with infinite charity.

We gather about You, O Chaste and Holy Mother, Virgin Immaculate, Patroness of our beloved land, determined to fight under Your banner of holy purity against the wickedness that would make all the world an abyss of evil, without God and without Your loving maternal care.

We consecrate our hearts, our homes, our land to Your Most Pure Heart, O great Queen, that the kingdom of Your Son, our Redeemer and our God, may be firmly established in us.

We ask no special sign of You, sweet Mother, for we believe in Your great love for us, and we place in You our entire confidence. We promise to honor You by faith, love, and the purity of our lives according to Your desire.

Reign over us, then, O Virgin Immaculate, with Your Son Jesus Christ. May His Divine Heart and Your most chaste Heart be ever enthroned and glorified among us. Use us, Your children of America, as Your instruments in bringing peace among men and nations. Work Your miracles of grace in us, so that we may be a glory to the Blessed Trinity, Who created us, redeemed us, and sanctifies us.

May Your valiant Spouse, St. Joseph, with the holy angels and saints, assist You and us in 'renewing the face of the earth'. Then when our work is over, come, Holy Immaculate Mother, and as our Victorious Queen, lead us to the eternal kingdom, where Your Son reigns forever as King. Amen.

(3) On September 15, 1956 Our Lady taught the seer this:

Prayer: By Thy Holy and Immaculate Conception, O Mary, deliver us from evil.

XIII Special Devotion Given To Seer(s)

(1) **Medal of Our Lady of America** - The medal of Our Lady of America, including the picture of Our Lady on one side and Coat of Arms of Christian Family on the other.

The one side bears the image of Our Lady of America and around it the words, *"By Your Holy and Immaculate Conception, O Mary, deliver us from evil."* The Coat of Arms of the Christian Family is on the other side of the medal. The Divine Indwelling is represented by the Triangle and the Eye on the red shield of the Precious Blood, through which sanctifying grace was made possible to fallen man. The sanctification of the family through imitation of the Holy Family is represented by the Cross and the two lilies, on each of which is depicted a burning heart. The flaming sword is a symbol of Divine Love so necessary to attain union with God, while the rosary indicates a most profitable means of drawing closer to the Holy Family, through devout meditation on the various mysteries. The scroll above bears the inscription, 'Gloria Patri et Filio et Spiritui Sancto' and the one below, 'Jesu, Maria, Joseph.' These aspirations are simply explanations of the whole theme and are also acts of praise to the Trinity and the Holy Family.

This medal is to be worn with great faith and fervent devotion to Our Lady for the grace of intense purity of heart and the particular love of the Holy Virgin and Her Divine Son.

(2) **Picture/Statue of Our Lady of America** - Our Lady also requested Pictures/Statues of Herself to be honored and venerated in every Christian home.

XIV Requests Made by Our Lady

(1) **Dedicate America to Purity** - September 26, 1956: *"I am Our Lady of America. I desire that My children honor Me, especially by the purity of their lives.*

"My child I entrust you with this message that you must make known to My children in America. I wish it to be the country dedicated to My purity. The wonders I will work will be the wonders of the soul."

(2) **Shrine in Washington, DC** - Our Lady often emphasized Her desire that the Shrine in Washington, DC, be made a place of special pilgrimage. She wishes to be honored there as Our Lady of America, the Immaculate Virgin.

(3) **Picture** - On November 15, 1956 Our Lady requested the seer to draw a picture of Her first appearance.

(4) **Statue** - On November 15, 1956 Our Lady also requested a statue be made according to the likeness of the picture, and placed, after being solemnly carried in procession, in the Shrine of the Immaculate Conception in Washington D.C.

"When a picture or statue of Myself as Our Lady of America is placed in the home and honored then will My Son bless His people with Peace." (February 22, 1972)

A statue of Our Lady of America has reportedly been cast by a California artist/sculpturist, and is now awaiting acceptance and approval by the visionary and Church authorities.

(5) **Medal** - Our Lady requested that a medal be struck and distributed depicting Our Lady as She appeared to the seer.

XV Specific Bible References - Not Reported
XVI Secrets Given to the Seer(s) - Not Reported

XVII Miracles Promised by Our Lady

On September 25, 1956 Our Lady promised that greater miracles then those granted at Lourdes and Fatima would be granted here in America, the United States in particular, if we would do as She desires. She said: *"I do not promise miracles of the body, but of the soul."*

XVIII Miracles Performed - Not Reported

XIX Miracles Promised not yet Performed

Unknown what is contained in the unpublished portions of the seer's diary.

XX Signs Promised - Not Reported
XXI Signs Given - Not Reported
XXII Predictions/Promises - Not Reported

XXIII Prophecies/Warnings of Chastisement

(1) In January 1957 Our Lady said: *"The Hour grows late. My Son's patience will not last forever. Help Me hold back His anger which is about to descend on sinful and ungrateful men. Suffering and anguish, such as never before experienced, is about to overtake mankind. It is the darkest hour. But if men will come to Me, My Immaculate Heart will make it bright again with the Mercy which My Son will rain down through My hands. Help Me save those who will not save themselves. Help Me bring once again the sunshine of God's peace upon the world. Hurry for the time is short, but the punishment will be long, and for many, forever."*

(2) In April 1957 Our Lady said: *"Unless My children reform their lives, they will suffer great persecution. If man himself will not take upon himself the penance necessary to atone for his sins and those of others, God in His Justice will have to send upon him the punishment necessary to atone for his transgressions."*

(3) *Unless My children in America do penance by mortification and self-denial and thus reform their lives, God will visit them with punishments hitherto unknown to them."* Further: *"There will be peace as has been promised but not until My children are purified and cleansed from*

defilement. My dear children, either you will do as I desire and reform your lives, or God Himself will need to cleanse you in the fires of untold punishment."

(4) On February 11, 1958 Our Lady said: *"My Immaculate Heart will win in the end, and the Spirit of Christ will dwell in the hearts of men. Those in whom the Spirit is not found will be condemned to eternal hell-fire."*

(5) Again on April 24, 1961: *"If My desires are not fulfilled, much suffering will come to this land."*

(6) On November 22, 1980 Our Lady gave this graphic and urgent warning: *"Unless the United States accepts and carries out faithfully the mandate given to it by heaven to lead the world to peace, there will come upon it and all nations a great havoc of war and incredible suffering. If however the United States is faithful to this mandate from heaven and yet fails in the pursuit of peace because the rest of the world will not accept or cooperate, then the United States will not be burdened with the punishment about to fall."*

(7) During Our Lady's last visit on January 3, 1984 the seer asked Our Lady if there will be a nuclear war. Our Lady responded: *"If My warnings are taken seriously and enough of My children strive constantly and faithfully to renew and reform themselves in their inward and outward lives, then there will be no nuclear war.*

"What happens to the world depends on those who live in it. There must be much more good than evil prevailing in order to prevent the holocaust that is so near approaching.

"Yet even should such a destruction happen because there were not enough souls who took My warning seriously, there will remain a remnant, untouched by the chaos who, having been faithful in following Me and spreading My warnings will gradually inhabit the earth again, with their dedicated holy lives."

XXIV Method of Appearance

(1) On September 25, 1956 the seer saw only a part of Our Lady's white gown and a small portion of Her blue sash.
(2) Thereafter Our Lady simply appeared to the seer in the form depicted on the Medal as Our Lady of America.

XXV Method of Departure

Our Lady simply vanished or faded out.

XXVI Confrontation w/Civil Authorities - NR

XXVII Confrontation w/Church Authorities - NR

XXVIII Request Chapel/Shrine Built

(1) On October 13, 1956 Our Lady said of the National Shrine in Washington, DC: *"This is My shrine. I am very pleased with it. Tell My children I thank them. Let them finish it quickly and make it a place of pilgrimage. It will be a place of wonders. I promise this: 'I will bless all those who, either by prayers, labor, or material aid, help to erect this shrine.'"*

(2) On November 15, 1956 Our Lady said She wishes to be honored there (National Shrine in Washington, DC) in a special way as Our Lady of America, the Immaculate Virgin.

XXIX Free Will/Choice

Although the diary does not report on this concerning Our Lady, yet Our Lord said to the seer in July 1954: *"I will not force your free will, for that is yours to use as you desire."*

XXX Seer(s)' Suffering/ Sacrifice - Not Reported
XXXI Healings Reported - Not Reported
XXXII Action Taken by the Church - Not Reported

XXXIII Bibliography

Our Lady of America 1960-1989
By: Sister Mildred Mary Neuzil
Published by: The Contemplative Sisters

Chapter 21

SEREDNE, UKRAINE
(1954-1955)

I Place - Seredne, Ukraine (also Dubovytsya)

II Dates of First and Last Apparition

First: December 20, 1954
Last: November 21, 1955

III Seer(s) - 1

Name: Hanya (Ann)
Birth: Unknown
Age at first apparition: Unknown
Status: Unknown

IV Total Number of Apparitions - 16

V Dates And Locality of Each Apparition

All apparitions occurred in the mountains of Seredne unless otherwise noted.

1954: December 20 (during Mass); later on an unknown date.
1955: Feast of the Purification of the Blessed Virgin Mary; First Sunday of Lent; Feast of the Annunciation; May 15, (during Mass); Feast of the Ascension; Last Sunday in May; June 5 and 6; Feast of the Sacred Heart; harvest time; Saturday before the Feast of the Assumption (during Mass); September 28; November 21 (during Mass).

VI Description of Our Lady

(1) On December 20, 1954 the seer saw Our Lady standing, clothed in a white robe with a blue sash. There was a crown of 12 stars around Her head which diffused light toward the heavens. Light radiating from Our Lady was so bright that the seer could not look upon Her.

(2) On the Feast of the Purification 1955 the seer saw the Mother of God clothed in somber hues with a large open wound in Her Heart along with several smaller wounds. Our Blessed Mother seemed sad and troubled, Her eyes cast toward the ground, She pointed to Her wounded Heart as She spoke to the seer.

(3) On the Feast of the Annunciation Our Lady held a rosary blue in color. On this occasion She knelt and prayed.

VII Title(s) of Our Lady - 1

No title is reported given by Our Lady, however, She does focus on the Immaculate Conception and appeared dressed as Our Lady of Lourdes.

VIII Brief Factual Review

First it is noted that all dates given are from the Gregorian calendar, which is the calendar we now use in the West. But in Ukraine they use the Julian calendar which is thirteen days late after our calendar. Thus the Ukrainian Uniates celebrate the Immaculate Conception on December 21st of our calendar. The Holy Year (commemorating the 100th anniversary of the proclamation of the dogma of the Immaculate Conception of the Blessed Virgin Mary) began on December 8, 1953 and ended December 25, 1954. This means that for Uniates, using the Julian calendar, it commenced on December 21, 1953 and concluded on January 7, 1955.

Seredne is located in the northwest region of the Ukraine, near the Polish border, which is known as the Ivanfrankivske region. The Ukraine was part of the USSR; but since the breakup of the USSR, Ukraine has become an independent state.

The seer receiving the visions and apparitions was named Hanya (Ann). The first vision occurred while Ann was in church attending Mass. Just before the consecration everything disappeared and then the seer saw the mountain of Seredne, the place where there were stalls and a spring. (Ann had never been to the hill of Seredne herself.) Our Blessed Mother was standing on the mountain clothed in a white robe and a blue sash. There was a circle of twelve stars around Her head which diffused their light towards heaven.

Our Lady complained that although She holds so many graces, yet She is unable to give them out, because nearly no one wants to receive Her graces. Our Lady said: *"Never have people fallen so low since the beginning of the world as at this time. This is the age of the Kingdom of Satan."*

Our Lady requested that a grotto be built on the spot where She was standing and that a statue of the Immaculate Conception be placed in it so that people would know where She had appeared. She also reported a spring be prepared where water could be blessed and further requested that a Ukranian priest bless the spring secretly on the Feast Day of the Immaculate Conception.

Later the seer did go up on the mountain of Seredne to the site where Our Lady appeared. It was only then that Ann informed the parish priest of Our Lady's request. After putting her off at first, the priest agreed to go to the mountain and bless the spring. This did occur on the Feast Day. After Mass in church, the parish priest did go up to the mountain and bless the spring on the mountain. Very few people were present, however, two other priests arrived shortly after the blessing. The people prayed and sang the 'Mnohaya Lita' (Many Years), confessions were heard and Holy Communion was distributed in celebration.

The seer had a total of sixteen reported apparitions and visions of Our Blessed Mother. Ann also had apparitions of Jesus on three separate occasions. Once she was shown the Holy Trinity in a vision on the mountain. St. Michael also appeared on one occasion.

Other signs were given to the seer, such as hearing a choir of angels sing; the mountain would visibly become aglow or illuminated; Our Lady appeared standing on the crescent of the moon with hosts of angels attending Her. Once the seer was shown the Sorrowful and Wounded Heart of Mary and on another occasion Our Blessed Lady was seen crushing the head of a black serpent. During several apparitions Our Lady walked on the mountain and lightning rays of gold showered from Her person like darts and fell upon the water and on the clumps of brushes along the way. The seer was favored with many other gifts, visions and graces.

Our Lady's message was for us to convert, do penance and pray, especially the rosary. She also warned of the great disaster at hand.

Although no healings were reported, yet Our Lady told the seer: *"Whoever comes in the spirit of penance for his sins and drinks this water with faith, shall be strengthened in body and soul and he shall not die when the catastrophe strikes"*, thus indicating healings would occur.

It is remembered that during the time of these apparitions (1954-1955) the Ukraine was under the yoke of the Soviet Republic. The Soviet government was aware of the happenings going on at Seredne because, as recently as July 1959, the communist press declaimed against the faithful pilgrims who were visiting the site of the apparitions. One report states that the communist press wrote:

"Priests have organized the Seredne Miracle . . . and have proclaimed a miraculous spring there as holy . . . The Faithful have begun to gather there. And National Uniates are spreading actively nationalistic Anti-Soviet propaganda."

During this time the Church was underground; yet it is reported that as early as the apparition on the Feast of the Immaculate Conception in 1954 "more and more people, men, women, children, came visiting Seredne hill from villages and cities of the neighboring districts."

No action by the Church is reported.

IX The Primary Messages - 3

(1) **Penance** - On the Feast of the Annunciation Our Lady said: *"Penance! Penance! Penance!"*

Then again during the first apparition, Our Lady said in part: *"...whoever comes in the spirit of penance for his sins . . . will be strengthened in body and soul . . ."*

(2) **Rosary** - Also on the Feast of the Annunciation Our Lady began to say the rosary on Her own rosary which was light blue in color. Usually the seer was praying the rosary when Our Lady appeared to her.

(3) **Spiritual Decline in the Church in Rome** - At harvest time during the thirteenth apparition, Our Lady said: *"Rome will be ruined. The Holy Father will be killed. Rome will rise and be renewed through the mountain of Seredne."* The seer then heard words from Jesus and understood the meaning of the words of Our Lady to be that this meant a spiritual ruin of Rome, in that many apostate priests were railing against the Holy Father. This was the spiritual ruin of Rome and symbolic killing of the Holy Father.

X Signs Preceding the Apparitions

Usually the seer was praying the rosary when Our Lady appeared. Also a brilliant light filled the grotto and Our Lady appeared in that light.

XI Other Visions During Apparitions

(1) Jesus appeared to the seer three different times, once before lent 1955, on May 1, 1955 and finally on the Feast of Christ the King in 1955.
(2) St. Michael appeared to the seer on the Saturday before the Assumption. He was of medium height, dark and of pleasant mien. He wore a short white tunic and his right hand held a flaming sword while his silvery wings flashed like the sun. He faced south and swung the sword three times. A blaze of fire trailed the sword as it flashed through the air.
(3) The Holy Trinity was shown to the seer during the apparition occurring on the last Sunday in May 1955. Above the head of the Blessed Virgin, appeared the Holy Trinity in dazzling light. The Persons of God the Father and God the Son were visible, above whom fluttered a dove;

Seredne, Ukraine

symbolic of the Holy Ghost. Countless angels were in attendance.
(4) On the Feast of the Purification Our Lady appeared with a large open wound and two smaller wounds on Her Immaculate and Sorrowful Heart.
(5) Angels appeared to the seer during several visions.
(6) The seer was given to see Our Lady crushing the head of a black serpent and once saw Our Lady standing on the crescent of the moon.

XII Prayers Taught to the Seer(s) - Not Reported
XIII Special Devotion Given to the Seer(s) - NR

XIV Requests Made by Our Lady

(1) Our Lady requested that a grotto be built on the spot where She appeared and that a statue of the Immaculate Conception be placed inside the grotto. This was done.
(2) She also requested that the spring be prepared and that the water be blessed by a Ukranian Catholic priest secretly on the Feast of the Immaculate Conception. This was done.
(3) During the apparition on the Feast of the Ascension, Our Lady requested that a priest be present and a cross placed on two spots on the mountain which Our Lady indicated.

XV Specific Bible References - Not Reported

XVI Secrets Given to the Seer(s)

No secret messages are reported other than the message that the priest bless the water secretly on the Feast of the Immaculate Conception.

XVII Miracles Promised by Our Lady - NR
XVIII Miracles Performed - Not Reported
XIX Miracles Promised not yet Performed - NR
XX Signs Promised - Not Reported

XXI Signs Given

(1) After the first apparition the mountain of Seredne would sometimes be aglow (become illuminated). Many people saw the unnatural light and came to the mountain to find the grotto and statue of Our Lady. People thus became convinced of supernatural happenings.
(2) On one occasion, Our Lady showed the seer Her wounded Sorrowful Heart.

(3) On May 15, 1955 the seer was given to see Our Lady crushing the head of a black serpent.
(4) On the last Sunday of May 1955 Our Lady was seen standing on the crescent of the moon with a host of angels in attendance.
(5) On one occasion Ann was shown the Holy Trinity.
(6) On the Feast of Pentecost June 5, 1955 the seer saw a huge star that shed its light directly on all the people gathered.
(7) Then on June 6, 1955 while praying the rosary the seer saw the words coming from the sincere hearts of the people changed into beautiful red roses which were gathered up by the angels and offered to Our Blessed Mother, who in turn pressed them joyfully to Her Heart.

XXII Predictions/Promises

During the first apparition Our Lady said: *"I shall remain on this mountain. From here I see the whole universe. I see many sinners and I shall distribute My grace from this spring from which the water flows. Whoever comes here in the spirit of penance for his sins and drinks this water with faith, shall be strengthened in body and soul, and he will not die when the catastrophe strikes."*

XXIII Prophecies/Warnings of Chastisement

At the first apparition Our Lady said: *". . . I greatly desire to help sinners, because disaster is at hand, just as the time of Noah people will be destroyed not by flood but by fire, because they have sinned against God."*

XXIV Method of Appearance

Usually a light would fill the grotto and Our Lady would be in that light. The seer could not always look directly at Our Lady because of the brilliant light.

XXV Method of Departure

She just disappeared.

XXVI Confrontation w/Civil Authorities

The Church was underground during these times and the communist government and press were aware of the events at Seredne and were trying to disparage these events.

XXVII Confrontation w/Church Authorities - NR

XXVIII Request Chapel/Shrine Built

Our Lady requested a grotto be built and a statue of the Immaculate Conception be placed inside at the spot where She first appeared. This was done.

XXIX Free Will/Choice

Our Lady said: *"You see that I hold so many graces, but am unable to give them out, because even though there are so many sons and daughters, almost all have turned from Me and do not beg for My graces."*

XXX Seer(s)' Suffering/Sacrifice

The Church was underground, the government and the press labeled the events at Seredne as Anti-Soviet propaganda and accused the priests of organizing the "Seredne Miracle." No doubt the seer had much to suffer during these years due to these events occurring at Seredne.

XXXI Healings Reported

None are reported, however, Our Lady promised healings through the faithful use of the blessed water to all who pilgrim to the mountain.

XXXII Action Taken by the Church - NR

XXXIII Bibliography

Vers Demain 1972 (July - August - September issue)
By: Vers Demain
Published by: Vers Demain

The Final Hour 1992
By: Michael Brown
Published by: Faith Publishing Company

Chapter 22

BUDAPEST, HUNGARY
(1955-1988)

I Place - Budapest, Hungary
(In a convent.)

II Dates of First and Last Apparition

First: 1955
Last: January 11, 1988

III Seer(s) - 1

Name: Sister Dolores (Until recently undisclosed)
Birth: Unknown
Age at first apparition: Unknown
Status: Unknown

IV Total Number of Apparitions - 27

Twenty are reported. There are at least seven other messages reported with no dates given. All apparitions occurred in a convent in Budapest, Hungary.

V Dates And Locality of Each Apparition

1955: September 24; October 29; October (date unknown).
1961: November 16.
1969: February 2.

1978: April 20.
1983: (Holy Year).
1984: (Holy Year).
1985: January.
1986: May 20; August 10; September 20, 24; October 16; November 7.
1987: February 17; September 18; October 27; November 22.
1988: January 11 (when an image of Our Lady with an apron full of small hearts was given to the seer).

VI Description of Our Lady

No description of Our Lady is reported as such. However it is reported that Our Lady appeared sorrowful to the seer. It is further reported that the picture appearing on the booklet **'Life Offering'** is based on an apparition of Our Lady. This picture depicts Our Lady as somber and sorrowful. She is wearing a white dress with a blue front apron and an embroidered white veil. Her head is surrounded by a halo of stars. Her apron is full of small red hearts. Her Immaculate Heart is radiating beams of light from Her breast. She is handing small hearts from Her apron to the Sacred Heart of Jesus to Her upper right, which has the Host as a background and is surrounded by the Crown of Thorns.

VII Title(s) of Our Lady - 1

On January 1985 Our Lady said: *"I asked to be addressed as the Mother of Jesus. This title is most pleasing to Me."*

VIII Brief Factual Review

Hungary, an Eastern European nation which was then under the control of the USSR, has since shaken off the communist yoke.

An anonymous nun in an unnamed convent in an unnamed place in Hungary kept a diary of messages received from Our Lord and Our Lady over a period of 33 years. It has recently been learned that her name is Dolores, however, it is her request to remain hidden.

During these years both Jesus and Mary gave her the mission to promote 'Life Offering' and to recruit volunteer souls to offer up their suffering, sickness and sacrifices for the greater glory of God and for the salvation of souls.

The declaration text of the 'Life Offering' was dictated to the seer, and Our Lady gave the seer five beautiful promises for those faithful souls who offer their lives to Our Lady. Our Blessed Mother said the 'Life Offering' must be made with humble heart, firm resolution and clear intent.

Our Heavenly Mother also taught the seer a prayer of contrition and told the seer that we should become united with Our Lady in prayer of sacrifice. Our Lady once said: "*My daughter, all My children can become saints if they try to do perfectly the task that God places before them.*"

Our Lady told the seer that she must make sure that the great grace of the "*Life Offering reach the souls who suffer greatly in body or soul, those that are incurably sick, the physically handicapped and the bedridden so their suffering will not be in vain.*" Our Lady went on to say: "*This suffering can become a fund of gold for all humanity as well as for yourselves, because in your hearts and souls you will receive peace, strength, relief and satisfaction, if you realize that patient acceptance of your sufferings will bring you great happiness in heaven.*"

Sister Dolores faithfully obeyed Our Lady's requests. The seer visited the critically ill in the hospitals, especially those who were neglected or ignored by their relatives and those who had no one. She reports that many had given up, knowing that no cure or relief was in view, and that their life and their suffering was meaningless, believing no one needed them anymore. But when she told them that they were indeed precious children of Our Blessed Mother and that Jesus searches for companion souls who will unite their sufferings with His, and that by their sufferings they can pay for their own sins and for the sins of others, and that at the hour of death they will go straight to heaven, without purgatory; they started to cry for joy because they realized that God and Our Blessed Mother loved them so. Some had thought that God was angry with them and was punishing them; some atheists had considered suicide. The seer witnessed firsthand the graces received by the way of the 'Life Offering'.

Our Lady gave the seer a "prayer for the sick", and also a prayer to say before Holy Communion. "*Unity is desired by God and must first be realized in the bosom of the Church,*" said Our Lady. During the Marian Year of 1987-1988 Our Blessed Mother requested her children to visit the Marian Shrines, which should be a meeting place for "*My life-sacrificing children.*"

In addition to the requested practice of 'Life-Offering', Our Lady also asked the seer that Her life-offering children extend the devotion to the Sacred Heart and Immaculate Heart from nine to eleven consecutive months. She asked for a rosary and the Litany of the most Sacred Heart of Jesus on First Fridays and on First Saturdays, as well as a rosary and the Litany of Loreto.

The messages have been translated from the Hungarian into other languages and the 'Life-Offering' apostolate has spread throughout the western world.

IX The Primary Messages - 5

(1) Sacrifice - Our Lady said: "*God is looking for souls who will* *sacrifice their lives for others, because only perfect, exalted love is able to save mankind and help souls reach eternity."*

Once Our Lady said: *"My dear children, you should burn with fervor to help save those who suffer in the slavery of sin."*

(2) Prayer - Our Lady told the seer: *"My children who offer your lives make the Act of Contrition every day!.."*

Our Lady dictated a prayer of contrition to the seer. On January 11, 1988 Our Lady said: *"...pray for fallen and faithless human brothers."* Again in January 1985: *"Pray daily for the Holy Father."*

(3) Pray the Rosary - On October 27, 1987 Our Lady said: *"...Pray the rosary daily!"*

(4) Fast - Our Lady said: *"Fast on Fridays as your health permits. The most effective fast is when you take only bread and water, but only those who can. Those who cannot do it because of their health can offer an hour's prayer vigil during the night preceding Friday."*

(5) Eucharist - On October 16, 1986 Our Lady confided to the seer with sorrow that many receive Communion with indifference and without a living faith. Then Our Lady said: *"You must firmly believe that Jesus is truly present in the Host as Man and God! You must believe that you really meet Him, and, more than that, unite with Him in the Eucharist."*

X Signs Preceding the Apparitions - Not Reported

XI Other Visions During Apparitions

(1) Jesus appeared to the seer on more than one occasion. He gave messages to her, and also requested that she spread the 'Life Offering' mission and recruit souls.
(2) During one apparition the seer was shown symbolically what Jesus is asking from us. She saw an image of Our Lady holding an apron full of small hearts which She places into the Sacred Heart of Jesus. In the background of the Sacred Heart is the Host surrounded by the Crown of Thorns.

XII Prayers Taught to the Seer(s)

(1) Text of the Life Offering (1955) -
Prayer: "My dear Jesus, before the Trinity, Our Heavenly Mother, and the whole Heavenly Court, united with Your most Precious Sacred Blood and Your sacrifice on Calvary, I hereby offer my whole life for the intention of Your Sacred Heart and of the Immaculate Heart of Mary. Together with my life I place at Your disposal all Holy Masses, all my Holy Communions, all my good deeds, all my sacrifices, and the sufferings of my entire life for the adoration and supplication of the Holy Trinity, for

unity in Our Holy Mother Church, for the Holy Father and for the priests, for good priestly vocations, and for all souls until the end of the world.

O my Jesus, please accept my life sacrifice and my offerings and give me Your grace that I may persevere obediently until my death. Amen."

(2) Prayers of Contrition -

Prayer: "O my Jesus, I love You over and above everything! For the love of You I am sorry for all my sins. O Merciful Love, I ask pardon for the sins of the world.

"United with the Immaculate Heart of Our Heavenly Mother, I ask pardon for all my sins and for all the sins of my brothers and sisters that have been and will be committed until the end of the world.

"My dear Jesus, united with Your Holy Wounds I offer my life to the Eternal Father according to the intention of the Sorrowful Mother.

"Virgin Mary, Queen of the World, Mediatrix of Humanity, our only refuge and hope, pray for us!"

(3) Prayer of the Sick - (Recommended by Our Lady.)

Prayer: "My Jesus, I know that You love me, and You love particularly those who are sick or suffering. I ask if it is possible to take away this chalice of suffering, but I say with You 'not my will but Thine be done,' as You said in the Garden of Gethsemane. My Jesus, strengthen and console me. Our Heavenly Mother, healer of the sick, pray for me to Your Holy Son. Amen."

(4) On August 14, 1981 Jesus taught the seer this:

Prayer: "Your warmest prayer should be: 'Come Holy Spirit, prepare the hearts for the coming reign of the two most Holy Hearts, inflamed with love, all over the world.'"

XIII Special Devotion Given to the Seer(s)

The primary mission given to the seer by Jesus and also by Mary: **Text of the Life Offering (1955)**

"My dear Jesus, before the Trinity, Our Heavenly Mother, and the whole Heavenly Court, united with Your most Precious Sacred Blood and Your sacrifice on Calvary, I hereby offer my whole life for the intention of Your Sacred Heart and of the Immaculate Heart of Mary. Together with my life I place at Your disposal all Holy Masses, all my Holy Communions, all my good deeds, all my sacrifices, and the sufferings of my entire life for the adoration and supplication of the Holy Trinity, for unity in Our Holy Mother Church, for the Holy Father and for the priests, for good priestly vocations, and for all souls until the end of the world.

"O my Jesus, please accept my life sacrifice and my offerings and give me Your grace that I may persevere obediently until my death. Amen."

This life offering must be made with humble heart, firm resolution, and clear intent. All prayer, good deeds, suffering, and work done with

Budapest, Hungary

pure intention have great merit, if they are offered together with the merits, the sufferings, and the blood of Jesus Christ.

It is recommended that you make this life offering as soon as you feel ready, and renew it from time to time.

"You can pray for your own earthly well-being or other intentions on First Fridays and First Saturdays. I would like to ask that you extend the nine occasions to eleven. For your own petition say a rosary and the Litany of the Most Sacred Heart of Jesus on First Fridays, and on First Saturdays also a rosary and the Litany of Loreto; but always, when you petition for something for yourself: Not my will, O Lord, but Thine be done! My life-offering children can also offer up the Mass with My priests. The wisdom of the Church prevails in the Mass when the priest remembers in prayer all the living and the dead."

XIV Requests Made by Our Lady

(1) Our Lady implores those who receive Holy Communion daily, or at least weekly, to offer their lives for the greater Glory of God and the salvation of souls; that is to make the 'Life Offering'.

(2) On February 17, 1987 Our Lady said: *"Visit My shrines often. My shrines should be the meeting places for My life-sacrificing children, and for all those who still have a living faith."*

(3) On November 22, 1987 Our Lady asked us: *"Greet each other thus: 'The flaming love of the Hearts of Jesus and Mary be in our hearts forever and ever. Amen.'"*

(4) On January 11, 1988 Our Lady requested that Her life-offering children sacrifice for the three following holy intentions:

1) For: adoration and consolation of the Holy Trinity, all the ingratitude, the many profanities, and the great multitude of sins of the world. 2) For unity. 3) For our fallen and faithless human brothers and sisters.

XV Specific Bible References

(1) I Corinthians 2:9
(2) John 19:30
(3) John 14:2
(4) John 17:21
(5) Matthew 16:26

XVI Secrets Given to the Seer(s) - Not Reported
XVII Miracles Promised by Our Lady - NR
XVIII Miracles Performed - Not Reported

XIX Miracles Promised not yet Performed - NR
XX Signs Promised - Not Reported
XXI Signs Given - Not Reported

XXII Predictions/Promises

Mary, Our Heavenly Mother, implores those who receive Holy Communion daily, or at least weekly, to offer their lives for the greater glory of God and the salvation of souls, that the souls of sinners may not be damned but receive, at least in their last hour, the graces of eternal life.

The five promises of our Heavenly Mother to those who offer their lives to Her:

1) Their names will be written in the Hearts of Jesus and Mary, inflamed by love.

2) Their life offering, together with the infinite merits of Jesus, can save many souls from damnation. All souls who will live until the end of the world will benefit from their life offering.

3) None of their family members will go to hell, even if it seems otherwise, because they will receive deep in their souls the grace of sincere contrition before the soul departs from their bodies.

4) On the day they offer their lives, their loved ones suffering in purgatory will be released.

5) I will be with them at the hour of their death. They will not know purgatory. I will carry their souls straight to the presence of the Glorious Trinity, where they will live with Me in a special place created by God and will rejoice forever.

XXIII Prophecies/Warnings of Chastisement - NR
XXIV Method of Appearance - Not Reported
XXV Method of Departure - Not Reported
XXVI Confrontation w/Civil Authorities - NR
XXVII Confrontation w/Church Authorities - NR
XXVIII Request Chapel/Shrine Built - NR

XXIX Free Will/Choice

(1) On October 27, 1987 Our Lady told the seer: *"Say always when you petition for something for yourself: Not my will, O Lord, but Thine be done."*

(2) The invitation to make the 'Life Offering', as requested by Jesus and Mary, clearly indicates that we have the freedom to choose to make this 'Life Offering'. Our Lady said that the 'Life Offering' must be made with humble heart, firm resolution, and clear intent.

XXX Seer(s)' Suffering/Sacrifice

The mission given to the seer to promote the 'Life Offering' apostolate is based on sacrifice and suffering with love. No doubt the hidden seer suffers daily for sinners in conformity with her own 'Life Offering'.

XXXI Healings Reported

The message is replete with words from Our Lady that by sacrifice with love for others we can, and do, convert other souls, thus affecting spiritual healings.

XXXII Action Taken by the Church

Not much is reported regarding action taken by the Church. However it is reported that the local bishop who supplied the Imprimatur to the booklet entitled: 'Life Offering', himself made his own 'Life Offering' as requested by Our Lady.

XXXIII Bibliography

Life Offering, to the Sacred Heart of Jesus, through the Immaculate Heart of Mary   1990
By: Sister Dolores (Diary)
Published by: Two Hearts Books and Publishers

Chapter 23

EISENBERG, AUSTRIA
(1955-1982)

I Place - Eisenberg, Austria

II Dates of First and Last Apparition

First: October 13, 1955
Last: December 22, 1982

III Seer(s) - 2

Name: Aloisia Lex
Birth: June 19, 1907
Age at first apparition: 48
Status: Deceased: December 28, 1984

Name: Anne Marie Lex (Aloisia's daughter)
Birth: Unknown
Age at first apparition: 6½
Status: Unknown

IV Total Number of Apparitions - 13

V Dates and Locality of Each Apparition

All apparitions occurred inside the seer's home or at the site of the "Grass Cross."

1955: October 13, another undated.
1956: September 6.
1965: May 27, May 30.
1968: Undated, another undated.
1969: February 12.
1971: December 7.
1975: December 22.
1982: December 22.
About 20 years after first apparition; one undated.

VI Description of Our Lady

(1) Our Lady appeared as Our Lady of the Rosary dressed all in snow white, with a golden belt and with a beautiful long rosary.

(2) The seer's daughter Annemarie, who also claims to have seen Our Blessed Mother in 1954 described Our Lady the same way.

VII Title(s) of Our Lady - 4

(1) On December 22, 1975 She appeared as Our Lady of the Rosary.

(2) On February 12, 1969 Our Lady told the seer *". . . I want to be known as the Mother of Mercy and Help of Christians, and be honored through the praying of the rosary and be known as the Queen of the Holy Rosary."*

VIII Brief Factual Review

Austria is located in South Central Europe with its southern border on Italy and the Balkan states, and adjoining Germany and Czechoslovakia to the North.

Aloisia Lex was born on June 19, 1907. She was 48 when these apparitions commenced in 1955. Aloisia was married to a farmer and was the mother of 11 children. She had been sick, confined to bed and unable to attend Mass at church for most of the 10 year period, since about 1945. Aloisia received her first apparition from the Blessed Virgin Mary in 1955.

However, prior to that date Our Lady already appeared to have designs on the Lex family. In 1947, Aloisia's father saw a white female figure covered by a veil at the same location where the Cross in the Grass was later to appear in 1956. As he came closer the figure disappeared. He reportedly was an upright, truthful and hard working man. He often spoke of this experience and said he did not understand. In 1948 he died.

All was forgotten until in 1954, when the youngest daughter, Annemarie had an experience. Annemarie was just 6½ at this time. It was September 8, 1954 (the calendered birth day of Our Blessed Mother), school had just begun, when little Annemarie announced to her mother that the "Heavenly Father" appeared to her last night all dressed in white, with a long rosary. The child did not know the difference between Our Lady and the Heavenly Father. Her mother dismissed this as the child's imagination. However later that same day Annemarie was playing with other children in the yard when they all heard what sounded like a big approaching storm, with blustering and whistling wind. The chickens were disturbed and formed into a circle. Then a big silver ball descended from the sky and suddenly Our Blessed Mother (called the Heavenly Father by Annemarie) was standing there at the same spot where the Cross was later to appear. Annemarie described Our Lady as being snow white, with a golden belt, with a long rosary. The rosary had a big cross with Jesus on the cross "full of blood." The child was frightened and felt shaky and cried. When she told her family of the vision in the garden, they would not believe her and scoffed at her. Her own brothers and sisters hit her. Annemarie showed her mother the exact spot of the vision. Everyone at school made fun of Annemarie. They thought she was crazy and laughed at her. They ridiculed her. Little Annemarie suffered a lot. These attacks lasted for five to six weeks.

Sometime later, after the Cross appeared in the Grass in 1956, Annemarie became sick with mumps and had a fever of 104 degrees Fahrenheit. The Blessed Virgin again appeared to Annemarie and said that She was going to take Annemarie with Her. Annemarie was frightened, and said: "No, no I don't want to die, no, no!" Aloisia was upset and decided to wrap Annemarie in blankets and take her outside to the Cross on the Grass because maybe our Blessed Mother would make her child well. Women from the village came running wondering what was happening. The Grass Cross elevated above the ground before their very eyes and was suspended in air. It seemed certain that Our Lady was there, and Annemarie was healthy again.

Although Aloisia had been sick and confined to bed since 1945, she was able more recently to get up and walk short distances with the help of a cane. Thus on October 13, 1955 Aloisia walked through the garden towards the pigs' barn accompanied by her dog. Suddenly she saw a white figure in the garden at the same place where Annemarie had earlier seen it. Aloisia reports that she saw rays of light come from the figure, but she didn't have the courage to go closer to the figure, then it was gone.

Just as had happened with Annemarie before, Aloisia's own family refused to believe her, the townspeople scorned the entire family and ridiculed them. Little Annemarie often told her mother: "See, they don't believe you either." In desperation Aloisia begged Our Blessed Mother for a sign so people would believe her. Aloisia attached a small picture of Our Lady to the pear tree in the garden.

It was nearly one year later when an amazing sign did appear in the garden at Aloisia's home. It was a Cross in the Grass in the garden. This Cross remains today in spite of numerous efforts to eradicate it. On September 6, 1956 (as on every September 6th), the parish celebrated Adoration Day at the church. It was always festive with priests from neighboring parishes participating. Aloisia had been unable to attend these services for several years due to her illness consisting of paralysis of her left side. She lay in bed and prayed and prayed. She was depressed. When she cried out and pleaded with God to let her go to church one more time on Adoration Day, suddenly a wooden cross with the corpus appeared in front of her bed. Aloisia was frightened. She looked at Jesus on the Cross, who then began to increase in size until He was a normal size person with His feet on the floor. Aloisia relates that she thought she had died. She looked into His face and He opened His eyes wide and smiled warmly at Aloisia. She was instantly healed, and relates she had seen the glory of God and was now a changed person. Then Aloisia asked Jesus to please forgive all her sins. Jesus spoke these words: *"Your sins are forgiven you, your family's and your deceased parents."* Then Jesus returned to His normal size on the cross, and the cross disappeared. Now she felt no pain whatsoever. All was healed. Aloisia felt great joy because she now was healed and could attend the Adoration Day services at church. On the way to church she met neighbors who were surprised and alarmed to see her up and around and going to church. She reports that she had such devotion and was so captivated by prayer that day that she did not want to leave the church. She stayed late after Mass and the Cross appeared to her again during Mass. She was awestruck yet puzzled. What happened to her this day was that she was totally healed of all infirmity and pain and felt she was not the same person as before.

When she returned home her family was upset, so she fixed lunch quickly and went out to feed the swine. As she went to the garden to gather some sweet turnips she was shocked to find a large yellowish brown Cross imprinted in the grass at the exact place where the Blessed Virgin had appeared to her and to Annemarie. She thought to herself this may be the sign she prayed for God to send. The distinctive shape of the Cross was withered grass, yet all the grass around it remained green. The Cross remains in this condition today. When she revealed the appearance of the Cross to her family they yelled at her and told her that now they would never have peace in their home. Again people laughed at her and made sport of it all. Some people even made crosses by their house the next day in mockery. Of course the children went to school and told all about the Cross in the Grass.

The school inspectors, Neuherz and Heissenberger, came with all the school staff to inspect the phenomenon. Inspector Neuherz suddenly appeared very pale, and then he asked Aloisia if she had seen the three bolts of lightening that just then struck the Cross. He had been skeptical but now he placed his hands on the grass burned by the lightening and said he was convinced of the truth of the Cross. He has always stood by his conviction.

Though it had been raining earlier, by September 14, 1956 the grass had completely dried. The Cross was cordoned off and policemen held 24 hour watch. It was also on September 14th, the Feast of the Triumph of the Holy Cross, that the authorities had all the grass under the Cross uprooted and laid out on the lawn, all in one piece. Aloisia reports that not one little spot was damaged on the Grass Cross. It was beautiful with roots intertwined like angel hair, yellow and clean. It would have been possible to lift the entire Grass Cross in one piece. People took part of the grass from the cross. The cross stayed open this way for three to four weeks, during which time none of the animals in the garden would step on the Cross, neither cows, nor chickens.

After four weeks the monsignor came to inspect the Cross. He had enclosed the area around the Cross with fine wire and covered it for protection. He locked the enclosure and kept the key to himself.

For about one year the grass grew around the Cross, but under the Cross no weeds or grass grew. It was barren.

After another year moss started to grow on the Cross. This moss covered the Cross for seven or eight years. Then someone poured weed-killer over the moss and burned it. The Cross looked devastated.

The following year daises started to grow over the whole garden, except on the Cross. It looked so striking; however, on October 31st someone again poured weed-killer on the Cross and on the daises. All the flowers died. This same activity was repeated the following year. Now the Cross was wasted with cracks and burned on the edges. The Cross was still very distinctive but desolate which made Aloisia cry.

Our Blessed Mother appeared to Aloisia and told her that this is what the world would look like after the Chastisement. All devastated and burned.

A year later moss started to grow in the Cross again. Only this time it was not real moss, and neither was it grass. It had little buds on the moss that seemed to want to start blooming. It was at this time that miracles, signs and wonders and conversions began to occur.

On March 19, 1968, St Joseph's Feast Day, the first 'Miracle of the Sun' happened. Fr. Lagler, the local parish priest, was there to witness this event, as were several hundred people. The sun became very big in the sky and swung back and forth in all colors. It looked like it would fall onto the crowd. The rays from the sun came down upon the Lawn Cross in all colors. People fell to their knees, many saw apparitions, Hosts, Chalices, and Monstrances. Others saw the head of Jesus crowned with thorns. Fr. Lagler saw a sword come down from the sky. These events have all been recorded.

Many miraculous physical healings and conversions are reported from 1968 onward. Whole families were converted on the spot after an encounter with the Lawn Cross. One person named Fuchs from Leutersdorf returned to the Sacraments and to the Church after 40 long, dry years. During one year alone 30 healings were recorded. And the miraculous healings and conversions are still going on.

Aloisia would tell the pilgrims who came for a healing to have great faith when praying and begging a healing from God.

Experts from the University of Vienna have examined the Cross and declared it to be an unexplainable phenomenon.

Sometime during 1968 Our Blessed Mother again appeared to the seer. Aloisia and some pilgrims had prayed for a long time hoping a 'Spring' with water would be found near the Cross. Suddenly Our Lady appeared and told the seer She would answer the prayer, that a small Spring will come forth near the Cross. Our Lady told Aloisia to wait, there would be a wet spot and then the water would spring out. On the third day it happened just as Our Lady said. They dug a hole about 1 meter deep which produced plenty of water for people to take home with them. All went well for two to three weeks, when two men were mocking the Spring and asked to dig the hole larger. As these two men began to dig the hole larger, the water stopped.

Our Lady again appeared to the seer and told Aloisia that the reason She stopped the Spring was that these two men were intent on poisoning the Spring. Then Our Lady, told the seer that there is enough healing water in the house from the tap, because that water comes from the same source, and flows through the Cross.

Again what Our Lady said turned out to be true. Soon miraculous healings occurred from water taken from the faucet inside the seer's home. Of course many people ridiculed the seer. Yet hundreds of healings are recorded using this tap water. Soon signs began to appear in the ice when the water was frozen. Even Fr. Lagler had made some joking remarks about tap water healing. Yet when he was gravely ill some people brought him frozen water from the faucet. There in the ice was a beautiful image of Our Blessed Virgin Mary. He was completely healed.

This tap water can be rubbed on the skin, used as ice packs, even drinking the water is recommended. It is reported that hundreds of healings have occurred; from ailments of the feet to cancer, and doctors have attested to these healings.

Aloisia always reminded everyone to thank God and Our Lady for healings received. She said that Our Lady especially requested that people give thanks and spread the healing news.

Jesus also appeared to this seer on more than one occasion and also gave messages to the seer. Jesus warned of dire consequences if mankind doesn't follow His holy instructions. Once He said in part: *". . . The earth will be barren. A tremendous sadness will befall on man. Heaven mourns with you . . ."*

Our Lady told this seer that the catastrophes are the beginning of the judgment. Everyone should be prepared. It was at this point that Our Lady gave the seer a secret to keep for now. This secret is not reported to have been revealed.

On December 22nd Our Lady appeared as Our Lady of the Rosary and called for prayer, sacrifice and penance, as She had requested at Fatima. However, Our Lady said: *"Before I said it was time, now I say it is high time. . ."*

During this same apparition Our Lady said that preparation for the destruction of the world was in high gear. Our Lady then announced the 'Big Storm of Prayer'. She said that only one thing can save the world and that is the Big Storm of Prayer. It had to be done in all the churches and prayer houses, and had to be announced by, and led by the priests. Only in this way could the worst be averted. Then Our Lady said if the will of God is not fulfilled again, then She could not help, which makes Her very sad. Our Lady said: *"If I cannot speak anymore, I will still be able to cry."* She also promised to *"Give signs to My select. . ."*

Our Lady's messages call for prayer, sacrifice and penance for atonement, begging for conversion, that we pray for the conversion of Russia, for peace in the world, for conversion of sinners, and for saving souls. Our Lady warned that humanity and the Church must meet a 'great Good Friday'; mass destruction of humanity and mass starvation. But She reassures us when She pronounces: *"But you My small flock, My select who pray the rosary daily and entrust themselves to Me and trust in Heavenly protection, have nothing to fear, whatever may come."*

Thus Our Lady said: *"Pray, pray, pray without ceasing."* (She needs our prayers.) *"The end battle will soon fall with the power of darkness. But you should not be afraid, for after each Good Friday follows a shining Easter Morning. The Easter Morning on which My Immaculate Heart will triumph, and the Cross of Truth will be victorious. The Cross will appear in the sky."*

Aloisia had many visions of crosses appearing in the sky. One such vision occurred on Ascension Day in the 1960's when it was shown to her by Our Lady that those who have always venerated the Cross will fall on their knees and look up to heaven with folded hands when the Cross appears in the sky. For these it will bring salvation, protection and blessing. For others who reject the Cross of Christ, it will bring tragedy, death and destruction.

It appears that this seer was requested to warn the world and the Church of impending punishment if God's will isn't followed and if these messages are not heeded. As proof of her mission a visible sign of the Cross was placed in the garden of this seer's home.

Jesus Himself on June 10, 1965 told Aloisia that: *". . . I, Christ your Lord shall reveal Myself, My Truth and My Justice to the world through visible miraculous signs and through catastrophic consequences of My Divine Power and the power of the forces of nature to give witness Myself to the truth and authenticity of this sign, and of the truth of My words, requests and warnings . . . "*

On February 12, 1969 Our Blessed Mother again appeared to this seer after Holy Mass inside the church. Suddenly the statute of Our Lady of Lourdes seemed to come alive and speak. Our Lady said that through Her power and the graces and the blessings of God, Her Immaculate Heart will triumph; and at the end the Cross and the Truth over the enemies of God will be triumphant, as it was with the Cross at Golgotha. This will occur when a Cross of Light appears in glory in the sky to give credence to the Holy Cross on the ground, then the Holy Spirit will renew the earth, which will be holy and blessed again, and will be prepared for the return of Christ.

Our Lady went on to say that God wants His Holy Church to be cleansed and sanctified again. The Church is in the fight for its life or death in the modern world, and many priests have fallen into lethargy, through confusion in this modern world. The leaders of the Church are faced with a serious decision. Either the Church becomes holy again or it is doomed to self-destruction. The Blessed Mother wishes that the Holy Father, with all the bishops, decide to eradicate the confusion out of the modern Church and all unite in the unity of the Holy Spirit. Our Lady exhorts us to pray, pray much for priests.

During this same apparition Our Lady also said: *"Much has been neglected. Only through prayer, sacrifice, repentance and reparation can the punishment be mitigated. With much prayer the sudden fall of these punishments can be postponed, but they cannot be completely prevented."*

Our Lady also said that the powers of the adversary in the world increases constantly. But She also said She will not abandon Her faithful children, that Her heavenly legions of angels stand prepared at all times to defend against the power of unholiness, unbelieving and the lie. Satan knows the enormity of what is at stake, that is why he fights to subdue the truth of the sign of the Cross on the ground and to undermine it. Then Our Lady assures us that She: *"will spread the mantle of My mighty protection over My children."*

Our Lady also told this seer that because many priests and lay people alike no longer believe in the Real Presence of Jesus in the Eucharist, that God reveals Christ visibly in the Host to an unbelieving world, so that they may believe.

On June 10, 1965 Jesus revealed to this seer 'His Last Offer of Love and Mercy', as reported. Priests and all the people must be prepared to submit to the Divine Will, recognize and glorify "this Holy Place," that is the Cross on the Lawn, through prayer, processions, and hymns of praise to implore heaven through this sign of the Cross, to make reparation to heaven in order to implore God for an extension of His days of grace.

On May 30, 1965 while Aloisia was at the Cross on the ground, Satan spoke to her, bragging that everything was proceeding according to his plan and that "... *daily I am taking my victims off the streets."*

Pastor Kroboth gave a memorial speech on December 31, 1984 eulogizing Aloisia Lex. He said her life was happy but filled with much work, concerns, suffering, prayers and sacrifices. She had much to suffer; it seemed her Good Friday never ended. She knew the Christian value of suffering and offered all her sacrifices and sufferings up for the conversion of sinners. She was a simple and humble woman who radiated goodness and calmness. A few days earlier, on December 24th, Fr. Kroboth brought her Holy Communion. She was happy and very thankful and full of adoration. Pastor Kroboth was impressed with Aloisia's special reverence for priests and for the priesthood. On December 24th they spoke of religious matters and Aloisia said that we have to stand faithfully by the Pope and the Church. This was the last discussion they had together before Aloisia died on December 28, 1984.

No official Church action is reported. There is no prohibition to visit the Lawn Cross or to pray there. Healings are constantly reported to the Chancery.

IX The Primary Messages - 6

(1) Prayer
(2) Rosary
(3) Sacrifice, Repentance and Reparation
(4) Penance
(5) Adoration of the Blessed Sacrament
(6) Suffering Church and Clergy

(1) Prayer - February 12, 1969 Our Lady said in part: *"... Without the recognition and glorification of the sign of the Holy Cross and without humility, prayer and penance, no one is worthy to believe in the authenticity of the occurrence..."*

Again: *"Much has been neglected. Only through prayer, sacrifice, repentance and reparation can the punishment be mitigated."*

Later, Our Lady said: *"Pray, pray much for priests. Pray that those priests who fall into confusion through the modern unChristian spirit, will be enlightened."*

Again Our Lady speaks: *"Pray also much for the poor souls, so many are forgotten by their relatives. You cannot get tired. I will send the heavenly assembly of angels to strengthen you in your prayers and to pray with you."*

It was also on February 12, 1969 that Our Lady pleaded for a strong wall of prayer. Our Lady speaks: *"I need a strong wall of prayer from the devout and faithful, prayers, with the rosary, in a storm of prayers to withstand the attack of the enemy of God and the haters of God, that at least those countries will be saved which are as yet free of communism — the enemy fights as never before to ruin the faith of mankind in God, and thereby to put Christian churches in danger, especially the Catholic Church, and the priests will have much to suffer under pressure from the godless communism."*

On December 22, 1975 the seer reports that Our Lady appeared as Our Lady of the Rosary. She said: *"Don't be afraid. I came to fulfill My promise. Do you remember the things I told you before?"* Our Lady then called for the same thing She asked for at Fatima, that is: prayer, sacrifice and penance. Then the seer reports: "Before Our Lady said: *'it is time'*; now She says *'It is high time'*."

Our Lady also told the seer that we are to pray for the conversion of Russia, for peace in the world, for conversion of sinners and for saving souls.

(2) Rosary - Firstly, Our Blessed Mother always appeared with a long rosary, and She specifically appeared as Our Lady of the Rosary on December 22, 1975. Thus giving ample assurance of Her desire that we pray the holy rosary.

February 12, 1969, Our Lady speaks: *". . . If, through meditation during the rosary, you honor My Immaculate Heart and therewith the Name of Jesus and the Sacred Heart of Jesus as being glorified, God's wrath is being averted. . . "*

Again, *"Pray much the rosary for the conversion of sinners and the unity in the Church and for peace in the world."*

Also on February 12, 1969 Our Lady said: *"If everyone who has not been praying the rosary would pick it up and start praying now, the danger could be partially prevented."*

Again: *". . . I want to be known as the Mother of Mercy and Help of Christians and be honored through praying of the rosary and be known as the Queen of the Holy Rosary.*

(3) Sacrifice, Repentance and Reparation - February 12, 1969: *"Only through prayer, sacrifice, repentance, and reparation can the punishment be mitigated."*

Later Our Lady also said: *"The sign of the Holy Cross on the ground and the powerful Miracle of the Sun — shall let the world and all mankind know that we are close to catastrophic times, which cannot be prevented if you don't do what I demand, and obey My urgent appeal for processions, prayer, penance, sacrifice and reparations. . . ."*

(4) Penance - February, 1969 Our Lady said in part: *"Be watchful and do penance! This danger can come upon you suddenly and overnight."*

On December 22, 1975 Our Lady recalled the Fatima message for prayer, sacrifice and penance. Later Our Blessed Mother told the seer that: *". . . through prayer, sacrifice and penance for atonement, and begging for forgiveness the affronts to God could be forgiven . . ."*

(5) Adoration of the Blessed Sacrament - February 12, 1969 Our Lady speaks: *". . . They should in special humility and veneration of the Blessed Sacrament of the Altar subject themselves humbly through My earnest warnings, to the Holy Will of God."*

Again: *"If the presence of Christ in the Holy Eucharist is thought little of, it will result in a weakened effect of the grace and blessing powers . . .the fruit of this is that people will go less and less to church and the Sacraments, because they lost faith in the presence of Jesus in the Eucharist."*

Our Blessed Mother adds: *"To prevent this, and a sign for all, Jesus shows His countenance visible in the Host. It is sad and grievous that God has to reveal Christ visibly to the unbelieving world. Therefore, the powerful sign of the visible countenance of Christ in the Host has to be especially watched, so that the faithful will believe in the presence of Christ in the Holy Eucharist of the Altar, and to practice humble reception of Holy Communion and Christ the Lord in the Sacrament of the Altar, out of love and thankfulness, be more and more venerated and glorified."*

(6) Suffering Church and Clergy - February 12, 1969 Our Lady speaks: *"God wants that His Holy Church will be cleansed and sanctified again—the unclean spirit has to be eliminated in the Church again, so that the graces of the Holy Spirit can once again work in the Church. The Church is in a fight of life and death; either the Church has to return to being a Holy Church, or it will, with the satanic plan of confusion, become unholy and unworthy and unity cannot be sustained. The leaders of the Church are faced with a serious decision."*

Then Our Blessed Mother adds: *"Pray that those priests who fall into confusion through the modern unChristian spirit, will be enlightened. I greet the bishops and priests and the entire people of God in the name of Jesus, that they will fulfill My intentions . . ."*

X Signs Preceding the Apparitions

No consistent sign precedes the apparitions although different signs were given just prior to some of the apparitions.

XI Other Visions During Apparitions

(1) Jesus appeared to this seer several times and gave messages to her.
(2) Satan spoke to Aloisia once while she was at the Cross in the Grass.
(3) This seer had many visions, some of which were during, or at the end, of the apparition. Especially she had many visions of the cross in the sky and also of the great purification.

XII Prayers Taught to the Seer(s)

Our Lady had requested a strong wall of prayer. Further a Prayer of the Holy Cross on the Ground and a meditation of the Holy Cross Rosary is reported. However, it is not clear from the reports whether these prayers are the seer's own meditations or given to the seer by Our Lady.

In either event they are spiritually uplifting:

(1) Prayer to the Holy Cross on the Ground

Prayer: Crucified Jesus! Through the place of graces at the site of the Lawn Cross, You have, oh Crucified Lord, brought to the attention of mankind Your terrible suffering and dying on the cross again.

We thank You from the bottom of our hearts for the place of graces at the site of the Lawn Cross, with what great Love You want to save mankind. With this place of graces of the Lawn Cross You put in the hands of humanity, which is blinded by sin, and in pride ignores Your work of redemption, a new saving anchor.

We pray that from this holy place many graces will flow forward into the hearts of people, that they will find their way to You, the Crucified, who is alone our salvation. We offer to You, Heavenly Father, the wounds, the painful sufferings, the precious blood, and the whole work of salvation of Our Lord Jesus Christ to You, to heal the woundedness of the souls of all people.   Amen.

(2) Holy-Cross Rosary - 1.) Apostles Creed 2.) Glory Be 3.) 3 Hail Mary's 4.) Glory Be

First Decade: Through the nailing of the right hand to the cross, under excruciating pain, Our Lord Jesus Christ spilled His most precious blood for us. (Meditate on this suffering)

  10x - Through Your Holy Cross grant us Mercy, Lord Jesus Christ.
   1x - Glory Be.
   1x - Holy Mary, Mother of Mercy, pray for us.
   1x - Holy Archangel Michael, pray for us.
   1x - Holy Archangel Raphael, pray for us.

Second Decade: Through the nailing of the left hand to the cross, under excruciating pain, Our Lord Jesus Christ spilled His most precious blood for us. (Meditate on this suffering)

  10x - Through Your Holy Cross grant us Mercy, Lord Jesus Christ.
   1x - Glory Be.

1x - Holy Mary, Mother of Mercy, pray for us.
1x - Holy Archangel Michael, pray for us.
1x - Holy Archangel Raphael, pray for us.

Third Decade: Through the nailing of the right foot to the cross, under excruciating pain, Our Lord Jesus Christ spilled His most precious blood for us. (Meditate on this suffering)

10x - Through Your Holy Cross grant us Mercy, Lord Jesus Christ.
1x - Glory Be
1x - Holy Mary, Mother of Mercy, pray for us.
1x - Holy Archangel Michael, pray for us.
1x - Holy Archangel Raphael, pray for us.

Fourth Decade: Through the nailing of the left foot to the cross, under excruciating pain, Our Lord Jesus Christ spilled His most precious blood for us. (Meditate on this suffering)

10x - Through Your Holy Cross grant us Mercy, Lord Jesus Christ.
1x - Glory Be.
1x - Holy Mary, Mother of Mercy, pray for us.
1x - Holy Archangel Michael, pray for us.
1x - Holy Archangel Raphael, pray for us.

Fifth Decade: Through the piercing of the right side and the Sacred Heart of Our Lord Jesus Christ, while hanging on the cross, all sins of this world were expiated and redeemed. (Meditate on this suffering)

10x - Through Your Holy Cross grant us Mercy, Lord Jesus Christ.
1x - Glory Be.
1x - Holy Mary, Mother of Mercy, pray for us.
1x - Holy Archangel Michael, pray for us.
1x - Holy Archangel Raphael, pray for us.

Prayer: You gave us, O Lord, in the Holy Cross a visible pledge of Your great Mercy, Graces, and Love. We beg of You: Help that we, through the intercession of the Mother of Mercy, seize this remedy of salvation and love, so that we might stay to Your right on judgment day.

XIII Special Devotion Given to the Seer(s)

Although not necessarily a devotion Our Lady did especially request a 'Big Storm of Prayer'. This was to be done by all the churches and prayer houses, it had to be announced by the priests. Priests had to lead the prayer and the people had to be appealed to for the Storm of Prayer. Only by this means could the worst be prevented.

XIV Requests Made by Our Lady

(1) Our Lady requested a 'Big Storm of Prayer'.
(2) Our Lady also requested processions in addition to prayer and sacrifice.

XV Specific Bible References - Not Reported

XVI Secrets Given to the Seer(s)

It is reported that Our Lady told the seer of the coming catastrophes, and asked the seer to keep it a secret for now.

XVII Miracles Promised by Our Lady

In 1968 after Aloisia and some pilgrims prayed at the Grass Cross that a Spring may be found, Our Lady appeared and said She would answer this prayer. True to Her word, three days later a Spring appeared near the Grass Cross.

XVIII Miracles Performed

(1) Spring appeared and gushed forth water near the Grass Cross.
(2) On September 6, 1956 the Grass Cross miraculously appeared in the seer's garden. Considering all attempts to obliterate it, and that it survives today as it was from the beginning; this could be considered to be a true miracle.
(3) The 'Miracle of the Sun' is reported to have occurred.

XIX Miracles Promised not yet Performed - NR

XX Signs Promised

In 1968 Our Lady promised to answer Aloisia's prayer that a Spring would be found near the Grass Cross. The sign appeared as promised when the Spring was found three days later.

XXI Signs Given

(1) The greatest sign given was of course the appearance of the Grass Cross in Aloisia's garden on September 6, 1956.
(2) On St. Joseph's Day, March 19, 1968 the first 'Miracle of the Sun' was witnessed by many.
(3) The Spring with running water appeared near the Grass Cross, a promised by Our Lady.
(4) Signs appeared in the frozen water (ice) taken from the faucet inside the seer's home. Signs such as images of Our Blessed Lady would appear in the ice witnessed by many, including the parish priest.

(5) It is reported that Jesus' image was visibly revealed in the Sacred Host.
(6) The Grass Cross was elevated and suspended in air in the presence of witnesses. This occurred at the time when little Annemarie had a fever of 104 degrees Fahrenheit and was afraid she would die. Her health was immediately restored.

XXII Predictions/Promises

(1) Our Lady promised to answer Aloisia's prayer and have a Spring with flowing water appear near the Grass Cross. It happened just as Our Lady promised.
(2) Our Lady promised that She would bless the tap water inside Aloisia's home after two men tried to poison the Spring. Many signs appeared in this frozen water and miraculous healing were reported attributed to this tap water.
(3) Our Lady predicted that Her Immaculate Heart would triumph and She promised to protect under Her mantle all the faithful who pray the rosary daily and believe in Her messages and entrust themselves to Her Immaculate Heart and to heavenly protection. She said She will take care of them and take them under Her special protection.
(4) She also predicted that after the purification of the upcoming 'Good Friday', that on Easter morning Her Immaculate Heart would triumph and the truth and the Cross would be victors, and the Cross will appear in the sky.

XXIII Prophecies/Warnings of Chastisement

(1) There are reports of Our Blessed Mother warning the seer of great catastrophes and of the judgment. These events were so horrifying that Our Lady told Aloisia to keep it a secret for now.
(2) On December 7, 1971 Our Lady said: *"The last days of grace are running out and a terrible punishment is close."*
(3) On December 22, 1975 Our Lady warned that disobedience against the Holy Will of God will bring about terrible disasters. She also warned of "massive starvation" during this same message.
(4) On December 22, 1982 this was the last appearance of Our Lady, and She said: *"Have no fear I have come to keep My promise which I gave to you over 20 years ago, to tell you when it is time. It is now high time; the world faces catastrophe. The powers act of themselves as if there is no tomorrow. The superior forces of godless communism will invade the free nations when they least expect it, for it knows no frontiers. That invasion will start the great world catastrophe."*
(5) Jesus also warned of the coming chastisement. When on June 10,

1965 He announced: *"Dark and sad hours will come over the world and mankind, the earth will become infertile, barren and deserted, sun and moon will lose their light. A great darkness will one day, break over the world. Truly I say to you, I Christ your King, shall then pronounce judgment of the world and of mankind through the revelation of My Truth and Justice, through the Holy Sign of the Cross, and through the Divine punishment. The Divine punishment has begun with the aid of the power of the forces of nature—the disasters, so that all of you may recognize and believe what this Sign of the Cross means to the world and mankind."*

XXIV Method of Appearance - Not Reported
XXV Method of Departure - Not Reported

XXVI Confrontation w/Civil Authorities

There is no report of Confrontation w/Civil Authorities as such. The school inspectors did inspect the Cross and thereafter the Cross received official protection from police guards. Although the Cross was vandalized repeatedly, no report indicates that any official action caused these events.

XXVII Confrontation w/Church Authorities

Again no confrontation is reported—the monsignor is reported to have inspected the Cross and to have enclosed it with fine wire, and also covered it, and kept the key to himself.

XXVIII Request Chapel/Shrine Built - NR
XXIX Free Will/Choice - Not Reported

XXX Seer(s)' Suffering/Sacrifice

(1) Aloisia was disbelieved by her own family (as was Annemarie before her).
(2) Also the townspeople ridiculed the seer and her entire family. Some people even made crosses at their own houses, to jeer at the seer.
(3) When the water from the faucet was used (after the Spring was closed down) the people again ridiculed the seer.
(4) Pastor Kroboth of St. Martin's Church recognized that this soul suffered much during her lifetime, when he gave the memorial address after Aloisia's death. The good pastor said that as a faith-filled woman she knew the value of suffering, the Christian value of suffering, so she

offered all her sufferings and sacrifices up for the conversion of sinners. He went on to say that she didn't have physical suffering alone, but spiritual anguish also from many, many sides. He concluded by saying that "she went home from darkness to light, from suffering to happiness, from time to eternity, from death to life, to eternal life. We want to thank her for her prayers, for the suffering she offered for sinners."

XXXI Healings Reported

(1) The record is literally filled with reports of healings and conversions. Many of the healings have been recorded with the local church authorities. The healings are apparently ongoing.

(2) Aloisia herself was healed miraculously when Jesus came out from the cross at the foot of her bed to heal her, so that she could once again go to church for Adoration Day.

(3) Daughter Annemarie was also returned to health dramatically, when the Grass Cross was elevated and remained suspended in the air.

(4) The reports indicate that on St. Joseph's Feast Day, March 19, 1968 the miraculous healings exploded. This was the day when the people first witnessed the 'Miracle of the Sun'. Some of the reported healings included:

a) On Holy Thursday, 1968 a family named Putcher came and made sarcastic remarks about the Cross. Suddenly the two daughters collapsed, and went through some trying days. Shortly thereafter the entire family converted and afterward warned everyone never to make fun of the Cross as they had done.

b) Another report of a man who came cursing and hollering at the Cross resulted in an instant conversion. He too was suddenly struck unconscious and remained so for over one hour. When he awoke he said he could not tell anyone what God had revealed to him while he was out. He cried a lot; he shook all over and said he had been to the "other side." After he collected himself he went back to the Cross and began to cry. He was converted.

c) Fr. Lagler had been gravely ill. Some people brought ice from the tap water which Our Lady said was blessed, because it flowed under the Cross. The ice had a beautiful image of the Blessed Mother. Fr. Lagler was instantly and completed healed.

d) A Mrs. Bernauer from Germany was cured of paralysis.

e) Another person named Fuchs had severe asthma and had not been to church, Confession, or Communion for 40 years. He came to the Cross during Holy Week 1968 and was told to return. In May he returned with his entire family. During this visit the 'Miracle of the Sun' occurred again, and he fell to the ground confessing: "God, I have to believe now, if I want to or not." He then ran to the Cross and knelt down. He was converted and announced: "I am a new man!" From then on his life changed drastically and within two months his asthma suddenly left him.

f) Another amazing healing happened to Herr Lazer. He was dying from stomach cancer. The doctors had sent him home to die. His family brought him from the hospice to the Cross. Aloisia went to the Cross with him and "prayed, prayed for a long time." His pain increased steadily.

Then they brought him back at midnight and his family prayed with him. He drank of the water. The miracle happened the next day. When he got up he was completely healed; and he was hungry.

XXXII Action Taken by the Church - NR

XXXIII Bibliography

Batschaft an die Kirche und die Volker
(Message to the Church and the People)
By: (Translated)
Published by: Druck and Verlag

Mutter Lex Erzahlt (Mother Lex Relates)
By: Aloisia Lex (Translated)
Published by: Rasenkreuz-Pilgerverein

Chapter 24

TURZOVKA, CZECHOSLOVAKIA (1958)

I Place - Turzovka, Czechoslovakia
(on Mt Okrouhlo)

II Dates of First and Last Apparitions

First: June 1, 1958
Last: August 9, 1958

III Seer(s) - 1

Name: Matous Lasuta
Birth: April 10, 1916
Age at first apparition: 42
Status: Unknown

IV Total Number of Apparitions - 7

V Dates and Locality of Each Apparition

All apparitions occurred in Turzovka unless otherwise noted.

1958: June 1, 7, 21; July 1, 7, 21; August 9.

VI Description of Our Lady

A beautiful Lady appeared to the seer within a light floating on a cloud about three and a half meters above the ground. She was young, slim and of extraordinary height. Her expression was serious yet majestic and She was smiling. A rosary hung from Her left arm. Her face was oval and very white, Her eyes were azure blue, and chestnut hair peeked out from behind Her veil. She radiated grandeur and majesty. She was clad in a snow white dress with a blue girdle and Her hands were joined, just as Our Lady appeared at Lourdes. She was about 17 or 18, of heavenly beauty and taller than any human being. Matous immediately knew that She was the Blessed Virgin Mary.

VII Title(s) of Our Lady - 1

Because of the many signs and wonders that have occurred, this site has become known has the Lourdes of Czechoslovakia, and Our Lady of Turzovka.

VIII Brief Factual Review

The Village of Turzovka, Czechoslovakia is located in the mountainous part of Slovakia not far from the Polish border. In 1958 Czechoslovakia was a Soviet satellite of Moscow, behind the iron curtain. Czechoslovakia has since split into the two separate states of Czech and Slovakia.

A mountain called Okrouhlo, which means 'round mountain', is about two miles through the forest near Turzovka. On the very top of the round mountain stood a pine tree to which was fastened a little wooden shrine with a picture of Our Lady of Perpetual Help. The shrine had been on the pine tree for many years and was well known to all who lived in the region, and was referred to as 'U Obrozku' which means 'to the picture'.

Matous Lasuta was born April 10, 1916. He lost his mother when he was four years old. He became employed as a hand boy by a pious family. Next he entered the military service. After his service in the military, he was married. He and his wife had four daughters, one of whom died. Matous became a woodcutter, however, he was promoted to forester in 1956. The 'U Obrozku' was situated in his forestry district. During his regular rounds through the forest he never forgot to stop and pray at the shrine. He kept the little shrine adorned with flowers in season.

On June 1, 1958 the 100th anniversary of the apparitions of Our Lady at Lourdes, and on the Feast Day of the Most Holy Trinity, Our Heavenly Mother first appeared to Matous at 'U Obrozku'. This occurred at 9:00 AM. Matous had never learned to pray the rosary, however, he was on his knees before the holy picture of Our Lady praying, when he saw a flash of light and felt his head spinning, the trees disappeared and then he saw a beautiful rose garden.

The rose garden was round and surrounded by a little white fence, in the center the roses were taller and from the center streamed a light brighter than the sun. In this light and floating on a cloud about three and a half meters above the ground was a beautiful lady, young, slim and of extraordinary height. Her expression was serious yet majestic and She was smiling. A rosary hung from Her left arm. Her face was oval and very white, Her eyes were azure blue, and chestnut hair peeked out from behind Her veil. She radiated grandeur and majesty. She was clad in a snow white dress with a blue girdle and Her hands were joined, just as Our Lady appeared at Lourdes. She was about 17 or 18, of heavenly beauty and taller than any human being. Matous immediately knew that She was the Blessed Virgin Mary.

She pointed Her right index finger to the ground. Matous looked and saw three boards which had become detached from the white fence. He understood that he was to fix Her garden fence so he picked up a little hammer and nails and nailed the boards back on. She seemed pleased.

Then Our Lady shook the beautiful rosary beads She was holding while She looked at Matous. He was ashamed and embarrassed because he knew She was asking him to say the rosary, yet he did not know how to pray the rosary, nor did he even own a rosary.

Our Lady then signaled Matous to look in the direction of the pine; he looked and saw a tableaux showing the globe, then all the different countries on earth were displayed. Different colors now appeared on the map, some green and some yellow. The water was blue. An inscription explained that the green spots indicate countries where the population is good and the yellow spots denote countries marked for destruction owing to the bad behavior of the people. The high country is more green and the flat land is more yellow. Matous sees the yellow invading and covering more countries while the green is retreating. The message was that the world is getting worse and worse. Then an inscription emerged forming the words: *"Do penance."*

By and by the yellow color had invaded all lands. Then powerful explosions burst forth over the water and land. A dense rain of small leaves fall to earth, and upon reaching the ground, these turned into flames. Soon all the touched soil is covered with fire.

Matous sees this as a punishment by God. From the indications on the map, Matous can make out which countries will be destroyed and which ones will be protected under Mary's mantle. However the seer is not permitted to communicate these precisions to any person except to the Holy Father in Rome. Then once more Matous sees the words: *"Do penance."* It is made known to Matous that what he had seen, he is to tell the world.

Towards the end of this first apparition Our Lady pointed across the trees. Looking in that direction Matous sees heaven descending to earth, then the seer sees Our Saviour in splendor with the cross beside Him. From Our Lord's heart three arrows of light stream forth, the one in the middle penetrates Matous and he falls to the ground. Matous feels that Mary was telling him: *"If you carry out My order, you will go there (heaven)."*

When the seer fully comes to himself, the Mother of God had disappeared; but She had left the rosary on the grass, which She previously offered to him. Matous picked up the rosary and to his great surprise was able to say the rosary, including all the mysteries. He immediately said the five Glorious Mysteries, at which moment he heard the bells from the church at Vipaka announce The Angelus at noon. He now realized the apparition had lasted three hours.

Matous reviewed his life and decided to humble himself and personally ask forgiveness of all whom he had hurt. That very day he visited the people to ask forgiveness. This lasted till midnight and the people he visited thought he was crazy. He did not want to have anything on his heart before he received Jesus in the Eucharist.

After this first apparition Matous received six additional apparitions. In each of the seven apparitions, Matous was given the message pictorially, and each time the subject matter was different.

On June 7, 1958 Matous received the second apparition and was given the message of the horrible spectacle of the sins of mankind.

Then on June 27, 1958 he was made to see the punishment that will strike the world if mankind does not return to God.

During the apparition of July 1, 1958 Our Lady showed Matous how the chastisement could be avoided or made lighter through prayer, the rosary and penance. Prayer can hold off the justice of God but such prayer must come from the heart, not proceed only from the intellect.

The features of the last three apparitions remain Matous' secret. These have not been revealed.

For several weeks after the apparitions Matous remained silent. He changed. He attended daily Mass. However the happenings leaked out and Matous was urged to tell all to the people.

On Sunday September 8, 1958 Feast of the Nativity of Mary, he went for the first time with a group of people to the place of the apparitions; to pray. After they finished praying Matous told the people: "In three days I will leave you."

In fact on the next Wednesday Matous was arrested and placed in jail. The rosary which Matous received from Our Blessed Virgin, and which he had always kept around his neck, disappeared mysteriously at the moment he was arrested. He was submitted to several trials in court. The judge offered to release Matous and to promote him and give him a raise in salary if he would only admit that he fell asleep and had a dream about Our Lady; but did not have an apparition. Matous asked the judge if he could renounce his own mother. Of course when the judge said he could not, Matous said neither could he renounce his own Heavenly Mother. As a result of this trial Matous was declared insane and confined to a mental institution. When he was released after ten months he was discharged from his job and lost all his rights.

The Church was suppressed in Czechoslovakia. The communist controlled government and Masonic influences were reportedly doing all in their power to make the memory of Our Lady of Turzovka "go away."

The communists became more aggressive in their efforts to stop devotion to Our Lady and also to prevent people from going to the place of the apparitions. The communist authorities had the pine tree cut down. They prohibited vehicle traffic to the site of the apparitions, but nevertheless more and more people kept coming up the mountain to pray and show their devotion to Our Lady of Turzovka.

The pilgrims who had received physical and spiritual health, in their gratitude, had erected little altars, crosses and statues on the mountainside. From the very wood of the pine tree which had been cut down, the villagers made a cross which was erected on the exact spot where the pine tree had stood. On 36 separate occasions since 1958 the communists broke down the altars, statues, crosses and candles that covered the mountainside at the apparition site. Still people from all over kept coming to Turzovka.

One year after Matous was released from the mental institution, he was rearrested and sentenced to three years in prison. After his release from prison, and during these more recent times, Matous is less bothered by the government police, although they still keep an eye on him.

At one point during the apparitions Our Lady indicated that a spring of healing water would come to flow in a place where no spring existed.

It is reported that for three consecutive nights a man by the name of Jaroslav Zaalenka had a vision in which a lady told him that he must go to 'U Obrozku' and dig there. On the third day he went there but did not know exactly where to dig. He started to dig, when the very lady of his vision, now present on the mountain said to him: *"Do not dig here, but over there where you see three ferns."* He went to that place and began to dig. Then the ferns mysteriously vanished. When he looked around for the lady, she too had vanished. From that moment a spring gushed there and exists today. Today there are seven springs on the mountain. Through the use of this spring water many physical and spiritual healings have been reported. For this reason this place has become known as the 'Lourdes of Slovakia'.

In addition to the healings, other phenomenon have been reported relating to the water. There have been several instances where miraculous images are formed within the ice when the water is frozen. Even more amazing when the ice thawed out and was refrozen sometimes other miraculous images depicting entirely different scenes appeared.

Numerous signs and wonders occurred, not only at the site of the apparition, but at other places. One such occurrence happened when passengers boarding the bus at Cadec headed for Turzovka included among their number a barefoot woman with a rosary on her belt. The driver asked her destination and she replied "Turzovka." He took a ticket from his book and gave it to her. She said she had no money. A passenger offered to pay her fare, but she declined because, "He had three children at home for whom he must care." So the driver offered to pay her fare. Again she declined telling him that he was single and wanted to get married and that he would have some very difficult times ahead. The passengers were amazed that she could so accurately relate such personal conditions. Thereupon all the passengers said they would each pay a portion of her fare but they wanted her first to show her identification. The lady replied that the driver had her ID in his pocket. The driver reached into his pocket and to his surprise pulled out a picture of the Blessed Virgin Mary. Thereupon the lady disappeared. Everyone on the bus was astonished.

On May 1, 1965 a great sign occurred at Turzovka, witnessed by some 1200 pilgrims and vacationers. On two opposite sides of the sky there appeared huge brilliant shrines. These two shrines then came together in the middle of the sky to form in brilliance a huge heart. On one side of the heart appeared the Immaculate Conception, while Our Saviour appeared on the other side. In front of Our Saviour was a big red cross. This lasted for ten minutes. People fell to their knees and prayed with great fervor.

There is a beautiful story reported concerning an exquisitely carved statue of Our Lady of Turzovka which is destined to be set in a prominent place in the new Basilica which is to be built on the mountain of the apparitions.

Alois Lasak, a retired coal miner who lived in Hlucin, some distance from Turzovka, felt drawn to Turzovka and would take the bus and visit the shrine at least once a month commencing in 1960. On one such visit in June, 1964 Alois saw blood flow from the crucified Christ on the cross which had been erected on the spot where the apparitions had occurred. Alois also saw Christ on the cross throw His head back and open His eyes, then bend His head forward and close His eyes again. This happened three times during this vision.

The next day Alois had another vision inside his own house. Our Lady appeared to him and commissioned him to carve a statue of Our Lady of Turzovka. She told Alois: *"What you see is to be done by you. This work once finished, you will deliver it to the believers. You must not fear, I shall help you. Even the face I shall supply."* During this vision Alois was also shown the passion of Christ. The vision lasted four hours and left Alois weak and trembling.

He had no experience in carving or sculpting and he was afraid. After talking to his wife he decided to visit the shrine again. When Alois arrived at 'U Obrozku' an aged man remarked: "Among you is a man who will carve a statue of Our Lady of Turzovka." This man then lead Alois to the cross (the very cross where Alois had the first vision).

Incidentally, in 1958 Our Lady had directed Matous to make a cross from the downed pine tree and to erect it on the spot where She had appeared. This was done, but the communists burned the cross. The pilgrims erected a new cross and placed the partially burned original cross on the new cross. The new cross was burned and again replaced always preserving the partially burned cross. This happened three separate times. It was to this third new cross that the aged man led Alois. Here the aged man insisted that Alois remove the partially burned cross and carve a small cross and a heart from it, and that these two objects should be placed inside the statue to be carved by Alois. It was done.

Someone obtained the wood for the statue, the cross and heart were placed into a cavity dug out inside the wood. After the wood was halved, the two halves were glued together and Alois proceeded to carve the statue—a feat which he completed in two months!

There are no reports of Church action, however, the bishop of the Nitra Diocese reportedly at first prohibited visits to the site, but later revoked this prohibition.

IX The Primary Messages - 6

(1) Do Penance - This message appeared in the very first tableaux that was shown to Matous during the first apparition. The inscription on the tableaux showed these words, not just once, but twice!

"Do penance! Do penance!" Also during the first apparition Our Lady said: *"As for penance, it must consist above all in abstaining from evil and in doing good."* Also Our Lady said that penance is not only for sinners but for all.

(2) Sin No More - The tableaux of June 7th showed the horrible spectacle of the sins of man. These sins surely are repulsive to God.

(3) Pray the Rosary - During the first apparition Our Lady presented a rosary to Matous, and even taught him to pray the mysteries of the rosary.

(4) Prayer - Our Lady told Matous that prayer can hold off the justice of God, but such prayer must come from the heart, not proceed only from the intellect, and it must not be said absentmindedly. And to the prayer must be added good works. These good works must not consist in a bare distribution of food, clothing or money, but the gifts must be accompanied by encouraging words, a smile, a friendly glance.

(5) **Conversion of Sinners** - Our Lady told Matous that mankind must come back to God and pray for conversion because the numerous sins of the world are urgently calling for the justice of God.

(6) **Chastisement** - On June 27th Matous was made to see the great punishment to befall the world if mankind does not return to God.

The description of the chastisement was made known to the seer; yet Our Lady also said that prayer can hold off the justice of God.

X Signs Preceding the Apparitions

Each of the seven apparitions occurred while Matous was in prayer before the image of Our Lady at the pine tree. It is reported that his head would turn and the natural background would disappear and then the apparition would take place.

XI Other Visions During Apparitions

(1) On June 1st Matous saw pictorially the increasing invasion of the nations by evil. He also saw a glimpse of heaven towards the end of the apparition and a vision of Jesus and the cross.

(2) It is reported that Matous was made to see a tableaux during each apparition, and each time the subject matter would be different.
On June 7th he was shown the horrible spectacle of the sins of mankind.
On June 27th he was shown the punishment that would strike the world if mankind does not return to God.

XII Prayers Taught to the Seer(s) - Not Reported
XIII Special Devotion Given to the Seer(s) - NR

XIV Requests Made by Our Lady

(1) Our Lady requested that a cross be made from the wood of the pine tree which the communist government had cut down, and that the cross be erected on the spot of the apparitions —this request was complied with.

(2) Our Lady made a request of Alois Lasak that he carve a statue of Our Lady. This request was not given to Matous. However the request has been accomplished and the statue has been completed.

XV Specific Bible References

None are reported, however, the last three apparitions have been kept secret which may or may not contain such Biblical references.

XVI Secrets Given to the Seer(s)

It is reported that Matous received seven apparitions and that in each he was shown a scene pictorially. Four of these have been revealed, but the last three apparitions remain Matous' secret. It is not reported whether Our Lady requested him to keep these secret or whether they concern him alone rather than messages for the world.

XVII Miracles Promised by Our Lady - NR

XVIII Miracles Performed

(1) On May 1, 1965 on two opposite sides of the sky there appeared huge brilliant shrines. These two then came together in the middle of the sky to form in brilliance a huge heart. On one side of the heart appeared the Immaculate Conception, while Our Saviour appeared on the other side. In front of Our Saviour was a big red cross. This lasted for ten minutes. People fell to their knees and prayed with great fervor.
(2) The water taken home from the Springs displayed miraculous images, after the water had been frozen. Several instances are reported where sacred images appeared in the ice. Then when the ice was melted and refrozen other and different images appeared.

XIX Miracles Promised not yet Performed - NR

XX Signs Promised

Our Lady told Matous that God's punishment will destroy about two thirds of humanity; however, as to the good survivors Our Lady said: *"All My children will receive and carry the sign of the cross on their foreheads. This sign only My chosen ones will see..."*

XXI Signs Given

(1) The barefoot woman on the bus going to Turzovka who identified herself by the use of a picture of the Blessed Virgin Mary; and then disappeared, may be taken as a sign that Our Lady did appear to Matous at Turzovka.
(2) Jaroslav Zaalenka had a vision for three consecutive nights wherein a woman told him to go to 'U Obrozku' and dig for water. When he got there that same woman also pointed to the place to dig where three ferns were growing. As he commenced to dig, the ferns vanished and when he turned to find the woman, she also had vanished. Jaroslav

found water at the spot indicated.

(3) There is an instance reported when Matous was detained by the police, who attempted to take his photograph (mug shot). Each time they took the picture of Matous, yet each time upon developing it, they found an image of Our Lady of Fatima and none of Matous.

(4) Alois Lasak had a vision at the apparition site and later Our Lady twice appeared to him, and requested that he carve a statue of Our Lady. Although he had no expertise as a carver, he got the job done, with Our Lady's help, in two month's time.

(5) Several cases of miraculous images being formed in the frozen water taken from the springs, are reported:

a) In 1963 a glass of the water belonging to Mrs. Agnes Koneana was frozen, and an image of the Blessed Virgin Mary was exquisitely shown in the ice. This was shown to some officials who just shook their heads. The iced water was allowed to thaw out and was refrozen. This time an image of a Chalice with a Host suspended above it appeared in the ice.

b) In the case of the glass of frozen water belonging to Mr. Hromek, a Monstrance appeared surrounded by brilliant rays. Many people came to see this.

c) In another case some people went to Turzovka on September 8, 1963 and brought water to keep in case of sickness. The water was placed into two bottles.

On January 24, 1964 a woman was in pain so they fetched the bottles and found the water was frozen. In the first bottle they saw the heights of Turzovka, and above it a Chalice with a silver cross in the center. In the second bottle was also shown the heights of Turzovka and above it a clock which showed the time as five minutes before 12:00 o'clock.

On February 7 1964 the ice now contained images of two Chalices with a silver disk inside. Then on February 15, 1964 the Easter Lamb appeared in the ice. On March 5, 1964 yet other images appeared in the frozen bottles of water. The first was the Immaculate Conception showing Our Lady with Her hands folded and a crown on Her head. The second showed Our Lady with a radiating heart standing on a pedestal.

XXII Predictions/Promises

(1) Our Lady predicted that the faithful survivors of the chastisement would have a sign of the cross on their foreheads visible only to Her faithful followers.

(2) It is reported in a little booklet entitled: "Turzovka the Slovakian Lourdes" by Johanna Schmidt that in 1920 Bishop Karl Kasper visited the

Mystic-Stigmatist, Theresa Neumann and informed her that he intended to travel to Lourdes. She reportedly replied: "In years to come there will be a second Lourdes in Slovakia and you will travel there as a pilgrim."

XXIII Prophecies/Warnings of Chastisement

(1) On June 27, 1958 Matous was made to see the punishment that will strike the world if mankind does not amend its ways and return to God.
God's punishment will strike out two thirds of humanity. Matous describes it thus:

    1) The sun will cease to warm, there will be cold summers with poor harvests.

    2) There will be terrible floods and other misfortunes through the elements.

    3) There will be earthquakes and mountains will move.

    4) Churches will collapse, houses will move and will be carried away by the floods.

    5) The nonbelievers will blaspheme in their despair.

    6) The air will be filled with demon-like forms, which are the incorporations of sin and vice. These phantoms will terrify humanity.

Our Lady also said: *"These days will start with rolling thunder and trembling of the earth. Then close well your habitation, pray, cross yourselves with the sign of the cross, repent your sins, call upon the Mother of God for help, and She will take you under Her protection."*

(2) On July 1st, 1958 Our Lady showed Matous how the Chastisement could be avoided or lessened through prayer, the praying of the rosary and penance. Our Lady also said: *"The angels who are entrusted with the work of destruction are ready, but the wrath of God can be stayed by praying the rosary, by penance and sincere repentance."*

(3) Our Lady told Matous that after the great punishment, then nature will calm down and a bright light will appear; but the world will not be recognizable. Everything will be destroyed. It will be difficult to find life and living beings. God will punish the wicked and those who will have blasphemed Him.

(4) What will happen to the good? Our Lady said: *"All My children will receive and carry the sign of the cross on their foreheads. This sign only My chosen ones will see. These chosen ones will be instructed by My angels how to conduct themselves. My faithful will be without any kind of fear during the most difficult hours. They will be protected by the good spirits and will be fed by heaven, from there they will receive further instructions. They will fall into a deathlike sleep, but they will be protected by the angels.*

"When they awake they will be like newly born. Their bodies will be beautiful and their souls will be steeped in God. Everything they do they will do for the Glory of God. The earth will be beautiful and My

chosen ones will see how God takes care of them.
"Love Me more from day to day! The more you love God and the more you love Me, the more courageous you will be during the days of fear."

XXIV Method of Appearance

It is reported that as Matous prayed before the shrine, he first saw a flash of light then the background would disappear and Our Lady appeared.

XXV Method of Departure

After Matous was made to see a pictorial scene, Our Lady would give messages and disappear.

XXVI Confrontation w/Civil Authorities

(1) Firstly, the communist controlled police arrested Matous and after standing trial he was interned in a mental institution.
(2) Then, the communists cut down the tree and thereafter destroyed the crosses, altars, statues and candles on 36 separate occasions.
(3) The communists tried to prevent all vehicle traffic from coming to the shrine.
(4) Matous was rearrested and sentenced to three years prison.

XXVII Confrontation w/Church Authorities

(1) Ecclesiastical opposition and obstruction is reported. It is reported that not only the civil authorities, but the Church authorities as well, were doing all in their power to have Turzovka forgotten and the authenticity of the apparition denied.
(2) The bishop of the Nitra diocese, Msgr. Netzey, first prohibited visits to the site of the apparitions, but later he revoked the prohibition.
(3) Interestingly enough, it is reported that infiltration by the Masons and the communists into the Catholic establishments, especially editorial staffs, has done much to promote a negative attitude towards these apparitions.

XXVIII Request Chapel/Shrine Built

There is no report that Our Lady requested a chapel; although She did request that Matous make a cross of the cut down tree and erect it on the spot where the pine tree stood.

On the other hand a Basilica is planned to be built on the site of the apparitions. The statue of Our Lady of Turzovka has already been carved and is to be placed in the Basilica.

XXIX Free Will/Choice

(1) Our Lady told Matous: *"Matous, what you have seen, make it known to the world."* Obviously he had the choice to obey her or not to do so.

(2) She also showed him heaven and told him: *"If you carry out My order, you will go there"* (pointing to heaven). Obviously She acknowledges Matous' free will.

XXX Seer(s)' Suffering/ Sacrifice

(1) Matous was ridiculed by friends, church and governmental officials. He was arrested and placed in a mental institution. When he was released he lost his job and all his benefits. He was rearrested and sentenced to three years prison. Indeed he suffered much.

(2) His mission given to him by Our Blessed Mother to spread the messages, was constantly hindered, frustrated and opposed by the police, who 36 times ravaged the shrine on the mountain side. Vehicles were prohibited. Both government and church authorities did their best to make the apparition story "go away." This has in the past caused, and continues to cause, Matous great distress.

XXXI Healings Reported

(1) Many healings have been reported, physical and spiritual. Some of these healings have been connected with the water taken from the springs. Many people were reluctant to publicly reveal their cures. The problem has been that no physician would dare certify a miraculous cure.

(2) There were two cases of miraculous cures of cancer reported, one in Prague and the other in Slovakia.

(3) During the three hours of ecstasy on June 1, 1958 Matous himself was cured of all his sickness including his chronic bronchitis.

XXXII Action Taken by the Church

(1) The bishop of the diocese first prohibited visits to the shrine, then later revoked this order.

(2) Reportedly that same bishop, Msgr. Netzey, was promoted to archbishop and intended to travel to Rome to present this matter to the Pope. However, he died unexpectedly without ever making the trip to Rome.

(3) Understandably, under a communist regime many obstacles were placed in the path of a fair, open and orderly process to determine the authenticity of these apparitions.

XXXIII Bibliography

This is Turzovka   1983
By: Stephen Senick S.J. translated by
Sr. Gabrielle Woyko O.P.
Published by: Slovak - Jesuit Fathers

Vers Demain   1970
July-August-September 1970 Edition
By: Louis Even
Published by: Vers Demain

Our Lady of Turzovka, Slovakia
(Audio Cassette)
By: Not Given
Published by: 101 Foundation Inc.

Chapter 25

GARABANDAL, SPAIN
(1961-1965)

I Place - Garabandal, Spain

II Dates of First and Last Apparition

First: July 2, 1961
Last: November 13, 1965

III Seers - 4

Name: Mari Loli Mazon
Birth: Unknown
Age at first apparition: 12
Status: Living

Name: Jacinta Gonzalez
Birth: Unknown
Age at first apparition: 12
Status: Living

Name: Mari Cruz Gonzalez
Birth: Unknown
Age at first apparition: 11
Status: Living

Garabandal, Spain

Name: Conchita Gonzalez
Birth: Unknown
Age at first apparition: 12
Status: Living

IV Total Number of Apparitions - 33

It is reported there were actually some 2000 apparitions at Garabandal from 1961 to 1965.

V Dates and Locality of Each Apparition

All apparitions occurred at the Pines in Garabandal unless otherwise noted.

1961: July 2, 3, 4, and the last two weeks of July. (It is reported that the visionaries went into ecstasy many times each day.) July 26 or 27 Conchita (in Santander), the other three seers (in Garabandal); the 29th & 31st; August 2, 3, 5, 6, 7; 8(twice w/second apparition in church); 16, 17, 19, 22; October 18.
1962: May 1 & June 18 (Archangel Michael); June 19, 20; 22 & 23 (Archangel Michael); July 3; July 18 (Archangel Michael); Sept. 12.
1963: June
1964: December 8 (inside church)
1965: January 1; June 18; June 19 (Archangel Michael); November 13
In addition to apparitions of Our Lady, it is reported that the Archangel Michael also appeared to the seers, on June 18, 27, 28 & July 1 & 2 of 1961.

VI Description of Our Lady

Our Lady wore a white robe and blue cloak and had a crown of golden stars. Her feet are not visible, Her hands are slender with a scapular on Her right wrist. The scapular is reddish-brown in color. Her face is long, Her nose is long and slender and Her mouth is delicate and very beautiful. Her lips are just a little bit full. She has a complexion that is quite dark but lighter than the angel's. Her voice is different from the angel's voice, it is a very beautiful voice, very unusual. Our Lady appears to be about 18.

The seers report there is no woman who is like Our Lady, either in voice or in any way at all.

Sometimes Our Lady carries the Child Jesus in Her arms. He is quite tiny, as tiny as a newborn baby. He has a round face with a sweet little mouth. His blonde hair is rather long; His hands are very small and He is dressed in a sort of sky-blue tunic. He appears to have the same complexion as Our Lady.

VII Title(s) of Our Lady - 1

Our Lady presented herself as Our Lady of Mount Carmel.

VIII Brief Factual Review

San Sebastian of Garabandal is a small village located in northwestern Spain in the Santander Province, in the heart of the beautiful Cantabrian Mountains.

June 18, 1961 was a Sunday. On that day the four girls, Mari Loli, Jacinta, Mari Cruz and Conchita, after Mass, picked apples from a tree without the owner's permission. Afterward they felt remorse. They sat on a rocky pathway, the 'cuadro', when suddenly a beautiful angel appeared surrounded by a great light. The pathway (cuadro) led uphill away from the village to a sunken lane, the 'calleja', which led to the hilltop area referred to as 'The Pines'.

The angel was wearing a long white robe, hanging loose and without a seam. His wings were rosy-hued, large and very beautiful, so reported the seers. The angel did not speak and quickly disappeared. The angel, later identified as St. Michael, appeared to the girls several times and finally on July 1, 1961 the angel announced that the Blessed Virgin Mary under the title of Our Lady of Carmel would appear to the seers on Sunday July 2, 1961. A plaque with roman numerals appeared to the girls beneath the angel. They asked its meaning and the angel said Our Lady would explain.

On July 2, 1961 the Blessed Lady appeared to the seers accompanied by St. Michael and another angel. Our Lady's first message for the world was given on July 4, 1961 and released publicly on October 18, 1961. During this apparition She explained the meaning of the plaque to the seers.

On January 1, 1965 Our Lady told Conchita during an apparition that Archangel Michael would appear to her on the following June 18, 1965 to deliver a final message from Our Lady for the entire world. And so it happened. On June 18, 1965 St. Michael appeared to Conchita at the 'cuadro' and delivered the message. Our Lady's last appearance to Conchita occurred on November 13, 1965. Locutions continued thereafter until February 13, 1966.

Commencing on May 1, 1962 St. Michael appeared to Mari-Loli and told her that he himself will give Holy Communion to the girls when the priest is absent from the village. St. Michael did exactly as he said on several occasions.

On June 22, 1962 St. Michael announced to Conchita the miracle of the 'Visible Communion'. Then on June 23, 1962 St. Michael told Conchita that Our Lady will set the date for the miracle of the 'Visible Communion'. During an ecstasy at 'The Pines' on July 3, 1962 Conchita had a locution which set the date for the 'Visible Communion' for July 18, 1962.

On July 18 (actually about 1:00 AM on July 19, 1962) Conchita received the Host from St. Michael. Because this promise of 'Visible Communion' was revealed by Conchita, a great crowd had gathered. One person took a photograph with light from a flashlight showing the Host on the tongue of Conchita. Those near to Conchita saw the Host suddenly appear on her tongue.

On July 19 and July 20, 1962 the girls received visions of possible future chastisements. On January 2, 1965 Our Lady told Conchita about the 'Warning' during an apparition. During this apparition Our Lady also revealed the nature of the Chastisement to Conchita.

The 'Warning' is to be a worldwide event whereby each person would have an interior experience after first seeing something in the air. This is intended to show us how we stand in God's eyes, and to urge us to convert. Mari-Loli knows the year of the 'Warning'.

During an apparition occurring August 8, 1961 the seers state that they saw a preview of the 'Great Miracle'. This 'Great Miracle' is to take place above 'The Pines'. It will occur within one year after the 'Warning' and it will occur on a Thursday evening at 6:30 PM between the 8th and 16th of April. It will coincide with an important event of the Church and be on the feast day of a Martyr of the Eucharist. Conchita knows the date of the 'Miracle' and must announce it eight days in advance. The 'Miracle' will be visible in Garabandal and the mountains surrounding 'The Pines'. The Pope and Padre Pio will also see the 'Great Miracle'.

A 'Permanent Sign' will remain forever at Garabandal as a result of the 'Great Miracle'. The 'Sign' will be supernatural in origin and will be something that has never been seen before on earth. It will be possible to film and televise the 'Sign' but no one will be able to touch it.

The 'Great Miracle' and 'Sign' will be sent as proof of the tender love of God and the Blessed Virgin for the world.

Afterwards, if the world does not reform, God will send a terrible Chastisement. This Chastisement is conditional. If the people return to God and reform the Chastisement can be averted.

On August 8, 1961 a priest, named Fr. Luis Andreu was present during an apparition at 'The Pines'. He observed the girls intently and suddenly exclaimed "Miracle!". Later the next morning on the way home Fr. Luis died in the town of Reinosa. Before he died he said "How happy I am! I'm overflowing with happiness! The Virgin gave me such a gift! I do not harbor the slightest doubt about the reality of what has happened to the children! It is the truth!" It is believed by some that on August 8, 1961 Fr. Luis saw the future 'Great Miracle at The Pines'.

During the apparitions, while in ecstasy, the girls were able to detect and recognize priests in the crowd. Sometimes the seers would walk (both forwards and backwards) in the dark without stumbling, sometimes their body weight would increase during an ecstasy. Other phenomena occurred while the seers were in ecstasy.

Our Lady kissed religious articles for the people in the crowd during some of the apparitions. She also taught the children to pray the rosary. Once She wore the brown scapular.

Our Lady told the seers that a time would come when they would doubt the messages and even doubt that Our Lady had appeared to them. This did happen. One of the seers, Mari Cruz, is said to have recanted. The other girls went through a period of grave doubt and depression.

Three of the girls now reside in the United States. They are married and have families. Mari Cruz resides in Spain, is also married and has children.

In 1961 a commission set up by the bishop returned a negative report. Thus far each commission has returned a negative report. However, the latest commission set up in 1986 has not returned it's decision.

IX The Primary Messages - 2

(1) Sacrifice, Penance, Visit Blessed Sacrament - On July 4, 1961 Our Lady gave the first message and told the girls to announce the message to all on October 18, 1961: *"Many sacrifices must be made. Much penance must be done. We must pay many visits to the Blessed Sacrament . . . But first of all we must be very good . . . If we do not do this, punishment awaits us . . . Already the cup is filling, and if we do not change we shall be punished."*

On January 1, 1965 the Blessed Virgin told Conchita that the Archangel Michael would appear to her on June 18, 1965 to deliver a final message in Mary's name for the entire world, because Her first message was not heeded.

(2) Eucharist, Prayer for Priests, Pray the Rosary - On June 18, 1965 the Archangel St. Michael appeared to Conchita and delivered the following message at approximately 1:00 AM on June 19, 1965: *"Since My message of October 18th has not been complied with and has not been made known to the world, I will tell you that this is the last one. Before, the chalice was filling, now it is over flowing. Many cardinals, many bishops and many priests are on the path of perdition and they take many souls with them. To the Eucharist there is given less and less importance. We should avoid the wrath of God on us by our good efforts. If you ask pardon with your sincere soul, He will pardon you. It is I your Mother, who through the intercession of Saint Michael, wish to say that you amend, that you are already in the last warnings and that I love you very much and do not want your condemnation. Ask Us sincerely and We will give to you. You should sacrifice more. Think of the Passion of Jesus."*

These were the two public messages given for the world at Garabandal.

Garabandal, Spain

X Signs Preceding the Apparitions

The visions to the seers were preceded by three interior calls, each becoming stronger than the last. After the third call the girls would run to the sunken lane where the visions first began, then crashing to their knees on the jagged rocks, they would enter into ecstasy. Their heads were thrown back, the pupils of their eyes were dilated and their faces imbued with an angelic countenance. They were insensitive to pin pricks, burns, physical contact or bright spotlights shown directly into their eyes. Their weight factor changed so much that two grown men had difficulty in lifting one 12 year old girl; yet the girls could lift each other, while in ecstasy, with the greatest of ease to offer a kiss to Our Lady.

XI Other Visions During Apparitions

(1) On November 13, 1965 at the final appearance of Our Lady, She appeared with the Infant Jesus. This had occurred more than once previously.
(2) St. Michael and Our Lady sometimes appeared during the same apparition.

XII Prayers Taught to the Seer(s) - Not Reported
XIII Special Devotion Given to the Seer(s) - NR
XIV Requests Made by Our Lady - Not Reported
XV Specific Bible References - Not Reported

XVI Secrets Given to the Seer(s)

(1) **Warning:** Mari Loli knows the year the warning will occur.
(2) **Great Miracle:** Conchita knows the date of the miracle.
(3) **Permanent Sign:** Conchita knows the date of the sign.
(4) **Chastisement:** During July 1962 Conchita, Mari Loli and Jacinta were shown a vision of the Chastisement.

XVII Miracles Promised by Our Lady

(1) The Great Miracle
(2) The Permanent Sign
(3) Announcement of the Miracle of the Visible Communion

XVIII Miracles Performed

The Visible Communion was given to Conchita by St. Michael and photographed. (July 18/19, 1962)

XIX Miracles Promised not yet Performed

(1) The Great Miracle
(2) The Permanent Sign

XX Signs Promised

(1) The Warning
(2) The Great Miracle
(3) The Permanent Sign
(4) Visible Communion

XXI Signs Given

(1) Visible Communion
(2) Celestial signs were witnessed in the sky above 'The Pines' by many on August 15, 1961.

XXII Predictions/Promises

(1) The Warning
(2) The Great Miracle
(3) The Permanent Sign
(4) Chastisement (conditional)
(5) Visible Communion (this has occurred)
(6) On the day of the Great Miracle a blind man named Joey Lomangino of New York will regain his sight.
(7) Only three Popes will be installed after Pope John XXIII till the 'end of time'.

XXIII Prophecies/Warnings of Chastisement

Conchita, Loli and Jacinta saw a vision of the chastisement. In describing the vision it is reported that it will be a direct intervention from God, it will be more fearful than anything we can expect, it will come when we least expect it and all Catholics should go to confession and receive Holy Communion. However, if the world changes and returns to God the Chastisement can be averted.

XXIV Method of Appearance

First the children receive interior calls. When they respond and go to the apparition place Our Lady is suddenly present to them.

XXV Method of Departure

The children often ask Our Lady to stay longer; when She leaves "She just vanishes into thin air."

XXVI Confrontation w/Civil Authorities - NR

XXVII Confrontation w/Church Authorities

(1) The local bishop was skeptical of the apparitions. A commission was appointed in 1961. In August 1961 the bishop sent a 'nota' to the parishes in his diocese containing an admonition to priests and laity to avoid the events and prohibited visiting priests from saying Mass at the village church in Garabandal.
In 1987 the new bishop lifted this prohibition and now permits visiting priests to say Mass at the village church.
(2) On August 30, 1966 the bishop and Vice General interrogated Conchita for seven hours. She said: "Everything was a lie..." Nonetheless Conchita never stops confirming the truth of the apparitions and asserts that the Warning and the Great Miracle will take place, as will the Chastisement, unless people convert.
(3) Jacinta, upon reaching the age of majority wrote a letter to the bishop declaring her formal retractions must be considered as null and void. Our Lady had told the seers that a time would come when they would have doubts of the apparitions and the messages.
(4) Each commission established returned a negative report. A new commission was established in 1986. The world awaits its decision.

XXVIII Request Chapel/Shrine Built - NR
XXIX Free Will/Choice - Not Reported

XXX Seer(s)' Suffering/ Sacrifice

(1) The mothers of several of the girls resisted them going to the site of the apparitions, because they at first did not believe the girls.
(2) Our Lady told the seers they would have doubts; this occurred and some recanted.

(3) On December 8, 1964 Our Lady told Conchita: *"you will not be happy on this earth, but in heaven."* It is obvious that extreme emotional and spiritual suffering was experienced by the seers.

XXXI Healings Reported

Healing, physical, emotional and spiritual are reported occurring all over the world.

One such healing involved a woman who had suffered an injury and lost one knee cap. Her name is Christina Wayo of Mkurdi, Nigeria. In July of 1961 she joined a pilgrimage to Garabandal. She had a stiff left leg and found it difficult to climb stairs.

On July 21, 1961 two girls helped her to climb the hill to The Pine trees where many of the apparitions took place. They helped her in her descent from the hill as well.

On that same afternoon of July 21st the group again climbed the hill but Christina stayed behind resting. Around 4:00 PM she decided to try to climb the hill alone. She tried crawling but became exhausted. Then she made a prayer mentally to Our Lady for help. Suddenly she felt a surge of power in her left leg, and walking upright on both legs she completed the journey to the top of the hill. She prayed at The Pines and made the difficult descent unaided. At the bottom people gathered around her. She found she could jump, kneel and bend her knees without difficulty.

Later, upon reexamining her left knee, it was found that she now had a kneecap on her left knee which had been surgically removed after her accident. X-rays confirmed this miracle. The details and records are in the Garabandal Miracle files in Madrid.

XXXII Action Taken by the Church

(1) The 1961 Santander Commission established and returned a negative conclusion.
(2) In 1962 and thereafter the bishop sent a 'nota' that no visiting priest may say Mass at the village church.
(3) A 'nota' from the bishop of July 8, 1965 states: "We have found no grounds for an Ecclesiastical Condemnation either in the doctrine or in the spiritual recommendations that have been divulged in the events and addressed to the Christian faithful..."
(4) From 1966 to 1983 the controversy as to whether the events were supernatural or not, continued. However at no time were the apparitions ever condemned.
(5) Reportedly another commission has been appointed, the outcome of which is now being awaited.

(6) May 30, 1983 Dr. Luis Morales delivered an historic address retracting his earlier negative judgment as a member of the first commission appointed in 1961. Dr. Morales' wife was dying. He called for the crucifix (the one which Our Lady kissed during one of the apparitions at Garabandal), to comfort his wife on her deathbed.

XXXIII Bibliography

Garabandal, the Village Speaks 1981
By: Ramon Perey
Published by: The Workers of Our Lady of Mount Carmel, Inc.

God Speaks at Garabandal 1970
By: Fr. Joseph A. Pelletier
Published by: Assumption Publications

Star on the Mountain 1969
By: Fr. Maternd Laffineur and M. T. Le Pelletier
Published by: Our Lady of Mount Carmel de Garabandal Inc.

The Apparitions of Garabandal 1966
By: A - de Bertodano
Published by: St. Michael's Garabandal Center for Our Lady of Mount Carmel, Inc.

Chapter 26

KESPEST, HUNGARY
(1961-1981)

I Place - Kespest, Hungary

II Dates of First and Last Apparition

First: 1961
Last: December 12, 1981

II Seer(s) - 1

Name: Karoly Kindelmann (Elizabeth)
Birth: June 6, 1913
Age at first apparition: 48
Status: Deceased: April 11, 1985

IV Total Number of Apparitions – 67

There may have been more visions, locutions, or apparitions recorded in the seer's diaries which are not reported in the book 'Flame of Love'.

V Dates and Locality of Each Apparition

All apparitions occurred inside the Chapel at the seer's home in Kespest unless otherwise noted.

1961: Once undated.

1962: April 13, 15, 30; May 4; twice undated in May; August 1, 8, 16, 31; September 7/8, 15, 29; October 13, 19, 25; November 6/7 (traveling); 17, 19; 22 (traveling); 30; December 1; 12 (traveling); once undated (traveling); 15 (traveling).
1963: January 8, 14; February 7, 12; March 11; May 19; July 12, 23, 26; August 26, 31; September 12-16; October 18; November 7, 27; December 10.
1964: January 17; April 15; May 16; August 27; December 6, 12.
1965: May 30; July 9, 17.
1966: April 9, 16; June 3.
1971: July 26.
1975: Once undated.
1980: August 15.
1981: January 1; March; April 12; November 20, December 12.

VI Description of Our Lady

No description is reported except that Our Lady was sobbing uncontrollably while giving a message.

VII Title(s) of Our Lady - 1

Mother of Sorrows.

VIII Brief Factual Review

The seer, Erzsbet (Elizabeth) Szanto, who was Mrs. Karoly Kindelmann by marriage, was born on June 6, 1913 in Kespest, Hungary (near Budapest). She was the youngest of 13 children, all of whom are now deceased.

Elizabeth became an orphan at age eleven. She completed only four years of school. Although Elizabeth desired to become a nun, she was never accepted. In 1930 she married and had six children. She became a widow in 1946 and had to strive to support herself and her six children.

She belonged to the Third Order Carmelites, although she came very close to giving up the practice of her faith, due to her difficult daily struggle for survival.

One Sunday she reluctantly went to church with her children, but her heart was not in it. Arriving home from Mass she found herself holding the 'Little Office of the Blessed Virgin'. As she began to read from it she was thrown into great spiritual anguish. She cried. The next day, July 16th was the Feast of the Queen of Carmel. Again she spent nearly the entire day at church. She went to confession, did the assigned penance, but she still felt a spiritual dryness. She spent most of that night in her garden crying. Next morning she went to Communion at Mass. She felt remorse and deep sorrow for her sins. Then she began to pray to Our Lord with fervor. In turn the scourged Jesus appeared to her. Now she was transported. She divided up her possessions and gave them to her family. She was determined to give all to God.

Commencing in 1961 Our Lord began to communicate with her while she prayed before the Blessed Sacrament. Some time later Our Blessed Lady also began to speak to her. Our Lady's first message was: *"Pray to My much offended Son. Console Him."* Elizabeth at first had inner locutions. However, the reports seem to indicate that visions, and perhaps apparitions, occurred later. During one period she reports that it was difficult to hear what Our Lady was saying because Our Blessed Mother was sobbing so much.

The primary mission given to Elizabeth by Jesus and Mary was to reveal, through the Holy Father, to all the world, the *"Flame of Love of the Immaculate Heart of Mary."* Our Lady said: *"I will place a torch in your hand (*which is the Flame of Love of the Immaculate Heart of Mary *), which must go from heart to heart."*

When the seer asked what is the 'Flame of Love', she was told by Jesus: *"My Immaculate Mother's Flame of Love is to you, what the Ark was for Noah."* Our Lady then added: *"My Immaculate Heart's Flame of Love is Jesus Christ Himself."*

The 'Flame of Love' then became the seer's Apostolate. A soul burning with the Flame of Divine Love wishes to ignite other souls, which may be done by example, by sacrifice, by prayer, by frequent visits to the Holy Eucharist, by attendance at daily Mass, by frequent reception of Communion, while turning to the Blessed Mother to flood its own soul with the Flame of Love to protect from evil.

Our Lord arranged for Elizabeth's devotions for each day of the week:

Monday Prayer for suffering souls.
Tuesday Prayer for members of family.
Wednesday Prayer for vocations.
Thursday Prayer of atonement to the Holy Eucharist.
Friday Meditate on the Passion of Jesus.
Saturday Honor the Mother of God.
Sunday No program given.

Our Lady's messages, in addition to teachings of the mission of the 'Flame of Love', were for prayer, fasting, sacrifice and for preservation of the family, in the main. Our Lady made several requests of the seer and also announced devotions and gave promises to all who would devoutly practice the announced devotions.

On several occasions her guardian angel appeared to the seer.

The seer did travel to Rome to present the messages concerning the 'Flame of Love' (from Jesus and Mary) to the Pope, but she was unable to have an audience with the Pope.

In Hungary the entire 'Flame of Love' movement and publication was suppressed. Nevertheless the bishop delivered the messages to the Vatican, and word is being awaited from Rome. No official Church action is reported.

The messages of the 'Flame of Love' have been translated into several languages and disseminated through various parts of the world. The seer Elizabeth died on April 11, 1985.

IX The Primary Messages - 4

(1) **Prayer** - In May 1962 Our Blessed Virgin said: *"Pray a great deal and offer Sunday particularly for this purpose."* Our Lady asked the seer to pray for the dying and to pray for priests.

(2) **Sacrifice** - On September 17, 1962 Our Lady asked Elizabeth to accept sacrifices which could save many souls. On June 23, 1963 Our Lady said: *"Sacrifice! Prayer! These are your mains!"*

(3) **Pray for Families** - On August 8, 1962 Our Lady said: *"Families are in disarray. They live as if they had no soul. I wish to warm homes and to keep families together with My Heart's Flame of Love. Let families pray that together we may hold back the punishing hand of My Son."* Again on January 17, 1964: *"I want to warn the world through you, and communicate My great worry about the great danger which is threatening it by the disintegration of the family sanctuary."*

(4) **Flame of Love** - Of course the primary mission given to the seer was that of the 'Flame of Love'. On April 13, 1962 (Good Friday) Our Lady said, while She was sobbing: *"My Carmelite daughter there are so many sins in the world! Help Me, all of you, to save souls! I will place a torch in your hand. It is the Flame of My Heart's Love. I am your kind and loving Mother, and if you put your trust in Me, I shall save you."*

X Signs Preceding the Apparition - Not Reported

XI Other Visions During Apparitions

(1) Jesus gave the seer many messages during this 20 year period.
(2) The seer's guardian angel appeared to her on at least one occasion.
(3) Jesus and Mary often gave the seer messages during the same vision or locution.

XII Prayers Taught to the Seer(s)

(1) On October 25, 1962 Our Lady asked the seer to add the following in the 'Hail Mary': HAIL MARY ... pray for us sinners *"and send forth the graces of your Flame of Love to all mankind"*... now and at the hour of our death. Amen. Then Our Lady added: *"It is not My intention to change the prayer venerating Me in the Hail Mary, but I want to shake up humanity with this supplication. This should be a permanent supplication."*

XIII Special Devotion Given to the Seer(s)

(1) **Flame of Love** - This was the primary mission given to the seer by Our Blessed Lady on April 13, 1962. *"I will place a torch in your hand. It is the Flame of My Heart's Love."* Again: *"The Flame of Grace which I give you from My Immaculate Heart must go from heart to heart.*

"I wish that the Flame of Love of My Immaculate Heart be known all over the world. I cannot suppress it any longer, it is flowing towards you. With the Flame of My Heart I will bind Satan. United with you, My Heart's Flame of Love will burn up all sins.

"The Flame of Love also extends to all the dying and the suffering souls in purgatory.

"My Immaculate Heart's Flame of Love is Jesus Christ Himself."
On April 15, 1962 Our Lady said: *"My Carmelite daughter, I ask the Carmelites to be the first who will receive the Flame of Love and give it to others."* On November 7, 1963 Our Lady implored the seer to spread Her Flame of Love all over the world.

(2) **Family Holy Hour** - Our Lady asked the seer *"...to regard Thursdays and Fridays as days of special graces, regard them as days of atonement to My Divine Son. The way to achieve this is with the Family Holy Hour. During this Hour of Reconciliation you should say various prayers (rosary) and sing hymns. Begin your worship by making the Sign of the Cross five times in honor of My Son's five Holy Wounds. Try to hold these reconciliation sessions in groups of two or three... You should make it a practice during the day of crossing yourself five times, one after another."*

XIV Requests Made by Our Lady

(1) April 15, 1961 Our Lady requested that the Carmelites be the first to receive the 'Flame of Love'.
(2) Our Lady (and Our Lord) asked the seer to keep night prayer vigils.

Our Lady said the night vigil is a very important exercise for the soul. On July 9, 1965 Our Lady said: *"My daughter, I want to ask you to tell your confessor about the nightly vigils. My intention is to save souls from damnation by your prayers during the night. I would like you to organize in each parish a group who do nightly vigils, so that not one moment would be without someone praying. This is an instrument I give into your hands. In this way you can save many souls from damnation. My Flame of Love will bind Satan."*

(3) On August 1, 1962 Our Lady said: *"I ask the Holy Father to designate Candlemas Day, February 2, as the feast of My Immaculate Heart's Flame of Love. I do not want a separate feast."*

(4) **Revitalize Carmelite Third Order** - In March 1981 Our Lady said: *"The Carmelite Third Order should be renewed all over the world as soon as possible and in many places. Mankind needs prayerful lay souls the most — mankind needs to heed My requests faithfully and devotedly."*

(5) On January 1, 1981 Jesus told the seer: *"In each parish a reparation group should be urgently organized. Bless each other with the Sign of the Cross."*

(6) Our Lady: *"Adore publicly the five Holy Wounds of My Divine Son Jesus, make the Sign of the Cross five times in adoration of My Son's Five Holy Wounds while offering yourself into the mercy of the Heavenly Father, together with My Holy Wounds, gaze into My Son's bloodshot eyes and reflect on the blows He received from you too."*

(7) On February 2, 1981 Our Blessed Lady was sobbing so hard that Elizabeth could hardly hear Her voice. This lasted for about 15 minutes. When the seer asked why Our Lady was sobbing, She responded: *"Because you are not doing everything I am asking you to do to save the world from terrible tragedies."*

XV Specific Bible References - Not Reported
XVI Secrets Given to the Seer(s) - Not Reported
XVII Miracles Promised by Our Lady - NR
XVIII Miracles Performed - Not Reported
XIX Miracles Promised not yet Performed - NR
XX Signs Promised - Not Reported
XXI Signs Given - Not Reported

XXII Predictions/Promises

(1) On September 7/8, 1962 during the night vigil, Our Lady said: *"From now on, during your night vigil, I will extend to all dying persons in*

your neighborhood the graces of the Flame of Love. This grace also applies to all those who know My Flame of Love and who keep the nightly vigil and pray..."

(2) On September 25, 1962 Our Lady said: *"From now on, if someone fasts for the soul of a departed priest, by that fast his soul will be freed from purgatory on the eighth day after his death. Anybody who observes this fast will free one soul from purgatory."*

(3) On October 13, 1962 Our Lady said: *"I will grant the grace that if anyone, anywhere, will say three Hail Mary's in reference to My Flame of Love, on each occasion a soul will be freed from purgatory. Furthermore, in the month of the Holy Souls (November) ten souls will be freed from purgatory for each 'Hail Mary'. Suffering souls will also feel the effect of the grace coming from My Motherly Heart's Flame of Love."*

Later on August 31, 1963 Our Lady said: *"Until now you have said three 'Hail Mary's,' honoring Me, to liberate one soul from purgatory. From now on, as a reward for your fervor, one 'Hail Mary' will liberate ten souls from the place of suffering."*

(4) On November 6/7, 1962 Our Lady said: *"From now on, if someone adores the Blessed Sacrament or just visits It, during this time* (of the visit) *the evil one will lose his power over all souls in that parish. Blinded, his power over those souls will stop."*

(5) On September 1, 1963 Our Lady said: *"Those families who keep the Holy Hour of Reconciliation on Thursdays and Fridays will receive special graces through which they can liberate a member of the family from purgatory by keeping only one strict day of fast on bread and water."*

(6) On August 15, 1980 Our Lady said: *"Priests, if they fast on bread and water on Mondays, will free a multitude of souls from purgatory, that week, at each Mass they say when they perform the transubstantiation."*

When Elizabeth asked Our Lady, how many souls, a thousand or a million? Our Lady replied: *"Even more! So many that it cannot be expressed in human numbers."*

(7) On another occasion Our Lady said: *"If you attend Holy Mass on a day of no obligation, the light of My Flame of Love will envelope those for whom the Mass is offered. During your participation in the Mass, the binding of Satan will increase in proportion to your fervor."*

(8) Our Lady also said: *"Those who fast on Mondays on bread and water shall liberate the soul of a priest from the place of suffering. It is not necessary to hunger, bread and water must be taken. Those who systematically observe the Monday fast, need to fast until only 6:00 PM. But in that case they should say one rosary (five decades) for the souls in purgatory on the same day.*

"Religious and lay people - who observe the Monday fast - will free great numbers of souls from purgatory at the moment they receive Holy Communion during that week."

XXIII Prophecies/Warnings of Chastisement

(1) **Prepare For the Hard Times** - Jesus gave messages to Elizabeth concerning the approaching hard times:
    a) May 19, 1963 - *"You see, the world now resembles nature prior to a storm. It is like a volcano exploding, choking with its infernal smoke, killing, blinding, laying in ruins every thing around it. That is the terrible state of the earth now. The crater of hate is boiling over. Its murderous sulfuric ashes want to turn the human soul, created in the image of God, colorless."*
    b) March 12, 1964 - *"Before the hard times befall you, prepare yourself for the vocation to which I have called each of you. Do not live in indifference and idleness. The approaching storm will carry away the idle, indifferent souls. Only the souls who are able to make sacrifices will be saved. The storm will start when I lift My hand. Give My warning to everyone, especially to priests. Let My warning shake you up from your indifference in advance."*

(2) Our Lady said: *"My children, My Holy Son's hand is prepared to strike. It is difficult to hold Him back. Help Me! If you ask for help from My Flame of Love, together we can save the world!"*

XXIV Method of Appearance - Not Reported
XXV Method Of Departure - Not Reported

XXVI Confrontation w/Civil Authorities

It is reported that the Flame of Love movement and publication were suppressed by the government's Office of Religious Affairs.

XXVII Confrontation w/Church Authorities

Although the seer did journey to Rome with her confessor and other priests, they were not given a hearing with the Pope. The seer saw several priests who summarily brushed her off, however, the diocesan bishop has conveyed the Blessed Virgin's request to the Sacred Congregation in the Vatican. There has been no reported response or action from the Vatican.

XXVIII Request Chapel/Shrine Built - NR
XXIX Free Will/Choice

Both Jesus and Mary respected the seer's free will in all requests made of her.

XXX Seer(s)' Suffering/Sacrifice

(1) The seer went to confession to several different priests. When she would tell of her visions, the priests would ridicule her and humiliate her. This caused great suffering to the seer.
(2) She was not given an audience with the Pope although she traveled to Rome with three priest companions expecting to be received. This was stressful to the seer.
(3) The government banned the publication of the *Flame of Love*. This caused great suffering to the seer, especially since it was her mission to spread the devotion given to her by Jesus and Mary!

XXXI Healings Reported - Not Reported

XXXII Action Taken by the Church

The local bishop sent the documentation for the Flame of Love to the Vatican, no action by the Vatican has been reported.

XXXIII Bibliography

The Flame of Love of the Immaculate Heart of Mary 1991
By: Diary of Elizabeth
Published by: Two Hearts Books and Publishers

Chapter 27

SAN DAMIANO, ITALY
(1964-1970)

I Place - San Damiano, Piacenza, Italy

II Dates of First and Last Apparition

First: October 16, 1964
Last: May 31, 1970 (last reported)
Note: It is reported that thereafter Our Lady continued to appear to Rosa until her death in 1981. However, no messages are reported for this period.

III Seer(s) - 1

Name: Rosa Quattrini (Mamma Rosa)
Birth: January 16, 1909
Age at first apparition: 55
Status: Deceased - September 5, 1981

IV Total Number of Apparitions - 185

(1) In all likelihood the total number of apparitions exceed the 185 reported.
(2) In the message of February 19, 1966 Our Lady said She would appear to the seer every Friday until the death of the seer, and thereafter She would appear at San Damiano every First Friday until the end of the world. The seer died on September 5, 1981.

(3) In May of 1970 the bishop forbade the publicizing of the messages received by the seer. She obeyed and privately recorded the messages received thereafter. The total number and contents of these messages is not known or reported.

V Dates and Locality of Each Apparition

All apparitions and messages from October 16, 1964 through September 2, 1968 occurred while the seer knelt and prayed the rosary near the pear tree in her own yard where the first apparition occurred. These are reported as follows:

1964: October 16, 23.
1965: August 20, 27.
1966: January 14, February 19, April 4, July 8, September 9, October 21, November 18.
1967: January 6, February 10, 11; March 1, 31; April 14, 21; May 12, 13, 26; June 2, 9, 30; July 13, 14, 16; August 5, September 6, 8, 22; October 15, 16, 27; November 22, December 15, 22, 29.
1968: January 5, 11, 12, 19, 21; February 2, 5; March 8, 15, 19, 22, 25, 29; April 5, 12,14, 19, 26, 27, 30; May 9, 10, 13, 17, 21, 23, 24, 26, 29, 30, 31; June 7, 18, 21, 24; July 5, 6, 12, 16, 19; August 5, 9, 15, 16, 21, 22, 23, 25, 30 - Total 87 apparitions.

{As of September 2, 1968 in obedience to the bishop's order, the seer ceased coming to the pear tree and instead received the messages inside her home from September 1968 until May 31, 1970 when the bishop forbade Rosa to disseminate the messages. The seer obeyed and privately recorded the messages thereafter. The reported messages for this period, i.e. September 1968 through May 1970 follow.}

1968 con't: September 15, 20, 29; October 11, 18, 25; November 1, 8, 11, 29; December 8, 10, 12, 20, 27.
1969: January 10, 12, 17; February 2, 14, 21; March 1, 14, 21, 31; April 11, 18, 25; May 5, 8, 9, 13, 16, 23, 24, 25, 30; June 1, 13, 14 , 29; July 1, 2, 4, 10, 11, 16, 18; August 1, 2, 4, 6, 8, 15, 16, 29; September 5, 6, 12; October 11, 13, 16, 17, 24, 26; November 1, 14, 29; December 6, 8.
1970: January 6, 9, 11, 23; February 20; March 6, 13, 19, 20, 25, 26; April 4; May 3, 6, 7, 14, 15, 19, 22, 23, 24, 25, 26, 28, 29, 30, 31 - Total 97 apparitions.

VI Description of Our Lady

On October 16, 1964 Mamma Rosa was reciting the Angelus, when she heard a voice calling from outside: *"Come! Come! I am waiting for you."* These words were repeated again.

Rosa went outside, holding her rosary and looking upwards, she saw a large golden and silver cloud surrounded by numerous stars and roses of many colors, position itself over the plum tree. A red globe came out of the cloud and descended upon the pear tree. Then the cloud disappeared and there was the Most Holy Virgin, surrounded by a great light. Bright luminous rays, full of rose petals, were shining from Her hands and falling to the ground. The Madonna was wearing a blue robe with a great white mantle and a white cincture.

VII   Title(s) of Our Lady - 3

(1) Miraculous Madonna of the Roses.
(2) On September 29, 1961 Rosa was miraculously cured by a stranger who came to the seer's door. This stranger (a lady) told the seer to see Padre Pio at San Giovanni Rotondo.
In the Spring of 1962 the seer complied and journeyed to see Padre Pio. While saying the rosary in the church at San Giovanni she suddenly was called by the name: *"Rosa! Rosa!"* She turned and was surprised to see it was the same stranger who then asked Rosa: *"Do you recognize Me?"* And Rosa responded: "Yes; you are the Madonna who cured me." Then the Madonna said: *"I am the Mother of Consolation and of the Afflicted."*
(3) On Oct 16, 1964 Our Lady announced: *"I am the Mother of Love."*

VIII   Brief Factual Review

Rosa Quattrini was born January 26, 1909 in the village of Santimento, Italy. Rosa had three sisters who all became nuns.

She married Giuseppe Quattrini and they had three children, each born by cesarean section. Upon the birth of her last child complications resulted requiring surgery. During the next nine years Rosa was in and out of the hospital because her wounds would not heal. On September 24, 1961 Rosa was discharged from the hospital as incurable. They could do nothing else to help her. At her home, Rosa was cared for by her aunt Adele.

On September 29, 1961, 5 days after being discharged from the hospital, a beautiful young lady came to the door requesting alms for Padre Pio. Aunt Adele told the young lady they had only 1000 lira in the home and needed it for Rosa because she was ill. At the lady's insistence Adele led her to Rosa's bedside. The lady asked Rosa if she had faith in Padre Pio. When Rosa said "yes" the lady replied: *"if you have confidence in Padre Pio he will cure you."*

As the noon bells rang the lady recited the Angelus with Rosa and helped Rosa get up out of bed and stated that Rosa should visit Padre Pio.

The lady then departed. Soon Rosa arose and went to the kitchen to do the dishes, suddenly she announced to Aunt Adele that she was cured.

The following Spring of 1962 Rosa went on a pilgrimage to San Giovanni Rotondo. While reciting the rosary in the church a lady called out, *"Rosa! Rosa!"* It was the same beautiful lady who had cured Rosa. The Lady identified herself as: *"I am the Mother of Consolation and of the Afflicted. After Mass I will accompany you to Padre Pio and he will give you a mission."*

When Rosa met Padre Pio he told her she must care for the sick, both physical and spiritual care. Rosa did this for 2 years and finally went to her own home to care for Aunt Adele who now was herself sick.

The apparitions began on October 16, 1964 while Rosa was inside her own home reciting the Angelus. Suddenly a voice called to her: *"Come, come I am waiting for you."* After a second call Rosa went outside and observed a large white cloud descend from the sky and position itself over the plum tree. A moment later a large red globe emerged from the cloud and settled over the pear tree. The cloud disappeared and there was the Madonna standing on the globe and surrounded by bright lights.

The Madonna spoke to Rosa and gave her this message: *"My daughter, I come from very far away. Announce to the world that all must pray because Jesus can no longer carry the cross. I want all to be saved; the good and the wicked. I am the Mother of Love, the Mother of all; you are all My children. That is why I want all to be saved. That is why I have come to bring the world to prayer because the chastisements are near. I will return each Friday and I will give you messages and you must make them known to the world."*

When Rosa said: "They won't believe me." Our Lady replied: *"Do not fear because now I will leave you a sign. You will see it. This tree will blossom!"*

Then Our Lady disappeared, in that same instant the pear tree burst into blossoms. The tree was still heavily laden with fruit and the new blossoms were so profuse that the leaves could scarcely be seen. A branch of the plum tree which had been brushed by Our Lady also blossomed the following day. During the next three weeks thousands of people came to see the trees which remained in blossom in spite of the heavy autumn rains.

Three cousins of Sister Lucia (of Fatima) came from Portugal to San Damiano at Sister Lucia's suggestion to witness the pear tree in bloom.

It is reported that Our Lady continued to appear to Rosa until Rosa's death in 1981. However, no messages are reported for this period. From the first apparition until September 2, 1968 Rosa would kneel at the pear tree and pray the rosary, then Our Lady would appear. As of September 2, 1968 the bishop ordered Rosa to cease kneeling before the pear tree. Rosa obeyed and thereafter the apparitions took place inside Rosa's own home on each Friday and on some Feast Days, on each of the First Fridays and First Saturdays and on all Marian Feast Days.

Rosa received, recorded and distributed Our Lady's messages until May 31, 1970 when the bishop forbade her to report or distribute messages. Again Rosa obeyed and thereafter privately recorded all further messages.

Our Lady referred to the garden where the pear tree grows as: *"I will be with you day and night in this sacred place, in this 'Garden of Paradise'. I will await you here."* (July 16, 1968)

On February 19, 1966 Our Lady said: *"I will come always; the Eternal Father has promised Me this; every Friday while My instrument is alive, then I will come every First Friday of the month until the end of the world."*

Two destructive attempts were made on the enclosure surrounding Rosa's Garden as well as on the plum tree. On December 28, 1968 a plastic bomb exploded in the enclosure causing a deep crater. During the night of May 13/14, 1969 the plum tree was sawed off almost completely. A certified arboriculturist from France stated the damage was such that the plum tree could not survive. During Mass the following day Rosa received a message from St. Michael to repair the plum tree. This was done and by August the plum tree yielded fruit.

On May 31, 1969 Our Lady referred to this damage when She said: *"My children do you not see how they damaged the place where I stand? What are you trying to do to Me? I have nothing in common with the trees."*

On October 21, 1968 Our Lady announced to Rosa that a well must be dug in the enclosure. Rosa and others present saw a yellow globe fall onto a spot behind the pear tree indicating the exact spot where the well was to be dug. After much hassle and after obtaining the advice and blessing of Padre Pio, the well was completed on October 26, 1967.

Our Lady instructed Rosa to obtain a specific tract of land near her own 'Little Garden of Paradise' and that a Basilica must be built therein containing 15 altars, one for each mystery of the rosary. The land now called 'City of Roses' consisting of 109 acres was purchased in 1974 to be used for the assigned purpose.

Our Lady's messages exhort us to prayer and penance, to pray the rosary, to embrace the cross and follow Jesus, to attend Holy Mass and receive the Eucharist frequently, to pray for the Church and for the Pope, to increase devotion to the Sacred Heart of Jesus and to the Sorrowful and Immaculate Heart of Mary, and to pray for family unity and for young people.

The messages warn of a great purification and of chastisements, and of a great war to come if people do not listen to Our Lady's messages. The chastisements are to come after a great epidemic. (December 12 1968)

Other presences heard or seen or mentioned during the apparitions include: The Most Blessed Trinity, the Eternal Father, Jesus, the Holy Spirit, St. Michael the Archangel, as well as other angels, St. Joseph, the Apostles, and Jacinta and Francisco of Fatima.

Some reported predictions made by Rosa have come true. The knowledge obtained by Rosa came through visions and dreams.

Many people have reported seeing visions while they were at San Damiano, some have seen the 'Dance of the Sun', others have smelled heavenly perfume and heard heavenly voices. Spiritual conversions and physical healings have been reported. Photographs depicting Our Lady and other images not explained through natural causes have been taken and preserved.

Our Lady requested Rosa to bring white handkerchiefs to the 'Garden of Paradise', and that the handkerchiefs were a great gift from Her to be kept on one's person and given to sick people to dry their tears.

Although the local pastor had confidence in Rosa, and publicly so stated and believed in the apparitions; and although Padre Pio believed in these apparitions, nonetheless the Church has not approved them.

Rosa died September 5, 1981. Padre Pio had previously died. Fr. Pellacani, the local pastor at the time the apparitions commenced, died on August 2, 1989. After the death of Father Pellacani the Church's attitude seemed to have improved towards these apparitions. Now all priests of the diocese may say Mass at the church, there are parks and areas provided for the pilgrims. A clinic has opened for the sick and needy, housing for the elderly and handicapped is being completed, and youth facilities have been constructed at the 'City of Roses' location.

IX The Primary Messages - 8

(1) **Prayer and Penance**
(2) **Pray the Rosary**
(3) **Embrace the Cross and Follow Jesus**
(4) **Increase Faith**
(5) **Attend Holy Mass and Receive the Eucharist**
(6) **Pray for the Church, the Pope and Priests**
(7) **Consecration to the Sorrowful & Immaculate Heart of Mary**
(8) **Family and Young People**

(1) **Prayer and Penance** - Mary urges us to pray. "*Be united in prayer, My sons, for union makes strength. It is by uniting in prayer that graces are obtained.*" (October 25, 1968)

(2) **Pray the Rosary** - On August 22, 1968 Our Lady said: "*Make hours of Adoration with the rosary in your hands and recite it often, with many hymns, songs and praise.*"

Our Lady said: "*I proclaim the crown of the rosary to all My children.*" (September 6, 1969) Again: "*I will put together all the rosaries that you recite and on the day that you leave this earth, I will take this rosary and draw you up above into My arms of a Mother who loves you.*" (October 24, 1969)

(3) **Embrace the Cross and Follow Jesus** - Our Lady said: *"Embrace the Cross, My children, and follow Jesus on the way of Calvary. Be humble, be poor in spirit, all charity for God and your neighbor. By following Jesus on the Way of Calvary, you will arrive at sanctity with Him."* (July 11, 1969)

(4) **Increase Faith** - *"My sons, increase your faith! Ask it of Jesus in the Eucharist."* (October 15, 1967) Again on February 21, 1969: *"With Faith, all understand the truth. Without Faith nothing is good, souls are cold, they have no remorse for what they are doing because they feel no love for Jesus or for Me."*

(5) **Attend Holy Mass and Receive the Eucharist** - Our Lady said: *"Go, go often to Holy Mass. It is the greatest Sacrifice and Jesus gives you many graces there."* (November 11, 1968)

"Jesus is real and alive in the Most Holy Sacrifice of the Altar." (May 13, 1968)

"Remain united to My Son, Jesus, especially in the Sacrament of the Eucharist. Receive Him every day because the moments are sad." (May 5, 1969)

(6) **Pray for the Church, the Pope, the Priests** - Our Lady said: *"My children, pray for the Holy Father, Paul VI and for the whole church. May the church of Peter triumph, such as Jesus founded it."* (October 25, 1969) *"And you, My sons of predilection, go to the feet of the Eucharistic Jesus. Make a good examination of conscience and reflect on My words. Think of all the harm and the many insults I receive from My privileged sons, I want to save you."* (August 30, 1968)

(7) **Consecration to the Sorrowful & Immaculate Heart of Mary** - Our Lady said: *"Console My Heart which is so transpierced. Make the consecration to My Sorrowful Heart in families. I will come into your midst to give you so many graces, peace and love, to console you in your sorrows."* (January 21, 1968)

"Announce, My sons, that I want celebrated the Sorrowful and Immaculate Heart of Mary. I want this to be a triumphant Feast Day." (January 19, 1968)

(8) **Family and Young People** - Our Lady said: *"Imitate the Family of Nazareth by example, humility, charity. You young people, imitate My Son, Jesus. Do as He did when He was on earth. He loved everyone, above all the poor. You also, mothers and fathers love your children."* (January 12, 1969)

"Blessed are the families in which the children and the elderly are united. I grant so many graces when they pray for their sons and love Me." (June 18, 1968)

"Young people! You must be the salvation of the world through prayer, through faith, through love and through pardon. Rush into My arms and rest upon My Heart." (May 24, 1970)

X Signs Preceding the Apparition

At the first apparition a cloud appeared over the plum tree, a large red globe emerged from the cloud and settled over the pear tree. When the cloud disappeared Our Lady appeared standing on the globe surrounded by bright light.

It is not reported whether this sign appeared at other apparitions.

XI Other Visions During Apparitions

(1) **The Most Blessed Trinity** - *"All the angels and saints of paradise are here with Me, with the Father, the Son, and the Holy Spirit."* (March 20, 1970)

(2) **The Eternal Father** - *"I am here in your midst with the Eternal Father who gives you abundant light, strength, intelligence, knowledge, and well being."* (June 1, 1969)

(3) **Jesus** - *"I am Jesus, I am your Brother who calls you to My Heavenly table to enrich you with graces and pardon."* (March 26, 1970)

(4) **The Holy Spirit** - On August 15, 1965 and September 8, 1967 the Holy Spirit was present under the form of a dove. The August 15, 1965 message includes: *"Look at this white dove."*

(5) **St. Michael and Angels** - *"I am St. Michael, your brother, who assists you every moment of your life and also at the hour of death, if you call me."* (July 13, 1967)

(6) **St. Joseph** - *"I am here in your midst with My Patriarch St. Joseph, who is the Patron of Christian Families of the entire world."* (March 19, 1970)

(7) **Apostles** - *"I am here with you, with My Son Jesus, and all the Apostles."* (June 29, 1969)

(8) **Children of Fatima** - On one occasion Rosa said: "The Heavenly Mamma is there, with Jacinta, Francisco and Lucia."

XII Prayers Taught to the Seer(s) - Not Reported
XIII Special Devotion Given to the Seer(s) - Not Reported

XIV Requests Made by Our Lady

(1) Our Lady requested that a well be dug here so that the water could serve many as the purification of soul and body. (October 21, 1966) This well was completed.

(2) Our Lady requested Rosa to obtain specified land and to build a Basilica with 15 altars, one for each decade of the rosary. The land was purchased in 1974. This land is named 'The City of Roses'. The

status of the Basilica is not reported.
(3) Our Lady instructed Rosa to bring white handkerchiefs which are specifically to be carried on one's person and used by many sick people. Our Lady said: *"My children, the handkerchiefs! This is a great gift I have given you, so great, so great!"*

XV Specific Bible References - Not Reported
XVI Secrets Given to the Seer(s) - Not Reported
XVII Miracles Promised by Our Lady - NR

XVIII Miracles Performed

(1) Our Lady cured Mamma Rosa when She came to Rosa's home in 1961.
(2) The pear tree (and one branch of the plum tree) miraculously blossomed on October 16, 1964.

XIX Miracles Promised not yet Performed - NR

XX Signs Promised

(1) Our Lady promised a sign at the time of Her first apparition October 16, 1964 that the pear tree would blossom and it did blossom instantly upon Our Lady's departure.
(2) Our Lady promised curative water at a well to be dug. This was also done.

XXI Signs Given

(1) Blossoming pear tree.
(2) Curative water from the well.
(3) In addition solar phenomena, signs in the sky, perfumes, heavenly voices, and inexplicable photographs have been reported.

XXII Predictions/Promises

(1) On September 29, 1961 the beautiful lady told Rosa that if Rosa has confidence in Padre Pio she would be healed. In fact Rosa was healed.
(2) There are a series of messages where Our Lady says She will return again with a great light to convert souls, and that She will return in triumph.
"All will be resolved in the Reign of Love. Jesus will return on this

earth. His Reign will be one of mercy, pardon and peace. Jesus will come with great retinues of martyrs. They will follow Him on the roads. (December 29, 1967)

"Do not fear My children, for I will come. Yes, I will come in your midst and all will see Me and all will believe." (September 12, 1969)

XXIII Prophecies/Warnings of Chastisement

Our Lady said: *"Jesus is merciful but He is also Judge. He allows things to go on, but then He will intervene through chastisements."* (July 11, 1969)

"Do you see the misfortunes everywhere? These are the beginning of the chastisements that the Eternal Father is sending." (May 7, 1970)

"If you continue this, there will be great, terrible scourges, shocks that will make the whole earth tremble. How many cities, how many countries will be destroyed, I come Myself to announce that scourges have begun and they will always become more terrible." (August 27, 1965)

"It has been a long time, years that I announced that there would be a great epidemic, but you never believe My words, the chastisements will come after the epidemic." (December 12, 1968)

"Go to confession, prepare yourselves with a good confession and Communion. Remain prepared for when these days of scourges come. If you are ready you will be united to Jesus. Call Him aloud 'Jesus, Mary, help us! Jesus, Mary, save us!' At the moment of trial take the crucifix in hand and emphatically call Jesus." (August 20, 1965)

"It is up to you to pray so that the scourges will not come." (April 4, 1966)

"Let us pray together in order that chastisements may be lessened." (May 9, 1968)

"It is up to you to soften the chastisements." (February 2, 1969)

XXIV Method of Appearance

On the first appearance a brilliant cloud appeared over the plum tree, a globe emerged from the cloud and settled over the pear tree. Our Lady emerged from this globe in splendid light. It is not reported whether later appearances by Our Lady repeated this method of appearance.

XXV Method of Departure

Our Lady just disappeared.

XXVI Confrontation w/Civil Authorities - NR

XXVII Confrontation w/Church Authorities

(1) The parish priest witnessed the blossoming of the pear tree and believed in the apparitions.
(2) However, in 1968 the bishop ordered Rosa to stop kneeling before the pear tree, and in May 1970 he ordered Rosa to stop reporting or distributing messages. Rosa obeyed the bishop.
(3) The bishop did open an investigation, but no one from the commission talked to Rosa or to the local parish priest.
(4) It seems that since the death of the parish priest in 1989, a more tolerant attitude has been taken by the Church.

XXVIII Request Chapel/Shrine Built

Our Lady instructed Rosa to acquire a specified parcel of land, 'The City of Roses', on which a Basilica is to be constructed with 15 altars, one for each decade of the rosary. In 1974 the land was purchased. Some improvements have been added to the land, however, a Basilica has not been built.

XXIX Free Will/Choice

The messages repeatedly urge us to abandon our sinful ways and choose to convert our hearts, to believe and live the messages and follow Jesus.

XXX Seer(s)' Suffering/Sacrifice

There is no doubt that the bishop's refusal to believe in Rosa and his orders stopping her from kneeling at the pear tree and later from reporting and sharing the messages, caused Mamma Rosa great distress.

XXXI Healings Reported

(1) First there was Rosa's own healing on September 29, 1961.
(2) Many physical, emotional and spiritual healings were reported. Sworn statements were given testifying to many such healings.
(3) Healing and cures were also attributed to the water in the well dug at the site of the apparitions.
(4) The 'Blessed Handkerchiefs' reportedly have been involved with healings.

XXXII Action Taken by the Church

(1) After the first apparition on October 16, 1964 the bishop set up an investigation. This resulted in a negative report. It is reported that neither Rosa nor the parish priest were interviewed.
(2) Upon the death of the parish priest in 1989 a more tolerant attitude has been adopted by the Church. All priests of the diocese may say Mass at the Church in San Damiano, and a permanent pastor has been assigned there. However, the Church has not approved these apparitions.

XXXIII Bibliography

The Most Holy Virgin of San Damiano
By: Editions du Parvis
Published by: JMJ Damiano Center

Miraculous Lady of the Roses
By: Not Given
Published by: Miraculous Lady of the Roses

The Most Holy Virgin at San Damiano
By: S. di Maria
Published by: Editions Du Parvis

Chapter 28

PORTO SAN STEFANO, ITALY
(1966 - 1979)

I Place - Porto San Stefano, Italy

II Dates of First and Last Apparition

First: April 24, 1966
Last: May 30, 1979

III Seer(s) - 1

Name: Enzo Alocci
Birth: February 20, 1931
Age at first apparition: 35
Status: Unknown

IV Total Number of Apparitions - 17

V Dates and Locality of Each Apparition

All apparitions occurred at Porto San Stefano unless otherwise noted.

1966: April 24 (grotto); June 2 (inside seer's house); July 31 (grotto); September 11 (grotto); December 4 (grotto).
1967: February 11 & April 16 & June 25 (grotto); July 14 (inside seer's house).

1968: September 14 (inside seer's house).
1971: October 24 & November 8 (both inside seer's house).
1972: May 8 & November 14 (both inside seer's house).
1973: March 27 & April 14 (both inside seer's house).
1979: May 30 (inside seer's house).

VI Description of Our Lady

On April 24, 1966 the seer was dazzled by a strong light, in the midst of that light a beautiful Lady appeared, dressed like a queen with a crown on Her head.

VII Title(s) of Our Lady - 1

On April 24, 1966 Our Lady said: *"I am the Madonna, the Queen of the World."*

VIII Brief Factual Review

Porto San Stefano is the main town of the municipality of Monte Argentario, an island part of Italy and located in the Tyrrhenian Sea.

Enzo Alocci was born February 20, 1931. As a child he attended school for a very few years; two or three. His only wish was to become a seaman, which he eventually did. After he became married he wanted to stay at home, so he found a job at the shipyard in Porto San Stefano. He was working there when the first apparition occurred.

It is reported that Our Blessed Mother once appeared to Enzo when he was but a child, yet he never forgot the vision. She simply smiled and disappeared.

Above the town of Porto San Stefano, on a mountain, Enzo's family owned a parcel of land (his home) and it was there that the seer received the first apparition on April 24, 1966. The apparitions have all been either at the grotto on that land or inside Enzo's home, except a few minor appearances reportedly took place at the Naval dockyard.

About six months after the first apparition, Enzo received the Stigmata. This occurred on September 11, 1966 when Jesus and Mary appeared at the grotto with four angels. Due to the wounds on his hands and feet he was not able to continue to do the heavy work at the shipyard. The family suffered greatly thereafter in trying to make ends meet. In the spring of 1972 Our Lady rendered the Stigmata invisible at the request of Enzo.

It is also reported that on March 27, 1966 (about one month before the first apparition of Our Lady) Enzo was digging near the grotto when he felt a strong puff of wind, raising his eyes he saw a lady dressed like a nun with a full skirt and barefooted. The lady asked Enzo to fetch her a glass of water. Enzo went to the house to get the water, when he returned he was surprised to find that the lady had disappeared.

On April 24, 1966 (the first apparition) Enzo was again digging near the grotto when he again felt a strong wind which pushed him towards the house. When he arrived at the house he was dazzled by a strong light, in the midst of which light a beautiful lady appeared, dressed like a queen with a crown on Her head. Frightened, Enzo asked who she was, and She answered: *"I am the Madonna, the Queen of the World."* And then She added: *"We will see each other again."*

On June 2, 1966 Our Lord and Our Lady appeared inside Enzo's farm house and blessed the water in the tap. That water remained perfumed all day.

There were seventeen reported appearances of Our Lady, nine of Our Lord and also there were appearances and messages from Archangels Michael and Gabriel. St. John of the Cross also appeared to the seer.

Jesus and Mary requested the seer to send the messages to the Pope. This was done on October 7, 1969 on March 13, 1971 and again on April 24, 1971.

On July 31, 1966 the Archangel Gabriel brought Enzo the Holy Eucharist at his home and gave him Communion. Our Lady also appeared and told the seer: *"If the world does not change in six or seven years I will send a warning..."* Immediately after the apparition Enzo touched and completely cured someone named Anna Maria who suffered from arthritis.

Enzo received several urgent messages warning of the coming chastisement if mankind does not repent and return to God. Our Lady also pleaded for prayer, the rosary, penance, and for us to suffer for poor sinners *"in the time that is left for you, and offer everything into My hands so that nothing will be lost."*

On June 25, 1967 Our Lady informed Enzo that She would appear to him in spirit on the 14th day of each month. On October 24, 1971 Our Blessed Mother said: *"Praise to the Most Precious Blood of Jesus, who with His own Blood has saved us!"*

On November 8, 1971 Our Lady said in part: *"Tell My children that there is no time left to ask requests ... only to pray for the salvation of souls."* At this time Enzo received a secret which was to be sent to Pope Paul VI. The seer reportedly said that included in the secret messages were all the dates of the warnings, punishments, etc.

A statue of Our Lady kept in the home of Enzo shed human tears on July 3, 4, 5, 6, and 7, 1972. Then again on July 11 and July 19. On October 16, 1972 the statue shed tears of human blood. It shed tears of human blood again on November 1, 17, 18 and on December 2, 6, 20, 1972. The statue again shed tears of blood in 1973. The shedding of tears and tears of blood was witnessed by many people and photographs were obtained. The lab test results reportedly were that the blood was human and belonged to 'A' group.

An eyewitness to the first occurrence of tears of blood on October 16, 1972 reports that she had felt a great urge to see the Stigmatist Enzo, so she wrote to him announcing that she would arrive at Porto San Stefano on October 16, 1972 and requested to see him.

When she arrived at Enzo's home shortly after 3:00 PM on October 16th the front door was wide open. Inside she found Rosa, the wife of Enzo in tears, along with other women from the neighborhood. Some minutes before this witness arrived the statue of Our Blessed Mother began to shed tears of blood. This witness goes on to say that it was almost unbelievable to see a stream of fresh red blood streaming down both cheeks and large drops of blood glistening in the orbits of both eyes. It reminded her of the message given to Enzo by Our Lady on May 8, 1972 when Our Lady said that She shed tears of blood because of the disastrous plight of the whole human race.

Often as people came to Enzo's house to see the miracle, he would fervently speak to them inviting them to convert and start a new life.

Our Lady's message of April 14, 1973 speaks of Her displeasure in the way the photographs of the statue shedding tears of blood had been distributed. She said: "*I repeat in this present day that I am very displeased that My pictures have fallen into so many diabolical hands of disbelievers and evil traffickers . . . My pictures should serve only to promote prayer and not to make commerce . . .*"

It is reported that Enzo did have an audience with the Pope. However, there is no report of any action taken by the Church.

IX The Primary Messages - 5

(1) Prayer - Our Lady said on November 8, 1971: "*Prayer, this is the salvation of many souls.*" Again: "*Pray much in My absence, a period of another six months. I want prayer and penance on the place of the Queen of the World.*"

November 14, 1972: "*Suffer, pray and do penance; if you do not do what I have already told you, you will all be lost.*"

March 27, 1973: "*The evil is very great. My dear son, where there is no prayer there does not exist love of charity.*"

April 14, 1973: "*Every day, offer to Me a prayer for the glory of the grotto and pray for peace and salvation of the world.*"

July 14, 1967: "*I recommend to intensify the prayers.*"

September 14, 1968: "*There are false prophets; pray, pray.*"

November 24, 1971: Archangel Gabriel told the seer: "*The true devotees are counted, they are indeed few in comparison to the wicked who are many. This comes about because many will not sacrifice themselves and do not pray. Evil increases and prayer becomes weaker and the devil steals by force.*"

Porto San Stefano, Italy

(2) **Rosary** - Our Lady said on October 24, 1971: *"My son, every mystery of the rosary should be said for sinners. My son, you must say every mystery of the rosary in this manner for the salvation of sinful souls."*

March 27, 1973: *"Always recite the beautiful rosary of Fatima, for this is the greatest rosary for the salvation of so many souls."*

(3) **Penance** - Our Lady said on November 8, 1971: *"My dear children, I repeat as I have always repeated that I do not want much of you, only penance, prayer to save all mankind."*

April 14, 1973: *"I will return to the grotto when there will be much prayer and penance and when the earth will be liberated."*

(4) **Suffer for Sinners** - Our Lady said on November 8, 1971: *"Now, My son, remain serene, suffer for poor sinners in the time that is left to you and offer everything into My hands so that nothing will be lost."*

November 14, 1972: *"It is necessary to suffer, pray and do penance. And also to save your own precious souls."*

(5) **Fight Immorality** - Our Lady said on March 27, 1973: *"Fight, My dear son, as always, the immorality! You must combat immorality without any human respect."*

November 8, 1971: *"Only amusements, wasting money at the expense of suffering souls! But soon, money and pleasures will come to an end."*

April 14, 1973: *"You must pray to combat immorality and to lessen so many punishments which are coming down on the whole world."*

May 30, 1979: *"Miserable, very miserable is this human generation which suffers the fate of a great corruption and depravation, on the road of evil towards a perdition without end, because this generation rose against God. My children, because of the Red Wolf, which hides himself in the shadow since a long time ago and who awaits the moment to tear its prey; My child it is time to tell all the peoples to unite in prayer and to make many sacrifices."*

X Signs Preceding the Apparition

(1) A strong wind preceded at least the first few appearances.
(2) A brilliant light lit the grotto, then Our Lady would appear in that light.

XI Other Visions During Apparitions

(1) Jesus appeared either alone or with Mary on several occasions: December 12, 1971; January 19, 1972; February 26, 1972; March 2, 1972 (twice); November 22, 1972; January 7, 1973; April 14, 1973; May 2, 1973; and on September 11, 1966 when Enzo received the Stigmata during this apparition.

(2) The Archangels Gabriel and Michael: They appeared alone or together on several occasions: July 31, 1966; November 10, 1966; April 16, 1967; November 24, 1971; December 1 and 5, 1971; December 1, 1972; February 14, 1973; and on September 11, 1966 when the seer received the Stigmata during this apparition.

(3) St. John of the Cross also appeared to the seer.

XII Prayers Taught to the Seer(s) - Not Reported

XIII Special Devotion Given to the Seer(s)

Although no new devotion is reported; on October 24, 1971 Our Lady said: *"Praise to the Most Precious Blood of Jesus, who with His own Blood has saved us!"*

XIV Requests Made by Our Lady

(1) Our Lady and Our Lord both requested the seer to transmit the messages to the Holy Father. This was done on October 7, 1969 again on March 13, 1971 and again on April 24, 1971.

(2) Our Lady requested the seer not to give the pictures of the statue shedding tears of blood and human tears to people who are only curious or wish to use or abuse these pictures in commerce.

XV Specific Bible References - Not Reported

XVI Secrets Given to the Seer(s)

(1) On November 8, 1971 Our Lady gave the seer a secret message. This message has not been revealed; although Enzo did say that included in this message were all the dates of the warning, punishments, etc.

XVII Miracles Promised by Our Lady - NR
XVIII Miracles Performed - Not Reported
XIX Miracles Promised not yet Performed - NR
XX Signs Promised - Not Reported

XXI Signs Given

(1) The statue of Our Lady shed human tears on July 3, 4, 5, 6, 7, 11, 19 of 1972.

(2) The statue shed tears of human blood on October 16, November 1, 17, 18, December 2, 6, 20 in 1972, and again in 1973.
(3) On June 21, 1966 Our Lady and Our Lord blessed the tap water in Enzo's house. The water remained perfumed all day.
(4) On September 11, 1966 Enzo received the Stigmata during an apparition of Our Lord and Our Lady. Also present were the Archangels Michael and Gabriel.
(5) On July 31, 1966 the Archangel Gabriel brought the Host to the seer and gave him Holy Communion.

XXII Predictions/Promises

(1) On July 31, 1966 Our Lady said: *"If the world does not change in six or seven years I will send a warning."*
On March 27, 1973 She appeared and reminded us it was precisely seven years since her first appearance to Enzo. She continued to give warnings to us to convert, do penance and pray.
(2) On November 14, 1972 Our Lady said: *"My son, we shall meet again in five months time, and when I shall come I shall make My appeal to all."*
On March 27, 1973 She again appeared and appealed to us to fight immorality and to pray, especially the rosary.

XXIII Prophecies/Warnings of Chastisement

(1) July 31, 1966. Our Lady said: *"If the world does not change in six or seven years I will send a warning: the earth will shake, the sun will spin on itself with big explosions, the moon will be in mourning. All this will happen in about half an hour. In that moment the sky will be free from all clouds and this miraculous phenomenon will be visible from every part of the earth."*
(2) December 4, 1966 Our Lady said: *"The chalice is full to the brim."*
To this Archangel Gabriel added on November 10, 1966: *"Big storms, floods, and earthquakes, are already on their way."*
(3) April 16, 1967 Our Lady said: *"God can no longer bear it, and the chalice is full to the brim. Patience a little longer to save many souls and not to make many innocent suffer."*
(4) May 8, 1972 Our Lady said: *"My word has not been heard; neither by My priests nor by the people. My Heart mourns knowing that for you I do not exist, but evils are already abroad with many grave episodes, revolutions, wars, diseases, hunger, and many grave errors that will explore the world."* Then continuing: *"Everything has been done by that infernal beast to draw you away from Divine Love; and My word to you has not been heard because that fiend has represented the world*

as something to be enjoyed. Scandalous pleasures, waste of money, egoism and indecent manners, these do not appertain to God and to heaven."
(5) November 14, 1972 Our Lady said: "*I am present this morning to say to you that the punishments are already on earth, and all are asking for favors instead of praying to correct these grave errors.*"
(6) April 14, 1973 Our Lady said: "*My Heart suffers, knowing that one day you will be overwhelmed with great punishments. Wickedness increases from day to day. What will become of you My beloved sons?*"
(7) December 1, 1972 Archangel Gabriel said: "*Italy is very far from the love of God ... but soon, very soon Italy will be destroyed with great punishments and there will be violent earthquakes . . .*"

XXIV Method of Appearance

It is reported that a strong wind first got Enzo's attention. Then when he went to the grotto he saw a brilliant light, from which Our Lady appeared.

XXV Method of Departure - Not Reported
XXVI Confrontation w/Civil Authorities - NR
XXVII Confrontation w/Church Authorities   NR
XXVIII Request Chapel/Shrine Built - NR

XXIX Free Will/Choice

Throughout the messages Our Lady exhorts us to give up our life of sin and return to God; thus necessarily requiring that we exercise our free will and choose to abandon sin and follow Jesus.

XXX Seer(s)' Suffering/Sacrifice - Not Reported

XXXI Healings Reported

(1) On July 31, 1966 it is reported that Enzo touched Anna Maria after the apparition and she was instantly cured of severe arthritis.
(2) Previously on June 2, 1966 Our Lord and Our Lady appeared to Enzo at his home and blessed the tap water inside. There are no cures reported by way of the blessed water — however, such cures have occurred at many other apparition sites.

XXXII Action Taken by the Church - Not Reported

XXXIII Bibliography

Porto San Stefano, Italy 1973 (July - August - September) and (October - November - December) issues
By: Vers Demain
Published by: Vers Demain

Message of Our Lady at Porto San Stefano, Italy 1980
(December 1980 issue)
By: Michael
Published by: Michael

Chapter 29

IMO STATE, NIGERIA
(1972 - 1989)

I Place - Owerre-Eberie, Orlu Imo State, Nigeria

II Dates of First and Last Apparition

First: 1972
Last: July 30, 1989 (last reported)

III Seer(s) - 1

Name: Innocent Okorie
Birth: Probable date 1937
Age at first apparition: 35
Status: Living

IV Total Number of Apparitions - 15

V Dates and Locality of Each Apparition

All apparitions occurred at Owerre-Eberie, Orlu-Imo State unless otherwise noted.

1972: Unknown dates
1974: August 26.
1976: August 5.
1977: May 9, 18.

1978: May 8; June 18; August 13.
1980: October 28.
1982: July 13.
1983: April 2-10.
1986: March 23
1987: May 25.
1988: November 24.
1989: July 30.

VI Description of Our Lady - Not Reported

VII Title(s) of Our Lady - 3

"I am the Queen of Heaven, the Mother of Mercy, Queen of the Whole World." This Our Lady told the seer on August 26, 1974.

VIII Brief Factual Review

Nigeria is located in Western Africa and borders on the Gulf of Guinea.

Innocent Okorie was born in 1937 to pagan parents. In 1944 he attended St. Mary's Catholic school at Umuowa. However due to his father's death in 1945 Innocent was forced to leave school. Later in 1948 he started school again at Owerre-Eberie.

Innocent learned to be an auto mechanic, as well as a commercial vehicle driver. During the years 1957 through 1961 he served as office boy and driver for Fr. Harkette's parish (Amigho parish). While serving Fr. Harkette, Innocent was inspired and participated in various religious activities and societies. In 1949 Innocent was baptized by Fr. Harkette. Later he opened his own business under the name "Holy Innocent's Technical Service and Trinity Motors." In 1958 he was married and now has nine children.

From early childhood on, Innocent received the torments of the passion of Christ; especially the flogging, which he received yearly during the Lenten season. Every attempt to treat 'the ailment' failed (treatment in pagan fashion) and his parents accepted it as an annual illness. During the flagellation Innocent was violently thrown to the ground and invisible forces flagellated him up to fifteen minutes at a time. At the end of the torment he would be exhausted and small marks of the flagellation were visible all over his body.

On Good Friday morning in 1971 he was violently thrown down from his bed and was flogged by unseen forces. He cried out and many people gathered around him. After some time he became helpless. His body was covered with tiny lacerations. Then blood came gushing from the palms of his hands, from his feet at the instep, and from his side. Blood also came from his head. He thus received the Stigmata. His wife and family were uncertain what to do; they decided to leave him at home and attend Good Friday services without Innocent. When they returned from church the bleeding and pain increased, now they were sure this was a sign from God.

On Holy Saturday the bleeding had stopped and after Easter the wounds disappeared (except for tiny spots resembling birth marks where the wounds had been and from which the blood had flowed).

This phenomena is repeated every Holy Week. Commencing on the First Friday of Lent the tiny marks become swollen and the wounds open and bleed profusely on Good Friday. The flagellation is repeated on every Good Friday, during which time vast numbers of onlookers witnessed flashes of light and also saw the lacerations on his body when the flogging stopped. Photographs of the wounds in his hands and feet show these wounds clearly.

It was during the Lenten period of 1972 when the Blessed Virgin Mary first began to appear to the seer by way of apparitions, visions and in dreams and began to give messages to him. Angels also appeared to him teaching him songs which he later taught to the members of his Block-Rosary Group.

From the time when Our Blessed Mother first appeared to Innocent, other phenomenon have been identified with him, such as flashes of light issuing from his chest, miraculous medals falling from above while Innocent is in devotion, (on one occasion 87 medals were picked up and counted). He also exhibited the characteristic of bilocation. It is reported that two different priests witnessed one bilocation. Innocent has also been given the gifts of taking photographs of Our Lady and Our Lord as they appear to him. When these photographs are developed and printed Our Lady and Our Lord appear clearly on the photographs for people to see.

Innocent receives messages from both Our Lord and Our Lady. The messages he receives are generally for the world, and he is encouraged to distribute them. This is being done through the Apparition Investigation Association. The messages contain many warnings, predictions and prophecies. Some of these predictions have already come to pass. Primarily the messages point out how mankind has failed to serve God and has fallen to evil influences in the world. We are urged to repent, change our hearts and return to God and ask for His forgiveness. If mankind does not heed these messages then the hardships will increase, the influence of evil will be greatly felt on earth and commencing in 1980 the catastrophes and natural disasters will increase and escalate until the year 1992. We are warned that starting in 1992 even more serious calamities will occur and that "the most terrifying things will happen." The messages also warn of great wars after the year 1992 passes and that *"faithful Christians will suffer greatly."* (November 24, 1988) The messages identify certain countries which will suffer much.

On July 13, 1982 the message predicted uncontrollable epidemics, and added that scientists shall not find the cause *"but it is for the murder of the unborn that your country and America, particularly the USA will receive the disaster. The increase in earthquakes throughout the universe."* Then Our Blessed Lady added: *"I am sorry for Canada and California. Men of science find the answer."*

However, Our Heavenly Queen also told Innocent on November 24, 1988: *"... therefore, My children, I mean those that call Me Mother, those that honor Me, those that love Christ more than all things. Come! Come! Cry with all your strength to the Eternal Father, He will answer you people..."*

In some of the messages we are told of the "Jaffret Club, Operation 666," which is now active on earth and which is an instrument of Satan. We are told to avoid this club and all of its members. Satan's power on earth is on the increase and we must constantly pray, pray the rosary, receive the Holy Eucharist, and humbly turn to God in order to secure our own salvation and that of others.

In December 1985 the seer is reported to have received a special gift from Jesus and Mary in that Lucifer was compelled to narrate to the seer the inner thoughts and activities which Lucifer used on mankind.

Innocent has also authored certain "Inspired Writings" which are being distributed at the request of Our Lady. At one point Our Lord and Our Lady dictated to the seer "The History of the IGBOS" which has also been printed for distribution. Briefly the Igbos (the Ancestors of Innocent's lineage) were from the tribe of Juda, who came to Nigeria, after the Assyrians had conquered and dispersed the Israelites. This reportedly occurred during the period 718 BC to 638 BC.

The last reported apparition of Our Blessed Mother to Innocent occurred on July 30, 1989. There may have been additional messages not reported. In fact it is reported that the apparitions and messages are ongoing. Also the seer continues to suffer the flagellation which last occurred on Good Friday, 1994.

No Church action is reported.

IX The Primary Messages - 6

(1) Keep the Commandments - On November 24, 1988 Our Lady told the seer: *"You have transgressed all the Commandments of God; none is left unbroken by you people, but the serious and persistent ones are: idolatry, profanation of Sundays and Holy Days of Obligation, and adultery/ fornication. Go around the whole world and learn that My Son, Jesus Christ is no longer respected, most serious is the insults heaped upon Him in the Blessed Eucharist."*

(2) Abandon Idol Worship/False Gods - *"People have now taken to different methods of idol worshipping... There can never be any methods,* *ways, procedures and processes used in the worship of idols that will please your God and Creator. Fly away from idol worship."* This Our Lady said on November 24, 1988.

During this message Our Lady also informed and warned of the destructive Jaffret Club, Operation 666. She states that the destructive marks of any member of this club are a distaste for prayer and a stumbling block for those who hunger for prayers and a hatred of those who love devotions and reparations. *"The pleasures of the world please the members of Operation 666 more than the things of God,"* She said.

On July 13, 1982 Our Lady explained the meaning of Operation 666 in the Jaffrets Club: *"First 6 means six great demons who are in charge of destruction. They are now on earth with a special mission to destroy. Second 6 means the six terrible days of darkness, and the last 6 means the great six to handle punishments.*

"The devil will greatly increase his miracles and wonders. This will bring to a great increase, the worshipping of God through false devotions and ceremonies. . . . Many people during their prayers meditate not on their God that they are praying to, but clutter their souls with thoughts for the things of this world. Sincere repentance is what the Eternal Father demands of you people.

Then on July 30, 1989 Our Lady said: *". . . Most top officials in the world today are members of the Club (666). Those that belong to that Club do not know Me, Mary in their spirit..."*

(3) Prayer - *". . . Let all these pray with all their strength, with humble contrite heart, cry constantly to your God for your sins and those of the whole world, so that the Eternal Father will forgive you people. . . "* Thus was the message on November 24, 1988. Again during Holy Week 1983 Our Lady said: *"Prayer is something prayed with quietness and humility — that is, with a repentant heart one comes to God."*

". . . Continue praying, continue doing penance, continue lamenting and making reparations to appease God, who is the Eternal Father. Let 'Hail Mary' always be on your lips, you must say at least three Hail Marys daily. When you are not able to recite the Chaplet, you can at least pray the three Hail Marys daily. Whoever does this will be given graces of repentance, amendment and reconciliation with Christ who is always ready to accept you whenever you come back to Him." (October 28, 1980) *"Pray always for the priests of My Son, Jesus Christ. Pray fervently for them so that victory will be truly yours."* (July 30, 1989)

Again on March 23, 1986 Our Lady spoke: *". . . The ways of the Church of My Son are the Chaplet, prayerful songs, the remembrance and mortification is the way to appease God, penance and sleeplessness* (vigils) *without making noises and remembrance of the sufferings of My Son Jesus Christ and the words of God* (the Bible) *because all these culminate in holiness."*

(4) Pray the Rosary - "*Pray the rosary and the 'Catena'. The rosary is the great weapon which My Son's church has been using to vanquish her enemies... Pray the fifteen decades daily ... as the rosary is prayed the power of Satan diminishes.*" (Holy Week 1983)

Again on March 23, 1986 Our Lady said: "*My children, begin now to do penance, begin to perform good deeds, say your prayers, pray the Chaplet so that victory shall be yours.*"

On May 9, 1977 Our Lady says: "*Pray hard, all the faithful. You will triumph.*"

(5) Pray for the Priests - "*Pray for the priests and do penance, for the Church is in real darkness, but she will eventually triumph because of the promise of Christ.*" Thus said Our Lady on May 18, 1977.

Again on August 13, 1978: "*...You are required to pray and do penance for them* (priests) *instead of degrading them . . .*"

On May 25, 1987 Our Lady taught Innocent a prayer for controlling the tongue and She said: "*. . . avoid slander but seriously avoid slandering priests who are servants of My Son . . .*"

(6) Penance and Reparation - On July 30, 1989 Our Lady spoke: "*The period now is that of life or death, sorrow or joy. The Eternal Father will give you whichever you want. Therefore lament greatly, do penance! Do penance! Do it seriously so that the Eternal Father will give you joy. The period of reparation has now come, the great period of penance has set in . . .*"

X Signs Preceding the Apparition - Not Reported

XI Other Visions During Apparitions

(1) Jesus appeared to Innocent and gave him lengthy messages and Jesus also dictated the history of the Igbos to the seer.
(2) In December 1985 Lucifer was compelled to narrate his thoughts and activities concerning mankind. It is not reported that Lucifer appeared to the seer.

XII Prayers Taught to the Seer(s)

(1) On October 28, 1980 Our Lady told the seer to ask for whatever he wants from God through God's Mother and it shall be given. She said "*always say this prayer:*"
Prayer: 'You are my Mother, Mary, help me to avoid all occasions of sin; that I may console Thee and Thy Son Jesus Christ; that I may accept all situations in life that are the will of God, so as to gain eternal happiness

through Thee and Thy Son. Amen.'

"*Then say this:* 'You are my Mother, Mary, I love You, help me to love You and Thy Son more with all my heart and all my understanding. I entreat Thee to guide and direct me to live a holy life and to become a saint. Amen.' *Say these prayers always.*"

(2) On May 25, 1987 Our Lady taught Innocent the Prayer to control the tongue.

Prayer for the Tongue: 'Oh my God, permit not Your Spirit living in me to allow me to utter abominable words through my mouth. That this same Holy Spirit living in me may not allow my tongue to deceive me nor bring about condemnation on me, rather, grant that my tongue may be a source of encouragement to those in afflictions and in needs; that it may be an instrument of consolation in the midst of the sorrowful. Grant that my words may be a compass to those in the danger of being lost and that at all times it may bring to Thee, my God, the glorification of Your Name. Accept my tongue as Your own, and all my thoughts as Your working instruments; that the words coming out of my mouth may yield good conduct, peace and truth. Help me to be meek and humble. Permit me not to talk without reasons, rather grant that I may be in constant conversation with Thee than with creatures. That my words may gather people together rather than scatter them. That it may bring about the conversion of the hardened hearts, the fallen; to the extent that they continue to worship and love Thee through Jesus Christ Our Lord, Amen.' *After this, say*: 'One Our Father, Hail Mary, and Glory be, etc'. *Then say:*"

Prayer: 'Open my lips, and proclaim the Blessed Virgin, conceived without sin. Oh Queen make haste and be my Mother. With Your mighty power, deliver me from the hands of the enemy. Glory be to the Father, and to the Son, and to the Holy Ghost. As it was in the beginning is now and ever shall be world without end. Amen.' {Alleluia should be added where and when appropriate.} ' Praise be to Thee my Lord, the Everlasting King. Amen. Praise be to Jesus, now and forever. Amen.'

(3) On August 26, 1974 Our Lady taught the seer to say:

Prayer: 'My Queen and Mother, I give my whole self to You without reserve. I shall give respect to my Lord today by keeping my eyes, ears, mouth, heart and my whole body pure. Since I am Yours, my good Mother, protect and lead me as Your own. Amen.'

She further added that in time of temptation say this prayer quickly:

'My Queen and Mother, remember that I am Your own. Protect me and lead me as Your own. Amen.'

XIII Special Devotion Given to the Seer(s)

(1) The prayer for the tongue given to the seer by Our Lady may well be considered a special devotion.

(2) Although no new devotion is taught the seer, the Blessed Virgin did request devotion to Her Immaculate Heart. On October 28, 1980 Our Lady said: *"My Immaculate Heart must triumph. Therefore if you people follow Me you shall triumph with Me."*

XIV Requests Made by Our Lady

On October 28, 1980 Our Lady requested the formation of the Association of the Children of Mary. At that time Our Lady also said: *"Those that shall start the association should be prepared to embrace sufferings, constant prayer and also be ready to work at all times. I shall transform them to have new life. Any person that propagates My name shall have life, for he shall see the Lord, for the Lord shall save such a person for the time of that preordained war which is now at hand."*

XV Specific Bible References - Not Reported
XVI Secrets Given to the Seer(s) - Not Reported
XVII Miracles Promised by Our Lady - NR
XVIII Miracles Performed - Not Reported
XIX Miracles Promised not yet Performed - NR

XX Signs Promised

(1) August 26, 1974: *"Tell the people that they will see a sign which I will give them in the sky on the 18th of July, 1975 at 10:00 AM. You will see changes in the sun. The sun will start turning and changing to different colors. I shall make the people see the Archangel Michael. He will take the form by which people know him. The people will recognize him and name him themselves..."*

This sign or phenomenon took place and it is reported that people who were aware of the message saw the sign and saw St. Michael in the sky.

(2) May 9, 1977: *"There will be changes in the rainy season and dry season and harmattan."*

Here it is noted that a similar message was given on August 26, 1974. It is reported these changes have indeed occurred.

XXI Signs Given

(1) On July 18, 1975 it is reported that the sign of the Archangel Michael, appeared in the sky, as promised, on August 26, 1974.
(2) It is likewise reported that the sign promised on May 9, 1977 also came to pass.

(3) This seer received the Stigmata and suffers the flagellation every Lenten season.

XXII Predictions/Promises

(1) August 26, 1974: *"Your country will be plagued with too much money next year. There will be hunger in the midst of money. The situation will be ushered in by a strange light, after that* (light), *for example gari which sells now 13 cups for 10 Koba, the following day* (after the light) *gari will sell for 10 Koba for one cup."*

This is reported to have come to pass as predicted. Both the strange light and the spiral inflation reportedly occurred.

(2) The great sign predicted for July 18, 1975 also occurred as predicted when St. Michael appeared in the sky.

(3) August 5, 1976 Our Lady predicted that the next Pope after Paul VI would not be a Roman, but if he was a Roman, he would not last. That before the next Pope would be elected there would be misunderstanding among the cardinals, and the next day the real Pope would be selected. That in the interim there would be a false Pope, that a cardinal would declare himself Pope. (This message was typed and circulated to bishops and priests during a bishop's conference before the death of Pope Paul VI). Pope Paul VI died in 1978 and his successor was a Roman (Pope John Paul I) whose reign lasted only 34 days before he died. Next a Polish Pope, John Paul II was installed. A false pope declared himself in Spain as Gregory XVII.

(4) November 24, 1988: *"Earth tremors and earthquakes will increase tremendously in different countries of the world. The devil will greatly increase his miracles and wonders, the most serious of all wars will set in after 1992, contagious diseases and different types of sickness shall set in to an alarming state, terrible thunder storms will set in and untold hunger will take its own share.*

"Recall to mind that from 1992 on, the most terrifying things will happen; when all these might have happened, faithful Christians will suffer greatly; for during then the enemies of Christ will turn out to a great number and will condemn the worship of God . . ."

(5) Our Lady predicted that the tribulations would start in 1980 and increase in the form of heat, famine, hunger, epidemics, that different types of disease and different types of death would appear throughout the world.

The messages say that it will be very difficult to cure or eradicate these diseases and they would never yield to any type of drug or therapy. That from 1984/85 serious things will happen such as earthquakes, landslides and great heat; but the most serious sufferings will befall the people in 1992 when terrible things will happen. 1992 marks the year of the beginning of the period of greatest suffering.

On March 23, 1986 Our Lady said: *"Look from now onwards till 1992 many governments will collapse. Different countries shall fall. Countries will wage wars against other countries, war will be widespread and life will be much harder."*

XXIII Prophecies/Warnings of Chastisement

Nearly every message reported contains one or more warnings of the coming chastisement; yet always tempered with a plea for conversion in order to lessen or eliminate the suffering.

August 26, 1974: *"Russia will cause war which will spread everywhere."*

May 9, 1977: *"There will be great flashes of lightning which will bring down light and consume many of the creatures of earth including human beings . . . different towns will experience earth collapse. All the hills in different towns will fall into the earth. The Almighty Father will order the earth to open up and swallow towns and hills. When all these things shall have come true then there will come some things . . . the sun ceases its light and there will be darkness everywhere."*

August 13, 1978: *"My children return to God. If you don't I will let fall the wrath of My Son which I have suspended for a very long time whereby life has looked normal for humanity. The punishment which will follow such an action on My part will be great, very great."*

October 26, 1980: *"Terrible sufferings will befall you in 1992 . . ."*

July 13, 1982: *"In America, towns, cities, hills and states will fall into the earth. In Europe, Africa and Asia hills and towns will fall into the earth. Pray hard in order to lessen the power, otherwise the Almighty Father will order the earth to open up and swallow cities, states, towns and hills. This must happen. Your country will witness different types of epidemic, uncontrollable epidemics; tears will be shed for many shall die, especially children. Scientists shall not find the cause, but it is for the murder of unborn that your country and America, particularly the USA, receive the disaster, the increase of earthquakes throughout the universe."*

Then Our Lady added: *"I am sorry for Canada and California. Men of science find the answer."*

May 25, 1987: *"It is long now that I have been hammering on 1992. If by 1992 you people failed to amend your ways, and then appease the Eternal Father, the punishment will grow tremendously, when the most serious sufferings, uncontrollable unrest and great bloodshed will set in . . ."*

Again: *"When your cup shall be filled, when fire rains down and consumes the whole world; not only consuming all the amassed treasures but both human and animal lives."*

Our Lady continues: *"But if you people do what I instructed you to do, it will then happen very little . . ."*

November 24, 1988: *"Rainfall will be accompanied with terrible landslides great earth tremors and earthquakes, the great heat which the sun will radiate towards the earth will set many towns on fire which will be accompanied by serious earthquakes and landslides."* Again: *"There will be terrible wars, such that had never been heard of; but the most serious of all wars will set in after 1992; when 1992 might have come to pass, faithful Christians will suffer greatly . . . this will lead to the period of the complete darkness* (the disappearance of the sun)."

July 30, 1989: *"The period of reparation has now come; from now till 1992 and beyond, great hardships and sufferings will set in. I give you warnings concerning all that will take place from the year 1992. This would mark the beginning of the period of greatest suffering."*

XXIV Method of Appearance - Not Reported
XXV Method of Departure - Not Reported
XXVI Confrontation w/Civil Authorities - NR
XXVII Confrontation w/Church Authorities - NR
XXVIII Request Chapel/Shrine Built - NR

XXIX Free Will/Choice

On May 18, 1977 Our Lady said: *"God has given you intelligence to do good things, to know what is good and bad. He has also given you the way to life which you must follow. There are two ways and everyone is free to choose. . ."*

XXX Seer(s)' Suffering/Sacrifice

(1) Throughout the messages Our Lady tells the seer that he will suffer much; that many will criticize him who do not believe the messages, and others will start to follow the messages and then will fall away. This all causes the seer great spiritual and emotional distress.
(2) This seer suffers the flagellation and the wounds of Christ.

XXXI Healings Reported - Not Reported

XXXII Action Taken by the Church

An association named the Pilgrimage Association and now known as Apparition Investigation Association has been formed to record and distribute the messages of Innocent Okorie. This is not an official Church action.

XXXIII Bibliography

Messages From Our Lord Jesus Christ and the Blessed Virgin Mary
By: AIA
Published by: AIA

The Review of Life (Part one & Part two)
Inspired writings of Innocent Okorie
By: Innocent Okorie
Published by: AIA

The History of the Igbos and the Chronology of Events
Revealed to Innocent Okorie The Stigmatist by Our Lord Jesus Christ and the Blessed Virgin Mary
By: Innocent Okorie
Published by: AIA

Chapter 30

AKITA, JAPAN
(1973)

I Place - Akita, Japan
(Convent of Handmaids of the Eucharist at Yuzawadai)

II Dates of First and Last Apparition

First: July 6, 1973
Last: October 13, 1973

III Seer(s) - 1

Name: Sister Agnes Katsuko Sasagawa (Servants of the Eucharist)
Birth: May 28, 1931
Age at first apparition: 42
Status: Living

IV Total Number of Apparitions - 3

V Dates and Locality of Each Apparition

All apparitions of Our Lady occurred inside the chapel at the convent in Akita unless otherwise noted.

1973: July 6; August 3; October 13.
In addition to the apparitions of Our Lady to the seer, the seer's own guardian angel also appeared to her and gave the seer messages.

The Statue of Our Lady wept human tears 101 times from January 4, 1975 to September 15, 1981; and human blood came from the wound on the right hand of the statue.

VI Description of Our Lady

In each instance the seer saw the wooden statue of Our Lady come to life, it was bathed in a brilliant light, then Our Lady spoke to the seer in a voice of indescribable beauty from the statue.

VII Title(s) of Our Lady - 1

(1) Generally known as "Our Lady of Akita."
(2) Our Lady did not announce a title during any of the messages to the seer. These messages were given by Our Lady from a wooden statue carved after the likeness of Our Lady of All Nations, when Our Lady earlier appeared to a seer in Amsterdam, Holland under the title (Our Lady of all Nations).

VIII Brief Factual Review

Japan is an Island nation located in the Pacific Ocean across the Sea of Japan from Korea, China and the USSR.

The seer, Agnes Katsuko Sasagawa, was born on May 28, 1931 in Joetsu City, Japan. She had been ill since childhood and at age 19 her lower limbs became paralyzed. In 1956 when she was 25 she was cured of this paralysis by drinking Lourdes water. In 1973, seventeen years later, she lost her hearing.

Sister Agnes joined the convent of the Handmaids of the Eucharist located at Akita, some 200 kilometers north of Tokyo. Bishop Ito was the founder of the Institute (Order) and it was upon his invitation that she joined the Handmaids. Her duties were to teach catechism and take care of the church in Myoko.

The first of the extraordinary events occurred on June 12, 1973 when Sr. Agnes saw a brilliant mysterious light emanate from the Tabernacle. This same phenomenon occurred again on each of the next two days. On June 28, 1973 a cross shaped wound appeared on the inside of the seer's left hand. The wound was painful and bled profusely. On July 5, 1973 her guardian angel appeared and prayed with Sr. Agnes.

On July 6, 1973 Our Lady spoke to Sr. Agnes from the statue for the first time. Also on July 6, 1973 other nuns first noticed a wound cross-shaped on the inside of the right hand of the statue of Our Lady. This wound bled human blood on four separate occasions, then on September

23, 1973 it completely disappeared. On that day when the wound disappeared; the statue began to "sweat" human perspiration.

Our Lady spoke from the statue to the seer on two other occasions: August 3 and October 13, 1973. Our Lady gave warnings of a terrible chastisement by fire which is to befall humankind to show God's anger caused by the gravity and multitude of sins committed by mankind.

Sister Agnes' guardian angel appeared to her several times and gave her messages. Her guardian angel told her she would be cured of her deafness, first temporarily, then permanently. In each case it happened as the angel predicted. In 1969 her guardian angel taught her to say the "Fatima Prayer" at the end of each decade of the rosary.

The statue wept human tears on 101 separate occasions, beginning January 4, 1975 and finally weeping on September 15, 1981.

On September 28, 1981 an invisible angel opened a visible Bible to Genesis 3:15 and explained to the seer the biblical relationship and meaning of the statue weeping 101 times.

Our Lady pleads for prayer, penance and sacrifice to soften God's anger and in reparation for the sins of mankind. On October 13, 1973 Our Lady said: *"If sins increase in number and gravity, there will be no longer pardon for them."*

These apparitions have been approved by the Church.

IX The Primary Messages - 3

(1) Prayer in Reparation:
Prayer for the Pope and Clergy: - July 6, 1973: *"My daughter, My novice, you have obeyed Me well in abandoning all to follow Me. Is the infirmity of your ears painful? Your deafness will be healed, be sure. Be patient. It is the last trial. Does the wound of your hand cause you to suffer? Pray in reparation for the sins of men. Each person in this community is My irreplaceable daughter. Do you say well the prayer of the Handmaids of the Eucharist? Then, let us pray it together:*

"Most Sacred Heart of Jesus, truly present in the Holy Eucharist, I consecrate my body and soul to be entirely one with Your Heart, being sacrificed at every instant on the altars of the world and giving praise to the Father pleading for the coming of His Kingdom.

"Please receive this humble offering of myself. Use me as You will for the glory of the Father and the salvation of souls.

"Most Holy Mother of God, never let me be separated from Your Divine Son. Please defend and protect me as Your special Child. Amen."

When the prayer was finished the Heavenly Voice said: *"Pray very much for the Pope, bishops and priests. Since your Baptism you have always prayed faithfully for them. Continue to pray very much ... very much. Tell your superior all that passed today and obey him in everything* that he will tell you. He has asked that you pray with fervor."

(2) Prayer, Penance, Sacrifice, Warning of Chastisements - August 3, 1973: *"My daughter, My novice, do you love the Lord? If you love the Lord, listen to what I have to say to you. It is very important... You will convey it to your superior.*

"Many men in this world afflict the Lord. I desire souls to console Him to soften the anger of the Heavenly Father. I wish, with My Son, for souls who will repair by their suffering and their poverty for the sinners and ingrates.

"In order that the world might know His anger, the Heavenly Father is preparing to inflict a great chastisement on all mankind. With My Son I have intervened so many times to appease the wrath of the Father. I have prevented the coming of calamities by offering Him the sufferings of the Son on the Cross, His Precious Blood, and beloved souls who console Him forming a cohort of victim souls. Prayer, penance and courageous sacrifices can soften the Father's anger. I desire this also from your community ... that it love poverty, that it sanctify itself and pray in reparation for the ingratitude and outrages of so many men. Recite the prayer of the Handmaids of the Eucharist with awareness of its meaning; put it into practice; offer in reparation (whatever God may send) for sins. Let each one endeavor, according to capacity and position, to offer herself to the Lord.

"Even in a secular institute prayer is necessary. Already souls who wish to pray are on the way to being gathered together. Without attaching too much attention to the form, be faithful and fervent in prayer to console the Master."

After a silence: *"Is what you think in your heart true? Are you truly deciding to become a rejected stone? My novice, you who wish to belong without reserve to the Lord, to become the spouse worthy of the Spouse, make your vows knowing that you must be fastened to the Cross with three nails. These three nails are poverty, chastity and obedience. Of the three, obedience is the foundation. In total abandon, let yourself be led by your superior. He will know how to understand you and to direct you."*

(3) Pray the Rosary, Warning of Chastisements - October 13, 1973: *"My dear daughter, listen well to what I have to say to you. You will inform your superior."*

After a short silence: *"As I told you, if men do not repent and better themselves, the Father will inflict a terrible punishment on all humanity. It will be a punishment greater than the Deluge, such as one will never have seen before. Fire will fall from the sky and will wipe out a great part of humanity, the good as well as the bad, sparing neither priests nor faithful. The survivors will find themselves so desolate that they will envy the dead. The only arms which will remain for you will be the rosary and the Sign left by My Son. Each day recite the prayers of the rosary. With the rosary, pray for the Pope, the bishops and the priests."*

"The work of the devil will infiltrate even into the Church in such a way that one will see cardinals opposing cardinals, bishops against bishops. The priests who venerate Me will be scorned by their conferees ... churches will be full of those who accept compromises and the demon will press many priests and consecrated souls to leave the service of the Lord.

"The demon will be especially implacable against souls consecrated to God. The thought of the loss of so many souls is the cause of My sadness. If sins increase in number and gravity, there will be no longer pardon for them.

"With courage, speak to your superior. He will know how to encourage each one of you to pray and to accomplish works of reparation.

"It is Bishop Ito, who directs your community." Our Lady smiled and then said: "You have still something to ask? Today is the last time that I will speak to you in living voice. From now on you will obey the one sent to you and your superior. (Until this message, Sr Agnes was unsure whom Our Lady was referring to as 'your superior'.)

"Pray very much the prayers of the rosary. I alone am able still to save you from the calamities which approach. Those who place their confidence in Me will be saved."

X Signs Preceding the Apparition

(1) On July 6, 1973 the seer suddenly felt the statue come alive and bathed in brilliant light, just before Our Lady spoke.
On October 13, 1973 the seer again saw the luminous light radiating from the Tabernacle and filling the whole chapel.
(2) The seer's guardian angel first appeared on July 5 and again on August 3 before Our Lady spoke. The angel also appeared during the October 13 message.

XI Other Visions During Apparitions

(1) The seer's guardian angel appeared and gave messages to her on each of the three occasions when Our Lady gave messages.
(2) The seer's guardian angel appeared to her at other times when Our Lady did not appear.

XII Prayers Taught to the Seer(s)

(1) On July 6, 1973 Our Lady instructed Sr. Agnes to add the word 'truly' to the Handmaid's Prayer of the Eucharist.
(2) In 1969 her guardian angel taught the seer to add the 'Fatima prayer' after each decade of the rosary.

XIII Special Devotion Given to the Seer(s)

Refer to Section XII above.

XIV Requests Made by Our Lady

(1) Prayer: July 6, August 3, October 13, 1973.
(2) Prayer: Penance, Courageous Sacrifice; August 3, 1973.
(3) Pray the rosary: October 13, 1973.
(4) Add the word '**truly**' to the Handmaid's Eucharist Prayer: July 6, 1973.

XV Specific Bible References

On September 28, 1981 the invisible angel opened a visible Bible to Genesis 3:15 and invited Sr. Agnes to read a passage (Genesis 3:15). The voice of the angel was heard explaining in sort of a preamble that the passage just read had relationship with the tears of Mary.

The angel continued: *"There is a meaning to the figure one hundred and one. This signifies that sin came into the world by a woman and it is also by a woman that salvation came to the world. The 'zero' between the two signifies the Eternal God who is from all eternity until eternity. The first one represents Eve and the last one the Virgin Mary."*

XVI Secrets Given to the Seer(s) - Not Reported

XVII Miracles Promised by Our Lady

Although Our Lady did not promise a miracle She did promise that the deafness of the seer would be healed. Agnes' guardian angel did predict, first a temporary, and then a permanent healing of the seer's deafness. It happened as promised.

XVIII Miracles Performed

Both the temporary and the permanent healing predicted by the seer's guardian angel came true as predicted.

XIX Miracles Promised not yet Performed - NR

XX Signs Promised

The seer's guardian angel predicted the cure of her hearing loss.

XXI Signs Given

(1) **Seer's Stigmata** - On June 28, 1973 the seer received a cross-shaped wound in her left hand which bled profusely. This wound disappeared completely on July 28, 1973.
(2) **Statue Wound** - On July 6, 1973 the statue of Our Lady had a similar cross-shaped wound appear on its right hand, which bled human blood. This wound remained until September 29, 1973.
(3) **Statue Perspires** - After the wound on the hand of the statue closed on September 29, 1973, the statue of Our Lady oozed a copious perspiration emitting a wonderful fragrance.
(4) **Worm** - On October 16, 1973 a single live worm appeared in front of each sister present; this was the beginning of a horrible stench coming from the confessional.
(5) **Dream of Snow** - On January 30, 1974 Sr. Agnes had a dream that the weight of the snow was collapsing the roof of the convent. It proved to be true just as she had dreamed.
(6) **Dream of Serpent** - On June 10, 1974 Sr. Agnes had a dream that a serpent was in one of the rooms at the convent. This also was true as dreamed.
(7) **Statue Weeps Tears** - The Statue of Our Lady wept human tears 101 times starting January 4, 1975 and ending September 15, 1981.
(8) **Genesis 3:15** - On September 28, 1981 the invisible angel opened a visible Bible and requested Sr. Agnes to read a passage from Genesis 3:15. Thereafter the angel explained to Sr. Agnes the meaning of the statue weeping 101 times.
(9) **Rosary of the Birds** - It is reported that on June 15, 1986 Sr. Agnes recovered a wooden rosary and Miraculous Medal which had been given to her some 11 years prior by Sr. Yasu Esumi, Mother Superior of the Nagasaki Junskin Convent. Sr. Agnes had lost this rosary somewhere on the grounds surrounding the Akita Convent.

It seems Sr. Agnes was accustomed to feeding the birds the left over crumbs of bread from breakfast at her second story window. If she left her window open the birds would fly inside and peck her on her cheek. On this occasion of June 15, 1986 Sr. Agnes closed the window in her bedroom in order to get a good sleep. Sr. Maria Theresa Kazuko Kaizu who had the room next to Sr. Agnes relates that before 5:00 AM she was awakened by a commotion outside Sr. Agnes' window. Sr. Agnes was also awakened and went to her window to find two birds (robins), fluttering in place with their wings vibrating while suspended in midair. Then Sr. Agnes noticed something shinning on the window sill. There she found the Miraculous Medal and wooden rosary on her window sill; the very ones lost for some 11 years. As soon as Sr. Agnes found these the robins flew away. The nuns of the convent now call Sister Agnes' rosary "The Rosary of the Bird" (Torino Rosario). The rosary and medal are kept at the convent as a reminder of God's love and Our Blessed Mother's special love for Her most holy rosary. (Mary's People Vol. 30 No. 52; Twin Circle Supplement-December 25, 1994)

XXII Predictions/Promises

Sister Agnes' guardian angel predicted her temporary healing and her permanent healing; both of which came true as predicted.

XXIII Prophecies/Warnings of Chastisement

(1) August 3, 1973: *"My daughter, My novice, do you love the Lord? If you love the Lord, listen to what I have to say to you. It is very important... You will convey it to your superior.*

"Many men in this world afflict the Lord. I desire souls to console Him to soften the anger of the Heavenly Father. I wish, with My Son, for souls who will repair by their suffering and their poverty for the sinners and ingrates.

"In order that the world might know His anger, the Heavenly Father is preparing to inflict a great chastisement on all mankind. With My Son I have intervened so many times to appease the wrath of the Father. I have prevented the coming of calamities by offering Him the sufferings of the Son on the Cross, His Precious Blood, and beloved souls who console Him forming a cohort of victim souls. Prayer, penance and courageous sacrifices can soften the Father's anger. I desire this also from your community ... that it love poverty, that it sanctify itself and pray in reparation for the ingratitude and outrages of so many men. Recite the prayer of the Handmaids of the Eucharist with awareness of its meaning; put it into practice; offer in reparation (whatever God may send) for sins. Let each one endeavor, according to capacity and position, to offer herself to the Lord."

(2) October 13, 1973: *"My dear daughter, listen well to what I have to say to you. You will inform your superior."*

After a short silence: *"As I told you, if men do not repent and better themselves, the Father will inflict a terrible punishment on all humanity. It will be a punishment greater than the Deluge, such as one will never have seen before. Fire will fall from the sky and will wipe out a great part* of humanity, the good as well as the bad, sparing neither priests nor faithful. The survivors will find themselves so desolate that they will envy the dead. The only arms which will remain for you will be the rosary and the Sign left by My Son. Each day recite the prayers of the rosary. With the rosary, pray for the Pope, the bishops and the priests.

"The work of the devil will infiltrate even into the Church in such a way that one will see cardinals opposing cardinals, bishops against bishops. The priests who venerate Me will be scorned by their conferees ... churches will be full of those who accept compromises and the demon will press many priests and consecrated souls to leave the service of the Lord.

"The demon will be especially implacable against souls consecrated to God. The thought of the loss of so many souls is the cause of My sadness. If sins increase in number and gravity, there will be no longer pardon for them.

"With courage, speak to your superior. He will know how to encourage each one of you to pray and to accomplish works of reparation."

"Pray very much the prayers of the rosary. I alone am able still to save you from the calamities which approach. Those who place their confidence in Me will be saved."

XXIV Method of Appearance

Generally the seer's guardian angel would first appear and speak to Sr. Agnes, then the wooden statue of Our Lady would come to life and become bathed in a brilliant light. It is then that Our Lady gave messages to Sr. Agnes. Sr. Agnes usually remained prostrate while Our Lady spoke.

XXV Method of Departure

After each message when Sr. Agnes looked up, the luminous splendor had completely disappeared and her guardian angel was no longer visible and the statue had resumed its normal aspect.

XXVI Confrontation w/Civil Authorities

Great opposition and criticism from all sides came after the publication (Catholic Groph) first informed the public about the weeping statue of Our Lady.

XXVII Confrontation w/Church Authorities

(1) The first inquiry commission concluded that Sr. Agnes was a psychopath from birth and had already manifested ectoplasmic powers which had

now resurfaced. This committee found that Sr. Agnes' experiences were without validity.

(2) On September 12, 1981 a second commission of 7 members was appointed by Bishop Ito. When the commission had concluded its inquiry four members voted in favor of recognizing the events as supernatural and three voted against. In spite of the majority, Bishop Ito used prudence and waited. On September 15, 1981 the statue again wept for the 101st and last time.

It was thereafter on September 28, 1981 that the invisible angel appeared and the visible Bible was opened to Genesis (3:15) when the angel explained to the seer the meaning of the statue weeping 101 times.

It was also thereafter on May 30, 1982 that Sr. Agnes was permanently cured of deafness as predicted by the angel. After this, sudden and dramatic healings occurred to many others. Finally on Easter Sunday, April 22, 1984 Bishop Ito issued his pastoral letter declaring the "events of Akita" to be supernatural.

In June 1988 Joseph Cardinal Ratzinger judged the Akita phenomenon and messages to be reliable and worthy of belief.

XXVIII Request Chapel/Shrine Built - NR

XXIX Free Will/Choice

(1) July 6, 1973 Our Lady said: *"My daughter, My novice, you have obeyed Me well in abandoning all to follow Me....it is the last trial. Since your Baptism you have always prayed faithfully for them..."*

Thus Our Lady recognizes that the seer had chosen of her own free will to abandon herself and to follow Our Lady and to be faithful in prayer.

(2) August 3, 1973 Our Lady said: *"My daughter, My novice, do you love the Lord? I desire souls to console Him to soften the anger of the Heavenly Father. I wish, with My Son, for souls who will repair by their suffering and their poverty for sinners and ingrates."*

Our Lady invites us to use our free will and to choose to make reparation for the sins of mankind. *"Is what you think in your heart true? Are you truly decided to become the rejected stone?"* Thus asked Our Lady. She recognizes that Sr. Agnes made a deliberate choice and decided to become the "rejected stone".

(3) October 13, 1973 Our Lady said: *"The priests who venerate Me will be scorned and opposed by their conferees. The demon will press many priests and consecrated souls to leave the service of the Lord."*

It seems that Our Lady especially invited priests and religious to use their free will and choose to remain faithful to the Lord.

XXX Seer(s)' Suffering/Sacrifice

(1) The seer willingly suffered deafness; not once but twice. She is a victim soul and accepts all suffering sent by God.
(2) She also suffered great pain from the bleeding wound to her left hand.
(3) The first investigation into the events resulted in Sr. Agnes being accused of being psychopathic and manifesting ectoplasmic powers. Of course these false accusations caused her great pain and suffering, even though Bishop Ito later declared the events as being supernatural in origin.

XXXI Healings Reported

Aside from the predicted and miraculous healings of Sr. Agnes herself, there have been many other healings.

One such healing occurred to Theresa Chun, a Korean, age 46, baptized Catholic on April 11, 1981. On July 3, 1981 she developed brain cancer without hope for cure. Treatment was of no avail and she fell into a coma. Theresa had no knowledge of the events occurring at Akita.

On October 15, 1983 some Korean pilgrims came to Akita and a priest, Father Oh, brought back photos of the Our Lady of Akita statue. He himself had witnessed the statue weeping on May 26, 1979.

Father Oh gave a photo of Our Lady to both Theresa's sister and to her Godmother. Theresa, however, was not shown this photo at this time. At the hospital certain treatments were proposed for Theresa, when Theresa suddenly began to speak like a child and said: "I do not wish it, Jesus will cure me." Thereupon her family placed all their hopes in Our Lady and they were not disappointed.

Within a space of six months Our Lady appeared to Theresa three times and she became completely cured. The first apparition was on August 4, 1981 when Our Lady appeared wearing a golden garment and held in Her arms a lamb as white as snow. She breathed three times on the forehead of Theresa, who reported the breath as alive, warm and so strong that she could see the wool of the lamb wave as Our Lady breathed on her. Those present heard Theresa cry out: "Lamb! Lamb! Lamb!", but they did not understand.

The second apparition took place on the Feast of The Assumption, August 15, 1981. Our Lady wore the same golden garment but no longer held the lamb. Our Lady first asked Theresa to say the morning prayer with Her, then ordered Theresa to rise. Theresa did get up but needed assistance from her sister.

The third and final apparition took place in the X-ray room of the hospital of St. Paul on December 9, 1981 while Theresa was being examined to see if she had been cured. This time Our Lady wore a garment of brilliant white. She looked at Theresa with a smile before going back towards heaven, all the while smiling.

The X-rays showed that Theresa was completely cured. The authorities of the local church recognized that the miraculous cure of Theresa Chun was due to the intercession of Our Lady of Akita, and sent a letter to the Vatican so stating.

After Theresa was cured her sister showed her the photo of Our Lady of Akita, and Theresa did not hesitate to recognize Our Lady of Akita as both the author of her cure and the Lady that had thrice appeared to her.

XXXII Action Taken by the Church

(1) By pastoral letter of April 22, 1984 Bishop Ito declared the supernatural character of events occurring in Akita and authorized veneration of the Holy Mother of Akita.
(2) In June 1988 Joseph Cardinal Ratzinger judged the Akita phenomena and messages as reliable and worthy of belief.
(3) Akita has approval of the Church.

XXXIII Bibliography

Akita, the Tears and Message of Mary
By: Teiji Yasuda. CSV. 1989
English Version by: John Haffert 1989
Published by: 101 Foundation, Inc.

The Meaning of Akita 1989
By: John Haffert
Published by: 101 Foundation, Inc.

Chapter 31

MILAN, ITALY
(1973 to Present)

I Place - Milan, Italy (and various other places)

II Dates of First and Last Apparition

First: July 7, 1973 (locution)
Last: December 31, 1994 (last reported)
Note: The locutions are reportedly ongoing.

III Seer(s) - 1

Name: Fr. (Don) Stefano Gobbi (Company of St. Paul)
Birth: March 22, 1930
Age at first apparition: 43
Status: Living

IV Total Number of Apparitions - 536

(Through December 31, 1994. This seer receives locutions only.)

V Dates and Locality of Each Apparition

1973: Thirty-two locutions in five locations in Italy: Milan, Spotorno, Dongo, San Vittorino, Ravenna.
1974: Thirty-five locutions in three countries: Rome, Milan, Arcade, Dongo, Italy; Lourdes, France; Fatima, Portugal.
1975: Twenty-four locutions in Milan, Italy.

1976: Twenty-five locutions, of which 24 were in Milan, Italy and one in Lourdes, France.
1977: Twenty-seven locutions: one in Mexico; one in Fatima, Portugal; one at Nijmegen, Holland; one at Montegiove, one in Rome and the others in Milan, Italy.
1978: Twenty-four locutions: Milan, Rome, Italy; Fatima, Portugal; Florida, USA; Nagasaki, Japan; Hong Kong, China; Czestochowa, Poland.
1979: Twenty-four locutions: Milan, Italy; Garabandal, Spain; San Miguel, Azores; Fatima, Portugal; Altotting, Germany; Nijmegen, Holland; Lourdes, France; Nairobi (Kenya) & Douala (Cameroon), Africa.
1980: Twenty-eight locutions: Milan and Rome, Italy; Salzburg, Austria; Cologne, Germany; Fatima, Portugal; New York (N.Y.), Inverness (Florida), and Chicago (Illinois), USA; Cebu and Manila, Philippines; Sidney and Melbourne, Australia; Calcutta and Bangalore, India.
1981: Twenty-one locutions: Milan, Valdragone (San Marino), Italy; Lome (Togo), Africa; Tananarive, Madagascar; Sao Paulo, Brasilia & Ponta Grossa, Brazil; Montevideo, Uruguay; Buenos Aires, Argentina; Santiago, Chile; Quito, Ecuador; Puebla, Mexico; New York (N.Y.), USA.
1982: Seventeen locutions: Milan, Rome, Valdragone (San Marino), Italy; Jerusalem, Israel; Munich and Blumenfeld, Germany; Split, Yugoslavia; Nijmegen, Holland; Paris, France; Fatima, Portugal.
1983: Twenty-four locutions: Milan, Pescara, Valdragone (San Marino), Italy; Toronto, Vancouver, Montreal, Canada; Saint Francis (Maine), and Fort Lauderdale (Florida), USA; Curacao (Antilles), West Indies; Enugu (Nigeria) and Grand Bassam (Ivory Coast), Africa.
1984: Twenty-one locutions: Milan, Dongo, Castelmonte, Zompita, San Marco, Valdragone (San Marino), Italy; Altotting, Germany; Strasbourg, France; Fatima, Portugal; London, England; Zagreb, Yugoslavia.
1985: Eighteen locutions: Milan, Dongo, Pescara, Castelmonte, Valdragone (San Marino), Italy; Cagliari, Sardinia; Fulda, Germany; Fatima, Portugal; Auckland, New Zealand; Perth & Melbourne, Australia.
1986: Twenty-four locutions: Milan, Dongo, Merine, Rubbio, Tivoli, Sant'Omero, Naples, Valdragone (San Marino), Italy; Fort Lauderdale (Florida) and Dallas (Texas), USA; Santiago, Dominican Republic.
1987: Twenty-seven locutions: Milan, Dongo, Rubbio, San Quirino, Valdragone (San Marino), Italy; Washington D.C., Denver (Colorado), Seattle (Washington) and Detroit (Michigan), USA; Ottawa, Canada; Tokyo & Akita, Japan; Seoul & Inchon, Korea; Taipei, Taiwan; Hong Kong.
1988: Twenty-six locutions: Milan, Dongo, Rubbio, San Marco, Italy; Porto Alegre, Manaus-Amazonas, Recife-Pernambuco, San Paulo-Itaici, Brazil; Marienfried and Heede, Germany; Le Bouveret (Vallese), Switzerland; Knock, Ireland; Vienna, Austria; Paris & Lourdes, France;

Madrid, Spain; Fatima, Portugal; Zagreb, Yugoslavia.
1989: Twenty locutions: Milan, Rubbio, Dongo, Sant'Omero, Valdragone (San Marino), Italy; Tindari, Sicily; Fatima, Portugal.
1990: Twenty-four locutions: Milan, Rubbio, Dongo, Valdragone (San Marino) Italy; Jauru, Brasilia, Sao Paulo, Brazil; Malvern (Pennsylvania), Saint David (Maine), Dallas (Texas), USA; St. Albert (Alberta) and Quebec, Canada; Fatima, Portugal; Vacallo, Switzerland; Budapest, Hungary; Mexico City, Mexico.
1991: Twenty-three locutions: Milan, Rubbio, Dongo, Valdragone (San Marino) Italy; Cagliari, Sardinia; Brasilia, Brazil; Olomouc (Moravia), Czechoslovakia; Salzburg, Austria; Berlin, Germany; Sastin, Slovakia; Velehrad, Bohemia; Budapest, Hungary; Birkenhead, Birmingham, England.
1992: Twenty-two locutions: Rubbio, Bologna, Sant'Omero, San Marco, Valdragone (San Marino), Italy; San Salvador, El Salvador; Managua, Nicaragua; Quito, Ecuador; Sao Paulo, Brazil.
1993: Twenty-four locutions: Rubbio, Sant'Omero, Dongo, Milan, Caravaggio, Valdragone (San Marino), Italy; Fatima, Portugal; Gap, France; Vallese, Switzerland; Sydney and Perth, Australia; Jakarata-Cisarua, Indonesia; Suva, Figi Islands; Beppu-Oita and Tokyo, Japan; Jauru and Sao Paulo, Brazil.
1994: Twenty-six locutions: Capoliveri, Caravaggio, Dongo, Milan, Rome, Rubbio, Sant'Omero, Valdragone (San Marino), Italy; San Leonardo, Sardinia; Ottawa and Saskatoon, Canada; Bogota, Columbia; Santiago, Dominican Republic; Ilobasco, El Salvador; Berlin, Germany; Tegucigalpa, Honduras; Lago de Guadalupe and Our Lady of Guadalupe Shrine (Mexico City), Mexico; Omaha (Nebraska), Effingham (Illinois) and Saint Francis (Maine), USA.

VI Description of Our Lady - Not Reported

VII Title(s) of Our Lady - 1

On January 1, 1990 Our Lady said: *"I am the Mother of the Second Advent."*
Note: Our Lady has announced Herself under numerous other titles which are not all included in this work.

VIII Brief Factual Review

Don Stefano Gobbi was granted a late vocation to the priesthood. On May 8, 1972 while on a pilgrimage to Fatima, Don Gobbi was praying in the little Chapel of the Apparitions. He was particularly praying for some priests who had given up their own vocations, and who were also attempting to associate themselves in a planned rebellion against the Church's authority. A strong interior force beckoned his confidence in the Immaculate Heart of Mary and further stressed that he be used as an instrument to gather priests, who would in turn accept Her invitation to consecrate themselves to Her Immaculate Heart, always strongly united to the Pope and to the Church and to bring the faithful to Her safe refuge. By this means a powerful cohort would be formed and would spread throughout the world.

Don Gobbi asked Our Lady for a sign of confirmation. She responded with a sign before the end of the month while he was at the Shrine of the Annunciation at Nazareth.

It was in this manner, from this simple incident that Father Gobbi's life mission was born; that of the Marian Movement of Priests. The movement, although having a modest beginning, has now reached worldwide membership of priests as well as laity. It is reported that some 60,000 priests are members and millions of lay people. The International headquarters is in Milan, Italy.

The requirements for membership are simple and straightforward: Consecration to the Immaculate Heart of Mary, unity with the Pope and Church, thus united leading the faithful to a life of entrustment to Our Lady.

The publication entitled "To the Priests, Our Lady's beloved Sons" has been published in most widely used languages. A great number of editions have been published. The publication contains forms for the Act of Consecration to the Immaculate Heart of Mary to be used by priests, forms to be used by religious and laity, and forms to be used by young people.

Don Gobbi received the first locution on July 7, 1973 on the Feast of the Immaculate Heart of Mary. This first message was brief and said in part: *"Renew your consecration to My Immaculate Heart. You are mine; you belong to Me."*

It was in the very next message that Our Lady announced: *"The Marian Movement of Priests is now born..."* (July 8, 1973)

Thereafter he received messages from Our Lady at different locations around the world. Many of the messages, if not most, were received on important Feast Days of Our Blessed Lady.

Also interestingly enough the messages take on a theme for each calendar year and the messages given seem to unfold a larger living message or pattern. Each year's messages are given an appropriate title in the publication which heralds the theme of the messages for that year. Each year's messages seem to build on the shoulders of the previous year's messages.

Therefore the theme's given are:
    (1) 1973 - The Movement is now born.
    (2) 1974 - Cenacles of Life with Me.
    (3) 1975 - Be Joyous.
    (4) 1976 - You must be Little.
    (5) 1977 - In Every Part of the World.

- (6) 1978 - Your Public Mission.
- (7) 1979 - The Signs of the Purification.
- (8) 1980 - Your Victorious Mother.
- (9) 1981 - The Light and Glory of the Lord.
- (10) 1982 - I am the Consoling Mother.
- (11) 1983 - Open Wide the Gates to Christ.
- (12) 1984 - I ask the Consecration of all.
- (13) 1985 - I am the Beginning of the New Times.
- (14) 1986 - Queen of Peace.
- (15) 1987 - The Rising Dawn. (Marian Year)
- (16) 1988 - Shed Light upon the Earth. (Marian Year)
- (17) 1989 - Come, Lord Jesus.
- (18) 1990 - Mother of the Second Advent.
- (19) 1991 - The Announcement of the New Era.
- (20) 1992 - Your Liberation is Near.
- (21) 1993 - The Time of the Great Trial.
- (22) 1994 - Open Your Hearts to Hope.

The primary messages, in addition to the plea for everyone to consecrate themselves to the Immaculate Heart of Mary, seem to be the messages given at Fatima. Pray, pray the rosary; strive to become holy, take part in the Sacraments and in the Holy Mass; do penance and fast; and form Cenacles of prayer groups.

Our Lady's theme of Her great love for Her priests is punctuated by Her warnings of the great apostasy and of the great chastisement to come soon. She pleads with the faithful cohort of priests, religious and laity to cling to Her during that period for protection and salvation.

Many of the messages are instructive, also many messages quote from or refer to Scripture or even explain or amplify the Scriptural passages referenced.

As the messages proceed, they discuss the Second Coming of Jesus and the Second Advent. A group of messages are apocalyptic in nature, some of which go on to explain the meaning of the numbers #333 and #666 and other things contained in Revelations.

On May 13, 1987 Our Lady said in part: *"The refusal to return to God through conversion has brought all humanity along the arid and cold road of hatred, of violence, of sin and of an ever increasingly widespread impurity. People no longer go to confession. They live and die habitually in mortal sin and every day how many souls go to hell, because there is no one to pray and sacrifice for their salvation. You are living in a humanity which has built a new civilization, atheistic and antihuman. People no longer love one another; they no longer respect the life and the good of their neighbor; the flames of egoism and hatred are extinguishing those seeds of goodness which are still springing up in the hearts of men. The poor are being* abandoned; the little ones are being ensnared and nourished with the poisoned food of scandal; the youth are being betrayed; homes are being profaned and destroyed. How great is your desolation! How dense is the darkness which surrounds you! Into what an abyss you have fallen!"

Then Our Lady added in part: *"But you are now beginning to live through that which I had foretold to you at Fatima ... As of now, the great events are coming about ... these are the times when, from your profound abyss of darkness and of desolation, I will lead you to the highest summit of light."*

Then again on August 15, 1988 Our Lady said: *"During this Marian Year I have intervened forcefully in the life of the Church and of humanity."*

On March 13, 1990 Our Lady reminded us of the Gospel reading: *"When the Son of Man returns, will He still find faith on earth?"* She also reminds us that at Fatima She foretold that a time would come when the true faith would be lost. Our Lady adds: *"These are the times."*

Our Lady goes on to instruct us in the causes of the loss of faith, which causes are the spread of errors taught by professors of theology in seminaries, by the open and public rebellion against the authentic Magisterium of the Church, and by the bad example given by the pastors who have allowed themselves to be completely possessed by the spirit of the world. Our Lady explains: *"this is why, in these times of yours, I have prayed everywhere. My Marian Movement of Priests is to form the little flock; gathered together and formed by Me to ever preserve the true faith."*

"This is My plan" Our Lady announced on September 8, 1990. *"The stronger My presence becomes among you, the more will the darkness of evil, of sin, of hatred and impurity withdraw themselves from you, because Satan is becoming more and more imprisoned and destroyed."* Our Lady said on January 1, 1993 that: *"the Great Trial has come for all of you; and for the Church;"* yet 1994 has been designated as 'Open Your Hearts to Hope' year.

It is reported that critics within the hierarchy of the Church, including cardinals, point to the abundance and sentimentalism of the messages. On the other hand the Pope and the Holy See, observant of the fruits the Movement has brought forth, have encouraged Don Gobbi, that is to say, no *official* approval has been given. Meanwhile, the locutions are even now ongoing.

IX The Primary Messages - 9

(1) Message to Her Beloved Priests - Our Lady brought into being the Marian Movement of Priests through Don Gobbi in 1973 and has since then given numerous messages for Her priests; messages of hope, of love, of mercy and many messages of instruction and guidance. Thus She told Her priests: *"I myself will take you by the hand."* (July 28, 1973)

"Therefore train yourself to remain in Me; in My Heart." (Aug, 24, 1973)

She urges the priests to defend the Pope, to obey Her orders and to fight the adversary (September 23, 1973). She is preparing Her loyal and faithful cohort for the time of the decisive battle, and meanwhile urges prayer and keeping the commandments.

On November 30, 1974 Our Lady said: *"There is only one sign which God gives to the world and to the Church of this day: I myself."*

Then on May 13, 1976: *"Each one must consecrate himself to My Immaculate Heart, and through you priests many of My children will make this consecration."* Again: *"I want you pure in mind, heart and body."* (February 11, 1977) For it is beneath the Cross of Her Son that Our Lady wants to teach Her beloved priests to love, to suffer and to be silent (April 8, 1977). *"Let yourselves be possessed by His Love."* (March 31, 1994)

Our Lady announces that She is involved in the maternal work of co-redemption and that She is the Mediatrix of Graces (July 13 and 16, 1980).

"Walk in the light of faith, walk in the light of grace, walk in the light of love," so She counsels on August 15, 1984. Again *"be My apostles in living and spreading what I have told you."* (September 20, 1984), and *"do battle by means of love, by means of prayer; and by means of personal immolation."* (October 24, 1984)

On June 19, 1993 Our Lady said: *"It is My work which I am carrying out in every part of the world in these last times. . . .It is My work because I Myself am accomplishing it and spreading it in a silent and hidden way."*

(2) Prayer - The messages are replete with appeals for prayer.

"Pray, pray, pray." (December 1, 1973) *". . . and now I repeat it: just pray and remain always in My Heart in prayer."* (October 23, 1974)

Frequently Our Lady urges the last hours of the year be spent in prayer. (December 31, 1982 and other dates)

On June 12, 1978 Our Lady said: *"First of all, have recourse to prayer. Pray more, pray with greater confidence, pray with humility and absolute self-abandonment."*

Then again on January 22, 1980: *"Pray more and more; multiply your Cenacles of prayer; multiply your rosaries; I ask you for prayer and penance for the conversion of sinners..."*

February 11, 1993: *". . . I again repeat to you My Motherly invitation to follow Me along the way of grace and purity of penance and prayer, in order to obtain the gift of healing and salvation."*

(3) Rosary - On October 7, 1979 Our Lady said: *"Your entire rosary, is like an immense chain of love and salvation with which you are able to encircle persons and situations, and even to influence all the events of your time."*

(May 1, 1983) *"Give Me the garlands of your rosaries, recited more frequently and with greater intensity."* On October 7, 1983 Our Lady asked: *"Why is the holy rosary so efficacious?"* and then went on to explain that it is because it is a simple prayer, a humble one, and it forms you spiritually in littleness, in meekness, and in simplicity of heart.

"The rosary brings you to peace. With this prayer you are able to obtain from the Lord the great grace of a change of hearts, of the conversion of souls, and of the return of humanity to God..." (October 7, 1986)

On January 28, 1975 Our Lady said: *"Pray with Me and through Me, with the prayer which is so simple yet so efficacious and which is the prayer I asked of you, the holy rosary."*

(4) Penance and Suffering - Our Lady urges Her beloved priests to be prepared to suffer and to come to Her Immaculate Heart for refuge.

"Offer up the holocaust of your suffering. The hours through which you are living are truly difficult and painful . . ." (June 12, 1978)

"Today there is need for a great chain of suffering, raised up to God in reparation!" (September 15, 1982)

On March 5, 1983 Our Blessed Mother instructed Her priests that the first stage of penance is that of renunciation and self denial, and the second stage is carrying one's cross properly. Then She added: *"Some of you will even have to shed your own blood in the decisive moment of this bloody purification."*

Then on September 15, 1986 Our Lady told Her Beloved Priests that She was forming them into suffering. Later on March 4, 1987 Our Lady instructed Her priests that penance is to be offered to Her Immaculate Heart in three different ways; first as an interior penance; then as a silent and daily penance; and also as an exterior penance.

January 1, 1993: *"Let frequent confessions be the remedy which you make use of against the spread of sin and evil."*

September 8, 1993: *"In these times when My adversary is succeeding in misleading many, through the wicked spirit of self-affirmation and rebellion, give a good example of humble and courageous obedience."*

May 1, 1994: *". . . above all I ask you to offer Me the fragrant and precious flower of your suffering."*

(5) Warnings of Apostasy - Our Lady warned Her priests of the great apostasy to come. On March 10, 1977 She said: *"Your suffering will of necessity grow greater as the great apostasy spreads more and more.*

"The Apostasy has now been spread into every part of the Church; betrayed even by some bishops, abandoned by many of its priests." (August 26, 1983). Again on September 6, 1986: *"The Church of Jesus is wounded with the pernicious plague of infidelity and apostasy; many bishops, priests, religious and faithful no longer believe and have lost the true faith; for this reason, the Church must be purified, with persecutions and with blood..."*

On December 3, 1986 Our Lady offered a remedy for the wound of apostasy, by the priests preaching more the truth which Jesus taught, and by them opposing anyone who teaches false doctrine, and further by speaking openly to the faithful of the grave danger encountered today in swerving from the true faith of Jesus and from the Gospel.

Later on June 11, 1988 Our Lady said: *"The great apostasy is spreading* more and more ... many bishops, priests, religious and faithful are victims of the great apostasy. In these times, in the Catholic Church, there will remain a little remnant who will be faithful to Christ, to the Gospel and to its entire truth."

On January 1, 1993 Our Lady warned that: "*Apostasy is spreading everywhere.*"

May 13, 1993: "*Satan has succeeded in entering into the Church, the new Israel of God. He has entered there with the smoke of error and sin, of the loss of faith and apostasy, of compromise with the world and the search for pleasure.*"

(6) Cenacles - Our Lady repeatedly requests that Cenacles of Prayer be established and multiplied.

On January 17, 1974 Our Lady requested that Her priests in the movement gather as Cenacles of Prayer. Then She said: "*Why do I want them to come together in Cenacles with Me? To remain with Me; above all to pray with Me; to love each other; and to await the decisive moment.*" She also said during this locution: "*Now that My Movement of Priests is spreading everywhere, these Cenacles must be multiplied.*"

Again on September 13, 1984 Our Lady expressed joy to be in Cenacle with Her Beloved Priests; She says: "*In Cenacle with Me; I form you in prayer which it now becomes necessary to employ . . . as the weapon against Satan and all the spirits of evil who, in these times, have been unleashed with great violence . . . ; I encourage you to continue along the difficult road of your times . . . ; I teach you to look on the evils of today with My motherly and merciful eyes. . .*"

May 1, 1993: "*. . . Let the Cenacles of Prayer which I have asked of you flourish everywhere . . .*"

May 30, 1993: "*I want to gather young people together in Cenacles, so that they may experience My Motherly presence.*"

June 19, 1993: "*It is My work which I am carrying out in every part of the world in these last times.*"

December 31, 1993: "*During these hours, share in My great concern and unite yourselves, each and all, to My prayer of intercession and reparation.*"

December 8, 1994: "*. . . I have formed you* (My Beloved Priests) *with particular care . . . to be the aposltes of these last times . . .*"

(7) Holy Mass/Eucharist - "*Holy Mass must be celebrated well, and it must be lived by My priests . . .*" (May 20, 1974), "*. . . lived interiorly by your life and at the moment of its celebration.*" (February 11, 1978)

On August 8, 1986 Our Blessed Mother instructs Her priests on Her role as "Mother of the Eucharist," explaining why She is the True Mother of the Eucharist, the Joyful Mother of the Eucharist and the Sorrowful Mother of the Eucharist.

(8) Purification - "*The Purification has already begun within the Church pervaded by error, darkened by Satan, covered with sin, betrayed*

Milan, Italy 329

and violated by some of its own pastors." (November 20, 1976)

On January 28, 1979 Our Lady said: *"Various signs indicate to you that the time of purification has come to the Church, the first of these is the confusion which reigns there. This in fact is the time of its greatest confusion, the second sign is the lack of discipline which is spreading in the Church, and which indicates to you that the final time of the purification has come."* (February 2, 1979) *"The third stage is division which indicates to you with certainty that the final moment of the painful purification has come."* (February 11, 1979) The *". . . fourth sign which indicates to you that the culminating period of the Church's painful purification has come, is persecution. The Church in fact is being persecuted in various ways."* (May 3, 1979)

However, on September 15, 1980 Our Blessed Mother said: *"All the sufferings of the Pope, of the bishops, of the priests, of the consecrated souls, and of the faithful are enclosed in My Heart."*

January 1, 1993: *"You have thus entered into the time of the great trial."*

May 13, 1993: *"You are living the bloody years of the battle, because the great trial has now arrived for all. There is now taking place that which is contained in the third part of My message which has not yet been revealed to you, but which will now become evident from the events themselves through which you are now living."*

May 30, 1993: *"The decisive time of the Purification and the great tribulation is the time of the Holy Spirit."*

January 1, 1994: *"My divine Motherhood is exercised today in preparing the way for His glorious return. As I was the humble and poor Mother of His First Coming, so too am I the glorious and powerful Mother of His Second Coming among you."*

(9) Angels - On September 29, 1994 Our Lady said: *"... the Archangels Gabriel, Raphael and Michael ... are the Angels of your time . . . To the Archangel Michael is entrusted the task of leading the battle against the armies of Satan . . . To the Archangel Raphael is entrusted the mission to help and heal those stricken and wounded . . . To the Archangel Gabriel is entrusted the great mission of announcing the return of Jesus in glory . . ."*

X Signs Preceding the Apparitions - Not Reported.
XI Other Visions During Apparitions - NR
XII Prayers Taught To The Seer(s) - Not Reported

XIII Special Devotion Given to the Seer(s)

(1) Although no new devotions were given to Don Gobbi, nevertheless Our Blessed Mother urged us *"to make use of the Consecration to My Immaculate Heart, the frequent recitation of the holy rosary, and the*

practice of the Five First Saturdays of the month in reparation for the offenses committed against My Motherly Heart." (August 4, 1979)
(2) Cenacles of prayer have been established throughout the world.

XIV Requests Made by Our Lady

The primary request made of Don Gobbi by Our Lady was to start the Marian Movement of Priests.

XV Specific Bible References

(1) Letter of Paul to the Thessalonians.
(2) Many references to the Apocalypse are contained in the messages.

XVI Secrets Given to the Seer(s)

No secrets are reported given to Don Gobbi; however, on May 13, 1990 during a message given to Don Gobbi at Fatima, Our Lady said: *"My third secret, which I revealed here to three little children to whom I appeared and which up to the present has not yet been revealed to you, will be made manifest to all by the very occurrence of the events."* (apparently a reference to Fatima)

XVII Miracles Promised by Our Lady - NR
XVIII Miracles Performed - Not Reported
XIX Miracles Promised not yet Performed - NR

XX Signs Promised

It is reported that when Don Gobbi received the first locution on May 8, 1973 he asked for, and shortly thereafter, received a sign of confirmation.

XXI Signs Given

On January 24, 1984 Our Lady reviewed the various signs She has given and continues to give around the world, such as fragrance of roses, the shedding of human tears and tears of blood, the visions, apparitions and messages given to seers around the world.

Then on September 15, 1987 during a locution in Akita, Japan, Our Lady stated She was weeping because humanity has not accepted Her invitation to conversion, because the Church is continuing along the road of division, because souls of Her children are being lost, because too few accede to Her request to pray or even to listen to Her.

XXII Predictions/Promises

(1) On September 19, 1988 Our Lady predicted certain events to happen in a ten year period when She said: *"In this period of ten years, all the secrets which I have revealed to some of My children will come to pass and all the events which have been foretold to you by Me will take place."* (This was reiterated on May 13, 1990)

(2) On November 12, 1988, Our Lady said: *"You are now entering into the most painful and dark phase of the purification and soon the church will be shaken by a terrible persecution, a new persecution, such as has hitherto been unknown."*

(3) On June 11, 1988 Our Lady predicted the great apostasy when She said: *"In these times, in the Catholic Church, there will remain a little remnant who will be faithful to Christ, to the Gospel, and to its entire truth. The little remnant will form a little flock, all guarded in the depths of My Immaculate Heart. This little flock will be made up of those bishops, priests, religious and faithful who will remain strongly united to the Pope, all gathered together in the Cenacle of My Immaculate Heart, in an act of unceasing prayer, of continual immolation, of total offering to prepare the painful way for the second and glorious coming of My Son Jesus."*

XXIII Prophecies/Warnings of Chastisement

The messages as early as 1973 warned of the coming tribulation; and they continue to sound warnings of the great chastisement to come.

(1) *"Times of great tribulations will unfold. . ."* (July 28, 1973)

(2) *"These are the times of the purification, these are the times when the justice of God will chastise this rebellious and perverted world, for its salvation."* (November 20, 1976)

(3) *"The times foretold by Me have come, . . . humanity is now on the brink of that destruction which it could bring upon itself by its own hand. Indeed that which was predicted to you by Me at Fatima, concerning the final closing of this age of yours, has already begun. How can I any longer hold back the hand of Divine Justice . . . Famine, fire and great destruction; this is what the scourge, which is about to strike humanity, will bring you!"* (January 22, 1980)

(4) *"You are close to the great chastisement . . ."* (September 8, 1985)

(5) *"These are the times of the great chastisement. The cup of Divine Justice is full, is more than full, is flowing over ... the most painful,*

most bloody hours are in preparation for you. The times are closer than you think . . ." (July 3, 1987)

(6) "I am leading you all to understand the signs of the great tribulation; all these signs are in the act of being realized in this time of yours; then, in your time, overturnings of the order of nature are multiplying, such as earthquakes, droughts, floods and disasters which cause the death of thousands of persons, followed by epidemics and incurable diseases which are spreading everywhere . . ." (December 31, 1987)

(7) Then on November 15, 1990 Our Lady said: "The great trial has arrived for all humanity. The chastisement predicted by Me at Fatima and contained in that part of the secret which has not yet been revealed, is about to take place. The great movement of Divine Justice and of Mercy has come upon the world."

(8) "You have entered into the times that have been foretold to you. You have entered into the last times." (December 24, 1990)

(9) Then on December 31, 1990 Our Lady said: "For this world, the moment of its chastisements has now arrived. You have entered the grievous times of the purification and sufferings must increase for all."

(10) December 8, 1993: "During these years you will see the great chastisement, with which the justice of God will purify this world, which has become a thousand times worse than at the time of the Flood, and so very possessed by evil spirits. . . . And so I am gathering My little children from every part of the earth, and enclosing them in the safe refuge of My Immaculate Heart, so that they may be defended and saved by Me, at the moment of the great trial which has now arrived for all . . . Thus in the very years when Satan is triumphing by leading humanity along the road of its own destruction, My Motherly Heart is also triumphing, as I bring My little children along the way of salvation and peace."

XXIV Method of Appearance - Not Reported
XXV Method of Departure - Not Reported
XXVI Confrontation w/Civil Authorities - NR

XXVII Confrontation w/Church Authorities

It is reported that theologians and clergy, including cardinals, criticize the messages as being too abundant and too sentimental. However, the Pope, it is reported, has encouraged Father Gobbi to continue to spread the messages because of the good fruits produced.

XXVIII Request Chapel/Shrine Built - NR

XXIX Free Will/Choice

By Our Lady's constant request to follow Her teachings which lead to Our Lord and to salvation, She clearly requests that we choose the true way back to God.

XXX Seer(s)' Suffering/ Sacrifice

Throughout the messages Our Lady reminds Her Beloved Priests that She calls them to suffer with Her on their journey. She also promises that Her cohort will be persecuted and suffer much.

XXXI Healings Reported - Not Reported
XXXII Action Taken by the Church - Not Reported

XXXIII Bibliography

To the Priests, Our Lady's Beloved Sons 1991   (12th Edition)
By: Father Stefano Gobbi
Published by: Marian Movement of Priests

Supplement to the 12th Edition   1992
By: Father Stefano Gobbi
Published by: Marian Movement of Priests

The Brief   1992
By: Marian Movement of Priests
Published by: Marian Movement of Priests

Supplement to the 14th English Edition 1994
By: Father Stefano Gobbi
Published by: Marian Movement of Priests

Supplement to the 15th English Edition 1995
By: Father Stefano Gobbi
Published by: Marian Movement of Priests

Chapter 32

BINH LOI, VIETNAM
(1974 - 1982)

I Place - Binh Loi, Vietnam

II Dates of 1st And Last Apparition

First: February 1974
Last: October 1, 1982
Note: October 1, 1982 was the last reported apparition, however, Our Lady is said to be appearing to the seers in Vietnam. Due to the difficulty in receiving communication from Red Vietnam this has not been confirmed.

III Seer(s) - 2

Name: Stephen Ho Ngoc Anh
Birth: Unknown
Age at first apparition: 23
Status: Unknown

Name: Theresa
Birth: Unknown
Age at first apparition: Unknown
Status: Unknown

IV Total Number of Apparitions - 37

Stephen - 17, Theresa - 20

V Dates And Locality of Each Apparition

Stephen:
1974: February - Tan Quy (at home of foster sister).
1975: October 12 - Tan Quy (at home of foster sister); December 21 and 22 - Tan Quy (at home of foster sister); Christmas Eve - Tan Quy (seer's parent's home); December 27 and 28 - Binh Loi (Shrine of Our Lady of Fatima).
1976: January 14, 1976 through October 14, 1979, Our Lady appeared to Stephen on the 14th day of each month at the Shrine at Binh Loi, Vietnam.
Theresa: *(All apparitions occurred at Theresa's home unless otherwise noted.)*
1977: May 6; September 2.
1979: October 13, 14; November 14.
1980: October 5, 13; November 8; December 28.
1981: February 9; March 29; April 12; July 2; September 29; October 14; November 26; December 27.
1982: January 25, 26; October 1.

VI Description of Our Lady

On October 12, 1975 Stephen reported that Our Lady appeared "all dressed in white." She was quite tall, approximately 1.8 meters (5'9"). Sometimes at least, She was holding a rosary. At times She was sad.

VII Title(s) of Our Lady - 2

(1) On September 2, 1977: *"I am the Virgin Queen Mary."*
(2) Mother of Vietnam.

VIII Brief Factual Review

Vietnam is located on the Asian continent and is part of the Malaysian Peninsula. When these reported events occurred a civil war was raging in Vietnam. The North against the South. The United States also became involved in this war.

Stephen Ho Ngoc Anh was only 18 when he joined the South Vietnamese Army in 1969. He was a paratrooper. He was dropped behind enemy lines to search for captured American soldiers and was himself captured along with some Americans and imprisoned by the North Vietnamese.

During his captivity he was cruelly beaten and tortured. His stoicism so infuriated his captors that he was given four injections, which in a short time, reduced him to a state of total disability. He also lost his ability to speak and communicated by written messages only. Through it all he never lost his faith in Our Lady. In 1973 Stephen was released by the terms of a truce.

At first he was placed in a hospital in Vietnam, then he was transferred to the USA. While in an American hospital, and while praying to Our Lady, a small boy came up to Stephen and said: "You must go home to be cured. Here although medical techniques are advanced, you will die." Shortly thereafter a friend of Stephen's died in the hospital so Stephen decided to heed the boy's words. He was pronounced 100% disabled, sent home to Vietnam and given a military pension, and also given a wheelchair. The discharge report from the hospital read: "Paralyzed in both legs and dumb."

In 1974 the Blue Army of Mary in Vietnam solemnly received a statue of Our Lady of Fatima which went to rest overnight in the hospital in Vietnam where Stephen was confined. The Chaplain arranged for a special blessing of all the patients in wheelchairs. When the statue came before Stephen he saw it shed tears. He reported this to the Chaplain in writing, but the Chaplain dismissed this claim.

The very next night Stephen could not sleep. At about 4:00 AM he heard a voice: *"Stephen, at Tan Quy where your family lives, an officer shot Me in the arm and broke it."* Again Stephen wrote a message to the Chaplain telling of this experience. The Chaplain did travel the five miles to the village of Tan Quy, and there the parish priest confirmed that on the previous day an officer did shoot the statue of Our Lady and broke it. This had also been previously reported to the local council.

During the next year, events in South Vietnam created uncertainty and many patients discharged themselves from the hospital, leaving only a small group of seriously handicapped, including Stephen.

Saigon fell on April 30, 1975. Stephen was seen by the invaders as he was cleaning up Our Lady's altar, for which he was punished and made to leave the hospital. Not knowing if his family was still in his village, he transported himself by wheelchair to the home of a Catholic nurse whom he had met earlier in the hospital. He stayed with that family until the end of 1975. He refers to the nurse as his "foster-sister." His devotion to Our Lady was strong and he continued to pray the rosary and ask for help from Our Lady.

On October 12, 1975 while he was praying the rosary, Our Lady appeared to Stephen for the first time. She was dressed all in white. She spoke to him: *"Tomorrow is the anniversary of My appearance at Fatima."* Then She added: *"I will cure you so that you can walk and talk again."* However nothing happened and he was not cured that next day. His foster-sister thought he was mad.

Then on December 21, 1975 Our Lady appeared to Stephen again.

She asked him to go out into the yard so She could give him a sign. He followed Her request and once outside he saw a large comet in the sky, with Our Lady in front of it with Her crown shining with light. The next day at the same hour he had his foster-sister come out to the yard and there the comet again appeared with Our Lady. His foster-sister saw the comet but could not see Our Lady.

On December 22, 1975 Our Lady appeared to Stephen and directed him to join his own family for Christmas. This he did.

On Christmas eve, Stephen was at home praying the rosary, while his family was attending midnight Mass. Our Lady again appeared to him. This time She spoke to him at length. She told Stephen: *"On October 12th, in order to test your faith, I promised to heal you, but although I did not do so, you always believed in Me. Now on December 28th at 9:00 AM I will make you walk and speak again at the Binh Loi Fatima Centre. You must go there the evening before and stay with Me the whole night. I will tell you what to do."*

Stephen was elated and invited his family and friends to attend the healing. He also requested that State and private doctors witness the healing. These requests fell on deaf ears. Of course, Stephen planned to go to the Centre as Our Lady requested.

However, because the bus driver refused to give Stephen a ride, Stephen had to travel the whole distance by wheelchair. When he arrived at the Centre he asked the archbishop of a nearby monastery to witness the miracle, which request was likewise declined. At the Centre he made arrangements with Fr. Vo Van Bo, the Director of the Centre, to be permitted to pray inside at the Shrine all night, however, one of the nuns locked the gates excluding Stephen because she did not get the message.

As Stephen began to pray the rosary outside the gate that night, he suddenly found himself inside the Shrine in a blaze of light. Soldiers, upon seeing the light, came running towards the Shrine with weapons in their hands. Stephen was afraid, but Our Lady reassured him: *"With My protection you need not be afraid."* The lights around him dimmed and the soldiers went away.

After the soldiers had gone, Our Lady turned to Stephen with a rosary in Her hand. She held it towards him and said: *"Stephen I am giving you these rosary beads. Take them and try to say the rosary and repent your sins. Tomorrow at 9:00 AM I will heal you and you will walk and speak again. Are you happy to accept all the sufferings that will come to you because of it?"* Stephen freely accepted. Then Our Lady spoke at length about the neglect of the special devotions to the Sacred and Immaculate Hearts. She said: *"These devotions have been almost forgotten, even by religious. People no longer remember God and their Blessed Mother, Mary. If they don't repent of their sins and say the rosary, the world will suffer great disasters; children too will be innocent victims of these disasters."* Then Our Lady took a letter from Her dress and held it in Her hand. She said: *"Take this letter now."* Stephen asked Our Lady if he should present the letter to the archbishop at the healing on December 28 1975. Our Lady said: *"No, read the letter, I will tell you later."* Then Stephen read the letter, memorized it, placed it into the envelope and handed it to Our Lady, who then said: *"Say to everyone; repent and do penance, pray and say the rosary constantly. If men repent, do penance, God and Our Lady will reduce the sufferings that should come to mankind at the end of the year of the dragon, that is 1977. If men do not repent and do penance these events will happen."* Then She added: *"You cannot disclose to anyone the contents of the three things set in the letter, even if the archbishop interrogates you, you cannot disclose, even if the fathers question you, you cannot disclose."* Then Stephen asked Our Lady when he could disclose the three things in the letter. Our Lady responded: *"I'll let you know on December 28, 1980 at 9:00 AM on the same day I cured you, come to the Fatima Centre to pray to Our Lady, and Our Lady will appear to you and give the letter to you again. Then you will open and disclose the three things in the year 1980."*

Suddenly the 5:00 AM bells rang and Stephen found himself outside the gates of the Shrine. Our Lady had gone. However, Stephen was dressed in the clean change of clothes he had brought with him. The clothes he had been wearing were neatly folded in his carry bag.

As time for Mass approached and priests arrived, Stephen told them of his experience. They were doubtful, yet nonetheless they permitted him to sit next to the statue of Our Lady during Mass. Although Fr. Vo Van Bo was not scheduled to say the 9:00 AM Mass, he did so, and announced to the 400 assembled parishioners that this Mass was being said in honor of Our Lady according to the intentions of a disabled veteran (i.e. Stephen).

When Communion time came Fr. Bo took the Host, dipped it into the Chalice, and gave it to Stephen. A Mass server then approached Stephen with a glass of water, as Mary had previously requested Stephen to take water after Communion. As the server approached, Stephen saw Our Lady instead who handed the water to him. Our Lady said: *"Take this and drink it all."* He drank and was filled with an immense desire to be healed. As Our Lady left he tried to reach and touch Her clothes, calling out to Her "Mother! Mother!" He had spoken his first words in five years. As he did so Stephen fell from the wheelchair, because he overreached the wheelchair. He was helped up by some witnesses and was taken to the Sacristy. As he sat in the Sacristy, he suddenly regained consciousness and said his first whole sentence: "Please leave me alone, I have to thank God and Our Lady." As he was saying these words to the priests and others in the Sacristy, the color came back into his legs and thighs and they became normal size. He stood up and was able to take his first steps in five years. He walked to Fr. Bo's House, some 200 yards distance.

Fr. Bo was anxious that the communist authorities would react if they found out about this miraculous healing. Yet he felt that he must speak to his parishioners. He simply said: "Our Lady has just cured Stephen Ho Ngoc Ahn, please go back to the church and thank God."

The Shrine at Binh Loi is located a few miles east of Saigon. Thereafter Our Lady began to appear to Stephen at the shrine on the fourteenth day of each month starting January 14, 1976. Our Lady had promised to appear to Stephen on the 14th day of each month at 10 AM. When asked by Msgr. Vincent how Stephen knows that Our Lady will appear on the fourteenth day of the month, Stephen answered: "Every day I get up at 5:00 AM and say the rosary, then make my meditation and pray. If there is anything I should know Our Lady communicates it to me then." Msgr. Vincent witnessed four apparitions including the one of February 14, 1976.

On May 14, 1976 Our Lady's message was very similar to the message given at Fatima in 1917: *"Say the rosary - Repent of your sins - Reform your lives."* This same message is repeated during most of the other apparitions. On May 14th Our Lady added that unless people understood the importance of this triple message and put it into practice, a great disaster would befall mankind such as had never been seen before!

On July 14, 1976 Our Lady again gave the triple message and warning of disaster, however, She added that mankind made God and Herself sad, especially the priests and religious because they do not follow Her messages.

The last reported message received by Stephen at Binh Loi was on November 14, 1979. It is reported that Our Lady used the word *"urgent"* four times, and also requested four times that the seer spread Her warnings.

The apparitions of Our Lady at the Binh Loi Fatima Centre have attracted great crowds despite communist persecution.

Sometime during 1979 or 1980 both Fr. Bo and Stephen were arrested and imprisoned. In an attempt to eradicate the evidence of the cure his captors once more used injections to make Stephen an invalid. They tortured him and broke his back and legs. He was paralyzed, made dumb and in addition he was blinded.

Again Our Lady promised to cure Stephen. Stephen wrote that he was to notify a certain Jesuit priest when the time came for his cure. It is reported that Our Lady did appear to Stephen again in prison in 1980 and again cured him. According to a fellow prisoner, (a Buddhist who converted to Catholicism), the guards taunted Stephen: "How did you get cured?" Stephen answered that Our Lady cured him. Then they would beat him savagely on his head and face. This was constantly repeated so that Stephen's face became disfigured, and kept bandaged.

One day Stephen announced: "In 10 days Our Lady will cure my face." On the appointed day the guards built a platform on which Stephen was placed so everyone could see him become humiliated. Suddenly Stephen cried out: "Look! Our Lady cures me!" Then he took the bandages off his face. All his wounds had disappeared. During this event and immediately after this spectacular miracle another sign occurred. There was a big blackboard in the yard of the prison camp, and by way of an invisible hand the following words were written on the blackboard in large letters: "ME SE CUU VIETNAM" which translates: "Mamma will save Vietnam."

On that very day Stephen was transferred to another prison. At present his whereabouts are unknown to the outside world.

The Buddhist prisoner was told by Our Lady a few days later: *"I will bring you out of jail."* He is now a free man living in the USA with his family. He is now a Roman Catholic.

In 1977 another phase of these apparitions began. Theresa is the wife of a South Vietnamese Lieutenant who was imprisoned since the fall of South Vietnam. Theresa belongs to the "Little Souls" established by Jesus through "Marguerite" in Belgium. The members chose St. Therese of the Child Jesus as their model. Theresa's apparitions started in May 1977 which occured shortly before Stephen's last known apparition from the Blessed Virgin Mary. Our Lord appeared to her several times but most messages came from Our Blessed Mother. In 1977 she received one message from God the Father which was given to her by the Holy Spirit. This message warned of three days of darkness which will come upon the world because of the great increase of sins committed. Also: *"My little child note very clearly this: What your Father wants from souls is this: give up all attractions of the earth, give up vulgar and ephemeral dreams, and direct your heart and mind to heaven where I am to give you real and everlasting happiness."*

On May 6, 1977 Our Lady appeared to Theresa and extolled the marvelous benefits and mysteries of the rosary. She said: *"Your rosaries are flowers from the heart, flowers of love that you offer Me to be used in My 'Co-Redemption' of mankind in the final hour."*

On September 2, 1977 Our Lady warned of the chastisement. She said: *"So now is coming the time for God to clean the earth. He commands the demons of hell to take out the wicked. He orders the angels to guard the righteous."* Then She warns the priests and religious to fulfill their total commitment to God, and says: *"This is the last message in Vietnam where I still mention about priests and religious..."* Also: *'When this message comes God's hour is close ... do not hope that He will wait longer."*

It was during this appearance that Our Lady gave instructions especially for the "Little Children".

On October 13, 1979 Our Lady appeared before a group of "Little Souls" in Theresa's home and repeated the three messages of Fatima. The next day, October 14th, Our Lady appeared at the Shrine.

On November 14, 1979 Our Lady appeared to Theresa and gave her a message urging her to send that particular message abroad. This message of November 14, 1979 reached the USA on Christmas Eve 1979. The message is to fulfill the three messages of Fatima. Further if the human race does not listen to Our Lady's request, it will suffer the extremely just sentence on the day 'God gets rid of all kinds of weeds'.

On December 28, 1980 Our Lady appeared to Theresa and explained that the promised revelation of her letter of December 28, 1975 did not occur because men did not respond to Her Motherly Love.

On February 9, 1981 Our Lady again appeared to Theresa and explained that the contents of the letter to have been revealed on December 28, 1980 were not revealed because mankind did not do its part, and after mankind does its part on earth, then the contents will be revealed that very day. Then She added: *"That is why I have to warn you to prepare yourselves and also to let mankind know clearly that Mary is the Mistress of space and time, and that mankind must return to My Heart where space and time lay."*

On October 5, 1980 Theresa and a group of Vietnamese "Little Souls" met clandestinely in Theresa's home for a prayer meeting and to consecrate the Vietnamese people and the land to Our Blessed Mother, when Our Blessed Mother suddenly appeared to them and said: *"I want to show the power of the Virgin Queen on this land so that the names of Jesus and Mary will be venerated by all ... The world is hungry and thirsty for true love. That is why I come to give it back, proving that I am the Mother of Mankind. The human race needs not only to be judged but also trained and selected. But now is the season of blessings, of graces for the earth, that is why the salvation is poured forth on the world in every aspect, every circumstance. Only the obstinate, perverse and rebellious elements will be eliminated. I will set up among My Vietnamese children a Broadcasting Station for the world, preparing the world for a movement in every aspect on the surface of the world."*

Then again on October 13, 1980 after Theresa and her "Little Souls" had conducted a special reparation vigil, Our Lady appeared to them and gave them a lengthy message.

Part of it reads: *"Today, the anniversary of the day I repeated the three messages of Fatima here, I give you this message:"*

Message of the Merciful Love: *"Jesus, My Son, asked Me to give this to you and to the world: 'I wish that one day the whole world will accept the merciful love with a childlike heart. I wish the conversion of all souls into children. I wish the Glorious Reign of the Hearts of Jesus and Mary in all souls.'"*

Then Our Lady said a most heartwarming sentence, in obvious appreciation for the special vigil of reparation: *"During the past two days you have consoled very much the Hearts of Jesus and Mary; and both of Us do not want to be surpassed in generous love by Our little children, that is why I proclaim to you children: My little children will triumph completely* behind Mary. During the last two days, the sufferings of the souls in purgatory have been greatly diminished, and today at noon, I have visited purgatory and brought a number of souls to heaven to enjoy the Holy Face of God. These souls in their lifetime have venerated Our Lady of Fatima. Also the sinners have been struck on the heart by the rosaries; those hearts which were dead by sin; and a number of sinful souls are being converted. Who can understand the power of love!" Again Our Holy Mother pleaded:

"Fulfill the three messages of Fatima so that the destruction does not happen to mankind. I promise before you children, if mankind faithfully fulfills the three messages of Fatima, I will use My Rights as Queen of Heaven and Earth to tear out the dark veil which covers mankind and lead the human race into the Glory of the Cross of Resurrection."

Later on November 8, 1980 Jesus gave a message to Theresa stating: "The works of the age have been put into the hands of Mary, Merciful Virgin Queen, My Mother."

On March 29, 1981 Our Lady gave Theresa a message imploring the people of Vietnam to venerate and call upon St. Joseph. She said: "Run to Joseph.

"In Vietnam, St. Joseph will perform this mission of 'Joseph the Provider'. I promise and guarantee this to all you children. Anyone who runs to St. Joseph will not be hungry, spiritually or materially."

Our Lady delivered a message to a group of "Little Souls" on April 12, 1981. She told them: "It is the time of the Mother Co-Redemptrix." She also said: "Proclaim to the world in order to participate with Me in the mystery of Co-Redemptrix, all the faithful must love the rosary."

Beginning with Her message of October 5, 1980 then on several other occasions, Our Lady referred to the "Broadcasting Station" of Vietnam to the world. It was on July 2, 1981 that Our Lady gave the message to the "Little Souls" in the home of Theresa: "How soon will the human race stop sinning? I announce news from heaven so hurry and obey My orders! When tumults happen, do not be surprised, for they are most efficient means to awake mankind from its drunkenness of materialism." In the same message Our Lady also said: "... regarding the atheists, you have only two choices: either resemble them and become atheists or openly oppose them."

This was Our Lady's first message at Her 'Broadcasting Station'.

The message of Our Lady given on September 29, 1981 implores us to make reparation, do penance and pray. Then Our Lady said: "The world today is needing your sacrifices and sufferings. When I lead you into this battle, I know Satan will make you suffer, but here is your shelter: My Immaculate Heart. A Heart that has been in perfect accord with the Redeemer's Heart."

On October 1, 1981 the Feast Day of St. Therese of the Child Jesus, Our Lord himself gave the "Little Souls" a message wherein He said that He had agreed to establish the "Legion of Little Souls" on earth to pray for the conversion of sinners.

On October 14, 1981 Our Blessed Mother appeared to Theresa and a group of "Little Souls" and told them that She was *"carrying the people and land of Vietnam in My Sorrowful Heart. I promise you trials and tribulations will transform those of the Vietnamese people into everlasting happiness."*

The message of November 26, 1981 given during an apparition to Theresa at 4:55 AM speaks of Our Lady's power to crush the head of Satan. She said: *"Mary, Queen of Vietnam, will show Her power on this small land, and you children will see your Mother crush the head of Satan."* Again: *"My work on earth is to prepare for the Kingdom of God to come. But the closer the end approaches, the more terribly the work of Satan emerges, that's why, once again, I command the world to venerate My Heart."*

Our Lady gave a Christmas message on December 27, 1981. She said that the hour is here when the Church will be purified, that will be the time man will recognize the Might of God. After that the Holy Ghost will pour down the fire of Love as a new Pentecost to transform mankind and the universe.

In Vietnam, the first three days of the lunar year are considered the New Year. Our Lady appeared and gave messages to the "Little Souls" on the first day (January 25, 1982) and on the second day (January 26, 1982).

On the first day Our Lady's message was to: *"repent, stay awake and pray ... because the Great Purification is coming ... because the devils and My enemies are looking around you ... pray much so that you can be saved. Don't wait! Repent! Stay awake! Pray!"*

The second day Our Lady said: *"Arrange your lives children in order to have more time for repentance and prayer. The hour of Purification will stormily come through really violent events. The New Deluge will soon come to purify the world. If My children do not trust the Heart of Merciful Mary, when the Deluge comes, the source of evil will break out flooding the world, and people will not have time to go into the Ark of Noah, because the Heavenly Father cannot delay anymore. He must purify the world to have a new Holy People in the New Sky. New earth."*

The final reported message of Our Lady was given to Theresa on October 1, 1982 the Feast Day of St. Therese. On this date St. Therese came with Our Blessed Mother and gave the gathered group a blessing.

Our Lady's message urged us to pray the rosary daily, pray especially for priests, pray for the world's fulfillment of the three messages of Fatima. She said: *"Oh! if you only understood the anger of God before the sins of your world today! At the present time, My children pray very little! Pray very much, very much, for the world, for everybody, because time left for you, children, to pray and do penance is running out!"*

The final chapter of Stephen's story must remain untold for now. Msgr. Vincent, who had received messages from Stephen and Theresa, messages which were somehow brought out of Vietnam, now states that he has received no messages since receiving Theresa's message of October 1, 1982.

IX The Primary Messages - 4

Our Lady pleaded with Stephen to tell everyone to heed the three messages given at Fatima, namely: Repent of your sins, reform your lives and pray the rosary regularly.

On November 26, 1981 Our Lady said: *"I wish that the messages of Fatima would become the heart and blood of man on earth, and then, I will be more actually present among mankind, I will be living within you, as if you, children, and I, your Mother are one."*

(1) Repent of your sins - On December 28, 1975 Our Lady told Stephen: *". . . People keep falling into sins, thinking not of God and Our Lady at all. If mankind does not repent and do penance, constantly pray and say the rosary, God and Our Lady will punish mankind . . ."*

Again on September 29, 1981 Our Lady said to Theresa: *". . . Make reparations, do penance and pray . . . "*

(2) Reform your lives - Our Lady gave the seer this message on May 14, 1976: *"Say the rosary! Repent of your sins! Reform your lives!"* She added that we all must repent of our sins, reform our lives and say the rosary devoutly.

On September 2, 1977 Our Lady's message was in part: especially to the *"LITTLE CHILDREN"*.

(a) Prepare everything necessary for each one of you, as I have instructed (blessed handkerchiefs and blessed candles).

(b) Increase praying for the sinners, the atheists, the erroneous, the Church, the whole humanity.

(c) Be firm in faith, love and hope. Keep constancy and action in all circumstances.

(d) Pray for and realize love, peace and joy in every attitude, in every moment and even in smaller acts.

(e) Get your soul and 'luggage' ready to be used any time (luggage is the TWO HEARTS OF MARY AND JESUS).

(3) Say the rosary regularly - Our Lady repeated the message that mankind must heed the three messages given at Fatima (as well as all others) namely that we REPENT OF OUR SINS, REFORM OUR LIVES, SAY THE ROSARY REGULARLY.

On April 12, 1981 Our Lady told Theresa: *"Proclaim to the world in order to participate with Me in the Mystery of Co-Redemption, all the faithful must love the rosary."* Again on May 6, 1977: *"Mankind has fallen into sin ... Save them by your love, particularly by rosaries you offer Me in their place."* And then *"when you make the rosary part of your life, you make Me part of your life. Some people dare to say the rosary is useless! Only those who do not want to be saved by the mystery of the rosary disregard it in this manner."*

(4) Pray for priests - On May 14, 1976 Our Lady complained to Stephen that mankind made God and Herself very sad, especially for their beloved children, the priests and religious; much as She had said on December 12, 1975 when She stated: *"They abandon God and Our Lady, in religious congregations too ... they are so indifferent."*

Our Lady admonished the priests and religious in a message given to Theresa on September 2, 1977: *"... My children priests, you chase and ruin the children I use to carry out the messages from heaven ... because you are obstinate, timid, fearful or you do not dare take responsibility!... I earnestly beg My children who have devoted themselves to God in the service of the Church ... you do not love God entirely. You have given too much love to creatures and to yourself ... This is the last message in Vietnam where I still mention about priests and religious."*

The final message reported of October 1, 1982 contains this message from Our Lady: *"Here is the greatest sorrow that smites My Heart, My children, and I want to rely on you to pray for the priests, so that they fulfill the three Holy Messages of Fatima. It is because I really love the priests of Jesus, My Son, that I eagerly beg them to fulfill the three Holy Messages of Fatima. I don't want to lose any priest. Children have you forgotten, long ago, to pray ardently for priests and religious orders? Pray hastily! Otherwise many priests and religious orders will become rotten and the Church will lack shepherds."*

X Signs Preceding the Apparitions

Stephen was praying the rosary each time Our Blessed Mother appeared to him.

Theresa, on the other hand, was usually praying with her fellow "Little Souls" when Our Lady appeared to her.

XI Other Visions During Apparitions

(1) In 1977 the Eternal Father gave a message to Theresa through the Holy Spirit. On this occasion the message was: *"My little children note very clearly this. What your Father wants from souls is this: give up all the attractions of the earth, give up vulgar and ephemeral dreams, and direct your heart and mind to heaven where I am, to give you real and everlasting forgiveness."*

(2) On November 8, 1980 Jesus appeared to Theresa and gave this message: *"... The works of the age have been put into the Hands of Mary, Merciful Virgin Queen, My Mother ..."*

Our Lord also appeared to the "Little Souls" on September 30, 1981.
(3) St. Therese of the Child Jesus appeared and gave a message to Therese and other "Little Souls" on September 30, 1981. On October 1, 1981 St. Therese appeared to them again.
(4) On December 21, 1975 and again on December 22, 1975 a comet appeared streaking across the sky with Our Lady in front of the comet. This was seen by Stephen and his 'foster sister'.

XII Prayers Taught to the Seer(s) - Not Reported

XIII Special Devotion Given to the Seer(s)

(1) On December 28, 1975 Our Lady complained about the neglect of the devotion to the Sacred Heart and to Herself in this twentieth century.
(2) Our Lady told Theresa that Our Lady was establishing, among Her Vietnamese children a Broadcasting Station for the world preparing the world for a movement.

XIV Requests Made by Our Lady

(1) On December 22, 1975 Our Lady requested that Stephen join his own family for Christmas. Stephen did this.
(2) On December 24, 1975 Our Lady requested that Stephen journey to Our Lady's Shrine at Binh Loi on December 27th and stay with Her that night. This he also did.
(3) On March 29, 1981 Our Lady requested that the "Little Souls" call upon St. Joseph in these words: *"Run to Joseph."*

XV Specific Bible References

On October 14, 1981 Our Lady spoke to Theresa: *"Now I want to remind you of the Old Testament. When you have time read it again: 'The Lord Yahweh ordered to make a snake and hang it up. Those who look at it will be saved.' Meditate upon it and pray with Me."*

XVI Secrets Given to the Seer(s)

On December 28, 1975 Our Lady permitted Stephen to read three messages in a letter which She handed to him. She told him that She would appear to him at the Shrine on December 28, 1980 at 9:00 AM and then permit him to disclose the messages. On December 28, 1980 Stephen was in a communist prison, however, Our Lady appeared to Theresa on that date and explained that Our Lady did not fail in Her promise, but that the knowledge of the message was not as important as the accomplishment on earth of its contents. Again on February 9, 1981 Our Lady told Theresa that: *"The promise given to Stephen to publish the letter on December 28, 1980 had also a parallel. There were to be preparations for the accomplishment of the letter's contents. When the facts officially happen on earth, the publication will be made: . . . on the same day and at the same hour!"*

Thus far the secret contents of the letter have not been made public.

XVII Miracles Promised by Our Lady

(1) On December 24, 1975 Christmas Eve, Our Lady made a promise to heal Stephen at the Shrine on December 28, 1975 at 9:00 AM. This occurred as promised.

(2) Later in 1979 or 1980 Stephen was arrested and imprisoned. This time the communists broke his back and legs and also blinded him. Our Lady promised to heal him and did so while he was in prison.

(3) In 1980, while Stephen was imprisoned, Our Lady promised to heal Stephen's face. At a public showing She healed his face. This healing was witnessed by a fellow prisoner who was a Buddhist, who has converted to Catholicism. He now lives in the USA.

XVIII Miracles Performed

(1) Stephen was healed on December 28, 1975.
(2) Stephen was healed again in prison in 1980.
(3) Stephen's face was later healed while imprisoned.
(4) On December 27, 1975 Stephen was miraculously brought into the Shrine, although all gates were locked. Our Lady even changed Stephen's clothes and then placed him outside the gates the next morning.

XIX Miracles Promised not yet Performed - NR

XX Signs Promised

(1) On December 21, 1975 Our Lady appeared to Stephen and told him to go outside where he would see a sign. This was the first occasion when Stephen saw the comet in the sky led by Our Lady.

(2) Our Lady also promised to heal Stephen on December 28, 1975. This promise was made on December 24th and was fulfilled just as She promised.

XXI Signs Given

(1) Prior to Stephen's return to Vietnam and while he was in a military hospital in the USA, a small boy came up to him and said suddenly: "You must go home to be cured. Here, although medical techniques are advanced, you will die." Stephen took this as a sign from Our Lady, went back home to Vietnam and was miraculously cured by Our Lady on December 28, 1975.
(2) In 1974 Stephen witnessed the statue of Our Lady of Fatima weep tears while in a military hospital in Vietnam.
(3) Our Lady gave Stephen the message that someone had broken an arm on Her statue. Upon checking this out, the Chaplain found this to have occurred just as She told Stephen.
(4) On December 22, 1975 and again on December 24, 1975 Our Lady promised, and did show Stephen a sign in the sky. It was a comet streaking across the sky with Our Lady leading it.
(5) On December 27, 1975 at the Shrine of Our Lady in Binh Loi, Our Lady suddenly transported Stephen inside through locked gates. She quelled the soldiers and then transported Stephen outside the gates the next morning, safe from harm. The next day She healed the seer.
(6) In 1980 while Stephen was in prison, his face was miraculously cured by Our Lady. At this time a writing miraculously appeared on the blackboard: "Mamma will save Vietnam."

XXII Predictions/Promises

(1) Our Lady promised to heal Stephen and did so as promised on December 28, 1975 during the 9:00 AM Mass.
(2) She promised and did cure Stephen again in 1980 and She also healed his face as promised.
(3) On March 29, 1981 Our Lady said: *"Anyone who runs to St. Joseph will not be hungry, spiritually or materially."*
(4) On October 13, 1980 Our Lady said: *"I promise, before you children, if mankind faithfully fulfills the three messages of Fatima, I will use My Rights as Queen of Heaven and Earth to tear out the dark veil which covers mankind and lead the human race into the Glory of the Cross of Resurrection."*

XXIII Prophecies/Warnings of Chastisement

(1) On December 28, 1975 Our Lady said: *"People no longer remember God and their Blessed Mother, Mary. If they don't repent of their sins and say the rosary, the world will suffer great disasters, children too*

will be innocent victims of these disasters."

(2) Again on May 14, 1976 Our Lady told Stephen that unless people understood the importance of the triple message of Fatima and put it into practice, a great disaster would befall mankind such as had never been seen before.

(3) Then on November 14, 1979 Our Lady appeared to Theresa and said: *"If the human race does not listen to My requests, it will suffer the extremely just sentence on the day God gets rid of all kinds of weeds. Remember! Publish My command positively."*

(4) On September 2, 1977 Our Lady said: *"The whole human race will be purged by the might of God. During this purge people will die like thatches. ...so now is coming the time for God to clean the earth. He commands the demons of hell to take out the wicked. He orders the angels to guard the righteous..."*

(5) On July 2, 1981 Our Lady warned: *"Amend your lives. Fulfill the three messages of Fatima and fulfill them in a hurry, for it might be too late to save the world from danger of destruction ... When tumults happen, do not be surprised for they are most efficient means to awake mankind from its drunkenness of materialism."*

(6) On the Vietnamese New Year Our Lady warned: *"Repent because the Great Purification is coming. The hour of Purification will stormily come through really violent events."*

XXIV Method of Appearance - Not Reported
XXV Method of Departure - Not Reported

XXVI Confrontation w/Civil Authorities

The record is filled with the atrocities visited upon Stephen by the communists. First they cruelly tortured, injected and disabled him. After he was cured they attempted to discredit Our Lady and they again arrested him (and Fr. Bo) and again tortured him, broke his back and legs and also blinded him. Our Lady again cured him and then he was secretly taken to an unknown prison by his captors.

XXVII Confrontation w/Church Authorities

(1) At first the Chaplain in the military hospital did not believe Stephen when he reported the statue of Our Lady was weeping tears. He later believed.
(2) Later Stephen requested the archbishop, and others in authority, to witness the promised healing of December 28, 1975. They all refused.
(3) No real confrontation w/Church authorities is reported.

XXVIII Request Chapel/Shrine Built - NR

XXIX Free Will/Choice

(1) Our Lady told Stephen on December 24, 1975 that She had tested him to see if he would continue to love Her even though he had not been cured as She promised on October 12, 1975. By his own free will, he kept believing.

(2) Then on December 27, 1975 Our Lady asked Stephen if he agrees to accept sufferings coming to him. He responded and said: "I will accept any suffering coming to me from anywhere." Clearly Stephen exercised his free will and just as clearly Our Lady respected his right to exercise his own free will.

XXX Seer(s)' Suffering/Sacrifice

Stephen is a victim soul. He suffered very much through his captivity and torture at the hands of the communist North Vietnamese, and he probably continues to suffer in unknown locations in Vietnam, if he is still alive.

XXXI Healings Reported

(1) Stephen was instantly healed on December 28, 1975.
(2) Stephen was healed again in 1980.
(3) Stephen's face was miraculously healed before witnesses in 1980, while in prison.
(4) Because it is difficult to get information out of Vietnam regarding these apparitions, it is unknown and unreported if other healings have occurred.

XXXII Action Taken by the Church - Not Reported

XXXIII Bibliography

Celestial Wonders in 1966 Red Vietnam
By: Khong-Trung-Luu
Published by: Legion of Little-Souls

Message of Our Lady of Fatima at Binh Loi
By: The Blue Army
Published by: The Blue Army

Chapter 33

EASTERN CANADA
(1974 - 1987)

I Place - Eastern Canada

II Dates of First and Last Apparition

First: September 6, 1974
Last: April 19, 1987 (last reported)
Note: The apparitions are reportedly ongoing.

III Seer(s) - 1

Name: Brother Joseph Francis (Name taken to protect anonymity)
Birth: May 21, 1944
Age at first apparition: 30
Status: Living

IV Total Number Of Apparitions - 43

Note: Apparently there are more apparitions than reported.

V Dates and Locality of Each Apparitions

(All apparitions occurred in Eastern Canada unless otherwise noted.)

1974: September 6.
1983: May 13; December 24.

1984: June 8 (Rome, Italy); July 6 (Fatima, Portugal).
1985: July 19, 22; August 18; October 4, 7, 25; November 2, 29; December 27.
1986: January 11, 25, 26; February 8, 11; April 12, 13; May 5, 11, Fatima, Portugal; July 31; August 9; September 1, November 2, 12, 29; December 8, 13, 25.
1987: January 1, 2, 10, 13; February 6, 14, 15, 19; March 4, 15; April 19.

VI Description of Our Lady

(1) At the first apparition on September 6, 1974 the seer describes Our Lady as all dressed in white under the identity of Our Lady of Fatima. Suddenly She covered Her face with Her hands as a person in grief. She cried abundantly, Her shoulders shaking with the sobs.

(2) Thereafter the seer usually described Our Lady of Fatima, sometimes showing Her Immaculate Heart burning with rays of light, and with light oozing around Her and different colored lights shooting around the room. Sometimes roses were hanging from Her mantle as tassels.

(3) On November 29, 1985 the seer saw Our Lady's face close up. Her face was more beautiful than anything. Her eyes were bluish-green crystal shining with beauty. She had a high forehead and reddish-gold hair. Her eyebrows were arched and Her nose was long and narrow but delicately shaped. Her mouth was a deep rose color and full.

VII Title(s) of Our Lady - 2

On August 24, 1985 Our Lady first showed Herself as: *"The Rose of Souls"* then on July 31, 1986 Our Lady said: *"I come as Our Lady of the Rose of Souls."*

VIII Brief Factual Review

Joseph Francis was born on May 21, 1944. He was one of a set of twin boys. He was not expected since the doctor heard but one heart beat. His arrival pleased his mother, but he was rejected by his own father. The family consisted of 11 children, seven boys and four girls.

Joseph Francis was sickly and at age of four he was hospitalized. It was during his stay in the hospital that he was "adopted" by a beautiful mysterious lady who came to visit him regularly. On the first occasion, She appeared at midnight and was seen by all the personnel at the hospital. Thereafter, She appeared to Joseph Francis alone. She would sing hymns to him and tuck him into bed. After he returned home from the hospital She continued to visit him. She urged him to ask permission to go to church with his own mother. Also, She taught him how to genuflect and how to pray. She would tell young Joseph Francis about Her 'Son' who was present behind the tabernacle door. Sometimes She complained that Her 'Son' was alone and felt lonely, and nobody paid attention to Him. She taught him the catechism and the mystery of the Eucharist. She told him that he would have to nourish himself with the Body of Christ because his life would be full of trials, his life would be that of the cross. She showed him how the Holy Family lived poor in material goods and rich in God. And that he would live his own life in material poverty alongside the greatest spiritual wealth.

He grew up showing a great lack of interest in temporal things; rather his interest was in prayer. He often withdrew into isolation in the woods where he 'sensed God's presence'. It was here that he had erected a wooden cross near his parent's home. On one occasion he showed the parish priest this cross in the woods. The priest quipped: "The cross will always be in front of you, you will often have to carry it..."

He was an eager apostle. Not only did he bring his friends into the Catholic Church, but he taught catechism to his dog. It worked! The dog became more docile.

Joseph Francis developed a great love, devotion and veneration for Our Blessed Mother. She was to mold him as a disciple-witness and victim soul. He tried to enter the priesthood but circumstances opposed this choice of vocation. He came into contact with the Blue Army and unsuccessfully tried to bring the Pilgrim Statue of Our Lady of Fatima to his own diocese. It was during these years that he had prophetic dreams, interior locutions, visions and dialogues with beings from heaven. It was on September 6, 1974 that he had his first apparition of Our Lady. These signs and events all pointed forward and converged on a new series of activities starting July 29, 1977.

It was in May 1974 that "something pulled at his heart" and made him order a wooden statue of Our Lady of Fatima from the Blue Army. When the statue arrived he was not satisfied because the statue was "not pretty at all." He decided to return it. However, during the following night, he could not sleep. He was resting in the room where the statue was placed. At some point during the night something unusual happened. Rays of light fell onto the statue, then a luminous cloud of light enveloped it. This lasted for a time. When the cloud lifted, a perfume of rose scent had filled the air. Now looking at the statue, he noticed how it had changed. It was beautiful! He discarded the idea of returning it and asked forgiveness from Our Lord and Our Lady for having been disrespectful towards the statue.

This same statue of Our Lady of Fatima first wept on July 29, 1977 at 5:00 PM as Joseph Francis was kneeling and praying at the foot of the statue. Thereafter this statue, along with a host of other statues, wept human tears as well as tears of blood; in Joseph Francis' home. Many people witnessed these various weepings. Photographs were taken on several occasions. Joseph Francis became Canada's Guardian of this Pilgrim Statue of Fatima and he traveled with Her. On some occasions, several statues and photographs displayed on the wall of the seer's room would weep simultaneously. Such was the case on December 24, 1983 when the statues of Our Lady of Fatima, of the Infant Jesus in the Crib, of Our Lady of the Abandoned and Unwanted, of Our Lady Crowned with Thorns, of St. Cecilia as well as photographs of Pope John Paul II, of Our Lady of the Sacred Heart, and of Padre Pio; all wept together. Again on June 9, 1985 numerous statues and pictures wept simultaneously!

It is reported that later when the seer moved to New Brunswick, some of his statues wept while kept in a little chapel in Petit Rocher, New Brunswick. The first weeping at this new location occurred on November 18, 1992. The statues also wept on November 20, and from November 26 to December 7, 1992. This weeping of the statue of Our Lady of Fatima occurred alongside the weeping statues of the Infant Jesus of Prague, the Baby Jesus in the Crib, the bust of the Sacred Heart and the bust of St. Therese of Lisieux. It is further predicted that when the next massive weeping occurs it will be just before certain major events which are to come upon the world.

On May 13, 1981 (the day an attempt was made on the life of Pope John Paul II), the statue shed tears and also dropped tears of blood. There were other occasions when the statues shed tears of blood. The wounds of Jesus crucified on the cross shed blood on April 6, 1984 and again on November 1984 on June 9 and on August 5, 1985. Also the bust of Jesus Crowned with Thorns shed blood on June 25 and again on April 5, 1985. Rosa Mystica statues, the statue of Our Lady of the Rose of Souls, the statue of Our Lady of the Ark, the statue of Our Lady of Fair Love, statues of St. Joseph with the Child Jesus, as well as pictures of Our Lady of Perpetual Help, St. Francis of Assisi and other statues and pictures belonging to this seer have been reported weeping while at the seer's residence. Our Lady told the seer the reason for the tears is that we do not listen to, nor act upon, Her messages and that Our Lady and Our Lord desire us all to convert and return to God's ways under Her mantle.

Joseph Francis was the object of repeated diabolical assaults. He was offered many material things if he would get rid of "that statue". The seer always managed to call on the help of Jesus and Mary and in this way the demon departed.

Joseph Francis was a victim soul and suffered for the conversion of many sinners. One night Our Lady asked him to pray for someone in order to save that person from damnation. In the days following Our Lady let him know that a young man had nearly committed suicide with a firearm while intoxicated. He was apparently saved.

Although it is not reported whether the seer was given the Stigmata; yet it is reported that he often suffered on Fridays.

After the first apparition of Our Lady in September 1974 there was a period of time when the seer received visions and dreams but no reported apparitions. It was during this period and thereafter when the statues wept with increasing frequency and intensity.

Jesus also appeared to this seer and gave him messages. Various saints including St. Joseph and St. Michael appeared to the seer. Sometimes these apparitions of the saints would occur with an appearance by Our Lady, and at other times not.

There was an occasion when Our Lady reportedly showed the seer a vision of aborted babies who were saved through adoption of these babies by prayer.

The primary messages given to the seer by Our Lady were to pray, pray the rosary, to forgive one another, to accept suffering for unity, and Consecration to the Sacred Hearts of Jesus and Mary. We are warned to never let pride lead us, for pride is the most dangerous fall of all.

Joseph Francis suffered much, not only physical pains, but he was also persecuted by lay people and clergy who did not believe in the apparitions nor the weeping statues. He was a victim soul. Articles appeared in newspapers quoting priests who are said to have stated that they gave no credibility to these weeping statues.

There have been reported healings, physical and spiritual. A testimony by Fr. Jerry (Gerald) McCormick is reported wherein he states that in August 1978 he witnessed the weeping statue in the seer's home. Fr. McCormick had left the priesthood two years previously, explaining he couldn't agree with the hierarchy. When he witnessed the tears forming and dropping from the eyes of the statue he was so overwhelmed that he took immediate steps to return to the priesthood. Two years later he was readmitted and has since celebrated Mass in the presence of the statue. He states he has personally witnessed this statue weeping approximately 25 different times.

Reportedly Jesus and Mary requested that the seer write a book of the messages. He also wrote a book of devotional poems in addition to the Book of Messages.

The Church has taken no reported action in this matter. It is further reported that the seer is again receiving visions and messages pertaining to the coming chastisement (especially when kneeling in front of the Rosa Mystica Statue). It is not reported whether these more recent events have triggered any further action by the Church.

IX The Primary Messages - 5

(1) Consecration to the Immaculate Heart - December 17, 1985

Our Lady said: *"My Immaculate Heart is your refuge. You will be able to endure whatever comes. Do not worry for heaven will never forsake you."* She urges us to consecrate our lives, our families and all that we love to Her Immaculate Heart, and we will surely find the road to heaven.

August 9, 1986 Our Lady said: *"If you pray the beautiful consecration prayer - you're offering everything up. Love one another and you would love Us."*

(2) Pray - December 27, 1985 Our Lady said: *"Pray, pray much for your families, your loved ones. Pray for enemies, forgive them. Pray for the souls in purgatory and pray to the hearts of Jesus and Mary."*

February 11, 1986 Again Our Lady: *"I love you. Pray for your priests. Pray for your bishop. Pray for the new bishop of your city and pray for all the bishops throughout the world . . ."*

January 25, 1986, *". . . allow peace to come into your life. Come to Us, come in supplication and prayer, for prayer weighs heavier than all the treasures of the world . . ."*

(3) Reparation, Sacrifice and Suffering - January 11, 1986 Our Lady said: *"Yes share this joy. Suffering elevates the fragrance of sweetness as the thorns will bud one day into roses. . . You too will help your brothers and sisters along the way. Turn nobody away. Remember the Heart of Jesus is also the Heart of your Mother. It's the door to eternal happiness, this is where you find true spiritual strength. Trust me and I will be with you always to console you, to guide you. My hand, My Heart are ever ready to guide you whenever you need Me. Just call Me by name."*

May 5, 1986 Our Lady said: *"Only reparation, sacrifice, fasting and prayer can overcome all the struggles and tribulations in the world.*

(4) Conversion - Two weeks after Easter Sunday in 1986 Our Lady said: *". . . Persevere, turn your back on sin, repent and please go to confession, go to Mass as often as you can . . ."*

August 9, 1986 - Our Lady said: *". . . Pray for the Pontiff, continue your fast days, continue with your prayers, your rosaries, but do this in love."*

(5) Pray the Rosary - August 9, 1986 Our Lady told of great tribulations and disasters that are not far off. She said only few can be averted by prayer and sacrifice offered up in love. Then She said: *"Please say the rosary every day. Pray for sinners, pray for everyone in the world..."*

X Signs Preceding the Apparitions

(1) On some occasions such as February 20, 1987 the seer would see a flash of light in his bedroom. Out of this light Our Lady would appear, usually dressed like Our Lady of Fatima.

(2) Although light is reportedly associated with each appearance, no specific sign is repeated.

XI Other Visions During Apparitions

(1) Jesus appeared to the seer many times, and gave messages to the seer. Sometimes Jesus appeared when Our Lady appeared and other times He appeared alone.
(2) Various saints and angels appeared to the seer including St. Michael, St. Joseph, St. Therese, St. Matthew, St. Francis, St. Benedict, St. Charbel, Padre Pio, St. Gabriel, St. Stephen, St. Agnes, and Francisco and Jacinta (the children of Fatima).
(3) The seer was also shown visions of heaven, hell and purgatory and other visions.
(4) Demons appeared to and tormented the seer on several occasions.

XII Prayers Taught to the Seer(s)

On December 27, 1985 Our Lady requested the seer to add these prayers in honor of Her seven sorrowful wounds, seven times:

Prayer: Pardon and Mercy through the merits of the Holy Wounds.

Then, after three (3) Our Fathers, three (3) Hail Mary's and three (3) Glory Be's say:

Prayer: Pardon and Mercy through the merits of the Holy Wounds, and with the Holy Wounds, and Thy Sacred Hearts heal all those who are sick in soul, spirit, body and mind. Then we are to say:

Prayer: For the souls that will die this day, and for those that died this past week, have mercy on their souls.

XIII Special Devotion Given to the Seer(s)

(1) Although not a new devotion, Our Lady urged us to unite with, and consecrate ourselves to, both the Most Sacred Heart of Jesus and Mary's Most Holy and Sorrowful Immaculate Heart.
(2) On June 28, 1987 Our Lord told the seer: *"I will grant all that is asked of Me through the invocation of My Holy Wounds..."*

XIV Requests Made by Our Lady

(1) It is reported that both Jesus and Mary requested books be published containing certain messages, prayers, etc. The books listed in Section XXXIII have been published.
(2) On December 27, 1985 Our Lady requested that certain prayers be added to the prayers honoring the seven sorrowful wounds of Our Lady.
(3) Our Lady and Jesus asked the seer to pray for a specific sinner. Later

he learned that a young man considering suicide was saved.
(4) Our Lady requested a statue be carved in Her image as Our Lady of the Rose of Souls.
(5) Our Lady requested that we pray while we are on our knees. (February 6, 1987)

XV Specific Bible References

November 29, 1985 Our Lady gave a message to the seer, then said: *"You can read it and understand it in the Apocalypse."*

XVI Secrets Given To The Seer(s)

It is reported that the seer was given three (3) secrets during the course of about one week in October/November 1986.

XVII Miracles Promised by Our Lady - NR
XVIII Miracles Performed

It could be said that the various weeping of statues, photos and pictures were miracles.

XIX Miracles Promised not yet Performed - NR
XX Signs Promised - Not Reported

XXI Signs Given

(1) Numerous weeping statues, photos and pictures (weeping both human tears and blood) over a seven year period. Reportedly, the weepings have begun to reoccur in 1992. This time human tears and oil wept from the statues.
(2) It is reported that beginning in August 1984 the seer was given the grace to take photos indoors (without flash) nor any artificial light; very nearly no natural light. Some of these photos are reproduced in the books titled under section XXXIII below.
(3) The reported changes of the original statue of Our Lady from one "not pretty" to the "most beautiful" statue, which change occurred before the very eyes of the seer.
(4) Reported fragrances of roses.

XXII Predictions/Promises - Not Reported

XXIII Prophecies/Warnings of Chastisement

(1) The seer reportedly received visions of the coming purification and chastisement; some were in dreams and others were not.
(2) On July 22, 1985 the seer received a message which related that the purification is coming much sooner because the state of the world is much worse.
(3) On October 25, 1985 the seer was permitted to see a part of the chastisement that is to come.
(4) On February 8, 1986 Our Lady said: *"The world has come to a crisis so bad, so severe, that the appointed time of the chastisement has been moved forward. Many will die. There will be blood on the streets, some good will die with the bad, some will be converted at the time..."*
(5) Again on February 11, 1986 Our Lady said: *"Soon, very soon, the chastisement, the purification is going to strike. I will help with My angels those who consecrate themselves every day to My Immaculate Heart..."*
(6) On September 1, 1986 Our Lady said: *"You have seen great scenes of tragedies mounting up. You saw great multitudes of people dying because the anger of God is approaching. Soon darkness will come in the daytime and cover up the sun ... but this is nothing compared to what is going to come. WAKE UP!"*

XXIV Method of Appearance

No repeated or unusual method of appearance is reported.

XXV Method of Departure

No repeated or unusual method of departure is reported.

XXVI Confrontation w/Civil Authorities - NR

XXVII Confrontation w/Church Authorities

(1) It is reported that the weeping statue was banned from an important diocese of Ontario, Canada.
(2) In 1985 the pastor of one church publicly protested against the statue. On October 12, 1985 an article appeared in the Telegraph Journal headlined: "CLERGY FROWNS ON WEEPING STATUE."
(3) Some priests witnessed the weeping statues and believed. Others believed without witnessing the actual tears. The seer's own spiritual

advisor Fr. Jean-Paul Belinger not only believed, but wrote the preface to books reporting on these matters.

XXVIII Requests Chapel/Shrine Built - NR
XXIX Free Will/Choice - Not Reported

XXX Seer(s)' Suffering/Sacrifice

(1) The seer suffered much during his childhood and was told that he would suffer much throughout his lifetime.
(2) On February 16, 1986 Our Lady said: *"You understand My son, why you're going through these agonies. It is the agony of a stronger suffering, of being the victim soul of love..."*
(3) The seer suffered much because of the frequent diabolical assaults.
(4) Of course, Joseph Francis also suffered when people and priests refused to believe the weeping statues and ridiculed him for his beliefs.

XXXI Healings Reported

(1) Many physical, emotional, and spiritual healings are reported. The books contain testimonials of some who claimed to have obtained a cure or healing.
(2) One such spiritual healing is dramatically presented in testimonial form by Fr. Jerry McCormick who had left the priesthood. He related that once he saw the statue of Our Lady of Fatima weep, he applied and was readmitted to the priesthood. He once celebrated Mass with the weeping statue present in the church. He testified that he has seen the statue weep over twenty-five (25) times.

XXXII Action Taken by the Church

No Church action is reported. There is no indication that any commissions were formed to investigate these happenings. The Church has not approved these messages or apparitions.

XXXIII Bibliography

The Messages   1988
By: Brother Joseph Francis
Published by: Les Editions Fatima - Quebec

Heart Prints   1987
By: Brother Joseph Francis
Published by: Les Editions Fatima - Quebec

My Very Own   1986
By: Jean-Yves Simard
Published by: Les Editions Fatima - Quebec

The Last Call   1985
By: Jean-Yves Simard
Published by: Les Editions Fatima - Quebec

Chapter 34

BETANIA, VENEZUELA
(1976-PRESENT)

I Place - Betania, Venezuela

II Dates of First and Last Apparition

First: March 25, 1976
Last: March 25, 1984 (last reported)
Note: The apparitions are reportedly ongoing.

III Seer(s) - 1

Name: Maria Esperanza Medrano de Bianchini
Birth: November 22, 1928
Age at first apparition: 47
Status: Living

IV Total Number of Apparitions - 12

Twelve apparitions reported on six different dates.

V Dates and Locality of Each Apparition

All apparitions occurred at Finca (the farm), Betania, Venezuela unless otherwise noted.

1976: March 25; August 22.

1977: March 25; November 27.
1978: March 25.
1984: March 25. (seven appearances)
Further apparitions were announced but not reported. (Seven apparitions were witnessed by the seer with over 100 people present.)

VI Description of Our Lady

(1) On March 25, 1976 Our Lady was bathed in light when She appeared to the seer.

(2) On March 25, 1984 She appeared seven times to the seer and to well over 100 other people. Our Lady is described as a remarkable formation of luminous fog that took on the shape of Our Lady. Most witnesses agreed that Our Lady was radiant with light. She wore a blue cincture and resembled Our Lady of Lourdes. She was accompanied by sweet perfume of roses.

VII Title(s) of Our Lady - 1

Mary, Reconciler of All Peoples and Nations.

VIII Brief Factual Review

Venezuela is located at the very top of South America, with its coastline on the Atlantic Ocean and Caribbean Sea.

It was on a farm in Betania, village of Cua, Venezuela that Our Lady appeared to Maria Esperanza beginning on March 25, 1976. Maria was born November 22, 1928. She had mystical experiences since childhood. At the age of twelve she contracted pneumonia, and in spite of the doctor's pessimism she made a remarkable recovery.

She became preoccupied with religious life and entered the Franciscan Order. In 1954 she experienced an apparition of St. Therese of Lisieux who told the seer that this was not her vocation and she is to work out her salvation as a wife and a mother.

On November 1st she met her future husband Geo under circumstances outlined in the apparition. They were married on December 8, 1956 in the Chapel of the Immaculate Conception in St. Peter's Basilica in Rome. They have seven children, six girls and one boy, all of whom are now married.

Maria is a devoted wife and mother. She was the recipient of many special gifts and phenomena, such as: reported clairvoyance, foretelling the future, levitations during Mass, transfiguration during prayer, mysterious reception of the Host and mysterious emission of sweet-smelling odors of perfume and roses, and bilocation. She also received the Stigmata, the wounds of Christ. The Stigmata came to her as a young woman while praying at Mass. She relates that she was talking to Our Lady and when she raised her eyes she saw before her St.Therese of Lisieux. St. Therese threw a rose to the seer who was then kneeling; as she jumped up to catch the rose she felt a stinging sensation and saw blood coming out of her hands. For some years afterwards the seer suffered the wounds of Christ on her hands, feet and side on Good Fridays.

Also amazing is the report that on 14 occasions a rose, an actual flower, stem and all, had broken through the skin of the seer's bosom and unfolded gloriously from her body. The local bishop is reported to have said: "Two doctors sent testimony saying a rose came out of her skin, there is a hole in the skin and a bruise and great suffering." Other reports state that as the seer was relating messages received from Our Lady, the seer's voice changed to a voice that was lower and sweeter.

The bishop personally interviewed 200 people, including psychiatrists, psychologists, engineers and lawyers and found no abnormality in Maria except "a profound spirit of prayer; very, very profound."

Maria reportedly communicated spiritually with Padre Pio, and also met with him in Italy on several occasions. It was told that Padre Pio once told some people that a young woman from Venezuela would be coming and about that time Maria did travel to see Padre Pio in San Giovanni Rotondo. When he came out of the confessional and saw her he blurted: "Oh, Esperanza!"

Maria had a dream about a plot of land which was to serve as a center for pilgrimage and especially for youth. Our Lady said She would come to this place. It is reported that the seer told this dream to Padre Pio. In any event Maria says that from 1957 until 1974 Maria and her husband, Geo searched for the land in her dream throughout Venezuela. Then in 1974 they found their "holy land"; an old sugar mill. They later discovered a Lourdes grotto on the land. They cleared a flat land out of the mountain by the grotto, next to a cascade, and this became their sanctuary.

It is here that Our Lady first appeared to Maria on March 25, 1976. Maria, Geo and a few friends were reciting the rosary in front of the grotto when Our Lady suddenly appeared. The first message was: *"My daughter, I have given you My heart. I give it to you. I will be your refuge."*

Our Lady then gave Maria a mission of service and sacrifice, kindness and fidelity. Then Our Lady said: *"I am the Reconciler of All Peoples and Nations."*

Our Lady is reported to have appeared again on the 25th day of March 1977 and also the 25th of March, 1978. The apparitions thereafter were sporadic. Others also claimed to have seen Our Lady.

The first time that the apparitions were seen by many people in Betania occurred on March 25, 1984 eight years after the first appearance. On March 25, 1984 Our Lady made seven appearances, each lasting 10-15 minutes, except the final apparition lasted one-half hour. It is reported that 108 people, in addition to Maria, saw Our Lady on that day. She appeared as a real person to many witnesses including professional people such as doctors, lawyers, a judge and an army general. Our Lady is described as radiant with light and wearing a blue cincture and resembled Our Lady of Lourdes. She gave a message: *"My children, I am Mary, Virgin Mother of Reconciliation of Peoples and Nations, and I come with My Son in My arms to reconcile you ... oh, sublime Hope of all. Pray the rosary."*

Her message calls for a deeper faith, a call to prayer and conversion, pray the rosary, more frequent reception of the Sacraments and a call to charity and social justice. Our Lady told Maria: *"Humanity was deteriorating due to infiltration of demagoguery, falseness, and social injustice."*

Maria saw difficult times ahead and warned that Russia may act "in a surprise way." She received messages of the warning of chastisements. She said justice is coming and a very hard time will come very soon; 1992, 1993, 1994; but it will make us better people.

According to the bishop many documented healings have been reported and many conversions.

Other phenomena reported included intense aroma of flowers and sound of hymns during the apparitions. During one of the Saturday Night Vigils very large letters 'MI' appeared in the sky. This was photographed and reportedly stands out like a neon sign. It was interpreted to mean 'Mary Immaculate'. The phenomena of the 'large blue butterfly' appearing and flying around the crowd and returning to the grotto was first witnessed on March 25, 1984 and reoccurred during Holy Mass on October 12, 1989.

On October 14, 1989 about 30 people claimed that they were seeing Our Lady in the grotto. It is reported that 1,000 people have seen Our Blessed Lady at Betania since 1976 and She is still appearing.

It is reported that the 'Miracle of the Eucharist' took place in Betania on December 8, 1991 the Feast of the Immaculate Conception.

Fr. Otty was celebrating a midnight Vigil Mass for the Feast of the Immaculate Conception. At the time of the Consecration, about 15,000 people present saw a radiant rose color light over the Host. None of the people at the altar saw this light.

At the time of Communion, Fr. Otty broke the Host in half and broke off a small particle of the Host to put into the chalice. To his great amazement the remaining portion of the Host from which the particle was taken, began to bleed. For three days, the Blood on the Host was fluid then it began to dry up. The blood did not seep through the Host nor did it stain the opposite side of the Host.

This 'Miracle of the Eucharist' has been examined in laboratories and has been found to be human blood. It has been photographed. Presently the 'Miracle of the Eucharist' is in the bishop's residence, and the bishop intends to construct a special altar in the Cathedral of the diocese for a permanent residence for the 'Miracle of the Eucharist'.

Bishop Pio Vello Ricardo undertook the investigation himself. He is a Jesuit with a background in mystical phenomena. He interviewed some 490 witnesses and has collected some 381 written statements. He found the crowds, the intensity of the prayer and remarkable fruits of conversion, prayers and cures all present at Betania, and he believed these apparitions were real and supernatural. After informing Rome, the bishop declared officially on November 21, 1987 that the apparitions are authentic and supernatural in character. He further adds: "I therefore officially approve that the place where they occurred to be considered a sacred place. May it become a place of pilgrimage, a place of prayer, reflection and cult; (it is my wish) that liturgical rites be celebrated there, above all the celebration of Mass and the administration of the Sacraments of Reconciliation and the Eucharist, in accordance with the laws of the Church and the diocesan norms for overall pastoral ministry." (Pastoral Instruction, 21 November 1987, p.12)

At the conclusion of this same instruction the bishop adds: "I give thanks to God for the privilege of a visit by the Blessed Virgin accorded to our diocese and to our country, because in this period of the history of our Church, marked by a new way of evangelization, (the visit) invites us to a renewal and deepening of our faith, the living out of our faith in total conversion, prayer and apostolic commitment; because in a divided world Our Lady shows herself as the 'Reconciler of Peoples'.

"May Our Lord grant us that same outpouring of the Spirit which He granted Elizabeth when she was visited by Mary."

This was the first Church approval of an apparition (aside from Akita, Japan) since the apparitions at Banneux and Beauraing, Belgium were approved.

Our Lady had made a request of the seer that a church be built to Our Lady the Reconciler of All Peoples and Nations. Bishop Ricardo welcomed Our Lady's request. A site for the building has been donated. Construction was to begin March 25, 1989 and was targeted to be completed on March 25, 1991.

IX The Primary Messages - 3

(1) Mission - Our Lady: *"My children, I call on you this day with the fullness of life to live with a clear conscience the responsibilities of the mission entrusted to you, with the virtues of faith, hope, and charity. I particularly recommend purity of intention, humility and simplicity. The Lord's laws and doctrines are a part of you ... the promise to keep the straight road of the innocents.."*

(2) **Prayer and Conversion** - Our Lady called for: prayer for the Church, priests, conversion of sinners and peace in the world. We are to help those still afflicted with evil and *"bring them forward to live in healthy environment and in Peace of the Spirit... A great moment is approaching, a great day of light"*, said Our Lady.

(3) **Social Justice** - Our Lady said that it was important to save God's children from *"the mocking and ridicule of the Pharisees of these apocalyptic times."* Our Lady told Maria that economics and material possessions have turned mankind cold and egotistical and that it was deteriorating due to *"the infiltrations of demagoguery, falseness and social injustice."*

X Signs Preceding the Apparitions

The phenomenon of the "large blue butterfly" began on December 8, 1977 and occurred several times. The butterfly comes from the grotto and circles the crowd and returns to the grotto as if to signal the presence of Our Lady.

XI Other Visions During Apparitions

(1) It was reported that during one Saturday Night Vigil very large letters 'MI' appeared in the sky and were successfully photographed. The interpretation by the witnesses was 'Mary Immaculate'.
(2) On October 14, 1989 about 30 people reported that they saw Our Lady at the grotto.
(3) Although it is not reported that St. Therese appeared during any apparition in Betania, yet it is reported that St. Therese appeared on two occasions to Maria; once to dissuade her from pursuing the religious life, and again when Maria received the Stigmata.

XII Prayers Taught to the Seer(s) - Not Reported
XIII Special Devotion Given to the Seer(s) - NR

XIV Requests Made by Our Lady

(1) Maria Esperanza had announced about four months earlier that October 12, 1989 was to be a special day at Betania, presumably Our Lady invited people to the grotto that day. The news attracted more than 12,000 people to the site on the announced day, causing traffic jams. On this day the 'large blue butterfly' made its appearance.
(2) It is also reported that Our Lady requested a church be built in Her honor.

XV Specific Bible References - Not Reported
XVI Secrets Given to the Seer(s) - Not Reported
XVII Miracles Promised by Our Lady - NR

XVIII Miracles Performed

'Miracle of the Eucharist' took place during Mass on December 8, 1991.

XIX Miracles Promised not yet Performed - NR
XX Signs Promised - Not Reported

XXI Signs Given

(1) It is reported that when Maria relates the messages received from Our Lady that Maria's voice changes to a voice that is lower and sweeter.
(2) The large letters 'MI' seen in the sky during one of the Saturday Night Vigils (October 14, 1989).
(3) People reported smelling fragrant scents at the time of and immediately after the apparitions had occurred.
(4) It is reported that the 'large blue butterfly' was a sign of Our Lady's presence.
(5) This seer reportedly received the Stigmata.
(6) The 'Miracle of the Eucharist' occured during Mass, December 8, 1991.

XXII Predictions/Promises

(1) Very hard times are coming in 1992, 1993 and 1994. The Father's justice is coming, Maria reported.
(2) About four months before October 12, 1989 Maria announced that this day was to be a special day at Betania. And so it was.

XXIII Prophecies/Warnings of Chastisement

Our Lady told Maria: "...*Mankind was abusing the graces received and is moving toward perdition, and if there is no change or improvement of life, you will succumb under fire, war and deaths. We want to stop the evil that suffocates you, the evil of rebellion, and overcome the darkness of oppression by the enemy. That is why, again, in this century, My Son arises...*"

XXIV Method of Appearance

It was reported on the first apparition that a fog first appeared and formed into the likeness of Our Lady, then She appeared in a brilliant light.

XXV Method of Departure

She just disappeared.

XXVI Confrontation w/Civil Authorities - NR
XXVII Confrontation w/Church Authorities - NR

XXVIII Request Chapel/Shrine Built

Our Lady requested a church to be built to Her honor. The local bishop approved and accepted this wish. Land was donated and construction was to commence in 1989.

XXIX Free Will/Choice

Our Lady states: "... *if there is no change and improvement of life*... " then a warning of punishment is given by Our Lady. Thus implying the freedom of choice open to us all. We are always given free choice and Our Lady respects our free will, yet always praying and urging that we make the right choice.

XXX Seer(s)' Suffering/Sacrifice

(1) The seer had the Stigmata and as such suffered the passion of Christ on Good Fridays.
(2) There are no reports of the seer suffering due to receiving the messages. Often there are nonbelievers who ridicule the visionaries.

XXXI Healing Reported

The local bishop reports there were many documented healings and many conversions. The bishop stated some cures in his statement: (1) advanced cancer of kidneys (2) sudden cure of two duodenal ulcers (3) disappearance of an ovarian fibroma (4) unexpected cure of vaginal mycosis.
These factors played an important role in the bishop approving these apparitions.

XXXII Action Taken by the Church

(1) Bishop Pio Vello Ricardo personally undertook the investigation and declared on November 21, 1987 after informing Rome, that these apparitions are authentic and supernatural in character.

(2) These apparitions were the first Church approved since Beauraing and Banneux, Belgium were approved in 1949; (aside from Akita, Japan).

XXXIII Bibliography

Apparitions in Betania, Venezuela
By: Sister M.C. Sims, CSJ
Published by: Star Litho, Inc.

The Final Hour 1992
By: Michael Brown
Published by: Riehle Publ. Co.

Apparitions of the Blessed Virgin Mary Today 1990
By: Rene Laurentin
Published by: Veritas

Queen Newsletter
(November-December 1989 issue) (May-June 1990 issue)
By: Roger M. Chorest SMM.
Published by: Not Given

Chapter 35

LE FRECHOU, FRANCE
(1977-PRESENT)

I Place - Le Frechou, France

II Dates of First and Last Apparition

First: June 10, 1977
Last: August 14, 1994 (last reported).
Note: It is reported that these apparitions are ongoing.

III Seer(s) - 1

Name: Msgr. Jean-Marie, SND   (Now Bishop Jean-Marie)
Birth: Unknown
Age at first apparition: Unknown
Status: Living

IV Total Number of Apparitions - 29
(Through August 14, 1994)

V Dates and Locality of Each Apparition

All apparitions occurred in the "Blessed Wood" at the Congregation of Notre Dame in Le Frechou, unless otherwise noted.

1977: June 10, 14; August 14, September 14.

1978: July 14, 15, 31.
1979: May 1, 14; July 26; November 1 (All Saints Day).
1981: June 10, August 14, October 14.
1982: January 31, February 1.
1983: April 14.
1993: On the 14th of October, November and December.
1994: On the 14th of January, February, April, May, June, July and August.

Note: In addition to the 29 reported apparitions, Our Lady also reportedly appeared on the 14th day of each month.

VI Description of Our Lady - Not Reported

VII Title(s) of Our Lady - 2

(1) On June 10, 1977 Our Lady announced: *"I am Mary, Mother of Mercy, and Mother of the Church."*

(2) October 14, 1993 Our Lady said: *" I am Mary Queen of Homes."*

VIII Brief Factual Review

Le Frechou is located in the Gascony region of France, just 22 miles from Agen.

Commencing on June 10, 1977 Our Blessed Mother began to appear to Father Jean-Marie, who is now His Excellency Bishop Jean-Marie (SND) Society of Notre Dame.

These apparitions have been ongoing even to this date. Usually Our Lady appears at midday. Sometimes Fr. Jean-Marie celebrates Mass in the presence of Our Blessed Mother.

On the first apparition of June 10, 1977 Our Lady announced She was Mary, Mother of Mercy and Mother of the Church. She said She would appear on the 14th day of each month. (However, She has also appeared on different dates). Our Lady also said that Her Divine Son had chosen this piece of land, this blessed wood, which is henceforth concentrated to Our Blessed Mother.

On November 1, 1977 Our Lady showed the seer the site, that is, the place in the woods (the Sanctuary), where the apparitions were to take place. The seer and all those present saw an immense and magnificent blue curtain manifest. This marked off the boundaries of the Wood of the Apparition. The curtain with harmonious folds opened, then closed again, and then disappeared. This in fact is the place where the apparitions have occurred.

Our Lord has also appeared to this seer. In fact the seer was given his

Le Frechou, France

mission by Our Lord and Our Lady. This mission known as the "Work of Le Frechou", is to increase and train young men and women in vocations. Though subject to many persecutions, it has nevertheless grown and developed in the Le Frechou Community.

On August 14, 1981 Our Lord said to the seer: *"Young men, young ladies, young and older ones, let nothing stop you, let nothing trouble you, let nothing turn you away from your vocation. Join Me at Frechou in the religious family I have wanted and which is dear to Me because it is wholly abandoned to My Most Blessed Mother. . . ."*

The Fraternite Notre Dame centered at Le Frechou, of which the seer is a member, ministers to all. This Society provides care to all without distinction of class, race or religion. It is reported that this Society does its work around the globe, and its sisters, brothers and priests minister to the most destitute, especially the abandoned children and those who have AIDS. The Society has established facilities such as schools, dispensaries and prayer groups in many places. The society has a presence in Haiti, Rwanda and other locations.

Our Lady's messages are for prayer, (especially the rosary), penance, charity and mercy.

Many 'signs and wonders' are reported. The 'Miracle of the Sun' first occurred on September 14, 1977 witnessed by many onlookers, and has been repeated thereafter. A statue of Our Lady has been seen to smile and to cry. On the very first apparition of June 10, 1977 Our Lady said: *"I am weeping over the Church, over Frechou, and over the world."*

It is reported that on June 11, 1978 Fr. Jean-Marie was lacking sufficient Hosts for Holy Communion; then unexplainably Hosts appeared, one by one, into the Ciborium. This grace was given to the seer on yet another occasion, Easter Sunday 1980. On this later date Our Lady announced: *"I shall show the entire world that it is My Son who has called you."* The seer reportedly has been given the gift of bilocation. Other people have also reported seeing Our Lady at Le Frechou on one or more occasions.

It is also reported that this seer has been given the Stigmata. On July 26, 1979 at the foot of the Altar, and at the words "Introibo Ad Altare Dei," Our Lady put the 'Mystical Ring' on the finger of Fr. Jean-Marie.

There are reports of many marvelous healings, including many spiritual healings and conversions.

On June 10, 1981 Our Lady requested a medal be struck according to Her indications. Then She gave the seer a list of graces and blessings attached to this medal to benefit those who wear the medal with confidence.

IX The Primary Messages - 3

(1)   **Prayer and Penance**
(2)   **Rosary**
(3)   **Charity and Mercy**

(1) Prayer and Penance - June 10, 1977: *"May this blessed wood, which is consecrated to Me, be a place of prayer, penance and mercy."*

November 14, 1993: *"A great deal, a very great deal of prayer is needed in Haiti . . ."*

December 14, 1993: *"Pray a great deal . . ."*

January 14, 1994: *"My little children, resume prayer. If you pray, you shall obtain light and your life on this earth shall be happier."*

(2) Rosary - October 14, 1981: *"Pray the holy rosary and do penance to obtain the conversion of the most obstinate sinners."*

June 14, 1993: *"Pray a great deal with the rosary in your hands."*

October 14, 1993: *"Pray a great deal with your rosary in hands."*

On February 14, 1994: *"Pray a great deal with the holy rosary in your hands."*

(3) Charity and Mercy - April 14, 1993: *"Care for the poor, the sinners, the neglected ones, the sick, the contagious patients, the disabled, the paralytics, the prisoners, the homeless, those with no families, those without love . . . Give them much love, so that when they see you, they may discover how Jesus loves them and how infinite is His mercy."*

December 14, 1993: *"You will always have the poor among you, do not despair. Give them much love. Give much of yourselves to them. Do not shut yourselves up in your riches, in your own well-being, in your own comfort. Think of the poor, of the unhappy. Come to their help."*

X Signs Preceding the Apparitions - Not Reported

XI Other Visions During Apparitions

(1) Jesus appeared to this seer and also gave messages.
(2) Fr. Jean-Marie received a number of visions apart from reported apparitions.

XII Prayers Taught to the Seer(s)

Although no new prayers are reported, yet Our Lady urged that the Angelus be recited in the morning, at noon, and at night.

XIII Special Devotion Given to the Seer(s)

Our Lady did not give a new devotion to this seer, but She did urge devotion to the Sacred Heart of Jesus:

June 14, 1993: *"My little children, look often at the picture of the Heart of Jesus, it will teach you, it will invite you to have a greater love for it. Even if you have sinned much; even if, for a long time, you kept away from it; even if you think you are alone and abandoned, look at it and you will understand how much it loves you."*

XIV Requests Made by Our Lady

(1) On June 10, 1977 Our Lady said: *"I desire My children to come here on pilgrimage. . ."*
(2) On June 10, 1981 Our Lady requested a medal be struck in Her honor.
(3) Then on October 14, 1981 Our Lady said: *"I desire that the recitation of the Angelus, in the morning, at noon, and at night, be restored."*
(4) Our Lady strongly urged us to look after the poor. (April 14, 1993 and December 14, 1993).
(5) Our Lady told the seer: *"Meditate often upon the Sorrowful Passion of My Divine Son."* (April 14, 1994).

XV Specific Bible References - Not Reported
XVI Secrets Given to the Seer(s) - Not Reported
XVII Miracles Promised by Our Lady - NR

XVIII Miracles Performed

(1) On June 11, 1978 the miracle of the Hosts which appeared one by one into the Ciborium. (This phenomenon was repeated on Easter Sunday 1980).
(2) The seer is reported to have (or had) the Stigmata.
(3) And on July 26, 1979 Our Lady Herself reportedly placed the 'Mystical Ring' on the seer's finger during Mass at the foot of the altar.

XIX Miracles Promised not yet Performed - NR
XX Signs Promised - Not Reported

XXI Signs Given

(1) Miracle of the Sun on September 14, 1977 and other times thereafter.
(2) The 'Blue Curtain' Our Lady showed on November 1, 1977 demarking the boundaries of the 'Wood of Apparitions'.
(3) Statue of Our Lady smiled on November 14, 1977 as the seer was

holding the statue and placing it on a pedestal.
(4) The statue of Our Lady also wept tears.
(5) On July 31, 1978 while Our Lady was appearing in the Wood, a group of pilgrims saw a magnificent cross and crown shining in the sky.
(6) During May 1979 reportedly some 80 people saw the Holy Face of Jesus during Adoration of the Blessed Sacrament.
(7) The seer is reported to have borne the Stigmata in his own flesh.
(8) On July 26, 1979 Our Lady placed the 'Mystical Ring' on the finger of the seer, during Holy Mass.
(9) It is reported that on June 11, 1978 Fr Jean-Marie lacked sufficient Hosts for Holy Communion, when Hosts unexplainably appeared one by one into the Ciborium.

XXII Predictions/Promises

Our Lady gave promises for those who accept and wear Her medal with confidence; promises of choice graces.

These graces extended to all people, but especially referred to children, young men and women, mothers, widows and widowers, the sick and infirm, religious men and women, and finally bishops and priests.

XXIII Prophecies/Warnings of Chastisement - NR
XXIV Method of Appearance - Not Reported
XXV Method of Departure - Not Reported

XXVI Confrontation w/Civil Authorities

The reports are that "all kinds" of persecutions were set upon the seer, in spite of which the "Work of Frechou" thrives. No mention is made of the source of these persecutions. (No reports with civil authorities known.)

XXVII Confrontation w/Church Authorities

The reports are that "all kinds" of persecutions were set upon the seer, in spite of which the "Work of Frechou" thrives. No mention is made of the source of these persecutions. (No reports with church authorities known.)

XXVIII Request Chapel/Shrine Built

On June 10, 1977 Our Lady indicated by Her presence the place where She wants Her sanctuary to be built.

XXIX Free Will/Choice - Not Reported

XXX Seer(s)' Suffering/Sacrifice

(1) First there are reports of persecution which will always result in suffering.
(2) Also this seer is reported to suffer the Passion of Jesus, in his own flesh; the Stigmata.

XXXI Healings Reported

A spectacular healing is reported to have occurred on March 13, 1978. Although the claim is that this healing is "incontestable", yet no details are accounted.

XXXII Action Taken by the Church - Not Reported

XXXIII Bibliography

Booklet, Background of the Apparition at Frechou
By: Fraternite Notre Dame
Published by: Fraternite Notre Dame

Various Newsletter Articles
By: Fraternite Notre Dame
Published by: Fraternite Notre Dame

Chapter 36

Philadelphia, Pennsylvania, USA
(1978 - Present)

I Place - Philadelphia, Pennsylvania, USA

II Dates of First and Last Apparition

First: February 15, 1978
Last: July 3, 1993 (last reported).
Note: These apparitions are reportedly ongoing.

III Seer(s) - 1

Name: Marianne   (This is a pseudonym)
Birth: Unknown
Age at first apparition: Unknown
Status: Living

IV Total Number of Apparitions - 110

(Locutions and visions only through July 3, 1993)

V Dates and Locality of Each Apparition

(All dates and locations are in Philadelphia, Pennsylvania)

1978: February 14, 17; March 24.
1979: April 6.
1980: March 12.
1982: February 28; August 15, 16; October 7, December 1.
1983: February 27.
1984: October 6.
1985: February 20; March 29; May 3; September 14; December 7.
1986: May 30; June 22; August 22; September 8; December 24.
1987: November 15.
1988: August 31; October 12.
1989: April 26; June 11; June 29; August 23; December 8.
1990: February 10, August 4, 10, 11; September 8, 29; November 10, 24; December 10, 13, 22, 29.
1991: January 5, 15, 19; February 16, 18, 23; March 1, 5, 9, 16; April 28; May 13; June 29; July 4, 12, 13, 20, 24; August 24; November 9, 20, 23; December 12, 14, 28.
1992: January 4; February 8, 11. (Note: The messages reportedly are ongoing and are being distributed; although not in bound volume form subsequent to February 11, 1992.) February 15; March 7, 14, 21, 26, 28, 31; April 5, 10, 30; May 1, 2, 30; June 20; July 16, 22, 25; September 1, 12, 19, 29; November 28; October 6, 7; December 10, 26, 29.
1993: January 1, 9, 16, 23; February 2, 10; March 29; April 17, 18; June 18; July 2, 3.

VI Description of Our Lady - Not Reported

VII Title(s) of Our Lady - 1

(1) On February 14, 1978 Our Lady said: *"I am the Lady of Light."* This was repeated on Aug 15, 1982.

VIII Brief Factual Review

Philadelphia, Pennsylvania is a state located in the northeast industrial region of the USA.

Marianne, a pseudonym given her by Our Lady, is an elderly woman who lives in Philadelphia. She was born on Palm Sunday, and was later told by Jesus this meant *"victory over the cross"*.

Marianne was cured of a terminal illness when she was only two years old, through the prayers of others. Later her own father was cured of cancer, also through intercessory prayers.

The life of Marianne has been one of suffering. From the time she was a child, poverty and illness plagued the family. Then in December 1945 doctors injured her spine during an operation, leaving her paralyzed and confined to a wheelchair. She eventually regained use of her legs. At first this was depressing to Marianne, but after she prayed to the Holy Spirit, her life began anew. She grew spiritually and has gained a fervor which remains with her to this day in spite of her sufferings.

In 1960 she made the Total Consecration to Jesus through Mary. Since then she has had many supernatural experiences including visions of Our Lady and of angels. Other visions and phenomenon are also reported.

One day while praying in church, Our Lady gave her a lengthy locution, explaining Marianne's future mission in life, and what was expected of her.

In 1977 the messages started as an 'Interior Voice'. Jesus instructed her to disseminate the messages throughout the world. Marianne asked for a confirmation of the validity of the messages, that the words not be those words used by Marianne in her own vocabulary. This was granted. With the help of her spiritual director and her mentor she was able to carry out her mission and disseminate the messages.

The first reported messages from Our Lady occurred in 1978. Our Lady stressed the insignificance of the "voice box," and the importance of the messages alone.

The messages themselves cover a wide range of subject matter and are ongoing to this day. Our Lady exhorts us to pray the rosary, to wear the scapular, to pray for and support the Pope, to repent and return to God. Our Lady also warns of the coming purification and chastisement. The messages announce that the hour of Mary's greatest victory is at hand. Many of the messages are instructive.

The messages given by Jesus to Marianne are likewise reported in the books containing Our Lady's messages.

Copies of the messages were provided to Pope John Paul II. On May 27, 1991 the Holy Father granted a private audience to Marianne. No Church action is reported.

IX The Primary Messages - 3

(1) Prayer - *"Time now on earth is very short, use all your time for prayer."* (April 6, 1979)

Then on February 20, 1985: *"My beloved priests, I beg on bended knees; pray, pray, pray the rosary, slowly with recollection on the mysteries."*

"The world is so easily gained as the people do not pray. Only prayer will now save you, nothing else!" (September 29, 1990)

On December 22, 1990 Our Lady said: *"My children, I plead with you, pray, adore God, serve God and all will be well."*

Again on March 1, 1991: *"My dear people pray, pray till all evil is *eradicated from the face of the earth."*

(2) Rosary - *"When fashioning a ring of love, do it through the rosary, the most powerful weapon on earth."* (March 12, 1990)

"Bright lights of glory shine around My children who pray the rosary with devotion, with great feeling, recollection." (October 7, 1982)

"Satan is now raging against My children of the rosary as he hates them with a vengeance." (August 31, 1988)

"Sweet children of the rosary, begin a new crusade of the rosaries, to reach your whole earth." (April 26, 1989)

Then on September 29, 1990 Our Lady announced: *"Give Me rosaries and I'll give you a happy life for all eternity!"*

(3) Sacrifice/Penance - On February 20, 1985: *"I appeal to you to reform and purify your sinful lives ... If you come back to Us repentant, Jesus will honor your trust and show His greatest Mercy."*

"The cruel world is on the brink of great tragedies, but people do not want to listen and do penance . . ." (December 14, 1991)

Then on June 29, 1991: *"Repent! Repent! I cry but no one listens . . ."*

X Signs Preceding The Apparitions - Not Reported

XI Other Visions During Apparitions

It is reported that through February 8, 1992 Marianne received 121 messages from Jesus. She also received messages from St. Joseph, the Holy Spirit and the Eternal Father.

XII Prayers Taught to the Seer(s) - Not Reported

XIII Special Devotion Given To The Seer(s)

Although no new devotions are reported, yet Our Lady did request devotions:
  (1) Litany of the Saints (December 29, 1990).
  (2) Consecration to the Immaculate Heart (February 11, 1992).

XIV Requests Made by Our Lady - Not Reported
XV Specific Bible References - Not Reported
XVI Secrets Given To The Seer(s) - Not Reported
XVII Miracles Promised by Our Lady - NR
XVIII Miracles Performed - Not Reported
XIX Miracles Promised not yet Performed - NR

XX Signs Promised - Not Reported
XXI Signs Given - Not Reported

XXII Predictions/Promises

(1) **September 29, 1990** - "*The next two years will be full of weal and woe as the anti-Christ sits on his throne and badgers the world.*"
(2) **December 12, 1991** - "*1992 will be a banner year as the trumpets have sounded and the angels are ready to descend and chastise evil people according to God's eternal plan fashioned in eternity.*"

XXIII Prophecies/Warnings of Chastisement

(1) **November 10, 1990** - "*Children, the rapid-changes in the world are leading straight to the holocaust of Armageddon, the last big battle of your era.*"
(2) **December 14, 1991** - "*The cruel world is on the brink of great tragedies, but people do not want to listen and do penance.*"
(3) **February 17, 1978** - "*Prepare yourselves for future shocks, know that they are coming.*"
(4) **February 19, 1978** - "*Prepare yourselves for a holocaust as you have never seen.*"

XXIV Method of Appearance - Not Reported
XXV Method of Departure - Not Reported
XXVI Confrontation w/Civil Authorities - NR
XXVII Confrontation w/Church Authorities - NR
XXVIII Requests Chapel/Shrine Built - NR

XXIX Free Will/Choice

The messages plead for all to pray, do penance and convert; obviously inviting us to choose to do as Our Lady asks.

On May 3, 1985 Our Lady said: "*It is up to you to be redeemed, fully purified, sanctified, or be condemned eternally to hell, the infernal abode of the damned.*"

XXX Seer(s)' Suffering/Sacrifice

The record reveals that Marianne suffered constantly from an early age. She was cured of a terminal illness when only two years old. Later she was paralyzed and confined to a wheel chair.

XXXI Healings Reported

(1) Marianne herself was healed of a terminal illness at age two, and then was again healed some years later through prayer.
(2) Her own father was also healed through intercessory prayer.

XXXII Action Taken by the Church - Not Reported

XXXIII Bibliography

Just Love My Jesus 1992
By: Marianne
Published by: Marianne

Chapter 37

Cuapa, Nicaragua
(1980)

I Place - Cuapa, Nicaragua

II Dates of First and Last Apparitions

First: May 8, 1980
Last: October 13, 1980

III Seer(s) - 1

Name: Bernardo Martinez
Birth: Unknown
Age at first apparition: About 50
Status: Living

IV Total Number of Apparitions - 6

V Dates and Locality of Each Apparitions

1980: May 8 & 16 (Cuapa, Nicaragua); June 8 & July 8 (vision in a dream at seer's home); September 8 & October 13 (Cuapa, Nicaragua).

VI Description of Our Lady

(1) May 8, 1980 Our Lady appeared during a second flash of light. She was standing above a white cloud, which cloud radiated light in all

directions. Our Lady's feet were bare, Her dress was long and white. She had a celestial cord around Her waist. Long sleeves. A pale cream veil with gold embroidery along the edge covered Her. Her hands were held together over Her breast. She looked like the Lady of Fatima statue. She extended Her arms and from Her hands emanated rays of light stronger than the sun, some of these rays of light touched the seer's chest.

(2) September 8, 1980, this time the Virgin Mary appeared as a child, beautiful but little, age 7 or 8. She did not have a veil, nor crown, nor mantle. No adornment and no embroidery. Her dress was long, with long sleeves, and the dress was girded with a pink cord. Her hair fell to Her shoulder and was brown in color. Her eyes were much lighter, almost the color of honey. All of Her being radiated light. She looked liked Our Lady, but She was a child.

VII Title(s) of Our Lady - 1

On May 8, 1980 Our Lady said: "*I am Mary, I come from heaven. I am the Mother of Jesus.*"

VIII Brief Factual Review

Nicaragua is located in Central America with shore lines on both the Atlantic and Pacific oceans.

The village of Cuapa, Nicaragua is located in a small valley in the municipality of Juigalpa in the Chontales (mountains). The inhabitants are mostly small cattle ranchers.

Bernardo Martinez was a humble and poor man. He was the keeper of the chapel (sacristan), sweeping the floors, dusting, cleaning and washing the altar cloths and albs. He had done so since he was old enough to use the dust cloth and broom, and always without pay. He had the keys to the chapel. This was his way to serve the Lord. He was ridiculed, scorned and called a fool for doing so; his own brothers would tell him that the reason he did not prosper financially was because of his involvement with things at the sacristy.

Bernardo remarks that after the events which occurred in the chapel, that everything changed for him. Now sweeping the chapel had become an honor, the altar cloths were washed in the blink of an eye, even before it could be noticed that they needed to be washed and ironed.

It was near the end of March 1980 when upon entering the sacristy, Bernardo found that someone had left a light burning. He was disturbed because he was responsible to control the costs of utilities; he had the keys. A few days later, he again found a light left on in the sacristy. He believed that the ladies upon leaving the sacristy had left the lights on. Therefore, he went to the homes of Mrs. Barea and Mrs. Martinez to confront them about the waste of electricity. But he realized when he talked to the women that they were not to blame.

Thereafter on April 15, 1980 Bernardo went into the chapel and saw the statue of Our Lady illuminated. He immediately thought some boys had broken some tiles from the roof which allowed the light into the chapel. However, when he went outside to look, no tiles were missing and also it was nighttime about 8:00 PM. When he went inside the chapel again, he looked closer at the statue and saw the hands, the feet, the neck; the light was actually coming from inside the statue. It was so bright that he could see and walk around without turning the lights on inside the chapel.

Now Bernardo understood this was not an ordinary thing, he thought that the Holy Virgin was angry with him because he had quarreled with the two women about leaving the lights on. Bernardo immediately decided to ask their forgiveness because he was so moved at seeing the lighted statue. It was getting time for the daily rosary so Bernardo rang the church bell to gather the people to pray the rosary. When the people arrived, Bernardo made a public apology to everyone he hurt, and they all forgave him.

After this public apology Bernardo told the people praying the rosary what he had seen, and asked them to keep it a secret. This did not happen and the news spread throughout the village. One of the nuns told the priest the entire series of events. The priest asked Bernardo what were the prayers he prayed and Bernardo answered that he prayed the rosary, three Hail Mary's, and a little prayer his grandmother taught him to say when he had any tribulation. Here is that prayer:

Prayer:
"It is Mary our Helper, sweet lighthouse of the sea.
Since I first learned to love, the love of my soul is She.
She each of my childhood stages did guide.
And for that, since childhood, my love for Her did abide."

The pastor then told Bernardo to pray to Our Lady and ask Her if there was anything She wanted "from us". Bernardo's prayer, however, in his humility was: "Please do not request anything of me, I have many problems in the church. Make your request known to some other person because I want to avoid any more problems." One day, Mrs. Consuelo Marin told Bernardo that she believed his story about the statue, and asked if Bernardo would request of Our Lady that she too could see the illuminated statue. This he agreed to ask of Our Lady.

It's now early May 1980 and Bernardo had become sad and despondent due to financial and employment worries; and also spiritual concerns. On the night of the 7th, he felt hot and was unable to sleep. The next day, May 8th he decided to go fishing where he would feel cool and tranquil. He left early that next morning, but about 1:00 PM it began to rain. So he sat under a nearby tree and prayed his rosary. The rain stopped about the time he finished the rosary. He then went off to pick some fruits, mangos and jocotes. He now remembered he had to feed the animals and then go to town to pray the rosary with the people at 5:00 PM.

As he was walking, he saw a flash of lightning but could see no sign of rain. Then another flash and Our Lady appeared to him. She was standing above a cloud which was over a little morisco tree. At first Bernardo wondered if someone had brought the statue from the chapel to trick him. She was in bare feet, Her dress was long and white, a celestial cord around Her waist and long sleeves. Her veil was pale cream with a golden embroidery along the edge. She looked like the statue of Our Lady of Fatima at the church; only this Lady was alive, She moved her eyes. Then Our Lady extended Her arms and from Her hands emanated rays of light which streamed out and touched Bernardo on his chest. He blurted out "What is your name?" Our Lady told the seer that Her name was Mary and *"I come from heaven. I am the Mother of Jesus."* When Bernardo asked what She wanted, Our Lady said: *"I want the rosary to be prayed every day."*

When the seer interrupted and said that they were praying the rosary every day already, Our Lady said: *"I don't want it prayed only in the month of May, I want it prayed permanently, within the family including the children old enough to understand; to be prayed at a set hour when there are no problems with work in the home."*

Our Lady requested: *"Renew the Five First Saturdays. You will receive many graces when all of you do this."* Bernardo remembered that before the war in Nicaragua, the people used to make the Five First Saturdays, but since the Lord stopped the war and bloodshed, the people had discontinued this practice.

Our Lady urged everyone to pray; pray the rosary, love each other and make peace. She also acknowledged that Nicaragua had suffered much since the earthquake and that the world is threatened with great dangers. If we don't change: *"You will hasten the arrival of third world war."* Before Our Lady departed, She told Bernardo to tell this message to believers and nonbeliever alike. Again, Bernardo pleaded with Our Lady to tell another person, but Our Lady said that Our Lord had selected Bernardo to receive the message. Interestingly enough just as Our Lady was departing, the seer asked Our Lady if Mrs. Consuelo Marin could see Her, but Our Lady responded that not everyone can see Her. He was told to notify Mrs. Marin that she will see Our Lady when she is taken to heaven; in the meantime, she is to pray the rosary. After this Our Lady raised Her arms towards heaven, looked upwards and then the cloud that held Her slowly elevated Her. Our Lady was in a ray of light and when She reached a certain distance, She disappeared.

Although Bernardo was instructed to tell the message, he resisted. He went to the chapel and prayed the rosary. He was concerned that the people would ridicule him even more now that he saw Our Lady and received messages. He kept praying the rosary and kept the messages secret. However, he was under great stress, he could not sleep at night and felt he had a weight on him. At night he would hear a voice telling him to reveal the messages, but he held fast for eight days. Then on May 16, 1980 while Bernardo was en route to give water to his calf in the pasture, he saw a lightning flash. Then another flash even brighter. It was from this light that Our Lady appeared. She looked just as She did at Her first appearance. Now Bernardo felt guilty because he had avoided going to the place of the first appearance so he wouldn't have to explain to Her why he didn't tell the messages. She had followed him here to the pasture, the seer thought: 'Surely She is angry with me now.' Our Lady asked Bernardo: *"Why have you not told what I sent you to tell?"* Bernardo responded that he was afraid people would laugh at him and think he was crazy. But Our Lady kindly said: *"Do not be afraid. I am going to help you, and tell the priest."* Then She disappeared with another flash of lightning.

Bernardo then completed his chores and went to the chapel and prayed the rosary. He decided to tell the message to only two people he trusted, namely Mrs. Martinez and Mrs. Marin. When he told them they reprimanded him for not obeying Our Lady. The seer reports that all his anxiety now left him. The next day Bernardo told everyone who came to his house. Some believed, others did not.

On May 19th Bernardo went to Juigalpa and told the priest about the apparitions and the messages. The priest listened and then told Bernardo to go to the site of the apparition and pray the rosary. The seer was told not to tell anyone what he saw or heard, but he could tell everyone of the message he already received.

On June 8th Bernardo went to the site of the first apparition because Our Lady told him that She would appear to him on the 8th day of each month. The seer and others present prayed the rosary, but Our Lady did not appear. During the night of June 8th Our Lady appeared to Bernardo in a dream; he was at the same place where he first saw Her. In the dream he prayed the rosary, then came the two flashes of lightning and She appeared. Our Lady gave the seer the same message as was given at the first appearance. However, She also answered some special requests that Bernardo gave Her from different people. Then raising up Her hand, Our Lady said: *"Look at the sky."* When the seer looked in that direction, he saw what looked like a movie screen presented to him. First, he saw a large group of people dressed in white walking towards the sunrise. They were bathed in light and were very happy and were singing. Light radiated from their bodies. In the midst of this scene, Bernardo heard Our Lady tell him that these are the first catechumens, and many of them were martyrs. She asked Bernardo if he would like to be a martyr. Of course he said yes, but at the same time he did not know the exact meaning of martyr. Next he saw another group of people dressed in white. Some of them had luminous rosaries in their hands. One carried a very large book. They prayed the rosary and Bernardo prayed with them. When the rosary was finished Our Lady said: *"These are the first ones to whom I gave the rosary. That is the way I want all of you to pray the rosary."* Afterwards he saw a third group dressed in brown robes. These Bernardo recognized as Franciscans, carrying rosaries and praying. Our Lady told Bernardo: *". . . they received the rosary from the hands of the first ones."*

A fourth group arrived, a huge procession, the people dressed as ordinary people, they carried their rosaries in their hands. Bernardo wanted to join them because they were dressed like him; however, they radiated light and their hands were white while Bernardo looked at his own hands and he saw them as black. Our Lady then told Bernardo: *"I have shown you the Glory of Our Lord and you people will acquire this if you are obedient to Our Lord, to the Lord's Word; if you persevere in praying the holy rosary and put into practice the Lord's Word."*

After this Our Lady departed as before, being elevated on the cloud. Bernardo reported this vision to the priest. The priest forbade him to reveal it to anyone. Bernardo objected but obeyed the priest. Some days later, on June 24th the priest relented and gave the seer permission to tell the people.

On July 8th the seer again went to the site of the first apparition; about 40 people were there with him. Again, Our Lady did not appear. That night Bernardo had a dream in which he was praying the rosary for a boy who was in jail in Cuapa. Then Bernardo found himself at the scene of the first apparition. He saw an angel at the place where Our Lady had appeared. The angel spoke and said: *"Your prayer has been heard."* The angel then told the seer to tell that prisoner's sister to go and console him on Sunday, and advise him not to sign the document presented to him and for her to go to the police headquarters on Monday and pay 1000 cordovas for his release. Then, still in his dream, Bernardo presented another petition from his own cousin who lives in Zelaya. The angel also gave advice for this problem of the seer's cousin. The angel told Bernardo to warn his other cousins that the first cousin would be assaulted, he would be shot in the left heel, and at a later time he would be killed.

The next day, Bernardo went to the first cousin's farm to warn him, but the cousin refused the warning. Everything predicted by the angel came true as stated. The boy was released from jail, the problem with one cousin was resolved as advised and the other cousin was shot in the left heel and later he was killed. Our Lady did not appear to Bernardo on August 8th. However he went to the site and found the river swollen and was unable to cross it. It is reported that the priest had a dream in which he saw the site of the apparition. Later the priest visited the place with the seer and the priest found the place in his dream to be the exact place of the first apparition.

On September 8, 1980 Our Lady again appeared to the seer; only this time She came as a child. In the seer's own words: "I saw Her as a child. Beautiful, but little!" Again the apparition was preceded by two flashes of lightning; there was no rain. The time of Our Lady's appearance was again at 3:00 PM. Our Lady repeated the message given at the first apparition; She spoke in a child's voice. Since people had been requesting that the seer ask Our Lady if She would let others see Her, Bernardo thought that he might convince Her to do so. So he asked Her to show Herself to everyone. Our Lady listened to the seer and then responded: *"No. It is enough for you to give them the message because for the one who is going to believe that will be enough, and the one who is not going to believe though he should see Me, he is not going to believe."* As Bernardo reflected on these words he understood that what Our Lady said was true. Then the seer asked Our Lady about the church which the people were talking about building. Our Lady said: *"No. The Lord does not want material churches. He wants living temples which are yourselves. Restore the sacred temple of the Lord. In you is the gratification for the Lord."* Bernardo then asked Our Lady whether he should continue in the Catechumenate; he was unsure what to do. Our Lady said: *"No. Don't leave. Always continue firmly in the Catechumenate. Little by little you will comprehend all that the Catechumenate signifies as community groups meditate on the Beatitudes, away from all the noise."* Our Lady announced She would appear on the 13th of October instead of the usual 8th day of each month. Then the cloud elevated and carried Our Lady up and away.

About 50 people accompanied Bernardo to the apparition site on October 13, 1980. They were praying the rosary, when all of a sudden a large luminous circle formed over the ground. Everyone present saw this sign. Looking upward, a circle of light had also formed in the sky. This circle in the sky gave off light in different colors which light did not come from the sun which was already setting.

After this sign, the seer saw two flashes of lightning. Then Our Lady appeared on a cloud as before. She extended Her arms and rays of light came from Her hands and reached all the people. Again, everyone wanted to see Her; but Our Lady simply said: *"No. Not everyone can see Me."* Nonetheless some people said they saw a shadow, like a statue, over the flowers. The seer then pleaded with Our Lady to show Herself so they would all believe. She did not answer, instead She assumed the pose of Our Lady of Sorrows, Her face turned pale, She looked sad and then Our Lady cried. This made Bernardo believe that he caused Her unhappiness and he pleaded with Our Lady to forgive him. Our Lady answered: *"I am not angry nor will I get angry."* When the seer asked why She was crying, Our Lady said: *"It saddens Me to see the hardness of those persons' hearts. But you will have to pray for them so they will change."*

Upon hearing these words the seer was so affected that he could not stop crying himself. Then Our Lady gave the seer a message pleading that we pray, pray the rosary, love one another, forgive one another, make peace and seek ways to please God. Again Our Lady warned of a coming third world war if people do not change. She said: *"Never turn to violence."* Then Our Lady taught the seer a prayer which She repeated three times before She departed.

Bishop Vega has appointed an Episcopal Conference to look into these alleged apparitions. The bishop has stated that he, himself, believes in these apparitions but does not wish much publicity because the Episcopal Conference of Nicaragua has not yet issued a statement confirming the judgment of Bishop Vega.

IX The Primary Messages - 4

(1) **Pray the Rosary** - *"I want the rosary to be prayed every day; I don't want it to be prayed only in the Month of May, I want it prayed permanently, within the family; including children old enough to understand; to be prayed at a set hour when there are no problems with the work at home."* (May 8, 1980)

In a dream the seer had on June 8, 1980 he was shown visions of groups of people whom Our Lady identified as those to whom She first gave the rosary and those who received the rosary from these first ones.

On October 13, 1980 (the final apparition) Our Lady told Bernardo: *"Pray the rosary, meditate on the mysteries. Listen to the Word of God spoken in them..."*

On May 8, 1980 Our Lady said: *"Pray, pray My son, the rosary for all the world..."*

(2) **Prayer** - Our Lady pleaded with us to pray for all the world, and even taught the seer a prayer to be invoked. On October 13, 1980 She said: *"Pray, pray My son for all the world. Great dangers threaten the world."*

(3) **Love and Forgive Each Other** - *"Love each other. Fulfill your obligations."* (May 8, 1980)

On September 8, 1980 Our Lady said: *"Love each other. Love one another. Forgive each other."*

Then at the final appearance on October 13, 1980 Our Lady again repeated: *"Love one another. Love each other. Forgive each other. Do not turn to violence. Never turn to violence."*

(4) **Peace** - Our Lady pleads with us to make peace with each other. *"Make peace. Don't ask Our Lord for peace because if you do not make it, there will be no peace."* (May 8, 1980)

Again on September 8, 1980 She said: *"Make peace. Don't just ask for it. Make peace!"*

During the last apparition of October 13, 1980 Our Lady said: *"Make peace. Don't ask for peace because if you don't make it, it does no good to ask for it. Fulfill your obligations."*

X Signs Preceding the Apparitions

The seer saw two separate flashes of lightning before each appearance. This was nearly a duplicate of the reported Fatima apparitions.

XI Other Visions During Apparitions

(1) In the July 8th dream, the seer was visited by an angel dressed in a long white tunic. The angel was tall and very young and his body appeared to be bathed in light.
(2) In the dream of June 8th, the seer was shown visions of three separate groups of people identified with the rosary.

XII Prayers Taught to the Seer(s)

Just before departing during the final apparition of October 13, 1980 Our Lady said: *"Invoke Me with these words"* and then She repeated this prayer three times: *"Holy Virgin, You are my Mother, the Mother to all of us sinners."*

XIII Special Devotion Given to the Seer(s)

No new special devotion was given to the seer; yet Our Lady urged us to renew the Five First Saturdays Devotion to Her Immaculate Heart. She reminded the seer: *"You received many graces when all of you did these."* (May 8, 1980)

XIV Requests Made by Our Lady

(1) Renew the Five First Saturdays Devotion. (May 8, 1980)
(2) On September 8, 1980 Our Lady requested the seer come to the apparition site on October 13th because She would appear then instead of October 8th. This occurred as She stated.

XV Specific Bible Reference

On May 8th Our Lady told the seer to read Bible citations when praying the rosary. No specific bible reference was given. The seer asked: "Where are the Biblical citations?" It is reported that Our Lady told the seer to look for them in the Bible.

XVI Secrets Given to the Seer(s) - Not Reported
XVII Miracles Promised by Our Lady - NR

XVIII Miracles Performed - Not Reported
XIX Miracles Promised not yet Performed - NR

XX Signs Promised

None were promised and when requested to show a sign by the seer, Our Lady said: *"No. It is enough for you to give them the message because for the one who is going to believe that will be enough, and the one who is not going to believe though he should see Me is not going to believe."* (Sept. 8, 1980)

XXI Signs Given

(1) July 8, 1980. In this dream the seer was given a sign that his friend in jail would be released to his friend's sister on the following Monday; the angel had said: *"Your prayer has been heard."* And it occurred as promised.
(2) On October 13, 1980 all those present saw a big luminous circle form over the ground, and looking upwards they saw a circle that had also formed in the sky.
(3) The statue of Our Lady in the chapel became illuminated.

XXII Predictions/Promises

In the dream of July 8, 1980 the seer was given a promise or prediction that the person he was praying for would be released from jail on the following Monday. It occurred in exact detail as given. Also in that dream the angel predicted a cousin of the seer would be shot in the heel and later killed. The seer tried to convince his cousin to take steps to avert the danger, but to no avail. The events occurred exactly as predicted.

XXIII Prophecies/Warnings of Chastisement

(1) May 8, 1980 Our Lady said: *". . .Tell believers and nonbelievers that the world is threatened with great dangers. I ask the Lord to appease His Justice, but if you don't change, you will hasten the arrival of the Third World War."*
(2) October 13, 1980 Again Our Lady said: *"Nicaragua has suffered a great deal since the earthquake and will continue to suffer if all of you don't change. If you don't change you will hasten the coming of the Third World War."*

XXIV Method of Appearance

Two flashes of lightning would alert the seer that Our Lady is present. Then Our Lady appeared over a cloud above the little morisco tree.

XXV Method of Departure

After the message Our Lady looked upward towards heaven and the cloud that held her slowly elevated Her until She disappeared.

XXVI Confrontation w/Civil Authorities

Although many people did not believe the seer and also ridiculed him, there are no reports of civil authorities becoming involved with these apparitions.

XXVII Confrontation w/Church Authorities

No confrontation reported. However, there was a case reported where the priest had a dream in which he saw the site of the apparition. This priest had not believed the seer; nevertheless, he asked Bernardo to take him (the priest) to the place without showing the priest the exact spot. The priest then silently went along and seemed to recognize something. It was then that the priest announced, "this is the place that was in my dream last night". He had indicated the exact spot of the first apparition. After this experience the priest seemed to change and believed not only that Our Lady had appeared to Bernardo, but that She would appear to him again. This occurred when She appeared to the seer again in September and October 1980.

XXVIII Request Chapel/Shrine Built

Although Our Lady told Bernardo on September 8th that: *"Our Lord does not want material churches, He wants living temples which are yourselves . . ."* yet She told the seer to donate the money given to him for the construction of the Chapel at Cuapa.

The bishop of Juigalpa believes in these apparitions and has already purchased the piece of land where Our Lady appeared with a view towards building a chapel or church.

XXIX Free Will/Choice

The seer is reported to have said: "The important thing is the message. We can accept it or we can reject it. We are free. The Lord respects our freedom."

XXX Seer(s)' Suffering/Sacrifice

(1) Firstly, the seer apologized to the ladies whom he had wrongly accused of leaving the lights on in the chapel, by a public apology.
(2) After the first apparition the seer could not find peace because Our Lady told him to reveal the message, but he was worried that people would ridicule him again, as they had done when he saw the statue glow.
(3) His own family scorned him because he did not prosper financially due to the time he spent in the Sacristy.

XXXI Healing Reported - Not Reported

XXXII Action Taken by the Church

The bishop believes in these apparitions and has purchased the land where the apparitions occurred. He has also appointed an Episcopal Conference to review and report on these happenings. No final action by the Church is reported.

XXXIII Bibliography

Apparitions of Our Blessed Mother 1982 at Cuapa, Nicaragua
By: Bishop Vega
Published by: The Blue Army

Chapter 38

El Escorial, Spain
(1980 - 1992)

I Place - El Escorial, Spain

II Dates of First and Last Apparitions

First: November 13, 1980
Last: April 4, 1992

III Seers - 1

Name: Amparo Cuevas
Birth: March 13, 1931
Age at first apparition: 49
Status: Living

IV Total Number of Apparitions - 30

V Dates and Locality of Each Apparitions

All apparitions were located in the field at Escorial, Spain unless otherwise noted.

1980: November 13.
1981: January 15; May 23; July 6; September 25; October 2, 14, 23; November 22; December 11, 18.
1982: January 15; March 19; April 2; July 3; November 19, 20, 26;

December 4, 22, 25.
1983: January 14, 22; February 5; March 27; July 20; November 5.
1989: February 4; July 1.
1992: April 4.
A total of 30 apparitions are reported; however, it is almost certain that there were more apparitions. It is reported that these apparitions are ongoing and take place on the First Saturdays.

VI Description of Our Lady

On one occasion, December 18, 1981 Our Lady of Sorrows appeared crying. Previously, the seer had never seen Her cry.

VII Title(s) of Our Lady - 1

It is reported that the Blessed Virgin Mary appeared as Our Lady of Sorrows on December 18, 1981.

VIII Brief Factual Review

Spain is located on the Iberian Peninsula of Europe. Gibraltar, the ancient guardian of the Mediterranean Sea is located on the southern tip of Spain, exposed to both the Atlantic Ocean and the Mediterranean Sea.

Amparo Cuevas was born on March 13, 1931 in the municipality of Penascosa, Spain. Her mother died when Amparo was just six months old. It is reported that even as a child Amparo suffered much. Her own stepmother sent the child to sell things on the street with instructions not to return home until all her wares were sold. As a result, it is reported that she frequently slept outside, under a tree and even covered with snow. Once when she was only nine years old, she had to be resuscitated. It is also reported that at home she slept inside a cupboard which was too short to allow her to stretch out. She had no bed. When she was ten years old, she was picked up for begging food on the street. In jail she survived on flour and water. Through all this, Amparo had a great love and devotion to the Blessed Virgin Mary. In a child's innocence, Amparo asked Our Lady: "Dear Mother in heaven, I would like to see my own mother. Take me where she is." Amparo believed Our Lady heard her prayer.

Amparo married Nicasio Barderas Bravo. Together they had seven children. The suffering of Amparo continued into her marriage. Her husband struggled with an alcohol problem and with nearly constant unemployment; although, it is reported that he has had a sincere conversion. The family has lived in El Escorial, located about 50 kilometers from Madrid, for some 20 years.

Amparo and her husband were both in poor health. In 1977 she went to Lourdes and was cured of her affliction of heart trouble. It is reported that in October 1980 Amparo first heard a voice which said to her: *"Pray for peace in the world and for the conversion of sinners. Love one another. You are going to have painful trials."* Soon thereafter Our Lady appeared to Amparo in an apparition showing Our Lady, Herself nailed to the cross. It was then that Jesus said to the seer: *"My daughter, this is the passion of Christ. You have to experience it in its entirety."* Amparo complained that she could not bear it. Then Jesus said to her: *"If you cannot bear it for a few seconds, (imagine) what I experienced on the cross for hours, dying for those very persons who crucified Me? You can save many souls with your pains."* Then Jesus asked if she accepted. She responded: "With your help Lord, I will bear it."

Later she received the Stigmata; the wounds of Christ's passion. Amparo said she was given the Stigmata so that one third of humanity may be saved from cataclysm of an unheard of magnitude. It was shortly thereafter on November 13, 1980 that Our Lady first appeared to the seer. Our Lady said She would appear on the First Saturdays. Our Lord thereafter also appeared to the seer. Our Lady continued to appear to the seer and to give her messages exhorting all to prayer, to pray the rosary, to accept suffering and do penance for the conversion of sinners. Our Lady also warned that we were being too materialistic as a society and further gave stern warnings of the coming Great Chastisement.

The seer was shown the horrors of hell, but was also shown heaven. These apparitions and messages reportedly have continued into the year 1992 and may be occurring at the present time (not all messages were available for this work).

The Church has not made a definitive judgment, although in 1985 the archbishop issued a statement to the effect that the supernatural character of the alleged apparitions and messages had not been established. He also requested that priests refrain from attending these manifestations. It is not reported whether a commission has been established.

IX The Primary Messages - 4

(1) Prayer - Our Lady pleaded for prayer during many of the messages.

October 14, 1981 *"I ask you, My sons and daughters, to pray much. My Son is awaiting your prayers. Pray My sons and daughters, pray much because many souls are condemned since they have no one to pray for them."*

July 3, 1982 *"Pray for those who do not pray, and do penance for those who do not do it."*

February 4, 1989 *"Therefore, My children, I ask that you form a 'Great Flock' and all join together to pray..."*

July 1, 1989 *"Pray, My children, today I promise to protect all of you with My cloak. Do not cease to pray, My children, for the enemy is on the watch for your souls..."*

(2) Pray the Rosary - The exhortation to pray the rosary was repeated most often in the messages.

November 22, 1981 *"Do not cease to pray the holy rosary which when prayed with devotion, is very powerful. I ask you this."*

October 2, 1981 *"Tell everyone to pray the rosary often so that they appease the wrath of God the Father."*

October 14, 1981 *"It is fitting that you pray the 15 mysteries. Hasten to save souls. With each rosary, many souls are saved. You must help My Son and you also console the Eternal Father."*

May 23, 1981 *"Tell everyone to pray the rosary in all parts of the world. The holy rosary is most pleasing to Me. Tell them it pleases Me very much if they would go from town to town praying the holy rosary. With it, all of humanity can be saved."*

July 1, 1989 *"Pray the holy rosary with much devotion, My children. The devil hates this prayer."*

February 4, 1989 *"Do not cease to pray the holy rosary with much devotion, and take refuge in My Immaculate Heart, for It will protect you, My children."*

(3) Penance and Sacrifice - November 20, 1982 *"It is necessary that you suffer. It is necessary so that one third (1/3) of humanity may be saved."*

February 4, 1989 *"Kiss the ground, My daughters, in reparation for so many, many sins that are committed by mankind ... and you My child, continue to be a victim of reparation for mankind..."*

On July 1, 1989 both Jesus and Mary appeared to the seer and pleaded for sacrifices, prayer and sufferings in reparation for the sins of mankind. On this date Our Lady said in part: *"Love the Church, My children, love the Pope ... part of Her (the Church) has fallen, only by sacrifice and prayer can she arise. I want you to be poor, humble and sacrificing..."*

(4) Conversion - April 2, 1982 *"Amend your lives, dress with decency and do not commit those sins of impurity."*

February 4, 1989 *"My Son is sick of the hypocritical souls and of the indifference that there is in the world. Be converted My children and repent of your sins."*

July 1, 1989 *"Give up material things My children, occupy yourselves with the only good which is Christ."*

X Signs Preceding the Apparitions - Not Reported

XI Other Visions During Apparitions

(1) Jesus appeared with Mary during some of the apparitions and also

gave messages to the seer.
(2) Jesus also spoke with Amparo on October 1980 just prior to Our Lady's first apparition to the seer.
(3) On November 19, 1982 St. Michael appeared and gave a message to the seer giving warnings of the Great Chastisement that is to come.
(4) The seer was shown a vision of hell and all its horror. She was also shown the place of heaven.

XII Prayers Taught to the Seer(s) - Not Reported

XIII Special Devotion Given to the Seer(s)

No special devotions are reported, yet Our Lady requested the devotion of Five First Saturdays to Her Immaculate Heart, earlier announced at Fatima in 1917.

XIV Requests Made by Our Lady

(1) On several occasions Our Lady requested that Amparo kiss the ground, *"for so many, many sins that are committed in the world."*
(2) In addition Our Lord Himself requested, *"that all men who can withdraw from the world and live in community."* (April 4, 1992) Our Lord also said during this apparitions: *"Live the Gospel, for the majority of mankind does not live the Gospel..."*

XV Specific Bible References - Not Reported
XVI Secrets Given to the Seer(s) - Not Reported
XVII Miracles Promised by Our Lady - NR
XVIII Miracles Performed - Not Reported
XIX Miracles Promised not yet Performed - NR
XX Signs Promised - Not Reported

XXI Signs Given

This seer received the Stigmata.

XXII Predictions/Promises

(1) December 18, 1981 *"The Holy Father, the Vicar of My Son, will have to suffer much because during a period the Church will be subject to great persecutions ... The Church will encounter a horrible crisis..."*

(2) *"There will be three days of darkness* (September 25, 1981), *during this time, each one will see what he has done during his whole life."* (January 14, 1983)

XXIII Prophecies/Warnings of Chastisement

These messages contain many strong warnings and graphic descriptions of the great punishment to come upon mankind due to our refusal to return to God.

(1) *"Tell this to everyone: 'Because they have not changed and continue abusing My Mercy, the world will be involved in a great war, various nations will be destroyed. There will be many killed. The clouds will fall from the heavens and they will embrace the earth. All this will be as horrible as the human race has ever experienced. The judgment of the nations is very near. God is going to punish as never before. There will be great misfortunes in the world, and some nations will experience great earthquakes. This is the punishment of the century.'* (November 20, 1981)

(2) *"The punishment will be worse than 40 consecutive earthquakes destroying the earth. It will be horrible and no one will escape it, no one."* (October 23, 1981)

(3) *"God will permit Satan to sow division between governments, societies and families. There will be much physical and moral suffering. God will abandon all of them and send them many punishments which are near and are horrible."* (December 11, 1981)

(4) *"The punishment will destroy two thirds of humanity."* (December 22, 1982)

(5) *"The end of the times has arrived, the end of the end."* (December 4, 1982) *"The end of time is near, it is horrible ... Our Heavenly Father wants to send His justice upon men, this time He will punish much more severely than when He punished with the Flood."* (January 15, 1982)

(6) On September 23, 1981 the seer reportedly received a message containing the exact date of the Great Chastisement. Again on December 25, 1982 and on March 27, 1983 the dates of the Chastisement were given.

Note: The date of the Great Chastisement was not reported, is not contained in this work, and is not known to this writer.

(7) *"The Chastisement is going to fall on mankind, My daughter ... great showers of fire will reduce the earth to ashes, and all those great works that men have made and that their hearts admire so much are going to be destroyed ... The earth will tremble and entire nations will remain lost under the rubble; therefore, I come with a sad heart, My daughter because I see the Chastisement that lies in wait for mankind; and men do not change!"*

XXIV Method of Appearance - Not Reported

XXV Method of Departure

In several of the messages, it is reported that Our Lady said: *"Kiss the ground My child in reparation for so many, many sins that are committed against My Immaculate Heart."* Our Lady then asked everyone to hold up all religious articles to be blessed, and announced that all will be blessed with a 'Special Blessing'. Then Our Lady disappeared.

XXVI Confrontation w/Civil Authorities - NR
XXVII Confrontation w/Church Authorities - NR

XXVIII Request Chapel/Shrine Built

It is reported that Our Lady asked that a chapel be built in Her honor. However, no report is given as to whether a chapel has been built.

XXIX Free Will/Choice

(1) When Jesus appeared to Amparo in October 1980 He asked her if she would accept the mission to suffer in reparation for sins committed. She accepted and thus used her own free will in choosing to follow Our Lord.
(2) The messages exhort us to conversion, prayer and penance. We must choose to follow these messages or to reject them. Again, we exercise our own free will.

XXX Seer(s)' Suffering/Sacrifices

(1) The seer suffered very much during her childhood and the suffering continued in other forms into her marriage.
(2) She was specially chosen by Our Lord to become a victim soul when He first appeared to her in October 1980 and asked her if she would accept the suffering of His passion. She accepted.
(3) She has received the wounds of Christ, the Stigmata *"... so that one third of humanity might be saved from a cataclysm without precedent"* (the seer's own words).

XXXI Healings Reported

No healings are reported. It is reported that the seer was healed of heart trouble at Lourdes in 1977.

XXXII Action Taken by the Church

The archbishop issued a statement on April 22, 1985 to the effect that the supernatural character of the reported apparitions and messages had not been established, and further requesting that priests refrain from attending these alleged apparitions. There is no report of appointment of a commission, nor is it reported that these apparitions are condemned.

XXXIII Bibliography

The Apparitions of the Blessed Virgin Mary Today 1990
By: Fr. Rene Laurentin
Published by: Veritas

The Appearance of the Blessed Virgin Mary at Escorial
By: Not Given
Published by: Not Given

Chapter 39

MEDJUGORJE, YUGOSLAVIA
(1981 - PRESENT)

I   Place - Medjugorje, Bosnia-Herzegovina, Yugoslavia

II   Dates of First and Last Apparition

First: June 24, 1981
Last: January 24, 1994 (last reported).
Note: It is reported that these apparitions are ongoing.

III   Seer(s) - 6

Name: Mirjana Dragicevic Soldo
Birth: March 18, 1965
Age at first apparition: 16
Status: Married/Living

Name: Ivanka Ivankovic Elez
Birth: June 21, 1966
Age at first apparition: 15
Status: Married/Living

Name: Vicka Ivankovic
Birth: September 3, 1964
Age at first apparition: 16
Status: Living

Name: Ivan Dragicevic
Birth: May 25, 1965
Age at first apparition: 16
Status: Married/Living

Name: Marija Pavlovic Lunetti
Birth: April 1, 1965
Age at first apparition: 16
Status: Married/Living

Name: Jakov Colo
Birth: March 6, 1971
Age at first apparition: 10
Status: Married/Living

IV Total Number of Apparitions - over 3,000

It is reported that there have been in excess of 3,000 apparitions. Some of the seers received fewer, while others received more apparitions.

V Dates and Locality of Each Apparition

The sheer volume of apparitions makes it non-feasible to set forth each apparition separately. The apparitions occurred on Mt. Podbrdo, on Mt. Krizevac, at St. James Church in the choir loft, in the room of apparitions above the rectory, in the homes of several of the seers, and at other places where the seers were then visiting.

VI Description of Our Lady

(1) In the first days of the apparitions, the children describe Our Lady: "Our Lady wore a grey dress with a white veil. She had a crown of stars, blue eyes, dark hair, and rosy cheeks. She was floating on a grey cloud not touching the ground."

(2) On special Feast Days, Our Lady appeared in golden splendor. On August 5, 1984 Our Lady was dressed in gold and declared that it was the 2,000th anniversary of Her birth.

VII Title(s) of Our Lady - 2

"*Our Lady, Queen of Peace*" on August 6, 1981 Our Lady so identified Herself to the children.

Then in December 1988, Our Lady said: ". . . *I came to you as your Mother, Queen of Peace.*"

VIII   Brief Factual Review

Medjugorje, Yugoslavia is a small village located in southwestern Yugoslavia in the Republic of Bosnia-Herzegovina, some distance inland from the Adriatic Sea, about midway between Split and Dubrovnick. Bosnia-Herzegovina became one of the separate break-away republics of former Yugoslavia when these severed republics declared their independent status. In 1981 Yugoslavia had a population of about twenty-three million people, consisting primarily of Serbians, Croatians, and Muslims, whose religious adherence was primarily Eastern Orthodox, Roman Catholic, and Islam, in that order.

Medjugorje itself is located in a Croatian Catholic region. Its population, including several surrounding villages and farms, was about 500 families in 1981. The people who live in and around Medjugorje are mostly farmers growing tobacco, grapes, and various crops and animals for their own use.

Medjugorje, a word of Slavic origin which means "among the hills", lies hidden among the Herzegovina Mountains and is located at the foot of Mt. Krizevac which rises some 1,600 feet above the surrounding land. It is upon this Mount that the population erected a huge concrete cross (some 14 meters/46 feet tall) in 1933 to commemorate the 1900th Anniversary of the Crucifixion of Jesus on Mt. Calvary.

Mt. Krizevac means 'Mount of the Cross' and is located about three miles south of and behind St. James Church.

Mt. Podbrdo meaning 'Foot of the Hill' and now labeled the 'Hill of Apparitions' is located a short distance southeast of St. James Church.

St. James Church, with striking twin towers, was completed in 1969 and is the Parish Church of the Parish of Medjugorje. In 1981 Fr. Jozo Zovko was the pastor at St. James, later he was replaced by Fr. Tomislav Vlasic. In 1981 Pavao Zanic was the bishop of the diocese centered in Mostar, and Archbishop Frane Franic was bishop of the neighboring diocese at Split. Bishop Zanic has since been replaced by Bishop Ratco Peric.

In 1981 Yugoslavia was under the control of a communist regime. Atheistic Marshal Tito had earlier broken away from Russian style communism and ruled Yugoslavia with his own iron hand. Tito died in 1980, however, the communist government continued in power. It was said that Yugoslavia was a bridge between East and West; that is, a communist country that looks to the West across the Adriatic Sea. Politically supported by the East and economically by the West, this small country had a foot in each camp but was not to be favored by either.

Added to these complications was the long standing animosity and distrust of the several ethnic and religious factions, who over the centuries, had brutalized each other. They never completely forgot nor forgave each other's behavior.

On the positive side since the election of Pope John Paul II in 1978 the

Church in Yugoslavia has made much progress; especially among the young Croats and Slovenes. It seemed to model itself after the Church in Poland. This factor led to rapidly declining relations between the Church and State. It reached a new freezing point in February 1981 when thousands of Croats commemorated the 21st year of Cardinal Stepinac's death at his tomb in the Zagreb Cathedral.

Now it seemed the stage was set and the actors were all in place. And it was in this setting that this drama of supernatural origin was to unfold on June 24, 1981 the Feast of St. John the Baptist. It is said that just as St. John the Baptist was the herald to prepare the way for the First Coming of the Christ, so now the Blessed Virgin is to herald the Second Coming of Jesus.

It is also reported that a few years earlier Padre Pio had prophetically told a group of pilgrims from Mostar that "The Blessed Virgin will soon be visiting your homeland."

On June 24, 1981 Our Blessed Mother appeared to some children in Medjugorje and continues to appear to some of these seers even today; some fourteen years later.

Actually the first apparition occurred near the neighboring village of Bijakovici and not in Medjugorje. It was Ivanka Ivankovic, aged fifteen, and her friend Mirjana Dragicevic, aged sixteen, who first saw the apparition about 200 yards above Bijakovici on the rocky slope of Mt. Podbrdo. At first they saw a luminous figure of a young woman apparently hovering above the ground. They became frightened and ran back to the village where they told Milka Pavlovic of their experience. The three of them went back to the site and found the apparition was still there.

Meanwhile, Vicka Ivankovic (also a friend of Ivanka and Mirjana) responding to a note left for her at her own home by these two friends, went up the pathway only to meet Ivan Ivankovic and Ivan Dragicevic, who then all went together up the hill. These last named children also saw the apparition which they described as seeing "just as clearly as I can see now." The apparition wore a grey dress with a white veil, had a crown of stars, blue eyes, dark hair and rosy cheeks. She was floating on a grey cloud not touching the ground.

Word spread fast. People were busy talking and were curious to see for themselves. The next day, June 25th after the day's work was done, Vicka and some other children and adults went up the hill again. This time Marija Pavlovic and Jakov Colo also went up the hill with the other children. This time not only did the apparition appear, but Our Lady beckoned the children to come to Her. The children ran to Her "as though we had wings in spite of the sharp stones and brambles." On this day (June 25th) the first message was given to the seers.

On June 26, 1981 Our Lady gave Her message of Peace, saying: *"Peace! Peace! Peace! Be reconciled! Only peace. Make your peace with*

God and among yourselves. For that, it is necessary to believe, to pray, to fast, and to go to confession." This was to be Our Blessed Mother's primary message.

On August 6, 1981 Our Lady said: "*I am the Queen of Peace.*" It was also on this day that the word "MIR" (meaning "Peace" in Serbo-Croatian) appeared in large letters of light in the sky above Mt. Krizevac. This sign was witnessed by some 150 people and was successfully photographed.

After these initial days, the apparitions continued but occurred at different locations. Since early 1982 the daily apparitions have been mainly within the grounds of St. James Church. Starting in April 1985 the apparitions of Our Lady took place in a small second story room above the rectory which became known as 'The Apparition Room'. Commencing in August 1987 the visionaries had the apparitions daily before the evening Mass in the choir loft of St. James Church. Apparitions have also taken place on Mt. Krizevac, Mt. Podbrdo, at various homes, and at different places where some of the seers were then visiting.

Since Her first appearance, Our Lady has been appearing almost daily; and over 3,000 times; to six regular visionaries who were together when they saw (Gospa) Our Lady on June 25, 1981. These visionaries are:

    Mirjana Dragicevic Soldo
    Ivanka Ivankovic Elez
    Vicka Ivankovic
    Ivan Dragicevic
    Marija Pavlovic Lunetti
    Jakov Colo

During the apparitions the visionaries feel themselves outside of time and space. They are in a trancelike state of ecstasy. Scientific teams from France and Italy have found the seers do not respond to bright lights, loud noises, or pin pricks while in this state. And they further found the visionaries responded together, within one-fifth of a second, when Our Lady appeared or departed!

It has been written that the messages have come in three phases: Phase I, from June 24, 1981 to March 1, 1984 Our Lady came to give individual help to the visionaries; Phase II, from March 1, 1984 to January 8, 1987 seemed to focus on messages for the parish; while Phase III, announced on January 8, 1987 presented special monthly messages on the 25th of each month thereafter, giving guidelines to the world on how to live the messages actively in our daily lives.

The first monthly message was given on January 25, 1987 thereafter, these special messages are given to Marija on the 25th of each month.

Our Blessed Mother showed the seers visions of heaven, hell, and purgatory.

Father Jozo Zovko had been in charge of the Medjugorje Parish only since November 1980. On June 24, 1981 the date of the first apparition,

Fr. Jozo was out of town preaching an eight day retreat. When he first talked to some of the visionaries a few days after the first apparition, he was skeptical. He was concerned that the children may be connected with drugs or that this may be a communist plot. He advised the children to pray more; nevertheless, he tape recorded all his conversations with the children. He later protected the children from arrest. He is now a strong supporter.

The communists, likewise, suspected a plot; one against the government on the part of the Croat clergy. On Saturday, June 27th the police made their first move when they took the children away for a medical check up. The children were released that same evening. The police again picked up the visionaries and tried to have them declared mentally unstable; but all to no avail.

Bishop Pavao Zanic of Mostar at first was happy about the apparitions and believed in them. However, there was some conflict in the Mostar Diocese because Bishop Zanic attempted to have secular priests fill vacancies while the Franciscans wanted those slots filled with their own clergy. Our Lady, reportedly, gave a message to one of the seers reprimanding the bishop. From that time forward the bishop has been vehemently against these apparitions.

Meanwhile, crowds were coming to St. James church and climbing Apparition Hill with the seers, all to the consternation of the communist authorities. Father Jozo was called to the communist headquarters several times and was told to issue an order forbidding the faithful from going up the hill and also to abolish the evening Mass. They accused Fr. Jozo of being "behind this whole thing". They said that they had evidence, both documents and witnesses, against him.

Father Jozo was tagged as a "Clerico-Nationalist" and on August 17, 1981 he was imprisoned in Mostar for a two-month period. Later he was picked up again, together with Fr. Ferdo. The Franciscan nuns were body searched while Fr. Jozo and Fr. Ferdo were hauled away to prison. The village was in shock! On October 22, 1981 Fr. Jozo was sentenced to prison for 3 1/2 years after a trial. It was charged that during his homilies he insinuated that being a Catholic was a hindrance to advancement in government employment; and that it was sometimes necessary to shed blood for one's belief; and further, that his sermons were in danger of awakening the whole Church throughout Croatia and Herzegovina.

Father Jozo was released early from prison. He has since been transferred to a nearby parish; and he was banned from saying Mass or preaching homilies at St. James Parish. However, since Bishop Zanic has been replaced as bishop of Mostar, it seems likely this ban may have little practical application; if, in fact, it is still in force.

Our Lady also promised to give each seer ten secrets which are to be revealed to the world through a priest of each seer's choice. Thus far, two of the children have received all ten secrets. The other four visionaries have received nine secrets and still have daily apparitions. The third secret, which is the same for all the seers, involves a permanent sign for all humanity. It will happen after the apparitions here cease for all the visionaries and will appear on Mt. Podbrdo. The sign will be miraculous in origin, visible, and beautiful. All the visionaries, except Marija, know exactly what the sign will be and exactly when it will occur.

Since the apparitions first started in June 1981 over twenty million pilgrims have visited this little village of Medjugorje. It has changed. Not only have many buildings been constructed to house the pilgrims and to provide various services, but also, since the church was unable to accommodate the pilgrims, a new round pavilion was added at the rear of the church where Masses and other events take place. Rows of confessionals have been added and many priests, including those accompanying the pilgrims, hear Confessions, and concelebrate the Masses. It is reported that the parishioners have gained great spiritual benefits, including many conversions. Though there are detractors among the clergy, yet a great number of clergy and religious believe in, and support, these apparitions. Some of these clergy have written books about Medjugorje. One book, published in 1992, was written by eighty-four priests who give witness of their own experiences in Medjugorje. It is said that various cardinals have visited Medjugorje incognito, and that Pope John Paul II is reported to have said: "Let them go to Medjugorje to pray, to fast, to convert, to confess, and to do penance."

Mt. Krizevac has a rocky pathway to the huge cross on its top. Artist, Carmelo Puzzolo of Italy, designed beautiful bronze Stations of the Cross which now adorn the pathway up the hill. On any given day, one can find groups of faithful praying the Stations along this pathway in many different languages.

Many signs and wonders have been reported. The 'Miracle of the Sun', photographs depicting Our Lady to the surprise of the photographer, rosaries changing from a silver to a gold color instantly, and pictorial messages in the clouds in the sky above the Hill of the Cross, are just a few samples of these signs. One of these amazing signs occurred when the letters MIR (meaning peace in Croatian) appeared above Krizevac Hill. Also reported are phenomenon of lights over the hills.

Numerous healings, physical, mental, and especially spiritual, have been reported. Scores of instant miraculous healings are reported.

A multitude of prayer groups as well as Medjugorje and Peace Centers have sprung up around the world; in many countries, including the USA.

Something is definitely going on in Medjugorje. Bishop Zanic appointed one commission who returned a negative opinion. The investigation has been taken out of this bishop's hands and a new investigative commission has been appointed by Archbishop Franic. No final decision has been given by the Church.

Now, mention should be made of the visionaries:

(1) Mirjana Dragicevic Soldo - Mirjana was born March 18, 1965 and was sixteen when the apparitions started. She was born in Bijakovici but was living in Sarajevo with her family in 1981 when the first apparition happened. She attended college in Sarajevo and was married in 1990. They have one child. Although she was a Catholic before the apparitions, her life has changed. She now spends a great deal of time in prayer.

Between June 24, 1981 and December 25, 1982 Our Lady appeared to this seer almost daily. On December 25, 1982 Mirjana received her tenth and last secret. She was the first seer to receive all ten secrets. She has said the ninth and tenth secrets are very serious. Our Lady told this seer that now is a time of grace and conversion. The main theme often repeated is for peace, penance, conversion, and prayer. Our Lady promised to appear to her on her birthday (the 18th of March) and in special times of need.

(2) Ivanka Ivankovic Elez - Ivanka was born June 21, 1966 and was fifteen when the apparitions started. Her father worked in Germany and her mother died just two months before the apparitions started.

She lives in Medjugorje and married Rajko Elez on December 28, 1986. Her first child Kristina was born November 11, 1987.

She also received her tenth and final secret on May 6, 1985. Since then, Our Lady appears to her only once a year, June 25th, the anniversary date honoring Our Lady as Queen of Peace.

Ivanka says that the apparitions have caused a complete change in her. Before the visions she prayed and went to Church because her parents asked her to, now "when I pray I know and feel I'm united with God and with Our Lady."

(3) Vicka Ivankovic - Vicka was born September 3, 1964 and was sixteen when the apparitions started.

She attended school in Mostar but quit when they tried to convince her to deny the existence of God. Her father also worked in West Germany.

She is very cheerful, yet she suffers much from various ailments. In early 1988 this seer was told by Our Lady that she would be cured of her physical ailments on September 25, 1988. Vicka wrote down this healing date and gave the envelope to a priest. The healing occurred just as Our Lady promised. In 1983 Our Lady began telling Vicka the life story of Our Blessed Mother. Vicka has been recording these messages which are to be released to the proper authorities when Our Lady informs the seer to do so.

Vicka's health is not good. She has gone for long periods of time without seeing Our Lady, as a sacrifice. She is a victim soul and often sees Our Lady in the seer's own home.

This seer says the reason why Our Lady has been appearing so often and for such a long period of time is that Our Lady desires to attract every living person to Her Son, Jesus. She wishes that no one be lost.

She has been given nine secrets thus far and she says some secrets are good and some are bad. Since April 17, 1985 she has been given messages about the future of the world. This seer reports experiencing heaven, hell and purgatory.

It can be said that Vicka's home is open to pilgrims. Each day she greets visitors in her yard and speaks and prays with them.

(4) Ivan Dragicevic - Ivan was born May 25, 1965 and was sixteen years old when the apparitions started. He lives in the village of Medjugorje.

In 1986 he reported for a one year mandatory term in the military service of Yugoslavia. During his tour in service, he did not receive any apparitions but did receive locutions from Our Lady. In early 1984 Our Lady told this seer that August 5, 1984 would be the 2000th anniversary of the birth of Our Lady. He is one of the seers to receive daily apparitions.

Ivan continues to reside in Medjugorje, however, he traveled to the United States in 1988 and appeared on EWTN television with Mother Angelica. In 1990, he again visited the USA and met with then President George Bush.

This seer was shown purgatory and states we should pray for the souls in purgatory to alleviate their suffering.

His message to us, that he has learned from the apparitions, is: "We should pray to God with our hearts."

Ivan says "I am confident now, I'm not afraid of death because I know who leads me. People in our parish and in the world should feel this way."

This seer leads and is involved with prayer groups, especially youth prayer groups.

He has received nine secrets. It is later reported that Ivan was married on October 23, 1994 to Laureen Murphy in Boston, Massachusetts, USA.

(5) Marija Pavlovic Lunetti - Marija was born April 1, 1965 and was sixteen when the apparitions started. She lives in Bijakovici and her home is en route to the 'Hill of Apparitions'.

From March 1, 1984 through mid-January 1987, Our Lady gave this seer special weekly messages, on Thursdays. Since the later date Marija has received special monthly messages for the world on the 25th of each month.

Marija visited the USA at the end of 1988 and again in early 1989. She is busy with prayer life and is involved in two youth prayer groups. She is married to Paolo Lunetti of Milan, Italy.

This seer says: "At the moment of death God gives everyone the grace to see his whole life, to see what he has done, they recognize the results of the choices on earth. Each person chooses for himself where he belongs. Every individual chooses for himself what he deserves."

She has received nine secrets.

(6) Jakov Colo - Jakov was born March 6, 1971 and was the youngest to see Our Lady. He was ten.

He attended school in Mostar and Citluk as was usual for children from Medjugorje of his age.

His mother died in 1983 followed by his father's death in 1986. Jakov was married on Easter Sunday, 1993 to Annalisa Barozzi.

He has been taken to heaven by Our Blessed Mother. He also saw hell and purgatory. Our Lady has told this seer much about the future of the world. He has received nine secrets.

Jakov says that Mass is an encounter with the living God. He begins and ends each day with prayer. He also says: "the Blessed Mother of Jesus is pure Love."

IX The Primary Messages - 6

The most oft repeated pleas from Our Lady in the 3,000 plus messages given are for: peace, conversion, penance, strict fasting, prayer from the heart, attendance at Holy Mass and frequent reception of the Eucharist, as well as praying the rosary and increasing our faith.

(1) Peace - Our Lady announced that She was our Queen of Peace. Her very first message was one proclaiming peace and this has been the primary and essential message given to the seers.

June 26, 1981 Our Lady said: *"Peace! Peace! Peace! Be reconciled! Only peace. Make your peace with God and among yourselves. For that, it is necessary to believe, to pray, to fast, and to go to Confession."*

October 1984 Our Lady said: *"When the Holy Spirit comes, peace will be established."*

Christmas Day, 1988 Our Lady said: *"Live peace in your heart and in your surroundings, so that all recognize peace, which does not come from you, but from God."*

October 25, 1990 again Our Lady: *"Today, I call you to pray in a special way and to offer up sacrifices and good deeds for peace in the world."*

March 1993 Our Lady said: *"I call you to pray for peace, for peace in your hearts, peace in your families and peace in the whole world because Satan wants war, wants lack of peace, and wants to destroy all which is good."*

(2) Prayer - In nearly every message Our Lady exhorts us to pray! April 19, 1984 Our Lady said: *"Pray, pray, pray!"* This message was repeated on June 21, 1984 and again on August 14, 1984 and many times thereafter.

January 16, 1986 again Our Lady: *"I am calling you to prayer. I need your prayer so that God may be glorified through all of you."*

February 25, 1988 again Our Lady: *"I am calling you to prayer and complete surrender to God."*

January 25, 1991 Our Lady said: *"Today, as never before, I invite you to prayer. Your prayer should be a prayer for peace."*

October 25, 1993 Our Lady said: *"These years I have been calling you to pray, to live what I am telling you, but you are living My messages a little. You talk but you do not live, that is why this war is lasting so long."*

January 25, 1994 Our Lady said: *"Dear Children, you are My little children. I love you. But, little children, you must not forget that without prayer you cannot be close to Me. In this time Satan wants to create disorder in your hearts and in your families. Little children, do not give in. You must not permit him to lead you and your lives. I love you and intercede for you before God. Little children, pray. Thank you for having responded to My call."*

(3) Conversion - The messages are replete with calls for conversion.

March 8, 1984 Our Lady said: *"Convert in the parish, that is My second wish, so that way all those who come here will be able to convert."*

May 23, 1985 Our Lady said: *"Open your hearts and surrender your life to Jesus so that He works through your hearts and strengthens you in faith."*

June 25, 1990 again Our Lady: *"I call all of you to a full conversion so that joy will be in your hearts."*

February 25, 1993 Our Lady said: *"I invite you all to conversion. I wish each of you decide for himself a change of life."*

(4) Penance and Fasting - Many of the messages urge us to fast regularly and to make sacrifices and do penance.

September 20, 1984 Our Lady said: *"Today, I call on you to begin fasting with the heart."*

March 27, 1986: *"Dear Children, I wish to thank you for all your sacrifices and also call you to the greatest sacrifice, the sacrifice of love. Without love, you will be unable to accept either Me or My Son. Without love you will not be able to convey your experiences to others. Therefore, dear children live love within your hearts. We are in the truth that God is love."*

May 25, 1990 again Our Lady: *"Consecrate the time to prayer and sacrifice. I am with you and desire you to grow in renunciation and mortification . . ."*

July 25, 1993 Our Lady said: *"Offer novenas, making sacrifices where you feel the most bound; I want your lives to be bound to Me."*

(5) Pray the Rosary - Our Lady urges us to pray the Family rosary daily!

August 14, 1984, Our Lady said: *"I would like the people to pray at least one rosary; every day . . ."*

October 8, 1984 Our Lady said: *". . . Every evening pray the rosary."*

June 12, 1986 again Our Lady: *"Today, I call you to begin to pray the rosary with a living faith - and that your rosary be an obligation which you shall fulfill with joy."*

(6) Attend Holy Mass - April 3, 1986 Our Lady said: *"Jesus is giving* you His graces in the Holy Mass; with love, come and accept Holy Mass."

May 16, 1985 again Our Lady: *"I am calling you to a more active prayer and attendance at Holy Mass. I wish your Mass to be an experience of God."*

April 3, 1986 Our Lady said: *"I wish to call you to a living of the Holy Mass. Jesus gives you His graces in the Holy Mass."*

X Signs Preceding the Apparitions

Three bursts of light precede Her coming, then Our Lady arrives on a cloud; elevated about three feet off the ground, and light emanates from Her.

XI Other Visions During Apparitions

(1) Baby Jesus — The Blessed Mother sometimes holds the Child Jesus in Her arms. This often happens at Christmas.
(2) Heaven, hell and purgatory — most of the seers have seen or have been taken to these places by Our Lady.
(3) Mirjana is reported to have seen Satan in June 1982.

XII Prayers Taught to the Seer(s)

(1) On October 25, 1988 Our Lady urged consecration to the Sacred Heart of Jesus and the Immaculate Heart of Mary. Our Lady gave the following consecration prayers to the children.

Consecration to the Heart of Jesus

O Jesus, we know that You are sweet,
That You have given Your Heart for us.
It was crowned with thorns by our sins.
We know that today You still pray for us
so that we will not be lost.
Jesus, remember us if we fall into sin.
Through Your most Sacred Heart,
make us all love one another.
Cause hatred to disappear among men.
Show us Your love.
All of us love You.
And we desire that You protect us
with Your Heart of the Good Shepherd.
Enter into each heart, Jesus!

Knock on the door of our hearts.
Be patient and tenacious with us.
We are still locked up in ourselves,
because we have not understood Your will.
Knock continuously, Oh Jesus.
Make our hearts open up to You,
at least when we remember the passion
which You suffered for us. Amen.

Consecration to the Immaculate Heart

O Immaculate Heart of Mary, overflowing with goodness,
Show us Your love for us.
May the flame of Your Heart, Oh Mary,
Descend upon all peoples.
We love You immensely.
Impress in our hearts a true love.
May our hearts yearn for You.
Oh Mary, sweet and humble of heart,
Remember us when we sin.
You know that we men are sinners.
Through Your most sacred and maternal Heart,
Cure us from every spiritual illness.
Make us capable of looking at the beauty of Your maternal Heart,
And that, thus, we may be converted to the flame of Your Heart.
Amen

(2) On Our Lady's visit on the fourth day of the apparitions, She recommended "the Medjugorje Prayer" consisting of seven Our Father's, seven Hail Mary's, seven Glory Be's and the Apostles Creed.

XIII Special Devotion Given to the Seer(s)

Again, no new devotions were given the seers; yet, Our Lady urged consecration to the Sacred Heart of Jesus and to the Immaculate Heart of Mary: "... *because I want to draw you closer to the Heart of Jesus.*"

XIV Requests Made by Our Lady

(1) That everyone pray "the Medjugorje Prayer" every day consisting of: 7 Our Father's, 7 Hail Mary's, 7 Glory Be's and the Apostles Creed.
(2) Our Lady requested Youth Prayer Groups be formed. This message apparently first came to Jelena Vasil, who was receiving locutions from Our Lady, and included a request to modify the 'Jesus Rosary'.

(3) On August 15, 1988 Our Lady asked, that starting *". . . from today on, I would like to start a 'New Year'— the year of the young people."*
(4) On July 25, 1993 Our Lady requested that novenas be offered.

XV Specific Bible References

Although specific Bible references are not reported, Our Lady did urge us to read and study Sacred Scripture, such as in the August 1993 message: *"Only by prayer can you understand and accept My messages and practice them in your life. Read Sacred Scripture. Live it!"*

XVI Secrets Given to the Seer(s)

Each of the six visionaries is to receive a total of ten secrets. Thus far, only Ivanka and Mirjana have received all ten secrets. The other seers have each received nine secrets. Some of the secrets are the same for each seer and some are not. It is told that the third secret is the same for all the visionaries and involves a permanent sign for all humankind. This sign will come after the apparitions have ceased for all the visionaries and it will appear over Podbrdo Hill. The sign will be miraculous in origin, visible and beautiful. The visionaries, except Marija, know what the sign will be and when it will occur.

Mirjana has said the seventh and eighth secrets are of a serious nature; however, due to prayers said by the people, the seventh secret has been alleviated though not completely eliminated. She said the grave ninth and tenth secrets concern chastisements for the sins of the world. Prayers and fasting can also reduce these chastisements.

Mirjana has been selected to make the secrets known. She will reveal to a priest of her choice (Fr. Petar Ljubiric) the contents of each secret, ten days before it is to occur. Fr. Petar, in turn, can spend seven days in prayer over the secret before publicly revealing the secret three days before it is to occur. He is to reveal the exact nature of each secret, including what, where, at what time, how, and for what period of time each event will happen.

The written secrets were given to Mirjana by Our Lady on a rolled-up parchment which is kept safe until the time comes to reveal the secrets to Fr. Petar. The writing on the parchment is not visible.

The first two secrets are a type of warning and proof that Our Lady did visit Medjugorje and these will be followed by the sign contained in the third secret. Mirjana urges us to "hurry and convert" before the signs occur because "after the visible sign the survivors will hardly have any time left for conversion."

It is reported that the events contained in the secrets will occur in the lifetimes of the visionaries.

XVII Miracles Promised by Our Lady - NR
XVIII Miracles Performed - Not Reported
XIX Miracles Promised not yet Performed - NR

XX Signs Promised

Our Lady promised a visible sign over Mt. Podbrdo for all humanity. This will appear after three warnings to the world which are to be in the form of events occurring on earth.

The purpose of the sign is as a testimony to the apparitions and in order to call us all back to God.

XXI Signs Given

Since the inception of these apparitions in 1981, many signs have occurred, witnessed by many and happening during the entire fourteen years.

(1) **Miracle of the Sun** - This phenomenon has been witnessed by many pilgrims and clergy at many different times. Thousands of people have looked at the sun with naked eyes without injury to their eyes. The first date when the 'Miracle of the Sun' occurred is reported to be August 2, 1981.

(2) **Cross on Mt. Krizevac** - At times the cross has changed form, has been seen to spin, has totally disappeared. At other times a luminous light or glow surrounds the cross. A shaft of light sometimes goes straight up from the cross.

(3) **Other Signs in the sky** - Some people have seen red hearts, a dove, a cross, angels, or the face of Jesus in the sky, usually, near the sun. Often the Host is manifested over the sun. A rainbow of different colors emanates from the sun and proceeds toward the large cross on Mt. Krizevac. Unusual cloud formations, such as scenes depicting "The Good Shepherd," have been seen and successfully photographed.

(4) **"MIR" in the sky** - On August 6, 1981 many priests and pilgrims, as well as some of the seers, saw the clear letters "MIR" appear in the sky over Mt. Krizevac. "MIR" in Serbo-Croatian means "Peace". One of the priests gave this testimony in writing, Fr. Umberto Loncar.

(5) **Rosaries turn gold color** - Since 1986, this phenomenon has been reported hundreds of times; especially from American pilgrims. The chain and/or other metal parts of the rosary turns into a gold color, which is permanent. There have been scientific studies without producing any solid proof of miracle. Yet, interestingly enough, new rosaries purchased in Medjugorje have turned before being used at all while old sterling silver rosaries used for many years have turned.

Medjugorje, Yugoslavia

Sometimes the chain between the "Hail Marys" is the only part to change to gold, other times the chain on each side of the "Our Fathers" is the only change. Sometimes the medal, or the crucifix, or the corpus changes. Reportedly, Our Lady told the seers this phenomena, as well as other signs, are given to bolster the faith of the people.

XXII Predictions/Promises

(1) Our Lady has promised to leave a visible sign for all humankind at Mt. Podbrdo, the site of the first apparitions.
(2) She also promised to disclose ten secrets to each of the seers. Thus far, two seers have received ten secrets and the other four have each received nine.
(3) In 1982 Our Lady said that even though this century is under the power of the devil, yet, when the secrets confided to the seers at Medjugorje have come to pass, then the power of the devil will be destroyed. This information was given to the Pope by letter on December 2, 1983 by Fr. Tomislav Vlasic.

XXIII Prophecies/Warnings of Chastisement

(1) Mirjana has said that the ninth and tenth secrets are serious, and have to do with the coming chastisement due to the sins of the world. Punishment cannot be avoided but can be diminished by prayer and penance, yet it cannot be eliminated.
(2) On the other hand, one of the evils contained in the seventh secret has been averted due to prayer and fasting.

XXIV Method of Appearance

It is reported that three bursts of light precede Our Lady's appearance, then a cloud appears before Our Lady clearly appears standing above the cloud.

XXV Method of Departure

Our Lady always departs with *"Go in the Peace of God."*

XXVI Confrontation w/Civil Authorities

(1) In the beginning the government was suspicious. The seers were

interrogated several times by the officials, subjected to various testing, all against their will. The government wanted to close down the apparitions because the crowds were a threat to them. They banned the children from the hill. However, as time went on, the financial benefit to the government had a soothing effect and they began to tolerate the pilgrims although activities were still being monitored by the military and secret police there in order to keep up to date on the happenings.

(2) Even so, Fr. Jozo was arrested, tried, convicted and sentenced to three years imprisonment for his alleged part in these apparitions. He actually spent eighteen months in prison. Others were also imprisoned.

XXVII Confrontation w/Church Authorities

(1) The bishop of the diocese, Pavao Zanic, spoke favorably at first of these apparitions. He found good fruit, faith, reconciliation, and conversions. Later, a debate arose concerning whether secular or Franciscan priests would staff the Franciscan parishes. Since then the bishop has opposed these apparitions.

(2) On the other hand, Bishop Frane Franic, Archbishop of the Diocese of Split is supportive.

(3) Generally, there seems to be a division with many clergy and religious, some believing in the apparitions and messages, while on the other hand, another group of clergy are opposed. This debate is still in progress and, occasionally, gets very heated. Most writers have supported these events. One book "In Testimony" is written by eighty-four priests who share their own positive testimony with their readers. Nothing less than what has been called "a campaign of disinformation" is reportedly going on. The assault comes from both the left and from the right; either the children have made up the whole thing or it is the work of the devil. That is the argument.

Monsignor Paul Hnilica, the Auxiliary Bishop of Rome, did his own investigation by visiting Medjugorje several times, he interviewed the seers, and also those who are close to the seers. He wanted to know what just cause there was to speak against Medjugorje. He wrote his testimony stating the children were not manipulated and that he sees a supernatural aspect to these events. He concludes that his own conscience requires him to speak out, that the voice of God is speaking with power in Medjugorje. "We must not and we cannot take the gifts of God lightly."

(4) At first, the pastor, Fr. Jozo was skeptical, but he prayed for discernment and is now a strong supporter. This cost him, not only his freedom when he went to prison; but also he was banished and transferred to another parish.

(5) Bishop Zanic appointed a commission. With hostility so visible, the Vatican removed the jurisdiction from Bishop Zanic and placed it with a convention of Yugoslavian bishops who are now investigating the authenticity of these apparitions.

It is said that Pope John Paul II has said that Medjugorje is a great center of spirituality and "let the people go there to pray, fast, and be converted."

XXVIII Requests Chapel/Shrine be Built - NR

XXIX Free Will/Choice

April 30, 1984 Our Lady said: *"I don't wish to force anyone to do that which he/she neither feels nor desires."*

January 2, 1986 again Our Lady: *"I call you to decide completely for God . . ."*

November 25, 1989 Our Lady said: *". . . Therefore, little children, I desire that your decisions be free before God, because He has given you freedom. Therefore, pray so that, free from any influence of Satan, you may decide only for God."*

XXX Seer(s)' Suffering/Sacrifice

(1) The children suffered very severely because many people, including the clergy and Bishop Zanic did not believe them. Some even attacked the children verbally.
(2) The children were arrested; picked up against their will; and made to undergo hours of tests and interrogation, all to their great pain.
(3) They also suffered to see Fr. Jozo and others being sent to prison; and further, to see Fr. Jozo banished to another parish.
(4) Reportedly Vicka has become a victim soul and has been asked to suffer for others.
(5) These six visionaries have been subjected to much publicity, many questions and generally much pressure from the pilgrims for some fourteen years. At the least, this must have produced much stress and strain and disrupted their lives. Yet, they have kept their honest and simple style of living.

XXXI Healings Reported

(1) All reporters agree that the most profound and amazing fruits of the apparitions and messages have been the avalanche of conversions. These include the fallen away, the lukewarm, the curious, the worldly,

as well as those who were nonbelievers and/or antagonists. The return to faith and to God began with the seers themselves, then with the parishioners, and quickly spread throughout the world. The conversions touched people of all ages, of all social strata, of all races, of nearly all countries and people of many different religious persuasions. And it is still going on!

Before the apparitions, the seers were generally lukewarm. The villagers had their share of conflict in relating to each other and to God. Since 1981 this has changed to a remarkable degree. The parishioners' lives are now centered on worship and doing the will of God. The attention is now on daily family prayer, the rosary, Mass, the Sacraments, Bible reading, and caring service to others.

Pilgrims, meanwhile, coming from all corners of the earth, have been drawn to Medjugorje. Many returning time after time and very few are disappointed. There are numerous reports of people going to confession in Medjugorje for the first time in ten, twenty, or even forty years! Many conversions are emotional and dramatic. There have been times when over 100 priests have heard confession simultaneously in many different languages.

A great number of prayer groups, especially youth prayer groups, have sprung up all over the world.

People have overcome debilitating addictions such as drugs and alcohol with the grace of God.

(2) In February 1983 Fr. Jozo was released from prison; and said a Mass in thanksgiving saying: "It was by your prayers I was set free."

(3) Additionally, there are numerous cures and physical and emotional healings reported. A few examples will suffice:

    a) Cvija Kuzman from Stolac had suffered eleven years from degenerative arthritis. In August 1981 she brought back some soil from Medjugorje. Her daughter made a paste of it and then applied the paste reciting seven Our Fathers, Hail Marys, and Glorias. She was instantly and permanently healed.

    b) On August 8, 1983 Maria Brumec was instantly cured of a fractured spine; Damir Coric, a hydrocephalic youth was instantly cured in the summer of 1981 when Vicka prayed over him; Iva Tole, who suffered from multiple sclerosis and who had to be carried into St. James Church, was instantly cured on September 13, 1981 and later that same day she climbed Mt. Krizevac to attend Mass said at the foot of the large cross. These three dossiers were submitted by Dr. Ludvik Stopar to Bishop Zanic. Other doctors have submitted dossiers for other alleged healings.

    c) Father Jozo, while exiled to Tihaljina, reportedly expressed his belief that the greatest miraculous healings taking place in Medjugorje were interior ones. Nonetheless, he relates the story of two women, both in wheel chairs, who came to Medjugorje to be healed. The elder woman was healed and returned to her home. The younger woman, named Manuela, remained in her wheelchair to give thanks and praise to God. Manuela was healed in her heart. She praised God for coming to her, for shedding light on the cross she carried and for showing her the value and meaning of suffering for the love of God. As Fr. Jozo says: "The Church was grateful for both blessings. Deeply grateful!"

XXXII Action Taken by the Church

(1) Bishop Zanic set up a commission to study these apparitions in January 1982.
(2) In May of 1986 in a rare case, the Vatican dissolved Bishop Zanic's commission and, at the Vatican's request, a new investigative commission was set up in January 1987 composed of bishops from Yugoslavia.
(3) Everyone, including clergy, may make pilgrimages to Medjugorje for spiritual growth and to help others. What is not permitted, is official pilgrimages such as those organized by the Church and led by the bishop; as this would infer Church approval prematurely.
(4) Although, neither the Church, nor the Pope, individually, has taken an official stand; yet it is believed, by many, that the present Pope is positive about events occurring in Medjugorje. Pope John Paul II is said to have responded to a question by saying: ". . . Let the people go to Medjugorje if they convert, pray, confess, do penance, and fast."
(5) Many priests, bishops, and even cardinals have concelebrated Mass at Medjugorje. Cardinal Timothy Manning of Los Angeles concelebrated at the evening Mass on December 4, 1988. This, of course, does not constitute church approval.

XXXIII Bibliography

In Testimony, Priestly Reflections on Medjugorje 1992
By: Eighty-four Priests
Published by: The Riehle Foundation

Medjugorje, the Message 1991
By: Wayne Weible
Published by: Paraclette Press

Words From Heaven 1990
By: Two Friends of Medjugorje
Published by: Saint James Publishing Company

Queen of the Cosmos 1990
By: Jan Connell
Published by: Paraclette Press

Medjugorje, its Background and Messages 1989
By: Mary Joan Wallace
Published by: Follow Me Communications

Eight Years, Latest News of Medjugorje 1989
By: Fr. Laurentin
Published by: The Riehle Foundation

Mary, Queen of Peace, Stay With Us 1988
By: Fr. G. Girard, Fr. A. Girard, Fr. J. Bubalo
Published by: Editions Paulines

Spark From Heaven 1988
By: Mary Craig
Published by: Ave Marie Press

Our Lady of Medjugorje 1988
By: Judith M. Albright
Published by: The Riehle Foundation

Chapter 40

KIBEHO, RWANDA
(1981 - 1989)

I Place - Kibeho, Rwanda

II Dates of First and Last Apparition

First: November 28, 1981
Last: November 28, 1989

III Seer(s) - 7

Name: Alphonsine Mumureke
Birth: 1965
Age at first apparition: 16
Status: Living

Name: Anathalie Mukamazimpaka
Birth: 1965
Age at first apparition: 16
Status: Living

Name: Marie-Claire Mukangango
Birth: 1961
Age at first apparition: 20
Status: It is later reported that Marie-Claire died in the summer of 1994

Name: Stephanie Mukamurenzi
Birth: 1968
Age at first apparition: 14
Status: Living

Name: Vestine Salima
Birth: 1958
Age at first apparition: 24
Status: Living

Name: Agnes Kamagaju
Birth: 1960
Age at first apparition: 22
Status: Living

Name: Emmanuel Segatashya
Birth: 1968
Age at first apparition: 15
Status: It is also later reported that Emmanuel was killed in 1994.

IV Total Number of Apparitions - over 30

(1) To Alphonsine - 10 It is also reported that she received apparitions almost every Saturday
(2) To Anathalie - 7 Also apparitions of Jesus
(3) To Marie-Claire - 5
(4) To Stephanie - 2
(5) To Vestine - 2
(6) To Agnes - 3 Also 3 of Jesus
(7) To Emmanuel - 1 Also 3 of Jesus

V Dates and Locality of Each Apparition

All apparitions occurred in Kibeho unless otherwise noted.

Alphonsine Mumureke   (Apparitions at Sister's School)
1981: November 28, 29.
1982: February 6, 16; October 2.
1986: Lent; October 3; December 3.
1988: November 28.
1989: November 28.
It is reported that Our Lady appeared to Alphonsine almost every Saturday.

Anathalie Mukamazimpaka
Apparitions of **Our Lady**:
1982: January 12; April 2; May 5, 31.
1983: Lent; October 3; December 3.
Apparitions of **Jesus**:
1983: May 31 - Reported as the last apparition of Jesus to Anathalie. Also reported are many apparitions of Jesus and Mary to Anathalie.

Marie-Claire Mukangango
1982: March 2, 27; May 8, 31; September 15.

Stephanie Mukamurenzi
1982: May 25; September 15. It is reported that Stephanie received a total of 15 apparitions.

Vestine Salima
1982: September 15. (Also reported as December 15, 1982)
1983: December 24. t is reported that Vestine also had private visions in 1980.

Agnes Kamagaju
Apparitions of **Our Lady**:
1982: June 4 (in seer's home, Kibeho). (Also reported as August 4, 1982); August 9.
1983: September 25.
Apparitions of **Jesus**:
1982: September 21.
1983: May 2; August 18, 29.

Emmanuel Segatashya
Apparitions of **Our Lady**:
1983: August 1.
Apparitions of **Jesus**:
1982: July 2; September 8; December 4.
1983: July 2.

VI Description of Our Lady

(1) On November 28, 1981 Alphonsine described Our Lady: "She was barefoot with a white dress with no seams and a white veil on Her head. Her hands were joined together and Her fingers turning toward heaven." Then the seer adds: "She was not really white like we see Her in the pictures. I could not determine the color of Her skin, but She was of incomparable beauty."

(2) It is also reported by some of the visionaries that the beauty of Mary cannot be described. Her voice is sweet, like beautiful music. Some of the seers saw Her dressed in white with a blue veil.

VII Title(s) of Our Lady - 1

On November 28, 1981 Our Lady told Alphonsine: *"I am the Mother of the Word."*

VIII Brief Factual Review

Rwanda is located near the center of Africa. It is often called the Switzerland of Africa because of its scenic mountains and vegetation. Since 1962 Rwanda has been an independent republic.

Five and a half million people inhabit Rwanda, the majority of whom are Christians. Most are engaged in farming. The Charismatic Renewal and the Marian Renewal are very appealing to the youth. The people love social relations such as singing and dancing.

It is reported that during the period between 1979 and 1981, a diabolic fury was going on in Rwanda. Savage mobs were destroying holy pictures and statues inside the churches and at other places throughout the country. Seemingly the authorities did nothing to stop this destruction.

It is also reported that during 1981-1982 natives throughout the country of Rwanda and in neighboring countries warned that something horrible and frightening was about to occur. They reported seeing strange sights in the skies above Rwanda. The sun would spin and pulsate and split into two separate suns. These, together with signs in the skies above Bantu and Watusi, were a portent of a major happening, even doom. The world was coming to an end, Jesus Christ was returning, and this was known to them because Our Lord's Mother was already there in Rwanda. Yes, ever since November 28, 1981 throughout Rwanda, it was heard: "Bikira Mariya Yabonekeye i Kibeho," which means: "the Virgin Mary is appearing in Kibeho." And during the very first apparition to Alphonsine, Our Lady said: *"Ndi Nyina wa Jambo"*, that is: *"I am the Mother of the Word."*

The apparitions of Our Lady began in 1981 at Sister's School in Kibeho. Sister's School is a college administered by nuns in a poor area. Three of the visionaries were boarders at the school when the apparitions began; namely, Alphonsine, Anathalie, and Marie-Claire.

There was a total of seven visionaries at Rwanda. The apparitions started on November 28, 1981 when Alphonsine saw Our Blessed Mother. The other seers later received apparitions of Our Lady as well as messages just as had happened to Alphonsine. By the end of 1983 the apparitions ceased, except those to Alphonsine continued until at least November 28, 1989. Jesus also appeared to several seers and gave messages to them.

The apparitions themselves usually lasted a long time, three to four hours, and even eight hours on one occasion. The apparitions are personal and individual; although occurring in public. Many of the apparitions took place on a platform and were witnessed by crowds. During the apparitions the seers sometimes take a position of meditation, sometimes blessing the people. Sometimes the seers take on an unnatural state during the apparitions, sometimes they lay on the ground, fall onto the ground without being hurt, and sometimes they make gestures with their entire body. It always took the seers a few minutes to return to normal after the apparition.

During the apparitions, the seers pray with great fervor, often reciting the entire rosary or other inspired prayers. Some of the prayers are songs taught to them by Our Lady.

All the seers claim to have experienced the 'mystical voyage' or a 'weekend with Our Lady'. They claim to have visited a different universe from our own, under the guidance of Our Lady. While on this voyage, the seer's body becomes cold and stiff. Once the seer returns, the body once again becomes warm. Often these experiences last more than one day. Alphonsine told Mother Superior and her companions not to worry about her from March 20 to March 21, 1982 because: "I will be like a dead person, but do not fear and do not bury me!" In fact during that entire period Alphonsine remained as a corpse, it was impossible to open her hands which were joined together. During these journeys, the children apparently saw heaven, hell and purgatory.

Jesus and Mary asked the visionaries to fast for long periods. During Lent of 1983 Anathalie fasted for 14 days, Emmanuel fasted for 18 days, and Agnes fasted for 8 days; a total of 40 days. In addition, Emmanuel was asked to remain silent and was unable to hear anything during this 18 day period.

The seers report that the beauty of Our Lady cannot be described. She is not white, not black, and not mixed color. She is above all so sweet, like beautiful music. Some saw Her dressed all in white, others with a blue veil.

The messages from Kibeho are said to be evangelical, universal, ecumenical, and urgent. Each seer is given a specific mission or message which is to be given to all people.

Here it may be noted that a terrible civil uprising occurred in Rwanda during the year 1994; causing many deaths and terrible sufferings by innocent people. The world watched in horror as the frightening punishment predicted by Our Lady, came to pass. Of special note, it seems that the visions that the seers record on August 19, 1982 and which frightened them so, have occurred in our own time — in dreadful accuracy and detail. Mankind must heed Our Lady's words!

Something can now be said about each seer.

Alphonsine Mumureke - She was the first seer to see Our Lady. It was on November 28, 1981 when Our Lady first appeared to her. She continued to see Our Lady and received messages until November 28, 1989. Even so, the seer may be having apparitions ongoing to this day.

Alphonsine was 16 when the apparitions started. She was serving table at Sister's School when Our Lady appeared to her. Our Lady asked her to join the Legion of Mary to better realize her vocation. The seer's mother was a Catholic. Our Lady's message to this seer is that the return of Jesus is near and that Our Lady comes to advise and help us to prepare for Her Son's return. Alphonsine prays: "Mother, place your image in my heart so that all those who see me can say, here is the child of Mary." Messages received by this seer are to pray and to suffer with Jesus, to pray the rosary and to detest and avoid sin.

During the apparition of February 6, 1982 it is reported that Alphonsine was cured of an illness affecting one of her eyes.

The apparitions to Alphonsine became quite regular, occurring nearly every Saturday. The apparitions occurred in the dormitory. In the beginning the Nuns (and everyone else) did not believe the seer. She was ridiculed and laughed at. This stopped abruptly on January 12, 1982 when Our Lady appeared to yet another girl at Sister's School.

Anathalie Mukamazimpaka - This seer was also 16 when Our Lady first appeared to her on January 12, 1982. She was born to Catholic parents, the fourth of eight children. She was in charge of the Legion of Mary and took part in the Charismatic Renewal at the school.

Everyone believed this seer because she was prayerful and more mystical than Alphonsine.

The messages given to this seer consist in the practice of humility, availability, charity, sacrifice and love of prayer life. We must return to God and abandon evil. Mary is our guide on the road leading to Jesus.

Anathalie herself has suffered much. She accepts everything with joy as coming from God. The last apparition of Our Lady to this seer was December 3, 1983 and the last apparition of Jesus to this seer was on May 31, 1983.

Marie-Claire Mukangango - This seer was 20 years of age when she first received the apparitions. She was also born into a Catholic family, the fifth of eight children. Her father had died and she had been teaching at an elementary school when she received the apparitions. The apparitions to this seer lasted from March 2, 1982 until September 12, 1982. Each apparition occurred at Sister's School. She had expressed decisive disbelief in the apparitions to Alphonsine and Anathalie, so everyone was surprised when she also reported having apparitions herself.

Our Lady chose Marie-Claire to spread a special message. Marie-Claire says repeatedly: "We must meditate on the Passion of Jesus and on the deep sorrow of His Mother. We must recite the rosary and the beads of the Seven Sorrows of Our Lady to obtain the grace of repentance."

On May 31, 1982 Our Lady told Marie-Claire: *"What I am asking is repentance. If people will recite these little beads of the Seven Sorrows, meditating on them, you will have the strength of repentance. Today many people do not know how to ask for pardon..."*

The Society of the Servants of Mary had already started to spread this special devotion of the little beads of the Seven Sorrows of Mary, however, this devotion has been neglected in our day.

Our Lady showed Marie-Claire many visions and scenes of the Passion of Our Lord. During Her last apparition on September 15, 1982 Our Lady gave Marie-Claire the mission to make known everywhere the devotion of the little beads of the Seven Sorrows. Our Lady said in part: *"You can make it known all over the world even though you will remain here. My grace is omnipotent."*

It was on this occasion that the seer fell seven times into a burning bush full of thorns. Our Lady said: *"I am asking people to correct themselves, to abandon impurity, to convert themselves, but they are refusing ... For this reason you have fallen seven times into the burning bush so that I can touch their hearts..."*

Our Lady asked this seer for prayers for the souls in purgatory (March 27, 1982).

This seer reportedly died in the summer of 1994.

Stephanie Mukamurenzi - This seer was the youngest of the seers, only 14 when she received the first apparition of Our Lady on May 25, 1982. These apparitions lasted four months, the last of which occurred on September 15, 1982. It was reported that she had 15 apparitions. Our Lady told this seer: *"You must be converted, you must pray and mortify yourselves. Satan tries to ruin you. God wants your prayer from the heart."*

The messages given to Stephanie consist of repentance, conversion, and prayer, with hope and from the heart. We must remain humble and available.

Vestine Salima - This seer was 24, born in 1958 of Muslim parents. Her mother had been born a Catholic, but had joined the religion of the father, Islamic. Vestine's parents were tolerant and permitted her to attend a Catholic school. After finishing elementary school, she joined a social center directed by the Sisters of Kibeho.

Vestine claims to have received apparitions since 1980 before Alphonsine received her first apparition on November 28, 1981 but she kept it a secret from everyone except one of her own sisters. Her first public apparition took place on September 15, 1982 and the last one occurred on December 24, 1983. It is reported that Our Lady chose Vestine to be a shepherd of the world. Whenever she spoke people were converted or renewed in their faith. Her own father was baptized a Catholic in 1983.

Our Lady told Vestine to always go out with a walking stick, for a shepherd always carries a stick. The messages given to Vestine were always accompanied with gestures from Vestine. These messages include detachment from goods of this world and search for goods prepared for us by God. The true meaning of the sign of our life is humility, availability, to pardon each other, sincere prayers and that we accept our daily crosses. The road to heaven is narrow while the road to Satan is wide. Here you can go fast because there are not obstacles.

Agnes Kamagaju - This seer was 22 when she received the first apparition of Our Lady on June 4, 1982. She was born of Catholic parents and attended only elementary school.

Our Lady appeared to her as the Mother of Heaven and also as the Immaculate Conception. The first apparition of Our Lady occurred on June 4, 1982 and the last one was on September 25, 1983.

During some of the apparitions to Agnes, it is reported that strange signs appeared in the sky. The sun would spin in the sky, sometimes two suns. Some people saw two lines dividing the sun into three parts. At other times the Cross of Jesus or the Crown of Thorns would appear to the right of the sun. Often this seer would ask for the blessing of Jesus and Mary, then a light rain would fall onto the ground.

The central point of the message to Agnes is that Jesus will return and that we must be prepared. We must accept, and not refuse, the cross which God sends us. Instead we are to pray for the grace of receiving it. On August 18, 1982 she received a message for the youth. The ideas and behavior of the youth are in contrast with what God expects. Youth should not use their bodies as instruments of pleasure. They forget that true love comes only from God.

Emmanuel Segatashya - Emmanuel was a pagan. This seer was 15 when he had the first apparition of Jesus on July 2, 1982. The last apparition of Jesus occurred on July 2, 1983 and the last apparition of Our Lady happened on August 1, 1983.

Emmanuel never went to school. He ran away from home and became a shepherd for a short time. At the time of the apparitions, the seer was living far outside Kibeho in the bush so he was not known to anyone in the area.

On July 2, 1982 he was walking towards Kibeho returning from a field of beans when Jesus appeared to him, and instructed him to bring the message to the people. Just three days later Emmanuel held a three hour conference talking about the Sacrament of Penance and how we are to prepare for the return of Jesus. People were shocked for Emmanuel was born to a pagan family. No one in his family knew how to read or write. They lived in an isolated village. The family did not even have a radio. He had never been inside a church and knew nothing of Christianity. He didn't even know how to make the Sign of the Cross. It is not surprising that people were amazed to hear of the great knowledge which Emmanuel displayed, considering his background.

On September 18, 1982 less than three months after his first apparition, he revealed a message for priests and religious. In less than one year he studied and learned the entire catechism. He was then baptized and confirmed. It has been reported that Emmanuel has done much apostolic work in nearby villages, and that he would soon become a priest!

The message to Emmanuel is that the world will come to an end. When Jesus returns to earth, each soul will find the body it had before. There is not much time left, Jesus will come and find everyone. Ask pardon and receive the Sacrament of Reconciliation and God will pardon us. We should pray together with fervor. The rosary is the strength of Christians. Emmanuel suffers a lot on Fridays. Jesus told Emmanuel that he must suffer every Friday to help Jesus save the world. The seer reveals that no one can love Jesus, adore Him, and yet live outside His Holy Mother. The Virgin Mary is the Mother of the Word, of mankind.

It is later reported that Emmanuel was killed in 1994.

On August 19, 1982 the apparition wept and all the visionaries present with Her also wept because Our Lady showed them some scenes and terrifying images of the future: deadly combat, a river of blood, people who were killing each other, abandoned corpses with no one to bury them, and a tree all in flames. The seers were crying and screaming and the people present (some 20,000) had an overwhelming impression of fear and great sadness. The recent civil war which resulted in the overthrow of the government also resulted in the deaths of hundreds of thousands of people, of monstrous sufferings by innocent victims, and displacement and massive migration by refugees into neighboring countries. The graphic scenes and description given by Our Lady to the seers on August 19, 1982 have been played out in painful detail, for all the world to watch in their own living rooms on their television sets!

On July 30, 1983 Msgr. Jean Baptiste Gahamanji, the bishop of Kibeho, issued a pastoral letter presenting background facts together with the messages the seers allegedly received. He stated that a judgment from the Church may take a long time and therefore invited all to be patient. On August 15, 1988 Msgr. Gahamanji approved the first stage of these apparitions. This permits public devotion. The bishop said: "Our Lady's message is prayer, conversion, and vigilance." The Church continues its review.

There have been reported miraculous healings occurring in Kibeho and other places relating to these apparitions.

Our Lady asked that a chapel be built at Kibeho which is to be called 'The Gathering of the Displaced'.

IX The Primary Messages - 6

The main and central message of Kibeho is the announcement that the return of Jesus is near, and that we must prepare now for Jesus' coming.

Each of the seven seers received messages.
- **(1) Prepare for the Second Coming of Jesus**
- **(2) Prayer**
- **(3) Reconciliation, Penance and Sacrifice**
- **(4) Conversion**
- **(5) Pray the Rosary and Seven Sorrows of Our Lady**
- **(6) Youth**

(1) Alphonsine - This seer's prayer to Our Blessed Mother is: 'Mother, Impress your image in my heart.' The message given to this seer is to prepare for the return of Jesus which is near. That the end of the world is not a punishment. We are asked to suffer with Jesus, to pray, and to be apostles to prepare for His return.

On November 28, 1989 (the last apparition reported) Our Lady told Alphonsine that everyone must be faithful to one's vocation, to the Church, and be faithful to the Gospel. Priests must offer themselves up while offering the Sacrifice of the Mass. Youth must not spoil their future by the wrong way of living - *"Don't lose heaven for the world! And pray, pray and pray!"*

(2) Anathalie - Before this seer blesses the people, she says: "Purify my hands, my heart, my whole being."

The messages given to this seer are: *"We must turn to God and abandon evil."* We must dedicate ourselves to prayer. We must develop in us the virtues of charity, availability, and humility. We must *"wash ourselves"*, that is receive the Sacrament of Reconciliation. We must *"get up"*, that is detach ourselves from the things of this world. And finally, Our Lady urges us to pass along the same road that Jesus traveled here on earth. *"The true road is the one of suffering."* (October 3, 1983)

(3) Marie-Claire - This seer prays: "Repent! Repent! The world has turned against God, we must repent and ask for pardon."

The messages given to this seer urge us to repentance, to conversion, to meditate on the suffering of Jesus, to pray the rosary daily and to pray the beads of the Seven Sorrows of Our Lady.

On May 31, 1982 Our Lady told Marie-Claire: *"What I am asking people is to correct themselves, to abandon impurity, to convert themselves, but they refuse."*

On March 27, 1982 Our Holy Virgin Mary invited Marie-Claire to pray for the poor souls in purgatory.

(4) Stephanie - Our Lady told this seer: *"God loves you already. It is the devil who wants to ruin you. You must refuse all means that he is using to catch you."*

The messages to this seer are for repentance, conversion; that we must remain humble and available. We must learn to pray with hope and from the heart.

(5) Vestine - Our Lady tells this seer: *"The road to heaven is through* *a narrow road. It is not easy to get through. The road to Satan is wide. You will go fast, you will run because there will be no obstacles."*

The messages given to this seer are to prepare for the return of Jesus. We must detach ourselves from the goods of this world and search for goods prepared for us by God. We must forgive each other, accept our daily crosses in union with Jesus and ask for pardon of our sins through the Sacrament of Reconciliation. We must live a life of humility and availability, of sincere prayer and sacrifice.

(6) **Agnes** - The central point of the messages to this seer is that Jesus will return and that we must be prepared. We must chose the only way, that of penance and detachment from things of the world and we must not refuse the cross which God sends us, but rather ask for the grace to receive our cross.

On August 18, 1983 Our Lady gave this seer a message for the youth. The message was that the behavior of youth and their ideas are in contrast with what God expects of them. They should not use their bodies as instruments of pleasure. Youth should pray to Mary, to show them the right way to God. No matter what vocation is pursued, everyone must be completely for God since our very body and soul depends on Him.

(7) **Emmanuel** - This seer said: "How can anyone love Jesus, adore Him, and live outside His Mother? The Virgin Mary is the Mother of the Word..."

The message to this seer is that this world will come to an end. We must prepare while there is still time. We must ask pardon for our sins and receive the Sacrament of Reconciliation. We should pray together with fervor and we should all pray the rosary. The rosary is the strength of the Christian. Nothing is more powerful for the conversion of a Christian than the rosary, prayer and practice of the virtues.

X Signs Preceding the Apparitions

(1) Alphonsine was the first visionary to see Our Blessed Mother. The seer reports that she was waiting tables when she heard a voice calling her: *"My daughter."* The seer turned, went to the corridor, and saw Our Lady. The seer knelt and asked: "Who are you?" Our Lady replied: *"Ndi Nyina wa Jambo"* (which means *"I am the Mother of the Word"*).

(2) Although many unusual signs appeared during the apparitions, no repeated sign is reported preceding the apparitions.

XI Other Visions During Apparitions

(1) Anathalie saw Jesus several times. Her last vision of Jesus occurred on May 31, 1983.

(2) Agnes saw Our Lord several times commencing September 21, 1982 through August 29, 1983.

(3) Emmanuel saw Our Lord from July 2, 1982 through December 4, 1982 during several apparitions.

(4) It is reported that Our Lady showed Marie-Claire many scenes of the Passion of Our Lord Jesus.

(5) Vestine was shown a vision of heaven and hell.

(6) On August 19, 1982 the seers wept with the apparition as they were shown terrible images of the future, such as deadly combat, a river of blood, abandoned corpses, and a gaping abyss. This apparition lasted eight hours and was witnessed by some 20,000 people. The seers were crying and screaming and the people present were overcome by a great impression of fear and sadness.

XII Prayers Taught to the Seer(s)

(1) Our Lady taught Marie-Claire a prayer to be recited when starting to pray the beads of the Seven Sorrows.

Prayer: My God, I offer to You these little beads of sorrow for Your greatest glory in honor of Your Holy Mother. I will meditate and share Your suffering. I beg for the tears that You spread in those moments to grant me and all sinners, repentance for sins.

Then Our Lady asked Marie-Claire to repeat the following prayer three times:

Prayer: To me a sinner, and to all sinners grant perfect contrition of our sins.

(2) Our Blessed Mother also taught the seer to sing prayers to Her:

To Alphonsine - Prayer: Mother of the Word, Mary, You are also Our Mother Mary. Dispenser of grace, Mary You have given us so many gifts. You have chosen us Mary, among all the children of our times. May You give us your blessing so that we may communicate this blessing to others. We, children of Kibeho, ask You for love as You Yourself have told us. Here is what it will be of me Mary ... for God is calling me. Come Yourself and give me strength Mary, give patience in the trials, Mary.

To Anathalie - You all come to Me, I am the best way to arrive to Jesus. God accepts all religions, but He wants His Son to be adored and His Mother to be respected, loved and prayed to. The rosary is a special prayer for turning to the Mother of God.

Our Lady taught the seer other prayers in song:

Prayer: Every son who loves Me, every son who prays to Me will have life everlasting. He who believes in Jesus and believes in God will have eternal life.

Also: **Prayer:** Mother who loves your sons, Mother of the Word, road leading to heaven, Mother of the Word. Mother of Mercy, Mother of the Word.

XIII Special Devotion Given to the Seer(s)

Our Lady taught the 'Little Beads of the Seven Sorrows' to Marie-Claire. Our Blessed Mother first gave a prayer to the seer to be recited to begin the Seven Sorrows (see section XII), then Our Lady also asked the seer to say a short prayer three times. This prayer likewise was given by Our Lady Herself (see section XII).

Next, Marie-Claire was told to recite the 'Little Beads of the Seven Sorrows' beginning with the Act of Contrition, and then announcing the Sorrows as she went along. The Seven Sorrows are:

a) **First Sorrow** - Simeon telling Mary that a sword will pierce Her soul.
b) **Second Sorrow** - The Holy Family traveling into Egypt.
c) **Third Sorrow** - The loss of Jesus in the temple.
d) **Fourth Sorrow** - Mary meeting Jesus on the Way of the Cross.
e) **Fifth Sorrow** - Mary at the foot of the cross.
f) **Sixth Sorrow** - Mary receiving the corpse of Her Son at the foot of the cross.
g) **Seventh Sorrow** - Mary at the tomb of Our Lord.

After each Sorrow, we are to say one 'Our Father' and seven 'Hail Marys'. Then, instead of the 'Glory Be To The Father', the following prayer is said: 'Mary full of Mercy, recall to our heart the suffering of Jesus during His passion.'

We are further told to meditate on the sufferings of Mary and on the suffering of Jesus and read short passages from the Gospel which refer to the sufferings of Jesus and Mary. After the Seventh Sorrow, three 'Hail Marys' and three 'Our Fathers' are said to conclude the 'Little Beads'.

XIV Requests Made by Our Lady

(1) Our Lady requested that Alphonsine join the Legion of Mary to better realize her own vocation.
(2) Marie-Claire was requested to spread the devotion of the 'Little Beads of the Seven Sorrows' in Rwanda and all over the world.
(3) Our Lady made special requests of the seers to take part in extraordinary fasting and in silence. During Lent of 1983 Anathalie was asked to fast for 14 days from February 16 until March 2, 1983. Emmanuel fasted 18 days from March 7 until March 24, 1983. Agnes fasted eight days. Altogether the fasting of the three seers amounted to 40 days; recounting the fast of Jesus.

XV Specific Bible References

It is reported that when praying the 'Little Beads of the Seven Sorrows', we are to read passages from the Gospel referring to suffering of Jesus and Mary.

XVI Secrets Given to the Seer(s) - Not Reported
XVII Miracles Promised by Our Lady - NR
XVIII Miracles Performed - Not Reported
XIX Miracles Promised not yet Performed - NR
XX Signs Promised - Not Reported

XXI Signs Given

(1) The teachers and pupils at the Sister's School had little confidence and at first did not believe that Our Lady was appearing to Alphonsine. They were saying: "We will believe in the apparitions only if Our Lady appears to someone else besides Alphonsine." When Anathalie also began to receive messages and see Our Lady, this was taken as a (sign) reply from heaven.

(2) All the seers claim to have visited a universe different from our own under the guidance of Mary. These experiences are sometimes called 'mystical voyages'. When these occur, the seer's body becomes rigid and cold and remains so during this 'mystical voyage'. When the occurrence ends, the seer's body 'comes back to life'. The seers describe the places they visit; the description of the places visited sound like heaven, hell and purgatory.

Our Lady showed Vestine a place of fire, but told the seer that hell is not fire, but the privation of seeing God. Our Lady told the seer that purgatory is a place of reconciliation before reaching God. Then the seer saw a place of splendid lights, of perfect joy, and perfect happiness.

(3) During the apparitions to Agnes, a number of extraordinary signs were seen by all those present. A sun spinning around and sometimes two suns. At times, people could see two lines dividing the sun into three equal parts. Other times the cross of Jesus or the Crown of Thorns would appear to the right of the sun.

(4) True Signs of the authenticity of the messages are reported to be the way in which the visionaries themselves talk and the content of the messages. For instance, Emmanuel was a pagan and had no knowledge or understanding of Christianity. He didn't even know how to make the Sign of the Cross and had never been inside a church before his apparitions. Yet, the people who first came to see him after the first apparition were amazed at his knowledge since he was talking about the Sacrament of Penance, about sin, and the return of Jesus. In less than three months, he revealed messages for priests and religious orders.

XXII Predictions/Promises

Jesus told Emmanuel that we will know His Second Coming is near when we see the outbreak of religious wars ... *"Then know that I am on My way."*

XXIII Prophecies/Warnings of Chastisement

On March 27, 1982 Our Lady told Marie-Claire: *"This world is on the edge of catastrophe."* Our Blessed Mother also told the seer that we must all be apostles to help Her save the world.

XXIV Method of Appearance - Not Reported

XXV Method of Departure

Alphonsine reported that after her first apparition of November 28, 1981 Our Lady "ascended towards heaven like Jesus".

XXVI Confrontation w/Civil Authorities - NR

XXVII Confrontation w/Church Authorities

Msgr. Jean Baptiste Gahamanji, the bishop of Kibeho, in his pastoral letter of June 30, 1983 talks about the usual attitude of Church authorities, the teaching of Scripture, and the need for prudence and patience. However, details of Church opposition are not reported.

XXVIII Request Chapel/Shrine Built

It is reported Our Lady asked for a chapel to be built in Kibeho which is to be called 'The Gathering of the Displaced', where all united could sing as did the first Christians, Maranatha . . . *"Come Lord Jesus".*

XXIX Free Will/Choice

On August 18, 1983 Agnes received a message from Our Lady for the youth, in which message Our Lady said: *"The behavior of youth and their ideas are in contrast with what God expects from us."* Thus clearly asking youth to make a decision of their own will and do what God expects of them.

XXX Seer(s)' Suffering/Sacrifice

(1) The seers actually suffer during the apparitions. They fall to the ground, and sometimes weep. On one occasion, the seers were shown terrifying visions of the future which caused them to cry and become extremely frightened.
(2) Each of the seers has had to endure suffering. It is reported that Anathalie especially had to go through a lot of suffering.
(3) It is also reported that Emmanuel suffered much every Friday. He was told by Jesus: *"You must suffer every Friday to help Me save the world."*

XXXI Healings Reported

(1) It is reported there are many conversions as well as physical and spiritual healings.
(2) Some of the seers themselves were baptized and converted to Catholicism; also, Vestine's father was baptized in 1983. He had been a Muslim.
(3) During an apparition occurring on February 6, 1982 Alphonsine was cured of an illness affecting one of her eyes.

XXXII Action Taken by the Church

(1) On July 30, 1982 the bishop of Kibeho, Msgr. Jean Baptiste Gahamanji, issued his pastoral letter setting forth the facts of the apparitions and asking for prudence and patience.
(2) The bishops of Rwanda have spoken favorably about these apparitions.
(3) A medical and theological commission has been formed by the local bishop to determine the authenticity of these events. No decision is reported.

XXXIII Bibliography

The Final Hour 1992
By: Michael H. Brown
Published by: Faith Publishing Company

A Message from Our Lady in the Heart of Africa
By: Father Gabriel Mendron
Published by: Not Given

The Apparitions of Our Lady of Kibeho
By: Not Given
Published by: O'Gormon's Limited

Video: Kibeho, Africa - Apparitions of the Blessed Virgin
By: Not Given
Published by: Marian Video

Chapter 41

DAMASCUS, SYRIA
(1982 - 1992)

I Place - Damascus, Syria

II Dates of First and Last Apparition

First: December 15, 1982
Last: November 26, 1992

III Seer(s) - 1

Name: Mirna (Myrna) Nazzour
Birth: Unknown
Age at first apparition: 18
Status: Living

IV Total Number of Apparitions - 16

Note: Some apparitions and messages from Jesus are reported.

V Dates and Locality of Each Apparition

All apparitions occurred at Damascus, Syria unless otherwise noted.

1982: December 15, 18.
1983: January 8; February 21; March 24; October 24 (two), 28; November 7, 25.

1984: September 7.
1985: May 1; August 4, 14.
1987: July 22.
1992: November 26.

VI Description of Our Lady

On December 18, 1982 the seer saw within the upper part of a large tree across the street, a large luminous white globe like a large diamond ball sitting on a tree limb. Then the ball opened splitting from the top and dividing into two half-moons. As these halves opened, a bow of light appeared over the top, and there inside the globe was the beautiful Lady. As the ball disappeared, the Lady seemed to be standing on the branch of the tree. The Lady was wearing a white veil that covered all Her hair and which became like part of Her dress that covered Her feet. A sky-blue cape wrapped around Her back over Her right shoulder and over Her left side. Only Her hands were visible. From Her right hand between the second and third fingers hung a long rosary. She floated above the street towards the seer leaving a stream of pure light behind Her. She shined as if She were covered with diamonds.

VII Title(s) of Our Lady - 2

Our Lady has become known as: "Virgin Mary of Soufanieh" or "Our Lady of Soufanieh."

VIII Brief Factual Review

Syria is located on the continent of Asia, and borders the Mediterranean Sea. Damascus, Syria is said to be the oldest continuously occupied city in the world. St. Paul (as Saul) went to Damascus to persecute those who followed Jesus. It was through the gates of Damascus to the house of Ananias that St. Paul was led after he found himself blinded by the light of truth. The house of the seer (Mirna Nazzour) is within sight of the house of Ananias. There are a variety of Orthodox, Catholic, and other churches in Damascus.

It is said that the split in the Roman Catholic Church between the East and West began in Bulgaria. In 726 AD, Emperor Leo III of Constantinople prohibited the use of images in the churches. St. John Damascene of Damascus defended the Roman Church in his famous letter "Apology for the Veneration of Things". This in turn led to a further rift between Patriarch Photius of Constantinople and Pope Nicholas, when Patriarch Photius in 866 AD accused the Pope of spreading false doctrines among the Bulgarians. The schism was completed when the East no longer accepted the Pontiff in

Rome as head of the Universal Church.

In 1979 Nicholas Nazzour, who was to marry the seer Mirna two years later, purchased several cheap copies of the icon of Our Lady of Kazan while visiting Bulgaria which copies were enclosed in damaged plastic frames. These were intended to be gifts to his family. Nicholas and Mirna were married in 1981. One of these icons was later attached to the wall next to Mirna's bed. It is interesting to remember that the original icon of Our Lady of Kazan had exuded oil some 200 years prior. A feat that was soon to be duplicated.

Mirna Nazzour, a Syrian Arab woman, was born in Lebanon. She was 18 years old in 1982 when these events first occurred. She was Roman Catholic and her husband was Greek Orthodox. They lived in Damascus, in the district of Soufanieh which was predominately Christian.

These events all started on November 22, 1982 when the seer, Mirna, had joined with a Moslem woman and an Orthodox Christian to pray over Mirna's sister Layla who was very sick. As they prayed, the Moslem woman saw light come from Mirna's hands. Then the seer's hands began to exude oil. Layla was instantly cured. Then later, on November 25, 1982, the seer's own mother was cured in the same manner.

On November 27, 1982 the three inch icon on the wall beside Mirna's bed began to exude oil; within the first hour it had filled four dishes of oil. The seer's hands also exuded oil. Later, oil was also to come from the face and eyes of the seer.

The oil was scientifically analyzed and found to be pure (100%) olive oil. Scientists agree that the human body cannot produce olive oil and no trickery was found. The state security police dismantled the icon which was found to be a piece of paper. After wiping it clean and observing the seer, the security police placed the icon back onto the wall, and promptly the icon began to exude oil.

Later the icon was relocated to the outside of the seer's home where it continued to exude large quantities of oil. (This was done at Our Lady's request). Still later the icon was removed to the Greek Orthodox Church where it promptly quit giving oil. When it was returned to the seer's house the oil resumed.

As time went on, the other icons which Nicholas purchased in Bulgaria also exuded oil as did copies of the icon made for distribution to the people. The original icon copy has quit exuding oil as of 1990. Today, Mirna still exudes oil from her hands, but not from her eyes or face except for one instance which occurred on November 26, 1991 when oil came from Mirna's face and hands simultaneously. This event was witnessed by many.

Also witnessed by many was the occasion when oil poured from a crucifix into the open hands of Mirna. Many amazing healings, physical, emotional, and spiritual are reported as resulting from application of the oil to the sick person.

On December 15, 1982 Our Lady first appeared to Mirna. However, the first message was not given until December 18, 1982 when Our Lady again appeared to the seer. Our Blessed Mother appeared dressed in white with a sky-blue cape and carrying a rosary in Her right hand. There are sixteen reported apparitions of Our Lady, the last being on November 26, 1992 when Our Lady said: *"Fear not if I tell you this is the last revelation before the Feast (Easter) is unified."*

Interestingly enough, the next date when the Orthodox and Roman Catholic Easter coincides on the same date will occur in the year 2001.

Jesus appeared to Mirna at least a dozen times. He also gave messages to her. One such message of November 26, 1987 was in part: *"Do not hate anyone, otherwise your heart will be blinded by My love. Love everyone just as you have loved Me. Especially those who hate and spread rumors about you. It is through them that you will earn glory . . ."*

Mirna would always go into ecstasy when she saw Jesus. When these visions occurred she would suffer severe pain in her eyes.

The primary messages received by Mirna were pleas for unity and for prayer, and for all to love and forgive each other. Mirna first received the Stigmata in 1983. Each year thereafter, during Holy Week she would receive the wounds of Christ in her hands, feet, and side. Later she would also receive the 'Crown of Thorns'. The pain and bleeding would usually last for six hours and then the wounds would close. On those occasions when Easter coincided on the same date for both the Orthodox and Roman Catholics, the bleeding would be more profuse. The last reported Stigmata occurred in April 1990.

Secrets were given to the seer by both Our Lady and Our Lord. On November 20, 1984 Our Lord Jesus told Mirna: *"I will take your eyes."* Mirna lost her sight and regained it three days later.

On December 31, 1982 after interviewing Mirna and Nicholas, the Patriarch of the Greek Orthodox Church in Damascus declared the Miracle of Damascus to be authentic. One priest, Father Elias Zahlaoui, relates his own personal witness to some of these events. Numerous members of the clergy from various Orthodox and Catholic Churches have apparently given their approval, albeit tacit, to the messages and to the contents of the book titled under section XXXIII below.

There seems to be another problem with Church authorities, and that is one of jurisdiction. There are three Patriarchs in residence in Damascus, namely: Orthodox, Syrian, and Greek Catholic. The Syrian Patriarch apparently has no jurisdiction because neither Mirna nor her husband belong to his flock. It seems that the Greek Patriarch has also declined jurisdiction because the family comes under the religious jurisdiction of the husband. In this case under the jurisdiction of the Patriarch of the Orthodox Church.

The icon which first exuded oil was taken in procession to the Orthodox Church of the Holy Cross but was later returned to the seer's home because the oil dried up while it was inside the church; yet resumed promptly when it was returned to the seer's home.

It seems likely that the Church will study these events further before a decision will be forthcoming. Mirna has traveled to Lebanon and to the United States. Wherever she traveled she would attend celebration of the Mass and usually her hands would exude oil. There were reported cures when oil was applied to sick persons during these visits, both in Lebanon and in the United States.

It should be noted that early in these events, a neighbor of the seer (who owned a camera shop) began to video tape the ecstasies which the seer experienced during the apparitions. These videos show Mirna actually receiving the Stigmata.

IX The Primary Messages - 3

(1) Forgive and Love - December 18, 1982 Our Lady said: *"Do good to evil doers. Do not treat anyone bad . . . Love one another."*

January 8, 1993 Our Lady said: *"The humble is thirsty for the remarks of others to correct his faults; whereas, the corrupt and arrogant* (one) *neglects, revolts, and becomes hostile. Forgiveness is the most preferable thing . . . Endure and forgive, endure much less than what the Father endured."*

Jesus also gave the seer messages on forgiveness.

(2) Prayer - March 24, 1983 Our Lady said: *"I say to you, pray, pray."*

Again on July 22, 1987 Our Lady said: *"Pray, pray, and pray . . ."*

Jesus also reminded the seer that we must pray with adoration.

(3) Unity - The main message that Jesus and Our Blessed Mother gave to the seer was one of unity.

On May 1, 1985 Our Lady said: *"My children, be united. My heart is wounded. Do not let My heart be divided because of your divisions."*

Then on August 4, 1988 Our Lady said: *"The Church is the Kingdom of heaven on earth. He who divides it sins. He who is happy with these divisions also sins."*

On August 14, 1988 Our Lady said: *"Happy Feast Day! 'My Feast' is when I see all of you gathered together. Your prayer is 'My Feast'. Your faith is 'My Feast'. The unity of your hearts is 'My Feast'."*

Jesus also gave the seer messages of unity.

X Signs Preceding the Apparitions

Prior to some of the ecstasies and apparitions, Mirna's hands would exude oil.

Damascus, Syria

XI Other Visions During Apparitions

Jesus appeared to the seer over a dozen times and gave her very important messages on unity and forgiveness.

XII Prayers Taught to the Seer(s)

(1) On July 22, 1987 the seer was taught a prayer: 'Our Father through the wounds of Your Beloved Son, deliver us.'

(2) On February 21, 1983 Our Lady said: "*I have a request to ask of you. Engrave these words in your minds and always repeat them:*"
Trinity Prayer:
"God saves me,
　　Jesus enlightens me,
　　　　the Holy Spirit is my life.
　　　　　　I am not afraid."

(3) On May 31, 1984 Jesus taught Mirna a prayer:
Prayer:
Sweet Jesus grant that I rest in
You above anything else.
Above all creation
Above all Your angels
Above all praise
Above all rejoicing and happiness
Above all glory and honor
Above all Heavenly Hosts.
For You alone are the Most High
You alone are the Almighty
And Good above all things.
May You come to me
And relieve me and release my chains
And grant me freedom
Because without You
My joy is not complete
Without You my table is empty.
"*Then I will come to say:*
　'Here I am because you called Me.'"

XIII Special Devotion Given to the Seer(s) - NR

XIV Requests Made by Our Lady

(1) Our Lady requested: *"Make a niche outside the house. Take out one stone and put Me in it."* After this message was received, one stone near the front door of the seer's house was removed and one of the icons was placed in that space with a marble dish under it. This icon exuded oil and filled the dish many times; an event that was also captured on video tape.

(2) Jesus also made requests of the seer: *"Go and preach to all nations, and tell them, without fear, that they have to work for unity."* In response Mirna traveled to Lebanon and to the United States to spread the messages of unity.

XV Specific Bible References - Not Reported

XVI Secrets Given to the Seer(s)

(1) On September 7, 1984 Our Lady confided a secret to the seer.

(2) Jesus also gave the seer secrets to give to three priests, namely: Fr. E. Zahlaoui, Fr. Malouli, and Fr. Paul Fadell.

XVII Miracles Promised by Our Lady - NR

XVIII Miracles Performed

(1) In light of the scientific conclusion that the human body cannot produce olive oil, the various times Mirna exuded olive oil from her hands and face are reported as being miraculous.

(2) Likewise, with the oozing icon exuding pure olive oil.

(3) Once oil poured from a crucifix into the hands of the seer.

XIX Miracles Promised not yet Performed - NR

XX Signs Promised

On November 20, 1984 Mirna was told that she would lose her eyesight. This occurred and for three days Mirna could not see, then her sight was restored.

XXI Signs Given

(1) Mirna received the Stigmata and suffered the Passion of Christ.

Damascus, Syria

(2) The exuding of pure olive oil from the icon and from the hands, face, and eyes of Mirna were likewise signs.
(3) A crucifix poured oil into the open hands of the seer.
(4) Mirna lost her eyesight for three days as predicted and then regained her sight, as was also predicted.
(5) It is reported that when Mirna came to California, oil came out of her hands almost everywhere she went.
(6) Many copies of the icon poured out oil and many people were cured.

XXII Predictions/Promises

Our Lady predicted Myrna would be blind for three days, then regain her sight. This occured as predicted.

XXIII Prophecies/Warnings of Chastisement - NR

XXIV Method of Appearance

(1) During the first few appearances Our Lady came in a ball of light which opened and from which Our Lady appeared.
(2) Later, Mirna would frequently exude oil before she went into ecstasy or had a vision.

XXV Method of Departure

Likewise, during the first few appearances Our Lady departed in that same ball of light.

XXVI Confrontation w/Civil Authorities

On November 29, 1983 a Syrian Security Police came to the seer's house and took the icon apart in order to discover how the oil came out from it. In doing so, they tore the top right hand corner of the icon and ripped the frame. The icon and frame are in this condition today. They found no trickery or device. It is reported that soon thereafter, one security policeman came back to Mirna's house and asked that oil be applied to his own body and a prayer be said for his own healing.

XXVII Confrontation w/Church Authorities

No confrontation is reported. There is a reported problem of jurisdiction. Just which Patriarch will look into these events and make the investigation is uncertain; although, it seems that the Orthodox Patriarch has the case.

XXVIII Request Chapel/Shrine Built

During the first message Our Lady said: *"I am not asking you to build a church for Me but a shrine."* A shrine has been built on the patio deck with a statue of the Virgin Mary over the spot where Our Lady first appeared.

XXIX Free Will/Choice

It was Jesus Himself who told the seer she could choose Jesus or decide not to. Clearly we have free will.

(1) September 7, 1987 Jesus said in part: *". . . I shall give you time to choose.*
(2) Then On September 26, 1987 Jesus said in part: *". . . I value your decision to choose Me, but not in words only. I want you to join My heart and your soft heart so our hearts will be united."*

XXX Seer(s)' Suffering/Sacrifice

(1) There was a time that neither the seer's husband nor her friends understood her. Nicholas thought that she was a 'Holy Relic' and her friends became angry with her because she continued to do housework with hands 'blessed by God'. Mirna answered: "I don't believe the Virgin Mary had a servant." This caused the seer to suffer.
(2) Mirna suffered the Passion of Christ during Holy Week when she received the Stigmata.
(3) The seer lost her eyesight for three days which caused her suffering.

XXXI Healings Reported

(1) On December 19, 1982 a nine-year-old boy, paralyzed with withered legs, who had never walked a day in his life, was brought to Mirna's house by his own father. Mirna and the father prayed over him, oil came from Mirna's hands. She anointed his legs and the legs straightened out instantly. The boy walked for the first time in his life. On that day, six other people came to Mirna's house on crutches and walked away without their crutches.
(2) Another amazing cure reported was that of Mrs. K. Okomosian who had a large tumor on her leg. Since 1973 she needed help to get around and was in constant pain. On December 14, 1982 she came to the

seer's house and prayed for a while, then left. Her leg did not feel the same. She went to meet some American ladies at a school. When she saw the children outside running she got an urge and started running after them and found she could outrun them. She was completely healed.
(3) On January 7, 1983 Safu Abu Fares, a Moslem woman who was completely blind recovered her sight while at the House of Soufanieh.
(4) It is reported that Samer Sayegh from Chico, California, who was crippled from birth with twisted legs, was instantly cured.
(5) Numerous other cures are reported.

XXXII Action Taken by Church

(1) It is reported that hundreds of priests and some bishops are closely watching these events.
(2) Many clergy, from different denominations, have given their support by being listed in the 'Book of Messages'.
(3) Documents, concerning these events, have been sent to the Vatican.
(4) Father Malouli obtained the 'Nihil Obstat' from his Major Superior for all messages from the beginning through August 14, 1987.
(5) On November 6, 1984 oil flowed from the icon and from Mirna's hands in the presence of the Vatican Pro Nuncio, Nicholas Rotunno, who also met secretly with Mirna.
(6) Nonetheless, no final decision has been given by the Church nor is it reported that any commission has been established.

XXXIII Bibliography

The Miracles of Damascus 1990
By: The Publican
Published by: The Messengers of Unity

Video - The Miracles of Damascus
Vol 1, Vol 2, Vol 3
Produced by: The Messengers of Unity

Chapter 42

SAN NICOLAS, ARGENTINA
(1983-1990)

I Place - San Nicolas, Argentina

II Dates of First and Last Apparition

First: September 25, 1983
Last: February 11, 1990

III Seer(s) - 1

Name: Gladys Herminia Quiroga de Motta
Age at first apparition: 46
Birth: July 1, 1937
Status: Living

IV Total Number of Apparitions - over 1800

It is reported there have been over 1,800 visions and apparitions from September 25, 1983 through February 11, 1990.

Note: The seer also received apparitions and messages from Jesus, totaling 68.

V Dates and Locality of Each Apparition

There are over 1,800 messages from Our Lady reported in the Book of Messages referenced in section XXXIII below. These messages are not restated in this work.

VI Description of Our Lady

The seer describes Our Lady at the first apparition as wearing a blue dress, with a Child in Her arms and a rosary in Her hand. She resembled the classical statues of Our Blessed Mother.

VII Title(s) of Our Lady - 1

'Mary of the Rosary of San Nicolas' (November 26, 1983).

VIII Brief Factual Review

Argentina is located on the South American continent, and encompasses most of the southern triangle that faces the Atlantic Ocean.

San Nicolas, Argentina, is located northwest of Buenos Aires. It is the Episcopal seat of the Suffragan of Rosario, which is also the archdiocese. The city of San Nicolas today exceeds 140,000 souls. Since these reported apparitions began in 1983 it has become known as the 'City of Mary'.

In 1884 a beautiful statue of the 'Virgin of the Rosary' was donated and brought to San Nicolas from Rome where it had been blessed by Pope Leo XIII. The Confraternity of the Rosary was initiated and a special feast of the 'Virgin of the Rosary' was inaugurated with a novena which was to become a yearly tradition. The statue was placed in the Cathedral at San Nicolas where it has always remained; however, due to a breakage of one of the hands it was placed in storage in the belfry of the Cathedral.

Gladys de Motta was born on July 1, 1937. She attended only four years of elementary school from age seven to eleven. This seer, a 46-year-old mother of two daughters, claims to have seen the Blessed Virgin Mary over 1,800 times since the first apparition of September 25, 1983. Gladys lives with her family on the outskirts of San Nicolas across the street from a wasteland known as the 'Campito', on the bank of the Parana River.

It all began when Gladys was in her own home praying the rosary on September 25, 1983 and the Blessed Mother appeared to her. No words were spoken. On October 13, 1983 Our Lady first spoke to the seer, and gave a Bible reference to her. There were to be many Biblical references given to the seer, both from the Old Testament and New Testament, during these 1,800 apparitions. For a period of time Our Lady appeared to Gladys on nearly a daily basis.

In November 1983 Father Perez, the pastor of the Cathedral, took Gladys to view the statue in the belfry, and the seer declared: "It is the same as what I see."

In the messages Mary announces that She is the Ark of the Covenant and the Woman Clothed in the Sun.

On November 17, 1983 Gladys sprinkled Holy Water on the apparition to test the source (much the same as St. Bernadette did in 1848 at Lourdes, France). Our Lady smiled at the seer. Gladys says she receives an 'interior call' like a tingling sensation when Our Lady is about to appear to her. (We are mindful of a similar report earlier from Garabandal, Spain.) On November 15, 1983 Our Lady said: *"I am the Patroness of this Region. Assert My rights."*

Early in the apparitions, Our Lady requested that a Sanctuary (Basilica) be built. On November 24, 1983 and again on January 4, 1984 a ray of light illuminated the exact spot where the Sanctuary was to be built. This was witnessed by the seer and others. The Sanctuary is now under construction, the cornerstone having been laid by Bishop Castogna, the bishop of San Nicolas. There have been more than one dozen messages recorded relating to the building of the Sanctuary.

Gladys has received the Stigmata. On October 23, 1984 her spiritual director sent a message to the bishop which read in part: ". . . I believe that she has been called to live the state of a victim. On this reality, the great sufferings of the Passion and her internal fire could take place . . ."

These words turned out to be prophetic, for three weeks later on Friday, November 16, 1984 Gladys first experienced the suffering of the Passion. The Stigmata appeared progressively on her wrists (not the palms of her hands). These renewed themselves every Thursday and Friday during Advent of 1984 and thereafter, during each Lenten Season.

Doctors, sent by the bishop, have carefully examined this phenomenon. First of all a red spot (hematoma) appears, then bleeding occurs, later the wounds close by themselves. The marks on her feet occur only on Good Friday and are not the characteristic wounds. Rather, the skin is colored red from the blood which shows on the surface but does not open or flow. Gladys' left foot comes to place itself on her right foot. The feet move as one and cannot be parted, as if both feet were nailed with but one nail.

Also, on Good Friday, her shoulder is marked with an extended, very painful spot, as she experiences the carrying of the cross.

On December 2, 1984 Our Lady requested a medal be struck honoring the Holy Trinity. Our Lady described both the obverse and reverse of the medal, and later, on September 25, 1985 Our Lady gave Gladys the meaning of the seven stars on the reverse side of the medal: *"These are the seven graces which My Son, Jesus Christ, is going to grant to those who wear it on their chest."*

The messages of Our Blessed Mother carry an urgent appeal to prepare for the Second Coming of Jesus. She sets forth the means and weapons to be used for our salvation in Hope and Trust. She urges us to pray, particularly the rosary, to do fasting, and to do penance. She asks for our conversion and for the conversion of the world, and finally, she asks for our prayers of Consecration to the Two Hearts as a means to achieve forgiveness and

San Nicolas, Argentina

love for all people. Many of these messages are supported with specific Scriptural references. There are eighty-nine references to the Old Testament and 148 references to the New Testament contained in the messages.

Our Lady warns that our youth are in peril: *"My daughter, I see the youth adrift. The devil corners them and leads them to sin. My children are harassed by evil, and the disorder of their spirits is complete. To all of them I say, to thank the Lord because of His patience and to ask Him for His protection. Read Ecclesiasties 17:25-26."*

Our Lady also commented on the individual mysteries of the rosary.

Jesus also appeared to the seer and gave her some sixty-eight messages. His messages were also concerning Faith and Hope: *"He who listens to My Words will find salvation. He who puts them into practice will live forever. Those who hope in God do not hope in vain."*

The last message from Jesus was on December 30, 1989. He said to the seer in part: *"Before, the world was saved by means of Noah's Ark; today, the Ark of My Mother. Through Her, souls will be saved, because She will bring them toward Me."*

The first remarkable cure occurred in October/November 1984. Gonzalo Miguel Godoy, age seven, was diagnosed with a tumor on the brain, evidenced as a result of a tomography. He was completely paralyzed. After a priest gave him the Last Rites and First Holy Communion and placed the boy under the protection of 'Our Lady of the Rosary of San Nicolas', he promptly improved and on November 19, 1984 a third tomography showed no evidence of the tumor; only a scar. This cure is presently under official investigation to determine whether it is to be proclaimed a miracle. Other cures are also reported.

It is reported that many people visit the Sanctuary. On the 25th day of each month, many thousands of pilgrims come to San Nicolas to take part in the procession and Mass. Outside the uncompleted Sanctuary is the venerated statue of 'Maria del Rosario de San Nicolas'.

The messages have been compiled by the Marian Information Center authorized by Bishop Castogna. The bishop has supported these events, authorized the dissemination of the messages, given his Imprimatur, laid the cornerstone for the new Sanctuary, celebrated the Mass on the 25th of each month, and has presided over a number of processions. It is reported that he also conversed with Pope John Paul II about these apparitions when the Pope visited Argentina. Bishop Castogna has appointed a commission of six priests as well as a team of medical experts. Finally, Bishop Castogna informed the Episcopal Conference of these events, and it is reported that many bishops are favorably impressed by the fruits. No official Church decision has been made.

It is also reported that Bishop Jorge Lopez, Archbishop of Rosario, visited San Nicolas as a pilgrim.

IX The Primary Messages - 9

The messages, totaling over 1,800, contain exhortations, statements, and warnings, as well as uplifting teachings and informative messages on Faith, Hope and Love.

The often repeated and urgent sounding messages may be summarized in several primary message categories:

(1) **Prayer**
(2) **Rosary**
(3) **Fast and Penance**
(4) **Conversion**
(5) **Forgiveness**
(6) **Eucharist**
(7) **Consecration**
(8) **Youth**
(9) **Spiritual Combat**

(1) **Prayer** - July 12, 1986 Our Lady said in part: *"Pray for the Pope, My most chosen son, who has given body and soul to the Lord and to Mary, Mother of Christ."*

March 24, 1987 Our Lady said in part: *"I tell those who are consecrated to Me. Renew yourselves with prayer, with intense prayer."*

December 8, 1983 Our Lady again: *"Today must be a day consecrated to prayer, do not let it pass without this."*

February 3, 1990 Our Lady speaks: *"I say to all mankind, be fervent and constant in prayer. Offer it to the Lord with love, with your heart, with suffering."*

March 25, 1988 Our Lady says: *"Prayer produces fruit beyond the imaginable. May the name of the Lord be called upon today and forever."*

Our Lady's last message of February 11, 1990 was: *"My children I invite you to live My instructions step by step; pray, repair, trust! Blessed are those who seek in prayer a refuge for their souls! Blessed those who repair the grave offenses that are inferred on My Son! Blessed those who trust in the love of this Mother! Whoever trusts in God and in Mary will be saved! Preach glory be to God."*

(2) **Rosary** - January 18, 1984 Our Lady said: *"Say the rosary and may the Lord see that with it goes your conversion."*

January 30, 1984 again Our Lady says: *"Summon as many as you can for prayer, say the holy rosary."*

June 14, 1985 Our Lady says: *"Say the holy rosary continuously, during the 24 hours of the 25th day of the month."* (repeated again on July 22, 1986)

November 19, 1988 again Our Lady: *"Gladys, the weapon that has the greatest influence on evil is to say the holy rosary."*

San Nicolas, Argentina

(3) Fasting and Penance - January 11, 1989 Our Lady said: *"Prayer, fast, penance, and above all conversion, I expect from them . . ."*

November 28, 1983 Our Lady said: *"Know how to carry your cross. Accept it as He accepted it."*

October 24, 1989 again Our Lady: *"The Lord will deliver the souls who return to Him repentant."*

(4) Conversion - February 24, 1984 Our Lady said: *"I want the conversion of the world . . ."*

January 18, 1987 Our Lady said: *"In a faithful heart, there will be no room for pride, nor for hatred, because it will be flooded with humility and love."*

August 26, 1988 again Our Lady: *"All must know My urgent call to conversion, My request of Consecration to the Sacred Hearts of Jesus and Mary."*

(5) Forgiveness - April 3, 1985 Our Lady said: *"He who curses, who hates, is only poisoning his own heart. Let no one curse; let no one hate. May there be in your thoughts, no ill thoughts. Forgive as the Lord forgives, love as the Lord loves you."*

January 15, 1989 again Our Lady: *"Where there is forgiveness, there is love; where there is love, there is no hatred, and where there is no hatred, peace reigns."*

October 10, 1988 Our Lady said: *"Charity is to forgive the offender, to bless those who curse you. He who has charity, loves his neighbor and whoever loves his neighbor, loves God. Pay attention to My message."*

(6) Eucharist - January 29, 1986 Our Lady said: *"Jesus reveals Himself, accessible to all."*

June 1, 1988 Our Lady said: *"I tell you brethren, Jesus' Eucharist is Live and Real Body! Adore Him and Love Him! My children, it is in the Eucharist where He again becomes Body and Blood and it is from the Eucharist that He wants to save the souls prepared to receive Him!"*

September 12, 1988 again Our Lady: *"Adore the Body and Blood of My Son in the Blessed Sacrament of the Altar."*

June 9, 1985 Our Lady said: *"In Holy Mass, one not only receives the Body and Blood of Christ symbolically, Christ Jesus is present, and He offers Himself truly."*

(7) Consecration - February 2, 1990 Our Lady said: *"I want my consecrated children to give the Mother whatever She asks. The consecration must be made on a special day of the Mother's. This is the consecration that I ask in my Sanctuary, that:*

    1) they devote at least one hour per day to prayer
    2) they receive Communion daily
    3) they be humble
    4) they be at the complete service of Mary
    5) they be pleasing to God each day by living as consecrated souls

6) they be united to the Love of Her Son
7) they ask for the grace to live under the Light of the Holy Spirit."

February 12, 1988 again Our Lady: *"When a heart opens to the Heart of the Mother, She goes in. When a Heart surrenders to the Heart of the Mother, the Mother shapes it and leads it to Her Son. In this heart there is purity, there is love, there is humility. It is the heart that loves and obeys the Son."*

March 24, 1987 Our Lady speaks: *"I tell those who are consecrated to Me; renew yourselves with prayer, with intense prayer. I wish perseverance, I wish fidelity. I wish true consecration. I want you with Me! You have come near to My heart, you have come into My heart, continue there. Offer, My children, together with your love, your spirit of penance."*

(8) Youth - September 21, 1987 Our Blessed Mother bewails the condition of youth: *"My daughter how sadly lost youth is! Drug addiction and easy life is the picture the evil one has set for the young. Sin, committed in very different ways, makes them stray further and further from God.*

"If only they turn their eyes toward the Mother of God, the Mother will make them find God again."

August 7, 1988 Our Lady said: *"Pray for all the children of the universe--for those in need of bread, for those who are deprived of love, and above all, of the Word of God. The one who reveals the Word of God to a child is truly a child of God."*

May 8, 1985 Our Lady said: *"I speak to My little children, the young; they who are in this corrupt and terrifying world! Do not let yourselves be trapped in the calamities you see before your eyes. Do not forget that they only lead to perdition as one is submitted to evil. For I want healing and pure hearts and minds. Pray that you may become a peace-wishing youth, surrendered to God."*

(9) Spiritual Combat - May 22, 1986 Our Lady speaks: *"The enemy is challenging Me pitilessly. He is tempting My children openly. It is a war between light and darkness, a constant persecution of My dear Church."*

October 10, 1984 again Our Lady speaks:*"Continually, you are attacked by the evil one but you will reject it all. Only this way will he lose his strength and be consumed."*

June 2, 1985 Our Lady speaks again: *"There are so many insane passions everywhere My children, that blindness has taken hold of people. Sin surpasses all measure. The devil wants to have full domination over the earth. He wants to destroy, but the Lord does not want the vanquished, but the victors. You must definitely overcome the wickedness that surrounds you."*

Message number #666 in the Book of Messages (see section XXXIII) September 11, 1985 quotes Our Lady: *"Daughter, the devil acts ferociously, do not be surprised. He attacks without pity, warping everything he can touch. Pray, because prayer strengthens."*

San Nicolas, Argentina

April 6, 1986 Our Lady said: *". . . A tempest has broken out, a terrible tempest, the work of the devil. It is that the Lord's Word is a stumbling stone for many sinners. But I repeat what I so often said to you; the work of God is great, there is no evil able to stop it!"*

February 17, 1989 Our Lady speaks: *"This is My time! The enemy has been attacked. His end is near and he is using, as a last resource, human weakness and pride! But I shall vanquish him. I have already started to overcome him. Now the world must know that the Mother of Christ will overcome Satan, because by Her side will be Her Son's humble ones! May My message be known."*

X Signs Preceding the Apparitions

(1) The apparitions and visions often occurred while the seer was praying the rosary, although this was not a sure sign that Mary would appear.
(2) Starting October 7, 1983, Gladys began to have an 'interior warning' which let her know that Our Lady would appear.
(3) Yet, at another time (November 27, 1983) it is reported that the seer feels a tingling sensation in her arms. "Then I know that She is coming. I close my eyes and She appears."

XI Other Visions During Apparitions

Jesus appeared to Gladys many times. There are 68 reported messages from Jesus.

XII Prayers Taught to the Seer(s)

(1) On December 6, 1988 the seer received this prayer from Our Lady:
Prayer:
"Glory to the Father: Father, I glorify You for everything that You have created.
Glory to the Son Jesus Christ: To You be glory for Your Sorrowful Passion, for abandonment to the Father, and for Your Resurrection.
Glory to the Holy Spirit: Glory to You for the Light which You gave to the world, for the Love which You spread in the world. Blessed be You, One and Triune God, because of Your great Mercy."

(2) On August 27, 1984 Our Lady exhorted us to pray in preparation for when Christ calls each of us to Him:
Prayer: "With Christ on my side my weakness disappears

His love nourishes me and multiplies my strength.
I give thanks to Jesus who has known how to awaken me."

(3) On December 12, 1983 Our Lady gave this prayer to Gladys:
Prayer: "Father, deliver us from all evil. With Your Holy Wisdom, Lord, save us from all sin. In the Name of all those who love You Lord, lead us on the right road. Amen."

Then Our Lady said: *"He who says this prayer during nine consecutive days, together with a rosary, will receive a very special grace from Me."*

XIII Special Devotion Given to the Seer(s)

(1) Although this is not a new devotion, Our Lady did invite us to consecrate ourselves to Her Immaculate Heart and to the Sacred Heart of Jesus. On one occasion (February 12, 1988) Our Lady spelled out in detail what it means to be truly consecrated to Her Immaculate Heart. (See Section IX - (7) above).

(2) Our Blessed Mother gave the seer several messages (and prayers) regarding the mystery of the Holy Trinity. Again, no new devotion was given to the seer, yet on May 21, 1989 Our Lady announced: *"I say to all mankind: the Blessed Trinity, through My Heart wants to reach all souls. The Perfect Love of the Father, and of the Son, and of the Holy Spirit, wants to purify you; respond to this invisible but real show of love, with a visible and sincere answer; your conversion."*

XIV Requests Made by Our Lady

(1) On August 31, 1984 Our Lady requested that during the month of September of each year, we dedicate ourselves to praying the holy rosary every day, praying for peace in the world, and for conversion. Our Lady said that on the ninth day of the month *"You will see that the Lord is working on your hearts."*

(2) On December 2, 1984 Our Lady requested that a medal be struck: *"You must strike a medal with My image and My words: 'Mary of the Rosary of San Nicolas': and on the reverse side, the 'Holy Trinity' with seven stars."*

Then on September 25, 1985 Our Lady said: *"My daughter, I am going to tell you the meaning of the seven stars. These are seven graces which My Son Jesus Christ is going to grant those who wear it on their chest."*

The medal has been struck and has been widely distributed.

XV Specific Bible References

Many of the messages are often accompanied with specific references to Holy Scripture and invitation to read that Scripture. There were eighty-nine references to the Old Testament and 148 references to the New Testament.

Old Testament	New Testament
Deuteronomy	Gospel of St. John
Ecclesiasties	Gospel of St. Luke
Isaiah	Gospel of St. Mark
Job	Acts of the Apostles
Proverbs	Apocalypse
Psalms	Hebrews
Wisdom	1st Peter
	1st Corinthians
	Romans

XVI Secrets Given to the Seer(s) - Not Reported
XVII Miracles Promised by Our Lady - NR
XVIII Miracles Performed - Not Reported
XIX Miracles Promised not yet Performed - NR
XX Signs Promised - Not Reported

XXI Signs Given

(1) **Aroma of Roses** - On November 12, 1983 the seer reported she experienced a great aroma of roses. At other times those around Gladys also smelled a sweet smell of roses.
(2) **Stigmata** - Through this great sign it is shown that the seer shares the Passion of Jesus with love.
(3) **Sanctuary** - On two separate occasions, Gladys was shown the exact location where the Sanctuary was to be built; each time a ray of light fell on that spot and seemed to disappear into the ground.
(4) **Rosary** - It is reported that a month before the apparitions started Gladys saw her rosary hanging in her room light up. Some neighbors also saw this sign. Thereafter, Gladys began to recite the rosary, first with these neighbors, then by herself.

XXII Predictions/Promises

On December 12, 1983 Our Lady gave Gladys a prayer (see Section XII above) and promised: *"He who says this prayer during nine consecutive days, together with a rosary will receive a very special grace from Me."*

XXIII Prophecies/Warnings of Chastisement

(1) February 21, 1985 Our Lady said: *"God save you My dears, in this time in which He is present. He will deliver you, since at every step you take you are exposed to this world's calamities . . . you must be warned, children, the plaque is big."*

(2) Then on May 18, 1985 Our Lady said: *". . . You are going through terrible situations, in which material things want to be above what is spiritual, and where brothers want to vanquish brothers, transforming thin love into hatred, without giving way to truth and the love that God places in each one."*

(3) November 19, 1987 Jesus said: *"Today I warn the world of what the world seems unaware: Souls are in danger, many will be lost! Salvation will reach few unless I am accepted as the Savior. The children of sin will grow in sin, if disbelief grows in them. The Heart of My Mother is the one chosen for what I ask to become reality. Souls will find Me through Her Immaculate Heart!"*

(4) In one of the early messages (December 27, 1983) Our Lady stated: *"All of humanity is contaminated."*

XXIV Method of Appearance - Not Reported
XXV Method of Departure - Not Reported

XXVI Confrontation w/Civil Authorities

No confrontation is reported. Rather, this city of 140,000 souls has accepted and embraced these phenomena. The municipality of San Nicolas has made a gift of the Campito to the Church. This is where the Sanctuary is being constructed.

XXVII Confrontation w/Church Authorities

Rather than confrontation, only true and genuine pastoral care in handling this matter is reported. Here is a list of the clergy-players.

(1) Bishop Castogna, the bishop of San Nicolas who was central in supporting and guiding the parties concerned in these matters.
(2) Father Perez the priest of the Cathedral of San Nicolas.
(3) Archbishop Jorge M. Lopez, the head of the Archdiocese of Rosario in which San Nicolas is located.

XXVIII Request Chapel/Shrine Built

Our Lady requested a chapel be built on the Campito on the bank of the Parana River. She repeated this request. On two separate occasions the seer (and others) saw a shaft of light at the exact spot where the Sanctuary is now being built. Our Lady's request was clear and certain. More than a dozen messages deal with construction of the Sanctuary.

The land was donated for the building project. Construction commenced October 13, 1987 with the first stage of construction being completed on October 5, 1988. This first part of the Sanctuary was blessed on March 19, 1989. On February 2, 1990 work began on the second phase of construction.

XXIX Free Will/Choice

(1) May 22, 1986 Our Lady stated: *"God gives freedom and prevents no one from making his own choice to become pure or live in sin. To grow in Christ, or to defeat oneself."*
(2) Again on January 30, 1984 Our Lady said: *"The Lord grants freedom of choice. He makes you see good and makes you see the evil, shows you the light and also the darkness. Those who want to be with Him must act according to His Commandments."*

XXX Seer(s)' Suffering/Sacrifice

Gladys received the Stigmata and suffered portions of the Passion of Christ during the Lenten Season.

XXXI Healings Reported

(1) It is reported that a large number of cures have taken place at the public Sanctuary. In the Book of Testimonies, consisting of 187 pages through the end of 1989 many pilgrims have related their cures and healings. A medical bureau studies these cures.
(2) Some of the cases reported stand out, such as the case of seven-year-old Gonzalo Godoy who was paralyzed from a brain tumor. He was totally cured. So also, nine-month-old Juan Olguin who contracted meningitis with cross paralysis. He was blind, deaf, mute, and unconscious in a comatose state for nine days. Following prayers addressed to 'Our Lady of the Rosary of San Nicolas', he awoke on the tenth day in perfect state of health. Truly amazing as reported.

XXXII Action Taken by the Church

The visionary remains secluded and obedient. Her parish priest provides spiritual advice. Bishop Castogna guides the fervor of the pilgrims and processions. The people support these events. Much good fruit is evident. Archbishop Lopez views these events favorably.

On September 25, 1984 Father Perez instituted the 'Perpetual Rosary' in the cathedral.

On December 28, 1987 Bishop Castogna authorized the first movement for a New Order to be in charge of the Sanctuary: 'The Daughters of Mary of the Rosary of San Nicolas'.

The bishop has named a commission to study these events. A first report of the commission was returned on October 25, 1985. It found that the personality of the seer was in good balance, in perfect harmony with reality, and the writings (messages) do not present any theological objection.

A pastoral program is now established and at present it is permitted to print images and the messages. Bishop Castogna gave his Imprimatur to publish the messages.

No final Church action has been taken.

XXXIII Bibliography

An Appeal From Mary in Argentina 1990
By: Fr. Rene Laurentin
Published by: Faith Publishing Company

Messages of Our Lady at San Nicolas 1991
By: Translated by E. DeNagy-Pol and Marie-Helene Gall
Published by: Faith Publishing Company

Chapter 43

KINSHASA, ZAIRE
(1984-1988)

I Place - Kinshasa, Bandalungwa, Zaire

II Dates of First and Last Apparition

First: February 6, 1984
Last: March 28(25), 1988

III Seer(s) - 9

Name: Umande Okita Sumbu Amini Fidele (Papa Fidele) (male)
Birth: September 19, 1913
Age at first apparition: 70
Status: Married/Living

Name: Hortense Yayi Bambile (female)
Birth: Unknown
Age at first apparition: 15
Status: Unknown

Name: Clementine Denise Tshimba (Nana) (female)
Birth: Unknown
Age at first apparition: 15
Status: Unknown

Name: Marie-Louise Wetsi (female)
Birth: Unknown
Age at first apparition: Unknown
Status: Unknown

Name: Danela Losala (female)
Birth: Unknown
Age at first apparition: Unknown
Status: Unknown

Name: Assissa Kishabongo (Mado) (male)
Birth: Unknown
Age at first apparition: 5
Status: Unknown

Name: Assissa Wasongo (Bruno) (male)
Birth: Unknown
Age at first apparition: 4
Status: Unknown

Name: Assissa Mulimbi (Leticia) (female)
Birth: Unknown
Age at first apparition: 2
Status: Unknown

Name: Umande Mulimbi (Celene) (Mother of the 3 children above)
Birth: Unknown
Age at first apparition: Unknown
Status: Unknown

IV Total Number of Apparitions - 11

(1) to Papa Fidele - three (3)
(2) to Hortense Yayi Bambile - two (2)
(3) to Clementine Denise Tshimba (Nana) - one (1)
(4) to Marie-Louise Wetsi - two (2)
(5) to Danela Losala - one (1)
(6) to Mado, Bruno and Leticia Assissa - one (1)
(7) to Umande Mulimbi (Celene) - one (1)

Reports indicate there were many more apparitions than reported.

V Dates and Locality of Each Apparition

(1) **To Papa Fidele** - Two apparitions, dates unknown, at the Mother House, #8 Rue Mapezo, Kinshasa.
March 28(sometimes reported as the 25th), 1988 at the Mother House, #8 Rue Mapezo, Kinshasa. (It is indicated there were more apparitions to this seer that are not reported.)
(2) **Hortense Yayi Bambile** - Before February 6, 1984 at Yayi's home. Again at 6:00 PM that same evening.
(3) **Clementine Denise Tshimba (Nana)** - February 6, 1984: Mother House of Chaste-Marie at #8 Rue Mapezo, Kinshasa.
(One week after February 6, 1984, this seer had an apparition of Jesus.)
(4) **Marie-Louise Wetsi** - After March 28, 1988: Mother House of Chaste-Marie at #8 Rue Mapezo, Kinshasa. One week after February 6, 1984 at the Mother House of Chaste-Marie at #8 Rue Mapezo, Kinshasa.
(5) **Danela Losala** - 1987: March 4-5, unreported location.
(6) **Mado, Bruno and Leticia Assissa** - 1986: At their home on Kimbondo Street, Kinshasa.
(7) **Umande Mulimbi (Celene)** - 1988: At the seer's home on Kimbondo Street, Kinshasa.
(It is also indicated that this seer had more apparitions of Our Lady. This seer was appointed as a "permanent visionary" by Our Lady.)

VI Description of Our Lady

(1) The Holy Virgin Mary appeared wearing a white robe, a white veil with a gold rosary in Her left hand, Her arms extended to welcome the people.

(2) When Our Lady appeared to the three Assissa children in 1986, the children saw a lovely play of sparkling stars take place before them; they also saw the sun and the moon. Then they saw white clouds in which a lovely white Lady appeared, all dressed in white with a long golden rosary shining on Her arm. A pleasant aroma of Bergamot was diffused in the room. The Lady was very refined and demonstrated maternal tenderness.

VII Title(s) of Our Lady - 3

In February 1984, Jesus Himself asked Nana (and several others), during an apparition, to honor Our Lady as the *Mother of God*. It is reported that Our Lady also identified Herself as *"The Mother of the Savior"*, and *"The Mother of the Redeemer"*.

VIII Brief Factual Review

Zaire is located in the central portion of Africa. Lingala is the language most widely used in the region where the apparitions occurred and of course Our Lady spoke to the seers in that language.

The Community of the Sons and Daughters of Mary, Mother of Charity (known as Mariechaste) or Chaste-Mary, is located at #8 Rue Mapezo, Kinshasa, Bandalungwa, Zaire. The founder of the Society of Chaste-Mary was Umande Okita Sumbu Amini Fidele, commonly known as "Papa Fidele." Papa Fidele, as well as the Mother House of the Society, were centrally involved in these reported apparitions. The parish located in the Bandalungwa Zone or Mayoralty is St. Charles Loanga. The pastor was Fr. Ive. The late Cardinal Malula was the archbishop of Kinshasa. Auxiliary Fr. Gossen was advocate and secretary of the Episcopacy of Zaire.

The Legion of Mary was strong in the parish and it is reported that the Society of Chaste-Mary did much good work in the region, such as evangelization resulting in many conversions, establishment of prayer groups and prayer meetings throughout the Archdiocese of Kinshasa, pilgrimages to the Grotto of the Virgin Mary and the spread of prayer, especially the holy rosary, throughout the archdiocese. The Society also successfully managed to inspire many young people to embrace religious vocations. Yet it is reported that the Society's progress was slow and all its works were accomplished in silence and poverty; which has helped to bring about unity. As Papa Fidele said: "Nevertheless, it is incumbent upon us to recognize that every human endeavor, especially if it is destined for God, must be put to the test in one way or another."

The Society was officially started on June 27, 1983 when Cardinal Malula, then the archbishop of Kinshasa, received a delegation from the Society and gave them his blessing, encouragement and permission to continue this apostolate. (The Society had been doing these good works previously). The cardinal placed two priests at the disposal of the Society; namely Fr. Rene Haes and Abbot Honore Nzenzg, in order to follow and guide the activities of the Society. The cardinal wisely counseled the delegation thusly: "My children to convert people and bring them to the path of eternal salvation is not an easy thing. Be careful that in saving lost sheep, you don't end up being lost yourselves. Pray a lot and little by little, you will manage to do some good by the grace of God."

From that time on the Society has become widely known throughout the world for its good work and good fruit produced from this good work.

Every member of Chaste-Mary is required to lead a holy life, keep the Commandments, attend daily Mass, receive the Sacraments, pray (especially the rosary), do penance and make sacrifice and do spiritual and corporal works of mercy. Everyone who wants to be saved may become a member of Chaste-Mary. Perhaps it is a small wonder God has looked favorably upon this Society, and has even sent Our Blessed Mother to appear and give messages of love and guidance to many associated with this Society.

It is reported that the messages given were for the Society, for the world, and some personal messages as well.

Papa Fidele was born in the St. Charles Mission in Kasongo Tongorie on September 19, 1913 and was baptized the same day after the 7:30 Mass. As a child, Fidele was sickly. The local priest advised his parents to dedicate their child to God and to the Virgin Mary if they wanted him to live. His parents did as advised, promptly making a novena of prayers. Fidele led a life of prayer, attended Sunday Mass with his parents walking one kilometer to attend daily Mass. When the child was 13 he became seriously ill which derailed his entry into the seminary. Fidele never went to the seminary, but instead got married to Helene Nojiki. Later Our Lady told him during an apparition that it was God's will that Fidele become married and not become a priest. After he became married, Fidele remained active in church work and spiritual activities. He was president of the Legion of Mary. He created the International Association for the Dead, and the Association of Christian Widows. Then came the creation of the Society of Chaste-Mary. The vows of the Chaste-Mary are chastity for one's station in life, obedience, poverty, humility and submission to the Church and Pope; and to act through solidarity and do everything through Mary, with Mary, in Mary and for Mary.

In the apparitions Our Lady stressed the familiar messages of conversion, prayer, recitation of the rosary, love of one's neighbor, forgiveness and reconciliation of all people. It is reported that one day during an apparition Papa Fidele asked Our Lady: "How could I deserve to be called Servant of Mary, a sinner like me? I consider myself unworthy when I consider the marvelous works accomplished by the great saints. . ." Our Lady responded: *"My Servant, do you think that what you do here is less important than what others have done? Don't you know that with your fervor and devotion to Me, you are serving not so much Me as My Son and My Father?"*

Our Lady told Papa Fidele that each apparition is related to the world situation in general and to the place of the apparition in particular. There is no longer peace in the world, instead armed conflicts break out everywhere. Man does not use his intelligence for the good of mankind, instead he uses it for the destruction of mankind. Meanwhile in Zaire man draws further away from God, no longer loves God or his neighbor, no longer has compassion for the unfortunate. Family conflicts, rebellion and injustice are the norm. Christians no longer attend Mass or receive the Sacraments. In short God is jeered.

On March 4-5, 1987 Our Lady told the seer Danela Losala, that apparitions are of three kinds:

(1) The visionary sees the apparition by means of his/her own eyes.

(2) The visionary sees the apparition, speaks to and hears the apparition speak, and afterwards relates the message.

(3) Our Lady or Our Lord introduce themselves into the body of the visionary and speak through him or her.

Our Lady's messages for the world are pleas for prayer, for penance and to forgive and love one another. On February 8, 1984 Jesus confirmed these messages and apparitions from Our Lady as being authentic and from God.

Our Lady warned the seers, and the Society through the seers, that they would suffer much from criticism, mockery and attacks, but to stand fast and persevere and pray unceasingly. She especially asked the Chaste-Mary to pray for the countries then at war. Of course the members complied with Our Lady's request and prayed. There were immediate results; cease-fire in Chad, as well as between Iran-Iraq and later independence in Nambia as well as cease-fire between the government forces and the rebels in Angola.

Our Lady also gave secrets to Papa Fidele. Jesus appeared to some of the seers and gave messages to them. Our Lady made several promises and predictions, all of which came true. Miracles and healings were performed through the seers.

Now we may look more closely at the seers and at the apparitions which the seers each personally received:

(1) **Papa Fidele** - This seer was the founder of the Society of Chaste-Mary, and is reported to have led an exemplary Christian life from early childhood right to the present. He was deeply devoted to the Blessed Virgin Mary. Our Lady had personal conversations with him and talked to him about his past and also about the future work he was to do. Fidele had a ministry and gift of healing. Reportedly people came from far and wide to have him 'lay hands' on them. Every work he did was done only after receiving the blessing of Church officials, and always carried out with much prayer and loving care. Our Lady referred to Fidele as 'Servant of Mary'. It is also reported that Our Lady appointed well over one dozen 'permanent visionaries' to whom She appeared and gave messages.

Our Lady's messages for the world were primarily for prayer, especially the rosary, conversion, love of one's neighbor, forgiveness and reconciliation of all people.

(2) **Hortense Yayi Bambile** - This seer was a girl of 15. It is reported that sometime "well before" February 6, 1984 Our Lady appeared to Yayi in her own home. The seer was cleaning the patio singing while she worked. Her family members suddenly heard her voice change and she began to sing in a marvelous voice. Then her face became transfigured. As her brothers and sisters drew nearer to her they heard her voice become gentle and unusual and then these words: *"Do not be afraid! It is I, the Holy Virgin Mary, here with you. I have come to cure the child. Take My girl to My servant Fidele at #8 Mapezo Street."* Then Our Lady left promising to return at 6:00 PM that day.

At 6:00 PM members of Chaste-Mary (including Fidele) met at Yayi's house. While they were praying the rosary Our Lady appeared and spoke to them. There was great joy because all those present heard Our Lady speak. The main message given was *"I will do extraordinary things at Mapezo."*

The seer complied and took 'the girl', Nana, to Papa Fidele to be cured.

(3) Clementine Denise Tshimba (Nana) - Nana was also a girl of 15 when these events occurred. It was Nana who was to be taken to Papa Fidele to be healed according to the message Our Lady gave to Yayi.

Nana was suffering from some kind of 'malady'. As early as April 13, 1983 it is reported that her behavior during Mass was such that she had to be removed. She screamed. She would cry for no apparent reason and would become angry over the smallest incident. She even barked like a dog. Her parents had taken Nana to prayer groups and hospitals but after months of fruitless efforts they decided to take her to Papa Fidele.

They arrived in Mepezo on February 5, 1984 which was a day devoted to Papa Fidele's healing ministry. The sick came up one at a time, and when it was Nana's turn she knelt and held the Crucifix like the others. But as soon as the Sign of the Cross was made on her forehead she resisted and with a sweep of her arm she knocked over the holy water. Papa Fidele then successfully exorcised Nana and the devils fled from her body after first throwing her to the ground.

That night Nana had a dream in which Our Lady appeared and said She would take Nana for two days and heal her. Upon awakening Nana told her family that Our Lady was going to come that day. The family was concerned and took her back to Papa Fidele on Mapezo Street.

Fidele was puzzled, however Our Lady spoke through Nana and affirmed that She was taking Nana for two days. Fidele pleaded with Our Lady to shorten the time, and Our Lady graciously promised to bring Nana back at midnight.

Just then Nana began to dance and sing; then she suddenly collapsed. No one could lift her or move her; yet Nana held the rosary in her hands and was praying. At exactly midnight, Nana suddenly sat up and began to sing. Nana began to speak English; a language she did not know and had never spoken before. Nana explained that Our Lady fetched her and took her to heaven, where she saw Jesus on the Cross. She was shown hell, where a great fire was burning. Our Lady told Nana to see what was there because "I was very stubborn". Nana was very scared and asked the Virgin Mary to take her home.

That night many miraculous healings were performed through Nana. One man had been blind in his left eye for 10 years; he was instantly able to see out of his left eye.

(4) Three Assissa Siblings:
    Mado - age 5 years
    Bruno - age 4 years
    Leticia - age 2 years

One day in 1986 these three children were home alone in the living room of their home. The door was locked by their mother who had gone to the market and a neighbor's house. These children were to receive two unusual visitors.

Suddenly the room became well lighted and a lovely play of sparkling stars appeared before their eyes, as well as the sun and moon. Then they saw a white cloud and a white Man appeared dressed in white and wearing sandals with straps reaching to his knees. A broad red cloth swung across his shoulder to his hip. He stood on the exposed electric wires on the floor. The parents had previously given the children strict orders not to touch those wires, because anyone touching the wires would receive an electric jolt. Of course the children were afraid that the white Man would be electrocuted. The white Man greeted the children in their own language and asked where was their father. When the children said their father had gone to work, the white Man said: *"You will tell him, when he returns, that the Lord Jesus Christ came to visit us. Go in peace."* He blessed them and left.

This visitor had scarcely left when the light display, the stars, the moon and the sun appeared again. Only this time a white Lady appeared from the clouds dressed all in white with a long golden rosary shining on Her arm. She smiled and greeted them, then asked them *"Where is your mother?"* The children answered that their mother had gone to the market. At that the white Lady took Leticia in Her arms and rocked her until the child smiled. Then the white Lady said: *"You will tell your mother that Mother Mary came to visit you. I will come back to see her another day. Go in peace."* She then left after blessing them.

When their Mother (Celene) Umande Mulimbi returned home she was amazed at the children's story; especially since the door was still locked. However Our Lady's promise to visit Celene did come true.

(5) Danela Losala - During the night of March 4-5, 1987 the Blessed Virgin Mary appeared to this seer and specified that apparitions are of three kinds:

a) The visionary sees the apparition by means of his/her eyes.

b) The visionary sees the apparition, speaks and hears the apparition speak, and afterward explains the experience.

c) The apparition is introduced into the body of the visionary and speaks through the seer.

(6) Marie-Louise Wetsi - On November 17, 1988 at the Mother House, both Jesus and Mary appeared to this seer. (Jesus had first appeared to this seer a week after the February 6, 1984 apparition of Our Lady to Nana.)

Jesus warned the people of the evils in the world and encouraged everyone to pray, to do penance, to love and honor His Mother, the Mother of God. He said He comes to bring peace and to ask for conversion. Then Our Lord said: *"It is through your prayers, sacrifices and penance that the world and your country will be saved. Recite daily the rosary."*

Our Blessed Mother asked that we pray unceasingly.

(7) Celene Umande Mulimbi - Our Lady also appeared to Celene Umande Mulimbi, the Mother of the three Assissa children, reportedly on several occasions and confirmed the promise Our Lady had made to the children at the earlier apparition to them. It is reported that Celene became a 'permanent visionary'.

It is also reported that when Our Lady appears to Celene, the seer goes into ecstasy and calls out to the children in a manner that indicates she can read their hearts. Celene is known to have said things like: "Why have you not left for school?" or "What have you stolen?" This has put the fear of God into the children's hearts, so it is reported.

IX The Primary Messages - 4

It is reported that in all apparitions the Holy Virgin called for conversion, recitation of the rosary, to love one's neighbor, to forgive offenses and to reconcile with everyone; all people, all families, all countries and nations in conflict.

(1) Conversion - On February 6, 1984 Our Lady expressed Her joy in the efforts the Society had undertaken towards converting poor sinners: *"I am delighted by the goal pursued by your Society and your prayers, that you pray for the conversion of the world. There is hardly a greater good in the world than the conversion of a man. I am very pleased with your ability to make Me known to the world and to spread My honor."*

A week after February 6, 1984 Jesus Himself appeared to the seer Marie-Louise Wetsi and said in part: *". . . I ask conversion of you. The Son of Man will return before long."*

(2) Prayer - Our Lady told Papa Fidele that we must pray for those who insult Our Blessed Mother because they do not know what they say or do; and the Holy Virgin remains always their Mother; the Mother of Mercy to all.

Jesus Himself on February 6, 1984 encouraged everyone to pray, to be penitent. He also said: *"The world is in danger because of your sin. Pray vigorously for your country. Pray as well for priests that they may live in respect of their commitment."*

When Our Lady appeared with Jesus, a week after February 6, 1984 to Marie-Louise Wetsi, She asked for prayers as well as other requests.

It is reported that the Society began to pray for the countries at war. They soon recognized some immediate effects, such as a cease-fire in Chad and between Iran and Iraq, and between the fighting factions in Angola. Later Nambia became independent.

(3) Rosary - Our Lady carried a golden rosary during the apparitions, even the time when She appeared to the three small children in their home, thus sending the message that She wants everyone to pray the holy rosary.

It is reported that Our Lady asked that the rosary be prayed each time She appeared to the various seers.

(4) Charity, Forgiveness and Reconciliation - It is reported that during each apparition Our Blessed Mother insisted that we pray the holy rosary, love one's neighbor, forgive all offenses and reconcile with everyone.

X Signs Preceding the Apparitions

A dazzling display of lights, stars, the sun and the moon in the living room of the three small children preceded the appearance of both Jesus and Mary.

XI Other Visions During Apparitions

(1) Jesus appeared to several of the seers.
(2) Nana was shown heaven and hell.

XII Prayers Taught to the Seer(s) - Not Reported
XIII Special Devotion Given to the Seer(s) - NR

XIV Requests Made by Our Lady

(1) Our Lady requested that the Chaste-Mary members consecrate themselves to Jesus and to Our Lady, especially for the countries that were at war.
(2) Our Lady asked Yayi to take Nana to Papa Fidele to be healed. This was done and on February 6, 1984 Nana was healed.
(3) Our Lady asked the three small children to tell their own mother that Our Blessed Lady would appear to the mother of the children. It happened as Our Lady said.

XII Specific Bible References

John 21, 15:24.

XVI Secrets Given to the Seer(s)

It is reported that Papa Fidele received secrets from Our Lady, some concerning the Society of the Chaste-Mary, some concerning the world and the Church, and others concerning him personally. These secrets have not been revealed.

XVII Miracles Promised by Our Lady

Our Lady told Wetsi that Our Lady would do *"extraordinary things at Mapezo."* Thereafter on February 6, 1984 Nana was healed at Mapezo.

XVIII Miracles Performed

It is reported that Nana performed 'many miracles' that night of February 6, 1984 after she was taken by Our Lady, herself cured and returned. She was also given the gift of speaking English, a language she never knew at all before.

XIX Miracles Promised not yet Performed - NR

XX Signs Promised

Our Lady promised to heal Nana and do extraordinary things in Mepezo. This She did.

XXI Signs Given

On February 6, 1984 while Our Lady took Nana to heal her, Nana's body became heavy and rigid until midnight when Our Lady returned Nana, cured of her malady.

XXII Predictions/Promises

(1) Our Lady promised the three small children that She would come back and see their own mother, Celene, another day. This did occur and Celene was appointed as a 'permanent visionary' by Our Lady.
(2) Later Our Lady told Celene, who had separated from her husband: *"Bear this cross, pray, your husband is going to convert."*

XXIII Prophecies/Warnings of Chastisement

A week before February 6, 1984 Our Lord Himself appearing with Our Lady said: *"The world is in danger because of your sins. It is through your prayers, sacrifices and penance that the world and your country will be saved. If not, My Father will punish the world and your country. Recite daily the rosary."*

XXIV Method of Appearance

When Our Lady and Our Lord appeared to the three small children, first they saw a light show of stars, the moon and the sun, then clouds appeared and the apparition emerged from the clouds.

XXV Method of Departure

In a 1986 apparition, Our Lady blessed the children with the sign of the cross and disappeared.

XXVI Confrontation with Civil Authorities - NR

XXVII Confrontation w/Church Authorities

No confrontations with Church authorities are reported. On the contrary, Cardinal Malula (now deceased) formed a theological and medical commission to study these apparitions. It was this same Cardinal Malula to whom Papa Fidele applied and received the permission and blessings to operate the Society. The cardinal even appointed two priests to guide and assist the Society.

Much prayer and many conversions have occurred and increased since these apparitions first started.

XXVIII Request Chapel/Shrine Built - NR
XXIX Free Will/Choice - Not Reported

XXX Seer(s)' Suffering/Sacrifice

Our Lady predicted that the seers and members of the Society would suffer due to the apparitions and messages. She told them that many would not believe. Our Lady told the seers: *"But stand fast, persevere and pray unceasingly."*

This happened just as She had told them. The seers and members of the Society were subjected to insults, mockery, disapproval, defamation and isolation. Of course this caused great emotional anguish to the several seers.

XXXI Healings Reported

(1) Firstly, Nana was healed on February 6, 1984.
(2) Then, Nana herself performed healings that night. One particular healing reported was of a man who had not been able to see out of his left eye for 10 years. The sight of his left eye was suddenly restored.

XXXII Action Taken by the Church

The late Cardinal Malula appointed a commission to study these events. No judgment is reported.

XXXIII Bibliography

A History of the Society and Report of the Apparitions at Mepezo (5 Volume Manuscript)
By: Society of Chaste-Marie
Published by: Society of Chaste-Marie

Chapter 44

OLIVETO CITRA, ITALY
(1985-1989)

I Place - Oliveto Citra, Italy

II Dates of First and Last Apparition

First: May 24, 1985
Last: January 9, 1989
Note: Some of these visionaries claim to have ongoing apparitions.

III Seer(s) - 10

It is reported there may be no fixed group of 'visionaries', although, reportedly, there are about thirty different people to whom Our Lady appeared several times, including the twelve boys who saw Her for the first time on May 24, 1985.

Those seers who seem to be most closely connected with these apparitions and the apparition site are:

Name: Dino Acquaviva (male) twin
Birth: Unknown
Age at first apparition: 15
Status: Living

Name: Carmine Acquaviva (male) twin
Birth: Unknown
Age at first apparition: 15
Status: Living

Name: Anita Rio (female)
Birth: Unknown
Age at first apparition: 24
Status: Living

Name: Sabrina DeBellis (female)
Birth: Unknown
Age at first apparition: 13
Status: Living

Name: Marco DeBellis (male)
Birth: Unknown
Age at first apparition: 11
Status: Living

Name: Umberto Gagliardi (male)
Birth: Unknown
Age at first apparition: Unknown
Status: Living

Name: Antonella Giordano (female)
Birth: August 5, 1973
Age at first apparition: 11
Status: Living

Name: Tarcisio DiBiasi (male)
Birth: Unknown
Age at first apparition: 16
Status: Living

Name: Mafalda Mattia Caputo (female)
Birth: Unknown
Age at first apparition: Unknown
Status: Living

Name: Antonia Ianecce (female)
Birth: May 3, 1974
Age at first apparition: 11
Status: Living

Note: An additional thirty or so people have been recorded by name at the parish as having received one or more messages. Some were pilgrims or tourists, others were just bystanders.

IV Total Number of Apparitions - 57

It is reported that Our Lady appeared hundreds, perhaps thousands of times, to hundreds of people. Not everyone received messages who reportedly saw Our Lady.

Of the ten seers identified above (section III), following are the reported number of apparitions; although it is further reported that these ten seers had many more apparitions which are not reported.

(1) Dino - 3
(2) Carmine - 3
(3) Anita - 4
(4) Sabrina - 6
(5) Marco - 6
(6) Umberto - 1
(7) Antonella - 4
(8) Tarcisio - 13
(9) Mafalda - 14
(10) Antonia - 3

Total: 57

V Dates and Locality of Each Apparition

(All apparition locations were at the gate of the castle unless otherwise noted).

Dino
1985: May 24; August 24, 25.
Carmine
1985: May 24; August 24, 25.
Anita
1985: May 24; 25 (seer's home), 28; August 5.
1988: January 1.
Sabrina
1985: June; November 13.
1986: February 2, 3.
1987: November 6.
1988: December 20.
Marco
1985: (Balcony).
1987: July 4.
1988: April 15; September 17; December 20.
1989: January 9.
Umberto
1985: June 2.

Antonella
1985: June 1.
1986: June 24; July 19; September 8.
Tarcisio
1985: May 24; December 15, 20.
1986: January 17; February 1; April 4, 12, 14; May 1, 7; June 5, 12.
1988: December.
Mafalda
1985: May 24; September 19; October 26; November 2; December 15.
1986: January 10; February 11; April; June 12, 13, 15, 16, 30; July 1.
Antonia
1985: Autumn.
1987: May 3; June.

VI Description of Our Lady

The most consistent description of Our Lady is of a young woman of indescribable beauty, dressed in a white robe, and wearing a blue mantle with a filigree gold border. A crown of stars encircled Her head. She carried an Infant in Her right arm. The Infant held a rosary in His hands. Some reported She was standing on a white cloud and a bright light came from Our Lady and descended on everyone at the gate.

VII Title(s) of Our Lady - 4

(1) On August 25, 1985 in answer to a question, Our Lady said: "*I am Our Lady of Consolation.*"

(2) On another occasion Our Lady said: "*I am the Madonna of the Castle.*"

(3) Our Lady revealed Herself to seer Renato Baron as: "*The Queen of Love.*"

(4) "*Our Lady of Graces*", thus Our Lady responded to a question from Dino Acquaviva on August 24, 1985.

VIII Brief Factual Review

Oliveto Citra is a small town of some 3,500 souls located in southern Italy near the city of Salerno.

In 1980, an earthquake damaged many houses as well as the local parish church named 'Our Lady of Mercy'. Across from the church stands an old castle built in 1145, which is locked and closed to visitors. An old stone stairway leads from the little square (Piazza Garibaldi) up to the fence and iron gate of the castle, which is now padlocked. This area near the gate is the site of the first and some of the later apparitions of Our Lady.

Today one can observe rosaries hanging from the bushes inside the gate, having been placed there by pilgrims, tourists or seers.

Oliveto Citra lies in the diocese of Campagna. At the time of the apparitions, the pastor of the parish was Monsignor Giuseppe Amato, affectionately known as "Don Peppino." Archbishop Guerino Grimaldi headed the Archdiocese of Salerno.

In May 1985, just before the apparitions, the voters elected a communist mayor and nearly all communists to the town council.

May 24th is the Feast Day of Saint Marcarius, the patron saint of Oliveto Citra. Many people had gathered at the square to celebrate the Feast Day which had taken the form of a civil, rather than a religious Feast Day because of the laxity of the people.

Twelve boys, ages 10-12, were playing in the square. They apparently got to the edge of the square nearer to the castle, when suddenly they heard a baby crying. The baby's voice came from inside the locked gate of the castle. Several of the boys were alarmed and ran back and forth to the square. One of the boys threw a rock. Again they ran off but returned right away.

It was then that some of the boys saw a light and the shape of a woman (with a child in her arms). This frightened the boys who again ran to the square but now went into the Ianecce Bar and reported what they saw. A barmaid named Anita Rio was curious. She followed the boys back to the gate. When she got to the gate she saw the apparition and described it as a young woman of indescribable beauty. Anita was frightened; however, Our Lady beckoned her with Her free hand and spoke: *"You will see Me at night."*

This so upset Anita that she was taken to a hospital that night where the doctor who examined her declared her to be healthy in body and mind. Anita saw the apparition and received messages several times thereafter, the last being in January 1988.

Some of the original twelve boys who saw Our Lady also received messages. Others, including residents of Oliveto Citra, tourists and pilgrims also claimed to have seen Our Lady. Some of these persons also received messages.

The thrust of the messages received, stress that we must pray, pray, pray! Especially the rosary. Prayer, penance, and conversion! She warns us that the world has lost its sense of the spiritual and that we must return to God or face sufferings. We are to pray for priests, for sinners, and for the conversion of mankind.

Our Lady asked that a chapel be built near the gate. This has been accomplished with a statue visible through the window displaying Our Lady as She appeared with the Christ Child in Her arms. This statue is made of multicolored marble, sculpted by artist Ludovico Bertoni.

Many healings and conversions are reported. People also report signs and wonders such as an intense red cloud which descended onto the castle. The Miracle of the Sun has been reported by many as well as an aroma of roses.

Our Lady gave secrets to some of the seers. The contents are not reported. All those who had seen or are now seeing Our Lady regularly, fast on Fridays and say the rosary every day. Many of these people meet every Saturday to pray together and to receive instructions for the growth of their spiritual life especially through personal prayer.

Albino Coglianesi, a middle aged man, was inspired to write the words to a hymn 'Queen of the Castle' which is regularly sung at the gate. He is on the Parish Committee for the Apparitions, though he had previously been chairman of the local Socialist Party.

The pastor, "Don Peppino" at first did not believe. He now believes that Our Lady has come to Oliveto Citra; but that She is not necessarily seen by all who claim to see Her. He takes written statements from persons who claim to have had an apparition and keeps these records. In April 1987 he blessed the new chapel next to the castle gate.

The archbishop has appointed a diocesan bishop to look into these matters. No decision is reported and the Church has not officially approved these apparitions or messages.

Monsignor Francino Spaduzzi, Vicar General of the Archdiocese of Salerno and a member of the commission, forbids priests and religious to bring pilgrims to Oliveto Citra, or to say Mass outdoors without the permission of the archbishop. It may be a long time before a decision is announced by the Church, either approving or disapproving these happenings.

Now we can look at the individual seers:

Dino Acquaviva and Carmine Acquaviva - These fifteen-year-old twin boys were part of the original twelve who first saw the apparition on May 24, 1985. They came to Oliveto Citra from Chicago in 1984 with their family. They speak both English and Italian. They both saw Our Lady that first night and described Her as dressed in white with a blue mantle and holding a baby in Her arms. Our Lady's first words were: *"Peace to you, children."* Dino, however, claims to have also seen the devil (or the head of the devil) just under Our Lady's feet. This frightened him.

Both Dino and Carmine continued to see Our Lady frequently at the castle gate. On August 24, 1985 Our Lady responded when Dino asked who She was by saying: *"I am Our Lady of Graces."* Thereafter, the twins have seen Our Lady two or three times a year.

Anita Rio - She was the barmaid who went to the gate with the twelve boys on May 24, 1985 and saw Our Lady that day. She said she went back to the gate several times that night and saw Our Lady before they took this seer to the hospital.

Anita was twenty-four, married, with a two-year-old daughter, named Sara. On the night after the first apparition May 25, 1985 Our Lady appeared to Anita in her own home. Thereafter, Anita saw Our Lady many times at the gate. She received messages. Our Lady requested prayer and also that a chapel be built. This request for a chapel was repeated during other apparitions.

Our Lady identified Herself as: *"Our Madonna of the Castle,"* and also gave the seer some secrets.

On May 28 Anita saw Our Lady and smelled sweet perfume. On August 5, 1985 Our Lady appeared to Anita dressed in shining gold, carrying roses, and announced that: *"Today is a day to celebrate, it's My birthday."* Since January 1988 Anita has not seen Our Lady.

In all, Anita was to receive thirty apparitions with messages concerning prayer, penance and fasting.

Sabrina DeBellis and Marco DeBellis - These two are sister and brother. Marco was eleven and Sabrina, thirteen. They lived in Oliveto Citra with their parents Agostino and Anna and little brother Andrea.

Marco first saw Our Lady in 1985 on the balcony of his family's apartment. She stood on a small cloud with the Child in Her arms. Since then Marco has seen Our Lady nearly every day. Our Lady has given messages to Marco asking him to be simple, humble, and obedient. She asks for prayer and says: *". . . The world stands already at the edge of the abyss . . ."*

On December 20, 1988 She told Marco: *"If you continue to follow the path you are on, the gates of Paradise will be open."* Marco last saw Our Lady on January 9, 1989.

Marco has also seen angels and claims the devil tried to pull him out of bed. The devil disappears when Marco swings the rosary at him. Marco has also received secrets from Our Lady.

Both Marco and Sabrina say the rosary every day.

Sabrina, on the other hand, first saw Our Lady in June 1985 at the gate of the castle. The vision lasted several hours. A man gave Sabrina three questions to ask of Our Lady. These were in German, although Sabrina does not speak German, Our Lady answered in Italian and requested that we *"Pray! Pray! Pray!"*

On November 13, 1985 Sabrina saw Our Lady and received a five point message in which Our Lady asked for prayer and that a chapel be built here. Our Lady appeared to this seer several other times, the last being on December 20, 1988 when Our Lady said: *"Have faith even when you do not see Me; I will stay close to you and give you signs that I am present next to you."*

In other messages Our Lady warns us that Satan is getting stronger and, therefore, we must pray more. Her central message is prayer and penance.

Their father, Dr. Agostino, saw Our Lady on July 20, 1985. Also, their little brother, Andrea, tells his family that he sees Our Lady. Their mother, Anna, has never seen Our Lady, but she sees a light at the castle every day and thinks it is Our Lady (or a sign).

Umberto Gagliardi - Umberto operates an Alfa-Romeo garage on the east edge of Oliveto Citra, and lives in an apartment in the same building with his wife and three teenage children.

Until June 1985 Umberto did not practice his Catholic faith. He went to Mass once a year. Although he heard about the apparitions in May, he was not interested. Then on June 2, 1985 he went to the square on his way to the pharmacy when suddenly he saw a luminous cloud in the shape of a woman. He was shocked. After that he went to the little square in the evenings. There he clearly saw Our Lady. She spoke to him and gave him messages and some secrets too. He has received predictions which he says have always come true. The main messages this seer received were for prayer and conversion.

Although not everyone believes that he sees Our Lady, his life has changed dramatically. He goes to Mass every Sunday, prays every day, says the rosary with his family at home and tries to live differently and to do no wrong to anyone. He claims he has seen Jesus four times.

Antonella Giordano - She was born August 5, 1973 to a poor family. She did not believe in the apparitions when she first heard of them in May 1985. Nonetheless, she went to the gate with her own mother a few days later. It was on June 1, 1985 that this seer first saw Our Lady at the gate. She was dressed in black, (as Our Lady of Sorrows), Her hands were joined and She was kneeling. After that the seer saw Our Lady many times, always dressed in white. She received a message during the first apparition to pray and to fast on Fridays.

Antonella sees Our Lady often, especially when she goes to the castle, which is about twice a month. Our Lady has given her three secrets and Our Lady will tell her when to reveal these secrets.

The messages given to this seer ask for prayer, especially the rosary, and prayer for others.

It is reported that in her own life, Antonella has remarkable spiritual maturity. She prays regularly, contemplatively, says the rosary daily, and fasts on Fridays.

Tarcisio DiBiasi - This seer is sixteen and lives in Oliveto Citra with his mother, grandmother, and his brother.

He was one of the original twelve boys who first saw Our Lady on May 24, 1985. He describes Her just as the others did. Our Lady's first words to him were: *"Pray!"* Then She smiled and said She had come to Oliveto Citra because there was so little faith. Tarcisio documented many of the apparitions and messages and gave them to the pastor. Some messages are personal to him. She tells him not to be discouraged and also that it is okay to choose to be a priest or choose to get married. The primary messages to this seer are for prayer, especially for others, and that many calamities and chastisements are coming. Some we can ward off with prayer.

He has been shown heaven and purgatory. On December 15, 1985 Our Lady said to him: *"Tell the pilgrims that I do not need flowers and candles, that I need prayers because the time left before the catastrophe is very short."*

He states that his life has been changed. Among other things, he stays away from boys who are bad company, and he thinks of a lot of ways he can help others. His neighbor's sufferings now become his own sufferings. Before the apparitions he did not go to church and he blasphemed. Now that has all changed.

Mafalda Mattia - This seer lives with her husband Eliseo and her son Vincenzo, one of the twelve boys who first saw Our Lady on May 24, 1985. They also have an adult daughter named Antonella.

From the very beginning Mafalda believed when her son told her that he had seen Our Lady. She went to the little square every evening to say the rosary, hoping she would see Our Blessed Mother. One night in June she did see a sign (a light that came towards her).

However, it was not till September 19, 1985 that this seer had her first apparition of Our Lady. On this first occasion Our Lady slowly emerged from the light wearing a grey gown and black mantle. She did not speak. Later on October 26, 1985 Our Lady again appeared, this time dressed in white, hands joined in prayer and holding a rosary. Mafalda, herself, was then praying the rosary.

Our Lady's message was to pray, to pray for the leaders of nations, for they have power in their hands but they don't pray. Also to pray for our brothers and sisters who suffer hunger. On October 29, 1985 Our Lady requested a chapel be built.

On January 10, 1986 Our Lady gave Mafalda a message for all humanity. Our Lady pleads with us for prayer, that time is short, that there will be earthquakes, disasters, and famines for the people on earth, that we must save ourselves with much prayer, by doing penance and by conversion.

Then, finally, on February 11, 1986 Our Lady urgently warned: *"... Do not ask, but be converted, and pray much; mankind is sliding toward a frightening precipice. Therefore, pray, do penance, and be converted..."*

Mafalda herself prays much, several hours a day, says the rosary and goes to daily Mass.

Antonia Ianecce - This seer is eleven and is a friend of Marco DeBellis. It is reported that she often has ecstasies during which she sees Mary or Jesus. On her birthday anniversary, May 3, 1987 Our Lady appeared to her and told Antonia that she was born in *"My month"* (May).

It is further reported that she received six secrets for the world, four for her family, and ten about her own future. She will not reveal any of them.

IX The Primary Messages - 3

(1) **Prayer** - Nearly every message given to nearly every person who claimed to receive messages, contained a plea for prayer. This was often stated as: *"Pray! Pray! Pray!"* (Thus a June 1985 message to Sabrina).

Again on June 13, 1986 Our Lady pleaded with Mafalda: *"I beg you; pray, pray, pray that their hearts be awakened from living in sin."*

Then to Tarcisio on May 7, 1986: *". . . Your prayer should not be only the rosary; your days should be a continuous prayer made up of good works, of love towards others and penance . . ."*

(2) **Rosary** - Again many of the messages to the identified seers and to others who claimed to have received messages contain exhortations to pray the rosary.

April 4, 1986 to Tarcisio, Our Lady said: *". . .When you recite the rosary you should think that in each mystery there is contained all the love and suffering of My Son and of Myself for all of you."*

Then to Mafalda on July 1, 1986: *"My children pray much and protect yourself by the recitation of the rosary."*

(3) **Penance** - July 10, 1986 to Sabrina: *"Pray, pray much for the sick, console the afflicted, and do penance."*

April 1986 Our Lady said to Mafalda: *"The threefold way to save yourselves from sin and punishment is: prayer, conversion, and penance."*

X Signs Preceding the Apparitions

A light is often reported preceding the vision of Our Lady at the gate. Not only have the identified seers so reported but also some pilgrims and tourists who claimed to have seen Our Lady have also claimed to see this light.

XI Other Visions During Apparitions

(1) Several of the seers also had apparitions of Jesus.
(2) Marco sometimes sees angels.
(3) Some of the seers were shown heaven, hell, and purgatory.
(4) Some of the seers have seen and have been tormented by the devil, as reported.

XII Prayers Taught to the Seer(s)

On February 8, 1986 Our Lady dictated a prayer to Sabrina:
Prayer:
Mother in heaven, have mercy on us.
We love You and we offer ourselves to You.
Protect us from evil.

Take care of us Mother in heaven and help us in all our problems. Mary, Queen of the Castle, lead us to heaven. Amen.

XIII Special Devotion Given to the Seer(s) - NR

XIV Requests Made by Our Lady

It is reported that Our Lady requested that we fast on Fridays.

XV Specific Bible References - Not Reported

XVI Secrets Given to the Seer(s)

Secrets were reported given by Our Lady to several of these seers: Anita, Marco, Umberto, Antonella, and Antonia.

XVII Miracles Promised by Our Lady - NR
XVIII Miracles Performed - Not Reported
XIX Miracles Promised not yet Performed - NR

XX Signs Promised

It was reported that the Madonna would give a sign on July 20, 1985. On that day about 2,000 pilgrims gathered. The visionaries announced that everyone would see the sign; and very soon they saw a luminous red cloud descend onto the castle. This red cloud was seen by many as far away as 10 kilometers.

XXI Signs Given

(1) The sign promised for July 20, 1985 was given (red cloud).
(2) There were reports by different people of sweet fragrances. A cross which had been damaged was reported giving off sweet odors.
(3) An invisible, but audible choir, taught Mafalda the melody to the hymn "Queen of the Castle". This occurred on October 19, 1985 at 8:45 PM.
(4) There were reports from various sources that on November 24, 1985 many people witnessed the 'Miracle of the Sun'.

XXII Predictions/Promises

(1) Our Lady told Anita that she would see Our Lady at night. And, true to form, Our Lady did appear to Anita the next night and also on other nights.

(2) A sign was promised for July 20, 1985. The red cloud appeared as the sign.

XXIII Prophecies/Warnings of Chastisement

(1) On January 10, 1986 Our Lady told Mafalda: *"The time left for you to pray is very short. There will be earthquakes, famines, and punishments for all the inhabitants of earth."*

(2) On another occasion, Our Lady warned: *"If people do not accept My plea for prayer, penance and conversion, terrible misfortunes will fall on the world, and with it the adults and the children also will be overturned."*

(3) On December 15, 1985 Our Lady told Tarcisio: *"You should tell the pilgrims that I do not need flowers and candles. Let them pray, for the time remaining before the chastisements is short."*

XXIV Method of Appearance - Not Reported
XXV Method of Departure - Not Reported

XXVI Confrontation w/Civil Authorities

The one 'civil' confrontation reported comes from an American-financed Pentecostal church (known as the 'Evangelicals') who, from time to time, come to the little square-gate area to heckle and shout abuses trying to drown out the Catholics who sing at the gate.

XXVII Confrontation w/Church Authorities

At first Monsignor Amato, the pastor of the parish of Oliveto Citra, was skeptical; but now he believes Our Lady does appear (at least to some of the claimed seers). It also appears that Archbishop Grimaldi is skeptical; yet he has appointed a commission to investigate.

Monsignor Spaduzzi, a member of the commission, forbids priests and religious to organize or accompany pilgrimages to Oliveto Citra, or to conduct outdoor Masses without the permission of the archbishop.

XXVIII Request Chapel/Shrine Built

Anita and several of the other seers received requests from Our Lady to have a small chapel built near the gate. The chapel has been built and was dedicated by Don Peppino.

XXIX Free Will/Choice - Not Reported

XXX Seer(s)' Suffering/Sacrifice - Not Reported

XXXI Healings Reported

(1) Monsignor Amato has remarked on the fruits manifested by way of conversions and cures.
(2) Several physical healings are reported. Two cases reported were of eye diseases that were cured.
(3) A seven year old boy from Naples, named Salvatore Grillo, was diagnosed on February 26, 1986 as "almost completely deaf". After praying to Our Lady of the Castle for a cure, the boy was cured. This was confirmed by his doctor on March 6, 1986.
(4) It is reported that an unusual number of young people addicted to drugs have been completely cured.

XXXII Action Taken by the Church

The chapel requested by Our Lady has been built and blessed and dedicated by "Don Peppino".

A commission has been appointed by Archbishop Grimaldi to investigate these matters.

Meanwhile, priests and religious are restrained from forming or accompanying pilgrims to the apparition site or to say Mass outdoors without the permission of the archbishop.

No decision has been made by the Church. The reports indicate it may be a long wait until a decision is made by the Church.

Meanwhile, pilgrims keep coming to Oliveto Citra. The rosary is prayed, the singing and other activities continue and hopefully the good fruits will become even more pronounced.

XXXIII Bibliography

Mary Among Us 1989
By: Fr. R. Faricy, SJ., and L. Pecoraio
Published by: Franciscan University Press

Oliveto Citra (Land of Mary)
Translated by: Sr. C. Metallo
Published by: Provincialate-Villa Rossello

Chapter 45

NAJU, KOREA
(1985-1994)

I Place - Naju, Korea

II Dates of First and Last Apparition

First: July 18, 1985
Last: February 3, 1994 (last reported)
Note: The apparitions are reportedly ongoing.

III Seer(s) - 1

Name: Julia Kim (in Korean - *Hong-Sun Yoon*)
Birth: 1947
Age at first apparition: 38
Status: Living

IV Total Number of Apparitions - 83

(Through February 3, 1994)

V Dates and Locality of Each Apparition

(All locutions and apparitions occured in the seer's home Chapel unless otherwise noted.)

1985: July 18; August 11.

1986: September 15; October 19, 20, 21, 22, 23, 24, 29, and 31; November 5.
1987: February 13, 25; March 13; April 18, 21, 23; May 12, 17; June 13, 14, 15, 27, 29, 30; July 15; August 11; October 19; December 11.
1988: January, 1, 10, 30 (AM) and (PM); February 4; June 5; July 24, 27, 29; November 6; December 8.
1989: January 8, 15, 29 (AM) and (PM); February 23; August 26, 29; October 14; November 26, 27.
1990: February 14; May 8; June 30; July 21, 30; August 15; October 4; November 11.
1991: January 29; March 10, 25; April 21; May 8, 16; August 27; September 17; October 19; November 4, 26; 28 at the site of the Basilica; December 5 at the site of the Basilica.
1992: February 11 (Manila, Philippines); May 31 (Lourdes, France).
1993: January 23; February 6 & 18; April 8 & 14; May 27 & June 27 (all in Naju, Korea).
1994: January 21 & February 3 (Naju, Korea).

VI Description of Our Lady

(1) Usually the statue of Our Lady (that wept) would suddenly become the living Blessed Mother. She wore a white dress with a white mantle stretching from head to feet. The hems of Her mantle were sparkling gold. She was about 5'5" tall, extremely beautiful and holding a rosary in Her right (sometimes left) hand. Sometimes She wore a sparkling laurel crown and carried the Baby Jesus. At other times (June 5, 1988), Her burning Immaculate Heart was red and looked like it was moving. Seven swords pierced Her Heart.

(2) On January 21, 1994 Our Lady wore a crown of 12 stars, a white dress with a blue mantle. She was holding a rosary in Her right hand.

VII Title(s) of Our Lady - Not Reported

VIII Brief Factual Review

The country of Korea is a peninsula located on the continent of Asia, and jutting out from mainland China, which is on Korea's northern border. The island empire of Japan is located directly east of Korea, across the Sea of Japan.

Naju is located near the southwestern tip of South Korea, about 200 miles south of its capital, Seoul. The population of Naju is about 80,000. Naju, written in Chinese characters, means "The Town of Silk."

The Catholic faith in Korea began in the 18th Century, brought from

China by some Korean scholars. In the 19th century Catholics were brutally persecuted. About 10,000 Catholics (including some French missionary priests) were tortured and martyred during the 19th Century. More than 100 of them were canonized in 1984 by Pope John Paul II.

Korea itself suffered much during the last 100 years, from foreign occupation, war, communist oppression and finally division of the country at the 38th parallel into North and South Korea.

When these apparitions began, the pastor of the Naju Parish (Holy Rosary) was Fr. Park (later Fr. Lazarus Lee became pastor). The Naju Parish belongs to the Kwangju Archdiocese, headed by Archbishop Gong-Hee Victorinus Yoon.

Fr. Raymond Spies, a Belgian missionary, is Julia's spiritual director and has her under obedience. At the request of Fr. Spies, Julia has kept a diary since January 1987.

Julia Kim was born in 1947. She is married to Julio Youn and is the mother of four children. Her full Korean name is Hong-Sun Yoon. The entire family was converted to Catholicism and were all baptized together on Easter Sunday, 1981.

Julia suffered much pain and many physical ailments since about 1976. Her friend Lubino had been suffering from bronchitis and asked Julia to pray for her cure. They prayed together for three days, after which Lubino was healed. As a gesture of appreciation, Lubino gave Julia a plaster statue of Our Blessed Mother. It is this same statue that began to weep tears on June 30, 1985 (and later, also tears of blood) for a total of 700 days from June 30, 1985 to April 6, 1992.

The tears of blood first started on October 19, 1986 and the last reported tears of blood occurred on March 25, 1991. Our Blessed Mother has revealed to the seer that She appears weeping tears and blood because She wants to show the human race and the Church Her sufferings caused by the many people who are in the state of grave sin which will provoke an imminent worldwide chastisement and bring many to eternal damnation if we do not quickly return to God, and implore His forgiveness and change our lives.

On July 18, 1985 Julia began to have apparitions of Our Lady. These generally occurred after Julia went into a "chapel room" in her own residence where the statue was kept. While Julia was praying, usually the rosary, the statue would come alive and Julia would go into ecstasy, then receive messages from Our Lady. Various clergy and others witnessed the ecstasies. The messages continued at least until February 3, 1994 and are perhaps ongoing. There is no indication that the visions and messages have ended or that they will continue.

Julia also had visions of Jesus and messages from Him. She also saw St. Andrew Kim, the first Korean priest and patron saint of Korea. In addition, she had visions of angels as well as of the devil. The devil tormented and physically abused her on some occasions. The last reported abusive encounter with the devil occurred on January 21, 1994.

On October 3, 1991 another phenomenon began to happen when a fragrant oil began to flow from the statue. This phenomenon reportedly continues even though the tears have ceased as of January 14, 1992.

Julia has suffered the wounds of Christ's Passion and received the Stigmata on at least four occasions: October 19, 1987, January 29, 1988, February 4, 1988, and January 29, 1989.

In addition to these sufferings, Julia also suffers as a victim soul for the babies that are aborted and for those causing the abortions. On July 27, 1988 Julia suffered not only the actual physical suffering of a woman giving birth, but also the suffering of the unborn child struggling against being put to death. She took the fetal position and rolled around the floor for hours. People present witnessed this and tried to help her. She screamed and begged while being the actual fetus: "Mommy! Mommy! Let me live!" Four times Julia underwent this ordeal. Our Blessed Mother only permitted this suffering after the seer agreed to it. Our Blessed Mother said: *"By your sufferings, many souls will be converted."* Then on July 29, 1988 Our Blessed Mother said: *". . . today 5,000 souls will convert and be offered to the Lord, thanks to your suffering."*

The messages urge us to pray, to pray for priests, to love and forgive one another, to do penance and sacrifice for the conversion of sinners. She also warned the world of an impending severe chastisement. It is to be inflicted on mankind due to the grievous sins committed unless we promptly convert, return to God and change our life-style drastically. She told us confession is a necessity and we are to have love and respect for Holy Communion. Our Lady told the seer (reminiscent of Akita, Japan): *"If one continues to accommodate to the things of the world without seeking those of heaven, then even if one repents, it will be too late."*

She also warned that Her priests must accept Her messages promptly: *"It is necessary that My beloved priests accept them promptly in order to prevent the chastisements which are going to follow."* And also: *". . . It is urgent that people put the messages into practice. . ."* (December 11, 1987).

Julia was also shown heaven, hell and purgatory. Our Lady requested a Basilica be built and even showed Julia the place where it was to be constructed.

Many phenomena are reported such as the 'Miracle of the Sun', the fragrance of roses, and other signs. In addition, a "Miracle of the Eucharist" occurred on four occasions: twice in Naju, once in Lanciano, Italy, and once in Rome. In each case the Host which Julia received at Communion bled inside her mouth profusely. These cases were witnessed inside the church by clergy and others. It is later reported that the miracle of the Eucharist has subsequently occurred three times in 1994.

Our Lady asked Julia to *"dig a spring here and I will invite all to come and drink from the Miraculous Spring of Mary's Ark of the Covenant."* This location is near Julia's home in Naju.

Although there is no final Church action as to the visions and messages, all the clergy connected with these happenings are reported to be very favorable. In July 1989 Archbishop Yoon stated to the gathered clergy that the fact of the tears is uncontestable. He further said that he was examining the fruits and he was asking Fr. Spies to keep him updated. Meanwhile, he would not prevent the messages from being distributed nor would he discourage pilgrims from praying before the statue.

Father Gobbi has visited Julia at Naju as has Fr. Laurentin. Julia traveled to Manila and met with Cardinal Sin. She has also traveled to Rome, and in 1992 Julia gave the Holy Father a replica of the weeping statue. She has traveled to other places to spread Our Lady's messages; namely, Japan and the USA.

There seems to be no negative feedback reported. The events are recent (and perhaps even current) yet there is a flow of optimism. We must await the Church's decision.

IX The Primary Messages - 5

(1) Prayer - Our Lady exhorts us to prayer in many of the messages, and urges us to pray for priests, peace, love, and the prevention of abortions.

July 18, 1985: *"Pray for the prevention of abortion and for those who carry out abortions."*

August 11, 1985: *"Pray for priests without ceasing."*

September 15, 1986: *"Pray without ceasing for the souls that are not turning away from the road leading to their perdition."*

April 18, 1987: *"Also pray for peace in this country and for the end of abortion."*

January 30, 1988: *"Now you must pray for the conversion of sinners and pray the rosary more fervently for peace in this country and in the world."*

October 14, 1989: *"Pray and offer sacrifices and reparations constantly for the Pope, the cardinals, bishops and priests."*

February 18, 1993: *"The prayers, sacrifices, and devotions offered for the conversion of sinners during the Holy Hours become reparations for their sins and sacrificial offerings to God's Justice."*

(2) Rosary - Our Lady often appeared with a rosary in Her hand, which gesture itself strongly urges and invites us to pray the rosary.

July 18, 1985: *"Pray the rosary all over the world for the prevention of wars and the conversion of sinners. This is your weapon."*

October 23, 1986: *"Offer more rosaries and sacrifices for world peace and human salvation."*

January 1, 1988: *"As I told you before, the rosary defeats devils. Tell* all the faithful to offer five more decades daily. If they pray the rosary for unity of this country, it will be saved from a calamity."

January 30, 1988: *"Now you must pray for the conversion of sinners and pray the rosary more fervently for peace in this country and in the world."*

Then on April 21, 1991 Our Lady said: *"I want all of you to wear the scapular with the intention of being with Me; pray the rosary fervently with all your body and mind and with love; live a completely consecrated life of prayers, sacrifices, and reparation."*

(3) Penance, Sacrifice and Reparation - October 20, 1986: *". . .You must offer prayers combined with sacrifices and self-denial, and also offer up poverty and penance gracefully."*

March 13, 1987: *Live a consecrated life filled with constant prayers, sacrifices, penance, and love."*

June 14, 1987: *"Even when you get pains from others, give them peace. Through sacrifice and penance do the things that can benefit them."*

January 1,1988: *". . . offer penances and prayers - make reparations for the sins of those who do wrong unknowingly."*

August 29, 1989: *"Pray, make sacrifices and do penance with a greater love in this time of darkness."*

January 21, 1994: *". . . Even if you suffer from persecutions and pains that are beyond imagination, I will help you at your side by amazing methods and will carry through My plan to the end and accomplish it."*

February 3, 1994: *". . . Now I want to combine all your prayers, sacrifices, penances, consecrations, self-denials, poverty and sufferings together, put them in the cup of My Immaculate Heart and offer them up to God's Justice which demands reparation."*

(4) Forgive and Love One Another - July 18, 1985: *". . . My Son becomes broken hearted when they hate each other and are unable to forgive each other; you must love one another . . . How can you say you love God and love Me when you cannot even love those in your family? Sanctify your family through love and harmony. This is what My Son Jesus thirsts for."*

March 13, 1987: *"There cannot be peace in the world because families are getting sick. The couples combined together to live a happy life are becoming isolated individuals, as they are unable to forgive and love each other and are becoming jealous, resentful and hateful of each other. My daughter see how serious family troubles are."*

Then on November 5, 1986 Our Lady said: *"Achieve unity by loving one another. I want you to trust each other, be respectful and faithful to each other, and fulfill your duties."*

(5) Avoid Satan's Influence - April 23, 1987 Our Lady asked that we pray for priests *"that they will not be infected with the world, but instead be faithful to their vocations."* Then She further said: *"This age is very evil* and filled with errors, and because of this, devils are so active and are employing all means to destroy priests."

January 30, 1988: "Because I called you to be apostles of My Immaculate Heart, devils will become more active and tempt you. Hold My hand tightly so that you may not fall into temptations."

November 11, 1990: "In this age, devils corrupt so many people's conscience, making them commit sins of impurity, even leading to murders; destroy human dignity by abortions, drag them into errors and all kinds of sins, such as corruption, injustice, curses, violent words, hatred, and revenge; and make them walk the way of selfishness. How sorrowful My Son feels when He sees all these children!"

On August 27, 1991 Our Blessed Mother said: "Now is the time for purification, but many children are confused because of the words that are not from God. My enemy, the devil, is promoting confusion and division at many places in the world by deceiving people with tricks and even by using supernatural phenomena . . . you must pray and love more fervently so that everyone can avoid condemnation and be saved. I will help you."

September 17, 1991: "The devil does his work through humans. Thus he employs all kinds of ways and means in using people around us to make us angry, resentful, unable to forgive and commit many mistakes; the good and the evil always coexist inside you, because your guardian angel and the devil confront each other; the angel helping you to do good and the devil afflicting you and tempting you to do evil all the time . . . Therefore, do not give a chance to the devil. Arm yourself with love and win the victory!"

May 27, 1993: "How corrupt and polluted this world is! Because people join forces with the devil through their pride, they, even without realizing themselves, become wolves that wear a sheep's skin and commit all kinds of blunders habitually, and drive numerous sheep into confusion. For this reason I want to call the souls who have been contaminated with these evils and are walking toward hell to My bosom of love and fill all their deficiencies."

January 21, 1944: "In this time of purification, so many children forget about the graces they have received, listen to false testimonies concocted by Satan, sidetrack from My way, and judge, criticize and condemn it. Because Satan is employing all the available means like false information and some supernatural phenomena even innocent people are being mislead. . ."

Then again Our Lady speaks: ". . .When you confront the devil and lead many souls to My Immaculate Heart, you are leading them to My Son. . ."

X Signs Preceding the Apparitions

On some occasions a light similar to sunlight was shining from the weeping statue. Then the statue seemed to turn into the living Blessed Mother and She began speaking to Julia.

XI Other Visions During Apparitions

(1) Jesus appeared to Julia several times, the first of which was on June 5, 1988. Jesus also gave messages to the seer. The last reported apparition of Jesus was on January 26, 1993 when He said: *"It is not too late yet. Come to My Bosom of Love in a hurry. If you repent hurriedly and come back to Me saying 'Yes' I will not question your past, but embrace you in My Sacred Heart . . ."*
(2) On October 24, 1986 she saw Fr. Andrew Kim while in ecstasy. He was the first Korean priest to be martyred. He was canonized in 1984.
(3) On June 30, 1990 Julia saw the Holy Spirit in the shape of a dove, who then shed light on all those present at the prayer meeting.
(4) Julia saw angels flying over her (February 25, 1987). Once she saw many angels dancing and heard music (September 17, 1991).
(5) On July 24, 1988 Julia was shown heaven, hell and purgatory.
(6) Satan appeared to Julia on more than one occasion. On some occasions he physically attacked the seer and also tried to persuade her to follow him and abandon her relationship with her spiritual director, Fr. Spies. Of course, Julia refused the devil's temptations. The last reported attacks occurred on January 21, 1994.
(7) Photographs taken by the seer and others showed the Host and Chalice which were not present on the scene when the picture was taken.

XII Prayers Taught to the Seer(s) - Not Reported

XIII Special Devotion Given to the Seer(s)

Although no new devotions are reported, yet Our Blessed Mother said if we observe the Five First Saturdays as She requested, She will secure all graces necessary for salvation (February 6, 1993).

XIV Requests Made by Our Lady

(1) On June 15, 1987 Our Lady said to Julia: *"Make a constant effort to blind Satan. On Thursdays offer reparations to the Blessed Sacrament."*
(2) On several occasions She requested that Her messages be made known. On November 27, 1989 Our Blessed Mother urgently said: *"... therefore, I demand that My messages be spread fast. When My messages are accepted by the Church and put into practice, the just anger of God will be softened, order and truth will be restored and the devils, who instigate confusion and cause winds, will be defeated."*

(3) On November 26, 1991 Our Lady requested that Julia: *"Dig a spring here and I will invite all to come and drink from the Miraculous Spring of Mary's Ark of Salvation in order to convert even the most evil of sinners."*

XV Specific Bible References

Although no specific references are reported, nonetheless, on May 16, 1991 Jesus told Julia: *". . . stay close to the Bible which contains the Sacred Truths, lead a life according to the Gospels . . ."*

XVI Secrets Given to the Seer(s) - Not Reported
XVII Miracles Promised by Our Lady - NR

XVIII Miracles Performed

The Miracle of the Eucharist occurred on four separate occasions to Julia prior to 1994.

(1) May 16, 1991 Julia received the Sacred Host during a Mass celebrated at the Naju church by two priests from the Philippines. Blood came from the Host inside Julia's mouth. This was witnessed not only by the two priests but also by scores of lay people.

(2) June 5, 1988, the Feast Day of Corpus Christi, Julia had been sick but put up with her suffering in order to attend Mass. When she received the Host and as she was standing, supported by two friends who helped her come to church, she felt her mouth being filled with blood. She also smelled blood. She felt as if she was floating on air, then Jesus spoke to her.

(3) June 1, 1992 Julia attended Mass in Rome, Italy in her hotel. Again, when she received Holy Communion, she smelled blood. The priest and Julia's husband saw the Host bleeding inside her mouth. Once again Jesus spoke to her.

(4) June 2, 1992 Julia, her husband, and Fr. Orbos (one of the Philippino priests who witnessed the earlier Miracle of the Eucharist in Naju) attended Mass in Lanciano, Italy, (the site of a Eucharistic Miracle 1,500 years ago) that to this day the Host that had changed into human heart muscle and human blood remains visible and intact. The Host and Blood are preserved inside the church at Lanciano.

When Julia received the Host during Mass she swallowed it, but a tiny piece of the Host remained on her tongue and began growing. She showed her husband. Then many people watched as the Host grew inside Julia's mouth and became bloody. Once again Jesus spoke to her: *"I am the Light. I am the Light of Love that chases away all darkness. I intend to let all of you receive My Light of Love and thus to*

repel the darkness in this world that is turning into a vast desert."
(5) The Miracle of the Eucharist occurred three times in 1994 as later reported.

XIX Miracles Promised not yet Performed - NR
XX Signs Promised - Not Reported

XXI Signs Given

(1) **Tears** - The statue of Our Lady first shed tears on June 30, 1985 and shed tears and tears of blood for 700 days from June 30, 1985 to January 14, 1992. No tears are reported since the later date.

(2) **Tears of Blood** - The statue first shed tears of blood on October 19, 1986. On July 5, 1989 the statue shed tears of blood for nearly three hours. This phenomenon occurred several more times.

(3) **Miracle of the Eucharist** - This miraculous sign happened to Julia on four separate occasions prior to 1994; two at Naju and two in Italy.

(4) It is later reported that the **Miracle of the Eucharist** has happened to Julia three more times during the year 1994.

    a) On September 24, 1994 in the Naju parish church witnessed by some 60 pilgrims from the Philippines and the USA.

    b) On November 2, 1994 in St. Anthony's church in Kilua, Hawaii. In this case a private Mass was celebrated by Fr. Martin Lucia, a well renowned Apostle of Perpetual Adoration. (It is of interest to note that Hawaii was the very first state to legalize abortion.)

    c) A seventh Eucharistic Miracle is reported having occured thereafter in Naju, Korea at a time when the Apostolic Nuncio was in Naju, visiting Julia Kim.

(Mary's Touch By Mail, St. Michael Center for the Blessed Virgin Mary: a newsletter dated January 1995.)

(4) **Fragrant Oil** - Starting May 4, 1992 the statue has exuded oil; this phenomenon is reportedly ongoing. The latest reported oozing of fragrant oil was on June 27, 1993.

(5) **Stigmata** - Julia suffered the Passion of Jesus and received the Stigmata on four occasions: October 19, 1987; January 29, 1988; February 4, 1988; and January 29, 1989.

(6) **Seer Suffers to End Abortions** - On several occasions, Julia took on the posture of an unborn baby (a fetus) and suffered the pains of a fetus undergoing an abortion. Her stomach also swelled and she suffered the pains of childbirth. On July 28, 1988 while Julia was suffering in the posture of a fetus, the baby cried out "No Mommy! No Mommy! No Mommy! I want to live! Mommy, let me live! Mommy, let me

live! Mommy! Mommy! Mommy!"
(7) **Fragrance of Roses** - This phenomenon was experienced by Julia and many others on several different occasions.
(8) **Miracle of the Sun** - This phenomenon was reported as being observed several different times. On December 5, 1991 it was further reported that the sun turned into an image of the Host. This was successfully photographed.
(9) **Photographs Showing the Sacred Host** - Several incidents are reported where the seer (and others) took photographs during or after the apparitions. To their amazement the picture depicted the Host and/or Chalice when the scene did not contain either. The latest reported incident occurred on June 27, 1993.

XXII Predictions/Promises

(1) On November 26, 1989 Our Blessed Mother said that: *"The numerous souls, who have brought about an imbalance in the universe because of their excessive pride will convert, and world peace will be realized through My fervent calls and tears, and through the prayers, sacrifices, and reparations by the little souls."*

(2) On February 18, 1993 Our Lady said: *"The Lord promised a plenary indulgence to those souls who make a sincere Confession, receive Holy Communion, and observe the Holy Hours well, by pouring down His spirit into them and bathing them in His Sacred Blood. This promise will surely be kept!"*

XXIII Prophecies/Warnings of Chastisement

(1) The messages evolve with an ever increasing reference to a great chastisement to come. The later messages seem to be more specific: Therefore, on June 23, 1993 Our Lady warns: *"Because people are not following the Lord's words and My messages, many chastising warnings are falling upon them: earthquakes, floods, droughts, traffic accidents, fires, famines, plagues, major destructions, many kinds of ecological disasters, abnormal climates; even so, they do not wake up, making My Heart burn so much that it even bleeds."*

And yet Our Lady holds out hope. Thus on June 27, 1993: *"If My words are well accepted and practiced, the chastisement which is to fall upon all of you will turn into the Second Pentecost and the Church will be renewed by the power of the Holy Spirit and the irresistible love."*

(2) February 3, 1994 Our Lady said: *"The cup of God's wrath is beginning to overflow, little by little; as I told you before, the natural order is now being disturbed and abnormalities are occurring frequently: floods,*

fires, famines, earthquakes, droughts, tidal waves, traffic accidents, large-scale destructions, many kinds of environmental disasters and unusual weather. Also many people are dying because of wars and incurable illness and contagious diseases. Through these signs you should know that the time of the Great Chastisement is near; you have seen immense conflicts and major events that have changed the world drastically. There have been many warnings but My children are not responding, therefore you need to offer up your bloody sufferings for the sake of the children of the world. Depending on whether you accept My words well or reject them, the time of the Second Pentecost and Purification can be advanced or delayed, therefore, become simple and innocent babies, listening to and rushing to this Mother. . ."

(3) August 15, 1990 Our Lady said: *"Now it is an age of sin and disorder . . . As a result a great calamity is looming over the human race. Even if I try to hold it off, it will not help, if the world does not repent."*

(4) Again on January 29, 1991 Our Lady speaks: *"There isn't much time left before the incredible punishment will fall even upon those countries which have been protected and intensely cherished so far. Thus the last hour of bleeding for purification is waiting for you. If you do not live according to the words of truth, you will soon suffer calamities and will surely regret it."*

(5) October 14, 1989: *"If I did not help you, the world would have become seas of fire already. But I will never leave you. Even when you walk in the middle of darkness, follow Me with confidence."*

XXIV Method of Appearance

While Julia was praying (usually the rosary) in the chapel in front of the statue, the statue itself became surrounded by a beautiful bright light. Then the statue seemed to become the live Blessed Mother who then spoke to the seer and gave messages to her.

XXV Method of Departure

When the message was over, the light disappeared and the appearance of Our Blessed Mother became that of the statue again.

XXVI Confrontation w/Civil Authorities - NR

XXVII Confrontation w/Church Authorities

There is no reported confrontation with Church Authorities. On the contrary the clergy involved are all reported to be supportive of these occurrences.

XXVIII Request Chapel/Shrine Built

Our Lady requested that a Basilica be constructed. She even showed the seer the location where the Basilica was to be built.

On November 28, 1991 Our Lady said: *"If you believe that good seeds will bear fruit a hundredfold and work entrusting everything to My Immaculate Heart, the Basilica of Mary's Ark of Salvation will be built."*

XXIX Free Will/Choice

Our Lady referred to the fact that God gave us free will in several of the messages such as on February 21, 1989 when She said: *". . . Because God gave humans free will . . ."*

XXX Seer(s)' Suffering/Sacrifice

(1) Julia suffered from various physical ailments; especially from the year 1972 onward.
(2) When the statue first shed tears, Julia would usually suffer more severely as a victim soul each time she prayed before the statue in the chapel.
(3) She suffered the Passion of Jesus and received the Stigmata on several occasions.
(4) Several times she suffered the pains of childbirth and of a fetus being aborted (July 27 and 29, 1988).
(5) She underwent the pains of the Crucifixion (April 2, 1987; August 27, 1989).
(6) On October 14, 1989 she underwent the sufferings of the Korean martyrs, such as application of leg screws and many debasing sufferings.
(7) Our Blessed Mother asked and received the seer's consent that she suffer for sinners, for priests, and to prevent abortions. Once Our Lady told Julia that 5,000 souls were converted due to the seer's sufferings.

XXXI Healings Reported

(1) Physical and spiritual healings are reported.
(2) Julia, herself, was healed in May 1985. Julia had left the hospital and prepared for death. She then said to Our Lord: "Lord I am yours if I die on the way. I am yours if I live. Accept my total suffering." God cured her.

XXXII Action Taken by the Church

In July 1989 Archbishop Yoon stated that the fact of the tears was incontestable. He requested that Fr. Spies keep him informed, which is being done by furnishing the archbishop with copies of all messages and videos taken during the apparitions. Also reports are sent to the archbishop of the number of clergy and pilgrims who gather and also what fruits are produced. Meanwhile, the archbishop will not prevent the messages from being distributed nor pilgrims from praying before the statue.

Fr. Gobbi of the Marian Movement of Priests has visited Naju as has Fr. Laurentin, the noted mariologist. Julia has traveled to Rome and presented the Pope with a replica of the statue. However, no decision has been made by the Church regarding the apparitions and messages. The report indicates that thus far everyone concerned has a "good feeling" about these events and messages.

XXXIII Bibliography

The Miracle in Naju, Korea 1992
By: Translator Sang M. Lee
Published by: Mary's Touch By Mail

Chapter 46

INCHIGEELA, IRELAND
(1985-1987)

I Place - Inchigeela, County Cork, Ireland

II Dates of First and Last Apparition

First: August 5, 1985
Last: March 8, 1987

III Seer(s) - 4

Name: Marie Vaughan
Birth: Unknown
Age at first apparition: 10
Status: Living

Name: Rosemary O'Sullivan
Birth: Unknown
Age at first apparition: 11
Status: Living

Name: Kelley Noonan
Birth: Unknown
Age at first apparition: 16
Status: Living

Name: Mrs. Mary Casey
Birth: Unknown
Age at first apparition: Adult
Status: Living

IV Total Number of Apparitions - 78

Marie - 19
Rosemary - 11
Kelley - 14
Mrs. Mary Casey - 34

In addition to the apparitions reported, it is also reported that from August 5, 1985 to April 1986 the apparitions to Marie and Rosemary occurred almost daily for the first two to three months. Thereafter they became intermittent. These all occurred at Gortaneadin. Starting in May 1986 Our Lady is said to have appeared every Wednesday.

Commencing on August 10, 1986 Our Lady also began to appear at Rossmore.

V Dates and Locality of Each Apparition

(All apparitions at Gortaneadin Grotto unless otherwise noted)

Marie Vaughan -
1985 - August 5 & 6.
1986 - April 27, May 19, 22, 23, June 12.
Rossmore Grotto - **1986** - August 10, 13, 14, 15, 17, 22.
Inchigeela Church - September 7.
Rossmore Grotto - October 5, November 11, 16.
Rossmore Grotto - **1987** - February 22, March 8.

Rosemary O'Sullivan -
1985 - August 5, 6, 8 15.
1986 - April 27, May 18, 21, 23, June 11.
Rossmore Grotto - August 10, 13.

Kelley Noonan
Rossmore Grotto - **1986** - August 10, 13, 14, 17.
Gortaneadin Grotto - August 17.
Rossmore Grotto - August 20.
Inchigeela Church - August 22.
Rossmore Grotto - August 24, October 26, November 16.
Inchigeela Church - November 30.
Rossmore Grotto - **1987** - January 1.
Gortaneadin Grotto - February 1, 22.

Mrs. Mary Casey
1986 - July 23, 30, August 6, 10, 13, 17, 20, 24, 31, September 3, 7, 10, 14, 17, 21, 24, 28, October 5, 7, 12, 15, 19, 28, December 8, 10, 25, 28, 31.
1987 - January 4, 11, February 8, 15, 22, March 8.

VI Description of Our Lady

At first a blue mist surrounds the statue; then instantly, the statue disappears and a beautiful lady about 17 appears dressed in a brilliant white gown, a blue sash, and a mantle of a delicate shade of blue drapes Her head. She has light brown shoulder-length hair and big blue eyes. When She smiles, dimples appear. Her hands are joined in prayer and clasp blue rosary beads. Our Lady moves, breathes and looks to the left and to the right. Sometimes She looks at the nearby stream. She always bows Her head at the name of Jesus.

VII Title(s) of Our Lady - 1

On June 11, 1986 Our Lady announced to Rosemary: *"I am the Queen of Peace."* This was repeated on July 23, 1986 to Mrs. Mary Casey.

VIII Brief Factual Review

Ireland is an island nation known as the Emerald Isle, home of St. Patrick, its patron saint. Ireland is part of Europe, itself being an island west of the British Isles in the Atlantic Ocean.

Inchigeela is a small village in Cork County, Ireland, about thirty miles west of Cork City. These events took place at two separate grottos: Gortaneadin Grotto on one side of the river and Rossmore Grotto across town. A few apparitions occurred in the Inchigeela Parish Church.

The three young girls, who received apparitions, namely Marie Vaughan, Rosemary O'Sullivan, and Kelley Noonan are each described as ordinary girls who come from practicing Catholic homes. The girls are described as pretty and the photographs also show them as beautiful girls. Marie is blonde, Rosemary is a brunette, and Kelly a flaming red head.

Marie Vaughan was ten years of age when she first saw Our Lady on August 5, 1985. Marie is the most outgoing and lighthearted of the three. On August 14, 1986 Marie saw the Sacred Heart of Jesus beside Our Lady whose Immaculate Heart was also visible. Marie was tested with some false apparitions in August 1986. This is when Our Lady said: *"The devil is going to try to make the three of you doubt."* (August 15, 1986). Marie also met her own guardian angel. Her last apparition was a silent one on March 9, 1987.

Rosemary O'Sullivan was eleven years old when she first saw Our Lady on August 5, 1985. She is shy and introspective. Our Lady called her "Rose", and appeared to her most frequently during the first six months. Her last reported apparition of Our Lady was on August 13, 1986.

These events started when Marie and Rosemary bicycled to visit the Grotto at Gortaneadin on August 5, 1985. The girls simultaneously saw the glowing figure of an exceedingly beautiful young Lady whom they immediately knew was the Blessed Virgin Mary. Frightened, yet fascinated, they hurried to Rose's house on their bicycles and related their experience to Rose's sister Mary.

Mary advised them to return to the Grotto again. This they did the next day, and while praying the rosary Our Lady appeared again and this time gave them a one word message: *"Peace!"* The apparitions continued until March 8, 1987.

Kelley Noonan was just turning sixteen when she first saw Our Lady on August 10, 1986. On this occasion the three girls had their first apparition of Our Lady together at Rossmore Grotto. Kelley also met her guardian angel. Her last apparition was on February 22, 1987.

All three girls are under the guidance of a spiritual director.

Mrs. Mary Casey is the mother of nine children. She and her husband are farmers. On June 25, 1986 she had her first apparition of Our Lady at Gortaneadin Grotto, and she received her first message on July 23, 1986. She said Our Lady spoke slowly and paused after every sentence and Her voice was as soft as music.

On August 13, 1986 this seer saw Our Lady descend a flight of stairs. Our Lady stood close to the people at the Grotto railing. This seer's last apparition occurred on March 8, 1987.

The girls would go into ecstasy and into a trancelike state during the apparitions. They were examined by a medical doctor while kneeling in this state and were not aware of the examination. The doctor could get no response from them and yet immediately after the experience they were completely normal.

At first only Rose and Marie received apparitions; reportedly, nearly daily for two to three months. These all occurred at Gortaneadin. Later commencing August 10, 1986 Kelley and the two other girls began to see Our Lady at Rossmore.

On the other hand, Mrs. Mary Casey received all of her apparitions and messages at Gortaneadin Grotto.

The messages were given over a period of time, from August 6, 1985 to March 8, 1987 and are reminiscent of earlier messages from Our Lady to other seers. We are urged to pray; pray the family rosary, pray for the souls in purgatory, sacrifice and do penance, live and keep the Ten Commandments, go to confession and receive Communion often.

Our Lady started every message given to Mrs. Mary Casey with the word *"Peace",* and often said that the youth must be encouraged to pray.

Mrs. Mary Casey saw Our Blessed Mother with the Infant Jesus in Her left arm and she also had a silent vision of the Sorrowful and broken Immaculate Heart of Our Blessed Virgin Mary.

It is reported that the three girls also saw Jesus, as well as angels who sometimes accompanied Our Lady. These angels of light would stand on either side of Our Lady during the apparition.

The girls also saw the devil during one or more apparitions.

Our Lady drew attention to two key passages in the Bible: **(1)** Matthew 7:15-20 (the warning about false prophets), **(2)** Matthew 6:34 (the futility of worry).

Our Lady said to tell the people to drink of the water because She blessed it. Finally, Our Lady asked each of these visionaries to spread Her messages. Mrs. Mary Casey attempts to do this by being available and talking to the pilgrims. She attends Gortaneadin Grotto on Wednesday and Sunday evenings for the public rosary.

The three girls are obedient to their spiritual director. They relate their story whenever asked with honesty and frankness. There has been some confusion in the media reporting, which has caused some suffering to these seers.

The Church has not acted, has not appointed a commission, nor has any official Church pronouncement been reported. The pattern that has developed at Inchigeela is that there is a small but steady flow of pilgrims to the Grottos where there is peace and quiet.

On February 23, 1986 the 'Miracle of the Sun' was witnessed by two nuns of an Irish Order who first saw the phenomenon while driving their car. They abandoned their car in the middle of the road and got out to watch the 'Miracle of the Sun'. Many others also stopped and watched.

The 'Miracle of the Sun' was reportedly repeated on March 2, 1986; only this time the Host and Chalice appeared and filled the sun. Then hands, visible to the wrists, were seen holding the Host over the Chalice. When these images disappeared, the sun was cut into quarters by two dark streaks. One vertical and one horizontal. These lines enlarged rapidly and became a Huge Cross in the sky with the sun at the intersection of the beams. This display was witnessed by about thirty adults.

There are several cases reported of miraculous physical cures and many spiritual healings and conversions are reported. The indications are that the waters from the Grottos are closely associated with the healings.

IX The Primary Messages - 5

(1) Prayer - Our Lady requested prayer and more prayer in the majority of the messages.

August 8, 1985 to Rose: *"Bring more children to pray; tell families to get together to pray the rosary."*

August 13, 1986 to Marie: *"The devil is trying to take over the world; you must pray more for sinners and for the souls in purgatory."*

August 17, 1986 to Kelley: *"Ask My people to pray; tell them to pray. This is the only way that they shall be saved."*

Mrs. Mary Casey received no less than one dozen messages urging us to pray; starting with the very first message given to this seer on July 23, 1986: *"I want people to pray more, more, more from the heart. I want people to behave and people to believe. God loves the people of Ireland."*

(2) **Rosary** - August 8, 1985 to Rose: *"Tell families to get together and pray the rosary."*

May 23, 1986 to Marie and Rose: *"If you love Me will you fast on Fridays and say three rosaries?"*

August 24, 1986 to Kelley: *"Thanks for praying the rosary!"*

Mrs. Mary Casey received over a half dozen messages exhorting us to pray the rosary. Thus, Our Lady pleads with Mrs. Mary Casey: *"Pray, pray, pray. I want the family rosary."* (August 13, 1986)

"Pray the rosary for peace and unity. Unforgiveness of heart is a barrier to peace." (August 20, 1986)

"Tell everybody to say the rosary. The rosary will overcome the problems Satan is causing." (August 24, 1986)

(3) **Penance and Fasting** - June 12, 1986 to Marie: *"I want the world to improve by prayer and penance. I want you to publish this."*

August 13, 1986 to Mrs. Mary Casey: *"By prayer and fasting you can prevent or even stop wars."*

(4) **Confession and Communion** - July 23, 1986 to Mrs. Mary Casey: *"I want people . . . Reconciliation and to receive the Sacrament of My Son more often."* This was repeated in essence in later messages.

(5) **Peace** - Our Lady brings a message of God's peace and love. The very first word uttered by Our Lady was: *"Peace"*.

Thereafter, She told the seers that She was the Queen of Peace. She told us to pray for peace and unity.

On January 1, 1987 Our Lady told Kelley: *"My child pray more for those in Ireland who have no faith and that Ireland may be united with peace."*

On August 15, 1986 Our Lady said to Mary Casey: *"By genuine prayer you can obtain peace of mind, peace of heart, peace in the home, peace in your parish, and peace in the world. Be on your guard against temptation. Pray for protection. Go in peace."*

Our Lady's first words to Mrs. Mary Casey were: *"I am the Queen of Peace!"* She began every message to Mrs. Mary Casey with the word *"Peace"*, and ended each message with the words: *"Go in peace."*

Then, On August 31, 1986 to Mrs. Mary Casey: *"With all the love and trust I have in young people, listen not to the language of hatred, revenge, retaliation. Go in peace."*

X Signs Preceding the Apparitions

The seers report that a glow of light surrounds the statue; the statue then disappears and Our Lady appears about three feet from the statue. After the apparition, the statue is in its proper place again.

XI Other Visions During Apparitions

(1) Several of these visionaries saw Jesus. On August 8, 1985 Rose saw Jesus, with angels around Him. On August 14, 1986 Marie saw the Sacred Heart beside the Immaculate Heart of Mary. On December 25, 1986 Mary Casey saw Our Lady with the Infant Jesus.
(2) Marie and Kelley met and saw their own guardian angel.
(3) The three girls saw angels, sometimes alone and sometimes the angels were with Jesus or Mary. On one occasion a male angel, aged about sixteen, was holding a candle.
(4) The three girls saw the devil as well.

XII Prayers Taught to the Seer(s) - Not Reported

XIII Special Devotion Given to the Seer(s)

Although not a new devotion, Our Lady told Marie on November 2, 1986: *"I wish that the Brown Scapular should be spread more."*

XIV Requests Made by Our Lady

(1) On May 23, 1986 Our Lady requested we fast on Fridays and say three rosaries.
(2) On November 2, 1986 Our Lady requested the Brown Scapular devotion be spread more.

XV Specific Bible References

(1) Matthew 7:15-20
(2) Matthew 6:34

XVI Secrets Given to the Seer(s)

No secrets are reported, although each seer received 'private messages'.

XVII Miracles Promised by Our Lady - NR

XVIII Miracles Performed

The 'Miracle of the Sun' occurred several times.

XIX Miracles Promised not yet Performed - NR

XX Signs Promised

On February 1, 1987 Our Lady showed Kelley two stone slabs of the 10 Commandments; clearly broken. She said She would repeat this apparition later in February.

True to Her word Our Lady again showed the Ten Commandments to Kelley on February 22, 1987 still broken, and said: *"Sons and Daughters of the world, I beg of you to recite and keep the Ten Commandments."*

XXI Signs Given

(1) February 23, 1986 'Miracle of the Sun'.
(2) March 2, 1986 'Miracle of the Sun', together with the Host, Chalice and Hands, and also the Cross appearing in the sun.
(3) On February 1, and again on February 22, 1987 Our Lady showed Kelley two stone slabs of the Ten Commandments; broken in both cases. She urged us to keep the Ten Commandments.
(4) It is reported that there were many other signs and wonders given in the sky over Inchigeela.

XXII Predictions/Promises

On August 15, 1986 Our Lady told Marie that: *"the devil was going to try to make the three of ye doubt."*

After a series of false apparitions Our Lady told Marie on August 17, 1986: *"This was a test to see if you knew the difference between love and hate."*

XXIII Prophecies/Warnings of Chastisement

(1) On August 8, 1985 Rose reports that Our Lady told her that we must pray much if we are to avoid catastrophe.
(2) On August 13, 1986 to Marie: *"The devil is trying to take over the world. You must pray more for sinners and for the souls in purgatory."*

XXIV Method of Appearance

At first a blue mist surrounds the statue and instantly the statue disappears and then a beautiful Lady appears. When She is present there is no statue, but She does not take the place of the statue.

XXV Method of Departure

When the apparition is concluded, Our Lady disappears and the statue is there again as before.

XXVI Confrontation w/Civil Authorities

Other than some confusing articles in the press and some mockery by busy people, there really is no confrontation with civil authorities reported.

XXVII Confrontation w/Church Authorities - NR
XXVIII Request Chapel/Shrine Built - NR

XXIX Free Will/Choice

Our Lady pleads with us to pray. On August 13, 1986 Our Lady told Mrs. Mary Casey: *"By prayer and fasting you can prevent or even stop wars."* Thus we have a choice to pray or not to pray.

XXX Seer(s)' Suffering/Sacrifice

The unfamiliar crowds, the doubting people, the interrogations and mockery the children endured, undoubtedly caused them suffering and pain. In spite of all, they have kept a high level of balance in their lives.

XXXI Healings Reported

It is reported that there were miraculous physical healings attributed to the water. Also, there were spiritual healings and conversions.

XXXII Action Taken by the Church

Other then the fact that the three girls have been obedient to their spiritual directors, there is no mention of any official Church action.

XXXIII Bibliography

Inchigeela, A Call to Prayer 1989
By: Mary O'Sullivan
Published by: Inchigeela Queen of Peace Group

The Final Hour
By: Michael Brown
Published by: Faith Publishing Company

Chapter 47

MELLERAY, IRELAND
(1985)

I Place - Melleray (Grotto), County Waterford, Ireland

II Dates of First and Last Apparition

First: August 16, 1985
Last: August 24, 1985

III Seer(s) - 3

Name: Ursula O'Rourke
Birth: Unknown
Age at first apparition: 17
Status: Living

Name: Tom Cliffe
Birth: Unknown
Age at first apparition: 12
Status: Living

Name: Barry Buckley
Birth: Unknown
Age at first apparition: 11
Status: Deceased

In addition to these three central visionaries, there were several other people present at the Grotto during the period from August 16th to August

24th, 1985 who reported having visions and apparitions, some of whom received messages. Of note is Michael O'Donnell who reported having visions of Our Lord's face and also of Our Lady at the Grotto on August 18, 1985. Our Lady spoke to him: *"Preserve Sunday for prayer."*

Also reported are several testimonies from various people who experienced visions and other phenomena subsequent to the week of August 16th to August 25th, 1985. Interestingly enough, on September 4, 1985 Msgr. Patrick Lannen visited the Grotto and to his surprise he saw visions of the Sacred Heart, St. Joseph, the Child Jesus, and finally Our Blessed Mother showed Herself. Although there were no words spoken, this Monsignor now believes; he admits having been a nonbeliever of these apparitions before this experience.

IV Total Number of Apparitions - 9

V Dates and Locality of Each Apparition

(All apparitions occured at Melleray/Grotto)
1985:
  Ursula - August 16
  Tom - August 18
  Tom and Barry - August 19 (2 times), 20, 21, 22, 23, 24.

VI Description of Our Lady

(1) First the statue of Our Lady moved back and forth, then the white gown of the statue started blowing as if in the wind. Her hands were joined in prayer and Her head moved in a slow reverent movement looking up to heaven. She wore a silver crown with gemstones on Her head and Her golden hair was flowing to Her shoulders. Sometimes Her fingers moved. She had a young tanned face, blue eyes and spoke in a low soft voice. Sometimes She prayed and sang with the people.

(2) On August 18th and again on August 19th Our Lady began to walk down some steps that had manifested. She wore a white robe and blue sash and brown sandals on Her feet. Her golden hair was flowing to Her shoulders and She wore one red rose in Her hair. The steps were brown clay with multicolored roses of all sizes on both sides of the steps. At the bottom of the steps She turned to the left a few paces to the water's edge in front of the boys.

VII Title(s) of Our Lady - 1

On August 24, 1985 at the request of a local nun, Tom Cliffe asked a question of the apparition: "Are you the Mother of Jesus Christ?" The apparition answered: *"I am."*

VIII Brief Factual Review

Melleray Grotto is a little Grotto located one mile below the Cistercian Monastery of Mount Melleray in the Knockmealdown Mountains in Waterford County, Ireland. High on the cliff face is set a statue of Our Lady of Lourdes, which is the site of the apparitions. By the side of the Grotto flows the small Monavugga River. The Cistercian Monks first came to this area in 1832 and eventually set up the statue of Our Lady.

Ursula O'Rourke, a seventeen-year-old local teenager was the first to see Our Lady. This happened on August 16, 1985 while Ursula was at the Grotto with her mother, her sister Mary, and her brothers John and Donal. To her amazement, she noticed that the statue of Our Lady was moving. When Ursula finally said: "Why me?" Our Lady smiled and when Ursula said: "Please bless all my family," Our Lady smiled even more.

When Ursula told her mother, they all went back right away to the Grotto to find Our Lady still there. This time, Mary, John, and Donal also saw Our Lady, but She did not speak. Ursula was to receive no messages directly from Our Lady; however, she was involved with messages given to the two boys.

On August 17, 1985 the statue again moved as witnessed by several people. There were no messages, only visions of Jesus and Padre Pio were given to various people.

The following day was Sunday, August 18, 1985. On this day Tom Cliffe, age twelve, came to the Grotto with his father and saw the face of Jesus on the statue. After he told his parents, the family returned to the Grotto and that is when Tom first saw the statue change and move back and forth and become a living person. Our Lady spoke to Tom, but he was so frightened that he did not hear clearly what Our Lady said. Either She said: *"I want to"* or *"I want you."* Tom said he did not want to come back because he was frightened.

It was on this same date that Our Lady also appeared to farmer Michael O'Donnell and said to him: *"Preserve Sunday for prayer."*

Commencing on August 19, 1985 Tom Cliffe and his eleven year old cousin Barry Buckley both saw Our Lady at the Grotto every evening for two and one-half hours, except on August 19th when Our Lady appeared to the two boys twice, about two hours each time. It seems that Barry called Tom to play for the day and they ended up at the Grotto. Shortly, after they started praying the rosary, they noticed the statue change and Her robe was blowing in the wind. Children were running around and it was noisy. Our Lady said: *"Behave."* When no one paid attention, tears flowed from the statue and splashed onto the ground.

Our Lady asked for prayer, then the boys received two biblical visions: one of the First Pentecost, and one of the Last Supper.

Because it was getting cold, the boys went home but returned to the

Melleray, Ireland 517

Grotto again at about 8:00 PM. This time Ursula joined them. Our Lady was now at the top of the Grotto standing on a manifested flight of stairs. She walked down the stairs and gave a message of peace and prayer. She also warned that people have to improve and pray, that people have ten years to improve and pray and if they don't, then this is what will happen. Then the boys received another biblical vision, this time of the Great Flood and Noah's Ark.

On August 20th Tom and Barry again received messages. Ursula was present also. Again Our Lady gave a stern warning that the world had ten years to improve. Then Tom received a biblical vision of the 'Doubting Thomas'. When the boys told Our Lady they had to leave She said: *"That is all right. I will see you tomorrow."*

Ursula and the two boys again went to the Grotto on August 21st. The Grotto was crowded and many cars and people were outside the Grotto unable to get in. This was the night the boys heard Our Lady singing: *"Peace is flowing like a river. . ."* This was also the first night that the public address (PA) system was rigged so the boys could speak into the microphone and let the crowds know what was happening and also speak out the messages as they were given to them.

Our Lady announced that She was pleased with Ireland and wanted the people of Ireland to convey Her messages. The boys then received another biblical vision; this time Our Lord was sleeping in the boat during a storm. This vision was described over the PA system. Then Our Lady said Her message was: *"for peace, prayer and no more fighting in the world."* The boys then received a biblical vision of the Nativity.

Then Our Lady told the boys: *"I will make a movement to the people."* This was announced over the PA system. Then things really began to happen. It seems that not only the two boys, but many people saw Our Lady move Her head towards the crowd on the road. The statue turned several times, people gasped as this happened and the boys announced what they saw over the PA system as it was occurring. Our Lady said She hoped most of the people saw Her. Suddenly the boys announced She was coming down the steps and looking towards the road. People backed away; but Our Lady assured the crowd through the boys: *"Be not afraid, I will never hurt you."* She also said: *"I want the people out on the road to see Me because I will leave soon."* And there were many who did see Our Blessed Lady that night.

The next night August 22nd Our Lady appeared and asked for more prayers and again asked for the hymn 'Peace is Flowing Like a River'. Her message was stern: *"The world must improve. . . If the world does not improve, the devil will take over God's Church in ten years."* It was then that Satan appeared at Our Lady's left side jeering at Her. This frightened the boys.

However, on the next night August 23rd Our Lady again reassured us with Her message: *"With your faith and prayers, you can overcome the devil."* Again She asked for more prayers and promised: *"I will show Myself to more people in more places."*

On August 24th Our Lady affirmed that She was the Mother of Jesus Christ. This was the final apparition to these two boys.

The Grotto today is much as it was then. Pilgrims constantly visit the Grotto. Many later visions of Our Lord, Our Lady, Padre Pio, and others have been reported. Also, the phenomenon of the 'Dance of the Sun' has been reported on several occasions. Rosary and prayer groups are set up Saturdays and Sundays. Numerous physical and spiritual healings are reported. The children were at first ridiculed. Many people refused to believe, but in spite of these obstacles, the children continued to do their part to spread the messages as Our Lady requested. The children each affirmed in writing their unwavering and solemn belief in the visions and the messages. Barry Buckley gave his written affirmation before a priest less than one month before his sudden death.

It is reported that the bishop is conducting an investigation. No decision is reported.

IX The Primary Messages - 4

(1) Prayer - Our Blessed Mother requested prayer in nearly every reported apparition when messages were given.

August 18: *"Preserve Sundays for prayer."*

August 19: *"I want Prayer."*

August 19: *"My message is Peace and Prayer."*

August 20: *"If the people would improve and pray, God would save Ireland."*

August 21: *"My message is peace and prayer and no more fighting in the world."*

August 22: *"I want prayer."*

August 23: *"I want you to pray harder. I want you to pray harder. With your faith and prayers you can overpower the devil."*

(2) Rosary - Each time Our Lady asked for prayer by saying: *"I want prayer"* the people would pray the rosary, after which Our Lady said: *"Thank you."*

(3) Conversion - August 19: *"God is angry with the world, the people will have to improve and pray. . ."*

August 20: *"The world must improve. The people must go to Mass more, and receive My Son more often. I want the people to believe."*

August 21: *"The world must behave. I want the world to believe Me."*

(4) Peace - August 19: *"I have a message: My message is peace and prayer."*

Again on August 21: *"My message is peace and prayer and no more fighting in the world."*

X Signs Preceding the Apparitions

Usually the boys saw the statue move back and forth, then the gown on the statue would blow in the wind just before they saw the apparition. Invariably they were praying the rosary when Our Lady appeared.

XI Other Visions During Apparitions

(1) Many people reported seeing visions of the face of Jesus, of Padre Pio, of some saints, and other visions.
(2) The boys were shown very powerful biblical visions during the apparitions: Pentecost - The Last Supper - The Great Flood and Noah's Ark - Jesus calms the storm - Doubting Thomas - Nativity scene - Passion scenes.
(3) August 22, 1985 the boys saw Satan appear to the left of Our Lady, jeer at Her, and then disappear.

XII Prayers Taught to the Seer(s) - Not Reported
XIII Special Devotion Given to the Seer(s) - NR

XIV Requests Made by Our Lady

(1) August 21 Our Lady asked time and again for the hymn 'Peace is Flowing Like a River.' Then She sang with the people. She also prayed with them.
(2) August 20 Our Lady said: *"I want the Irish people to spread My messages in the world."*
(3) August 21 She repeated: *"I want the people of Ireland to convey My messages to the world."* And further: *"I want Ursula to help you make the people believe. I want all of you to tell the world. You have ways yourselves of telling the world."*

XV Specific Bible References

Although no Bible passages were quoted or referenced, the two boys received several powerful biblical visions:
(1) August 19 - First Pentecost - Last Supper - Great Flood and Noah's Ark.
(2) August 20 - Doubting Thomas scene.
(3) August 21 - Jesus calms the storm.
(4) Nativity scene. (Tom saw the first part and Barry saw the scene continue from where Tom's vision left off)

XVI Secrets Given to the Seer(s) - Not Reported

XVII Miracles Promised by Our Lady

On August 21 Our Lady said: "*I will make a movement to the people.*" She did turn to the crowd on the road just as She said and many people on the road saw Her then.

XVIII Miracles Performed

The reports of the statue which moved and became animated at each apparition.

XIX Miracles Promised Not Yet Performed - NR

XX Signs Promised

On August 21 Our Lady said: "*I will make a movement to the people.*" She did turn as promised toward the crowd (on the street outside the Grotto). She also moved Her hands. Many saw Her that evening.

XXI Signs Given

(1) The various visions seen by the seers and others such as the face of Jesus, Padre Pio, saints and others.
(2) The movement of the statue back and forth and finally the statue itself becoming animated.
(3) The biblical visions given the two boys.
(4) During the apparition of August 19th, the two boys were dressed in tee shirts and they were visibly cold. Our Lady sent down jets of warm breeze which kept the boys warm for half an hour.
(5) Many other signs were reported occurring after the original apparition period such as the 'Miracle of the Sun'.

XXII Predictions/Promises

(1) August 20, 1985 Our Lady said: "*The world has ten years to improve. It must improve ten times.*"
(2) August 21, 1985 Our Lady said She would show Herself to the people in the street outside the Grotto; and She did as promised. Many people saw the statue turn that night.
(3) August 23, 1985 Our Lady said: "*I will show Myself to more people in more places.*" Again, She kept Her promise. The reports of Marian Apparitions all over the world have escalated since 1985 and are reported to be ongoing at the present time.

Melleray, Ireland

XXIII Prophecies/Warnings of Chastisement

(1) August 19, 1985: *"God is angry with the world. The people will have to improve and pray. My message is for all the people of God's Church. The people have ten years to improve and pray and if not then this is what will happen."*

It was at this point the boys received the biblical vision of the Great Flood and Noah's Ark.

(2) August 20, 1985 again Our Lady said: *"The world has ten years to improve. It must improve ten times."*

Later, after this message and during this same apparition, the boys received a vision of Doubting Thomas.

(3) August 21, 1985 during this apparition Our Lady showed the boys the vision of Jesus subduing the storm as if to remind us that God could still turn back the catastrophe overshadowing the world, if we would only turn to Him.

(4) August 22, 1985 Our Lady said: *"The world must improve and the world must believe. If the world does not improve the devil will take over the Church. If the world does not improve the devil will take over God's Church in ten years."*

The boys were then given a vision of Satan jeering Our Blessed Mother to Her left side.

XXIV Method of Appearance

Invariably the boys were praying the rosary, when the statue began to move back and forth. Then Our Lady was there.

XXV Method of Departure

After the apparition was concluded, Our Lady disappeared and the statue was there as before.

XXVI Confrontation w/Civil Authorities - NR
XXVII Confrontation w/Church Authorities - NR
XXVIII Request Chapel/Shrine Built - NR

XXIX Free Will/Choice

The messages clearly tell us we must improve in ten years or certain events will happen, we have a choice to do as She says or not to listen to Her.

XXX Seer(s)' Suffering/Sacrifice

It is reported that Tom was so frightened the first time Our Lady spoke to him: *"I want you,"* that he said he would not return. However, he did come back to the Grotto with his cousin Barry.

Both boys were very frightened when they saw the vision of Satan. These events undoubtedly caused them pain and suffering.

XXXI Healings Reported

Many physical and spiritual healings are reported. The local Committee for the Grotto has documented alleged cures for a variety of illness and disease; even cancer.

XXXII Action Taken by the Church

As reported a tremendous atmosphere of prayer developed since the apparitions. People pray at the Grotto every day and night. There are Sunday rosaries and hymns. All night vigils are held on Saturday nights.

The bishop is conducting an investigation. The children have given their solemn affirmation in writing. It appears that many good fruits are evident, but no decision has been given by the Church.

XXXIII Bibliography

Our Blessed Mother Is Speaking To You, Are You Listening?
Her Message From Melleray, Grotto. 1990
By: W. Deevy
Published by: W. Deevy

The Final Hour   1992
By: Michael Brown
Published by: Faith Publishing Company

Our Blessed Lady Speaks From Melleray, Grotto - (Video)

Our Lady Speaks From Melleray, Grotto - (Audio)

Chapter 48

SEVEN HILLS, OHIO, USA
(1985 - PRESENT)

I Place - Seven Hills, Ohio, U.S.A.

II Dates of First and Last Apparition

First: 1985
Last: January 31, 1994 (last reported)
Note: It is reported that these apparitions are ongoing.

III Seer(s) - 1

Name: Maureen H.
Birth: Unknown
Age at first apparition: Unknown
Status: Living

IV   Total Number of Apparitions - 283

(1) Locutions began in 1985 and are reported continuing. The first reported message is one received June 30, 1989.

(2) Messages received during locutions for the period June 30, 1989 through October 5, 1991 number some seventy one (71). Locutions and messages from Jesus are also reported during this time period.

(3) Apparitions and locutions with messages received from Our Lady during the period March 4, 1993 through January 31, 1994 number some two hundred and twelve (212). The seer also received messages from Jesus during this time frame.

(4) The apparitions and messages are reported ongoing.

V Dates and Locality of Each Apparition

(All apparitions, locutions and messages are received at Seven Hills, Ohio.)

1989: June 30; July 1 (twice); August 9, 18, 20, 28; September 17, 18; October 14 (twice), 20; November 3 (2), 15, 17.
1990: February 1 (four times), 3, 25; March 14, 15, 17, 19; April 4, 12, 26; May 4, 17, 26, 28, 30; June 2, 5, 7 (twice), 11 (twice), 12, 14, 16, 17, 20, 24, 29 (twice), 30; July 1, 9, 11, 13, 25; August 6, 8, 16 (twice), 19, 23, 28; September 16 (twice); October 21; November 24; December 4, 28.
1991: February 4, 5, 7; April 7; October 3.
1992: None reported.
1993: March 4 (twice), 7, 8, 14, 18, 21, 23, 25, 28; April 1, 5, 8, 9, 15, 21 (three times), 25 (twice); May 1 (twice), 2, 9, 13, 16, 20 (twice), 23, 27, 30; June 3, 6, 10, 13 (twice), 17 (twice), 19, 27 (twice); July 4, 8,9, 11, 15, 17 (twice), 18, 21, 22, 25, 29; August 1 (twice), 5, 8, 9, 12, 14, 15, 19, 22 (twice), 26, 27 (twice), 28 (twice), 29 (three times), 30; September 2 (twice), 3, 5 (twice), 6 (twice), 9, 10 (twice), 11 (twice), 12 (twice), 13, 15, 16 (twice), 17 (twice), 18 (twice), 19, 20, 21, 22, 23 (twice), 27, 28, 29 (twice), 30 (three times); October 1, 2 (twice), 3 (three times), 4 (three times), 5, 6, 7, 10, 11, 12, 14 (twice), 17, 19, 21, 22, 23 (twice), 24, 25, 27, 28 (twice); November 2, 4 (twice), 5, 6 (twice), 7, 8, 9, 11, 13, 14 (twice), 16, 18 (three times), 19, 20, 21 (twice), 25 (three times), 27 (twice), 28 (twice), 29; December 1, 2 (twice), 3 (twice), 4, 5 (twice), 8,9, 11, 12, 15, 16, 17, 18, 21, 22 (twice), 23, 25, 26, 27, 30, 31 (twice).
1994: January 1 (twice), 6 (twice), 8, 9, 11, 13, 14, 15, 16, 19, 20, 22 (twice), 23, 24, 27 (twice), 28, 29 (twice), 30, 31.

VI Description of Our Lady

Our Lady is reported to have appeared to this visionary in a marvelous array of adornment. Usually She was dressed in white with a blue veil. However, Our Lady often presented Herself dressed in grey, in blue, in pink or in gold. Most often She carried a rosary, sometimes Her Immaculate Heart was exposed; other times She was seen carrying a Crucifix, standing in front of the Cross or standing on the globe. Our Lady sometimes was wearing a crown, and once was seated on a throne. In 1994 Our Lady was seen carrying a rosary of the 50 States of the USA.

Our Blessed Mother reportedly appeared to this seer as Our Lady of

Grace, Our Lady of Fatima and Our Lady of Guadalupe. She has also presented Herself carrying the Baby Jesus in Her arms. Our Lady always bows before the Eucharist in the Monstrance prior to imparting Her message.

VII Title(s) of Our Lady - 3

(1) Our Lady is reported to appear under the title of Protectress of the Faith.
(2) She has announced Herself as Queen of the Most Holy Rosary and as Mary, Queen of Heaven and Earth (March 21, 1993).

VIII Brief Factual Review

Seven Hills is a smaller community located near Cleveland, Ohio, which in turn is sited on the southern shore of Lake Erie. The state of Ohio is located in the Northeastern Region of the USA.

The seer is a middle aged mother of four grown children, who wishes to remain anonymous (Maureen H.). She reportedly is a suffering soul who is dedicated to praying the rosary. It is reported that Our Blessed Mother usually appears to this visionary while the seer is praying the rosary.

It is also reported that the Episcopate has some reservations as to the authenticity of the messages, however many serious and convinced clergy reportedly believe in these events. At least one well noted author-cleric has announced his personal and private belief in these events. No church conflict as such is reported.

The seer has been receiving locutions from Our Lady since 1985, however the first message was received on June 30, 1989 and the first apparition of Our Lady occurred on March 4, 1993. The apparitions and locutions are ongoing. Jesus has also appeared to this seer and has given messages to her. St. Joseph, St. Michael, as well as other saints and angels have appeared to this seer sometimes accompanying Our Blessed Mother. Other times they appear without Our Lady.

Commencing with the first apparition of March 4, 1993 and typically thereafter, Our Lady appears to the seer, then gives her a private message, requests her to pray with Our Lady for a specific purpose, and then imparts the message. Our Lady generally blesses all present before She departs.

Our Lady appears in a variety of splendid attire, sometimes She cradles the Baby Jesus. She usually carries a rosary and at times wears a crown. At times Her Immaculate Heart is exposed. She appears under the title of Our Lady Protectress of the Faith, however, She has announced Herself as Mary, Queen of Heaven and Earth. Our Lady's messages are more akin to teachings. They stress Holy Love and Holy Humility all according to the Will of God. The messages urge us to live a life of reparation, purity, prayer and holiness, to pray the rosary and to forgive one another. We are taught that through Holy Love and Eucharistic Adoration we become aware of and are given defense against the temptations and insidious snares of Satan. Our Lady said: *"Pride is from Satan, Pride is self-love,"* whereas: *"Holy Love is the Refuge of My Immaculate Heart."*

Our Lady dictated the 'Four Steps to Holiness'. The first step is to choose holiness, the second is a decision to abandon sin, the third is to choose God's will and to abandon our own will, while the fourth step is to surrender our will to the Will of God. Our Lady also gave prayers to the seer. She referred to Sacred Scripture and also gave some predictions and promises.

At the beginning of each apparition Our Lady would usually invite the seer to pray with Our Lady for different purposes, such as: for people in turmoil, government leaders, unbelievers, peace, priests, conversions, to end abortion, for the remnant Church, and for lukewarm souls.

Our Lady announced that Christ had established the 'Mystical Church of Atonement' on earth and gave messages explaining the same. A Church which will rise from the ashes of complacency and self-fulfillment. Our Lady urges and invites all to offer prayers of atonement for our nation; that it change from decadence to holiness.

'Mary's House of Prayer' located in Seven Hills is the focus for 'Our Lady's Blessing Point' and is also where Our Lady announced the discovery of the Maranatha Spring. Maranatha means 'Come, Lord Jesus' in Aramaic. Our Lady has urged many to come to the Maranatha Spring, as people will receive blessings and the water will heal souls.

IX The Primary Messages - 7

(1) Prayer - Our Lady exhorts us to pray in a great number of the reported messages, one of Her most oft-repeated pleas: *"Pray! Pray! Pray!"* Thus, also on March 7, April 8, May 2, June 13, July 25, August 22, October 10, and December 16 of 1993; and January 5, 1994.

On November 8, 1993 Our Lady said: *"Prayer is a grace at work. I encourage you to pray, pray, pray."*

On June 27, 1993: *"... Pray fervently from the heart."*

September 30, 1993: *"Persevere in prayer ...."*

November 29, 1993: *"When you pray for the conversion of souls, pray that they respond to the graces in their lives."*

January 28, 1994 on this date Our Lady encouraged us in prayer: *"You have no petition I do not lay before the throne of God by My own hand."*

August 28, 1989: *"Pray and sacrifice all you can for the hour grows late."*

(2) Rosary - Our Lady carried a rosary during nearly every apparition, including the first reported apparition of June 30, 1989. In addition Our

Lady requested that we pray the rosary during several of the appearances:

June 5, 1990: *"Each day I intend to bind more and more souls to My Immaculate Heart through the golden chain of the rosary."*

August 23, 1990: *". . . Here is the weapon that can stop World War III. Pick it up and do not put it down. The rosary can bring all hearts to faith, love and peace."*

October 7, 1993: *"Rosaries that are prayed from the heart, are a great, great weapon in My hands against all evil."*

June 10, 1993: *"You have the most powerful weapon on earth at your fingertips; the rosary. But you must use it!"*

(3) Eucharist - Our Lady Herself showed a deep respect and reverence for the Eucharist, for whenever She appeared to this seer, Our Lady typically bowed before the Eucharist before any words were said or messages given.

In addition Our Blessed Mother urged Adoration of the Eucharist.

August 14, 1993 Our Lady first venerated the Eucharist, then turned to the seer and said: *"Let us give praise, honor and glory to Jesus King of Kings, Son of Man."*

June 13, 1993: *". . . Spend many hours in front of My Son's Eucharistic Heart, and pray, pray, pray!"*

September 19, 1993: *"Give praise and thanksgiving to Jesus, present in the Holy Sacrament of the Altar."*

November 25, 1993: *". . . These chains hold the world close to the grace of My Heart. One is the rosary, the other is faith-filled reception of the Eucharist."*

(4) Conversion and Forgiveness - November 17, 1989: *"Pray that every heart is reconciled with God and with his neighbor. Do not be afraid to change, to convert."*

May 20, 1993: *"Pray for the grace of forgiveness."*

July 8, 1993: *"There are many who think they love, but are deceived, for they have not forgiven; learn to come to My Heart for all the grace you need to love and to forgive."*

July 9, 1993: *"Pride is the root of unforgiveness. If souls could forgive, they would be able to love, therefore, pray always for forgiveness and show others how to forgive."*

September 10, 1993: *". . . It is only through Holy Love that the grace of conversion is effected . . . My call to you to conversion is a call to be a reflection of God: a reflection of Holy Love."*

November 11, 1993: *"Pray that the Holy Spirit lead you in forgiveness of others and forgiveness of yourself, so that this foreboding obstacle to holiness be forever removed from your life."*

December 31, 1993: *"Think only good of each other. Love each other as you love yourselves. This is the path of conversion and peace."*

(5) End Abortion - August 28, 1989, Our Lady said: *"Think of all the people who were slain in their mother's wombs before they could live* *to glorify God."*

March 14, 1990, Our Lady laments: *"You do not understand what jeopardy this country has placed herself in by adopting abortion as legal. Everyday the abyss between heaven and all countries engaged in genocide widens. Pray, pray, pray. Much atonement must be made to Our Hearts in order to avoid grave consequences."*

May 4, 1990: *"My Own Immaculate Heart feels most strongly the ravages of abortion. All the souls of the aborted infants pray in unison with you."*

(6) Reparation and Atonement - Our Lady announced that Jesus desired that 'His Mystical Church of Atonement' be established at Mary's House of Prayer in Seven Hills and that the Church of Atonement be extended all over the world. The work and purpose of this Church of Atonement is for prayers of atonement to be offered for this country and for many specific dire needs and special intentions of Our Lady. This mission was first given to the seer in a vision.

October 20, 1989: *"My Son grows anxious to construct this Church of Atonement."*

October 14, 1989: *"I seek these special souls to further this prayer movement to advance the cause of Prayer Rallies of Atonement across all the earth and to encourage prayer of atonement."*

August 20, 1989: *"I have invited all to come to offer prayers of atonement for this country."*

February 1, 1990: *"My Son, dear children is calling all souls into this Church of Atonement."* During this apparition Our Lady reminded the seer of the vision which first announced the Church of Atonement. Our Lady said of the vision: *"The Church stands empty in a desolate area as a beacon of light amidst darkness. You must call the people to the Church."*

April 12, 1990: *"Many graces await those who have been faithful to prayer and sacrifice and are assisting in the construction of the Church of Atonement."*

May 26, 1990: *"Each soul who enters the Church of Atonement is a living sign of faith, love, and peace to all the world."*

June 14, 1990: *"Know that your mission in this life is to strengthen and support the roots of love of the Church of Atonement on earth."*

September 16, 1990: *"The Hearts of Jesus and Mary are closest to the souls in the Church of Atonement, for these are the ones attempting to die to self."*

December 28, 1990: *"This movement was founded in grace, is perpetuated in grace and will proceed in grace."*

On December 4, 1990 Our Lady told the seer that the Consecration to the Cross was the key to the Church of Atonement:

Prayer: 'My Jesus, I consecrate myself this day to Your Holy Cross. Just as You took upon Yourself that great Cross for the sake of humanity, so I now too embrace the crosses in my life.

'Everything I suffer I give back to You, my sweet Jesus, to atone for my sins and those of all the world. I will begin and end each day at the foot of Your cross together with Our Blessed Mother and Saint John, our brother. My only pleasure will be to comfort You, my Sweet Savior. Amen.'

November 24, 1990 Our Lady gave promises to all who enter into Christ's Church of Atonement. *"They will receive special graces in their lifetime, they will have a deeper understanding of the sacred mysteries, they will be given wisdom and knowledge beyond their own. They will be given special insight as to the state of their own soul. In heaven the Lord God is reserving special rewards for the Congregation of His Church of Atonement. I am making these promises, My daughter for the hour grows late, and My Son wishes more and more souls be drawn through the grace of My Heart into the Church of Atonement."*

(7) Defend Against Satan - September 2, 1993: *". . . All manner of evil will come against the faith in the end. It is by means of the solemn refuge of My grace-filled Heart that My children will persevere. No one is immune from Satan's attacks. Even the most holy will be severely put to the test. But I mean to defend those who call upon Me."*

September 12, 1993: *". . . My children I come to ask that you make of your hearts burning vigils of faith, ever mindful of Satan's attempts to undermine the true faith by the means of his deceit."*

November 16, 1993: *". . . This is how Satan plants doubts. They begin small and grow bigger. His (Satan's) plan being to choke out My work at the House of Prayer. Always the malefactor comes to twist and deceive and cause misunderstanding . . ."*

January 19, 1994: *". . . There is no merit in any cross unless it is accepted by the soul. Struggles against any cross are inspired by the evil one. All conflicts, all wars are against Holy Love and inspired by evil."*

X Signs Preceding the Apparitions

Some of the apparitions were preceded by a bright light.

XI Other Visions During Apparitions

(1) The Infant Jesus appeared with Our Lady sometimes.
(2) Angels, at times the seer saw a group of angels. Often times Our Lady was accompanied by one or two angels.
(3) St. Joseph appeared once as did St. John Bosco.
(4) St. Michael the Archangel appeared to the seer and also gave her messages.
(5) Our Blessed Mother appeared with Her Immaculate Heart exposed.

XII Prayers Taught to the Seer(s)

This seer claims that Our Lady, as well as Jesus, dictated several prayers to her. Some of these prayers are published in a booklet entitled: 'Mary's Prayer Book.' The prayers are:
(1) Key to the Immaculate Heart of Mary. (August 28, 1989)
(2) A Special Consecration of Atonement to the Hearts of Jesus and Mary. (November 5, 1989)
(3) Consecration to the Cross. (December 4, 1990; The Key to the Church of Atonement)
(4) Prayer for Perfection. (October 23, 1993)
(5) Meditations on the mysteries of the rosary. (January 26, 1994)
(6) Jesus gave the seer a prayer on March 1, 1990 and again on June 27, 1990.

XIII Special Devotion Given to the Seer(s)

Although not a devotion as such, Our Lady dictated the 'Four Steps to Holiness' to the seer; the messages being given during four separate apparitions:
(1) **1st Step** - The soul must choose holiness. (November 21, 1993)
(2) **2nd Step** - The soul must choose to abandon sin. (Nov. 25, 1993)
(3) **3rd Step** - The soul abandons his own will and chooses God's will. (November 28, 1993)
(4) **4th Step** - The soul accepts everything in the present moment as the will of the Eternal Father. The soul makes his will one with God's will. (December 1, 1993)

XIV Requests Made by Our Lady

(1) Maranatha Spring - Our Lady requested the area She indicated be probed until the Spring was found. She requested that the Spring be named Maranatha 'Come Lord Jesus' Spring.
(2) Mystical Church of Atonement - Our Lady told the seer that Jesus desired this Church be established and She invited all to join and to have Prayer Rallies of Atonement.
(3) Mary's House of Prayer - Our Lady requested this to be established at Seven Hills, and invited all pilgrims to come and pray at Mary's House of Prayer and at the Maranatha Spring.
(4) 3:00 PM Prayer - Our Lady specially requested that the people gather and pray the Divine Mercy Chaplet at 3:00 PM, then go in procession to the Stations of the Cross and pray the Stations.

XV Specific Bible References

- **(1)** Acts 4:27-31
- **(2)** Amos 9
- **(3)** 1 Corinthians 13
- **(4)** Ephesians 4:1-4; 4:14-16; 5:1-3; 6:10-20
- **(5)** Jonah - Chapter 3
- **(6)** John 3:11-24; 4:7-21; 4:34-38; 5:25-30; 7; 15:1-17
- **(7)** Jude 17-25
- **(8)** Luke 6:27-38; 8:4-8; 8:11-15; 21:1-28
- **(9)** Matthew 5:3-12
- **(10)** Peter 2:11-17
- **(11)** Psalm 23; 32:10-11
- **(12)** Thessalonians 2:1-7

XVI Secrets Given to the Seer(s) - Not Reported
XVII Miracles Promised by Our Lady - NR
XVIII Miracles Performed - Not Reported
XIX Miracles Promised not yet Performed - NR
XX Signs Promised - Not Reported

XXI Signs Given

- **(1)** The seer reports that on March 21, 1993 during an apparition, the rosary beads Our Lady carried turned into drops of blood.
- **(2)** Our Lady showed Her Immaculate Heart during several apparitions.
- **(3)** On July 1, 1989 Our Lady appeared and showed the seer a rosary with the 50 United States of America on the 'Hail Mary' beads; and requested prayers for each of the 50 states.

XXII Predictions/Promises

- **(1)** On November 24, 1990 Our Lady promised specific and special graces during their lifetime for all those who are disposed to enter Christ's Mystical Church of Atonement. She also promised special rewards in heaven for the whole congregation of the Church of Atonement.
- **(2)** On May 20, 1993 Our Lady said: *"All countries that have been graced by My presence in the form of an apparition will suffer more or less in the coming retribution in proportion to their response to My call to holiness. Every site of My apparitions on earth will continue to be a blessed fountain of grace and peace throughout much of the Purification. Jesus gives souls every chance to respond to conversion."*

(3) On September 27, 1993 Our Lady promised that the waters from Maranatha Springs *"will heal souls."*
(4) Then on October 3, 1993 Our Lady stated: *". . . Each one that comes, that is, to be part of the remnant church, will receive a special angel for protection."*

XXIII Prophecies/Warnings of Chastisement

(1) On July 1, 1990 Our Lady warned: *"This Country will suffer greatly in the future unless you begin at once to make atonement to Our Hearts."*
(2) Yet She also said: *"I promise you, bring this nation to the Church of Atonement, and the Chastisement fast approaching will be mitigated; even eliminated."* (April 26, 1990)
(3) Then on March 4, 1993 Our Lady said: *"The hour of God's retribution is at hand, when all man's effort toward worldly gain will turn to dust."*
(4) And: *". . . there are many bitter trials ahead. There is no peace, save in the grace of My Heart."* (August 3, 1993)

XXIV Method of Appearance

It is reported that sometimes a bright light precedes Our Lady's appearance.

XXV Method of Departure

(1) Our Lady always blesses all those present just before She leaves.
(2) On at least one occasion (September 23, 1993) it is reported that after Our Lady disappeared a cross of light remained in the air for a period of time.

XXVI Confrontation w/Civil Authorities - NR
XXVII Confrontation w/Church Authorities - NR

XXVIII Request Chapel/Shrine Built

(1) Our Lady requested Mary's House of Prayer and outlined specific devotions She wanted.
(2) Our Lady also told the seer that Jesus requested the establishment of the Mystical Church of Atonement.

XXIX Free Will/Choice

(1) August 1, 1993 ". . . *You must make a choice between good and evil, for certainly those* (who fail to make a choice) *will find their indecision a condemnation.*"
(2) Again on August 30, 1993 ". . . *the door to the soul is free will.*"
(3) Then on September 18, 1993 Our Lady compassionately says: "*My little children, please understand that it is the soul's own will that leads it away from the Refuge of My Heart.*"
(4) December 8, 1993 ". . . *the way to Holy Love is through the door of the soul which is free will. It is surrendering your will until it becomes one with God's will.*"

XXX Seer(s)' Suffering/Sacrifice - Not Reported
XXXI Healings Reported - Not Reported
XXXII Action Taken by the Church - Not Reported

XXXIII Bibliography

Holy Love 1994
By: Not Given
Published by: The Message of Christ's Mystical Church of Atonement

The Message of Christ's Mystical Church of Atonement
By: Not Given
Published by: Mary's House of Prayer

Mary's Prayer Book
By: Not Given
Published by: Mary's House of Prayer

Chapter 49

UNDISCLOSED LOCATION IN THE USA
(1987)

I Place - Undisclosed location in Northeastern USA

II Dates of First and Last Apparition

First: February 8, 1987
Last: August 11, 1987

III Seer(s) - 1

The seer is anonymous and her identity is protected by Our Lady.

Name: Mariamante (means: "Lover of Mary" in Latin.)
Birth: Unknown
Age at first apparition: (A mother in her mid-thirties)
Status: Living

IV Total Number of Apparitions - 52

Also over 60 apparitions of Jesus are reported — some during the apparitions of Our Blessed Mother and some of Jesus alone.

Undisclosed Location, USA

V Dates and Locality of Each Apparition

(All dates and locations are in the local parish church or in the seer's home, unless otherwise mentioned as different.)

1987: February 8, 11, 12, 13, 14, 15 (twice); 16, 19, 20, 22 (twice); 23 (twice); 25, 26, March 1,2, 5, 7, 10, 16, 18, 19, 23, 25, 27, 31, April 9, 13, 16, 17, May 2, 19, June 4, 10, 11; 13 (Padua, Italy at St. Anthony's Church); 18, June 24, 28, July 2, 5, 8, 12, 14, 16, 24, 31, August 3, 10, 11.

VI Description of Our Lady

(1) On February 19, 1987 Our Lady appeared wearing a crown and dressed in white flowing robes.
(2) After the first few apparitions Our Lady would usually appear with the Christ Child in Her arms.
(3) Sometimes Our Lady wore a white veil and at times She would appear in a traditional image, such as Our Lady of Mt. Carmel or Our Lady of Sorrows.

VII Title of Our Lady - 2

(1) Our Lady appeared under the title "Mother of God."
(2) Also as "Queen of Heaven and Earth" as She announced on February 19, 1987.

VIII Brief Factual Review

The reports and facts identifying the location where the apparitions are said to have taken place are very sparse. The location probably is within one of the States located in the north-central/eastern part of the USA, according to the reports.

Likewise the visionary is not identified by her true or real name. Our Lady Herself promised to protect the true identity of the seer for good and prudent reasons.

What is reported is that the seer is a young mother in her mid thirties with a husband and three children, aged seven, three, and one. The seer was born into a Catholic family, but did not attend Catholic schools. Her religious education was limited to CCD classes. She did receive some instruction when she joined the Franciscan Third Order.

When these apparitions began, her spiritual director wisely forbade the seer to read any other writings on private revelations or mystical experiences, contemporary or otherwise, in order to retain the purity and integrity of the messages. The seer is called "Mariamante" which means 'Lover of Mary' in Latin.

Our Lord and Our Lady gave this visionary the mission to form a silent movement known as the Apostolate of Holy Motherhood consisting of mothers doing their ordinary duties within their own families, yet meanwhile participating in contemplative prayer for purity, for conversion, for gifts of the Holy Spirit, and other holy causes. The three basic rules of the Apostolate which the members (mothers as well as clergy and others) are to embrace are the following:

(1) They must devote their time, energy and resources, including their very selves, to the greater Glory of God and to the pursuit of the Divine Will in their lives.

(2) They must be consecrated to the Blessed Virgin Mary under the title "Mother of God".

(3) They must seek to fulfill their daily duties, that as mothers and wives in an exemplary manner of holiness by pursuing the contemplative life in their homes.

This is to be a spiritual movement and not an organization as such. Children are to be esteemed by parents as precious, which will be brought about, in part, by a renewed devotion to the Christ Child. The graces dispensed through this Apostolate will help to alleviate the suffering of innocent children in the world. Especially those who are suffering from spiritual hunger or abandonment.

These series of apparitions commenced on February 8, 1987 and continued, almost daily, until August 11, 1987. There are also reports of later apparitions. Also, these apparitions were preceded by a series of visions given to the seer in late 1986 and early 1987:

(1) In December 1986 the seer saw a vision of Our Lord as an adult dressed in flowing robes.

(2) Later she saw Our Lord's face in death while He was hanging on the cross.

(3) In January 1987 she saw visions of Our Blessed Mother with Her Immaculate Heart exposed.

(4) The seer also had visions of several saints such as St. Catherine of Sienna, St. Clare of Assisi, and St. Anne.

Later Mariamante pondered that since St. Catherine was single, St. Clare was a nun, and St. Anne was a mother that perhaps she was given these visions for her own reflection and meditation.

The apparitions received during this period from February 8, through August 11, 1987 were of Our Lady usually holding the Christ Child, and of Our Lord alone as an adult or as the Christ Child. The last several apparitions were of Our Lord and Our Lady with the Sacred Heart and the Immaculate Heart exposed.

Messages were given by Our Lady, by the Christ Child and by Our

Lord shown as the Sacred Heart. Once the seer asked Our Lady: "How do I know this is from You?" And Our Lady replied: *"You will know this is from Me by the truth in it."*

Mariamante promptly sought and obtained a spiritual advisor and confessor to whom she revealed every vision and all other events as requested by Our Lady and Our Lord.

The book of messages contains the Nihil Obstat and Imprimatur which Our Lady promised to accomplish in Her message of February 23, 1987.

The messages themselves focused on the Apostolate of Holy Motherhood and stressed purity, prayer, the rosary, reception of the Sacraments, allegiance to the Holy Father, the need to acquire the virtues and gifts of the Holy Spirit, and adoration before the Blessed Sacrament.

On February 24th Our Lady said: *"For as love is the queen of all virtues, so humility is the king."*

Our Lady especially requested that kindness be taught and shown to children. On February 15, 1987 Our Lady said: *"Mothers teach your children to be kind to one another. The important lessons are learned at home. Do not expect others to teach your children. That is your responsibility and should be your great joy."* Then on February 13th, Our Lady said: *"Be attentive to your children, they are most important. They will live during the Reign of My Immaculate Heart."*

We are told in the messages that it is due to the prevalent sin in the world, that the world now requires a tremendous diffusion of grace, and massive and instantaneous conversions. This new Apostolate has been formed to offer prayer power and suffering to help convert mankind.

In 1987 the Holy Father declared a Marian Year, to which Our Lady alluded in Her message of February 22, 1987: *"The Holy Father has declared this a Marian Year. This is at the inspiration of the Holy Spirit. . ."*

On April 17th Our Lady stated that the visions would end for a time; a time when the seer was to have great doubts and when she would be disregarded by many. This was to be a period of cleansing and sanctification, after which would come a glorious period. And so it happened.

The seer would go into ecstasy during the visions, especially during visions received inside the church after Mass. In order to protect her identity, the seer's spiritual director directed her to leave church immediately after Mass. Thereafter the visions would occur after she got home.

On one occasion while the seer was in rapture, she composed prayers and poems which she wrote down after coming out of that state.

Several noted clergy and theologians have stated their support for this Apostolate; yet no Church action has been reported. Often new Apostolates take a great amount of time to get into motion. Only time will tell what will finally happen.

IX The Primary Messages - 6

There seems to be no doubt that the heart and core of the messages, and the very purpose of the visions was to establish the Apostolate of Holy Motherhood as revealed by the Christ Child in the message of March 25, 1987 which is set out in full in section XIII below.

(1) Purity - On February 8, 1987 the very first message, Our Lady said: *"Evangelical purity is to be practiced especially among women and priests, all who are called to be spouses of Christ."* Then again: *"You are being made pure by the graces in the confessional. It is not necessary to discuss the impurity in today's society in depth or publicly."*

On February 11th Our Lady said: *"Pray for and practice purity. The world depends upon it now."*

(2) Rosary - Our Lady would often tell the seer to: *"Finish your rosary"* at the end of the vision, just before Our Lady departed.

On February 13th Our Lady said: *"Say a fifteen decade rosary daily. This is most pleasing to God."*

Again on February 15th Our Lady said: *"Humility and purity are what is needed now in the world. Say many rosaries for this purpose."*

On February 22, 1987 Our Lady said: *"I wish that I could persuade all My priest sons to return to their rosaries. The rosary is most powerful now."*

On February 23, 1987 Our Lady said: *"Pray the rosary always, it will help you to understand many things."*

(3) Prayer - On February 13th Our Lady said: *"Heaven is most distressed with the state the world is in. It is very bad right now. Only prayer and penance can change this."*

Again on February 14, 1987 Our Lady said: *"Pray for the world. It is urgent now. The world is facing a great catastrophe beyond known proportion due to impiety and impurity."*

On February 23rd Our Lady said: *"Continue to pray for all priests as they need your prayers right now."*

On March 27th Our Lady informed us: *"Prayer is the prerequisite to spiritual favors and gifts and must be asked for by someone."*

On June 28, 1987 Our Lady pleads: *"Pray in reparation to My Immaculate Heart for sin in the world, especially those sins against purity and blasphemies against My Divine and Adorable Son."*

On July 5th Our Lady said: *"I urge you to pray always. Make your life a prayer, a hymn of love for God and to God."*

On July 14th Our Lady said: *"Pray for children, all children throughout the world. Pray that families will have great reverence for new life, great reverence for children who are fashioned in My image."*

(4) Sacraments - On March 1st Our Lady said: *"I wish all My children would make use of this Sacrament and go to Confession frequently. Frequent,* regular Confession will make them grow in holiness."

On March 31st Our Lady said: *"As sinners you are all in need of constant help and support of the Sacraments. You must always turn to them for your strength, particularly, of course, the Sacrament of Penance and Holy Eucharist."*

Finally on July 29th Jesus told the seer: *"The frequent reception of the Sacrament of Reconciliation and Penance, and Holy Communion are the surest and safest way to Me . . ."*

(5) **Eucharistic Adoration** - On February 14th Our Lady said: *"The Eucharist must be adored. Adore the Eucharist. The Eucharistic Heart of Jesus is the greatest gift God has given to men. Sadly, it is now not appreciated."*

Then on July 12th Our Lady said: *"Praise Him always. Give Him thanks. Adore Him with all your hearts. Love the Blessed Sacrament and spend time in adoration daily in His presence."*

(6) **Allegiance to the Holy Father** - On February 22, 1987 Our Lady said: *"The Holy Father has declared this a Marian Year. This is at the inspiration of the Holy Spirit. He is the sovereign leader of the Church. He has been given this inspiration by God Himself. Follow his inspiration."*

Then on June 24th Our Lady said: *"The Holy Father is leading many of My children back to Me and My Divine Son. He is the crowning glory of My movement, the Pope I love so dearly, and the one to whom you must refer for all guidance in matters of faith and morals."*

X Signs Preceding the Apparitions - Not Reported

XI Other Visions During Apparitions

(1) The Child Jesus appeared during many of the apparitions of Our Blessed Mother. Jesus gave messages to the seer.
(2) Jesus appeared with His Sacred Heart exposed and gave messages to Mariamante.
(3) Our Lady showed Her Immaculate Heart to this seer.
(4) On February 11th St. Bernadette and St. Anne appeared to this seer during a vision of Our Lady.
(5) It is reported that in December 1986 and early in 1987 before the main visions occurred, the seer had several visions of Jesus, Mary, St. Catherine of Sienna, St. Clare of Assisi, and St. Anne.

XII Prayers Taught to the Seer(s)

(1) On May 19, 1987 Our Lady requested that the seer prepare in prayer before the Feast of the Pentecost *". . .with a special Novena to the Holy Spirit which will be given to you."* Then Our Blessed Mother

gave the seer this prayer to repeat for nine days before and after the Feast; first in petition, then in thanksgiving:
Prayer:
> 'Come Holy Spirit, enlighten my heart
> to see the things which are of God;
> Come Holy Spirit into my mind,
> that I may know the things that are of God;
> Come Holy Spirit into my soul,
> that I may belong only to God.
> Sanctify all that I think, say, and do,
> that all will be for the Glory of God.   Amen.'

(2) It is also reported that Mariamante composed poems and prayers while in ecstasy. Furthermore, the seer is reported to have received inspiration for a special prayer of Consecration that seems appropriate to the Apostolate.

XIII Special Devotion Given to the Seer(s)

(1) Apostolate of Holy Motherhood of Catholic Families - The establishment of this Apostolate was the primary purpose of the messages.

On February 23, 1987 Our Blessed Mother said: *"An Apostolate of Motherhood will grow out of these writings, and will be an Apostolate of prayer and duty in the home done in accord with the will of God and for the love of God. I will be the model for these mothers in their daily lives, and they will imitate My Virtues. This is necessary to combat the tide of evil which has swept across families and destroyed so many homes."*

Then on March 25, 1987 Our Lord Himself, under the mode of the Christ Child, gave the seer the details of this Apostolate: *"The Apostolate will be approved by the Holy Father and will be promulgated amongst the families of My Church in the four corners of the earth. It will do great good and help much in stemming the tide of evil ravaging so many families today. There will be three basic tenets that they, the members, must follow:"*

1) They must devote their time, energy and resources, including their very selves, to the greater Glory of God and the pursuit of the Divine Will in their lives.

2) They must be consecrated to the Blessed Virgin Mary under the title "Mother of God."

3) They must seek to fulfill their daily duties as mothers and wives in an exemplary manner of holiness by pursuing the contemplative life in their homes.

The major points of the Apostolate stressed in the messages are:
    a) An Apostolate of Mothers consecrated to the Mother of God
    b) Contemplative Prayer
    c) Eucharistic Adoration

d) Practice of Evangelical Purity
e) Pursuit of the Divine Will
f) Devotion to the Christ Child
g) Devotion to the Sacred Heart and to the Immaculate Heart
h) Devotion to daily duty
i) Devotion to the Holy Family
j) Fidelity to the Holy Family
k) Wearing the Scapular and Sacred Heart Badge
l) Practice Nine First Fridays and Five First Saturdays
m) Fifteen decade daily rosary
n) Daily prayers for purity

(2) **Devotion to the Christ Child** - Although not a new devotion, yet Jesus Himself urged this devotion.

February 21, 1987 Jesus said: *"Devotion to Me as a Child is important for it manifests the tenderness of My love. Pray to Me as the Christ Child. This is most pleasing to Me. Cultivate this devotion."*

(3) **Scapular** - Again this is not a new devotion, however, Our Lady encouraged us to wear it.

February 19, 1987 Our Lady said: *"The Scapular of Mt. Carmel is a sign of My protection. Wear it always. It will help you to do good, because it is a sign of My love and will remind you of Me often."*

XIV Requests Made by Our Lady

(1) Contemplative prayer.
(2) Wear the Scapular of Mt. Carmel.
(3) Pray to the holy angels: *"for guidance and wisdom to do God's will in your daily duties and they will help you to follow His will."* (February 24, 1987).

XV Specific Bible References

Although no specific Bible reference is reported, yet on July 5, 1987 Our Lady said: *". . Look to Him in the reading of Holy Scriptures, meditating upon His holy words . . ."*

XVI Secrets Given to the Seer(s) - Not Reported
XVII Miracles Promised by Our Lady - NR
XVIII Miracles Performed - Not Reported
XIX Miracles Promised not yet Performed - NR
XX Signs Promised - Not Reported

XXI Signs Given - Not Reported

XXII Predictions/Promises

(1) Our Blessed Mother promised to protect the seer's anonymity. On February 13, 1987 Our Lady said: *"I will protect you always from the public eye."* She kept Her promise.
(2) On February 22, 1987 Our Lady said: *"The time is at hand for the instantaneous conversion of the multitude. This I will accomplish through tremendous outpouring of grace upon the earth given at the hands of God to Me for this purpose."*
(3) On February 23, 1987 Our Lady promised to obtain the Imprimatur for the book of messages. This was done as promised.
(4) Again on February 23, 1987 Our Lady promised: *"An Apostolate of Motherhood will grow out of these writings."*
(5) On March 1, 1987 Our Lady predicted that: *"Nearly everyone working for My cause, the Triumph, will be experiencing some harassments now in accord with the importance of their mission for which I have entrusted them. Do not fear this. Consider it part of your sanctification."*
(6) On June 7, 1987 the seer reported that a prophecy, given to her by Our Blessed Mother earlier, regarding what would occur on Pentecost, was fulfilled.

XXIII Prophecies/Warnings of Chastisement

(1) On February 14, 1987 Our Lady said: *"The world is facing a great cataclysm beyond known proportion due to the impiety and impurity. The message of Fatima contains all that is necessary for you to know in this time."*
(2) Later on March 5th the Christ Child warned: *"Oh, pray for the world, especially now when it is so urgent. The cries of the innocent call out to Me. So much injustice cannot continue for long. It must be changed, and very soon, or a grave chastisement will come to all the world; this is the way it must be. Heaven can tolerate no more. Either change or this will come about."*

XXIV Method of Appearance - Not Reported

XXV Method of Departure

Usually Our Lady would say one of the following salutations just before She departed:

(1) *"Go in Peace."*
(2) *"Go finish your rosary."*

XXVI Confrontation w/Civil Authorities - NR

XXVII Confrontation w/Church Authorities

(1) No confrontation as such is reported.
(2) The seer was forbidden by her spiritual director from reading any writings of private revelation, either contemporary or otherwise, as well as any classical mystical writings in order to retain the purity and integrity of these messages.
(3) The manuscripts of the messages were submitted to a number of theologians, some of which have responded. The responses have been favorable.

XXVIII Requests Chapel/Shrine Be Built - NR

XXIX Free Will/Choice

Both Jesus and Our Blessed Mother gave messages to the seer recognizing that we have freedom to choose.
(1) March 2, 1987 the Christ Child said: *". . . How you answer is up to you. Now is the time to make your choice."*
(2) On August 10, 1987 Our Lady said: *"Are you willing to participate in this salvific action by your own sufferings and crosses which God chooses to send you?"* Thus, clearly giving the seer a choice.

XXX Seer(s)' Suffering/Sacrifice

There are repeated references in the messages that sacrifice and suffering are necessary before the glory can be enjoyed.
On August 10th Our Lady specifically asked the seer if she was willing to undergo suffering and crosses which God may send. The seer answered in the affirmative. She has suffered much in carrying out the Apostolate given to her, in living her state of life and in exercising her called-for daily duties. This is what Our Lady asked of the seer and seems to be consistent with the messages given at Fatima.

XXXI Healings Reported - Not Reported

XXXII Action Taken by the Church

No official church action is reported. No edicts and no formal declarations are reported.

The book of messages received the Imprimatur and several noted author-theologians have commented favorably on these messages.

XXXIII Bibliography

The Apostolate of Holy Motherhood 1991
By: Not Given
Published by: The Riehle Foundation

Chapter 50

HRUSHIV, UKRAINE
(1987)

I Place - Hrushiv, Ukraine, USSR

II Dates of First and Last Apparition

Marina Kizen
First: April 26, 1987
Last: Unknown

Joseph Terelya
First: May 12, 1987
Last: May 16, 1987

III Seer(s) - 2

Name: Marina Kizen (Kizyn)
Birth: Unknown
Age at first apparition: 11
Status: Living

Name: Joseph Terelya
Birth: October 27, 1943
Age at first apparition: 43
Status: Living

IV Total Number of Apparitions - 8

(1) To Marina Kizen - 1 reported
(2) To Joseph Terelya - 7 reported
(3) It is reported that thousands and perhaps tens of thousands saw Our Blessed Mother above the Holy Trinity Church in Hrushiv during the 1987 apparitions.

V Dates and Locality of Each Apparition

1987: Marina Kizen - April 26 at Holy Trinity Church.
1987: Joseph Terelya - May 9, 10, 11, 12, 13, 14, 16 at Holy Trinity Church.

It is reported that Our Lady appeared daily at Hrushiv, from April 26, 1987 through August 15, 1987.

Then the apparitions reportedly resumed in Hrushiv in April 1988, and lasted through July 7, 1988.

Reports are that the apparitions occurred in nine to thirteen other shrines scattered across the Ukraine during the period from August 15, 1987 to April 1988, and again in those other shrines after July 7, 1988 when the apparitions ceased at Hrushiv.

VI Description of Our Lady

(1) Initially Our Blessed Lady appeared over the Cupola of the Holy Trinity Church. First an aureole of light was seen, then, within this light was a movement of different colored lights, yellow, gold, and silver. Suddenly, Our Lady appeared floating above the church. Reports describe Her dressed in white or dressed in gold with a flaming red dress, always holding a rosary in Her right hand. She had gentle features. Her face was clear and bright and Her eyes were dark blue. She was about 18-21. Her head was covered with a blue veil. On one occasion, May 16, 1987, Our Lady raised Her left hand and kissed Her own rosary. On the Feast of the Ascension in 1987, Our Lady held the Child Jesus in Her arms.

(2) On February 12, 1972 when Our Lady appeared to Joseph Terelya in prison (Cell #21), Our Lady wore a heavy pleated dark blue dress and a kerchief with fringes, like the Carpathian Mountain women would wear.

(3) During more recent visions Our Lady is reported to have appeared to Joseph Terelya in Canada. On September 18, 1992 She appeared dressed in black with a white mantle over Her head. In Her hands, as always, She held a rosary; this time the rosary was black with white beads.

VII Title(s) of Our Lady - 1

Although the record does not include Our Lady's designation of Her own title, yet it is reported that during one of the visions, Joseph Terelya heard angelic choirs singing: *"Most Holy Mother of God, save us."*

Also, throughout the biography of Joseph Terelya, Our Lady is referred to as "Mother of God".

VIII Brief Factual Review

The village of Hrushiv (Hrusia) is located in the Ukraine, a part of the USSR when these apparitions occurred in 1987-1988. Hrushiv is located about midway between Urgord and L'vov, and had a population of about 2,000 families. The people work in collective farms or in factories. They cultivate potatoes, beets and other vegetables, and grains. They also raise animals for their own use.

Tradition has it that Our Blessed Lady first appeared in Hrushiv some 350 years earlier, at a time when local wars were being fought. In honor of Our Lady's visit the villagers planted a willow tree on the spot of that earlier apparition. At the end of the 18th century, a spring suddenly appeared beneath the willow tree. People used the water from the spring for healing and that place soon became a place of pilgrimage. An icon of Our Lady was placed above the willow tree. The authorities were opposed to the notoriety and arranged to have the spring contaminated.

In the mid 1800's there was an outbreak of cholera in Hrushiv. Many people died. A local woman claimed Our Lady appeared to her in a dream and told her to have the spring reclaimed and for Holy Mass to be said there and then the cholera epidemic would end. These requests were complied with and the epidemic ended.

Following a vision of three tongues of fire above the spring, a small chapel was built on the site in honor of the Holy Trinity. A larger church was later built, which still stands today, and is the site of the first apparition of 1987.

Then on May 12th, 1914 (two weeks prior to the outbreak of World War I), Our Blessed Lady appeared to twenty-two people. She asked for continued prayer, hope, fasting, and penance. Our Lady said that there would be a war, that Russia would become a godless country and that Ukraine as a nation would suffer terribly for eighty years and would have to endure three wars but would be free afterwards.

It is remembered that Ukraine was the first nation to consecrate itself to the Immaculate Heart of Mary; some 950 years ago.

After the Bolshevik Revolution the Ukraine came under the control of the communist regime which ran the USSR. In 1958 the Soviet authorities closed the chapel of the Holy Trinity. It was boarded up and all use of the chapel was prohibited. Moreover, it is reported that the authorities erected a fence and dug a ditch around the chapel. Visitors could only look through a hole in the door of the chapel through which they could see a gold painted wooden icon inside.

On April 26, 1986 the world was told of a terrible nuclear catastrophe which occurred at the Chernobyl Nuclear Plant located in the Ukraine.

The Holy Father in Rome had meanwhile declared a Marian Year for 1987-1988.

And so it happened that on April 26, 1987 (exactly one year to the day) after the Chernobyl Nuclear Disaster, Our Blessed Mother manifested Herself above the balcony of the Holy Trinity Chapel to an eleven-year-old girl named Marina Kizyn (Kizen).

Marina was walking to school from her home when she noticed a strange light hovering over the chapel. As she drew nearer, the vision unfolded. Contained within the strange light she saw the figure of Our Blessed Mother holding a Child in Her arms. Our Lady was dressed in black and told Marina that the Ukrainians, because of their long-suffering, have been chosen to lead the Soviet Union back to Christianity. At this Marina became frightened and rushed back to her home to tell her mother and sister. Her mother and sister quickly went to the chapel with Marina where they also saw the vision. Her mother said to Marina: "This is the Blessed Mary, kneel and pray." The vision remained over the chapel for several days before it dimmed.

Of course this news shook the village and news spread quickly and crowds soon came to see for themselves. People came from far off regions as well as from nearby villages. There are reports from many different people, from all walks of life, who saw Our Lady appear above the chapel in a bright light. Some children reported seeing "angels that fly".

Our Blessed Lady appeared continuously for some three weeks—during which time tens of thousands of pilgrims reported seeing Our Lady and many heard Her messages. There are reports of members of the KGB and the Militia (who were there to control, divert or disperse the crowds) seeing the apparition and becoming instant believers. It is also reported that there were conversions and even baptisms of many of the curious pilgrims of other faiths (or of no faith) once they witnessed the apparitions. It was apparently not unusual for 40,000 to 80,000 people to be at the apparition site every day during this initial three week period. On one of the days of the apparitions in May 1987, it is reported that there were 52,000 embroidered prayer towels left as tokens of reverence and love, which fairly implies that at least 52,000 people were present that day. Further, it is reported that the apparitions continued thereafter until August 15, 1987 and therafter resumed again in Hrushiv in April 1988 and lasted through July 7, 1988. Meanwhile apparitions were reported at other shrines in the Ukraine during the period August 15, 1987 to April 1988.

Although many pilgrims saw the apparitions and heard the messages it seems that the central visionary (and the one who recorded and wrote a book of the messages) was Joseph Terelya. Joseph Terelya was a Catholic activist who had promoted the underground Church in the dark days, and had spent over 20 years of his life imprisoned for his beliefs. His story is truly a heroic and courageous account of a dedicated disciple of Our Lady and of Our Lord.

Joseph Terelya was born in a tiny mountain hamlet called Dovhe. He was raised by his grandmother. His own mother and father worked for the communists, with assignments which included suppressing the underground Catholic Church. He was first arrested at age eighteen on September 4, 1962. Thereafter, he was arrested, tortured, imprisoned and escaped many times before his final release in 1987, shortly before the first apparition at Hrushiv. While imprisoned Our Blessed Mother appeared to Joseph in Cell #21 on two separate occasions; February 12, 1970 and February 12, 1972. She saved his life, gave him much good counsel, and gave Joseph a variety of predictions. She even predicted the date of his final release from prison. All came true as Our Lady foretold.

On September 18, 1987 Joseph was deported from the Soviet Union and stripped of his citizenship. He now lives in Canada and has told his story and makes appearances at various conferences and gatherings. He has spoken before the U.S. Congress and has had private meetings with Pope John Paul II. It is reported that Our Lady has resumed the apparitions to Joseph Terelya as of 1992 in Canada.

Joseph Terelya first obtained knowledge of the April 26th, 1987 apparition on or about May 9th. After some trepidation he did journey to Hrushiv. His reports concerning the visions and messages occurring during May 11th-16th, 1987, are related below:

(1) May 11, 1987: On this date the apparition appeared as the afternoon liturgy began and lasted throughout the entire day. At one point Our Lady held Her left hand on Her Heart and tears filled Her eyes. Also on this day, many students came to the site of the apparitions, followed by their teachers. The message given on this date by Our Blessed Mother was a request for diligent prayer, for conversion, for prayers for the Holy Father, and She urged us to carry our rosary and to pray the rosary every day. She said difficult times were coming and that the rosary is a powerful weapon against spiritual adversaries. Our Lady implored us to ". . . *lead a pure and sinless life, . . . prepare for great persecutions and new sacrifices."*

Our Lady also said: *"There is a greater need for lay apostles than ever before. Help the Pope and the third secret of Fatima will be revealed to you. We are living in the times of the Father. The third secret is all around you. The times of God have begun."*

It is reported that various sects espousing Fundamentalism and Pentecostalism were eager to openly declare these events as not being supernatural. This, of course, bolstered the KGB and the government itself who were concerned on the one hand, yet eager on the other hand, to work to condemn and to explain away all these events as some kind of gigantic fraud perpetrated by the Vatican. In spite of these obstacles it is reported by Joseph: "I saw plenty of non-Christians converted instantly".

There is a report that an officer in the Militia saw the apparition light up and fired a shot at the light. The officer reportedly was instantly struck unconscious. His arm turned black as though electrocuted. Witnesses state a ray of light came from the apparition and struck the officer down. Other strange and even mystical events are reported.

(2) May 12, 1987: On this date the crowd was quiet and peaceful. There were many members of the media and press present for this apparition. It is reported that one reporter from the 'Literary Gazette' exclaimed: "I see the Mother of God!" When Joseph asked if she would write that, she replied that she already had instructions on how to write her article.

Meanwhile, the Militia and the KGB did their best to prevent the crowds from coming to the site. One report states that cadets cut a large tree to fall across the road in order to block the pilgrims, but the wind shifted suddenly and the tree fell directly upon the military vehicles of the cadets instead of on the roadway.

On this date Our Blessed Mother appeared again holding the Christ Child. She told the crowd: *"The Infant is protecting you and I am giving you grace and strength . . . In ten years your people will be free and your enemies will never defeat you."* Then again: *"My daughter Ukraine, I have come to you because you have remained faithful to Me amidst this desolation, and devout people will spread news of Me everywhere."*

Our Lady also warned of a great conflagration. She warned: *"If people do not convert to Christ, there will be war."*

(3) May 13, 1987: On this date Our Lady appeared and implored us to pray constantly, to pray the rosary, do penance and be merciful. Then: *"You can save the world by your prayers."*

She also admonished us: *"How many warnings must mankind be given before it repents? If Russia does not accept Christ the King, the entire world faces ruin."* Our Lady concludes: *"Through you and your martyred Church will come the conversion of Russia, but hasten and pray very much, especially the rosary!"*

It is reported that on this date of May 13th, being the 70th Anniversary of Our Lady's first appearance at Fatima, a local TV program presented a few scenes from Hrushiv in order to ridicule these events. The TV station was flooded with calls from people who claimed to have seen on their TV screens in their own home, an image of the person of Our Blessed Virgin Mary instead of the news report!

(4) May 14, 1987: This day's crowd was estimated at 20,000 people. Many people saw Our Lady and heard Her messages. (Other pilgrims reported seeing the Crucified Christ). She held the Child Jesus in Her arms and bowed to the crowd. Her face was widened into a smile and She looked everyone directly in the eye. Then She spoke and delivered an unusually long message.

Our Lady said Her Heart was turned to Ukraine because it had been faithful to God. She urged us to *"not neglect prayers to the Archangel Michael,"* and to pray especially for the dead.

Again, Our Blessed Mother warned the world: *"The wicked world is gorging itself on depravity and impurity. The people are falling into the hands of Satan. They are blinded by unceasing idolatry. How many come as false Messiahs and false prophets! So I warn you to be diligent."*

She concluded with a message of encouragement and hope: *"You can achieve the destruction of all the arms that have been arrayed by the unbelieving nations through prayer and fasting, through the action of all people who have accepted Christ."*

(5) **May 16, 1987:** It had become a part of the daily routine for Joseph Terelya to address the crowds, to lead the rosary and to defy the KGB. So it was on this day. Joseph had led the rosary and given his talk to the crowds who were staring at the dome of the church. Suddenly someone called out: "It's Her!" and Our Blessed Mother once more appeared. First an aureole of light surrounded the dome, then a brilliant light appeared within the aureole, and moved to a position directly over the church. The light expanded and within the light was the form of a Woman holding a child in Her arms. There was a great feeling of peace and serenity. Then Our Lady raised Her left hand and kissed Her rosary. Now She was ready to speak.

Our Lady's opening message was to *"Repent and love one another."* Again, She warned of the difficult times coming, and implored us to pray and work for good.

She also gave private messages to Joseph and then Joseph was given a vision. He was also given messages of prophecy during the vision. The prophecies were apocalyptic in nature. She predicted: *"In two years you won't be here. . . ";* and sure enough Joseph was deported and now lives in Canada. Then Joseph heard a woman's voice while the vision was in progress. These are the words he heard: *"You have seen the godless East and West. The difference is that in the West godlessness is not officially recognized, but the goal of godlessness in the East and West is the same. In order to save Russia and the whole world from godless hell, you must convert Russia to Christ the King. The conversion of Russia will save Christian culture in the West and will push for Christianity throughout the world. But the Kingdom of Christ the King shall establish itself through the reign of the Mother of God."*

Additional apparitions occurred in Hrushiv after May 16, 1987 however, no messages are reported. Of course we are all now aware of the collapse of, not only the USSR, but also of all the nations in the Eastern

Block which were behind the 'Iron Curtain'.

These reported apparitions seem timely and portend the breakup of the Soviet Union and therefore freedom for the Ukraine; and only then the conversion of the Russian people.

It has been reported that Our Lady has again appeared to Joseph Terelya in 1992 and given him messages; this time in Marmora, Canada where Joseph now resides.

On September 13, 1992 Our Lady appeared all in light, dressed in white, a sky-blue mantle on Her head, and wearing a red cloak. She held a rosary in Her right hand and appeared with tears in Her eyes. She asked that a small chapel be erected on the hill between the 10th and 11th Stations of the Cross. She urged us to pray, to pray the rosary, and to fast three days a week: Wednesday, Friday, and Sunday.

On September 18, 1992 Our Lady is reported to have appeared again to Joseph; this time dressed in black, with a white mantle over Her head and a rosary with black and white beads in Her hands. Again She pleaded for prayers and conversion. She gave stern warnings of terrible events to come if the world does not return to God, and She also warned us of evil influences that are acting now in our world. *"Now understand, that the devil uses invisible evil spirits, who act upon visible servants throughout the world . . ."*

It is not reported whether these apparitions are even now ongoing. Nor is it reported whether there has been any Church action taken regarding the events that occurred in Hrushiv or in Canada.

IX The Primary Messages - 5

(1) Prayer - Our Lady repeatedly urged us to pray and to do so constantly.

May 11, 1987 Our Lady said: *"Proclaim the Word of God among those who have denied His Son. Pray! Pray for those who are leading immoral lives. Pray constantly and everywhere."*

Again on the same date: *"Pray for the Holy Father, pray together at one time . . ."*

Then on May 13th Our Lady said: *"Who wants to receive the grace of God should pray constantly. Pray for ravaged Russia. You can save the world by your prayers."*

May 14, 1987 Our Lady spoke: *"Do not neglect your prayers to the Archangel Michael; pray especially for the deceased . . ."*

On May 16th Our Lady said: *"I come to you in tears to implore you to pray, work for good, and labor for the glory of God."*

Later during a vision that same day: *"Pray to the Sacred Heart of Jesus . . ."*

During the apparitions reported in September 1992 occurring in

Canada, Our Lady urged prayer; prayer for the Pope and for unity.

(2) **Rosary** - May 11, 1987 on this occasion Our Blessed Mother urged us to: *"Pray the rosary, teach your children to pray the rosary. It is powerful against the Anti-Christ."*

Later during this same apparition: *"Pray the rosary daily, especially for the deceased."*

May 13th, Our Lady reminded us: *"Remember that the rosary will preserve mankind from sin and perdition."*

(3) **Teach Children to Pray** - During these apparitions Our Lady repeated Her strong plea that we teach our children to pray.

May 14, 1987 Our Lady said: *"Teach the children, for this will save them from the Anti-Christ. This is your heavenly defense."*

(4) **Repent, Sacrifice and Penance** - May 11, 1987 Our Lady said: *"Sacrifice is a chief commandment declared by Jesus Christ. Remember that sin is the forbidden luxury and that sacrifice allows you to become a sincere participant in the sufferings of Jesus. . ."*

Later on this date: *"Suffering and prayer will overcome everything."*

May 14th, on this date Our Lady said: *"The Kingdom of Heaven on Earth is at hand. But it will come only through repentance and penance."*

May 16th Our Lady said: *"All Christians should repent and, through purification from sin, stop the godlessness in Russia from continuing to spread through the world."*

(5) **Lead a Pure and Sinless Life** - May 11, 1987 Our Lady said: *"Lead a pure and sinless life . . . Do not overindulge in drink, do not smoke, do not go to sinful dances."*

May 14, 1987 on this occasion Our Lady said: *"Cast from your shrines any signs of Satan that have been forced upon you. The churches are weeping and perishing. Lead a pure and sinless life!"*

X Signs Preceding the Apparitions

(1) An aura of light appeared luminous above the chapel. Within this aura a smaller, yet more intense light moved and oscillated and settled over the Cupola. It was from this more intense light that Our Lady emerged and appeared.
(2) Other accounts describe how Our Lady's arrival was heralded by an iridescent pulsating light from which She would emerge floating in the air above the church building.

XI Other Visions During Apparitions

(1) Several pilgrims claimed to have seen Jesus Crucified during an apparition.
(2) Joseph Terelya reports having several visions where he was shown

various apocalyptic scenes.
(3) Our Blessed Mother did appear to Joseph in 1970 and 1972 while he was in prison.

XII Prayers Taught to the Seer(s)

On May 14, 1987 Our Blessed Mother said: *"All of you must say this prayer: 'O my God I am heartily sorry for having offended You and I confess all my sins.'"*

XIII Special Devotion Given to the Seer(s) - NR

XIV Requests Made by Our Lady

(1) On May 11, 1987 Our Lady said: *"When you pray during Mass use the sign of the Cross 33 times."*
(2) Our Blessed Mother urged us to forgive injuries. On May 11th She said: *"I turn to you and ask you to forgive your enemies; to be a beacon in the dark!"*
(3) On September 13, 1992 Our Lady requested we observe three days a week for fasting: Wednesday, Friday, and Sunday.

XV Specific Bible References

Although there were messages that contained quotes from Scripture and there were prophecies of an apocalyptic nature, even so there were no specific Bible references reported.

XVI Secrets Given to the Seer(s)

As one apparition faded (either May 11th or 13th, 1987), Joseph received a vision of the faces of nineteen different people on a screen. Some were members of the KGB, government officials, priests and one cardinal. Joseph later met this cardinal.

Our Lady told Joseph to keep secret the identity of these nineteen faces. Through this vision Joseph received some understanding of the great peril facing the Church.

XVII Miracles Promised by Our Lady - NR

XVIII Miracles Performed

Our Blessed Mother appeared to Joseph in prison Cell #21 on February 12, 1970 and miraculously saved him from freezing to death.

XIX Miracles Promised not yet Performed - NR
XX Signs Promised - Not Reported

XXI Signs Given

(1) It is reported some of the children saw angels flying.
(2) The great crowds saw their entire surroundings enveloped in a luminosity during the apparitions; including leaves, twigs, the people, and everything around them.
(3) Other pilgrims saw a massive cross in the sky; in that cross people would appear.
(4) On May 13th, while the government television was reporting on the Hrushiv appearances in order to demean them, many viewers saw the image of Our Lady on their TV screens in their homes.

XXII Predictions/Promises

(1) On May 12, 1987 Our Lady said: *"In ten years your people will be free and your enemies will never defeat you."*
(2) On May 13, 1987 She said: *"If Russia does not accept Christ the King, the entire world faces ruin."*
(3) Our Lady also predicted the date Joseph would be released from prison. It came to pass as promised.
(4) In the early 1970's, Our Lady told Joseph: *"There will be major changes within your own nation (USSR)."* Of course we have seen this happen in our own day.

XXIII Prophecies/Warnings of Chastisement

(1) In a vision on May 12th Our Lady looked ahead and said to Joseph: *"I see fire. The villages are burning. Water is burning. The very air is on fire. Everything is in flames. If people do not convert to Christ, there will be war. There shall be a great conflagration."* (This was more graphically reiterated during a vision on May 13th.)
(2) On May 14th Our Lady said: *"The Anti-Christ is sowing envy and dissension. The seal of the devil has been placed on the foreheads of many; the red five-pointed star, the mark of Satan."*
(3) On May 14th Our Lady warns: *"Repent and love one another. The*

times are coming which are spoken of as the end times, as has been foretold. See the desolation that surrounds us, the sloth, the genocide, the many other sins."

(4) On one occasion Our Blessed Mother said: *"If the Russian people do not accept Christ as King, there will be a Third World War."*

(5) On September 18, 1992 Our Lady told Joseph: *"I have come because there are terrible events that will befall a godless humanity . . . the time is at hand. So many events of greater or lesser magnitude have already affected many nations. But there is an event coming that will shake the entire world, a great war, the greatest that has ever been until now is imminent . . ."*

XXIV Method of Appearance

(1) An aura of light would illuminate the chapel and the surrounding area—when a brighter light within this aura danced around until it was positioned over the Cupola—then Our Lady would appear from this light.

(2) When Our Lady appeared to Joseph Terelya in prison he first became aware of an intense flash of light in the cell, then a warmth, and then he saw Our Lady.

XXV Method of Departure

Joseph reports that when Our Blessed Mother visited him in prison, a powerful flash of light preceded Her disappearance.

XXVI Confrontation w/Civil Authorities

(1) From the beginning, when Our Lady first appeared to Marina on April 26, 1987 the communist government, the KGB, and the Militia did everything in their power to prevent the pilgrims from coming to the site of the apparitions and also to discredit the apparitions themselves.

This included boarding up the chapel, digging a ditch around it, cutting off the roads, falling trees across the roads, harassing the pilgrims and keeping up their high profile visibility among the crowd during the apparitions. In spite of these, and other efforts, the crowds kept coming. People saw and heard Our Lady; and conversions happened.

Meanwhile, the political attack was just as furious, the media including TV, audio, and the press were told what to report. Accusations of false reports and of fraud and trickery were alleged, blaming the entire happenings on the Vatican. This, likewise, was all to no avail. On May 13th people saw Our Lady appear on their TV screens in their own homes; yet the TV program was in fact a propaganda message against the apparitions. No one has been able to explain this happening.

(2) It is noted that one militia man who shot at the apparition was instantly struck down.

(3) It is also reported that some militia men were converted on the spot when they saw Our Blessed Mother.

(4) The original seer, Marina, was subjected to a variety of psychological testings and other harassments.

XXVII Confrontation w/Church Authorities

(1) There is no report of any confrontation with the Catholic Church although some Christian sects spoke out against these apparitions.

(2) In 1946 the Kremlin imprisoned the entire Hierarchy and decimated the clergy of the Ukrainian Catholic Church. Thereafter, the Catholic Church, was in Diaspora (underground).

(3) The Orthodox Church was permitted by the government, however it was controlled and limited.

(4) The Pope declared 1987-1988 a Marian Year.

XXVIII Request Chapel/Shrine Built

Although it is not reported that Our Lady requested a chapel at Hrushiv; nonetheless, on September 13, 1992 Our Lady appeared to Joseph at Marmora, Canada and did request a wooden chapel be built between the 10th and 11th Stations of the Way of the Cross there in Marmora, Canada.

XXIX Free Will/Choice - Not Reported

XXX Seer(s)' Suffering/Sacrifice

(1) The principal seer, Joseph Terelya, suffered greatly through his repeated imprisonments and torture. On at least one occasion Our Lady saved him from freezing to death in prison Cell #21. This occurred before the apparitions at Hrushiv commenced in 1987.

The persecution by the KGB, the Militia, and Government Officials, were not only ongoing, but intensified when Joseph went to Hrushiv and took an active role in praying with, and speaking to, the crowds. Although this undoubtedly caused him suffering, he never diminished in his discipleship. Joseph is presented to us as an unwavering, heroic activist who endured and accepted all sacrifices and sufferings heaped on him while defending and building up the Faith.

(2) Marina was subjected to ridicule and contempt. Rumors spread that she was dumb from birth and only began to speak after seeing Our Lady. Of course this was not true. This must have caused her to suffer humiliation and embarrassment. The authorities even accused Marina's mother of coaching her to say that Our Lady appeared to her.

XXXI Healings Reported

(1) The record is replete with reports of many instant conversions. These occurred amongst nonbelievers as well as among people of other faiths. It is reported that Jews and Muslims were converted and were baptized on the spot! Joseph reports that several thousand families were converted to Christianity during the year 1987 alone.
(2) The reported miraculous cures were numerous and included various types of physical healings, such as cancer, eczema and others.

XXXII Action Taken by the Church

There are no reports of any church investigative commission being set up, or any church action. The 'Chronicle of the Catholic Church' in Ukraine has prudently announced that "the Catholic Church has never been in a rush to recognize miracles".

XXXIII Bibliography

Witness 1991
By: Joseph Terelya with Michael H. Brown
Published by: Faith Publishing Company

Recent Marian Apparitions
By: Not Given
Published by: Craig Lodge, Dalmally

Chapter 51

BESSBROOK, NORTHERN IRELAND (1987 -1988)

I Place - Bessbrook, County Armagh, Northern Ireland
(Lourdes Grotto at Sts. Peter and Paul Church)

II Dates of First and Last Apparition

Mark Trainor
First: May 30, 1987
Last: January 1,1988 (last reported)

Beulah Lynch
First: June 2, 1987
Last: November 11,1987 (last reported)

Note: It is reported that these apparitions are ongoing.

III Seer(s) - 2

Name: Mark Trainor
Birth: Unknown
Age at first apparition: 17
Status: Living

Name: Beulah Lynch
Birth: Unknown
Age at first apparition: Mid 40's
Status: Living

IV Total Number of Apparitions - 28

Mark Trainor — 15
Beulah Lynch — 13

V Dates and Locality of Each Apparition

(All apparitions listed here occurred at the Grotto, unless otherwise noted.)

Mark Trainor:
1987: May 30, June 3, 4, 7, 9, 10, 12, 13, 14, 16, 20, 24, 27, 28.
1988 January 1 (Galway, Ireland).
Beulah Lynch:
1987: June 2, 5, 6, 7, 9, 11; July 9, 10, 14, 20; August 6, 20, and November 11.

No other apparitions or messages are reported; however, it is reported that apparitions and messages to both of these seers are ongoing.

VI Description of Our Lady

(1) Mark Trainor described Our Lady on May 30, 1987 (his first apparition): First a light arrived, then the seer saw a beautiful Lady dressed in snow white, looking at the seer. Her hair was golden and very wavy. Her eyes were blue and Her lips were red. Her skin was pale yellow. She was beautiful. She was wearing a golden crown and She was smiling.

Sometimes Our Lady appeared to Mark covered with pink roses. At other times She was sad; sometimes She cried, not only ordinary tears but also tears of blood, which stained Her face and gown. On at least one occasion Our Lady appeared holding the Baby Jesus in Her arms. At Our Blessed Mother's request, Mark once held the Baby Jesus.

(2) Beulah Lynch first saw Our Lady on June 2, 1987 and described Her thus: " Our Lady appeared splendid, unspeakably beautiful, surrounded by light, young, and motherly, about 18-22. She had dark hair parted in the middle and was carrying a rosary. Our Lady usually wore white."

Sometimes Our Lady appeared sad, weeping and wounded; even tormented. She appeared to this seer with bloody wounds for 14 consecutive days which made Beulah dread going to the Grotto.

VII Title(s) of Our Lady - 2

(1) On June 2, 1987 (first apparition to this seer) Our Lady told Beulah: *"I am the Immaculate Conception."*
(2) Our Lady also identified Herself to Beulah on several different occasions when She said: *"I am the Mother of Christ."*

VIII Brief Factual Review

Bessbrook is located in County Armagh in the Eastern portion of Northern Ireland and not far from its common border with Ireland itself. It is said that St. Patrick himself established what is today the Archdiocese of Armagh.

Historically the town had been owned by the Richardson family. They owned the King's Mill and everything else in town. Reportedly the town was idyllic, with rows of red brick houses, a central park and lake. No 'pub' nor 'betting office' was found in town. The last of the Richardson family died in the late 1930s.

On January 5, 1976 the image of an ideal town was shattered when ten Protestant mill workers were killed in retaliation for the killing of two Catholic mill workers the previous day. The mill was closed and replaced with a military base; one of the largest such military bases in Ireland.

Northern Ireland is politically a part of England, not of Ireland. We are aware of the current foment in Northern Ireland, a clash said to be between Catholics and Protestants, struggling for the independence of Northern Ireland from England or to keep the status quo.

It is well known and well reported that extreme forces on both sides of the struggle have caused much destruction of human life and property in Northern Ireland over the past decades, and it is still going on. More recently in August-September 1994 the IRA announced a unilateral truce and a stop to all military action. Perhaps the parties to this conflict are now awaiting a healing conference regarding the future of Northern Ireland. The parties would seem to include Ireland, Northern Ireland, England and the two factions actively engaged in the conflict in Northern Ireland.

It was in this background setting that two different people, one a teenage boy and the other a housewife in her 40's, began to receive apparitions of Our Blessed Virgin Mary at the Lourdes Shrine at Saint Peter and Paul Church in Bessbrook.

Mark Trainor first saw Our Lady at the Grotto on May 30, 1987. A year earlier when Mark was 16 years of age, his father died at the young age of 39. Up to this point the family had always practiced their Catholic religion, attended Mass and prayed the family rosary every night. After the death of his father Mark turned away from the Church.

It was on the anniversary of his father's death, one year later on May 30, 1987 while Mark was taking care of his father's grave site, when Mark heard a voice calling him to go to the Church. At first he resisted, but finally he did go, only to be beckoned to go on to the Grotto. When he got to the Grotto, instead of seeing the statue of Our Lady, he saw only a bright light. Then the "most beautiful person that I have ever seen was standing by the wall. She didn't look like a statue or picture. She was alive. She was breathing. She walked and She smiled." So Mark reported.

Our Lady appeared to Mark several more times during 1987, but She did not speak to him until January 1, 1988. On that occasion Mark was in Galway in the south of Ireland.

Mark says that Our Lady came to show him that God is real. She urged us to pray, especially the rosary and to fast on Wednesdays and Fridays. (Because Judas betrayed Jesus on Wednesday and Jesus died on the Cross on Friday.)

Usually Our Lady appeared to this seer dressed in a snow white gown. Sometimes She held the Baby Jesus. Once She carried in her arms the broken body of Her Son Jesus. She kissed the wounds on the hands of Jesus. She usually wore a crown and on June 4, 1987 Mark was shown the Immaculate Heart of Mary. Sometimes Our Lady was sad and appeared crying. On June 9, 1987 She cried tears of blood which stained Her cheeks. On June 3, 1987 Our Lady appeared with the Child Jesus in Her arms. It was on this occasion that Our Lady offered a white robe to Mark. He was too nervous to reach out for it.

Mark has also received frequent inner visions starting in November 1987. These visions usually displayed scenes of natural disasters, such as earthquakes and the country filled with soldiers who seemed to be clones. He saw clocks with black faces and white hands spinning. Also he saw a map of Great Britain and Ireland, except Scotland was not joined and England and Wales were not on the Map.

This seer has also had apparitions of Jesus and has been shown the Sacred Heart of Jesus. He has also seen the devil.

He says his spiritual life has changed since he received these apparitions; and changed dramatically! He now visits the Blessed Sacrament and attends daily Mass. He prays the daily rosary and other prayers. He travels throughout the world speaking about the apparitions and talking to youth about Jesus and Mary. Our Lady asked Mark to end each of his talks by praying the Apostles Creed. He has complied with Our Lady's request. He is considering becoming a priest, although he has made no decision.

Beulah Lynch received her first apparition on June 2, 1987 when she visited the Shrine after Mass. During the very first message Our Lady identified Herself as the *"Immaculate Conception"* and requested *"more prayers."* She warned that the world is in great danger and that a great catastrophe will happen in the world. In order to avoid or lessen this great danger the world must *"behave"* and *"change"* and people must pray, do penance, fast, and return to God. Our Lady requested especially that people pray five decades of the rosary each time they visit the Grotto. She repeatedly urged more prayer and that more people come to the Grotto.

Sometimes Our Lady appeared sad, even tormented. For 14 consecutive days Our Lady showed Herself to Beulah with bloody wounds. This upset the seer. Our Lady explained the meaning of the bloody wounds; caused by the sins of the world.

Beulah was also given many visions of an apocalyptic nature, and like the other seer, Mark, she continues to see Our Blessed Lady.

This seer's life has also been changed due to these apparitions. She goes to confession once a month, attends daily Mass, attends Bible study, and goes before the Blessed Sacrament.

She says that her prayer life has deepened and that she is trying to come closer to God.

It is reported that both Mark and Beulah continue to receive visions and messages, although messages after 1988 are not reported.

Their spiritual advisor, Fr. Gerard McGinnity, reports that both seers are obedient and cooperative. He has a positive impression of these events and accepts the genuineness of what they claim. The Church asks us to be patient and to keep an open mind. There is one report that a commission was established to investigate. No Church decision has been announced.

There are reports of many signs and wonders, such as the 'Miracle of the Sun', the sky changing colors, and other such phenomena. Also reported are cures and many conversions. Many people have returned to the Sacraments, even after 16-18 years. Many youth are converted, family unity has returned, and attendance at Mass has dramatically increased. These evidence good fruit coming from these events.

IX The Primary Messages - 4

(1) **Prayer** - As frequently occurs in many of the apparitions and messages around the world, here also Our Lady constantly repeats Her request for prayer.

> June 2, 1987 *"I want more prayer. I want more prayer, pray harder. Tell a priest. I want more people to worship here."*
> June 9, 1987 *". . . I want prayer."*
> June 28, 1987 *"I want people to pray at the Grotto."*
> August 6, 1987 *"Nothing matters but prayer and God."*

(2) **Conversion** - On June 11, 1987 Our Lady announced that *"the world must behave. The world must change."*

> Then on August 6, 1987 She said: *"Abandon yourselves to God. Open your hearts and allow Me to come in . . ."*

(3) **Penance and Fasting** - July 10, 1987 *"Tell the people to come and*

pray—pray, fast, and do penance . . ."

Then on July 28, 1987 Our Lady said: *"Thank you for your sacrifices."*

November 11, 1987 Our Lady said: *"I cannot hold back any longer, I cannot save the world; the people must save the world. The people must come to the Grotto for prayer, fasting, and penance before the chastisement starts."*

(4) **Rosary** - Not only did Our Lady hold a rosary during some of Her appearances thus clearly recommending the rosary, but on July 28, 1987 She also said: *"It's God's will each time you come to the Grotto. You must say the five decades of the three most beautiful mysteries. Graces will be given to you at the Grotto."*

X Signs Preceding the Apparitions

One of the seers, namely Mark Trainor, states that when Our Lady appears the light arrives first, then She appears. In contrast to the times when Jesus appears, He and the light come together.

XI Other Visions During Apparitions

(1) Both Beulah and Mark claim to have seen Jesus on more than one occasion. Our Lady carried the Child Jesus in Her arms on some occasions.
(2) Both seers were shown many visions, usually of an apocalyptic nature.
(3) Both of these seers saw demons appearing to them as terrifying animals.
(4) The seers were shown the Sacred Heart of Jesus and the Immaculate Heart of Mary.

XII Prayers Taught to the Seer(s) - Not Reported
XIII Special Devotion Given to the Seer(s) - NR

XIV Requests Made by Our Lady

Our Lady requested us to fast every Wednesday and Friday.

XV Specific Bible References - Not Reported
XVI Secrets Given to the Seer(s) - Not Reported
XVII Miracles Promised by Our Lady - NR
XVIII Miracles Performed - Not Reported
XIX Miracles Promised not yet Performed - NR
XX Signs Promised - Not Reported

XXI Signs Given

(1) Our Lady appeared crying tears during more than one apparition.
(2) On one occasion (June 9, 1987) Our Lady shed tears of blood which stained Her cheeks as the tears flowed down.
(3) These seers each received several visions which were apocalyptic in nature.
(4) Signs and wonders such as the 'Miracle of the Sun' are reported.

XXII Predictions/Promises

Our Lady promised that many graces will be given to the people who come to the Grotto and pray the rosary there.

XXIII Prophecies/Warnings of Chastisement

June 11, 1987 *"The world must behave, the world must behave. A great catastrophe will happen to the world . . ."*
July 10, 1987 *"The world is in great danger. God is not pleased . . ."*
August 20, 1987 *"A great disaster will happen to the world. . . ."*
November 11, 1987 *". . .You cannot know the wrath of God. God is very, very angry because of the sins of the world. I cannot hold back any longer, I cannot save the world. . ."*

XXIV Method of Appearance

First the light would be seen by the seer (Mark Trainor), then Our Lady would appear.

XXV Method of Departure - Not Reported
XXVI Confrontation w/Civil Authorities - NR
XXVII Confrontation w/Church Authorities - NR
XXVIII Request Chapel/Shrine Built - NR
XXIX Free Will/Choice - Not Reported
XXX Seer(s)' Suffering/Sacrifice - Not Reported

XXXI Healings Reported

There are reports of cures, of many conversions. Many people, especially the youth, returned to the Sacraments and now attend Mass regularly.

XXXII Action Taken by the Church

Fr. McGinnity, the spiritual director of these two seers, relates that they are obedient and cooperative.

It is reported that these apparitions are under investigation by the Church; however, no formal Church action is reported.

XXXIII Bibliography

**Messages Conveyed by Our Lady
at the Grotto in Bessbrook Chapel
During the Summer of 1987**
By: International Medjugorje Centre
Published by: International Medjugorje Centre

The Final Hour
By: Michael Brown
Published by: The Riehle Foundation

Our Lady's Messages at Bessbrook, Northern Ireland
(Audio)
By: International Medjugorje Centre
Produced by: International Medjugorje Centre

Chapter 52

BALLINDAGGIN, IRELAND
(1987-1989)

I Place - Ballinacoola Well, Ballindaggin, County Wexford, Ireland.

II Dates of First and Last Apparition

First: August, 1987
Last: October 29, 1989

III Seer(s) - 1

Name: Joanne Farrell
Birth: Unknown
Age at first apparition: 9
Status Living

IV Total Number of Apparitions - 87

V Dates and Locality of Each Apparition

(All apparitions were at Ballinacoola Well unless otherwise noted.)

1987: August: 2 appearances at the Well and 1 appearance in the seer's bedroom; September 8, 16, 17, 22, 30; plus three others, dates unreported; October 20, 21, 29; plus two others, dates unreported; November 1, 3, 11, 19, and 25.
1988: April 27; May 6, and 22; June 22; July: one during Mass at

Baltinglass; plus one other date unreported; August 14, 21, 23; plus one other date unreported; September 3, 4, 6, 8, 20, and 29; October 6; December 12.
1989: January 10, plus 2 others, date unreported; May 6, 14, 17, 18 (two apparitions); June 12 (two apparitions), 14, 18, 19, 21, 28, 30; plus one other date unreported; July 4, 8, 9, 14, 15, 16, 19, 20, 23, 26, 27, and 30; August 6, 9, 13, 15, 16, 20, 27; September 3, 8, 9, 10; 21 (at school), 22 (in seer's bedroom), 23 (at seer's home); October 6 (at the Grotto within the Convent grounds at Baltinglass); 13 (in Kilkenny); 20 (at the Grotto in Grange Convent); 29 (at Grantstown Augustinian Priory, Wellington Bridge).

VI Description of Our Lady

(1) This seer describes Our Lady as beautiful. She has blue eyes, wears a white dress with a blue cloak, gold rosary beads, with 2 roses on Her feet. She carries a golden rose in Her hand, and sometimes wears a golden crown. Our Lady appears with Her Immaculate Heart exposed during some of the apparitions.

(2) On August 13, 1989 Our Blessed Mother appeared attired as Our Lady of Fatima. She was dressed in gold, with a gold crown and three doves at Her feet; angels hovered in the background.

VII Title(s) of Our Lady - 1

Our Lady introduced Herself to the seer with the specific name of 'Our Lady, Queen of the Golden Roses'.

VIII Brief Factual Review

Ballinacoola Well is located in County Wexford, Ireland, about four miles south of Bunclody. Ballinacoola Holy Well has a tradition of being 'a special place' dating back to the end of the last century. The locals especially, have recited the rosary at the Holy Well every August 15th. The Holy Well itself is located in the parish of Ballindaggin. The Well bears a plaque stating that in 1896 an emigrant priest named Fr. James H. O'Neill, from the USA, blessed the spring water in the Holy Well. A shrine was erected at the Well which is regarded as a holy place by all who know it. There have been many accounts of the healing powers of the water. A stream flows through the area.

Joanne Farrell is the third eldest of six children. She was nine years old when the visions of Our Lady began in August 1987. However, it is reported that Joanne actually saw Our Lady at the Holy Well in July 1986. It seems that many reports of apparitions in Ireland were being discussed at Joanne's school. She asked her mother to take her to the Well. The family went to the Holy Well for the first visit ever in July 1986. The children played and some prayers were said. As the family was leaving Joanne told her mother that Our Lady had appeared and that Joanne could see angels in the sky. Joanne became so frightened that her mother had to lift her up into her arms. A friend of Joanne who was also at the Well reported that she also saw Our Lady. Joanne's mother was naturally puzzled as to whether these were real or imaginary, but confirmation by the other girl that day and other later events have convinced her that Joanne was actually seeing Our Lady.

Mystical experiences continued for Joanne. She saw Jesus, angels and saints in the sky on her way to school. She saw Jesus crucified on the cross on the school shed. She also says she saw Satan at school.

Joanne's mother decided not to take Joanne to the Well again for a whole year. The year went by and it was in 1987 that Joanne went on vacation 'Holidays' to visit her grandmother. When she returned home in July 1987 Joanne told her own mother that Our Lady had again appeared to her and asked her to come to the Holy Well and that Our Lady would have three messages for her.

After some discernment and prayer, Joanne's mother took Joanne to the Holy Well in August 1987. It was during this visit to the Well that Our Lady again appeared to Joanne and gave her the first three of many messages. From that time on Our Lady appeared to Joanne nearly every time this seer visited the Holy Well until September 10, 1989. On September 8, 1989 Our Lady told the seer that September 10th would be the last time She would appear to Joanne at the Well. As it turned out the last appearance at the Well was in fact on September 10, 1989; however Our Lady has appeared to Joanne at the seer's home, and at various Grottos as well as at the school several times since then. The last reported appearance was on October 29, 1989.

Soon after the first messages, word got around and people began to flock to the Holy Well to pray the rosary and witness Joanne during the apparitions. Sometimes Joanne receives an inner urging or message that Our Lady is calling her to the Well. When Joanne arrives at the Well Our Lady thanks her for coming and proceeds with the message. It is reported that Our Lady uses a form of Old English used in the 17th Century in many of the messages. For this reason some of the messages may be hard to understand at times. On the other hand, it is pointed out that this fact lends credence to these experiences since it seems unlikely that this young seer would have knowledge of this old dialect.

There were some 87 apparitions of Our Lady reported. Also, sometimes Jesus appeared to the seer, as did St. Joan of Arc, St. Therese, St. Martin, St. Michael, and Padre Pio. Our Lady is described as beautiful. She has blue eyes, wears a white dress and blue cloak with two roses on Her feet and holds a rosary. Sometimes Our Lady appeared with Her Immaculate Heart exposed. Our Lady usually appeared while the rosary was being prayed. She has announced Herself as 'Our Lady, Queen of the Golden Roses'. At least once Our Lady came as Our Lady of Fatima.

The messages ring a familiar tone, calling for increased prayer, especially the family rosary and for conversions. Our Lady dictated several prayers to the seer. She sometimes gave the seer questions and would then give the answers. Our Lady often requested that Joanne pick up a stone from the stream. Sometimes Joanne would find a prayer written on the underside of the stone itself. Once Our Lady said that the stone is a relic and may be used much like the spring water is used for blessings and cures. It all depends on our faith in God. Our Lady requested that the sick be blessed with the water. She also requested that songs (hymns) be sung at the Well.

On September 22, 1987 Our Lady told Joanne *"I might give a sign."* It was on August 20, 1989 that Our Lady did give a sign. The Holy Eucharist, the Host, appeared unsupported against a dark background outside the blue wall of the Well. This event was successfully photographed. When Joanne asked Our Lady about this photograph, Our Lady responded: *"This is the Sign."*

Our Lady requested that we fast on Wednesdays and Fridays. She frequently challenged us: *"Ask the people: do they believe in Christ or in Satan?"*

Our Lady frequently pointed out the evil in the world and urged us to return to God. On June 18, 1989 Our Lady appeared at the end of the rosary and said: *"You have not prayed enough to the Father. I will help you with your prayers, offer up your love to the Father as a servant."* Then Our Lady started crying, with blood as tears. Joanne asked Our Lady why She was crying and Our Lady replied: *"For the sufferings of the people."*

On November 25, 1987 after praying the rosary, the seer experienced the whipping that Jesus suffered. The people prayed and gradually it stopped.

On February 20, 1988 Our Lady gave a prayer for members of Joanne's family; her mother and sisters Olivia, Maria, Catherine and all the babies.

On September 29, 1988 Our Lady requested a church be built at the Well, and that her messages be spread. At the end of each apparition Our Lady would usually invite all to return to the Holy Well. She thanked the people for their prayers, hymns and the flowers they brought to Her.

No church action is reported.

IX The Primary Messages - 5

(1) **Prayer** - A great number of the messages contain requests for prayer, especially to pray from the heart; and also thanking the people for their prayers.

August 1987: This is the date of the first recorded messages. Our Lady said: *"The world is precious to Me, I want you to pray a lot more; I care for the world."*

Then on a Sunday in August 1987, Our Lady spoke: *"Tell the world to pray."*

November 3, 1987: *"You must pray more, everyone."*

August 1988 Our Lady: *"We must pray harder for the world; we must pray to God a lot more if we want to stop the wars and fights."*

August 13, 1989: *"I want prayers and peace. That's all I ask of you."* Then on August 16, 1989 Our Lady urged: *"I want peace. I want you to have prayer and peace in your families."* This message was repeated on August 27, 1989.

On October 6, 1989 Our Lady said: *"I have come here today because you have chosen My place to pray at. I hope you will continue praying at My place of prayer at the Grotto."*

Then on October 29, 1989 which is the last reported message, Our Lady pleads: *". . . I plead with you to pray with your hearts. Pray, My children, pray. God Bless, I love you, I will never abandon you."*

(2) **Rosary** - Our Lady nearly always appeared during, or at the end of, the rosary being prayed at the Well. Our Lady also carried a rosary, thus amply indicating Her approval of the rosary. On May 6, 1989 She blessed the people's rosary beads.

June 12, 1989 Our Lady reminded Joanne: *"You promised you would keep God's Word by saying morning and evening prayers, and the family rosary."*

August 27, 1989 Our Lady gave this brief message: *"My dearest children, My message is Peace and Prayer. My Son's message is Love one another. The Father's message is pray the rosary!"*

(3) **Conversion** - November 19, 1987: *"God wants us to be truthful, be honest, don't be evil."*

May 6, 1988: *"You must pray really hard if you want safety from God. You must love people and be kind to people and you must make peace with the world."*

August 1988: *"The world is in bad need of help and it is for us that it is in need. You must be friendly and kind to people. You must take Communion, you must talk to Jesus, the Apostles; you have to be good."*

Then on July 20, 1989 Our Lady said: *"Turn back to the Lord, and He will forgive you."*

(4) **Fast and Sacrifice** - During the first reported message of August 1987 Our Lady said: *"Jesus died on the Cross for us and suffered a lot of pain, so we have to suffer on this earth and do something back for Him."*

July 23, 1989: *"The Father wants you to fast and repent on Wednesdays and Fridays, and wants you to have devotions to His Sacred Son."*

(5) **Holy Spirit** - Our Lady often asked the Holy Spirit to come down on the people praying at the Well.

On a Sunday in September of 1987 when Joanne asked "What is the Holy Spirit like?" Our Lady responded: *"It comes in the center of a cloud like a dove, with rays of sunshine."*

On September 17, 1987 Our Lady spoke: *"The Spirit comes down on us all."*

June 22, 1988 Our Lady announced: *"The Lord be with you. The Holy Spirit is with you all. Have trust in God and in the Holy Spirit."*

X Signs Preceding the Apparitions

(1) Our Lady usually appeared to the seer at the Holy Well upon conclusion of the rosary.
(2) On at least one occasion Joanne had an 'inner calling' from Our Lady beckoning her to the Well.

XI Other Visions During Apparitions

(1) Jesus
(2) St. Joan of Arc, St. Therese, St. Martin
(3) Padre Pio
(4) St. Michael the Archangel, Joanne's guardian angel, and a host of other angels
(5) Satan

XII Prayers Taught to the Seer(s)

Not only is it reported that Our Lady gave Joanne prayers, but so did St. Martin, St. Michael, and St. Joan of Arc. Our Lady gave prayers to the seer during ten different apparitions:

(1) September 30, 1987 {one prayer}.
(2) October 20, 1987 {one prayer}.
(3) October 1987 {one prayer}.
(4) October 29, 1987 {one prayer}.
(5) November 19, 1987 {one prayer}.
(6) February 20, 1988 {five prayers were given for Joanne's family members plus six other prayers}.
(7) August 12, 1988 {three prayers}.
(8) January 10, 1989 {ten prayers}.

(9) May 14, 1989 {one prayer}.
(10) September 22, 1989 {one prayer}.

XIII Special Devotion Given to the Seer(s) - NR

XIV Requests Made by Our Lady

(1) Fast and repent on Wednesdays and Fridays.
(2) Wear the Miraculous Medal.
(3) Drink the water from the spring.
(4) Sing hymns to Our Lady.

XV Specific Bible References - Not Reported
XVI Secrets Given to the Seer(s) - Not Reported
XVII Miracles Promised by Our Lady - NR

XVIII Miracles Performed

(1) Our Lady asked the seer to pick up a stone. A prayer was written on the stone: *"I, the Lord, by God, is man by Virgin. Amen."*
(2) The Host miraculously appeared unsupported at the wall of the Well. This was successfully photographed.

XIX Miracles Promised not yet Performed - NR

XX Signs Promised

On September 22, 1987 Our Lady told the seer: *"I might give a sign."*

XXI Signs Given

(1) On August 20, 1989 Our Lady gave the sign consisting of the Host suspended at the wall of the Well.
(2) The prayer that had been written on the stone which Our Lady asked Joanne to pick up seems to be a sign of Our Lady's presence.

XXII Predictions/Promises

On September 8, 1989 Our Lady told Joanne that She had a sad message for the seer: the message being that September 10, 1989 would be the last time Our Lady would appear to Joanne at the Well. It happened as predicted.

XXIII Prophecies/Warnings of Chastisement - NR

XXIV Method of Appearance

Our Lady usually appeared right after the rosary was prayed.

XXV Method of Departure

Our Lady usually gave a blessing to all those present and then disappeared.

XXVI Confrontation w/Civil Authorities - NR
XXVII Confrontation w/Church Authorities - NR

XXVIII Request Chapel/Shrine Built

On September 29, 1988 Our Lady said that She hoped that someday a church like the one at Lourdes, would be built at the Well.

XXIX Free Will/Choice

In October 1987 Our Lady said: *"Do ye wish to serve God, or evil?"* Clearly it is our choice. We have free will.

XXX Seer(s)' Suffering/Sacrifice

The seer suffered the "whipping" which Jesus suffered.

XXXI Healings Reported

Our Lady said that the waters taken at the Well would heal; it depends on our faith in God.

XXXII Action Taken by the Church - Not Reported

XXXIII Bibliography

Apparitions at Ballinacoola Well,
Ballindaggin, Co. Wexford
By: Not Given
Published by: Not Given

Chapter 53

GORTNADREHA, IRELAND
(1988-1992)

I Place - Gortnadreha, County Mayo, Ireland

II Dates of First and Last Apparition

First: January 21, 1988
Last: January 25, 1992 (last reported)
Note: The apparitions are reportedly ongoing.

III Seer(s) - 1

Name: Christina Gallagher
Birth: Unknown
Age at first apparition: Mid-thirties
Status: Living/married

IV Total Number of Apparitions - 34

This seer had other visions and locutions from Our Lady which were not reported. It is further reported that visions and locutions from Our Lady are ongoing.

V Dates and Locality of Each Apparition

(All dates and locations take place inside the seer's home in County Mayo unless otherwise stated.)

1988: January 21, (Dublin, Ireland at a friend's house); January 27, February 4, 22, 24, 25, 28; March 6, 16, (twice); March 23, 30; May 22; June; July 14, (two messages); July 23; August 11, 15, 17; September 24; October 15; December 25; Unknown date.
1989: May 30.
1990: Two appartions; (dates not reported).
1991: August 8, 20, 22; November 1.
1992: January 11 (Knock, Ireland); January 25.

VI Description of Our Lady

Our Lady is 19-23, has a round face, deep brown to black hair, large blue eyes, a tan complexion without blemish, slim nose and not very big lips, but filled out. She is beautiful.

Usually Our Lady appeared dressed in a white dress and blue mantle; however, on the third apparition, February 4, 1988 She was wearing a cream color cloak with a gold seam around the edge.

Our Lady is described as radiantly beautiful. She radiates light. The light comes from within Her. Her clothes seemed to be normal, yet the light radiated right through Her clothes. When Our Lady opened out Her mantle, it glowed in the light which extended outward. Our Lady's hands were joined, then She extended Her hands. On one occasion She held a glass globe in Her hands. Another time Our Lady placed one of Her hands over Her heart and with Her other hand She swayed Her mantle towards the seer three times.

VII Title(s) of Our Lady - 1

During the third apparition on February 4, 1988 Our Lady said: *"I am the Virgin Mary, Queen of Peace."* These words were repeated on February 22, 1988.

VIII Brief Factual Review

County Mayo is located in western Ireland and encompasses the land shoulder jutting out from the mid-western shore of the Island. The famous apparition site located at "Knock" is situated in County Mayo.

Christina Gallagher is from Gortnadreha, Knockmore, in County Mayo. At the time the apparitions commenced in 1988 she was a mother and homemaker in her mid-thirties with two teenage children.

Christina reportedly began having mystical experiences early in her life. While still in her early teens, she asked Jesus to grant her two special favors. One was to heal her own mother who was seriously ill at the time. The other was to teach Christina to read and write. Reportedly, these two favors were granted. Her mother came out of a coma and fully recovered. And Christina, who had a great fear of papers and books, suddenly discovered she could read and write.

Although she always had a strong, yet simple faith in God, it was not until 1985, when an experience in County Sligo dramatically altered her life and increased her faith. County Sligo is located just north of County Mayo. When Christina first heard of the apparitions reported at Cairn's Grotto in Sligo, she decided to visit Cairn in search of peace. That first night at Cairn's Grotto she saw a light approach rapidly, it grew to the size of the moon and turned red in color. Many others saw this same light. Thereafter, she went often to Cairn's Grotto to pray. One evening, as she was praying the rosary at the Grotto, she saw the Head of Jesus crowned with thorns. This scene affected her very profoundly. She said that she looked at a real living person in agony. Further, she knew that Jesus was suffering due to our sins. This made her remorseful and full of sorrow.

About six weeks after the vision of the Crucified Christ, she had terrifying experiences in the early morning hours in her own home when Satan appeared to her.

Christina had her first apparition of Our Lady on January 21, 1988. She had gone to Dublin to visit a relative and as they were sitting and talking, the thought came to Christina of the peace she experienced at Cairn's Grotto a few years prior. The instant she looked up she saw Our Lady before her standing in midair, a little above the floor. She was radiantly beautiful. No message was given during this first apparition. The person with Christina did not see Our Lady but could feel Her presence.

Upon her return home to County Mayo, Christina told several people of her apparition; and they each gave her a silent odd look.

The next apparition happened a week later in the kitchen of Christina's own home. This time St. Bernadette accompanied Our Lady. Again, no messages were given.

On the third apparition, February 4, 1988 Our Lady identified Herself as *"Virgin Mary, Queen of Peace."* These were the first words the seer heard Our Lady speak. Christina was so profoundly affected that she found herself pleading: "Holy Mother, please don't leave here, take me with you now!" Our Lady eloquently responded with a smile: *"My child, when your work is completed, I will come for you."*

The apparitions occured frequently during 1988. They became less frequent thereafter. Starting in 1989, the seer had a combination of apparitions, locutions, and visions. Jesus also appeared to the seer and gave messages to her. The apparitions during 1988 reportedly occurred at the seer's home, in a local church, at Cairn's Grotto and at other places. At the end of each message, just as Our Lady was ready to depart, She usually imparted a blessing upon the seer.

Meanwhile, Christina was having a difficult time with these events.

She had her household and family responsibilities and she was disbelieved and even mocked by many people. This made her doubt her own sanity. Her spiritual director, Fr. McGinnity, listened to her, prayed with her, and through discernment was able to alleviate the seer's misgivings. She has constantly kept him current in all matters and has been obedient for her part.

Christina was given several secrets by Our Lady. Jesus also revealed secrets to the seer consisting of strong warnings of future purifications. She has been given three dates which she is not allowed to reveal. The seer has said that the chastisements would begin to unfold in 1992 and would probably be completed by the year 2000. The message of December 25, 1988 states in part: *"In the year 1992, many will cry out to their Lord and He will not hear them."* This has been misconstrued and has caused some confusion.

The seer was shown visions of heaven, hell, and purgatory. Our Lady told Christina: *". . . Now the biggest disaster is abortion, which has drawn down the Hand of God."* On September 21, 1990 Jesus told the seer: *"The three sins which grieve My Heart most deeply at this time are abortion, the killing of the innocents; the sacrifice of the innocents to Satan; and the immoral abuse of the innocents."* Christina also was allowed to see many angels and saints including St. Catherine, St. Brigid and Padre Pio.

The primary focus of the messages are for prayer, especially the rosary, Confession, the Mass and Eucharist, to love one another and return to God. Our Lady also told of the value of suffering and asked us to fast and do penance. She requested we pray the rosary; 15 decades from the heart every day, for the lost souls and for the clergy and religious. Our Lady told the seer that She has a plan for Ireland. Ireland can be saved.

Our Lady requested the seer to establish a 'House of Prayer' for priests. It would be a place where priests and people would gather to pray. Some efforts have been made by the seer in furtherance of this request.

Christina has been told by Our Lady that all the people of the world will be given a warning, through a sign. The sign itself consists of an inner awareness. We will know it is from God and we will see ourselves as God really sees us. If the sign is not accepted the chastisement will follow.

There were several severe apocalyptic messages and warnings of the coming chastisement given to the seer. On July 23, 1988 Our Lady said in part: *"My child, the Purification will come."* On August 8, 1991 Christina received a severe message. Then on August 20, 1991 she received a vision and message. She was told to give the message to her spiritual director with instructions for him to read the Seven Seals of God (Rev 8), especially the Seventh Seal! Then a few months later on October 18, 1991 Jesus gave the seer a stern message which is in part: *"Your cries will be heard now if you throw yourselves under My Mercy and turn away from sin and your evil ways."*

Our Lady requested the seer to have a special medal struck. The medal is named the 'Matrix Medal'. On the obverse side a cross is depicted with Our Lady on Her knees praying before the Cross. The reverse shows the two Hearts of Jesus and Mary weeping tears of blood. This medal has been struck and several hundred thousand have been distributed worldwide. The seer reports the medal is also for protection, protection in the times of the great chastisement, as well as during the present time.

Many physical, spiritual, and emotional healings are reported after wearing or otherwise invoking Our Lady through the 'Matrix Medal'.

Christina has traveled extensively throughout the world with her spiritual director Fr. McGinnity. Several theologians have spoken favorably of these events. Many good fruits are seen. These apparitions are under investigation by the Church. There is no report of any decision by the Church.

Meanwhile, Christina is a victim soul who has consented to suffer for conversions. In 1989 Jesus asked the seer: *"Will you allow Me to suffer in you?"* The seer told Jesus: "I am hungry for suffering because it is only through suffering that I can come close to my dear Jesus and strip myself of weakness."

IX The Primary Messages - 6

(1) Prayer - The messages are replete with invitations to, and exhortations for, prayer.

February 24, 1988 Our Lady said: *". . .You must pray and make sacrifice for them. Through prayer people will be able to see and understand."*

March 30, 1988 Our Lady said: *"Tell all My children of Ireland that they must pray, fast, and do penance, if there is to be peace."*

Then on July 7, 1988 Our Lady speaks: *"Pray for strength to overcome darkness. Pray to My Heart . . ."*

On July 14, 1988 Our Lady pleads: *"Please pray more!"* On August 15, 1988 Our Lady told the seer to: *"Ask My Son to forgive those who offend His Divine Heart. It is full of mercy. He will not hold back when you ask forgiveness in prayer."*

Then on September 24, 1988 Our Lady asked for more prayer: *"I ask you to try to pray more."*

August 20, 1991 Our Blessed Mother pleaded: *"Pray in meditation on the passion of Jesus. The clock, its alarm is set. The hour is close. Pray! Pray! Pray!"*

Finally, on August 22, 1991 Our Lady urges: *"Yes I desire many works and much prayer. My child pray, pray, pray! The devil wants to destroy My plan for Ireland and the world. By your prayer, sacrifice, and suffering offered to Jesus, My Son will disarm all his snares."*

(2) **Rosary** - During these apparitions Our Blessed Mother especially stressed praying the rosary.

February 4, 1988 Our Lady said: *"Pray the rosary from the heart, all three mysteries, for nine days. Offer up these prayers to My Son's Heart and to the Holy Spirit for enlightenment. If you do that, you will understand."*

Again on February 22, 1988: *"Tell them I want the rosary said, all three mysteries, in My Church once a week, and from people's hearts, and in the people's own homes on the remaining days of the week. I want it offered for peace and the conversion of sinners. It is urgent."*

On May 22, 1988 Our Lady said: *"Pray the rosary to Me, from your heart. . . . Pray My beautiful rosary."*

Later on July 7, 1988 Our Lady requested that we: *"Pray the rosary for some of My lost souls . . ."*

Again, on August 11, 1988: *"Say My beautiful rosary to My Immaculate Heart."* And on August 15, 1988 Our Lady urged: *"My child, say My rosary every day."*

Later on August 22, 1991 Our Lady continues to urge us to: *"Pray My beautiful rosary with love from your heart . . . Pray My beautiful rosary often."*

(3) **Penance, Fast, and Sacrifice** - February 24, 1988 Our Lady speaks: *". . . Their faith is lukewarm. You must pray and make sacrifice for them."*

March 30, 1988 Our Lady said: *"Tell My people they must pray, fast, and do penance, if there is to be peace."*

Then on July 14, 1988: *"Please pray more, and fast for three days. The more you suffer, the greater the sacrifice."*

On October 15, 1988 Our Lady said: *"Pray to God fervently and make sacrifice."*

Finally, on November 1, 1991 Our Lady said: *"Sacrifice yourselves for My Son, Jesus, for those whose hearts are in darkness."*

(4) **Confession** - February 24, 1988 Our Lady speaks: *"Mass is so pleasing to Me and My Son, but more people need to go to Confession."*

February 28, 1988 Our Lady said: *"Repent, go to Confession. Unburden yourselves of all sin and receive My Son's Body and Blood worthily."*

August 15, 1988 Our Lady again: *"My children have abandoned the Sacrament of Confession. Do they not know they cannot be set free of Satan's influence and work without asking forgiveness?"*

(5) **Eucharist** - February 28, 1988 Our Lady said: *"My child, tell all My children to come back to Me and My Son . . . Repent, go to Confession and receive My Son's Body and Blood worthily."*

July 1, 1988 Our Lady again: *"Pray to God for them; especially those in religious life. Some of these do not believe that Jesus' Body* and *Blood are present in the Consecration of the Mass. They do not believe that bread and wine are changed into His Body and Blood."*

(6) **Mass** - On February 24, 1988 Our Lady said: *". . . Mass is so pleasing to Me and My Son . . ."*

Then again on July 14, 1988: *"Don't go to Holy Mass out of habit. Love My Son when you are at Holy Mass. . . ."*

August 11, 1988 Our Lady said: *"My children go to Holy Mass. Offer it to My dear Son, to console His Heart . . ."*

X Signs Preceding the Apparitions - Not Reported

XI Other Visions During Apparitions

(1) Jesus appeared to the seer several times and also gave messages to her.
(2) Several saints appeared to Christina including St. Catherine of Siena, St. Bernadette, St. Brigid and Padre Pio.
(3) Angels also appeared to the seer.
(4) Satan appeared to Christina.
(5) The seer was shown visions of heaven, hell, and purgatory.
(6) During different visions the seer experienced various other reported phenomena, such as seeing babies about to be aborted.

XII Prayers Taught to the Seer(s) - Not Reported

XIII Special Devotion Given to the Seer(s)

(1) Although no new special devotion is reported, yet on March 16, 1988 Our Lady requested a special 'Matrix Medal' be struck with the bleeding Sacred Hearts of Jesus and Mary on the obverse side. Our Lady said: *"Pray, pray, pray and make sacrifice to My Son's Heart."*
(2) Then on August 11, 1988 Our Lady said in part: *"My child, live the consecration to My Immaculate Heart."*

XIV Requests Made by Our Lady

(1) **House of Prayer** - Our Lady requested that the seer set up a 'House of Prayer' and explained to the seer on August 22, 1991 that Our Lady desires this 'House of Prayer for Priests' to be set up where priests and lay people can meet and pray together. Some efforts have been made to acquire property and establish this House of Prayer.
(2) **Matrix Medal** - On March 6, 1988 Our Lady requested that Christina cause to have struck a 'Matrix Medal'. On the obverse: *"I would like My Son's Cross on it, with Me on My knees, praying for My children."*

On the reverse: *"I would like two Hearts, weeping tears of blood,"* thus Our Lady requested. The medal has been struck and distributed. Many favors, as well as healings, have been reported and attributed to the Matrix Medal.

(3) On March 16, 1988 Our Lady especially requested that Christina *"fast three times a week until Easter for a private intention."*

XV Specific Bible References

On August 20, 1991 the seer had a vision with a message from Our Lady telling her to relay the message to her spiritual director, that he is to read the Seven Seals of God, especially the Seventh Seal. (Rev 8)

XVI Secrets Given to the Seer(s)

Christina was given secrets concerning a punishment to come. She is not permitted to tell the contents, although the seer has said that everything she has been shown or told about, she feels will be accomplished before the year 2000.

XVII Miracles Promised by Our Lady - NR
XVIII Miracles Performed - Not Reported
XIX Miracles Promised not yet Performed - NR

XX Signs Promised

The seer has been told that all people of the world will be given a warning, through a sign. Everyone will experience an inner awareness, and will know that it is from God, and will see themselves as they really are.

It is up to each one of us to help as many as possible through our prayer so they will change and be saved by God.

If the sign is not accepted, chastisement will follow.

XXI Signs Given - Not Reported

XXII Predictions/Promises

On December 25, 1988 Our Lady said: *"In the year 1992, many will cry out to their Lord and He will not hear them. Sin is the reason for all disaster, illness and suffering."*

XXIII Prophecies/Warnings of Chastisement

February 28, 1988 Our Lady speaks: *My children, you have not much time until My Son's hand will come over the earth in Justice."*

March 30, 1988 again Our Lady: *"My Son's hand is about to come over the earth in Justice."*

And then on July 23, 1988 She said: *"The Purification will come."*

December 25, 1988 Our Lady said: *God is angry with the world and with the Irish people — in the year 1992 many will cry out to their Lord and He will not hear them. Sin is the reason for disaster, illness, and suffering."*

Then on May 30, 1989 Our Lady said: *"The Purification is on the way."*

On August 20, 1991 Christina had a vision and a message from Our Lady: *"The world is held up by pillars. The pillar is Jesus Christ. The pillars are about to fall. My Divine Son is soon releasing His hand, the pillar of God; the clock, its alarm is set, the hour is close. Pray, pray, pray!"*

On January 30, 1991, and again on October 18, 1991 Jesus gave messages to the seer concerning the coming Purification.

XXIV Method of Appearance

The seer reports: "When Our Lady arrives everything is tranquil, and the whole world is gone into stillness."

XXV Method of Departure

Our Lady usually gives the seer a blessing before She departs.

The seer reports that "Then the light begins to get less, and She begins to fade, and soon She is gone."

XXVI Confrontation w/Civil Authorities

No such confrontations are reported. However, what is reported is that many people disbelieve the seer and humiliate her. Also there are reports of false "new" messages distributed and falsely attributed to the seer. These alleged "new" messages are subsequent to the publication of the book listed in section XXXIII below. None of these "new" messages are contained in this present work.

XXVII Confrontation w/Church Authorities

Again, no such confrontations are reported. Several priests and at least one noted theologian reportedly have responded favorably to these events and messages.

XXVIII Request Chapel/Shrine Built - NR

XXIX Free Will/Choice

(1) December 25, 1988 Our Lady speaks: *"He has given all free will to accept or reject My messages."*
(2) On September 24, 1988 Our Lady told the seer: *"If you accept all God permits you in suffering, many will be saved."* Thus, clearly giving the seer a choice to accept or decline. The seer, of course, accepted.

XXX Seer(s)' Suffering/Sacrifice

(1) The seer is disbelieved and even mocked by some people. This causes her severe pain.
(2) Our Lady and Our Lord have requested that the seer fast and sacrifice for the conversion of sinners. She accepted and thus is a victim soul to some degree.

XXXI Healings Reported

Healings are reported from around the world. There are testimonials attributing the healings to the Matrix Medal.

The healings range from broken bones to ulcers. A person from an undisclosed location in California reportedly had a sudden conversion after wearing the medal and praying the Chaplet. He went to Confession for the first time in some 30 years.

XXXII Action Taken by the Church

Christina has had a spiritual director (Fr. McGinnity) since the early apparitions, and has been obedient to him. Fr. McGinnity usually accompanies the seer on speaking engagements.

Several members of the clergy and theologians have been favorably disposed.

It is reported that these apparitions are under investigation by the Church. No official decision has been reported.

XXXIII Bibliography

Please Come Back to Me and My Son 1992
By: R. Vincent
Published by: Ireland's Eye Publications

Jesus and Mary Speak in Ireland
By: Not Given
Published by: Not Given

The Final Hour
By: Michael Brown
Published by: The Riehle Foundation

Chapter 54

SANTA MARIA, CALIFORNIA, USA
(1988 - PRESENT)

I Place - Santa Maria, California

II Dates of First and Last Apparition

Carol Nole
First: March 24, 1988
Last: September 2, 1988
Note: Carol received locutions only

Barbara Matthias
First: March 24, 1990
Last: May 13, 1990 (last reported)
Note: The apparitions are reportedly ongoing.

III Seer(s) - 2

Name: Carol Nole
Birth: Unknown
Age at first apparition: Unknown
Status: Living

Name: Barbara Matthias
Birth: January 20, 1947
Age at first apparition: 41
Status: Living

IV Total Number of Apparitions - 74

Carol Nole — 28
Barbara Matthias — 46 published through May 13, 1990.
(Note: The apparitions to Barbara have reportedly been occurring daily and are ongoing. None of the messages to Barbara have been published subsequent to the message of May 13, 1990.)

V Dates and Locality of Each Apparition

Carol Nole — Santa Maria
1988: March 24, 25; April 9, 19, 20, 25, 28; May 2, 4, 5, 14, 15, 19, 23, 27, 31; June 3, 8, 11, 28; July 9, 16, 18, 28; August 6, 11, 29; September 2.
Barbara Matthias — Santa Maria
1990: March 24, 28, 31; April 1, 2, 3, 4, 5, 6, 7, 8, 9, 10, 11, 12, 13, 14, 15, 16, 17, 18, 19, 20, 21, 22, 23, 24, 25, 26, 27, 28, 29, 30; May 1, 2, 3, 4, 5, 6, 7, 8, 9, 10, 11, 12, 13.

VI Description of Our Lady

(1) The seer Barbara Matthias reports that most of the time Our Lady appears barefooted on a cloud in a brilliant white light. Usually Our Lady is dressed in all white with gold trim on Her mantel and a gold belt around Her waist. Her hair is chestnut brown. She has rosy cheeks and a delicate mouth. Her eyes are a beautiful penetrating gray-blue and Her voice is the most gentle loving voice this seer has ever heard.
(2) On special occasions or Feast Days (such as the Queenship of Mary, August 22nd) Our Lady appears crowned with 12 golden stars and wearing a jewelled gown. She appears to be about 20 years of age.
(3) Sometimes Our Lady appears holding the Infant Jesus in Her arms. Also angels and saints sometimes appear with Her.

VII Title(s) of Our Lady - 2

(1) *"Our Lady of the Immaculate Heart"* was the title announced by Our Lady to Barbara on March 28, 1990 and repeated again on April 1, 1990.

(2) On April 11, 1990 Our Lady proclaimed to Barbara: *"I am the Queen of the Universe."*

VIII Brief Factual Review

The State of California is located on the West Coast of the United States, with its shoreline on the Pacific Ocean. Santa Maria is located in Santa Barbara County along the Central Coast of California, and lies within the Santa Maria Valley, approximately 170 miles north of Los Angeles. The population of the Valley is over 100,000, while Santa Maria itself has about 60,000 people.

Historically Santa Maria was first named Grangeville, then renamed Central City in 1874, and finally was given the present name of Santa Maria in 1882. El Camino Real (US Highway 101), the route of Blessed Junipero Sera's Missions, traverses the Valley. This region is situated between Mission Santa Ynez and Mission San Luis Obispo. Many of the surrounding places bear the names of Our Lady or the names of various saints (as do many cities in California).

Today there are three Catholic parishes serving the immediate Santa Maria area: St. Mary of the Assumption, St. Louis de Montfort, and St. John Newman. Santa Maria is located in the diocese of Los Angeles, in the Santa Barbara Pastoral Region, and on the boundary with the Monterey Diocese to the North. Archbishop (now Cardinal) Roger Mahoney heads the diocese of Los Angeles, with Bishop Patrick Zieman being the auxiliary bishop in charge of the Santa Barbara Pastoral Region until his appointment as bishop of the Santa Rosa Diocese in September 1992. Also in September 1992 Msgr. John W. Rohde took over Bishop Zieman's role of administrating the Pastoral Region as the Episcopal Vicar. Msgr. Rohde is now Rector of St. Vibianas Cathedral in Los Angeles. Locally the Pastor of St. Louis de Montfort had been Fr. Anthony Runtz, CJ, later to be replaced by Fr. G. Garcia, C. J. Currently Fr. Mark Newman, CJ is the pastor. Bishop Thaddeus Shubsda was bishop of the Monterey Diocese. He later died, in January 1991, after which Bishop Sylvester Ryan took his place as bishop of the diocese of Monterey.

There are reports of a tradition of prophecy relating to the future of the Santa Maria Valley. Earlier prophecies declared that "Many will come from the north and the south to find refuge and solace here." Furthermore the people of this region were to be a beacon and light for all in need of help; that is a "Light on the mountain top".

There was also reported a history of active prayer groups and small 'Faith Communities' meeting and praying together in their homes and churches along this entire Central Coast from Monterey to Santa Barbara. Reportedly some of the prayer group participants began receiving locutions and prophetic messages from Jesus and from Our Lady, as early as 1985.

One such prayer group receiving messages was the Montfort Prayer Group, of which Charlie and Carol Nole (the first seer) became members.

It was in this atmosphere that Carol was to receive her first interior locution from Our Lady on March 24, 1988. Carol Nole was in her forties when she received her first message from Our Lady. She is described as an attractive and caring person who gives priority to helping the sick and the afflicted. She has three children from a prior marriage, and is now married to Charlie Nole who has five children, also from a previous marriage. Both of their prior marriages have been annulled by the Church.

In the first message of March 24th which was received inside the St. Mary of the Assumption Church, Our Lady assured Carol that She would receive funds needed for a planned pilgrimage to Medjugorje. Of course she got the money and went to Medjugorje. Then on April 9, 1988 Carol received another message from Our Lady which was a request that a Cross be built on a hill on the north side of town. Carol received another message on April 19, 1988 giving her a specific design for the Cross, which was to be 75 feet in height. On April 28th the seer received a message to *"take the canyon road to find the area where the two paths intersect"*, which was to reveal the location where the Cross was to be erected.

On the following Saturday morning Charlie, Carol, and others went to the designated area in search of the "right hill" on which the Cross was to be built. Each of the people that day experienced an "intense heat radiating from the ground" as they came to a certain spot on the ground. They stopped, prayed a rosary together and marked that place with stones. Since that time Carol has never had another message about the site of the Cross. They believed they had found the place selected by Our Lady for construction of the Cross. It should be mentioned that the 'Hill of the Cross site' is located across the Santa Maria River and within the boundaries of the Monterey Diocese.

On April 4, 1988 Carol received a message from Our Lady: *"Many will come and many will stay in My City of Peace."* Interestingly enough on June 7, 1988 the Santa Maria City Council formally declared Santa Maria to be "The City of Peace" by Resolution duly and officially adopted. Carol received a total of 28 reported messages from March 24, 1988 through September 2, 1988. It is reported that the messages have stopped as of this later date.

A model of the Cross was built and set up for public display and comment. Meanwhile the owners of the land on which the Cross is to be erected were contacted in order to negotiate for the purchase of the land. This was met with a cool response, later to become ice cold, from the landowner, Newhall Land and Farming Company. The land has never been acquired.

Meanwhile the prayer groups, the Cross Committee, as well as other interested groups, began to experience division and conflict within their own ranks.

During the next 1½ years, people gathered along Highway #166 across from the selected hill to pray and plan for the acquisition of the land and for the erection of the Cross. Local clergy continued to suppress all activities while the landowners placed 'No Trespassing' signs on the land and prohibited all entry onto the land. Yet people kept coming to the roadside to pray, to be healed and to be converted.

One such pilgrim who had come to pray along the side of the road, near the 'Hill of the Cross' site, was Barbara Matthias. Barbara was born on January 20, 1947 in Brazil and was baptized when she was six years old. She is described as a humble and pious person. Of slight stature, the result of Turner's Syndrome. It is reported that she made two unsuccessful attempts at religious life and that she had two unfortunate marriages.

On March 24, 1990 Barbara made a pilgrimage to Santa Maria. It was at the side of the road near the site of the hill, that the seer received her first apparition of Our Lady. This date was the Feast of the Annunciation as well as the second anniversary of the 'cross messages' given to the seer Carol Nole. Our Lady appeared to Barbara again on March 28, 1990; and has continued to appear and give daily messages to Barbara, which are ongoing to this day.

The first person Barbara told of her apparitions was Charlie Nole. It should be noted that he is the husband of the seer Carol Nole as well as coordinator of the Cross Project. Charlie promptly took Barbara into his own home for discernment and for Barbara's own protection. It wasn't long before serious conflicts arose. It is reported that Barbara was moved to Southern California against her own free will; however, three days later she returned to Santa Maria and continued to receive daily apparitions.

During the apparitions Barbara is in a state of ecstasy. These periods of ecstasy lengthened from minutes to three hours and later progressed to nearly six hours. Presently the time this seer remains in ecstasy has decreased to one or two hours.

It is reported that Barbara had mystical experiences earlier in her life. The first occurred when she was six years old when a voice told her that her father would die the next day. This did occur as predicted. In 1974 she heard a voice while at Mission San Luis Rey. The voice directed her to hold the hands of Our Lady's statue. When she did this the hands became like flesh and Our Lady spoke to the seer. She was directed by Our Lady to a certain place in the Mission Rose Garden where Barbara saw the two-dimensional face of Jesus surrounded by a bright light. Jesus asked Barbara to tell people that He waits for their love, and that He would see her in two years. In 1976 two years later, Barbara saw Jesus inside St. Francis Church in Vista, California. He was walking in front of the altar. He again spoke to Barbara.

Signs and wonders are reported during the apparitions such as the 'Miracle of the Sun' witnessed by many. Rosary links turn to gold color, extraordinary photos are taken. Instant cures and conversions are also reported. In addition many good fruits are evidenced by an explosion of prayer groups and a more active faith demonstrated by the parishioners.

Other conflicts and confusion developed. An issue arose regarding pledges and money being pledged for the Cross Project without the clergy's approval. Also there was some conflicts which arose through an alleged lack of obedience on the part of Barbara. This was later rectified.

At one point Barbara was publicly scandalized and persecuted. She suffered much, not only from her physical condition, but also from lack of employment and decent housing for herself. This has apparently been partially alleviated in that the seer now has suitable housing and support.

After Bishop Shubsda, Bishop of the Monterey Diocese, died in January 1991 Bishop Sylvester Ryan was appointed Bishop of the Diocese. Of course the messages of the Cross which Carol Nole received were being investigated by that bishop's commission because the site of the 'Hill of the Cross' is located in the Monterey Diocese. Barbara, on the other hand, had not been part of that investigation.

Carol Nole's messages are primarily concerned with the Cross Project. On the other hand, Barbara Matthias' primary messages are pleas for prayer, especially the rosary, for fasting and reparation for the sins of mankind, and for conversion of heart.

However, Our Lady also had messages for Barbara concerning the Cross Project. Our Lady said that *"Her Immaculate Heart is filled with pure love for the people of Santa Maria and for the great project you have undertaken for Me. . . . the Cross will be a symbol of faith, love, and peace."* Later Our Lady said: *"When I look down on Santa Maria and your valley, I see a city of peace and hope."* Then on April 6, 1990 Our Lady said: *"My children, I want the Hill of Peace to be consecrated to My Immaculate Heart."*

Our Lady also requested that a chapel be erected on the *"Hill of Peace"*, as well as Stations of the Cross. Our Lady also requested daily and frequent adoration of the Blessed Sacrament. On May 8, 1990 Our Lady said: *"There are three things to keep the devil away: the Holy Name of Jesus, the rosary, and the Brown Scapular of Carmel."* Our Lady also gave secrets to Barbara.

In 1991 a group of faithful supporters of Barbara, including author Jerrie Castro, and nurse practitioner, Anna Marie Mangdenberg arranged to have Barbara undergo an independent investigation by qualified experts, with the consent of her spiritual director and with specific permission from Our Lady. Extensive and yet very intensive tests were conducted on Barbara by a scientific team established at the University of California San Francisco Medical Center.

On February 10, 1992 Msgr. Rohde, who had since been appointed Vicar of the Santa Barbara Pastoral Region, reported the preliminary findings of the scientific team that examined Barbara. In his report he recites in part: "I am satisfied with the sincerity of Barbara Matthias. I am satisfied that her state of ecstasy has been verified by medical science. Based on the medical, and psychiatric evaluations, I am satisfied she is not faking or pretending the experience; that she is not psychotic; and that no organic etiology accounts for her experience." Barbara Matthias is under the pastoral care of the Church through her spiritual director. The independent investigation by qualified experts is ongoing at this time. Final judgment always rests with Church Authority. And so it is; no final decision has been made by the Church.

Canon Rene Laurentin, world renowned theologian from France, has visited Barbara and Carol in Santa Maria twice. He has also written a book on these events. Canon Laurentin stated that Barbara illustrates the words of the Gospel: "Blessed are the poor," that further discernment must continue, and that Barbara has an authentic supernatural life which lends credence to the authenticity of the ecstasies. All in all the clergy seems favorably impressed with this seer.

IX The Primary Messages - 7

(Six to Barbara Matthias, and one to Carol Nole.)

Carol Nole Messages - The messages this seer received concerned the 'Cross Project'.

On April 9, 1988 she received a request for the Cross to be built *"on the north side of town on the hill directly in line with the back of Scolari's market. It will be 75 feet in height and will have golden stained glass where the nail holes were. It must radiate love and peace over your valley."*

Later on April 28th she was given directions to find the exact location of the hill where the Cross was to be built.

Barbara Matthias' Messages - The messages given to this seer generally speak of peace, hope, love, and conversion. Our Lady said She sees Santa Maria as a place of preparation for heaven. She also urges us to pray, especially the rosary and to do penance, reparation, and fasting.

(1) Prayer - On March 28, 1990 Our Lady said: *"You must pray, fast, and make reparation for sin . . ."*

Then on April 2, 1990: *"Satan seeks to ruin the carrying out of this project. . . Pray much for the defeat of Satan."*

April 7, 1990: *"Do not give lip service to your prayers. Mean what you are saying in each word of each prayer you pray . . ."*

Again on April 12th: *"Each of you must spend a great deal of time in prayer . . ."*

April 19, 1990: *"Pray much for world peace. Peace must be in*

(2) **Rosary** - On the very first apparition to this seer Our Lady said: *"Pray the rosary often; very often. I, your Mother, hold the world and all My children's needs in My Immaculate Heart. Love My Son unconditionally."* (March 24, 1990)

April 1, 1990: *"Pray the rosary. Each bead of the rosary, said with a sincere and loving heart, is a flower of love for Me."*

On April 6, 1990 Our Lady held up Her beautiful rosary and said: *"My children, this is to be your major weapon against Satan and the evils of the world."*

April 26, 1990: *"I would like you to say fifteen decades of the rosary daily so all My plans for peace will go smoothly."*

Then on April 27, 1990 Our Lady announced: *"I don't want anyone to be deprived of the graces received from the prayer of the rosary. For those who teach others how to pray the rosary, I have promised to come for them at the hour of their death and that there will be many conversions in their families."*

(3) **Sacrifice and Reparation** - April 4, 1990 Our Lady speaks: *". . .This ladder (to heaven) is composed of prayer, penance, sacrifices, fasting and love . . ."*

Then on April 17, 1990 Our Lady said: *". . . Through your prayers, sacrifices, and fasting the project of the Cross will be completed . . ."*

(4) **Fasting** - *"Keep praying, fasting, and turning your hearts to My Son and Me. . . "* (March 31, 1990)

On April 7, 1990 Our Lady requested: *"I desire that you fast, especially on Wednesdays and Fridays . . ."*

(5) **Conversion** - March 31, 1990: *"You must keep your hearts open like little children who love and depend on their Mother."*

April 4, 1990: *"You are modern day Apostles who must live the Gospel life by following the example of My Son on earth."*

April 25, 1990: *"The world is in turmoil now because in many places Jesus and I have been forgotten. Pray, because these souls must awaken quickly before it is too late. They must turn their hearts back to Jesus and Me. Time is shorter than they realize."*

(6) **Cross Project** - Our Lady has demonstrated Her great love and joy for this Cross Project through several messages.

March 24, 1990: *"I love you so very much. Have patience, the Cross will be erected here in My Son's time."*

March 28, 1990: *"Believe that this project will be a source of holiness for all who desire to love Me with their heart and allow My graces to transform their lives . . ."*

Again on April 1, 1990: *"The Cross will be a symbol of faith, love, and peace . . ."*

On April 23, 1990 Our Lady said: *". . . I have been preparing you in so many ways for when the Cross will be erected. The Cross is a symbol of courage and life for all the world. . ."*

April 30, 1990: *"My children I desire you to make St. Joseph your patron of Our Cross Project just as Your Mother of the Immaculate Heart is Your Patroness."*

On May 1st Our Lady requested Stations of the Cross to be placed on the 'Hill of Peace' where the Cross is erected. She also requested a Chapel to be built on the 'Hill of Peace'.

Finally on May 9, 1990 Our Lady: *"My children, when the Cross is erected on the hill and Our Holy Project is completed, I desire that once a year on the Feast of St. Francis, that you bring your animals to the hill to be blessed . . ."*

X Signs Preceding the Apparitions - Not Reported

XI Other Visions During Apparitions

Given to Barbara Matthias:
(1) The Infant Jesus appeared with Our Lady on April 7th and again on April 12th and 19th, 1990.
(2) St. Michael appeared with Our Blessed Mother on April 25, 1990.
(3) On April 30, 1990 Our Lady brought St. Joseph with Her.
(4) Angels also appeared with Our Lady during several of the apparitions.

XII Prayers Taught to the Seer(s) - Not Reported

XIII Special Devotion Given to the Seer(s)

Given to Barbara Matthias:
(1) Although not a new devotion, on April 20, 1990 Our Lady requested that we: *"wear the St. Benedict medal. This medal has the power of exorcism attached to it."*
(2) On May 8, 1990 Our Lady said: *"Wear the Brown Scapular. I promise that whoever wears the Scapular will receive Eternal Life in heaven."*

XIV Requests Made by Our Lady

Given to Barbara Matthias:
(1) The primary request was that a Cross be erected on the top of the selected hill.
(2) On April 6, 1990 Our Lady requested that the 'Hill of Peace' to be consecrated to Her Immaculate Heart.
(3) On April 30, 1990 Our Lady requested that St. Joseph be taken as the

patron of the Cross Project.
(4) Our Lady requested a chapel be built on the 'Hill of Peace'.
(5) On May 1, 1990 Our Lady asked for the Stations of the Cross to be placed on the Hill of Peace.
(6) On May 4, 1990 Our Lady asked that a statue of the Infant of Prague be placed in the Chapel after it is constructed.
(7) Then on May 6, 1990 Our Lady requested the Blessed Sacrament be exposed for a certain time daily in the Chapel.
(8) That we wear the Brown Scapular. (May 8, 1990)
(9) That we wear the St. Benedict medal. (April 20, 1990)
(10) That we fast on Wednesdays and Fridays. (April 7, 1990)

Given to Carol Nole:
(1) It was to this seer that Our Lady first gave the message to erect the 'Cross on the Hill'.

XV Specific Bible References - Not Reported

XVI Secrets Given to the Seer(s)

Barbara received five secrets, three of which have been revealed.

XVII Miracles Promised by Our Lady - NR
XVIII Miracles Performed - Not Reported
XIX Miracles Promised not yet Performed - NR
XX Signs Promised - Not Reported

XXI Signs Given

(1) The Miracle of the Sun occurred on several occasions during apparitions and was witnessed by many people who were present along the road.
(2) There are reports of other signs and wonders, such as pilgrims seeing everything around the hill becoming enveloped in a golden cloud, including the people, cars, etc. Even airplanes flying near the site were reported turning to a golden color while flying over the hill.
(3) On one occasion Our Lady showed Barbara the 'Door to Heaven', and said: *"The secret to opening this door is to love Me, remain faithful, and avoid the things of the world which are hindrances to eternal life in heaven."*
(4) There are reports of other persons actually seeing Our Lady. One was a boy of 11. Another young man (Juan Diaz) began to pray in tongues when he saw Our Lady and also saw the Crucified Christ while on the side of the road near the hill site.

XXII Predictions/Promises

Clearly Our Lady has stated that the 'Cross Project' will be completed.
- **(1)** On March 24, 1990 Our Lady told Barbara: *"Have patience, the Cross will be erected here in My Son's time,"* and that the *"Cross will be a symbol of faith, love, and peace. . . "* (April 1, 1990)   And finally *". . . through your prayers, sacrifices, and fasting the Project of the Cross will be completed."* (April 17, 1990)
- **(2)** Our Lady promised that the faith of the people of Santa Maria would always be strong, just like She had earlier promised that the faith of the people of Portugal would always be strong. (April 30, 1990)

XXIII Prophecies/Warnings of Chastisement

April 16, 1990: *"Now is the time of Mercy; tell people who are away from Jesus and Me to turn their hearts back to Us immediately. We want all to be saved; woe to souls who have abandoned Us deliberately and remain in this state. Warn them, tell them before it is too late. It will be horrifying for them. Concern yourselves with living each moment as if it were the last moment you have here to do Our will . . . When you realize the seriousness of the end times, and realize the fate of those against Us is eternal . . . In the end times there will be family dissensions. Members of families will hate each other, quarrel and plan evil for each other. This will be the work of Satan. You My children must not let dissensions arise in your families. You must avoid the work of Satan who wishes to enter your hearts and homes. I will protect you. Ask for My graces to overshadow you and your request will be granted. I have accounted the seriousness of the end times, so that it will be a time of victory for you, if you are faithful."*

XXIV Method of Appearance

A bright light first appears. Our Lady appears within this light, which continues to surround Her during the apparition.

XXV Method of Departure

The bright light fades back and upward until it disappears and the apparition ends.

XXVI Confrontation w/Civil Authorities

Conflicts and confrontations arose involving private groups and individuals rather than official civil governmental authorities.
- **(1)** The owners of the land on which the hill site was selected, namely

Newhall Land and Farming Company, refused negotiations for the sale and purchase of the land; and eventually ended by placing 'No Trespassing' signs on the land and forbidding entrance onto the land. This resulted in the seer and the pilgrims meeting along the roadside near the hill site. These roadside meetings were found to be a safety hazard by the Highway Patrol and thus were further curtailed.

(2) There were conflicts which arose between the various groups concerning raising funds for the Cross Project, building a cross on an alternate site, publication of Carol's messages and finally conflicts with the seer Barbara, all causing much pain, suffering, and mental anguish to the seers.

(3) It is reported that the seer (Barbara) was publicly scandalized and persecuted and actually forced to leave town.

XXVII Confrontation w/Church Authorities

(1) The seer Barbara was accused of being disobedient to Msgr. Rohde. This event seemingly occurred through some confusion in communication of Msgr. Rohde's request to the seer. However, once the facts were given the light of day this charge was entirely removed by written statement from Msgr. Rohde.

(2) There are reports of prayer groups becoming divided and decimated over the issues of the Cross Project, the messages, and the seers. One prayer group was evicted by the pastor of one parish and was required to find other meeting places.

(3) Yet the record speaks of the great beneficial influence given by Bishop Zieman, by Msgr. Rohde, and also by Canon Rene Laurentin. The clergy did guide and encourage the various factions to unity, successfully; given the many reported good fruits which have resulted. On August 22, 1992 (Feast of the Queenship of Mary), Msgr. Rohde moderated a public meeting for unity 'Bringing Believers Together' at St. Joseph High School in Santa Maria with well over 400 people in attendance.

XXVIII Request Chapel/Shrine Built

On April 30, 1990 Our Lady said: *"I would like a chapel to be built on the Hill of Peace. I want all to come and worship My Son and to venerate Me, your Mother."*

XXIX Free Will/Choice

On May 10, 1990 Our Lady spoke: *"My children, your life is what you make of it. You were given free will because My Son desires you to love and follow Him freely in love. Since you have control over your free will you can make your life a 'Little Heaven upon Earth' by following Jesus and Me, or a 'Little Hell upon Earth' by choosing evil. What will you choose for your life?"*

XXX Seer(s)' Suffering/Sacrifice

(1) The seer Barbara suffered greatly due to her poverty and physical handicaps.
(2) She also suffered public scandals and persecutions; as well as privations in her employment and living conditions.
(3) The confusion surrounding the charge of disobedience and its later clarification caused her to suffer much.
(4) The conflicts and divisions involving the Cross Project, the prayer groups and others, gave grief and suffering to both seers, i.e. Carol and Barbara.

XXXI Healings Reported

Physical healings have been reported; although not officially documented. In addition there are reports of conversions and a profusion of spiritual good fruits.

XXXII Action Taken by the Church

(1) No official Church decision has been made in the case of either Carol or Barbara concerning the messages or Cross Project.
(2) Bishop Zieman has publicly announced that the Cross Project has given the faithful a common goal to unite and pray together.
(3) Both Bishop Zieman and Msgr. Rohde have been supportive and have participated in various functions.
(4) Canon Rene Laurentin, a world renowned Mariologist, has visited these two seers in Santa Maria twice and seems supportive; yet awaiting further discernment.
(5) Finally the extensive investigation of Barbara by a team of scientific, theological and medical experts produced a preliminary report which cleared Barbara of any fraud or deficiencies which would rule against the authenticity of her messages. Msgr. Rohde made a public report of these findings and was encouraged by Barbara's own spirituality. Professor Dr. Mark Miravalle also reports positively about Barbara's spirituality.
(6) The clergy seems to be positive, yet discerning of these apparitions. More time is needed for the Church to make a final determination.

XXXIII Bibliography

Mary's Plan - The Madonna Comes to Santa Maria 1993
By: J. Ridley Castro
Published by: Queenship Publishing Company

The Way of the Cross in Santa Maria 1993
By: Fr. Rene Laurentin
Published by: Queenship Publishing Company

The Cross Will Be Built 1989
By: Not Given
Published by: The 'Cross of Peace' Project

Chapter 55

Cuenca, Ecuador
(1988 - 1990)

I Place
(1) Cuenca, Ecuador
(2) Mexico City, Mexico
(3) Garden in El Cajas, Ecuador

II Dates of First and Last Apparition
First: August 28, 1988
Last: March 3, 1990

III Seer(s) - 1
Name: Patricia Talbott (Pachi)
Birth: Unknown
Age at first apparition: 16
Status: Living/Married

IV Total Number of Apparitions - 33

V Dates and Locality of Each Apparition

(All apparitions took place in Cuenca unless otherwise noted.)

1988 - August 28 (seer's bedroom); date unknown (seer's bedroom); September (Cathedral); October 7 (Cathedral, Mexico City); October 8 (once at Shrine & once at Basilica, Mexico City); October 11 (Church on Tepeyac Hill, Mexico City); November 4 (seer's bedroom);

December 1 (Chapel at Dominican High School); December 15, Seer's bedroom; December 24 (once - seer's bedroom; once - Church of Servants of Mary); December 25 & 26 (seer's bedroom); December 26 (Virgen de Bronce Church); December 27 (Church of Carmelite Sisters at San Rogue).
1989 - January 16 (seer's bedroom); February 1 & 17(seer's bedroom); All the following occured in El Cajas: June 15; July 16 ; August 5 & 28; September 7 & 9; October 7; {November 4 & 8(seer's bedroom)}; December First Saturday; December 8, 12, 24.
1990 - January 6, February 2, & March 3 all at El Cajas.

VI Description of Our Lady

(1) **Cuenca - First Apparition August 28, 1988.** The seer's bedroom is flooded with a bright light, within which is a beautiful Lady.
(2) **Mexico City Apparitions October 8, 1988.** Our Lady is barefooted and standing over a cloud. A blue veil covers Her head and flows down to Her ankles. She wears a white skirt with a red blouse. Her eyes are big and long; the color of honey. Her hair, which comes out on both sides of the veil, is also honey colored. Her nose is small and straight and Her lips are thin. Her face is fine and Her skin is golden. She has a crown of twelve stars vertically around Her head. Her arms are extended outwards and down, and She is holding a rosary in Her hands with the cross near Her left hand. The rosary is a brown color and the cross has a metal Christ.
(3) Sometimes Our Lady wore a crown of roses around Her forehead and a rose on each foot. On special occasions, such as Her birthday on August 5th, Our Lady is dressed completely in white.

VII Title(s) of Our Lady - 1

"I am The Guardian of the Faith." Our Lady stated this title at the first apparition and during later apparitions as well.

VIII Brief Factual Review

Ecuador is located on the South American continent, in the bulky northwest portion of the continent, with a Pacific Ocean shoreline.
Patricia Talbott was the third eldest child born to Fernando and Carmen Talbott. They lived in Cuenca, Ecuador. Patricia was 16 when the apparitions first took place. She was in high school and active in a group which traveled to other countries modeling clothes.
The first apparition occurred in Patricia's bedroom on August 28,

1988 when she was awakened from a dream and saw her room filled with a bright light. She saw the figure of a beautiful lady who spoke to her. The apparitions and messages continued until March 3, 1990. Several apparitions occurred in Mexico City while Patricia was on a modeling trip during the period from October 7th to October 11th 1988.

After returning to her home, the apparitions and messages continued in the seer's bedroom and in various chapels and churches. On June 15, 1989 Our Lady led Patricia to a mountain area called El Cajas, a place where Our Lady appeared thereafter. For the final six months of the apparitions, Our Lady appeared on the First Saturday of each month at El Cajas. Her final appearance was on March 3, 1990.

On one occasion Patricia was miraculously given a Host on her tongue. Our Lady gave the seer a secret in Mexico City on October 11, 1988 during an apparition. This secret concerns: "bad things that are going to happen in the world, and what is asked for is conversions", so Patricia is quoted as saying.

On November 4, 1988 Our Lady gave Patricia the date of the great chastisement which is to occur on earth. She also warned of a Third World War being near, if we do not convert. Our Lady said the earth would leave its orbit for three days and that these will be terrible days of darkness. Families should stay inside and continuously pray. Our Lady said great times of tribulation are coming. Natural catastrophes and those created by men are near. We should pray for the clergy. We should pray and convert. In February 1990 Our Lady told the seer: *"It will be 10 very sad years. Time is short."*

During the last apparition of March 3, 1990 Our Lady said: *"At the end of all the apparitions of the world, I will leave a great sign in this place and in all those where I have been. Good-bye My little ones. Good-bye My children."*

Jesus appeared and spoke to Patricia several times during this 18 month period during which Our Lady's apparitions occurred.

Many people traveled up the mountain to El Cajas for the apparitions on the First Saturday of November and December 1989; and also on the First Saturdays of January, February and March 1990. Over 100,000 people were reported during the February and March apparitions. During this period (February - March 1990) several statues and images of Our Lady and of Jesus shed tears and exuded oil and bled human blood. Some of these statues and images were on Patricia's altar in her home, while other weepings occurred at different homes in Cuenca.

On March 3, 1990 Our Lady told Patricia that She would no longer appear to the seer but would be with her always and would console her in time of great need. Since that time Patricia has had several locutions from Our Lady. Patricia was given the mission to spread Our Lady's messages and to help the poor. On January 19, 1991 Patricia married Andres

Cordova. Together they devote their time and energy, fulfilling the mission given to Patricia.

The Church has not made a definitive decision. The first commission established in January 1989 concluded that the commission could not say that the apparitions of Our Lady were supernatural or from heaven. After pilgrimages to El Cajas in February - March 1990, the bishop reopened the case. The outcome is awaited by the world.

IX The Primary Messages - 9

(1) **Prayer** - The messages are permeated with Our Lady's requests for prayer. She says that we are to pray much for: peace in the world, conversions, priests, bishops and clergy, an increase in religious vocations, children who have gone astray, the sick and the souls in purgatory. She asks us to pray to Her and She will intercede for us with God, Our Father.

Further She says, pray slowly because prayers said in a hurry do not reach heaven. Abandon yourselves more to prayers of contemplation, pray to your guardian angel and to the angels, and finally pray the rosary every day and form prayer groups.

(2) **Rosary** - Our Lady says the rosary is the most complete prayer after the Holy Mass. It is our shield against the evil one who is active. She asks us to wear always the rosary on us which will protect us against evil. On Christmas day 1988 Our Lady said: *"The rosary is the most complete prayer. Do not ask yourself why you pray it. Let it be your shield against the evil one who is at work. Do not detach yourselves from it."*

On February 22, 1991 Patricia experienced a locution. Our Lady said among other things: *"I promise all those children who will pray the rosary with great devotion that, in the 5th mystery Archangels Michael, Raphael and Gabriel will sign the cross on their foreheads."*

(3) **Holy Mass and Eucharist** - Our Lady urges us to participate in Holy Mass as frequently as possible; daily. She said: *"Go to Mass and visit the Blessed Sacrament."*

(4) **Penance and Fasting** - Our Lady said repent, fast and do penance. Fast on bread and water at least once a week. She also stated *"Do not forget that with prayer and fasting you can deter wars and natural catastrophes."*

(5) **Works of Mercy** - Our Lady said: *"Be united, love your brothers, fulfill the works of mercy, My little ones."* Again: *"Do works of mercy among lonely people, visit the elderly, the sick . . . Help those who are in most need, and give alms in the temple to your Father."*

(6) **Satan's Role in the World Today** - Our Lady said: *"For there is a hell as there is a heaven, but there is only one King, God the Father, for Satan exists who contains hatred, perversion and all that does not give peace to your hearts."* Again: *"Do not let Satan penetrate your hearts."*

Our Lady said: *"Satan wants to destroy the mission which heaven has granted you, children of Light."* She also requests that we pray much for priests because Satan is penetrating into the depths of the Holy Church.

Our Lady says that other great victories for Satan are divorce, abortions, together with modern fashions, styles, music and drugs.

She warns us: *"Satan will entangle you, do not allow him to take My Son's place."* She stresses that Satan is especially active among the youth today. Our Lady says: *"Satan's hand is in the youth, you must take Satan's hand off and put the hand of My Son upon the hearts of the whole world."*

(7) **Merciful Heart of Jesus** - Our Lady spoke often of the Merciful Heart of Jesus, and that we were living in a time of mercy. She said: *"Love the Heart of My Son and His mercy and love My Immaculate Heart."*

Jesus also appeared to Patricia as the Merciful Jesus and said: *"I am the Merciful Jesus, I am great in heart. Ask children, I would like the day of My Mercy to be celebrated."* On April 2, 1989 (the First Sunday after Easter Sunday) Jesus appeared to Patricia and said: *"Today is the day of My Mercy. You do not know that My Heart is big. I want to help you, My little ones, ask, My children. This day is universal because I am universal."*

(8) **Conversion** - Our Lady's messages contain many urgings for conversion of heart. She continuously reminds us that through conversion, prayer and fasting we can hold back the hand of God! She asks for faithful conversion.

"Little children, I need speedy conversion, prayer, and more than anything, a faithful conversion from a humble heart. Why do you take so long to change, do not leave to tomorrow what you can do today." Again: *"All that I have told you is because God the Father has asked Me to. Children the time is short, very short. Conversion must be faithful. Remove all evil sentiments because Satan penetrates in them. Remove them with the presence of God in your souls. Children give thanks to God for what you have."*

(9) **Guardian Angels and Angels** - On one occasion Our Lady said: *"Today, I am accompanied by the Archangels Michael and Gabriel, you must pray to your guardian angel every day that he protect you. Intercede to St. Michael the Archangel that you be not tempted by the devil, and to Archangel Gabriel for truth."*

X Signs Preceding the Apparitions

(1) On the occasion of the first apparition, Patricia's bedroom was flooded with light before Our Lady appeared.
(2) Patricia would usually see a bright light, or feel the wind blowing or experience a deep calling within herself just before the apparition.

XI Other Visions During Apparitions

(1) Patricia saw angels as well as her own guardian angel, and also the Archangels, Michael and Gabriel. She also saw St. Francis of Assisi. On one occasion the seer saw the Holy Family in their home at Nazareth.
(2) Patricia reports that once, when she was praying late at night, Our Lady appeared to her and said: *"For there is a hell as there is a heaven, but there is only one King, God the Father . . ."* Patricia then went on to describe hell as a terrible place, like a big volcano where you see souls that hate each other. Purgatory was like coming out of the volcano. She could see hands reaching out and trying to get out. While she was in purgatory she heard a voice asking her to pray for them because they can't do anything without our help.

XII Prayers Taught to the Seer(s) - Not Reported
XIII Special Devotion Given to the Seer(s) - NR

XIV Requests Made by Our Lady

(1) Our Lady requested that Patricia come to El Cajas for six consecutive First Saturdays to receive apparitions and messages.
(2) Our Lady outlined to Patricia the description and dimensions of the Sanctuary She wanted built at El Cajas.
(3) Our Lady gave Patricia a special mission to care for the poor.
(4) At the first apparition Our Lady requested that Patricia make an altar in her own bedroom.
(5) On December 1, 1988 Our Lady requested a public rosary be prayed on December 8, 1988 in an open coliseum.
(6) On December 26, 1988 Our Lady requested that Patricia and her prayer group visit all the churches in that city that very same day.
(7) On July 16, 1989 Our Lady requested that a procession to El Cajas take place on August 28, 1989 to commemorate the first anniversary of the apparitions.
(8) In February 1989 Our Lady asked for a pilgrimage to all the houses where statues had exuded oil, telling all that special graces were to be given in those homes.

XV Specific Bible References

On one occasion Our Lady told Patricia: *"All that I tell you is in Sacred Scripture."*

XVI Secrets Given to the Seer(s)

On October 11, 1988 during an apparition in the chapel on Tepeyac hill in Mexico City, Our Lady said: *"Now, daughter, now I will reveal to you My Great Secret which corresponds to the one revealed to the other visionaries. This secret you cannot write nor tell to anyone until I permit you."*

Patricia reportedly later said: "She gave me the secret that there are bad things going to happen in the world, and what is asked for is conversion. I asked Our Lady if I could tell anybody about the secret and the Virgin said *"No,"*— because it was too strong a message and it would create panic. And so, I said, I can't just forget about this. And the Virgin said: *"One month ahead of time I'll tell you so you can say it."*

Later Our Lady told Patricia certain parts of the secret could be revealed. The secret contains three parts, each part has something to do with future events which will be chastisements for our world, the seer has reported.

It was also on October 11, 1988, after Our Lady gave the seer the Great Secret, that Our Lady gave the seer the Host on the seer's tongue in a miraculous manner.

XVII Miracles Promised by Our Lady

On Patricia's altar in her own bedroom she kept a statue of Our Lady of Fatima. It stood on a little wooden box. On November 8, 1989 Our Lady told Patricia: *"Get up and see inside the little box under the feet of the little statue. There is My Sacred Son."* Patricia opened the box and found a Sacred Host inside. Our Lady told Patricia that St. Michael had placed the Host there and that the seer was not to show the Host to anyone without using great discretion.

XVIII Miracles Performed

(1) On October 11, 1988 Our Lady miraculously gave the Sacred Host to Patricia on the seer's tongue.
(2) On November 8, 1989 Our Lady asked the seer to look into the box, where Patricia found the Sacred Host. Our Lady told Patricia that St. Michael had placed the Sacred Host there.

XIX Miracles Promised not yet Performed - NR

XX Signs Promised

On March 3, 1990 the final apparition to Patricia, Our Lady said: *"At the end of all the apparitions in the world, I will leave a great sign in this place and in all those where I have been."*

XXI Signs Given

(1) On the first Saturday of December 1989 a phenomena occurred at El Cajas that was witnessed by many. The clouds parted and a great light formed the image of Our Lady of the Miraculous Medal in the sky.
(2) On January 15, 1989 pictures and statues on Patricia's altar began to exude oil and tears.
(3) On June 15, 1989 as Patricia and some friends were searching for the place to establish the Sanctuary, which Our Lady asked Patricia to find, and as they drove up the mountain, they saw a strange light in the sky. The light was in the shape of an arrow, pointing to a place high in the mountains. They also heard bells. Both the light and the bells were so unusual, that they thought this may be the sign so they followed the light until it appeared to point downward toward a huge rock in the middle of a large open area — this was El Cajas, the site high in the Andes Mountains (11,000 feet above sea level) which Our Lady had selected for Her final apparitions.
(4) In February 1990 statues of Our Lady again began to weep.
(5) A Host appeared in a box in the seer's bedroom as predicted by Our Lady.
(6) Our Lady miraculously gave the seer the Sacred Host on the seer's tongue.

XXII Predictions/Promises

(1) On one occasion Our Lady said: *"Satan will reach the summit; but I am the woman the Father announced who will crush the head of the serpent that is Satan."*
(2) On February 2, 1990 Our Lady said: *"We have begun the hard times. It will be ten very sad years. Time is short."* However Our Lady also said: *"Little children, know that all you do benefits the world. Your prayers, penance and fasts are helping to prevent the third world war. Everything is as I have told you, all in your hands."*
(3) On November 4, 1988 Patricia was given the date of the Chastisement, which she cannot reveal. The date is to be revealed 30 days before the chastisement.

XXIII Prophecies/Warnings of Chastisement

(1) Our Lady not only revealed to Patricia the Great Chastisement, but also gave her the date of the chastisement which she cannot reveal without Our Lady's permission, and then only 30 days before the event.

(2) On the 26th of December 1988 Our Lady gave Patricia a message for Bernardita, a friend and companion of Patricia.

In this message Our Lady said: *"Bernardita, you know a part of the sacred chastisement. This is the sign. You My beloved daughter know already one of the ten sacred secrets. It is the dream, when in reality your spirit came out from your body and you saw all that can happen in that day. Do not talk about it until I ask you. My little soul I grant you that one month before the thing happens you can notify all My children. But, this will happen only if you have a complete vision from your Heavenly Father. If the contrary happens, you cannot reveal anything. I love you, and only if the Father permits will you, one month before, tell the little souls from the entire world."*

The message explains a dream which Bernardita had in November and of which she had told Patricia. Reportedly Our Lady told Patricia that *"she (Patricia) might be leaving before you Bernardita,"* which both Patricia and Bernardita understood to mean that Patricia may not be here on earth to transmit the message.

(3) As for the chastisements themselves, Our Lady said that: *"Great Catastrophes are coming upon humanity, the Third World War threatens the world, natural catastrophes created by man are coming. You must be strong with a faith that is like a rock."* And again: *"the war is near. It will be started with false peace treaties, treaties in which we should not place our trust. Many countries would be involved, among them China, Romania, Russia, and the United States."*

"Your prayers, penances, and fasts are helping to prevent a Third World War. Pray for the countries from South, catastrophes come there. Pray for Panama, Nicaragua, El Salvador. Repent, fast, make penance. Pray for the Soviet Union, Russia, the United States, Czechoslovakia and China. These are countries that will be involved in the Third World War."

"The Third World War is near. Natural catastrophes, earthquakes, floods such as humanity has never seen before, because of so much sin in the world. You know that you are surrounded by much sin. Convert your heart. Give it to Me. Have Peace!"

XXIV Method of Appearance

(1) At the first apparition, Patricia's bedroom was flooded with light, Our Lady then emerged from this light and spoke to the seer.

(2) Thereafter Our Lady appeared to Patricia, usually while the seer was at prayer.

XXV Method of Departure

Usually Our Lady would bless everyone present as She departed.

XXVI Confrontation w/Civil Authorities

(1) In September 1989 Patricia signed a 'vow of silence'. It reportedly was believed that a vow of silence was necessary because of the adverse publicity which these events had received. Newspaper articles were attacking everyone involved in the events surrounding the reported apparitions; factions were forming and the atmosphere was apparently not healthy for Patricia or the Church in Cuenca. Nothing more specific is mentioned in the published work as to further actual involvement with Civil Authorities.
(2) On August 28, 1989 Our Lady Herself, on the occasion of the first anniversary of Her appearance to Patricia, said: *"My children you do not know the sorrow the inhabitants of this city cause Me. You have not received with simple hearts the Love of My Son and My Love. My children I will be with you for a very short time, due to the ingratitude of the people of Cuenca. I leave you with great sorrow in My heart. I will be on this hill for six months for My pilgrims. The apparitions will be just once a month. My people of Cuenca have received Me with great rejection. I ask you My children, those who have worked with Me, to continue sharing that devotion with My little ones."*

XXVII Confrontation w/Church Authorities

(1) There were differing opinions, concerning the authenticity of the apparitions, held by members of the Episcopal Conference of Ecuador, which standing alone may not amount to confrontation with Church authorities.
(2) However, a Carmelite Priest, Father Lorenzo, whom Patricia sought out to be her confessor because of a vision and message from Our Lady, whom our Lady identified as *"an old priest almost blind"* in the seer's dream, at first agreed to be her spiritual director; however, when later contacted by Patricia, he excused himself because his superiors would not permit him to communicate with the seer.

XXVIII Request Chapel/Shrine Built

During the time when Patricia was receiving locutions but not seeing

Our Lady, the Virgin gave Patricia descriptions and dimensions of the Sanctuary She wanted to be built at El Cajas; a Sanctuary *"in which the Father, Son and Holy Spirit will be adored."* Our Lady also said it would take much time before this would come to be, and there would be many difficulties before it could happen.

XXIX Free Will/Choice

(1) On August 28, 1989 Our Lady sadly complained that the people of Cuenca had received Our Lady with great rejection, thus at least implying that we have the choice of believing or rejecting Her. In this instance there was a consequence for the great rejection, that being that the messages became less frequent and were curtailed in duration to six months.

(2) It was only after Patricia decided against a modeling career that Our Lady appeared to her and said she had made the correct choice. The choice is always our own.

XXX Seer(s)' Suffering/Sacrifice

(1) When the archbishop's negative conclusion was announced to Patricia on April 18, 1989 this was very painful to her and to her family. This was especially so in light of the fact that the apparitions continued thereafter until March 3, 1990 and gathered ever increasing numbers of pilgrims.

(2) Patricia's choice to give up her modeling career was a correct decision but caused her much pain.

XXXI Healings Reported

(1) No doubt Patricia and many of her close friends and members of her prayer groups received spiritual healings.

(2) Our Lady told Patricia that the oil exuded from the statues and pictures would be a blessing to the sick. On February 17, 1989 Our Lady asked for a pilgrimage to all the houses where Her statues exuded oil, stating that special graces were being given in those homes.

XXXII Action Taken by the Church

(1) The first commission appointed to investigate the apparitions resulted in a report stating that the commission was not able to say that the manifestations of the Holy Virgin were supernatural.

(2) In February 1990 after more apparitions and after many thousands of pilgrims traveled to El Cajas, a second commission was appointed.

The outcome of this commission is being awaited.
(3) Meanwhile Patricia has signed a 'vow of silence' promising not to speak publicly about the apparitions.

XXXIII Bibliography

I Am the Guardian of the Faith 1991
By: Sister Isabel Bettwy
Published By: Franciscan University Press

Chapter 56

AGOO, PHILIPPINES
(1989-1993)

I Place - Agoo, La Union, Philippines

II Dates of First and Last Apparition

First: March 31, 1989
Last: September 8, 1993

III Seer(s) - 1

Name: Judiel Nieva
Birth: October 29, 1976
Age at first apparition: 12
Status: Living

IV Total Number of Apparitions - 53

V Dates and Locality of Each Apparition

All apparitions occurred at the hillside of Barangay San Antonio, Agoo, La Union, unless otherwise noted.

1989: March 31; April 7; September 8; October 7.
1992: February; March 31; April 4; May 13, 16, 23, 30; June 11, 20, 27; July 4, 11, 18, 25; August 1, 8, 22, 25; September 5, 8, 19, 26; October 3, 17, 24, 31; November 7, 14, 21; December 8, 12, 19, 26.
1993: January 2, 19, 23, 30; February 6, 11; March 6, 25; April 3; May 1; June 3; July 3; August 7; September 1, 8 (twice).

VI Description of Our Lady

(1) On Her first public appearance to Judiel on March 31, 1989 Our Blessed Mother was sitting with the Baby Jesus on Her lap. Her Immaculate Heart was visible on Her chest and radiated a bright light.

(2) On April 7, 1989 a bright light flashed and angelic voices were singing the Alleluia and Salve Regina (as had also occurred on March 31), when suddenly Our Lady appeared in a long white dress, standing on top of a cloud. Her mantle touched the cloud at Her feet. Only Her toes could be seen. There was a shining star on the hem of Her dress, but the brightest star was on Her forehead. At Our Lady's feet on the cloud were seven roses. Above Her head was a beautiful crown, and above the crown was a halo of 12 stars. Rays of light emanated from Her entire body.

The seer reports that Our Lady's face and Her eyes, and everything about Her, was heavenly beautiful and could not be described or compared with anything here on earth. Her eyes were bluish-brown.

Our Lady's hands were outstretched and in Her right hand She held a rosary with beads of pearls, while in Her left hand She held a Brown Scapular. Her Immaculate Heart was exposed at Her breast. She wore a tassel with three rings at the tip. One ring was a rope with a ball and the others were knotted.

VII Title(s) of Our Lady - 12

During the several apparitions at Agoo, Our Lady announced Herself under a variety of titles:

(1) *"I am the Immaculate Queen of Heaven and Earth."* (September 8, 1991)
(2) *"I am the Mother of Sorrows."* (September 19, 1992)
(3) *"I am Your Beloved Mother."* (October 31, 1992)
(4) *"I am Your Mother, the Mother of All Sinners."* (November 7, 1992)
(5) *"I am Your Mother, the Co-Redemptrix."* (November 21, 1992)
(6) *"I am Your Mother, the Stella Maris."* (December 12, 1992)
(7) *"I am Your Mother of Mercy, the Refuge of Sinners."* (December 19, 1992)
(8) *"I am Your Mother, the Mother of God."* (January 9, 1993)
(9) *"I am the Immaculate Conception."* (December 8, 1992 and February 11, 1993)
(10) *"I am the Queen of Victory."* (January 2, 1993)
(11) *"I am the Mediatrix of all God's Gifts, Peace and Grace."* (February 6, 1993)
(12) *"I am the Morning Star."* (November 14, 1992)

VIII Brief Factual Review

Agoo is a town of some 40,000 people, located in La Union north of Manila, on the Island of Luzon, in the Philippines. At the time of the apparitions the primary source of income was tobacco; there was no major industry in Agoo.

The Philippines is the only country in Asia which is predominately Catholic. The region in and around Agoo is well known for the intense spiritual fervor of its inhabitants. It is said that many 'Healers', as well as priests, religious and bishops have come from this region.

The landscape around Agoo is reported as being breathtaking, remote, rugged, arid, and barren; yet beautiful. The site of the reported apparitions is Barangay San Antonio up in the hills some two kilometers from the center of town. This place is now called 'Apparition Hill'. The hill has a steep 45 degree slope upon which pilgrims gather to take part in these apparitions.

In 1978 a church and shrine were completed and dedicated to 'Our Lady of Charity', to commemorate the 400th Anniversary of the coastal settlement known as Puerto de Japon. This landmark Shrine of Our Lady of Charity was later elevated to the status of Basilica Minor. The killer earthquake of 1990, which damaged many public buildings and houses, also damaged the Basilica. The Basilica reopened in December 1992 after repairs were made. The home of Judiel's parents was also damaged in the earthquake of 1990. It is also being reconstructed.

Bishop Salvador Lazo was bishop of La Union province when these apparitions occurred.

The visionary Judiel Nieva reportedly first started receiving private apparitions of Our Lady in 1987 when he was only 10 years old and in sixth grade. These initial visions took place in the privacy of his own home. Later Our Blessed Mother instructed the visionary (and some of his friends) to go up to the small spring of water in the hills above Agoo, the site of San Antonio. It was at this 'sitio' of San Antonio that the first of the public apparitions began on March 31, 1989 when Our Lady appeared to the seer atop a guava tree on a rise high above the spring.

Judiel Nieva was born into a family of eight (he was seventh). His parents Pedro and Julia operated 2 stalls in the local market. The children were all expected to help. Once Judiel claims to have seen Jesus crucified hanging on the cross as the seer stepped out of his parent's stall. It is reported that everyone in Agoo knew Judiel because he was reputed to have special powers, even as a child of ten. He was sought out as a healer. Even then Judiel prayed a lot. He was said to be a psychic and could tell if a person was a nonbeliever, even from a distance. Yet the local parish priest of Agoo thought Judiel was making up these things. The name 'Judiel' reportedly means 'Bearer of God's Mercy'.

Judiel reports that the first public apparition of March 31, 1989 was preceded by a bright light, then he heard voices and sounds of trumpets, while angels descended from heaven towards him singing *"Alleluia"* and *"Salve Regina."* The angels formed an inverted letter 'V' with three angels on either side and St. Michael at the apex of the 'V', with a white dove above his head. The Holy Family appeared on a cloud, St. Joseph with a shepherd's staff and Our Lady was sitting on a rock holding Baby Jesus on Her lap.

The angels identified themselves, each representing a day in the week:
St. Michael - Sunday, holding a weighing scale and a sword.
St. Gabriel - Monday, holding a plum and a book.
St. Raphael - Tuesday, holding a fish and a sword.
St. Uriel - Wednesday, holding a weighing scale.
St. Setiel - Thursday, holding an incensor.
St. Judiel - Friday, holding a music book and bouquet of flowers.
St. Barachiel - Saturday, holding a small child.

Then Our Blessed Mother stood up and spoke. Her Immaculate Heart was visible on Her chest, and radiated light towards the spring, while the Infant Jesus waded in the water. Our Lady promised to visit Judiel every First Saturday and on Her Feast Days. She asked the people to return.

As it happened Our Lady appeared nearly every Saturday as well as on Her Feast Days. The visionary wrote down on paper the messages from Our Lady as She gave them to him. The notes are reported to be hastily but carefully written out, seemingly beyond the capacity of this sixth grader. The grammar was almost perfect. On one occasion the seer even made a drawing of Our Lady as She appeared to him. He signed the sketch with his inverted signature.

Judiel reports that as each apparition day approaches he begins a period of meditation and fasting. During this time he does not speak to anyone nor does he appear in public. Between apparitions, he sees many pilgrims.

More recently some unidentified persons have been abusive to the seer. He reportedly has received death threats. Accordingly, he has remained more private and is protected by male friends; 'bodyguards', when he is in public.

Many signs and wonders occurred during Our Blessed Mother's appearances. Usually Our Lady's presence was first felt through an extraordinary fragrance of roses. Even the ground itself at the apparition site seemed fragrant. People would kiss the ground when this occurred.

Generally the most spectacular phenomena occurred on the First Saturdays and on Her Feast Days. The miracle of the 'Dancing Sun' was witnessed by many thousands of people; on more than one occasion. First the sun turned from its radiant glare (which the naked eye could not normally endure) to a softer glow covered by a disc. Then different colors would radiate from the sun, spinning these rays of predominately blue, red, green, and yellow colors onto the crowds as colored discs. These colors would remain on the objects touched (in disc form) for several seconds. Images of angels, the Holy Family, Jesus, Mary and Joseph would appear from the pulsating sun. Other people reported seeing a mysterious blue light when Our Lady appeared.

Our Lady appeared at times shedding tears, sometimes tears of blood flowed profusely from Her eyes. On Aug 1, 1992 during an apparition, an angel appeared and gave the seer Mystical Holy Communion.

It is reported that on December 13, 1992 a Host was placed on Judiel's tongue by Fr. Cortez, when it turned into what looked 'like flesh and blood' to those nearby who witnessed this event. This event occurred in the cloistered Mary Consolatrix Convent in Naguilian and was witnessed by the nuns and by Fr. Roger Cortez. On December 10th Fr. Cortez had requested to meet with Judiel, and this meeting was arranged at the convent for the 13th. Not only did the seer receive mystical Communion, witnessed by Fr. Cortez and the nuns, but the statue of Our Lady (which was carved according to the description as Our Lady appears to Judiel, and which statue Judiel had brought with him to the convent) also shed tears to the amazement of the nuns and Fr. Cortez. Fr. Cortez had interviewed the seer before these miraculous signs occurred and stated that Judiel's answers were sincere and not contrary to Church doctrine. From that time on Fr. Cortez became Judiel's spiritual director. For their part the cloistered nuns have taken on the task to document the ongoings at Agoo and also to transcribe the messages received in 1992 from the hand written notes of Judiel. The nuns witnessed the apparitions of 1992 and 1993 only.

On February 6, 1993 the statue shed tears of blood after the regular First Saturday apparition at Apparition Hill. Later that night the statue was brought to the bishop's palace in San Fernando. Bishop Lazo is reported as saying that on that very night the statue shed tears of blood while in the palace, which the bishop witnessed with his own eyes. He said that the room was filled with the fragrance of flowers and "we knelt and prayed." The bishop is further reported as saying he placed his own fingers on the blood on the face of the statue and tasted the blood. It was salty. A photograph depicts the smeared bloody face of the statue after the bishop placed his fingers on it. Unconfirmed reports are that the National Bureau of Investigation in Manila tested the blood and found it to be human blood of type 'O'. It is reported that Our Lady appeared to Judiel shedding tears of blood on October 7, 1991, on May 23, 1992, and again on June 19, 1993.

Our Blessed Mother announced Herself as the Immaculate Queen of Heaven and Earth. She usually appeared carrying a rosary and sometimes a Scapular. The Child Jesus was often present as were various saints. Angels always accompanied Our Lady. Our Lady is described as a heavenly beauty to behold. She wore a large white dress with a long mantle which touched the cloud upon which She stood. Only Her toes could be seen. At the hem of Her dress was a shinning star, with a brighter star on Her forehead. Above Her head was a beautiful crown and above the crown was a halo of 12 stars. Her eyes were bluish-brown and Her Immaculate Heart was exposed. A flash of light generally preceded the appearance of Our Lady.

Our Lady's messages are simple and repetitive with a sign of urgency. She urges us to act immediately because it may be *"too late . . . very, very short time"* and *"very, very near."*

The primary messages are for prayer, especially the holy rosary, for penance, conversion, and for consecration to the Immaculate Heart of Mary and the Sacred Heart of Jesus. She implores us to heed Her messages—and if we do, God's wrath will be appeased and peace will come instead of sufferings and tribulations.

On March 31, 1992 Our Lady gave the seer the 'Seven Keys to Heaven' and pleaded with Judiel to pray the 15 decades of the holy rosary daily even while travelling so that he will be protected from all dangers of body and soul.

Seven Keys To Heaven

(1) Attend daily Mass.
(2) Visit the Blessed Sacrament often.
(3) Wear the Brown Scapular (cloth)
(4) Pray the 15 Mysteries of the holy rosary with the Litany and the Hail Holy Queen.
(5) Do the Way of the Cross.
(6) Go to confession regularly.
(7) Make Communion of Reparation on First Fridays and First Saturdays.

Our Blessed Mother urges us to teach our children to pray the holy rosary, and to pray for all those who are suffering around the world. We are to pray "more and more," do penance and sacrifice, and we are to be humble and live in humility.

On October 31, 1992 Our Lady said in part: *"Carry your cross not out of compulsion, for through the Cross, God is being glorified in every person."* Then on February 6, 1992: *"Your measure of happiness in heaven will depend upon the degree of grace you attained on earth."*

Our Lady gave secrets to the seer, which have not been revealed. She also gave promises to the seer which were performed. The seer was shown heaven, hell and purgatory. Judiel was also given prayers by Our Lady.

Warnings of suffering and of the coming chastisement if we do not amend our lives and return to God, were also given by Our Lady. On

April 4, 1992 Our Lady said: *"1995 will be the year of sorrows. My children, babies and little children will die of an unknown disease. This is not a punishment but an act of mercy to spare them from the coming chastisement, which is too horrible."*

On September 8, 1993 Our Lady told Judiel that this was Her last public appearance to him, but *"I will appear to you in private."*

While the apparitions were ongoing, large crowds were present during each apparition. Tens of thousands of people converged on this small community causing traffic jams extending for scores of miles. Many of those present reported seeing signs and wonders such as the spinning sun, the aroma of roses, the blue light and images in the sky.

On February 11, 1993 Bishop Salvador Lazo formed a committee to study these happenings and report to him. It was also reported that another and different commission was appointed to investigate these events concerning Judiel as well as those events witnessed by Fr. Roger Cortez. Meanwhile in Manila, Rev. Socrates Villegos, spokesman for Cardinal Sin said that the Church would be cautious and that it may take years of study and examination to come to a final conclusion. No final Church action is reported.

The first healing reported by the cloistered nuns was that of a six year old boy who was born blind and had his sight restored miraculously and instantly during the February 11, 1993 apparition. The nuns at the Convent also have said that the most touching healings they observed were the many conversions taking place in the hearts of many of the devotees. It is reported that at one time a priest heard confessions continuously from early evening into the wee hours of the morning.

IX The Primary Messages - 4

(1) Pray - Our Blessed Mother begs and pleads for prayer in nearly every message given to this seer.

September 8, 1991: *"Repent, My children, repent. Pray hard. Pray! Pray the holy rosary. Pray for the conversion of sinners."*

May 13, 1992: *"Pray especially for poor sinners. Your time is running out. Repent while the wrath of God has not yet come. Pray, pray, pray."*

May 30, 1992: *"Tell the people especially those with families that the family that prays together stays together and there will be peace in their families and in the whole world. Pray, pray, pray."*

July 25, 1992: *"Pray, pray, pray with all your heart. I will help you. I will pray but everything does not depend only on Me. It depends also on your faith, faith of those who pray. Faith is impossible without prayers."*

September 19, 1992: *"I am asking you again to pray and I will repeat it every time. Pray, pray the holy rosary every day."*

November 14, 1992: *"I am your Mother. Love each other; forgive each other; Pray, pray, pray. I love you so much."*

December 26, 1992: *"Gather together and pray in unison. Storm heaven with your prayers. It will give you strength to intercede for each other and every one of you. And this will be the triumph of My Immaculate Heart."*

January 23, 1993: *"I invite you to pray within your heart. I would like you to be closer to God through prayer and faith and to completely surrender to God. Only in that way will I be able to help you and to protect you from every attack of evil. Love one another. Forgive each other."*

September 8, 1993: *". . . Come to Me to pray with Me with rock solid faith and pray from the depth of your hearts."*

(2) **Pray the Rosary** - Our Lady's most urgent plea in nearly every message was that we pray the 15 decades of the holy rosary every day.

April 7, 1989: *"Pray the fifteen mysteries of the holy rosary every day to obtain peace for the world and the conversion of sinners."*

July 4, 1992: *". . . Pray the holy rosary; Satan will be defeated because he hates hearing the name of My Son and My Name. The 15 Mysteries of the holy rosary depicts the life, passion, and death of My Son. . . . teach your children how to pray the holy rosary; the holy rosary is a complete form of prayer . . ."*

September 19, 1992: *"I am asking you again to pray and I will repeat it every time. Please pray, pray, pray the holy rosary everyday. The devotions to My rosary is a great sign of predestination."*

October 24, 1992: *"My child, I love you all. I am begging you to pray the rosary and to wear the brown Scapular with lively faith."*

January 30, 1993: *"—You must lift up your hearts and think more of your eternal destiny rather than the pleasures in this world which are temporary. Please pray the rosary everyday."*

March 6, 1993: *"My children, I need your help. Please pray the rosary every day and repent of your sins . . ."*

September 8, 1993: *"My children, listen, you see how hard Satan is working to destroy unity in the whole world especially between the priesthood and the flock, and in families between man and children. Satan works to take away peace and unity, to stir up trouble all over the universe. We have to launch a counterattack. This will be only through the holy rosary. So pray the whole mysteries of the rosary daily because this is the most evangelical prayer . . ."*

(3) **Fast and Penance** - May 16, 1992: *"I will appear to you every Saturday. Pray more, do penance and sacrifice."*

August 22, 1992: *"Pray hard My children, and do penance. At the end, My Immaculate Heart will triumph."*

August 29, 1992: *"As much as possible do fasting and sacrifice, especially on Wednesdays and Fridays."*

January 9, 1993: *"Pray and fast and repent for your sins and do penance."*

(4) Repentance and Conversion - October 7, 1991: On this Feast of the Holy Rosary, Our Lady said: *"I am waiting My children. Repent before the punishment comes."* Then Our Lady cried tears of blood!

September 5, 1992: *"Confess your sins My children . . . return to My Son completely."*

December 8, 1992: *"I am calling you to reconciliation with God. I want to be with you to convert and reconcile with everyone."*

February 6, 1993: *"The only word I wish to say is conversion for the whole world. I ask only for conversion of heart. Be ready for everything and be converted."*

February 11, 1993: *"Hasten your conversion. Do not wait for the sign that will be given to unbelievers. If you believe, this is the opportunity to be converted."*

March 25, 1993: *"The only word I wish to say is: conversion to God. (Again) . . . the only word I wish to say is: conversion of the people."*

X Signs Preceding the Apparitions

A bright light accompanied by angels in song preceded the appearance of Our Lady in some of the reported apparitions.

XI Other Visions During Apparitions

(1) The Infant Jesus was present during several apparitions.
(2) Fr. Patrick Peyton appeared with Our Blessed Mother on June 27, 1992, the year after his own death.
(3) Seven angels (named) appeared with Our Lady on March 31, 1989.
(4) The Immaculate Heart of Mary was shown several times.
(5) The seer was shown visions of heaven, hell, and purgatory.
(6) Our Lady appeared weeping tears of blood.

XII Prayers Taught to the Seer(s)

(1) On August 7, 1993 Our Lady said in part: " . . . *God bless you always My children. Please sing this to Me. Dona nobis pacem Mater."*
(2) On September 8, 1990 Our Lady gave Judiel the following prayers:
   Prayer: O Holy Mother of God, we humbly approach Your Immaculate Heart under Your title as Immaculate Queen of Heaven and Earth to pray and intercede for the forgiveness of all our sins. Help us feel sorry for having offended Our Lord and ask pardon through the merits of His Sacred Wounds. We beg You also to pray for our material and spiritual needs.
   Prayer: O Holy Virgin Mother, the evil forces of the prince of darkness are all around seeking to ruin our souls through their malice

and wickedness. We entreat You, therefore, with Your spouse, St. Joseph, to send all Your holy saints and angels to protect us, to keep us away from all dangers and accidents, from our enemies, visible and invisible and from all temptations of sins. Help us to become worthy to love, serve, obey, and glorify the Name of Jesus forever and ever. Amen.

Pray: Our Father, Hail Mary, and Glory Be.

Memorare To Jesus, Mary, And Joseph

Prayer: Remember, Oh Merciful Jesus, Immaculate Virgin Mary and glorious St. Joseph, that no one has ever had recourse to Your protection or implored Your assistance without obtaining relief. Animated with this childlike confidence but weighed down by my sins, I prostrate myself before You. Oh reject not my petitions but graciously hear and grant them. Amen.

Chaplet

On the big rosary beads:

Prayer: Immaculate Queen of Heaven and Earth, Fountain of all Graces, Comforter of the Afflicted and Refuge of Sinners, You are the only hope and salvation in the hour of darkness when the wrath of God is unleashed to cleanse this sinful world.

On the small beads:

Leader: Through Your love and maternal protection of the whole world.

Response: Pray for us sinners especially in the hour of our needs.

Ejaculation

Alleluia, Alleluia, Ave Maria, gratia plena, Dominus tecum, benedicta tu in mulieribus, Alleluia. (Say it three times after the end of the rosary.)

After the Ejaculation, say at least fifteen decades of the rosary everyday. After the fifteen decades of the rosary, say the Litany of the Blessed Virgin Mary and the Hail Holy Queen.

Thanksgiving Prayer

Prayer: O Lord Jesus, thank you again for this wonderful day and this holy night. Thank you for all the graces and blessings we have been receiving and for Your guiding light. I offer You, through the Immaculate Heart of Mary and St. Joseph all our worldly possessions, our homes, our families, our thoughts, words, actions and our very own free will and our whole body and soul that You may dispose of them according to Thy Will. Amen.

(3) September 8, 1992 Our Lady of Agoo through an angel gave this message to the seer in La Union: **"Pray the Creed fervently."**

Profession of Faith to Mary

1. I believe in the Mother of Christ, in Her Immaculate Conception, Perpetual Virginity, Divine Maternity, Glorious Assumption and Universal Mediation.
2. That since the fall of man, Mary is predestined to be the Mother of God, the Mother of the Church and of mankind.
3. That Mary is the Spouse of the Holy Spirit and the Mediatrix of all God's Gifts, Peace and Graces.
4. I believe that Mary was conceived without Original Sin and is honored as Queen of Angels and Saints; all generations shall call Her Blessed.
5. That Mary will save mankind and the world through the Brown Scapular and the Holy Rosary.
6. I also believe that Mary was commissioned by Christ to be the only hope and salvation when the wrath of God is unleashed to cleanse this sinful world; the key, the gate and stairway to the Kingdom of God.
7. That Mary is predestined to crush the head of the serpent with Her heel, a victory over all sins and evil.
8. I believe that Mary is the Woman in the Scriptures, clothed with the sun, the moon under Her feet and on Her Head a crown of twelve stars, and is to reign as the Immaculate Queen of Heaven and Earth for ever and ever. Amen.

Consecration

Prayer: Oh, Holy Mother of God, we humbly approach Your Immaculate Heart under Your title as Immaculate Queen of Heaven and Earth to pray and intercede for the forgiveness of all our sins. Help us feel sorry for having offended Our Lord and ask pardon through the merits of His Sacred Wounds. We beg You also to pray for our material and spiritual needs.

Prayer: Oh, Holy Virgin Mother, the evil forces of the Prince of Darkness are all around seeking to ruin our souls through their malice and wickedness. We entreat You, therefore, with Your Spouse, St. Joseph, to send all Your holy saints and angels to protect us, to keep us away from all dangers and accidents, from our enemies, visible and invisible, and from all temptations of sins. Help us also to become worthy to love, serve, obey and glorify the name of Jesus, forever and ever, Amen.

Pray: Our Father, Hail Mary and Glory be.

(4) On March 31, 1992, Our Lady gave Judiel the following:

Seven Keys To Heaven
1. Attend daily Mass.
2. Visit the Blessed Sacrament often.
3. Wear the Brown Scapular. (cloth)
4. Pray the 15 Mysteries of the holy rosary with the Litany and the Hail Holy Queen.
5. Do the Way of the Cross.
6. Go to confession regularly.
7. Make Communion of Reparation on First Fridays and First Saturdays.

"One day through the Rosary and the Scapular, I will save the World."

XIII Special Devotion Given to the Seer(s)

The Seven Keys to Heaven may be considered a special devotion.

XIV Requests Made by Our Lady

(1) That we teach our children to pray the holy rosary.
(2) On August 29, 1992 Our Lady requested a procession and vigil be held at the apparition site.
(3) On February 11, 1993 Our Lady said: *"My child, please tell the priests to do the Seven Keys to Heaven."*

XV Specific Bible References - Not Reported

XVI Secrets Given to the Seer(s)

On June 19, 1992 a secret was given to Judiel which was not to be revealed.

XVII Miracles Promised by Our Lady - NR

XVIII Miracles Performed

(1) On August 1, 1992 an angel appeared during an apparition of Our Blessed Mother and gave Holy Communion to Judiel from a Host and Chalice suspended in midair. (We are reminded of Fatima.)
(2) The statue of Our Lady was reported to have shed human tears and

also tears of blood on more than one occasion.
(3) On December 13, 1992 the 'Eucharistic Miracle' occurred witnessed by Fr. Cortez and the nuns at the convent.

XIX Miracles Promised not yet Performed - NR

XX Signs Promised

(1) On September 5, 1992 Our Lady said: *"On September 8th I will give a great sign . . ."*
(2) On January 23, 1993 Our Lady said: *"On February 6th I will give great and special signs to the people coming here to Agoo."*

XXI Signs Given

(1) During the apparition of October 7, 1991 Our Lady cried tears of blood, then again on June 19, 1993 and May 23, 1992.
(2) A sweet fragrance usually was present before and during Our Lady's apparitions.
(3) On August 1, 1992 during an apparition, an angel appeared in white sparkling clothes floating in the air. The Sacred Host and Chalice appeared in midair and the angel then gave Judiel the Mystical Holy Communion.
(4) The 'Miracle of the Spinning Sun' occurred several times witnessed by many people.
(5) The statue of Our Lady shed tears on December 13, 1992 at the convent witnessed by the nuns and by Fr. Cortez. This phenomenon reoccurred.
(6) Also on December 13, 1992 the 'Miracle of the Eucharist' occurred when the Host inside Judiel's mouth swelled and became flesh and blood. This was also witnessed by the nuns at the convent and by Fr. Cortez.

Fr. Cortez presided at a Mass on this date at the convent after the nuns discovered the statue weeping tears. After Judiel received Communion he went to his pew when he felt liquid drip from his mouth. Also, the Host had swelled. The person next to Judiel alerted Fr. Cortez who asked Judiel to "spit out" the Host. The Communion Host had been transformed into pulsating flesh and blood. Fr. Cortez realized this was a 'Eucharistic Miracle'. Fr. Cortez wanted to have the Host preserved but Our Lady told Judiel he must swallow it. As a concession however the nuns were permitted to impress the bloody Host onto their white handkerchiefs. Each nun did receive an imprint on their handkerchiefs. The last nun to do so saw Judiel put the Host back into his mouth. It slowly turned back into a white Host, whereupon this nun witnessed Judiel swallow it. Fr. Cortez and the nuns then asked Judiel to open his month. There was no trace of blood or flesh or Host.

The events of December 13, 1992 apparently made believers out of Fr. Cortez and the nuns. It was then that Fr. Cortez volunteered to be Judiel's spiritual advisor and the nuns took on the job of transcribing the handwritten messages and distributing the messages for the year 1992.

XXII Predictions/Promises

(1) On May 16, 1992 Our Lady said: *"I will appear to you every Saturday."* She kept Her promise.

(2) On September 5, 1992 Our Lady said: *"On September 8, I will give a great sign."* Many people witnessed the 'Miracle of the Sun'.

(3) Then on December 8, 1992 Our Lady said: *"The Triumph of My Immaculate Heart will coincide with the Second Coming of Jesus in Glory to make all things new."*

(4) On January 2, 1993 Our Lady said: *"I promise to act, build their lives step by step, to those who consecrate themselves to My Immaculate Heart."*

(5) On January 23, 1993 Our Lady said: *"On February 6th I will give great and special signs to the people coming here to Agoo."* On February 6th Our Lady cried tears of blood. Also on this day the statue of Our Lady wept tears of blood which was witnessed by Bishop Lazo. The 'Miracle of the Sun' was also witnessed that day by a great number of pilgrims.

(6) On March 6, 1993 Our Lady said: *"September 8, 1993 will be the last apparition."* The public apparitions to Judiel have ended as of September 8, 1993.

(7) On February 6, 1993 after the apparition, Bishop Salvador Lazo brought the statue of Our Lady back to the bishop's palace. It was on this very night that Bishop Lazo witnessed the statue cry tears of blood. The bishop smeared his fingers on the blood and tasted it; salty. Reportedly the blood was tested and declared to be human blood of type 'O'.

(8) Many people witnessed blue lights streak across the sky during the apparitions.

XXIII Prophecies/Warnings of Chastisement

(1) April 4, 1992: *"1995 will be the year of sorrows. My children, babies and little children will die of an unknown disease. This is not a punishment but an act of mercy to spare them from the coming chastisement which is too horrible."*

(2) **May 23, 1992:** *"If you do not help Me, the wrath of God shall fall upon mankind. I can hardly hold the hand of My Son. If you do not repent, it will happen very soon. It may happen within two years."*

(3) **June 11, 1992:** *"If the world does not change, I will send the warning. The earth will shake, the sun will spin with a big explosion and the moon will appear in the morning; the sun at night. The miraculous phenomenon will be visible all over the earth and all will happen within half an hour. Big storms, floods, volcanic eruptions, earthquakes and changing weather conditions are already on the way."*

(4) **November 14, 1992:** *". . . Forgive each other and make peace. It is not enough to ask for peace but make peace. Do not turn peace to violence. Ask for faith that you may be patient. If you do not change your ways, you will provoke the Third World War."*

(5) **January 9, 1993:** *"The world must change. A great catastrophe will happen to the world. Tell the people to pray and be converted."*

(6) **February 6, 1993:** *". . . Nations formerly appealed to God in their hour of need, but such is not the case today. How can nations expect God's help and blessing upon their undertakings if they ignore Him? And so My children, without the grace and friendship of God among nations Satan will reign. There will be terrible wars among nations and peace will be obscured. You must seek peace. I am Your loving Mother, Queen of Peace and I will grant peace to each and everyone of you and to the whole world."*

XXIV Method of Appearance

The seer would usually see a flash of bright light and then Our Blessed Mother would appear.

XXV Method of Departure - Not Reported

XXVI Confrontation w/Civil Authorities

Judiel has been harassed by aggressive elements of some different religious groups, he even received threats on his life.

XXVII Confrontation w/Church Authorities

(1) Bishop Lazo witnessed the statue of Our Lady shed tears of blood at his own palace on February 6, 1993.

(2) Fr. Cortez witnessed the statue shed tears and also witnessed the 'Miracle of the Eucharist' on December 13, 1992 at the convent. The nuns witnessed the same. Fr. Cortez is now Judiel's spiritual director and the nuns transcribe the messages which Judiel received in 1992.

(3) Bishop Lazo appointed a committee to investigate these matters on February 11, 1993.
(4) Another commission was formed by the Catholic Bishop's Conference of the Philippines and is to be headed by Bishop Manuel Sobrevinas.
(5) The Church officials in Agoo, as well as Metro Manila, have noted apparent increase in devotions and conversions. On March 6, 1993 more than 100 priests travelled to Agoo to assist the local priest in hearing confessions of the pilgrims; 24 hour confession services were reportedly set up.
(6) Bishop Lazo cautions that regardless of the apparent good fruits, nonetheless the cause is still uncertain and is now under investigation.

XXVIII Request Chapel/Shrine Built

On September 8, 1991 Our Blessed Mother requested that a chapel be built at the apparition site; and that the Blessed Sacrament be exposed for adoration by the faithful.

XXIX Free Will/Choice

Our Lady repeatedly urges us to choose to return to God and abandon sin.

XXX Seer(s)' Suffering/Sacrifice

(1) On September 1, 1993 Our Lady told Judiel: *"You are My chosen one to suffer martyrdom of the heart for the sins of others."*
(2) Judiel suffered when he was harassed and when he received threats on his life.

XXXI Healings Reported

(1) The first reported healing was that of a six-year-old boy who had been born blind and received his eyesight during the apparition of February 11, 1993.
(2) Many conversions of the heart are reported. A remarkable increase of confessions, rosaries, vigils, and attendance at Mass is reported.

XXXII Action Taken by the Church

(1) Bishop Lazo heads one commission established February 11, 1993.
(2) Another commission formed by the Catholic Bishops' Conference of the Philippines, and headed by Bishop Sobrevinas is also investigating these events.

(3) Cardinal Sin's spokesman cautions patience, as does Bishop Lazo.
(4) No final Church action is reported.

XXXIII Bibliography

The Blessed Mother's Messages at Agoo,
La Union, the Philippines
By: Prepared by the Nuns at Mary Consolatrix Convent
Published by: Mary Consolatrix Convent

The Messages of the Blessed Virgin Mary,
the Mother of God, The Immaculate
Queen of Heaven and Earth 1994
By: Francis L. Panes, MD
Published by: Francis L. Panes, MD

Daily Inquirer, Philippines (Various articles)

Malaya, Philippines (Various articles)

Chapter 57

SCOTTSDALE, ARIZONA, USA
(1989 TO PRESENT)

I Place - Scottsdale, Arizona, USA
(Maria Goretti Church)

II Dates of First and Last Apparition

First: December 19, 1989
Last: February 11, 1993 (last reported)
Note: The apparitions are reportedly ongoing.

III Seer(s) - 4

Name: Gianna Talone (Sullivan)
Birth: March 12, 1957
Age at first apparition: 32
Status: Married/Living

Name: Annie Ross (Fitch)
Birth: May 18, 1963
Age at first apparition: 26
Status: Living

Name: Wendy Nelson
Birth: August 15, 1969
Age at first apparition: 20
Status: Living

Name: Mary Cook
Birth: December 28, 1963
Age at first apparition: 25
Status: Living

IV Total Number of Apparitions - 137

(1) Gianna Talone (Sullivan): 131
(2) Annie Ross (Fitch): 3   Although only two apparitions are reported, it is also reported that Annie saw Our Lady throughout 1990 and until September 1991.
(3) Wendy Nelson: 1
(4) Mary Cook: 2

V Dates and Locality of Each Apparition

Gianna Talone (Sullivan):
1989: December 19, 25, 28.
1990: January 11, 18, 25; February 1, 8, 15, 22; March 1, 4, 8, 22, 29; April 19, 26; May 3, 10, 17, 23, 31; June 7, 21, 28; July 5, 12, 19, 26; August 2, 8, 16, 23, 30; September 6, 20, 27; October 4, 18, 25; November 7, 14, 20; December 6, 13, 20.
1991: January 3, 10, 17, 24, 31; February 14, 21, 28; March 14, 21; April 4, 11, 18, 25; May 9, 16, 23; June 6, 20, 27, 28; July 4, 25; August 1, 8, 15, 29; September 5, 12, 19; October 3, 17, 31; November 7, 14, 21; December 5, 12, 19.
1992: January 9, 16, 23, 30; February 6, 13, 20, 27; March 5, 12, 19, 26; April 2, 9, 23, 30; May 7, 21, 28; June 4, 11, 18; August 6, 13, 27; September 3, 10, 17, 24; October 1, 8, 15, 22, 29; November 5, 12, 19; December 3, 10, 17.
1993: January 7, 14, 21, 28; February 4, 11.

Reportedly Gianna received locutions and messages from Our Lady before this seer had the first apparition of Our Lady. Reportedly Gianna receives daily apparitions of Our Lady at her own home as well as at the Thursday Night Prayer meeting.

Annie Ross (Fitch):
1989: December and October, Maria Goretti Church.
1990: Unknown date - Maria Goretti Church.

Wendy Nelson:
1990 Unknown date - Maria Goretti Church.

Mary Cook:
1990: Two apparitions in 1990 at Maria Goretti Church.

VI Description of Our Lady

First the statue glows, becomes animated, then Our Lady comes out of the statue. Our Lady does not appear or look like the statue; rather She appears dressed in dazzling white.

Our Lady is young (18-25), slender with long, thin fingers, dark hair, gray-blue eyes, fair complexion, rosy cheeks and a small chin. She wears a white dress and a light veil. The dress has no belt or ornament except for gold embroidery at the collar. The seers agree that Our Lady is so beautiful that all descriptions are inadequate.

VII Title(s) of Our Lady - 1

On July 25, 1991 Our Lady announced: *"I am your Mother of Joy."* This title was stated earlier as well.

VIII Brief Factual Review

Scottsdale, Arizona is located some 20 miles east of Phoenix in south central Arizona. The population of Scottsdale is some 100,000 people. It is an upscale community where many retired people reside and is located near several college communities. Scottsdale is part of the two million population of greater Phoenix. Nearly half the population of Arizona lives in this region known as the Valley of the Sun, a flat desert circled by pinkish mountains. A stark and beautiful landscape. Much of the land in Arizona, and especially in this region, belongs to the Pima Maricopa Indians and to the Apache Indians. The Salt River Indian Reservation contains a large acreage just east of Scottsdale; very near the Maria Goretti Church. The parish church, about 20 years old, has a unique design. Some 2600 families belong to the parish, including many youth who attend colleges in the area.

The pastor of Maria Goretti Church is Fr. Jack Spaulding. He had previously been Chancellor of the Diocese, then later He became Vicar. In his earlier years in the priesthood he learned to communicate with the deaf through sign language. He is even now able to celebrate Holy Mass in sign language using his arms and hands in addition to his voice. Fr. Jack was destined to play an important part in these events, even from their very beginnings.

Fr. Jack first went to Medjugorje on the 6th anniversary of Our Lady's appearance in Medjugorje, June 25, 1987, to film a television show. In October of that same year he returned to Medjugorje with a group of parishioners. Mary Cook (destined to be one of the future seers) had a conversion experience during this trip to Medjugorje.

Fr. Jack returned to Medjugorje three times during 1988: first in March, again in June and finally for the closing of the Marian Year in August. Another one of the future seers (Gianna Talone) accompanied Fr. Jack on the June 1988 pilgrimage and reportedly was told by Wayne Weible while in Medjugorje that: "You will play a very significant role in Our Blessed Mother's plan."

Meanwhile in Scottsdale several of the young people who were destined to receive messages (and apparitions) from Our Lady confided to Fr. Jack that they were "hearing voices" and having other unusual experiences. From these visits emerged what was to be known as 'The Group of Six', consisting of Gianna Talone, Mary Cook, Steve Nelson, Wendy Nelson, Susan Evans, and Jimmy Kupanoff. This group was later increased to nine when Stefanie Staab, James Pauley, and Annie Ross were added. Reportedly Gianna previously had a vision identifying this group.

The prayer groups, and most especially Our Lady's Thursday Night Prayer Group, played—and continue to play—an important role in these events. This Thursday Night Group was started on December 3, 1987. On June 6, 1988 Gianna was the first prayer group member to receive a message from Our Lady during a Thursday Night Prayer Meeting. Gianna's first public message from Our Lady occurred later on July 14, 1988.

The first reported apparition of Our Lady occurred in the Maria Goretti Church during the Thursday Night Prayer Meeting of December 19, 1989. Annie Ross first saw Our Lady on December 28, 1989. The seers state that the statue of Our Lady first glows, then Our Lady appears. Seemingly She steps out of the statue. However, She is not attired like the statue. They describe Our Lady as young and slender with long, thin fingers, dark hair, gray-blue eyes, fair complexion, rosy cheeks, a small chin, and about 18-25 years old. She wears a white dress and a light veil. The dress has no belt or ornament except for gold embroidery at the collar. She appears as a living person and She is so beautiful that all descriptions are inadequate.

Commencing in April 1990 two additional visionaries, namely, Wendy Nelson and Mary Cook also had apparitions of Our Lady. Wendy had only one apparition; Mary Cook had two apparitions. Annie Ross is reported to have seen Our Lady throughout 1990 and until September 1991. The apparitions and messages given through the Thursday Night Prayer Group are reportedly ongoing to date.

In addition Gianna is reported to have had several apparitions of Jesus and states that she receives 'Lessons' from Jesus. These 'Lessons' are published.

Fr. Jack reports that sometimes during his homily at Mass celebrated at the Maria Goretti Church during the Thursday night services, Our Lord will "take over" the homily and Fr. Jack will merely be the instrument used to speak the words that Jesus places on Fr. Jack's lips. It is also reported that sometimes Our Lady will "take over" the homily instead of

Jesus. These messages, through February 11, 1993 (both from Our Lord and Our Lady) are reported in published form.

The apparitions given to the four visionaries reportedly take place inside the Maria Goretti Church during the Thursday Night Prayer Meeting. The attendance at these Thursday night services have increased to some 500 people. The service consists of a 15 decade rosary, Holy Mass, followed by healing prayers. Witnesses report that Gianna and Annie both go into ecstasy and respond at the same instant in the same manner although they may not see each other. It is during these ecstasies that Gianna usually receives messages. The other seers have also received some messages. While the messages from Our Lord are in 'Lesson' form, those from Our Lady are more maternal and stimulate prayer, trust, confidence, and love for one another.

The messages themselves are collected, typed and readied for publication by a friend of Fr. Jack and the visionaries, namely, Carole Ameche. Carole also is a confidant to the seers and helps them in other ways.

Both Our Lord and Our Lady have given secrets to Gianna which have not been revealed. Also Our Lady requested the seers to "give 3 years to Our Lady." This each of them has done. It is reported that Our Lady taught prayers to the seers as part of the messages. Each seer has been assigned a different symbol representing a virtue. Gianna, and to a lesser degree some of the other seers, reportedly suffer physical pain during Lent. This pain was especially severe for a period of 40 days during Lent of 1989.

Many conversions and inner healings have been reported. In addition several physical healings are reported in published form as having occurred in Scottsdale. Some happened during the Thursday Night Prayer Meetings during 'Hands On' prayers.

In 1989 Bishop Thomas O'Brien, the bishop of Phoenix, formed a commission to investigate these events. Later in October of that year the commission returned its findings to the bishop. The commission concluded that the messages are "explainable within the range of ordinary human experience" and that "we don't think there are any hoaxes or that there was any attempt to deceive anybody."

Bishop O'Brien followed the findings of October, 1989 by announcing that the prayer meetings and public devotions at Maria Goretti Church may continue, however, there is to be no claim of miraculous intervention due to the fact that the findings are absent of any external evidence that the messages come directly from Our Lord or from Our Lady.

Since these findings were given, it is reported that apparitions have continued to take place regularly at the Thursday Night Prayer Meetings. Annie and Gianna reportedly experience some kind of ecstacy during these alleged apparitions.

A renowned priest-author seems to be favorably impressed with these events. Both Fr. Faricy and Fr. Laurentin have interviewed the seers and have also interviewed Fr. Jack Spaulding. No final action by the Church has been given. Meanwhile, the alleged apparitions and messages continue and are distributed in published form. Many good fruits seem to be evident. We must pray, discern and await further action by the Church.

Now let's look closer at the individual seers.

(1) Gianna Talone (Sullivan) - Gianna was born on March 12, 1957. She is a pharmacist by profession. The symbol given to her is divine love and mercy.

Reportedly Our Lady first spoke to Gianna on June 4, 1988 in Medjugorje. Thereafter, she received messages (locutions) from Our Lady starting July 14, 1988 and eventually Our Lady began to appear to her on December 19, 1989 during the Thursday Night Prayer Meetings in the Maria Goretti Church. Gianna continues to receive messages from Our Lady on Thursday nights.

Additionally Gianna claims that she also receives apparitions of Jesus; and Jesus gives her messages which are recorded as 'Lessons'.

Both Gianna and Annie claim they have embraced Our Lady, that Our Lady hugged and kissed them, and that they were also allowed to kiss Our Lady during the apparitions.

Gianna has received 8 secrets from both Our Lady and Jesus. This seer also states that St. Joseph spoke to her and that now she prays to St. Joseph everyday. During Lent in 1989 Gianna suffered for 40 days. She also suffered at other times during Lenten seasons. It is reported that the devil attacks her at night; sometimes she awakens with bruises on her body.

This seer was married to Michael Bianchi which marriage was annulled by the Church. Gianna now attends daily Mass, spends much time in prayer, and receives spiritual direction from Fr. Ernest Larkin, a Carmelite theologian. Gianna continues to see Our Lady daily (except on Fridays as a penance), and also receives messages frequently from Our Lord.

It is reported that Gianna recently remarried and now lives in Emmittsburg, Maryland with her husband, Dr. Sullivan. It is reported that Gianna continues to receive apparitions and messages.

(2) Annie Ross (Fitch) - Annie was born May 18, 1963. Her symbol is humility.

Her first experience happened on March 31, 1989 while she was alone at home, when a female voice spoke to her: *"My child I want you to write."* She heard this voice again while she was in the Maria Goretti Church when the statue of Our Lady of the Americas was being dedicated. Annie concluded the voice to be that of Our Lady. These communications continued and Annie did start to write. As she finished writing she had a feeling of great peace. She had been filled with much anger and hate and now found herself wanting to pray for the people who had hurt her.

She had her first apparition of Our Lady on December 28, 1989 while praying the rosary during the Thursday Night Service at Maria Goretti Church. On this date Our Lady also appeared to Gianna. Our Lady spoke to each seer separately.

Annie relates that during the rosary a brilliant light surrounded the statue of Our Lady. Then Our Lady seemed to step out of the statue. Our Lady does not look like the statue, but "She is so beautiful."

In October 1990 Our Lady told Annie that She would no longer appear to the seer regularly, only on the seer's birthdays and in times of difficulty.

Annie has a special task to pray for priests and religious. She, too, now attends daily Mass and is steeped in prayer.

(3) Wendy Nelson - Wendy was born August 15, 1969. Her brother Steve was also a member of the original group of six. Her symbol is strength.

This seer's experience began in 1987 when she heard a voice while at her own home in which the voice said: *"Will you give Me everything?"* She believed this to be the voice of Jesus. She went to Fr. Jack Spaulding and told him of the voice. Meanwhile, others also had reported to Fr. Jack. In August 1988 Fr. Jack had a meeting with 'the original six'.

Wendy spent about 1½ years during 1987/88 living at the Mission of Charity Congregation in Phoenix as a lay person helping the nuns. This is one of Mother Theresa of Calcutta's congregations.

This seer claims to have seen Our Lady on only one occasion during the Thursday Night rosary at Maria Goretti Church in 1990. Wendy says Our Lady is beautiful. She describes Our Lady as young, about 20, dressed in blue with blue eyes and brown hair visible under Her veil. First Wendy saw a very bright light surround the statue of Our Lady, then Our Lady came out of the statue. Our Lady did not speak to Wendy.

Wendy now attends daily Mass, spends time each day before the Real Presence, prays the rosary and attends the Thursday Night Prayer Service.

(4) Mary Cook - Mary Cook was born on December 28, 1963. Her symbol is hope. In April 1988 Mary made a pilgrimage to Medjugorje. After confession there, she realized that she had to change her life. When she returned she quit her job, moved back home to Wisconsin and began to read the Medjugorje messages. It was soon after this that Mary heard a voice *"Would you leave your family for Me?"* And later: *"Write to Fr. Jack."* Thereupon she returned to Scottsdale and was one of the 'Group of Six' who meet together with Fr. Jack in August 1988.

She states that since then, Jesus speaks to her nearly every day. These happenings have caused distrust and even division within her own family.

This seer states that she saw Our Lady twice during 1990 at the Thursday Night Services at Maria Goretti Church. She is also overwhelmed by the beauty of Our Lady.

She now teaches preschool, attends daily Mass, adores frequently before the Blessed Sacrament, and she is a Eucharistic Minister in the parish, like most of the others in the group.

IX The Primary Messages - 4

It is remembered that Jesus reportedly gave messages (and continues to do so) to Gianna, which messages are published in four volumes under the title 'I Am Your Jesus of Mercy' and described as 'Lessons From Jesus'. These 'Lessons From Jesus' are not covered in this work.

(1) Prayer - As Our Blessed Mother so frequently has done in other apparitions around the world and throughout the years, She likewise urges and exhorts us to pray; in nearly every reported message from Scottsdale.

July 14, 1988: (the first recorded message) Our Lady says: "... *Open your hearts to Jesus. He wants to fill you with His grace. Pray, pray, pray!*"

September 17, 1988: "*Please pray for unbelievers; the people who cannot be happy or peaceful because they will not surrender themselves to Jesus.*"

May 11, 1989: "*Pray, pray My children, for His Spirit to guide you. Center on My Jesus and you will find His truth and His peace.*"

August 31, 1989: "*I invite you to more prayer. Honor My Son with your prayer. Pray for peace. Pray that your heart may continue to be converted.*"

December 24, 1989: "*Prayer is the key to all success. The success of My plan relies on your prayers and devotions to My Son. Continue to pray and live in His faith. You gain His power through prayer.*"

February 22, 1990 : "*Pray the rosary and reform your lives.*"

March 29, 1990: "*Continually pray and pray, and believe in My Son's mission.*"

May 10, 1990: "*Pray, pray, pray. Prayer is the only way to peace in the world.*"

September 6, 1990: "*Please pray for peace. Pray! Pray! Pray! Focus all your attention on My Son ...*"

February 28, 1991: "*Satan is the enemy who seeks to destroy all goodness and that of nature. He wishes to cause harm to you. Prayer is your protection, and God is your peace. Do not give up hope. Pray as little ones, and know your prayers are heard.*"

April 11, 1991: "*Pray, pray, pray. Never cease praying. Please pray for My beloved priests and remain obedient to the Church.*"

November 21, 1991: "*Please, please, pray for peace of mankind. Your humanity is now in danger.*"

February 13, 1992: "*Please pray for My priests. Pray, pray, pray. Never cease praying.*"

April 30, 1992: *"Pray for your enemies, and bless those who persecute you . . . So send a loving prayer to your enemies . . ."*

May 28, 1992: *"Pray, My little ones, pray! The evil one is trying to cause destruction. Only prayer and love are the swords to freedom and justice in God."*

August 6, 1992: *"Pray! Pray! Pray! I need your prayers in the critical time of My plan. Please continue to open your hearts to My Son."*

January 28, 1993: *"Pray for peace in your hearts. Pray to be able to accept change in your life. I ask you to pray for acceptance of the will of God in your life."*

(2) Love One Another - August 25, 1988: *"You will experience happiness by loving one another . . . You will experience happiness by loving one another, because Jesus lives in everyone and by loving one another, you love Jesus and His treasures will be given to you."*

September 7, 1989: *"I ask you to fight Satan by loving and accepting one another. Be strong and accept one another. Much glory will be given to you who persevere."*

December 28, 1989: *"Love one another always. Love all of different faiths. Never deny anyone your love, for all belong to the Father. Never condemn! Always, always love. Be patient and peaceful children."*

May 3, 1990: *"Love and accept one another for who they are. Do not reject one another. Look beyond personality and see the beauty of creation from My Son."*

July 25, 1991: *"You must be like children in your love for one another. There is far too much hatred among men. I ask you to love one another unconditionally . . ."*

January 23, 1992: *". . .Begin first to love your family. Be love to one another, then you can love your fellow brethren. Beware, Satan is trying to cause division and disrupt unity not only in the family, but in the world. Form together in love as a strong unit and you will have the shield to protect you against his attempts."*

November 19, 1992: *"You can heal one another by reaching out in love. Reach out in love to the anger and hurts of your brothers and sisters. Then you will have peace in your world."*

(3) Conversion - July 30, 1988: *"My children you know that all you need do is walk in God's way and heed His Commandments and you will prosper, but you cannot and you wonder why. It is because you will not abandon yourself to Jesus. You want to control. If you allow Jesus to be the center of your lives and accept what He brings, He will bless you and all your work, and you will prosper."*

September 29, 1988: *"True happiness comes from surrendering yourself to Jesus, by opening your hearts to His words. If you will allow Jesus to be at the center of your life and dwell on Him all your problems will be minor. Dwell on Jesus, not your problems."*

November 10, 1988: *"Be serious about your conversion, not gloomy, but serious."*

June 15, 1989: *". . . Make the commitment daily to be open hearted to My Son. He will fill you with His love."*

February 8, 1990: *"Open your hearts daily. Continually love and accept My Son's peace by accepting His will for you."*

August 2, 1990: *"God is good and gives all good things to you. Live daily for Him. Give to Him all of your heart."*

August 22, 1991: *"Please be pure, have faith and trust in My Son. Fidelity to God will keep your hearts pure, and simpleness is the way."*

February 6, 1992: *"Do not be preoccupied with worry. Trust in My Son. Surrender unto Him all your worries, concerns and fears and be at peace."*

October 8, 1992: *". . . There needs to be great conversion and change of hearts. Unity and harmony, I need you—Pray, pray, pray. Take heed to change your hearts and return back to God."*

(4) Penance and Fasting - June 22, 1989: *"I ask you to begin fasting for My Jesus. There are many ways to fast. Go slowly and do not attempt to fast on bread and water if you have not fasted before."*

March 1, 1990: *"Always do penance with joy. Offer everything to God. I ask of you penances, prayers, fasting and self denial . . ."*

February 4, 1993: *"Use the Sacrament of Reconciliation, fast and give My Son what He has given you. He loves you."*

X Signs Preceding the Apparitions

A radiant light would surround the statue of Our Lady before the apparition.

XI Other Visions During Apparitions

(1) Jesus appeared to Gianna.
(2) Gianna also claims to have seen His exposed Sacred Heart.

XII Prayers Taught to the Seer(s)

Several prayers are contained in Volume III of 'I am Your Jesus of Mercy', preceded by the statement: 'These prayers are for all and must not be restricted by a copyright'.

Prayers From Our Lady

Prayer: Jesus, I adore you.
In You I hope.
In You I trust.
In You I have faith.
For it is in You alone, all things are possible.
You are our Living God. Amen.

Prayer: Sacred Heart of Jesus, I consecrate to You my mind (pause and sign of cross on forehead), my words (pause and sign of cross on lips), my body (pause and sign of cross on heart), my heart (pause and sign of cross on left shoulder), my soul (pause and sign of cross on right shoulder), in order that Your will be done through me this day.

XIII Special Devotion Given to the Seer(s) - NR

XIV Requests Made by Our Lady

Our Lady requested each youth in the group to devote three years to Our Lady's plan. All accepted.

XV Specific Bible References - Not Reported

XVI Secrets Given to the Seer(s)

Gianna is reported to have received a total of eight secrets; some from Jesus and some from Mary.

XVII Miracles Promised by Our Lady - NR
XVIII Miracles Performed - Not Reported
XIX Miracles Promised not yet Performed - NR
XX Signs Promised - Not Reported

XXI Signs Given

Fr. Jack Spaulding's voice audibly changes during his homily at the Thursday night Mass on those occasions when Jesus 'takes over'.

XXII Predictions/Promises

Earlier Our Lady promised Gianna that Our Lady would appear to

Gianna (and to others). This occurred as promised when Our Lady first appeared to Gianna on December 28, 1989.

XXIII Prophecies/Warnings of Chastisement - NR

XXIV Method of Appearance

The seers see a bright light behind and around the statue, then Our Lady appears in this light.

XXV Method of Departure

At the end of the apparition Our Lady is said to disappear by rising, and a luminous cross manifests itself for a short time afterward.

XXVI Confrontation w/Civil Authorities - NR

XXVII Confrontation w/Church Authorities

(1) Fr. Jack Spaulding seemingly supports these apparitions and messages. Fr. Robert Faricy and Sister Lucy Rooney state, "We believe strongly in the authenticity of the Scottsdale apparitions and messages." However, these supportive statements are submitted to the final judgment of the Church.
(2) There are no dissenting clergy reported.
(3) Bishop O'Brien appointed a commission to investigate these matters. The judgment of the commission was that the messages were explainable within the range of ordinary human experience and that no fraud or deceit was shown on the part of the seers. The bishop held that prayer meetings and public devotion may continue at the Church; but there may not be any unequivocal claim of miraculous intervention. The seers and the parishioners reportedly have accepted this judgment.

XXVIII Request Chapel/Shrine Built - NR

XXIX Free Will/Choice

On June 15, 1989 Our Lady said: *"Remember you have the choice every day to open your hearts. . ."*

XXX Seer(s)' Suffering/Sacrifice

(1) Gianna is said to suffer during Lent. And during Lent 1989 she

suffered for a period of 40 days, as reported.
(2) Our Lady reportedly told Annie she would suffer from the unbelief of others. This has occurred to this seer as well as some of the other seers, who have been mocked for their spiritual commitments.

XXXI Healings Reported

(1) Fr. Laurentin's book 'Our Lord and Our Lady in Scottsdale', chronicles a diverse group of reported healings. These range from recovery after heart surgery, cancer cures and total remission and healing in a case involving Crohn's Disease.
(2) More impressive are the reports of conversions among the parishioners and the pilgrims who visit. The attendance at the Thursday Night Service has increased to fill the Church; some 500 people attend. Other prayer groups have formed.
(3) Also, it is reported that Gianna travels and speaks and prays over people at seminars and conferences; promoting evangelization.
(4) Finally the four volumes of the books containing the messages and "Lessors" have apparently played an important part in the conversion of some readers. This is reported in Fr. Laurentin's book, wherein several testimonials are listed.

XXXII Action Taken by the Church

Bishop O'Brien's acceptance of the report of the commission he appointed to investigate their matters produced a judgment declaring that the messages were explainable within the range of human experience and further that no fraud or deceit was present in the seers; and that the prayer meetings and devotions may continue at Maria Goretti Church. However, there may be no unequivocal claim of miraculous intervention. In short, there is no final judgment of the Church. Meanwhile, the seers and the parishioners accept the bishop's judgment.

XXXIII Bibliography

Our Lord and Our Lady in Scottsdale 1992
By: Fr. Rene Laurentin
Published By: Faith Publishing Company

Our Lady Comes to Scottsdale 1991
By: Fr. Robert Faricy, SJ &
Sr. Lucy Rooney, SND de N
Published by: The Riehle Foundation

I am You Jesus of Mercy (Vol. I) 1989
By: Not Given
Published by: The Riehle Foundation

I am You Jesus of Mercy (Vol. II) 1990
By: Not Given
Published by: The Riehle Foundation

I am You Jesus of Mercy (Vol. III) 1991
By: Not Given
Published by: The Riehle Foundation

I am You Jesus of Mercy (Vol. IV) 1990
By: Not Given
Published by: Queenship Press

Chapter 58

LITMANOVA, SLOVAKIA
(1990 - PRESENT)

I Place - Litmanova, Slovakia
(In a wooden shed on Mount Zvir)

II Dates of First and Last Apparition

First: August 5, 1990
Last: July 1994 (last reported)
Note: The apparitions are reportedly ongoing.

III Seer(s) - 2

Name: Katarina (Katika) Ceselkova
Birth: Unknown
Age at first apparition: 13
Status: Living

Name: Iveta (Ivetka) Korcakova
Birth: Unknown
Age at first apparition: 13
Status: Living

IV Total Number of Apparitions - 69

V Dates and Locality of Each Apparition

(Note: All apparitions occurred at the little wooden shed on Mount Zvir, unless otherwise stated.)

1990: August 5, end of August; September 30; October 1, 2; November 1, 4, 11, 18, 21, 25; December 2, 8, 9, 16, 23, 24, 25, 26, 30.
1991: January 1, 6, 13, 20, 27; February 2 (twice), 17, 24; March 3; April 7; May 5; June 9; July 7; August 4; September 8; October 6; November 3; December 8.
1992: January 5; February 9; March 8; April 5; May 3; June 7; August 8; September 6; October 4; November 8; December 6.
1993: January 3; February 7; March 7; April 4; May 9; June 6; July 4; August 8; September 5; October 3; November 7 (in the Bishop's chapel in Presov); December 5.
1994: January 9; February 6; March 6; April 3; May 8; June 6; July 7.

VI Description of Our Lady

(1) Usually Our Lady wore a white dress, with a light blue cloak and veil, sometimes with a blue belt, holding a rosary (sometimes blue and sometimes white) in Her hands, and without shoes on Her feet. Very often Our Blessed Mother would appear wearing a shining crown. She once appeared holding a white lily in Her hands. She often smiled at the children. The seers report that She is beautiful.

(2) On February 17, 1991 Our Lady reportedly appeared dressed in black and holding a wooden rosary of contrition in Her hands. Later on February 24, 1991 She told the children that the reason She wore black was because of war and the killings in the Persian Gulf.

VII Title(s) of Our Lady - 6

(1) On December 2, 1990 Our Lady announced: *"I am the Immaculate Purity and come from heaven."* This title was repeated by Our Lady on December 23, 1990. However, She added: *". . . but also the Queen of the Rosary"*.

(2) Then on March 3, 1991 Our Blessed Mother explained that in heaven She was a Servant, Mother and Queen; Servant of God, Mother of My Son, and Queen of All People.

VIII Brief Factual Review

Slovakia is one of the surviving two countries resulting from the breakup of Czechoslovakia. The other survivor is Czech. Slovakia borders Poland on the north and Ukraine on the east. Litmanova is a remote mountain village located in the eastern regions of Slovakia, near the Polish border.

The apparition site itself is located 700 meters up Mount Zvir and consists of an old wooden shed, which is now bedecked with garlands of flowers and icons, but which was previously used to tether the cows of the families of both of the seers. These seers, both 13 when the apparitions first started, come from large, poor families. Their names are Katarina Ceselkova and Iveta Korcakova.

On August 5, 1990 these two seers together with Mikulas Ceselka went up Mount Zvir for a day's outing. Towards evening they heard strange noises and took refuge in a little old wooden shed on the mountainside. They said a short prayer three times: "Mary, our Mother, cover us with your protective coat." As they began to talk about returning to church and religious classes, a brilliant blaze suddenly surrounded them. They were fearful, and now pledged to go to church every day for a week. Their fear subsided. Just then a ball of light (the blaze) formed in the middle of the shed, and in this light Our Lady appeared. She was wearing a white dress, blue cloak, a veil, a crown on Her head and carrying a rosary. She didn't speak to them during this apparition. However, She did follow the children part way down the mountain, even as the children ran home in fright.

Their parents did not believe the children at this point. Instead Katarina's mother prayed to Our Lady for a sign either confirming or denying the truth of the vision. The next night Our Lady appeared to Katrina's mother in a dream, during which dream Our Lady told Katarina's mother not to doubt the girl's words. Later in August the three children and their parents went together to the old wooden shed on Mount Zvir. After saying the short prayer as before, Our Lady appeared to the two girls. Mikulas could not see Our Lady.

It is reported that though both girls see Our Lady, only Iveta hears the messages, which she gives to the local pastor, who, in turn, relates the messages to the people.

Great crowds began climbing up the mountain. They recite the rosary en masse. Usually Our Lady appears during the time the rosary is prayed. A custom has developed where the people gather after church and make a procession-pilgrimage up Mount Zvir, singing hymns and then reciting the rosary. Usually a fog or a bright light will appear before the apparition. It is reported that as of the first anniversary of the apparition, August 5, 1991 over 500,000 people made the pilgrimage to Mount Zvir. On one of the anniversary dates in 1993 over 100,000 people were present for the apparition.

On March 3, 1991 Our Lady announced that She would only be

appearing on the First Sunday of each month.

Reportedly there was a spring near the place where the apparitions first occurred. Scuffles broke out as people vied to get the water for blessings and cures. It is reported that Our Lady soon told the seers that all of Mount Zvir's water had the power of healing. This released tension, as people dug for water at other places on the Mount.

Some Slovaks say that Litmanova is fast becoming a new Medjugorje in the very heart of former communist territory, Eastern Europe. Under communist rule, the people resorted to teaching their children the liturgy in their own homes. When freedom came, faith was also freed. It is reported that the faith of the people is recovering, partly due to Mary's appearances.

The Slovak Church has reacted cautiously to these events. Two of the Greek Catholic priests who have worked in the village refuse to believe in these events. The local Greek Catholic Ordinary, Bishop Jan Hirka of Presov agreed to allow a monthly Mass at the hilltop shrine. In May 1993 the bishop set up a commission of seven priests and theologians. On November 7, 1993 a date when Mary was to appear at the site, the commission appointed by the bishop, took Iveta and Katarina to the bishop's chapel in Presov, to see if Our Lady would appear. She did. Some 20,000 people had gathered outside while this was happening. The message was: *"My dear children, I love you and I am happy to be here with you. The King of Love would like for you during this time to meditate upon His great sufferances. Through them He wants to bring your souls back to life. Reflect more upon the words of your Mother."*

There seems to be some degree of turmoil and dissent concerning these alleged apparitions. In 1991 Bishop Hirka issued his pastoral letter, recalling therein the saying of St. Augustine, that the doubts of Thomas were "more helpful than the faith of all the other Apostles." The bishop went on to say that not everyone must believe in these apparitions, but those who wish to can believe them, the Church will allow all attitudes and respects the feelings and convictions of all."

The pastor of the local parish is a young Brazilian priest, Fr. Polykarp Jacos. He goes to the mountain with the visionaries each month, says Mass there, and receives the messages from the seers. He is a great supporter of these events and has launched a program for spiritual renewal in the parish, such as: Holy Mass, rosary, fasting on Wednesdays and Fridays, confessions, and meditation on the messages during the month. Fr. Jacos says: "Pray according to Mary's intentions."

These apparitions and messages have affected the people of this village profoundly. Everyone knows the children and their families. People also know about Katarina's mother's dream. The parents of both seers are now deeply religious, attending Mass and confession frequently.

The apparitions are reportedly ongoing, occurring on the First Sunday of each month. The messages themselves call for prayer, especially the rosary, for conversion, for fasting on Wednesdays and Fridays, and for penance. During many of the apparitions the seers presented petitions from various people; usually requesting healings. Our Lady usually suggested prayer and Masses for the sick person, and that some of the water from Mount Zvir be used for blessing, drinking or bathing, in order to produce the asked-for healing. On some occasions She also requested that the sick person choose one Apostle, and pray to him. As Our Blessed Mother has said at other apparition sites, so She says here: *"Some of them will be cured."*

On December 30, 1990 Our Lady requested a medal be struck in Her honor. Her initials were to be above Her shining heart together with a lily (the sign of Her purity) on one side of the medal. On the other side of the medal a depiction of Herself with Her Divine Son Jesus. These medals are to be distributed to those who venerated Jesus and Mary, and the people who wear this medal and invoke Her as 'Immaculate Purity' honoring Her purity could expect help whenever they ask.

Our Lady did also warn that: *". . . a disaster impends over Slovakia . . ."*, but if the people prayed and devoted themselves to God, the catastrophe could be averted. Our Blessed Mother taught the seers a short prayer to appeal to Her when they are tempted.

On April 3, 1994 Our Lady said in part: *"I want to teach you to live for love. I invite you to God's mercy and want to give you a bit of joy from heaven."* (So simple yet so profound!)

No final Church action has been announced.

IX The Primary Messages - 5

(1) Prayer - May 5, 1991: *"This month your prayers will particularly be heard, but the prayer must originate in a pure and sincere heart. When praying you should know and think about your words. . ."*

October 6, 1991: *"Dear children, I wish that you pray together for the conversion of sinners this month . . ."*

January 3, 1993: *"I will fill you with the love of My Son because that's the only way you can accept every grace and pray with every thought and deed of yours."*

October 3, 1993: *"My beloved, I would like us to be connected through prayer especially this time. Let the Holy Ghost into your prayer. You don't know how many special graces for your souls, meditation over the mysteries of the holy rosary will bring. Please, let's pray for the conversion of sinners."*

March 6, 1994: *"Many of you pray perfunctorily and experience nothing through prayer. To pray profoundly, we need to apply ourselves altogether; all we have and all we are . . ."*

(2) Rosary - Our Blessed Mother always carried a rosary when She appeared to these seers. It is also worthy to note that Our Lady usually appeared while the rosary was being prayed by the faithful.

November 1, 1990: During this apparition Iveta asked Our Lady why She appeared to be so very sad. Our Lady is reported to have responded that the reason for Her sadness at that time was because Katarina had not prayed the rosary every night to do penance for her sins as Katarina had promised Our Lady.

December 2, 1990: During this apparition Our Lady reportedly stressed the importance of the rosary and deplored that there was so much hate among people and that people sought material riches more than anything else.

December 23, 1990: On this occasion the seer reportedly asked why Our Lady was always recommending the rosary. The Virgin Mary responded and told the seers that the rosary was Her prayer so that anyone who prayed the rosary was thereby praying for all God's graces.

December 25, 1990 Our Lady said: *"I love all the people who pray the rosary, but also all nonbelievers that offend Me and My Son Jesus."*

February 9, 1992: *"My dear children, try to be God's grace to everyone. Pray the holy rosary and pray for the youth because it is necessary."*

(3) Conversion - April 4, 1993: *"My dear children, I'm begging you again, change your lives and completely devote them to God because that's the only way your lives will be eternal."*

September 5, 1993: *"In the name of the Holiest God, I beg you, change your lives! Lay your old life onto My heart, and from My Son learn to live eternally."*

(4) Penance and Sacrifice - December 16, 1990: *"All the people need in order to guarantee themselves beautiful and joyous holidays is to have done penance and to pray the rosary."* As Our Blessed Mother spoke these words, with Her fingers She pointed to Her Heart.

August 4, 1991: *"My children, do not sin, for you don't know how much you thereby harm yourselves. I wish you to pray and offer sacrifices."*

May 9, 1993: *"Please bring sacrifices for others with love; totally donate yourselves to Jesus. You don't know how much sacrifice this world needs."*

(5) Fasting - December 13, 1990: During this apparition Our Lady besought the people to pray more earnestly and to fast on Wednesdays and Fridays.

July 4, 1993: *"Little souls, double your prayers and begin truly fasting. You don't know how much I need your praying and fasting to convert the strays . . ."*

X Signs Preceding the Apparitions

An intense light ("blaze") surrounded the seers, and in this light the

Litmanova, Slovakia

Blessed Mother would appear. Other times a fog developed and Our Lady would appear when the fog cleared.

XI Other Visions During Apparitions

On November 18, 1990 Our Lady appeared with the Child Jesus in Her arms.

XII Prayers Taught to the Seer(s)

(1) On July 7, 1991 Our Lady told the girls: *"When you are tempted, realize I've always been with you and pray: 'Immaculate Purity, help me preserve purity of my heart!'"*

(2) On April 4, 1993 Our Lady taught the seers this short **prayer:** *"Thy will be done everywhere and in everything, for in Thee resides eternal peace."*

XIII Special Devotion Given to the Seer(s) - NR

XIV Requests Made by Our Lady

(1) Fasting Wednesdays and Fridays.

(2) On December 30, 1990 Our Lady requested a medal be struck and distributed in veneration of Our Blessed Mother. On one side of the medal were to be the initials of the Blessed Virgin Mary above Her shining Heart, and a lily (a symbol of Her Purity); on the other side of the medal was to be an image of Jesus and Mary.

(3) Our Lady gave several suggestions to many of the people requesting a healing, such as: prayer and especially the rosary on Mount Zvir; wash or drink the holy water from the Mount; choose one of the twelve Apostles and pray to him daily; change your life-style and return to God.

XV Specific Bible References - Not Reported

XVI Secrets Given to the Seer(s)

It is reported that on April 7, 1991 the Virgin Mary gave a secret to Iveta; Our Blessed Mother was sad when She did so. No report of the contents of the secret is given.

XVII Miracles Promised by Our Lady - NR

XVIII Miracles Performed - Not Reported
XIX Miracles Promised not yet Performed - NR
XX Signs Promised - Not Reported

XXI Signs Given

(1) The water found on Mount Zvir near the place of the first apparition has healing graces. Our Lady later told the seers that all water on Mount Zvir had the power of healing.
(2) Katarina's mother had a dream the night after the first apparition. In this dream Our Lady appeared and told her not to doubt the girls. Our Lady was wearing a green wreath, which She explained She wore because She is Virgin with a pure heart.

XXII Predictions/Promises

(1) Our Lady told several people asking for healings that if they prayed the Family Rosary and had the sick person take some of the water from Mount Zvir, that the healing would occur if the parents firmly believed that the healing would take place.
(2) On February 2, 1991 Our Lady said: *"My dear child, you may know it is My holiday today. My hands are replete with gifts. I shall perform numerous miracles, sinners will convert and the sick will find that really rich are those who possess spiritual wealth and that material possessions do not matter to them. And those bearing pride in their hearts will see they have nothing to take pride in. I say this to you as your Mother."*
(3) On September 8, 1991 Our Lady said in part: *"However more saddened am I to have to tell you the following on My holiday: 'God's visit is near; search for love!'"*

XXIII Prophecies/Warnings of Chastisement

(1) November 11, 1990: *"I can't stand looking at the sins in Slovakia any more; My children have plenty of everything but fail to venerate Me and My Son. My Son will send down a disaster onto Slovakia unless people turn to Him and begin praying earnestly . . ."*
(2) Again on December 2, 1990 Our Lady again stressed the importance of the rosary and deplored that there was so much hate among people and that people sought material riches more than anything else. She reminded them of the pending disaster, which could be put off only if people amended their lives.
(3) January 20, 1991 Our Lady grieved over the slaughter in Bosnia. She said that war was of Satan, who has prevailed in the world for years.

Then: *"A disaster impends over Slovakia."* It all depends on whether or not the people prayed for Her help. If people devoted themselves to God and implored *"Thy will be done, Lord,"* the catastrophe would be averted.

XXIV Method of Appearance

Either an intense light ("blaze") would appear while the rosary was being prayed out of which light Our Lady would appear, or sometimes a fog developed and Our Lady appeared as the fog dissipated.

XXV Method of Departure

While the people prayed Our Lady gradually disappeared.

XXVI Confrontation w/Civil Authorities

The seer's own parents did not believe them at first. It was only after Katarina's mother had a dream, during which dream Our Blessed Mother appeared and told her not to doubt the girls.

XXVII Confrontation w/Church Authorities

On the one hand Fr. Polykarp Jacos, the pastor of the local church is supportive of the seers. He goes with them to Mount Zvir, he says Mass on the Mount as permitted by the bishop, and has reportedly launched a program of spiritual renewal in the parish.

On the other hand it is reported that the Greek Catholic clergy and Orthodox clergy are more cautious. In 1991 the Greek Catholic Bishop Jan Hirka appointed a commission of seven priests and theologians.

XXVIII Request Chapel/Shrine Built

Although no such request is reported, nonetheless the little wood shed is bedecked in flowers, icons and pictures, a virtual shrine. Also the Stations of the Cross were erected on the way up Mount Zvir.

XXIX Free Will/Choice - Not Reported

XXX Seer(s)' Suffering/Sacrifice

As often happened during the early stages of apparitions, the seers' own parents did not believe them at first. Of course, this would cause suffering to the girls.

XXXI Healings Reported

(1) During numerous apparitions Our Lady was asked to cure different people. She usually said that the person must have a strong belief that healing will occur; then She recommended prayer and use of the water from Mount Zvir.

(2) There are several testimonials of reported cures, however the reports are not clearly linked to Mount Zvir or to the waters from Mount Zvir.

XXXII Action Taken by the Church

Bishop Hirka has appointed a commission to investigate and report on these events. No report of commission action or further Church action is given.

XXXIII Bibliography

Litmanova's News   1994
Virgin Mary's Messages from Litmanova
By: Translated from Slovic to English
Published by: Not Given

Echo of Medjugorje (January-February 1994, #109)
By: Echo of Medjugorje
Published by: Echo of Medjugorje

Mary's People August 28, 1994
By: Mary's People
Published by: Supplement to Catholic Twin Circle and the National Catholic Register

Chapter 59

HILLSIDE, ILLINOIS, USA
(1990 - PRESENT)

I Place - Hillside, Illinois, USA
(Queen of Heaven Cemetery)

II Dates of First and Last Apparition

First: August 15, 1990
Last: May 25, 1994 (last reported)
Note: The apparitions are reportedly ongoing.

III Seer(s) - 1

Name: Joseph Reinholtz
Birth: Unknown
Age at first apparition: 81
Status: Living

IV Total Number of Apparitions - 222
(through May 25, 1994)

The apparitions are reportedly ongoing so that it is nearly certain that more apparitions have occurred than are reported.

V Dates and Locality of Each Apparition

All apparitions listed occurred at Hillside, Illinois before the Crucifix at Queen of Heaven Cemetery unless otherwise stated.

1990: August 15 and November 1st.
1991: August 15, September 21 (inside the seer's home), September 28 (Medjugorje); October 9, 16; 17 (inside the seer's home), 26, 27, 28, and October 30; November 1, 7, 8, 9, 10, 11, 13, 14, 15, 16, 17, 18, 20; 21 (inside the seer's home); 22, 23, 24, 25, 28, 29, and November 30; December 1, 2, 4, 5, 6, 7, 8, 9, 11, 12, 13, 14, 15, 18, 19, 20, 21, 22, 23, 25, 26, 27, 28, 29, 30.
1992 January 1, 2, 3, 4, 5, 6, 8, 9, 10, 11, 12, 13, 15, 16, 17, 18, 19, 20 (once at the Crucifix & once at the seer's home), 22, 23, 24, 25, 26, 27; 29 (Our Lady of Lebanon Church), 30, 31; February 5, 9, 12, 13, 14, 16, 19, 21, 22, 23, 24; 26 (the seer's home); March 1, 4, 5, 8, 11, 12, 15, 16, 18, 19, 22, 25, 28, 29; April 1, 5, 6, 8, 9, 12, 15, 17, 19, 21, 25, 28; May 2, 5, 10, 13, 16, 20, 23, 26, 30, 31; June 2 (once at the Crucifix & once at Our Lady of Lebanon Church); 7, 9, 13, 16, 20, 23, 28, 30; July 4 (twice); 7, 11, 14, 18, 22, 23, 25, 28; August 1 (twice); 8, 15 (twice); 16, 21, 29; September 6, 8, 13, 20, 27, 28; October 2, 21, 25, 31; November 7, 15, 22, 29; December 6, 12, 19, 25, 27, 31.
1993: January 9, 16, 24; February 6, 21; March 6, 20, 25; April 5 (Medjugorje), 25; May 20, 30, 31; June 8, 25; July 25; August 15 (twice), 25; September 25; October 8, 10, 11, 13, 14, 16 (all in Medjugorje), 25; November 1, 25; December 25.
1994: January 25; February 25; March 25; 31 (Medjugorje); April 1, 2; 3 (Medjugorje); April 25; May 25.

VI Description of Our Lady

Our Lady arrives in a brilliant light during the recitation of the rosary, accompanied by two or three, and sometimes four angels. She is usually dressed in white, wearing a cape. At times She is dressed in blue or gold or grey. Sometimes She wears a crown of gold. Our Blessed Mother often holds Her Divine Son.

She is described as very, very beautiful, about 18, approximately 5'4" tall, with beautiful blue eyes and black hair. The seer reports that Her eyes penetrate and look right straight at him. "It's like a line that comes right at you", reports the seer. The seer reports that Our Lady always carries a rosary in Her hand.

VII Title(s) of Our Lady - 3

(1) On December 2, 1991 Our Lady announced: *"I truly am the Mother of God . . ."* It was repeated again on December 28, and December 30, 1991.
(2) On November 23, 1991 Our Lady came as Queen of Peace. This title was repeated again on December 11, and 28, 1991, and on January 20, and February 23rd of 1992.
(3) On January 12, 1992 She announced: *"I am the Queen of the Rosary"*, repeated again on January 29, 1992.

VIII Brief Factual Review

Hillside, Illinois is a suburb of Chicago, located south of the windy city. The Queen of Heaven Cemetery located in Hillside, and more specifically in the military section of the cemetery is the focal point of the events and apparitions occurring to Joseph Reinholtz.

These events really began in 1987, when Joseph Reinholtz, an 81-year-old retired railroad worker made a pilgrimage to Medjugorje. He had suffered sporadic blindness and heard of healings and blessings that were given by Our Blessed Mother in Medjugorje. During this trip Joseph met Vicka (one of the visionaries in Medjugorje). After Vicka prayed over him, Joseph promised he would dedicate the remainder of his life to praying and working for the terminally ill.

After returning home, Joseph regained his vision while praying before his statue of the Virgin Mary inside his own home. The first object he saw when he regained his sight was the statue of Our Lady which was then weeping tears. The statue wept for three days and three nights.

In April 1989 he returned to Medjugorje in thanksgiving, when he again met with Vicka. She told Joseph that the Lord had chosen him for a special work he was to do when he got home. Vicka directed Joseph to look for a Crucifix 15 feet tall located between two trees, one of which was triple-branched. After finding this Crucifix, Joseph was to pray before it. Upon arriving home Joseph immediately began to search for the Crucifix and eventually found a 15 foot fiberglass Crucifix in the military section of the Queen of Heaven Cemetery. The triple-branched tree is now named the 'Trinity Tree'. During the next year Joseph privately prayed daily before the Crucifix. Joseph reports that during this period he saw the Crucifix bleed. Reportedly photos were successfully taken of this phenomenon.

Then on August 15, 1990 Our Blessed Mother appeared to Joseph as he was praying before the Crucifix. Our Lady appeared again to Joseph on November 1, 1990. This time She was accompanied by St. Michael the Archangel and three other angels. Our Lady reportedly gave Joseph messages asking the world to sacrifice and pray from the heart.

News of the apparitions began to spread throughout the area prayer groups. More people came to pray daily before the Crucifix between 9:00 AM and 10:00 AM; the time when Our Lady would appear to Joseph. Strong fragrances of rose scent, rosaries turning gold color, and stories of healings and conversions were spreading. When the media got hold of the story, the crowds increased. Then the archdiocese moved the Crucifix next to a large parking lot in another part of the cemetery, where it remains today. Even so the crowds increased to as many as 10,000 on the Feast of the Assumption, August 15, 1991.

Also, it was on August 15, 1991 that Joseph began to receive messages from Our Lady. The routine is that each day between 9:00 AM and 10:00 AM people gather. First they pray the 'Peace Rosary'. When Joseph arrives the Joyful Mysteries are said, because Joseph promised to pray the Joyful Mysteries daily for the terminally ill. Children lead the fifth decade. Our Lady usually arrives during or after the fifth decade. After the apparition, Joseph turns to the crowd and announces the messages and blesses the children and the terminally ill.

Joseph reportedly returned to Medjugorje again in September 1991, October 1993, and in March 1994 and received messages from Our Lady during these pilgrimages.

Our Lady appears in a brilliant light during the recitation of the rosary. She always carries a rosary in Her hands. She is usually dressed in white (but at times in blue, gold or grey) and sometimes wears a crown of gold. Often Our Lady holds the Infant Jesus. She is described as very beautiful, about 18 years old and about 5'4" tall, with beautiful blue eyes and black hair. She looks directly at the seer. At times She weeps tears.

She has announced Herself as the Queen of Peace, Queen of the Holy Rosary and Mother of God. Our Lady has told Joseph She will appear at the Crucifix every morning, which She does. At times She has appeared to Joseph at his home, at a church, and on four occasions She appeared to the seer in Medjugorje.

The messages Our Lady gave to this seer are strikingly similar to those given at many other apparition sites. Our Lady calls for prayer, especially prayer for peace, for the recitation of the rosary, for conversion, forgiveness, reconciliation and penance. She also warned of great chastisements should we fail to heed Her messages.

There are reports of many unusual phenomena such as the strong scent of roses during the apparitions, rosary links that change from silver to gold color, and unusual photographs showing Our Lady hovering above the Crucifix. Also reported are many healings and conversions. The seer himself is considered to be a devout and holy man.

Although the archdiocese moved the large Crucifix near a parking lot in the cemetery, apparently to accommodate the crowd, it has also issued a statement to the effect that it has no evidence that any unusual or supernatural events are taking place at the cemetery. Yet it at once encourages people to gather at the Crucifix and pray. We must await future Church action, if any.

IX The Primary Messages - 5

(1) **Prayer** - Nearly every reported message contains pleas from Our Blessed Mother, for prayer and more prayer; and for a wide range of beneficiaries, people and purposes.

November 1, 1991: *"Pray! Pray! Pray! Continue to pray, fast, and bring everything you have to Me. I will intercede and bring everything to God. All our little ones are in very, very difficult situations because the devil is around them. You must go on praying to achieve Our goals."*

November 10, 1991 Our Lady said: *" I am very sad about the condition of the world. We must continue to pray, pray, pray."*

December 5, 1991 Our Lady requests: *"Devote three hours of your time to prayer. Try to do it throughout the whole day. Holy Mass and the prayers of Our rosary are allowed in the prayers of the three hours."*

December 14, 1991 again: *"It is through prayer we can avoid war and can have the peace that we need throughout the world. I need your prayers more desperately than ever before."*

December 28, 1991: *"When you go home, continue to pray before the Crucifix. Your prayers mean a lot when you pray before My Son."*

January 9, 1992: *"Continue to pray for priests, bishops, cardinals, and for unity in all churches throughout the world, and in families."*

March 4, 1992: *"Banish from your heart hatred, bitterness, preconceived judgment. Pray for your enemies."*

March 19, 1992: *"You must pray for them (souls in purgatory) because they have terrible sufferings. They cannot pray for themselves. They are quite helpless and depend on our prayers to be freed from their sufferings. Help these souls!"*

April 15, 1992: *"Families are divided. There is no unity within families. Pray to your guardian angels. They are beside you always. Pray to them for guidance and protection from the evil spirits which are all about you."*

January 9, 1993: *"Pray beloved children and do penance, because you have now entered into the time of the great chastisement which the Lord will send, and do not let yourselves be seized by fear or discouragement."*

October 16, 1993: *"Keep up the practice of daily, devout, humble, confident prayer. You know how much prayer your particular work permits."*

January 14, 1994: *"My children, resume prayer. If you pray, you shall obtain light and your life on this earth shall be happier."*

(2) **Rosary** - Our Lady always carried a rosary in Her hands during

the apparitions. She also prayed with the seer and those present during the apparitions. In addition Our Lady urged us to pray three rosaries (15 decades) every day.

August 15, 1991: *"I ask you for three rosaries each and every day; the Joyful, Sorrowful, and Glorious Mysteries."* This message was repeated several times during the course of the reported apparitions.

November 18, 1991: *"Time is running out and we must think a little more. Pray the rosary more fervently."*

February 23, 1992: *". . . Pray the rosary. Give time to the rosary . . ."*

March 22, 1992: *"Pray and let the rosary always be in your hands as a sign to Satan that you belong to Me."*

April 9, 1992: *"Teach children how to pray the rosary."*

April 15, 1992: *". . . not enough to pray the rosary. There must be a complete reversal of the new trends in the Church in which the weapon I gave mankind, the most holy rosary, is being ignored. It must be prayed every day. Not only one rosary must be said, no, but all three mysteries consisting of fifteen decades because there are many upon your earth who make up for those who refuse to the pray the rosary."*

July 25, 1992 Our Lady repeated to this seer the 15 Promises that Our Blessed Virgin earlier gave to St. Dominic and Blessed Alan, for Christians who recite the rosary.

April 25, 1994: *"Pray your rosary every time you find yourself being attacked by Satan . . ."*

(3) Conversion - September 21, 1991: *". . . Today I bless you in a very special way with My Motherly blessing that God will give you the gift of conversion. Decide seriously to dedicate time to God . . ."*

November 20, 1991: *"The whole world must come to conversion. Everyone must find salvation before it's too late."*

December 7, 1991: *"I invite you to convert and go to confession once a month."*

February 9, 1992 Our Lady said: *"I am very sad because My heart bleeds for many conversions."*

March 22, 1992: *"I am calling you to a complete surrender to God. . . Put your life in God's hands."*

August 15, 1992: *"Conversion demands a frequent pondering of the word of God . . . Without frequent Confession conversion is impossible."*

February 25, 1994: *"We must use our free will to choose to surrender what we want in order to do what God wants."*

(4) Forgiveness, Penance and Sacrifice - December 12, 1991: *"Today I invite you to works of mercy. I will accept your sacrifices and prayers to God."*

On January 26, 1992 Our Lady urged us to reconciliation, to penance and said that much conversion had to be done.

March 1, 1992 Our Lady said: *"I ask you all to do something a little extra during this Lenten season, to repent and come to conversion by reconciliation, by making a good confession, and do penance."*

April 12, 1992: *"I desire sacrifices from you in order that I may help you drive Satan away from you."*

April 19, 1992: *"Forgive one another. Forgive everybody. Recommend them to the Father with joy; pray for them. Then wish them a great blessing, joy and great love."*

November 1, 1993: *"What I ask is sacrifice, prayer, mortifications, devotion to Me your Mother, revival and propagation of the rosary everywhere."*

(5) **Holy Mass, Reconciliation and Eucharist** - August 15, 1991 *"The Mass is the center of your life."*

April 5, 1992: *"I call you to live the Holy Mass. There are many of you who have experienced the beauty of the Mass. There are some who come unwillingly . . . Jesus is giving you His graces in the Holy Mass. Let us live conscientiously the Holy Mass. Let everyone come to the Holy Mass be joyful. You should have great love and accept the Holy Mass so that He may always pour abundant gifts into your hearts."*

July 7, 1992: *"The Sacrament of Reconciliation and Eucharist are very special weapons that Jesus gave to His Church to overcome the kingdom of sin and darkness."*

May 25, 1994: *"At the very foundation are the Sacraments of Confession and Holy Communion, the holy rosary. . ."*

X Signs Preceding the Apparitions

A brilliant light preceded Our Blessed Mother. Sometimes three flashes of light appeared to the seer as Our Lady arrived.

XI Other Visions During Apparitions

(1) Our Lord Jesus.

(2) Infant Jesus.

(3) St. Michael the Archangel; whom the seer described as being a very huge angel. He is apparently 7' to 8' tall. His wings are large and protrude above his head and almost down to the ground.

(4) Our Lady was usually accompanied by two or three angels; sometimes as many as five angels.

XII Prayers Taught to the Seer(s) - Not Reported
XIII Special Devotion Given to Seer(s) - NR

XIV Requests Made by Our Lady

(1) That we pray 15 decades of the rosary each day, and also seven Our Fathers, seven Hail Marys, seven Glory Be's, and one Apostles Creed daily.
(2) That we kneel or stand when we pray the Sorrowful Mysteries.
(3) That we pray the prayer to St. Michael every day.
(4) That we pray for the release of the souls in purgatory.
(5) On December 5, 1991 Our Lady said: *"Devote three hours of your time to prayer. Try to do it throughout the day. Holy Mass and the prayers of Our rosary are allowed in the prayers of three hours."*
(6) On March 4, 1992 Our Lady made a special request for the Lenten Season: *"Renounce all passions and inordinate desires during this Lenten season. Avoid television, particularly evil programs, excessive sports, the unreasonable enjoyment of food and drink. Difficulties will persist. Banish from your heart hatred, bitterness, and preconceived judgment."*
(7) Our Lady also asked for *"modesty in dress"*. (February 5, 1992)

XV Specific Bible References

(1) On February 9, 1992 *"Read the Book of Revelations."* (repeated again on February 16, 1992)
(2) Book of Genesis - Chapter 1 to 50. (March 15, 1992)
(3) March 25, 1994 - Proverbs Chapter 13, Verse 24.

XVI Secrets Given to the Seer(s) - Not Reported
XVII Miracles Promised by Our Lady - NR
XVIII Miracles Performed - Not Reported
XIX Miracles Promised not yet Performed - NR

XX Signs Promised

In April 1989 when Joseph returned to Medjugorje, it is reported that Vicka (one of the seers in Medjugorje), told Joseph that he, Joseph, was to look for a Crucifix 15' tall between two trees, (one of the trees was three-branched), when he returned home. And when he found this Crucifix he was to go to it and pray before it.

These events all occurred as announced.

XXI Signs Given

(1) The first object Joseph saw when his blindness was cured was his own

statue of Our Blessed Mother weeping tears in his own home. The statue wept for three days and three nights, as reported.
(2) It is also reported that the seer saw blood on the Corpus of the large Crucifix.
(3) On October 16, 1991 during an apparition, it is reported that Our Lady said: *"Bring that little boy closer to Me."* When the family lifted the boy up to the cross, he looked straight at the cross. When they set the boy down he is reported to have said: "Mommy and Daddy, I seen the Blessed Mother!"
(4) Other phenomena are reported such as a strong scent of roses when Our Lady appears, rosaries turning a gold color and photographs taken at the Crucifix which reportedly show golden images of Our Blessed Mother hovering near the Crucifix.

XXII Predictions/Promises

(1) On October 28, 1991 it is reported that Our Lady said that She would be at the Crucifix every morning. The reported appearances do occur in the mornings.
(2) On February 5, 1992 Our Lady pronounced: *"Many fashions will be introduced. I ask for modesty in dress. The sins of the flesh will take most souls to hell . . ."*
(3) On July 25, 1992 Our Lady gave this seer the 15 promises (earlier given to St. Dominic and to Blessed Alan) for those who recite the rosary.

XXIII Prophecies/Warnings of Chastisement

December 8, 1991: *"It is time for you to choose the Light of the World, or the Prince of Darkness. Peace or new catastrophes will affect the whole world."*

December 29, 1991 again: *"You have many hardships to go through. The wars still continue. They will continue unless you know how to pray."*

January 29, 1992 Our Lady: *". . . If people amend their lives, Our Lord can save the world. The Lord will chastise the world as never before. There is need of reflection, from all generations, upon the existence of hell."*

April 9, 1992: *"Prepare yourselves for great persecution and new sacrifices. . ."*

XXIV Method of Appearance

Our Lady would appear during or at the end of the fifth decade of the rosary. A brilliant light would precede Her, then She appeared before the Crucifix.

Sometimes the seer also saw three flashes of light just before Our Lady arrived.

XXV Method of Departure

When Our Lady departs a beautiful glow of light surrounds Her and the angels accompanying Her.

XXVI Confrontation w/Civil Authorities - NR
XXVII Confrontation w/Church Authorities - NR
XXVIII Request Chapel/Shrine Built - NR

XXIX Free Will/Choice

(1) On November 24, 1991 Our Lady said: *"I invite you to decide for Paradise. It is very difficult for those who have not decided for God."*
(2) Then on December 8, 1991 Our Lady said: *"It is time for you to choose the Light of the World or the Prince of Darkness."*
(3) On January 8, 1992 She said: *". . . Decide for God . . ."*
(4) February 25, 1994 Our Lady said: *"We must use our free will."*

XXX Seer(s)' Suffering/Sacrifice

Our Lady often told the seer how much She appreciated and acknowledged the sacrifices that people made in coming to the Crucifix in the rain and cold weather.

XXXI Healings Reported

(1) It is reported that many healings and conversions have occurred. No specific testimonials are reported.
(2) Joseph himself was cured of his blindness.

XXXII Action Taken by the Church

The archdiocese accommodated the crowds by moving the Crucifix to a more suitable location near a parking lot in another part of the cemetery.

Also the archdiocese allows the people to gather at the Crucifix and pray.

The Archdiocese of Chicago issued a statement saying that it has no evidence that any unusual or supernatural phenomenon was taking place at the cemetery. There has been no other official Church action reported.

XXXIII Bibliography

At the Cross Her Station Keeping, Vol I 1992
By: Not Given
Published by: At the Cross

At the Cross Her Station Keeping, Vol II 1994
By: Not Given
Published by: At the Cross

Mary's Newsroom, Vol. 5 Number 4 May 1993
By: Not Given
Published by: Mary's Newsroom

Chapter 60

DENVER/GOLDEN, COLORADO, USA
(1991 - PRESENT)

I Place - Denver & Golden (Mother Cabrini Shrine), Colorado, USA

II Dates of First and Last Apparition

First: April 12, 1991
Last: May 20, 1994 (last reported)
Note: These apparitions are reportedly ongoing.

III Seer(s) - 1

Name: Veronica Garcia
Birth: Unknown
Age at first apparition: Unknown
Status: Married/living

IV Total Number of Apparitions - 289
(reported through May 20, 1994)

V Dates and Locality of Each Apparition

Most of the apparitions occurred at Mother Cabrini Shrine, however, this seer also received apparitions in her own home, at her place of employment, inside various churches, while traveling and also at various

Denver/Golden, Colorado , USA

other places to which she travelled on her announced mission.

1991: April 12; May 11; June 11; July 11; August 13; September 12; October 15; November 11; 26; December 12.
1992: January 14, 17, 24, 30; February 2, 5, 13; March 2, 10, 11, 12, 13, 15, 17, 19, 20, 21, 24, 27, 29; 30, 31, once undated; April 4, 7, 12, 17, 18, 19, 21, 25, 26, 30; May 2; 4 (twice), 5, 10,11, 14; 19 (twice); May 20, 22, 23, 24, 26, 27, 29; June 3, 5, 10, 14, 15, 18, 20, 28; July 1, 2, 5, 7, 12, 16, 17, 20; 25 (twice); August 1, 5, 9, 15, 20, 26, 27, 30; September 3, 13, 15, 18, 20, 29; October 3, 7, 10, 11, 13, 15, 22, 23, 31; November 7, 12; December 2, 7, 9, 13, 19, 20, 25.
1993: January 1, 10, 18; March 9, 14; April 4, 9, 11, 20, 25; May 9, 15, 16, 17, 19; June 12, 13, 25, 30; July 3, 11, 17, 19; August 6, 8, 11, 15, 16, 17; September 11, 12, 19, 21; October 10, 13; November 2, 6, 14, 17, 24; December 8, 25.
1994: January 1, 3, 4, 5, 6, 7, 8, 9, 10, 11, 12, 13, 14, 15, 17, 18, 19, 20, 21, 22, 23, 24, 25; 26 (twice); 27, 28, 29, 30, 31; February 1, 2, 3, 4; 5 (twice); 7, 8, 9, 10, 11, 12, 13, 14, 15, 16, 17, 18, 19, 20, 21, 22, 23, 24, 25, 26, 27, 28; March 1, 2, 3, 4, 5, 6, 7, 8, 9, 10, 11, 12, 13, 14, 15, 16, 17, 18, 19, 20, 21, 22, 23, 24, 25, 26, 27, 28, 29, 30, 31; April 1, 2, 3, 4, 5, 6, 7, 8, 9, 10, 11, 12, 13, 14, 16, 17, 18, 20; 21 (twice); 22, 23, 24, 25, 26, 27, 28, 29, 30; May 1, 2, 3, 4, 5, 6, 7, 8, 9, 10, 11, 12, 13, 14, 15, 16, 17, 18, 19, 20.

VI Description of Our Lady

(1) On December 12, 1991 this seer first saw Our Lady "In the lights".
(2) Thereafter on April 12, 1992 Veronica saw Our Lady "in full blown living color" for the first time.
(3) On June 6, 1992 this seer saw Our Lady come out of a statue of Our Lady. She was dressed in an ivory dress with a blue mantle, the inside of the mantle was red in color. She had a wreath of red roses around Her head. Our Lady's Immaculate Heart was exposed sending forth rays of light.

VII Title(s) of Our Lady - 1

On December 12, 1992 being the very first time Our Lady appeared as a full apparition to this seer, Our Blessed Mother announced: *"I am your Mother."* This sentence was repeated by Our Lady during many later apparitions to this seer.

VIII Brief Factual Review

Denver, Colorado, commonly known as the 'Mile High City' is located in the Rocky Mountains in the West-Central portion of the USA. Golden is about 20 miles west of Denver. It is here that the Mother Cabrini Shrine is located.

Veronica Garcia was only two years of age when her own mother died, leaving Veronica and two other daughters. Her grandmother was the one who raised her. When Veronica was seven her father remarried. Veronica had problems adjusting to the new family; she ran away from home when she was only 14. She was returned home by the authorities in short order. Thereafter Veronica continued her education but became involved in a life of dissipation. At 24 she married and had one daughter. This marriage failed and after some years Veronica remarried on October 10, 1981. This marriage is intact.

Veronica's parents were always supportive through the difficult years. In 1987 her stepmother adopted Veronica and also adopted her two adult sisters. At about this time her stepmother tried to bring Veronica in closer contact with God in Veronica's own life. Soon Veronica was exposed more and more to spiritual activities, such as Bible studies and prayer. In 1988 her aunt went to Medjugorje where her aunt's rosary turned a gold color.

In October 1989 Veronica also made a pilgrimage to Medjugorje where she made her first confession in 20 years; this was at the foot of the Cross on Apparition Hill. She knew she was fully forgiven by Our Lord and her own dramatic conversion was now under way in earnest. In October 1990 she returned to Medjugorje where she received a memorable blessing from Father Jozo.

Soon thereafter Veronica began to have mystical experiences. In 1991 she saw the Crucified Jesus in a dream. Other things reportedly happened to her. She would be awakened at night to receive messages (locutions) from both Jesus and Mary. These messages comenced April 12, 1991. At first these messages were in the form of poetry; later the messages became instructive, yet always loving and caring in content.

It was in December 1991 that Veronica first saw Our Blessed Mother "in the lights". Thereafter in April 1992 she had her first full fledged apparition of Our Lady.

At Veronica's request Our Lady taught her to say prayers which Our Lady later prayed with this seer.

Nowadays this seer attends daily Mass and receives Holy Communion, weekly confession and daily prayer, especially the rosary. Veronica is not only a wife and mother, but also is employed as a legal secretary; and also travels often to fulfill the mission given to her by Jesus and Mary. Her mission is to spread the messages and to gain souls to return to God.

Our Lady requested that Veronica come to Mother Cabrini Shrine on the second Sunday of each month. Our Lady also told Veronica that she would suffer in carrying out her mission: *"People will try to discredit you."*

The messages given to this seer are for prayer, prayer for priests, the souls in purgatory and many other named purposes; to recite the rosary, attend Mass and receive the Eucharist daily, and make frequent confessions. We are to totally trust Jesus and convert. The messages are all given in a loving, gentle and caring mode. As Father Hefferman, the seer's spiritual director, is reported to have said: "The messages are universal in scope and full of love for God." Yet the messages are also instructive. On August 26, 1992 Our Lady said: *"The trials will become harder the further you get from the world and the closer you get to His Heart."* Then on January 17, 1994 Our Lady again: *"If you are full of worldly desires you are empty of spiritual needs."* Then on February 11, 1994 Our Lady said: *"Be silent long enough and open enough to realize that what you need is what Jesus Christ has been waiting to give you from the beginning. . . Depression, anxiety and loneliness come from being in the dark too long."* On March 11, 1994: *"Do not allow your pride and strong will to stand in the way of His Mercy and Compassion for you; Your first step is to trust Him."* Again on March 12, 1994: *"When you are able to unite your suffering with the Passion of Jesus Christ, you will become a true disciple and image of your Saviour."*

Although the apparitions are reported as ongoing, there is no report of any commission being appointed by the Church. Father B.F. Hefferman is Veronica's spiritual director. She has reportedly been obedient to his spiritual direction. Father Richard Foley, SJ penned the Introduction to the second volume of messages. Both of these clergyman seem favorably impressed with this seer; however, as they point out, we must await and submit to the decision of the Church.

It is interesting to note that this seer reportedly received apparitions and messages at Mile High Stadium and at Cherry Creek State Park in August 1993 when Pope John Paul II visited Denver for the International Youth Conference.

It is later reported that on October 2, 1994 the seer received a message from Our Lady which requested people to resume prayer and to *"come back to the Cabrini Shrine."* Our Lady also said that on the second Sabbath of December She would reveal Her final message *"from this place,"* and that She will continue with daily messages until the end of the year to encourage all to heed Her call. Then She invited all to come to the Shrine on the second Sabbath of each month to pray out of faith and love for Jesus.

IX The Primary Messages - 8

(1) Prayer - The messages are replete with pleas from Our Blessed Mother; pleas to pray constantly, to remain in prayer, to pray from the heart, to pray for priests, for sinners, for the souls in purgatory and to pray together as a family daily.

March 19, 1992: *"Prayer together is one of the strongest blessings you can give each other."*

March 27, 1992: *"Pray, yes pray, but then turn the prayer into action."*

May 10, 1992: *"Extend today's prayer to your families for unity."*

June 18, 1992: *"You must always pray for the safety, health and protection of My most beloved shepherd (the Pope)."*

July 5, 1992: *"Begin and end every day with prayer. . ."*

On July 7, 1992 Our Lady told the seer that prayer from the heart comes in three stages:

- Stage One begins with prayer to the Holy Spirit to prepare you.
- Stage Two places you in front of your Jesus. . .
- Stage Three is a prayer of thanksgiving to God the Father.

October 11, 1992: *"I come asking your prayers for the innocents, those who have had their very life taken before they could sing their songs of praise on this earth for their Creator."*

September 21, 1993: *"Pray to the Holy Spirit every day for His gifts of wisdom, asking for discernment between things that are of God and things that are not."*

March 4, 1994: *"Pray, for it is through prayer that you will find peace. Without prayer, peace is impossible. That is why Satan tries to keep you from prayer and attempts to fill your lives with worldly thoughts and desires."*

(2) Rosary - May 10, 1992: *"Clutch the rosary firmly in your hand."*

October 7, 1992 *"The recitation of the rosary has the power to stop wars, bring peace, convert souls, and prevent disasters."*

November 7, 1992: *"These are serious times. Prayer from your heart is the only way. The rosary is most powerful."*

(3) Attend Holy Mass and Receive Sacraments - May 14, 1992: *"Receive the Sacrament of Reconciliation as often as possible and continue going to daily Mass.*

September 3, 1992: *"I ask for you to use the Sacrament of Reconciliation weekly so that you may be sure to stay on the path that has been lit for you . . . Keep your soul in peace and your aim steady. Prayer, peace, reconciliation, penance and daily Mass are your weapons against attack."*

February 26, 1994: *"When you come before My Son in the Most Holy Eucharist open your hearts to receive His love as He embraces you."*

March 29, 1994: *"Reconciliation at this time is crucial if you are to be *freed from the weight of sins that have kept you from His bond of love."*

(4) Adoration of the Blessed Sacrament - September 3, 1992: *"Be in adoration before your Jesus as often as possible."*

October 10, 1993: *"Come before the Blessed Sacrament, for your Jesus awaits to hear the utterings of your heart. Share all with Him, asking for His blessings which He anxiously awaits to bestow upon you."*

April 16, 1994: *"Consume Him and be consumed. Adore Him and be fed by Him. Damaged souls will thrive in the reality of His Love in the Most Blessed Sacrament of His Life. Here He is, come to Him!"*

April 23, 1994: *"I ask you to spend more time in preparation to be with your Jesus in the Blessed Sacrament."*

(5) Trust in Jesus - March 21, 1992: *"Your Lord will not fail you, He will never forget His promises, and He is never late. Those who trust in His ways, walk in His light; and those who walk in His light, will see the Eternal Glory of heaven."*

May 19, 1992: *"All He wants you to do is trust in Him, to love Him unquestionably. . . Do you not know He will provide all of your needs?"*

October 11, 1992 *"You must become as children; leave your egos, your love of self behind you and recognize that it is your Lord who is in control. He alone knows what is best for your souls. He provides the nourishment and love that is necessary for your salvation. Trust in Him."*

July 19, 1993: *"Do not question, rather rejoice, for He has protected you in order for His plan to be fulfilled. Worry not what others think. Trust in He who is your salvation, and His rock of love on which you stand shall not crumble."*

January 4, 1994: *"I ask of you to find ways in which to be kinder to each other. Do not allow your anger to take control of your actions. Turn your back on greed and jealousy of one another. Trust in your Jesus. All has been provided according to your individual needs."*

(6) Simplicity and Humility - May 19, 1992: *"Love simplicity, Live each day in humility and thankfulness to your Lord. Keep your eyes on Him, your purpose always being to serve Him. In simplicity and humility He was born."*

May 19, 1993: *"Humility will come with the realization of your nothingness; a solid foundation of faith, hope and love will yield a harvest of humility, patience, perseverance and obedience."*

June 13, 1993: *". . . Rid yourself of your ego that stands in the way of doing the work the Father has called on you to do. Beware of this ego that will lead you to false humility."*

May 11, 1994: *"As you meditate on the life of Jesus, contemplate on His humility. Strive for that type of humility in all you do."*

(7) Unity - May 10, 1992: *"Extend today's prayer to your family for unity, then unity will spread within the Church, which will, in turn, spread between all the divided churches."*

May 15, 1993: *"My children must stop fighting amongst themselves. It saddens Me so to see this discord, lack of unity, greed that is coming from within even My most important, most essential, if My plans are to be fulfilled."*

(8) Mission - This seer was reportedly given a mission by Jesus and Mary to spread these messages and to travel and evangelize, urging people through these messages of love, to convert, acquire the virtues and to trust in Jesus and to return to God.

March 15, 1992: *"My child don't be so concerned about understanding everything. There will be times when you will be called upon to do the Father's will and you will be nothing more than an instrument. Oh, My daughter, there is so much to be done. Take My hand and trust. Ask God for the graces you need to do the work you have been called to do . . . The work ahead will not always be easy for you, nor will it always seem to make sense to you. Trust in Him. Trust in Me. Just as there will be hard times My daughter, there will be times of great outpouring of graces."*

March 29, 1992: *"I am sending you out among My children now, take heart, I will be with you and will guide you in what you must tell them. You will watch the hearts open, and many will return to Christ. It is important that you always pray first before you do anything in God's name."*

X Signs Preceding the Apparitions

It is reported that at times Veronica "felt Our Lady coming" to the seer. Such was the case on May 2, 1992 at the Des Moines Conference, when the missionary Image of the Tilma of Our Lady of Guadalupe was brought in procession, the seer "felt" that Our Lady was coming to her and the seer's heart began to beat rapidly. It was then that the seer saw the statue of Our Lady, above the Tilma, starting to glow; then Our Lady came out from the statue.

XI Other Visions During Apparitions

(1) Jesus appeared to Veronica and also gave her messages.
(2) Satan appeared to this seer.
(3) Our Lady exposed Her Immaculate Heart on several occasions.
(4) Many angels appeared with Our Lady; once it is reported that there were hundreds of angels present at the altar during the Consecration of the Mass.
(5) St. Michael the Archangel also appeared to this seer.
(6) Veronica was shown a vision of purgatory and hell during an apparition on November 8, 1992.

XII Prayers Taught to the Seer(s)

(1) On July 16, 1992 the seer claims to have received the following prayer from Our Lady by locution:
   Prayer: Dear Mother, I come before You now. Please hold me. I come wanting to give myself completely to You, but I am afraid. I know that fear is not of God. Please, Dearest Mother, crush this fear. Ask God to give me the graces I need to totally abandon myself, with full confidence that my Jesus will catch me when I fall into His Heart of Mercy. Strengthen my faith; increase my hope; unite my love. I ask this in Jesus' name. Amen.

(2) It is reported that Our Lady taught this seer to say the 'Glory Be' prayer as follows:
   Prayer: Glory be to the Father!
   Glory be to the Son!
   Glory be to the Holy Spirit!
   As it was in the beginning;
   As it is now; and
   As it evermore shall be;
   World without end.   Amen.

(3) On October 3, 1992 Our Lady taught the seer:
   Prayer: My Jesus, my Saviour, protect us within the
   circle of Your Blood.
   My Rock and my Fortress, place me within the
   circle of Your Love;
   My Lord and my God, unite me within the
   circle of Your life.

XIII Special Devotion Given to the Seer(s) - NR

XIV Requests Made by Our Lady

(1) On May 4, 1992 Our Lady requested that the seer: *"Please take Jesus to My imprisoned children."*
(2) Our Lady also requested that we consecrate ourselves daily to the Sacred Heart of Jesus and the Immaculate Heart of Mary.
(3) On August 8, 1993 Our Lady invited all to begin a prayer novena of one daily rosary for the protection of Her beloved sons; the priests.

XV Specific Bible References

(1) Psalm 46:10.
(2) Our Lady referred the seer to the reading of Holy Scripture.

XVI Secrets Given to the Seer(s) - Not Reported
XVII Miracles Promised by Our Lady - NR
XVIII Miracles Performed - Not Reported
XIX Miracles Promised not yet Performed - NR
XX Signs Promised - Not Reported

XXI Signs Given

There are several reported instances when Veronica received personal signs and charisms.

XXII Predictions/Promises

On December 25, 1993 Our Lady predicted: *"I shall be with you daily for the next year and then I will come no more to this special place, to this, My messenger of His Love."*

XXIII Prophecies/Warnings of Chastisement

On November 2, 1993 Our Lady warned: *"Time is running My small ones, the chastisements have begun. It will only be those who have accepted this invitation of Life that will be saved from certain ruin."*

XXIV Method of Appearance

Although there is no consistent method of appearance reported, yet on at least one occasion the seer had a premonition that Our Lady was about to appear, and then, Our Lady appeared coming out of a statue of Our Lady.

XXV Method of Departure

It is reported that on July 7, 1992 as Our Lady left, a beautiful, bright, complete rainbow appeared where She had been.

XXVI Confrontation w/Civil Authorities

Veronica was rejected, maligned and misunderstood by many. Some charge her as a fake copycat visionary. It is reported that damaging fabrications have been disseminated about her, all in an attempt to destroy her status as a genuine seer. This, of course, has caused great suffering to the seer. Our Blessed Mother forewarned Veronica: *"Many people will try to discredit and persecute you."*

It is reported, that in spite of all this, Veronica accepts these attacks with serenity and forgiveness.

XXVII Confrontation w/Church Authorities - NR
XVIII Request Chapel/Shrine Built - NR

XXIX Free Will/Choice

August 26, 1992 Our Lady said: *"You must remember that your Father would never interfere with your free will. He allows trials to happen so that when your choosing is for Him, it becomes a pure love that has not been forced."*

March 26, 1994 Our Lady said: *"I am asking you today not to delay any longer in your decision for God. Every day that passes without your decision, is a day that takes you further away from His love."*

XXX Seer(s)' Suffering/Sacrifice

The ridicule and attacks on the seer, of course, cause her much suffering and pain.

XXXI Healings Reported

Conversions have been reported both at the Shrine, during and after the apparitions, as well as during traveling sessions when the seer carries out the mission given to her.

XXXII Action Taken by the Church

There are not reports of any commission being appointed nor any official Church action.

XXXIII Bibliography

Messages of Love, 1992
By: Veronica Garcia
Distributed by: *Bridgeway*

Messages of Love, Volume II, 1993
By: Veronica Garcia
Distributed by: *Bridgeway*

AFTER-WORD

A central and important lesson we may learn experiencing these various apparitions of Our Blessed Virgin Mary is that Our Lady's messages and Her attention are totally directed towards, and focused upon Her Divine Son, Our Lord Jesus Christ. She neither asks for, nor retains, any glory for Herself, as an end.

It is true that Our Lady tells all the visionaries (and all of humanity) over and over again, that She loves us and will never abandon us and will always be with us. She is our Mother. Likewise She invites us to love Her and to follow Her messages. We can all identify with the love between a mother and her child. Her messages however, consist of loving and caring motherly pleas, constantly urging us to amend our lives, to pray always, to do penance and make sacrifices and to convert and return to Our Lord, for it is only through Our Lord Jesus Christ that we obtain salvation and eternal life.

Clearly, She is sent to us by God to help us in these difficult days. Our Blessed Mother is in Heaven. She is alive today; and will live forever. Of this we are convinced in faith and in fact, every time Our Blessed Virgin Mary presents Herself to some visionary upon this earth. She moves, She talks, She walks, She sings, She prays, She smiles; and gives us true messages from God.

Our Lady has partially revealed to us Her own personality, and has given us reassurance and reason to hope for Eternal Life; in fact, She has given us a glimpse of Paradise, which is Her permanent residence.

We believe, and the Church teaches, that Our Blessed Virgin Mary was conceived without sin (the Immaculate Conception); that She was ever Virgin and that She gave birth to Her Divine Son Jesus (the Nativity); that She was assumed into Heaven, body and soul (the Assumption); and that She was crowned Queen of Heaven (the Coronation). Further, She has the highest place in Heaven for a creature, as Queen of Heaven, Queen of the Angels, and Queen of all the Martyrs and Saints. It is little wonder that Almighty God should send His most precious jewel as His own faithful

Ambassador in times of great need, peril and turmoil on this, His earth. Our Lady assures us that we are all Her children; those who love Her and believe in Her, as well as those who despise Her. Our Lady loves us and prays for us all; and She has done so for 2000 years, unceasingly interceding for us before the Throne of the Most Holy Trinity.

During the many reported apparitions Our Lady has shown us Her own emotions, Her virtues of character, Her brilliant spirit, Her intellect and Her own person and personality. We may ponder: 'Does She not show us and share with us Her very own soul?' We are so privileged and blessed to be part of Her Heavenly existence, with the promise and prospect of our own Eternal Life.

All the visionaries agree that Our Blessed Mother presents Herself to them as so beautiful as to be beyond compare (a beauty that radiates from within Her); this is true and real whether Her eyes be blue or brown, whether Her hair be blonde or dark, and whatever mode of dress or adornment covers Our Lady. And Her voice is Heavenly; indescribably beautiful. We are reminded of Our Lady's splendor and beauty so melodiously described in Song of Songs, Chapter 2:14:

>'Show me Your face,
> let me hear Your voice,
>   for Your voice is sweet and
>   Your face is beautiful.'

During some of the apparitions Our Blessed Mother has cried and has appeared sad as well as happy. Sometimes She would pray with the seers, and sometimes She would sing with the crowds and actually request specific songs. Our Lady displayed a vast knowledge of the future. She made accurate predictions, as well as promises to some of the seers. She gave secrets to many of the seers and also gave warnings of events to come. Our Lady often quoted from, or referred to, certain passages in Sacred Scripture. Through Our Blessed Mother, God performed many wondrous signs and miracles, as well as miraculous healings, some of which are happening at various apparition sites even to this very day. She displayed Her great love and generosity in especially blessing the waters and springs at several of the apparition sites. Our Lady gave prayers and special devotions to some of the seers; and also exposed Her Immaculate Heart to several of the visionaries. Her message is Love. What a splendid pinnacle of womanhood is Our Blessed Mother!

It seems fair to say that Our Lady's personality is truly that of a loving and caring mother. One who unselfishly gives and sacrifices for all of us in order that we may one day be with Her and Her Divine Son Jesus and all the angels and saints in Heaven. How marvelous this Love! Could we but imitate and share in such Love, the world would truly be transformed!

The Church teaches that Our Blessed Mother has all the virtues *par excellence*; and is full of grace. She has in fact revealed to the seers some glimpse of Her virtues. Her humility, charity, compassion, faith, kindness, mercy, purity, piety, modesty, goodness, truth, generosity, fortitude, justice and patience can be gleaned from Her demeanor during the several apparitions and from the messages given to the visionaries by Our Blessed Virgin Mary. Would that one day Our Blessed Mother will be loved as much on earth as She is loved in Heaven.

This current work consists of some 60 apparition sites of Our Blessed Mother occurring during this 20th Century. About 8,000 apparitions are reported for these 60 sites alone. More than one hundred other locutions and apparition sites were reviewed and omitted from this work, for several different reasons. No judgment or inference, pro or con, is made regarding any such cases not reported here.

— Furthermore some apparitions were omitted because published sources were not available for various seers receiving apparitions, locutions or messages, some of which are ongoing to this day.

— Several of the cases reported in this work, and several other seers not reported here, have received or may be presently receiving, apparitions and/or messages from Jesus. Of course, the messages from Jesus are of primary importance, however, this work focuses mainly on Our Lady's apparitions.

— In addition there are many 20th century 'Mystics' who have received, or are presently receiving, messages from Our Lord and from Our Lady which are not reported here. Also silent apparitions, such as those occurring at Knock, Ireland and Zeitun, Egypt are not included in this work.

— Finally many important apparitions and messages occurred during the 19th Century and earlier, none of which are reported in this work. This does not lessen the importance of those apparitions or messages. Especially noted are the apparitions occurring at Mexico City, La Salette, Rue de Bac and Lourdes. Perhaps other works in print, or to be published, consider these various apparitions not included in this work.

In a word, this 20th Century has been rich in reported apparitions of Our Blessed Mother and of Our Lord; perhaps like no century before. We must pray for our Church, for our clergy and for our religious leaders, and also for these seers, visionaries and locutionists, who are very frequently under great stress; on the other hand we must give thanks to God for these apparitions, and messages which Our Blessed Mother is permitted to give to us. It is good for us to pray for discernment and guidance in these matters. May we always remain open and receptive to the graces which God sends to us.

Peter Heintz

TIME-LINE
A Guide to Apparitions

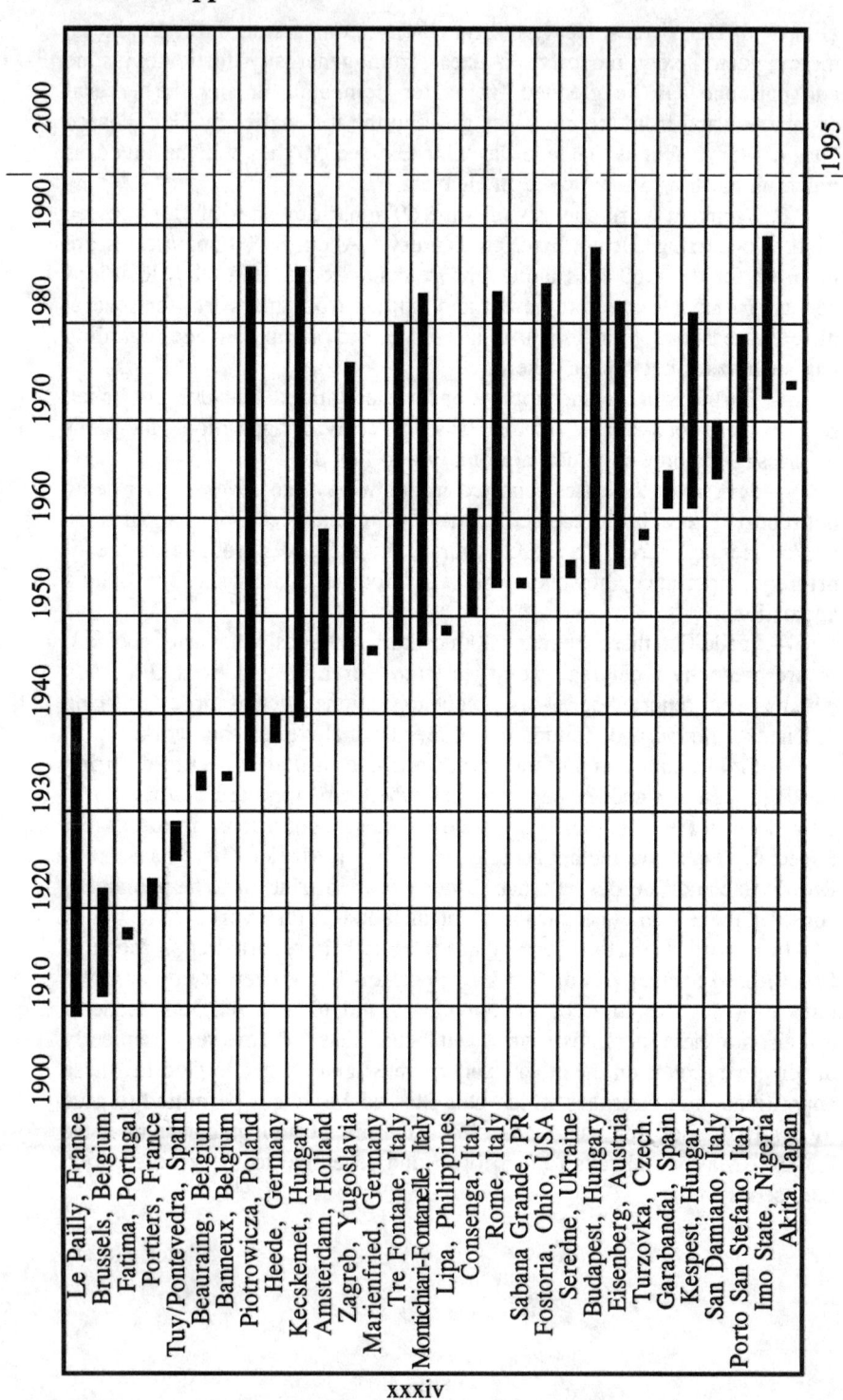

Location	Period
Le Pailly, France	1906–1938
Brussels, Belgium	1908–1920
Fatima, Portugal	1915
Portiers, France	1918–1922
Tuy/Pontevedra, Spain	1925–1926
Beauraing, Belgium	1931
Banneux, Belgium	1931
Piotrowicza, Poland	1937–1985
Heede, Germany	1937–1940
Kecskemet, Hungary	1938–1985
Amsterdam, Holland	1945–1959
Zagreb, Yugoslavia	1945–1975
Marienfried, Germany	1946
Tre Fontane, Italy	1947–1980
Montichiari-Fontanelle, Italy	1947–1983
Lipa, Philippines	1948
Consenga, Italy	1951
Rome, Italy	1952–1983
Sabana Grande, PR	1953
Fostoria, Ohio, USA	1954–1955
Seredne, Ukraine	1954
Budapest, Hungary	1961–1987
Eisenberg, Austria	1956–1982
Turzovka, Czech.	1958
Garabandal, Spain	1961–1965
Kespest, Hungary	1961–1981
San Damiano, Italy	1961–1970
Porto San Stefano, Italy	1964–1978
Imo State, Nigeria	1972–1988
Akita, Japan	1973

xxxiv

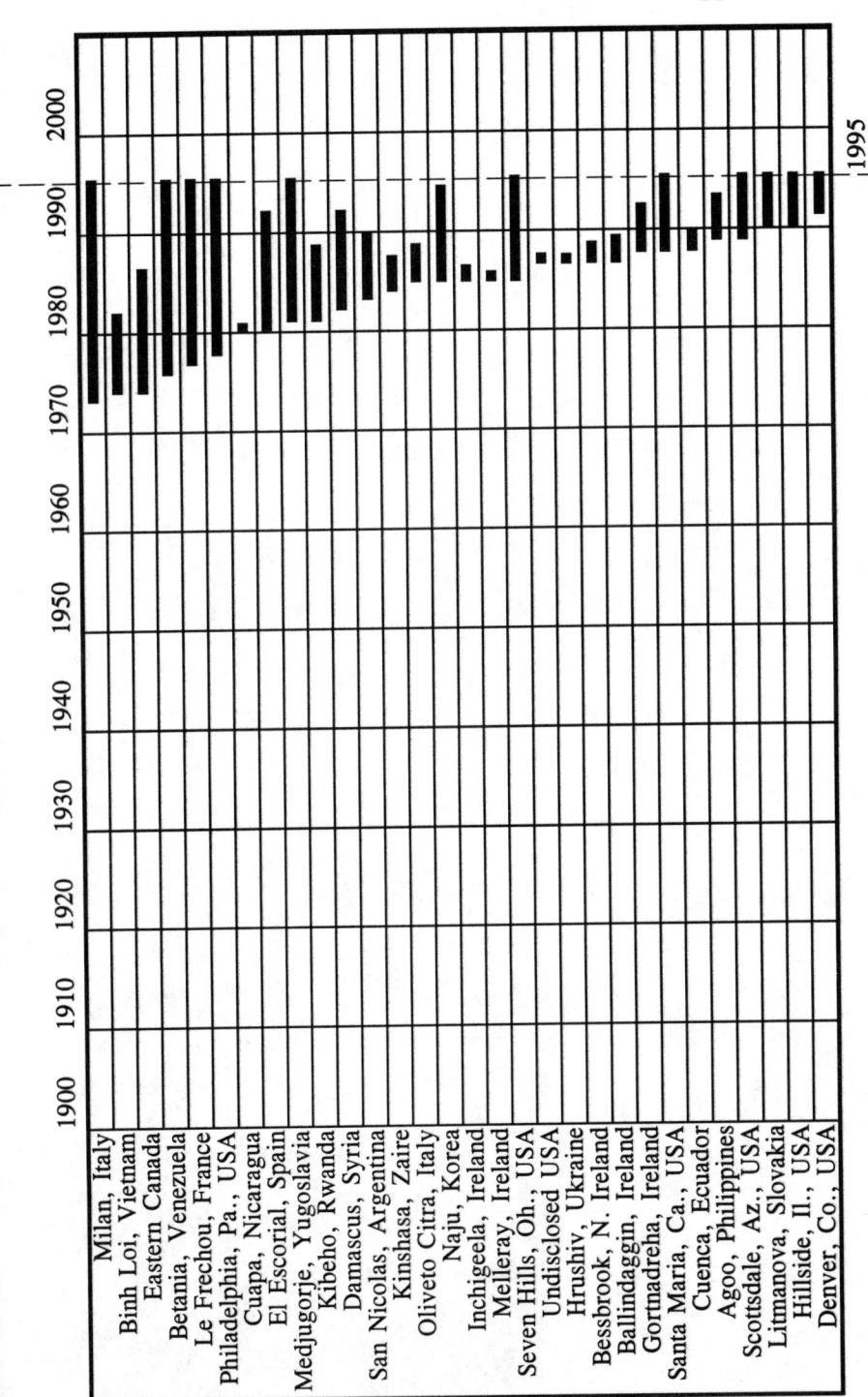

Time-Line
A Guide to Apparitions

Location	Years
Milan, Italy	~1970–1993
Binh Loi, Vietnam	~1978–1982
Eastern Canada	~1972–1985
Betania, Venezuela	~1976–1993
Le Frechou, France	~1975–1993
Philadelphia, Pa., USA	~1977–1993
Cuapa, Nicaragua	~1980–1982
El Escorial, Spain	~1980–1993
Medjugorje, Yugoslavia	~1981–1987
Kibeho, Rwanda	~1981–1989
Damascus, Syria	~1982–1990
San Nicolas, Argentina	~1983–1988
Kinshasa, Zaire	~1986–1988
Oliveto Citra, Italy	~1985–1993
Naju, Korea	~1985–1988
Inchigeela, Ireland	1985
Melleray, Ireland	1985
Seven Hills, Oh., USA	~1984–1993
Undisclosed USA	1988
Hrushiv, Ukraine	1987
Bessbrook, N. Ireland	~1987–1988
Ballindaggin, Ireland	1988
Gortnadreha, Ireland	~1988–1990
Santa Maria, Ca., USA	~1988–1993
Cuenca, Ecuador	~1988–1990
Agoo, Philippines	~1989–1993
Scottsdale, Az., USA	~1989–1993
Litmanova, Slovakia	~1990–1993
Hillside, Il., USA	~1990–1993
Denver, Co., USA	~1991–1993

xxxv

WORLD MAP
A Guide to Apparitions

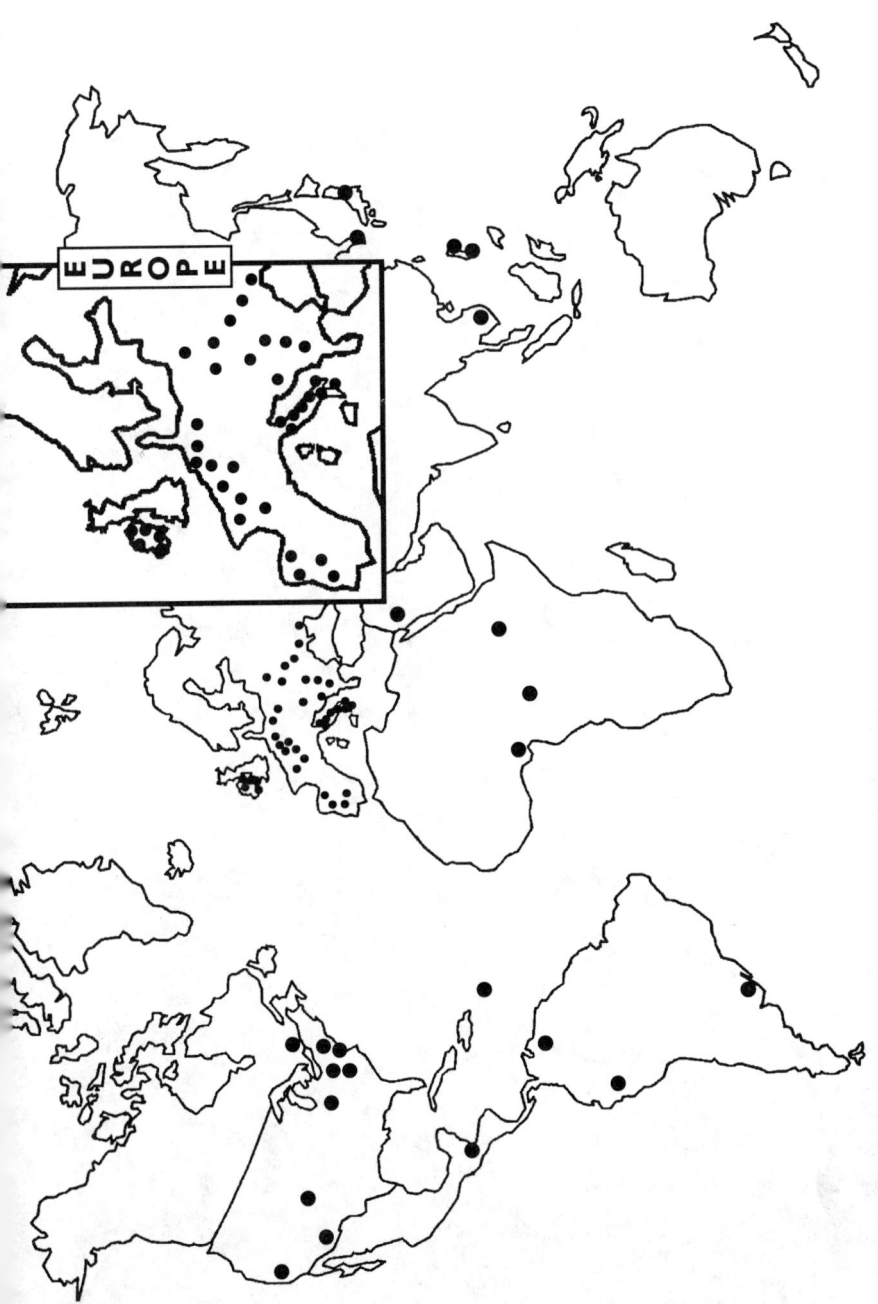

A Guide to Apparitions of our Blessed Virgin Mary, PART I: 20th Century Apparitions

TOPICAL INDEX

- A - Apparition Sites
- B - Church Approved
- C - Clergy/Religious
- D - Country
- E - Description of Our Lady
- F - Devotion/Mission
- G - Healings Reported
- H - Host Miraculously Received
- I - Prayers Taught the Seers
- J - Predictions/Promises
- K - Prophecies/Warnings of Chastisement
- L - Primary Messages
- M - Request Chapel/Shrine Built
- N - Secrets Given to the Seers
- O - Seers
- P - Statue Phenomena
- Q - Stigmata
- R - Titles of Our Lady

A - Apparition Sites

1. Agoo, Philippines 612
2. Akita, Japan 308
3. Amsterdam, Holland . . . 100
4. Ballindaggin, Ireland. . . 567
5. Banneux, Belgium 68
6. Beauraing, Belgium 57
7. Bessbrook, N. Ireland . . 559
8. Betania, Venezuela 362
9. Binh Loi, Vietnam. 334
10. Brussels, Belgium 14
11. Budapest, Hungary 216
12. Consenga, Italy 165
13. Cuapa, Nicaragua 384
14. Cuenca, Ecuador 600
15. Damascus, Syria 442
16. Denver/Golden, Co., USA 664
17. Eastern Canada 351
18. Eisenberg, Austria 224
19. El Escorial, Spain 396
20. Fatima, Portugal 22
21. Fostoria, Oh., USA 198
22. Garabandal, Spain 256
23. Gortnadreha, Ireland . . . 575
24. Heede, Germany 85
25. Hillside, Il., USA 653
26. Hrushiv, Ukraine 545
27. Imo State, Nigeria 296
28. Inchigeela, Ireland 505
29. Kecskemet, Hungary . . . 91
30. Kespest, Hungary 266

──── TOPICAL INDEX ────
A Guide to Apparitions

31 Kibeho, Rwanda 425	(Le Frechou, France) . . 371
32 Kinshasa, Zaire 465	2 Fr. (Don) Stefano Gobbi,
33 Le Frechou, France 371	Company of St. Paul
34 Le Pailly, France 1	(Milan, Italy) 320
35 Lipa, Philippines 151	3 Fr. Pere Lamy, Oblates of
36 Litmanova, Slovakia 643	St. Francis de Sales
37 Marienfried, Germany . . . 122	(Le Pailly, France) 1
38 Medjugorje, Yugoslavia . . 404	4 Brother Joseph Francis
39 Melleray, Ireland 514	(Eastern Canada) 351
40 Milan, Italy 320	5 Sr. Agnes Katsuko
41 Montichiari/Fontanelle, Italy . 139	Sasagawa, Convent of the
42 Naju, Korea 491	Servants of the Eucharist
43 Oliveto Citra, Italy 478	(Akita, Japan) 308
44 Philadelphia, Pa., USA . . 378	6 Sr. Dolores
45 Piotrowicza, Poland 76	(Budapest, Hungary) . . . 216
46 Portiers, France 39	7 Sr. Elena Aiello
47 Porto San Stefano, Italy . . 287	(Consenga, Italy) 165
48 Rome, Italy 176	8 Sr. Elena della Croce, Maid
49 Sabana Grande, Puerto Rico 184	of Jesus in the Most Holy
50 San Damiano, Italy 275	Sacrament of the Altar
51 San Nicolas, Argentina . . 452	(Rome, Italy) 176
52 Santa Maria, Ca., USA . . 586	9 Sr. Josefa Menendez, The
53 Scottsdale, Az., USA . . . 629	Society of the Sacred Heart
54 Seredne, Ukraine 209	(Portiers, France) 39
55 Seven Hills, Oh., USA . . 523	10 Sr. Maria das Dores,
56 Tre Fontane, Italy 131	Sisters of St. Dorothy
57 Turzovka, Czechoslovakia 242	a (Fatima, Portugal) . . . 22
58 Tuy/Pontevedra, Spain . . 50	b (Tuy/Pontevedra, Spain) 50
59 Undisclosed, USA 534	11 Sr. Maria Natalia, Order of
60 Zagreb, Yugoslavia 115	the Sisters of St. Magdalene
	(Kecskemet, Hungary) . . 91
B - Church Approved	12 Sr. Mildred Mary Neuzil,
	Cloistered Sisters of the
1 Akita, Japan 319	Precious Blood
2 Banneux, Belgium 75	(Fostoria, Oh., USA) . . 198
3 Beauraing, Belgium 66	13 Novice Teresita Castillo,
4 Betania, Venezuela 370	Convent of Discalced
5 Fatima, Portugal 36	Carmelites
6 Tuy/Pontevedra 55	(Lipa, Philippines) 151
C - Clergy/Religious	**D - Country**
1 (Bshp) Msgr. Jean-Marie,	Argentina
Society of Notre Dame	San Nicolas 452

xl

Topical Index
A Guide to Apparitions

Austria
  Eisenberg 224
Belgium
  Banneux 68
  Beauraing 57
  Brussels 14
Canada
  Eastern Canada 351
Czechoslovakia
  Turzovka 242
Ecuador
  Cuenca 600
France
  Le Frechou 371
  Le Pailly 1
  Portiers 39
Germany
  Heede 85
  Marienfried 122
Holland
  Amsterdam 100
Hungary
  Budapest 216
  Kecskemet 91
  Kespest 266
Ireland
  Ballindaggin 567
  Gortnadreha 575
  Inchigeela 505
  Melleray 514
Italy
  Consenga 165
  Milan 320
  Montichiari-Fontanelle . . 139
  Oliveto Citra 478
  Porto San Stefano 287
  Rome 176
  San Damiano 275
  Tre Fontane 131
Japan
  Akita 308
Korea
  Naju 491

Nicaragua
  Cuapa 384
Nigeria
  Imo State 296
No. Ireland
  Bessbrook 559
Philippines
  Agoo 612
  Lipa 151
Poland
  Piotrowicza 76
Portugal
  Fatima 22
Puerto Rico
  Sabana Grande 184
Rwanda
  Kibeho 425
Slovakia
  Litmanova 643
Spain
  El Escorial 396
  Garabandal 256
  Tuy-Pontevedra 50
Syria
  Damascus 442
Ukraine
  Hrushiv 545
  Seredne 209
United States
  Denver/Golden, Co. . . . 664
  Fostoria, Oh. 198
  Hillside, Il. 653
  Philadelphia, Pa. 378
  Santa Maria, Ca. 586
  Scottsdale, Az. 629
  Seven Hills, Oh. 523
  Undisclosed, USA 534
Venezuela
  Betania 362
Vietnam
  Binh Loi 334
Yugoslavia
  Medjugorje 404
  Zagreb 115

TOPICAL INDEX
A Guide to Apparitions

Zaire
Kinshasa 465

E - Description of Our Lady

Pages: 2, 15, 23, 40, 51, 58, 69, 86, 92, 102, 116, 122, 132, 140, 152, 166, 177, 185, 199, 210, 217, 225, 243, 257, 267, 276, 288, 309, 335, 352, 363, 384, 397, 405, 427, 443, 453, 467, 481, 492, 507, 515, 524, 535, 546, 560, 568, 576, 587, 601, 613, 631, 644, 654, 665.

F - Devotion/Mission

1 Apostolate of Holy Motherhood
Undisclosed, USA 540

2 Beads of the Seven Sorrows
Kibeho, Rwanda 437

3 Brown Scapular
Inchigeela, Ireland 511
Santa Maria, Ca., USA . 594
Undisclosed, USA ... 540

4 Cenacles of Prayer
Milan, Italy 328

5 Chaste Mary
Kinshasa, Zaire 468

6 Communion of Reparation and Consecration to the Immaculate Heart of Mary (Five First Saturdays)
Beauraing, Belgium ... 62
Consenga, Italy 169
Cuapa, Nicaragua 392
El Escorial, Spain 400
Fatima, Portugal 29
Gortnadreha, Ireland .. 581
Imo State, Nigeria 303
Lipa, Philippines 159
Marienfried, Germany . . 127
Milan, Italy 329

Naju, Korea 498
Philadelphia, Pa., USA . 381
San Nicolas, Argentina . 460
Tuy-Pontevedra, Spain . 53

7 Congregation of the Servants of Jesus and Mary
Le Pailly, France 1

8 Consecration to the Sacred Heart of Jesus (Five First Fridays) and Immaculate Heart of Mary
Binh Loi, Vietnam 346
Consenga, Italy 169
Eastern Canada 357
Le Frechou, France ... 374
Medjugorje, Yugoslavia . 416
Portiers, France 45
Rome, Italy 181
San Nicolas, Argentina . 460
Tre Fontane, Italy 135

9 Cross Project
Santa Maria, Ca., USA . 593

10 Devotion to the Christ Child
Undisclosed, USA 540

11 Family Holy Hour
Kepset, Hungary 270

12 Flame of Love
Kespest, Hungary 270

13 Four Steps to Holiness
Seven Hills, Oh., USA . 530

14 Great Double Novena to Honor the Sacred Heart of Jesus and the Immaculate Heart of Mary
Kecskemet, Hungary . . 94

15 Honor Our Lady on Saturdays
Lipa, Philippines ... 159

16 Hour of Grace at Noon December 8th
Montichiari/Fontanelle, Italy . 145

xlii

—— TOPICAL INDEX ——
A Guide to Apparitions

17 **House of the Kingdom of God and the Reconciliation of Souls**
   Rome, Italy 181
18 **Last Marian Dogma (Co-Redemptrix, Mediatrix, Advocate)**
   Amsterdam, Holland . . 111
19 **Life Offering**
   Budapest, Hungary 220
20 **Merciful Heart of Jesus**
   Cuenca, Ecuador 604
21 **Mystical Church of Atonement**
   Seven Hills, Oh., USA . 525
22 **Rosa Mystica Devotion to the Immaculate Heart of Mary for Religious Communities**
   Montichiari-Fontanelle, Italy 145
23 **Seven Keys to Heaven**
   Agoo, Philippines 623
24 **Sorrowful and Immaculate Heart of Mary**
   Brussels, Belgium 18
   San Damiano, Italy 281
   Zagreb, Yugoslavia 119
25 **Storm of Prayer**
   Eisenberg, Austria 236
26 **Work of Frechou (Vocations)**
   Le Frechou, France 372
27 **World Wide Communion of Reparation**
   Montichiari-Fontanelle, Italy 145

G - Healings Reported

Pages: 13, 20, 35, 49, 55, 65, 74, 83, 90, 98, 130, 138, 149, 164, 183, 196, 215, 223, 240, 254, 264, 285, 294, 318, 350, 360, 369, 377, 383, 403, 421, 440, 450, 463, 477, 490, 503, 513, 522, 558, 565, 574, 584, 598, 610, 627, 641, 652, 662, 673.

H - Host Miraculously Received

1 **Conchita Gonzalez**
   Garabandal, Spain 262
2 **Enzo Aliocci**
   Porto San Stefano, Italy . 293
3 **Bishop Jean-Marie**
   Le Frechou, France . . . 375
4 **Judiel Nieva**
   Agoo, Philippines 624
5 **Julia Kim**
   Naju, Korea 500
6 **Sr Lucia dos Santos**
   Fatima, Portugal 32
   (also Jacinta Marto & Francisco Marto received contents of the Chalice) . 32
7 **Maria Esperanza**
   Betania, Venezuela 368
8 **Patricia Talbot**
   Cuenca, Ecuador 607
9 **Novice Teresita Castillo**
   Lipa, Philippines 160

I - Prayers Taught the Seers

Pages: 18, 28, 43, 53, 62, 72, 94, 111, 126, 169, 180, 203, 219, 235, 270, 301, 312, 357, 374, 392, 415, 436, 447, 459, 487, 530, 539, 554, 572, 620, 638, 649, 671.

J - Predictions/Promises

Pages: 11, 19, 32, 47, 63, 73, 82, 89, 97, 112, 119, 128, 137, 146, 161, 171, 182, 194, 214, 222, 238, 251, 262, 271, 283, 293, 304, 315, 331, 348, 368, 376, 382, 393, 400, 419, 439, 449, 461, 475, 488, 501, 512, 520, 531, 542, 555, 565, 573, 582, 596, 607, 625, 639, 650, 661, 672.

TOPICAL INDEX
A Guide to Apparitions

K - Prophecies/Warnings of Chastisement

Pages: 12, 19, 33, 82, 89, 97, 112, 120, 128, 146, 161, 171, 182, 194, 206, 214, 238, 252, 262, 273, 284, 293, 305, 315, 331, 348, 359, 368, 382, 393, 401, 419, 439, 462, 475, 489, 501, 512, 521, 532, 542, 555, 565, 583, 596, 608, 626, 650, 661, 672.

L - Primary Messages

1 Adoration of the Blessed Sacrament
- Denver/Golden, Co., USA . . 669
- Eisenberg, Austria 234
- Garabandal, Spain 260
- Undisclosed, USA 539

2 Angels
- Cuenca, Ecuador 604
- Milan, Italy 329
- Montichiari/Fontanelle, Italy . 144

3 Charity-Love
- Banneux, Belgium 71
- Cuapa, Nicaragua 391
- Cuenca, Ecuador 603
- Damascus, Syria 446
- Kinshasa, Zaire 474
- Le Frechou, France 374
- Naju, Korea 496
- Portiers, France 42
- Scottsdale, Az., USA . . 637

4 Church-Clergy
- Akita, Japan 310
- Amsterdam, Holland . . . 110
- Binh Loi, Vietnam 345
- Eisenberg, Austria 234
- Garabandal, Spain 260
- Imo State, Nigeria 301
- Milan, Italy 325
- San Damiano, Italy 281
- Seredne, Ukraine 212

- Undisclosed, USA 539

5 Conversion
- Agoo, Philippines 620
- Ballindaggin, Ireland . . 571
- Beauraing, Belgium . . . 60
- Bessbrook, No. Ireland . 563
- Betania, Venezuela 367
- Binh Loi, Vietnam 344
- Cuenca, Ecuador 604
- Eastern Canada 356
- Eisenberg, Austria 233
- El Escorial, Spain 399
- Fatima, Portugal 25
- Heede, Germany 87
- Hillside, Il., USA 658
- Hrushiv, Ukraine 553
- Imo State, Nigeria 299
- Kibeho, Rwanda 434
- Kinshasa, Zaire 473
- Le Pailly, France 8
- Litmanova, Slovakia . . . 648
- Medjugorje, Yugoslavia . 414
- Melleray, Ireland 518
- Sabana Grande, Puerto Rico 188
- San Damiano, Italy 281
- San Nicolas, Argentina . 457
- Santa Maria, Ca., USA . 593
- Scottsdale, Az., USA . . 637
- Seven Hills, Oh., USA . 527
- Turzovka, Czechoslovakia 249

6 Eucharist
- Amsterdam, Holland . . 104
- Budapest, Hungary 219
- Cuenca, Ecuador 603
- Denver/Golden, Co., USA 668
- Garabandal, Spain 260
- Gortnadreha, Ireland . . 580
- Hillside, Il., USA 659
- Inchigeela, Ireland 510
- Kecskemet, Hungary . . 94
- Milan, Italy 328
- Rome, Italy 179
- San Damiano, Italy 281
- San Nicolas, Argentina . 457

TOPICAL INDEX
A Guide to Apparitions

Seven Hills, Oh., USA .	527
Undisclosed, USA	538
7 Fasting	
Agoo, Philippines	619
Ballindaggin, Ireland . .	571
Bessbrook, No. Ireland .	563
Budapest, Hungary	219
Cuenca, Ecuador	603
Gortnadreha, Ireland . .	580
Inchigeela, Ireland	510
Litmanova, Slovakia . . .	648
Medjugorje, Yugoslavia .	414
San Nicolas, Argentina .	457
Santa Maria, Ca., USA .	593
Scottsdale, Az., USA . .	638
8 Forgiveness	
Cuapa, Nicaragua	391
Damascus, Syria	446
Hillside, Il., USA	658
Kibeho, Rwanda	434
Kinshasa, Zaire	474
Naju, Korea	496
San Nicolas, Argentina .	457
Seven Hills, Oh., USA .	527
9 Humility	
Betania, Venezuela	366
Denver/Golden, Co., USA	669
Kibeho, Rwanda	434
Lipa, Philippines	157
Portiers, France	42
10 Mass	
Cuenca, Ecuador	603
Denver/Golden, Co., USA	668
Gortnadreha, Ireland . .	581
Hillside, Il., USA	659
Medjugorje, Yugoslavia .	414
Milan, Italy	328
Rome, Italy	179
San Damiano, Italy . . .	281
Zagreb, Yugoslavia . . .	118
11 Modernism	
Le Pailly, France	8
12 Peace	
Cuapa, Nicaragua	391

Inchigeela, Ireland	510
Medjugorje, Yugoslavia .	413
Melleray, Ireland	518
13 Penance	
Agoo, Philippines	619
Akita, Japan	311
Bessbrook, No. Ireland .	563
Consenga, Italy	167
Cuenca, Ecuador	603
Eisenberg, Austria	234
El Escorial, Spain	399
Fatima, Portugal	25
Garabandal, Spain	260
Gortnadreha, Ireland . . .	580
Hillside, Il., USA	658
Hrushiv, Ukraine	553
Imo State, Nigeria	301
Inchigeela, Ireland	510
Kibeho, Rwanda	434
Le Frechou, France	374
Le Pailly, France	8
Lipa, Philippines	157
Litmanova, Slovakia . . .	648
Medjugorje, Yugoslavia .	414
Milan, Italy	327
Montichiari/Fontanelle, Italy	143
Naju, Korea	496
Oliveto Citra, Italy	487
Philadelphia, Pa., USA .	381
Piotrowicza, Poland . . .	80
Porto San Stefano, Italy .	291
Rome, Italy	179
Sabana Grande, Puerto Rico	188
San Damiano, Italy	280
San Nicolas, Argentina .	457
Scottsdale, Az., USA . .	638
Seredne, Ukraine	212
Turzovka, Czechoslovakia	248
Zagreb, Yugoslavia . . .	117
14 Prayer	
Agoo, Philippines	618
Akita, Japan	311
Amsterdam, Holland . .	105
Ballindaggin, Ireland . .	570

xlv

TOPICAL INDEX
A Guide to Apparitions

Banneux, Belgium	71	San Damiano, Italy	280
Beauraing, Belgium	60	San Nicolas, Argentina	456
Bessbrook, No. Ireland	563	Santa Maria, Ca., USA	592
Betania, Venezuela	367	Scottsdale, Az., USA	636
Binh Loi, Vietnam	345	Seven Hills, Oh., USA	526
Budapest, Hungary	219	Tre Fontane, Italy	134
Consenga, Italy	167	Turzovka, Czechoslovakia	248
Cuapa, Nicaragua	391	Tuy/Pontevedra, Spain	52
Cuenca, Ecuador	603	Undisclosed, USA	538
Damascus, Syria	446	Zagreb, Yugoslavia	117
Denver/Golden, Co., USA	668	**15 Purity**	
Eastern Canada	356	Betania, Venezuela	366
Eisenberg, Austria	232	Fostoria, Oh., USA	201
El Escorial, Spain	398	Hrushiv, Ukraine	553
Fatima, Portugal	25	Porto San Stefano, Italy	291
Fostoria, Oh., USA	201	Undisclosed, USA	538
Garabandal, Spain	260	**16 Reconciliation**	
Gortnadreha, Ireland	579	Agoo, Philippines	620
Heede, Germany	87	Binh Loi, Vietnam	344
Hillside, Il., USA	657	Denver/Golden, Co., USA	668
Hrushiv, Ukraine	552	Gortnadreha, Ireland	580
Imo State, Nigeria	300	Hillside, Il., USA	659
Inchigeela, Ireland	509	Inchigeela, Ireland	510
Kecskemet, Hungary	94	Kibeho, Rwanda	434
Kespest, Hungary	269	Kinshasa, Zaire	474
Kibeho, Rwanda	434	Undisclosed, USA	538
Kinshasa, Zaire	473	**17 Reparation**	
Le Pailly, France	8	Akita, Japan	310
Le Frechou, France	374	Consenga, Italy	167
Lipa, Philippines	157	Eastern Canada	356
Litmanova, Slovakia	647	Eisenberg, Austria	233
Marienfried, Germany	125	Fatima, Portugal	26
Medjugorje, Yugoslavia	413	Imo State, Nigeria	301
Melleray, Ireland	518	Kecskemet, Hungary	94
Milan, Italy	326	Montichiari/Fontanelle, Italy	143
Montichiari/Fontanelle, Italy	143	Naju, Korea	496
Naju, Korea	495	Porto San Stefano, Italy	291
Oliveto Citra, Italy	487	Portiers, France	42
Philadelphia, Pa., USA	380	Santa Maria, Ca., USA	593
Piotrowicza, Poland	80	Seven Hills, Oh., USA	528
Portiers, France	42	Tuy/Pontevedra, Spain	52
Porto San Stefano, Italy	290	Zagreb, Yugoslavia	117
Rome, Italy	179	**18 Rosary**	
Sabana Grande, Puerto Rico	188	Agoo, Philippines	619

— TOPICAL INDEX —
A Guide to Apparitions

Akita, Japan	311	Seredne, Ukraine	212
Ballindaggin, Ireland	571	Seven Hills, Oh., USA	526
Banneux, Belgium	71	Tre Fontane, Italy	134
Beauraing, Belgium	60	Turzovka, Czechoslovakia	248
Bessbrook, No. Ireland	564	Tuy/Pontevedra, Spain	52
Binh Loi, Vietnam	344	Undisclosed, USA	538
Budapest, Yugoslavia	219	Zagreb, Yugoslavia	118
Consenga, Italy	167	**19 Sacrifice and Suffering**	
Cuapa, Nicaragua	391	Akita, Japan	311
Cuenca, Ecuador	603	Ballindaggin, Ireland	571
Denver/Golden, Co., USA	668	Banneux, Belgium	71
Eastern Canada	356	Beauraing, Belgium	60
Eisenberg, Austria	233	Budapest, Hungary	218
El Escorial, Spain	399	Consenga, Italy	167
Fatima, Portugal	25	Eastern Canada	356
Fostoria, Oh., USA	202	Eisenberg, Austria	233
Garabandal, Spain	260	El Escorial, Spain	399
Gortnadreha, Ireland	580	Fatima, Portugal	25
Heede, Germany	87	Fostoria, Oh., USA	201
Hillside, Il., USA	657	Garabandal, Spain	260
Hrushiv, Ukraine	553	Gortnadreha, Ireland	580
Imo State, Nigeria	301	Hillside, Il., USA	658
Inchigeela, Ireland	510	Hrushiv, Ukraine	553
Kibeho, Rwanda	434	Kespest, Hungary	269
Kinshasa, Zaire	473	Kibeho, Rwanda	434
Le Frechou, France	374	Litmanova, Slovakia	648
Le Pailly, France	7	Marienfried, Germany	125
Lipa, Philippines	157	Milan, Italy	327
Litmanova, Slovakia	647	Naju, Korea	496
Marienfried, Germany	125	Philadelphia, Pa., USA	381
Medjugorje, Yugoslavia	414	Portiers, France	42
Melleray, Ireland	518	Porto San Stefano, Italy	291
Milan, Italy	326	Rome, Italy	180
Montichiari/Fontanelle, Italy	143	Santa Maria, Ca., USA	593
Naju, Korea	495	**20 Simplicity**	
Oliveto Citra, Italy	487	Betania, Venezuela	366
Philadelphia, Pa., USA	381	Denver/Golden, Co., USA	669
Piotrowicza, Poland	80	Lipa, Philippines	157
Porto San Stefano, Italy	291	**21 Spiritual Combat**	
Rome, Italy	179	Consenga, Italy	167
Sabana Grande, Puerto Rico	188	Cuenca, Ecuador	603
San Damiano, Italy	280	Naju, Korea	496
Santa Maria, Ca., USA	593	Porto San Stefano, Italy	291
San Nicolas, Argentina	456	San Nicolas, Argentina	458

TOPICAL INDEX
A Guide to Apparitions

Seven Hills, Oh., USA . 529
22 Unity
    Amsterdam, Holland . . . 110
    Damascus, Syria 446
    Denver/Golden, Co., USA 669
    Tre Fontane, Italy 134
23 Youth
    Kibeho, Rwanda 434
    Hrushiv, Ukraine 553
    San Damiano, Italy 281
    San Nicolas, Argentina . 458

**M - Request Chapel/
Shrine Built**

Pages: 12, 34, 65, 74, 98, 113, 129, 137, 148, 163, 183, 196, 208, 215, 253, 285, 369, 376, 394, 402, 439, 450, 463, 489, 503, 532, 557, 574, 597, 609, 627, 651.

N - Secrets Given to the Seers

Pages: 9, 18, 30, 46, 54, 62, 72, 81, 88, 111, 127, 135, 145, 160, 193, 213, 237, 250, 261, 292, 329, 346, 358, 417, 448, 474, 488, 511, 554, 582, 595, 606, 623, 639, 649.

O - Seers

Agoo, Philippines
    Judiel Nieva 612
Akita, Japan
    Sr. Agnes Katsuko
        Sasagawa 308
Amsterdam, Holland
    Ida Perleman 100
Ballindaggin, Ireland
    Joanne Farrell 567
Banneux, Belgium
    Mariette Beco 68
Beauraing, Belgium
    Albert Voisin 57

Fernande Voisin 57
Gilberte Voisin 57
Andre Degeimbre 58
Gilberte Degeimbre 58
Bessbrook, No. Ireland
    Beulah Lynch 560
    Mark Trainor 559
Betania, Venezuela
    Maria Esperanza
        Medrano de Bianchini . . 362
Binh Loi, Vietnam
    Stephen Ho Ngoc Anh . . 334
    Theresa 334
Brussels, Belgium
    Berthe Petit 14
Budapest, Hungary
    Sr. Dolores 216
Consenga, Italy
    Sr. Elena Aiello 165
Cuapa, Nicaragua
    Bernardo Martinez 384
Cuenca, Ecuador
    Patricia Talbott (Pachi) . 600
Damascus, Syria
    Mirna (Myrna) Nazzour . 442
Denver/Golden, Co., USA
    Veronica Garcia 664
Eastern Canada,
    Brother Joseph Francis . 351
Eisenberg, Austria
    Aloisia Lex 224
El Escorial, Spain
    Amparo Cuevas 396
Fatima, Portugal
    Jacinta Marto 22
    Francisco Marto 22
    Lucia dos Santos
        (Sr. Maria das Dores) . 22
Fostoria, Oh., USA
    Sr. Mildred Mary Neuzil 198
Garabandal, Spain
    Conchita Gonzalez 257
    Jacinta Gonzalez 256
    Mari Cruz Gonzalez . . . 256

––––– TOPICAL INDEX –––––
A Guide to Apparitions

Mari Cruz Gonzalez . . . 256
Mari Loli Mazon 256
Gortnadreha, Ireland
  Christina Gallagher . . . 575
Heede, Germany
  Anna Schulte 85
  Greata Gansferth 85
  Margaret Gansferth 85
  Susanna Bruns 85
Hillside, Il., USA
  Joseph Reinholtz 653
Hrushiv, Ukraine
  Joseph Terelya 545
  Marina Kizen (Kizyn) . . 545
Imo State, Nigeria
  Innocent Okorie 296
Inchigeela, Ireland
  Kelley Noonan 505
  Marie Vaughan 505
  Mrs. Mary Casey 505
  Rosemary O'Sullivan . . 505
Kecskemet, Hungary
  Sr. Maria Natalia 91
Kespest, Hungary
  Karoly Kindelmann
    (Elizabeth) 266
Kibeho, Rwanda
  Agnes Kamagaju 426
  Alphonsine Mumureke . . 425
  Anathalie
    Mukamazimpaka 425
  Emmanuel Segatashya . . 426
  Marie-Claire
    Mukangango 425
  Stephanie Mukamurenzi . 426
  Vestine Salima 426
Kinshasa, Zaire
  Clementine Denise
    Tshimba (Nana) 465
  Danela Losala 466
  Hortense Yayi Bambile . 465
  Kishabongo Assissa
    (Mado) 466
  Marie-Louise Wetsi . . . 466

Mulimbi Assissa (Leticia) 466
  Umande Mulimbi
    (Celene) 466
  Umande Okita Sumbu
    Amini Fidele (Papa
    Fidele) 465
  Wasongo Assissa (Bruno) 466
Le Frechou, France
  (Bishop) Msgr. Jean-
    Marie 371
Le Pailly, France
  Fr. Pere Lamy 1
Lipa, Philippines
  Novice Teresita Castillo 151
Litmanova, Slovakia
  Katarina (Katika)
    Ceselkova 643
  Iveta (Ivetka) Korcakova 643
Marienfried, Germany
  Barbara Reuss 122
Medjugorje, Yugoslavia
  Ivan Dragicevic 405
  Ivanka Ivankovic Elez . . 404
  Jakov Colo 405
  Mirjana Dragicevic
    Soldo 404
  Marija Pavlovic Lunetti . 405
  Vicka Ivankovic 404
Melleray, Ireland
  Barry Buckley 514
  Tom Cliffe 514
  Ursula O'Rourke 514
Milan, Italy
  Fr.(Don) Stefano Gobbi 320
Montichiari/Fontanelle, Italy
  Pierina Gilli 139
Naju, Korea
  Julia Kim 491
Oliveto Citra, Italy
  Anita Rio 479
  Antonella Giordano 479
  Antonia Ianecce 479
  Carmine Acquaviva . . . 478
  Dino Acquaviva 478

xlix

―― TOPICAL INDEX ――
A Guide to Apparitions

Mafalda Mattia Caputo . 479
Marco DeBellis 479
Sabrina DeBellis 479
Tarcisio DeBiasi 479
Umberto Gagliardi 479
Philadelphia, Pa., USA
  Marianne 378
Piotrowicza, Poland
  Wladyslaw Biernacki . . . 76
Portiers, France
  Sr. Josefa Menendez . . . 39
Porto San Stefano, Italy
  Enzo Alocci 287
Rome, Italy
  Sr. Elena Patriarca
    Leonardi 176
Sabana Grande, Puerto Rico
  Isidra Belen 184
  Juan Angel Collado 184
  Ramonita Belen 184
San Damiano, Italy
  Rosa Quattrini (Mamma
    Rosa) 275
San Nicolas, Argentina
  Gladys Herminia Quiroga
    de Motta 452
Santa Maria, Ca., USA
  Barbara Matthias 587
  Carol Nole 586
Scottsdale, Az., USA
  Annie Ross Fitch 629
  Gianna Talone Sullivan . 629
  Mary Cook 630
  Wendy Nelson 629
Seredne, Ukraine
  Hanya (Ann) 209
Seven Hills, Oh., USA
  Maureen H. 523
Tre Fontane, Italy
  Bruno Cornacchiola . . . 131
  Carlo Cornacchiola 132
  Gianfranco Cornacchiola 131
  Isola Cornacchiola 131
Turzovka, Czechoslovakia

Matous Lasuta 242
Tuy/Pontevedra, Spain
  Sr. Maria das Dores
    (Lucia dos Santos) . . . 50
Undisclosed, USA
  Mariamante 534
Zagreb, Yugoslavia
  Julia 115

P - Statue Phenomena

1 Agoo, Philippines 624
2 Akita, Japan 314
3 Binh Loi, Vietnam 348
4 Consenga, Italy 171
5 Cuapa, Nicaragua 393
6 Cuenca, Ecuador 607
7 Damascus, Syria 448
8 Eastern Canada 358
9 Hillside, Il., USA 660
10 Le Frechou, France 375
11 Le Pailly, France 10
12 Lipa, Philippines 160
13 Melleray, Ireland 520
14 Montichiari-Fontanelle, Italy 146
15 Naju, Korea 500
16 Porto San Stefano, Italy . . 292

Q - Stigmata

1 **Amparo Cuevas**
  El Escorial, Spain 400
2 **Barbara Reuss**
  Marienfried, Germany . 128
3 **Bertha Petit**
  Brussels, Belgium 19
4 **Enzo Alocci**
  Porto San Stefano, Italy 292
5 **Gladys Herminia/
  Quiroga de Motta**
  San Nicolas, Argentina . 461
6 **Innocent Okorie**
  Imo State, Nigeria 303
7 **Julia Kim** Naju, Korea . . 500

1

—— TOPICAL INDEX——
A Guide to Apparitions

8 Maria Esperanza
   Betania, Venezuela 368
9 Mirna (Myrna) Nazzour
   Damascus, Syria 448
10 Msgr. Jean-Marie
   Le Frechou, France . . . 375
11 Sr. Agnes Sasagawa
   Akita, Japan 314
12 Sr. Elena Aiello
   Consenga, Italy 171

R - Titles of Our Lady

1 **All Wonderful Mother**
   Marienfried, Germany . 123
2 **Co-Redemptrix, Mediatrix, Advocate**
   Amsterdam, Holland . . 103
3 **Guardian of the Faith**
   Cuenca, Ecuador 601
4 **Help of Christians**
   Eisenberg, Austria 225
5 **I Am the Major Angel**
   Sabana Grande, Puerto Rico 185
6 **I Am Your Mother**
   Denver/Golden, Co., USA 665
7 **Immaculate Conception**
   Agoo, Philippines 613
   Bessbrook, No. Ireland . 561
   Brussels, Belgium 15
   Montichiari/Fontanelle, Italy 141
   Seredne, Ukraine 210
8 **Immaculate Mother of Jesus Christ**
   Portiers, France 41
9 **Immaculate Queen of Heaven & Earth**
   Agoo, Philippines 613
10 **Immaculate Purity**
   Litmanova, Slovakia . . . 644
11 **Immaculate Virgin**
   Beauraing, Belgium . . . 59
   Fostoria, Oh., USA . . . 200

12 **Lady of Light**
   Philadelphia, Pa., USA . 379
13 **Madonna of the Castle**
   Oliveto Citra, Italy 481
14 **Madonna, the Queen of the World**
   Porto San Stefano, Italy . 288
15 **Mary, Mediatrix of Grace**
   Lipa, Philippines 152
   Montichiari/Fontanelle, Italy 141
16 **Mary, Mother of the Church**
   Montichiari/Fontanelle, Italy 141
17 **Mary, Mother of Mercy and Mother of the Church**
   Le Frechou, France 372
18 **Mary of Grace**
   Montichiari/Fontanelle, Italy 141
19 **Mary of the Rosary of San Nicolas**
   San Nicolas, Argentina . 453
20 **Mary, Queen of Heaven and Earth**
   Seven Hills, Oh. 525
21 **Mary, Queen of Homes**
   Le Frechou, France . . . 372
22 **Mary, Reconciler of All Peoples and Nations**
   Betania, Venezuela . . . 363
23 **Mediatrix of all God's Gifts, Peace and Grace**
   Agoo, Philippines 613
24 **Mediatrix of All Grace**
   Lipa, Philippines 152
25 **Mediatrix of Graces**
   Marienfried, Germany . 123
26 **Miraculous Madonna of the Roses**
   San Damiano, Italy 277
27 **Morning Star**
   Agoo, Philippines 613

TOPICAL INDEX
A Guide to Apparitions

28 Mother of All Peoples
  Rome, Italy 177
29 Mother of Consolation and of the Afflicted
  San Damiano, Italy 277
30 Mother of Exalted Love of God's Creatures
  Zagreb, Yugoslavia . . . 116
31 Mother of God
  Agoo, Philippines 613
  Banneux, Belgium 69
  Beauraing, Belgium . . . 59
  Hillside, Il., USA 655
  Hrushiv, Ukraine 547
  Kinshasa, Zaire 467
  Le Pailly, France 2
  Portiers, France 41
  Undisclosed, USA 535
32 Mother of God and of Justice
  Rome, Italy 177
33 Mother of Jesus Christ
  Bessbrook, No. Ireland . 561
  Budapest, Hungary 217
  Cuapa, Nicaragua 385
  Melleray, Ireland 515
34 Mother of Joy
  Scottsdale, Az., USA . . 631
35 Mother of Love
  San Damiano, Italy 277
36 Mother of Mercy
  Agoo, Philippines 613
  Eisenberg, Austria 225
  Portiers, France 41
  Imo State, Nigeria 297
37 Mother of My Divine Son Jesus Christ
  Litmanova, Slovakia 644
  Montichiari/Fontanelle, Italy 141
38 Mother of Pure Love
  Zagreb, Yugoslavia . . . 116
39 Mother of the Redeemer
  Kinshasa, Zaire 467

40 Mother of Your Redeemer and God
  Portiers, France 41
41 Mother of the Savior
  Banneux, Belgium 69
  Kinshasa, Zaire 467
42 Mother of the Second Advent
  Milan, Italy 322
43 Mother of Sinners
  Agoo, Philippines 613
  Portiers, France 41
44 Mother of the Sorrowful Heart
  Brussels, Belgium 15
45 Mother of Sorrows
  Agoo, Philippines 613
  Kespest, Hungary 267
46 Mother of the True Way to the Father
  Sabana Grande, Puerto Rico 185
47 Mother of Vietnam
  Binh Loi, Vietnam 335
48 Mother of the Word
  Kibeho, Rwanda 428
49 Our Lady of Akita
  Akita, Japan 309
50 Our Lady of All Nations
  Amsterdam, Holland . . . 102
51 Our Lady of America
  Fostoria, Oh., USA . . . 200
52 Our Lady of Consolation
  Oliveto Citra, Italy 481
53 Our Lady of Divine Indwelling
  Fostoria, Oh., USA . . . 200
54 Our Lady of Fatima
  Fatima, Portugal 23
  Tuy/Pontevedra, Spain . 51
55 Our Lady of Graces
  Oliveto Citra, Italy 481
56 Our Lady of the Immaculate Heart
  Santa Maria, Ca., USA . 587

Topical Index
A Guide to Apparitions

57 Our Lady of Mount Carmel
 Garabandal, Spain 258
58 Our Lady Queen of the Golden Roses
 Ballindaggin, Ireland . . . 568
59 Our Lady Queen of Peace
 Medjugorje, Yugoslavia . 405
60 Our Lady of the Rosary
 Eisenberg, Austria 225
 Fatima, Portugal 23
 Tuy/Pontevedra, Spain . 51
61 Our Lady of the Rose of Souls
 Eastern Canada 352
62 Our Lady of Sorrows
 Consenga, Italy 166
 El Escorial, Spain 397
63 Our Lady of Soufanieh
 Damascus, Syria 443
64 Our Lady of Turzovka
 Turzovka, Czechoslovakia 243
65 Protectress of the Faith
 Seven Hills, Oh., USA . 525
66 Queen of All People
 Litmanova, Slovakia . . . 644
67 Queen of Heaven
 Beauraing, Belgium . . . 59
 Imo State, Nigeria 297
68 Queen of Heaven and Earth
 Agoo, Philippines 613
 Seven Hills, Oh. 525
 Undisclosed, USA 535
 Zagreb, Yugoslavia 116
69 Queen of Love
 Oliveto Citra, Italy 481
70 Queen of the Most Holy Rosary
 Eisenberg, Austria 225
 Litmanova, Slovakia . . . 644
 Hillside, Il., USA 655
 Seven Hills, Oh., USA . 525

71 Queen of Peace
 Gortnadreha, Ireland . . . 576
 Hillside, Il., USA 655
 Inchigeela, Ireland 507
 Medjugorje, Yugoslavia 405
72 Queen of the Universe
 Santa Maria, Ca., USA . 587
73 Queen of Victory
 Agoo, Philippines 613
74 Queen of the Whole World
 Imo State, Nigeria 297
 Porto San Stefano, Italy . 288
75 Refuge of Sinners
 Agoo, Philippines 613
 Portiers, France 41
76 Rosa Mystica, the Mystical Rose
 Montichiari/Fontanelle, Italy 141
77 Rose of Souls
 Eastern Canada 352
78 Servant, Mother and Queen
 Litmanova, Slovakia . . . 644
79 Servant of God
 Litmanova, Slovakia . . . 644
80 The Sign of the Living God
 Marienfried, Germany . . 123
81 Victorious Queen of the World
 Kecskemet, Hungary . . . 92
82 Virgin of Light
 Sabana Grande, Puerto Rico 185
83 Virgin Mary of Soufanieh
 Damascus, Syria 443
84 Virgin Mary, Queen of Peace
 Gortnadreha, Ireland . . . 576
85 Virgin Mary, the Spouse of God
 Sabana Grande, Puerto Rico 185
86 Virgin of the Poor
 Banneux, Belgium 69

Topical Index
A Guide to Apparitions

87 **Virgin Queen Mary**
Binh Loi, Vietnam 335
88 **Virgin of Revelation**
Tre Fontane, Italy 132
89 **Virgin of the Rosary**
Sabana Grande, Puerto Rico 185
90 **Your Beloved Mother**
Denver/Golden, Co., USA 665
Agoo, Philippines 613
91 **Your Mother, Mother of My Son Jesus**
Lipa, Philippines 152
92 **Your Mother, Queen of Peace**
Medjugorje, Yugoslavia 405
93 **Your Mother the Co-Redemptrix**
Agoo, Philippines 613
94 **Your Mother, the Stella Maris**
Agoo, Philippines 613

Oh God, since You chose the Archangel Gabriel from among the angels to announce the mystery of Your Incarnation, mercifully grant that we who solemnly keep his feast on earth may feel the benefit of his patronage in heaven. Who live and reign forever. Amen

3 years. (449)
{plenary, once a month under the usual conditions}